THE  MAD® BATHROOM COMPANION

THE GUSHING FOURTH EDITION

Also available from MAD Books

MAD About the Oscars

MAD About Comic Strips

The MAD Bathroom Companion—Turd in a Series

The MAD Monster Book of Horrifying Clichés

MAD About the Mob

MAD About Super Heroes

MAD: Neumanisms

The MAD Bathroom Companion Number Two

The MAD Bathroom Companion

MAD About TV

MAD About the Movies—Special Warner Bros. Edition

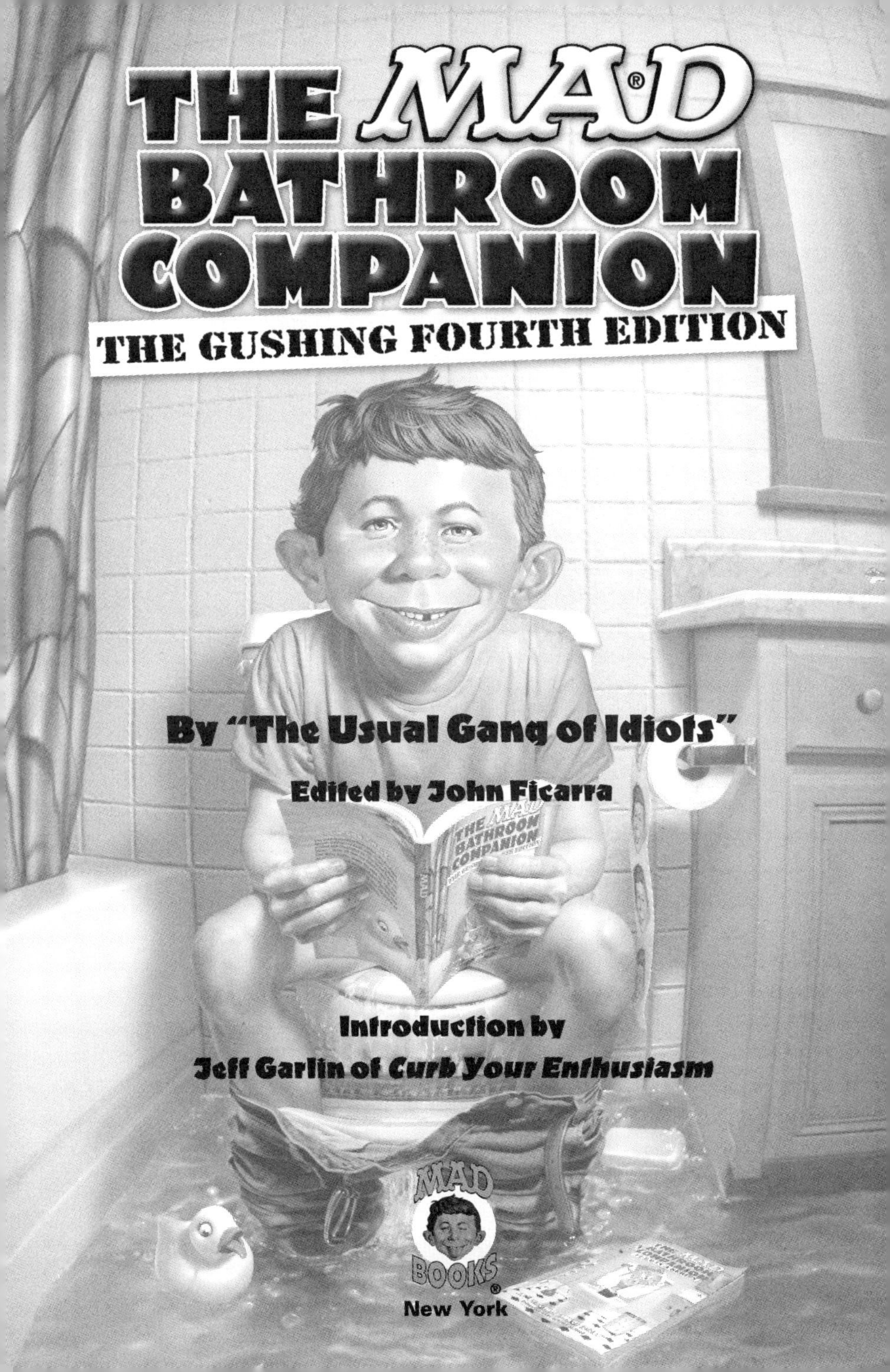

THE MAD® BATHROOM COMPANION

THE GUSHING FOURTH EDITION

By "The Usual Gang of Idiots"

Edited by John Ficarra

Introduction by

Jeff Garlin of *Curb Your Enthusiasm*

MAD BOOKS®

New York

MAD BOOKS

William Gaines Founder
John Ficarra Editor
Charlie Kadau Senior Editor
Charles Kochman Editor—Licensed Publishing
Sam Viviano Art Director
Patricia Dwyer Assistant Art Director

ADMINISTRATION
Paul Levitz President & Publisher
Georg Brewer VP—Design & Retail Product Development
Richard Bruning Senior VP—Creative Director
Patrick Caldon Senior VP—Finance & Operations
Chris Caramalis VP—Finance
Terri Cunningham VP—Managing Editor
Dan DiDio VP—Editorial
Alison Gill VP—Manufacturing
Rich Johnson VP—Book Trade Sales
Hank Kanalz VP—General Manager, Wildstorm
Lillian Laserson Senior VP & General Counsel
David McKillips VP—Advertising & Custom Publishing
John Nee VP—Business Development
Gregory Noveck Senior VP—Creative Affairs
Cheryl Rubin VP—Brand Management
Bob Wayne VP—Sales & Marketing

CONTRIBUTING ARTISTS AND WRITERS
"The Usual Gang of Idiots"

Compilation and new material © 2004 by E.C. Publications, Inc. All Rights Reserved.

MAD, Boy's Head Design, and all related indicia are trademarks of E.C. Publications, Inc.

Published by MAD Books. An imprint of E.C. Publications, Inc., 1700 Broadway, New York, NY 10019.
A Warner Bros. Entertainment Company.

ISBN 1-4012-0326-4

Printed in Canada

First edition
10 9 8 7 6 5 4 3 2 1

Visit *MAD* online at www.madmag.com

Though Alfred E. Neuman wasn't the first to say "A fool and his money are soon parted," here's your chance to prove the old adage right—subscribe to *MAD*! Simply call 1-800-4-MADMAG and mention code 5MBB1. Operators are standing by (the water cooler).

CONTENTS

"One Day in the Pasture," written and illustrated by Don Martin (*MAD* #101)
"Badly Needed Warning Labels For Rock Albums," by Desmond Devlin (*MAD* #262)
"*MAD*'s Great American Scavenger Hunt," by Mike Snider, illustrated by Sergio Aragonés (*MAD* #261)
"*MAD*'s Index," by Mike Snider and Frank Jacobs (*MAD* #282)
"Video Maladies," by Duck Edwing, illustrated by Duck Edwing and Harry North (*MAD* #265)
"Talk About Cheap!" written and illustrated by Paul Peter Porges (*MAD* #280)
"Horrifying Clichés," by May Sakami, illustrated by Paul Coker, Jr. (*MAD* #142)
"In the Hospital," written and illustrated by Don Martin (*MAD* #104)
"Further Additions to...*MAD*'s Table of Little-Known and Very Useless Weights, Measures & Distances," by John Ficarra, illustrated by Bob Clarke (*MAD* #237)
"The Lighter Side of...Outdoor Gardening," written and illustrated by Dave Berg (*MAD* #178)
"This Issue's Proposed *MAD* Medals...to be Presented to Deserving Working People," written and illustrated by Al Jaffee (*MAD* #213)
"When Roger Rabbit Technology Takes Over Hollywood's Films," by Stan Hart, illustrated by Bob Clarke (*MAD* #285)
"A Portfolio of *MAD* Placelies," written and illustrated by Max Brandel (*MAD* #111)
"A *MAD* Look at Musicians," written and illustrated by Sergio Aragonés (*MAD* #112)
"Later On in the Hospital," written and illustrated by Don Martin (*MAD* #104)
"The *MAD* Guide to...Yuppies, Yullies and Yuffies," by Frank Jacobs, illustrated by George Woodbridge (*MAD* #261)
"Footnotes to Hollywood," by Paul Peter Porges, illustrated by Paul Coker, Jr. (*MAD* #176)
"Spy vs. Spy," by Duck Edwing, illustrated by Bob Clarke (*MAD* #280)
"Things to Do on the Day After," written and illustrated by Al Jaffee (*MAD* #249)
"*MAD*'s Helpful Hints on Breaking Up With a Girl," by Larry Siegel, illustrated by Jack Rickard (*MAD* #245)
"Modern Merit Badges," by Stan Hart, illustrated by George Woodbridge (*MAD* #248)
"Still Later On in the Hospital," written and illustrated by Don Martin (*MAD* #104)
"Customized Academy Awards For Current Movie Trends," written and illustrated by Michael Montgomery (*MAD* #263)
"A *MAD* Peek Behind the Scenes at a Ripoff Mail-Order House," by Dick DeBartolo, illustrated by Jack Davis (*MAD* #281)
"The Lighter Side of...Making Extra Money," written and illustrated by Dave Berg (*MAD* #182)
"*MAD*'s Modern Believe it or Nuts!" by Frank Jacobs, illustrated by Bob Clarke (*MAD* #251)
"Reprieve It For Beaver," by Dennis Snee, illustrated by Angelo Torres (*MAD* #262)
"A *MAD* Look at Ms. Liberty," written and illustrated by Sergio Aragonés (*MAD* #265)
"Meanwhile at the Sculptor's Studio," written and illustrated by Don Martin (*MAD* #105)
"A *MAD* Look at Airline Safety Instructions," written and illustrated by Al Jaffee (*MAD* #251)
"The *MAD* Stress Chart," by Desmond Devlin, illustrated by Paul Coker, Jr. (*MAD* #257)
"Spy vs. Spy," by Duck Edwing, illustrated by Bob Clarke (*MAD* #282)
"Comics For Publications That Don't Have Comics," by Frank Jacobs, illustrated by Bob Clarke (*MAD* #88)
"*MAD*'s Heavy Metal Quiz," by Chris Hart, illustrated by Rick Tulka (*MAD* #288)
"The Lighter Side of Air," written and illustrated by Dave Berg (*MAD* #197)
"A Psalm for the Modern Television Preacher," by Barry Liebmann, illustrated by George Woodbridge (*MAD* #249)
"A *MAD* Peek Behind the Scenes at a Madonna Video," by Charlie Kadau and Joe Raiola, illustrated by Mort Drucker (*MAD* #304)
"If 'Hollywood Hype' Were Used For Everyday Dramatic Occasions," by Frank Jacobs, illustrated by Jack Rickard (*MAD* #221)
"The *MAD* People Watcher's Guide to a Political Convention," by Mike Snider, illustrated by Harvey Kurtzman (*MAD* #281)
"Late One Night...," written and illustrated by Don Martin (*MAD* #106)
"Stages in the Life of an Ad Campaign," by Charlie Kadau, idea by Marc I. Whinston, illustrated by Brian Buniak (*MAD* #277)
"A Portfolio of...Shape-ly *MAD* Verse," by William Garvin (*MAD* #104)
"The *MAD* Television Writer's Rule Book," by David Allikas, illustrated by Jack Davis (*MAD* #255)

"The Brick Layers..." written and illustrated by Don Martin (*MAD* #106)

"A *MAD* Look at Moving," written and illustrated by Sergio Aragonés (*MAD* #270)

"*MAD*'s Plan For Improving Movie Theatres," by Frank Jacobs, illustrated by Harry North (*MAD* #280)

"This Issue's Proposed *MAD* Medals...to be Presented to Deserving Actors," written and illustrated by Al Jaffee (*MAD* #214)

"Gift Catalog For Spoiled Rotten Pets," written and illustrated by Paul Peter Porges (*MAD* #282)

"Secret Supermarket Rules," by Charlie Kadau, illustrated by Paul Coker, Jr. (*MAD* #278)

"You Know It's REALLY OVER When...," by Al Jaffee and Gloria L. Rich, illustrated by Jack Rickard (*MAD* #143)

"Another Visit With a Sculptor," written and illustrated by Don Martin (*MAD* #108)

"Greeting Cards for Very, Very Special Occasions," by Frank Jacobs, illustrated by Bob Jones (*MAD* #285)

"*MAD* Looks at Handshakes," written and illustrated by Al Jaffee (*MAD* #279)

"*MAD*'s Modern Day Tongue Twisters," by David Ames, illustrated by George Woodbridge (*MAD* #267)

"The Sham-Jock Catalog," by Frank Jacobs, idea by James Kasmir, illustrated by Bob Clarke (*MAD* #249)

"Alf's Celebrity Cat Cookbook," by J. Prete, illustrated by Sam Viviano (*MAD* #282)

"Some Classic Examples of World Class Boredom," written and illustrated by Paul Peter Porges (*MAD* #285)

"The Paperhanger," written and illustrated by Don Martin (*MAD* #112)

"New Uses for Arm & Hammer Baking Soda," by Mike Snider, illustrated by Bob Clarke (*MAD* #261)

"The *MAD* Non-Smokers Hate Book," written and illustrated by Al Jaffee (*MAD* #144)

"*MAD*'s 'Do-It-Yourself' Job Application Letter," by Tom Koch (*MAD* #197)

"The Lighter Side of...Guilt," written and illustrated by Dave Berg (*MAD* #211)

"Spy vs. Spy," by Duck Edwing, illustrated by Bob Clarke (*MAD* #286)

"Instructional Sports Videos We'd Like to See," by Mike Snider, illustrated by Jack Davis (*MAD* #269)

"A *MAD* Look at Sharks," written and illustrated by Sergio Aragonés (*MAD* #180)

"One Day at the Ocean," written and illustrated by Don Martin (*MAD* #138)

"A *MAD* Look at the Silent Thinking Audience," by Paul Peter Porges, illustrated by Paul Coker, Jr. (*MAD* #213)

"*MAD*'s Guide to Making It in the Business World," by Larry Siegel, illustrated by George Woodbridge (*MAD* #279)

"One Beautiful Evening Last May," written and illustrated by Don Martin (*MAD* #177)

"The Movie Sequel Graveyard," by Frank Jacobs, illustrated by Bob Clarke (*MAD* #277)

"Practical Uses for Well-Trained Porcupines," written and illustrated by Paul Peter Porges (*MAD* #279)

"The Great Zucchini," written and illustrated by Don Martin (*MAD* #177)

"Truly Logical Transformers," written and illustrated by Al Jaffee (*MAD* #257)

"*MAD* Close-Ups," by Paul Peter Porges, illustrated by Harry North, Esq. (*MAD* #197)

"Spy vs. Spy," by Duck Edwing, illustrated by Bob Clarke (*MAD* #285)

"A *MAD* Look at Hands Across America," written and illustrated by Sergio Aragonés (*MAD* #266)

"Join *MAD*'s Trendy Book of the Month Club," by Larry Siegel, illustrated by Bob Clarke (*MAD* #256)

"The Lighter Side of...Celebrations," written and illustrated by Dave Berg (*MAD* #214)

"*MAD*'s Aptitude Test Number Three...Will You Make a Good Athlete?" by Frank Jacobs, illustrated by George Woodbridge (*MAD* #245)

"*MAD* Re-examines More Wise Old Sayings," by Tom Koch, illustrated by Paul Coker, Jr. (*MAD* #285)

"The Yellow Pages Through History," by Tom Koch, illustrated by Bob Clarke (*MAD* #211)

"*MAD*'s 12-Point Plan For Improving America," by Tom Koch, illustrated by Mort Drucker (*MAD* #293)

"One Afternoon Down Home," written and illustrated by Don Martin (*MAD* #183)

"Drawn Out Dramas," illustrated throughout by Sergio Aragonés

Introduction

I'M going to take you behind the scenes on *Curb Your Enthusiasm*. Way behind the scenes. To a place no one has ever gone. We are going into the bathroom of our trailer. On *Curb*, (we call it *Curb*), we have two trailers. One is for wardrobe, make-up, and production. The other is for the creative producers and actors. Larry David was becoming disenchanted with the status of the bathroom. I say bathroom because there is a shower in there. Anyway, Larry was upset. So he had some rules put up in the bathroom. These are the rules:

If you plan to use the bathroom:

- *Flush on contact. "Courtesy Flush."*
- *Please use air freshener.*
- *Men—wipe the toilet rim after use.*
- *Be scrupulous in your flushing.*
- *Make a visual check of the toilet after you flush.*
- *After washing your hands, make sure the sink area is dry and clean.*
- *The garbage can is for paper products only. No lunches or other degradable waste.*
- *In addition, if the garbage is overflowing, stomp it down with your shoe.*
- *Do not leave reading materials.*

Well, there they are. The reason I am publishing them is because I hate them.

I'm hoping that a public outcry will force their removal. If you don't think they're outrageous then let's go over them, shall we?

Flush on contact. "Courtesy Flush."

I don't know about you, but when I'm done making a doody I want everyone to know—like an announcement.

Please use air freshener.

Is this environmentally sound? I don't think so.

Men—wipe the toilet rim after use.

Two thoughts. First, I'm on autopilot with this one. I'm married. I've been yelled at enough. Secondly, why shouldn't women wipe the toilet rim after each use? Even if they don't get anything on the rim, it would still make for a cleaner rim.

Be scrupulous in your flushing.

The only detail I care about is how big my doody is. I get excited. I'm sad to flush. I don't like goodbyes.

Make a visual check of the toilet after you flush.

See above. I like checking before I flush.

After washing your hands, make sure the sink area is dry and clean.

I don't know about you, but after I clean the sink area, I feel like washing.

The garbage can is for paper products only. No lunches or other degradable waste.

Who eats lunch while making a doody?

In addition, if the garbage is overflowing, stomp down on it with your shoe.

Stomp down my lunch with my shoe?!?! No way!

Do not leave reading materials.

Actually, this one was specifically designed for me. I can't take a dump without reading. I also think that I'm not alone here. That's why I leave it there for others to enjoy.

The only warning I can give you is that this book is too good to leave behind. Someone will take it. So carry this book wherever you poop and then take it with you—especially if you work on *Curb*. If you don't, you'll find it scrupulously flushed or stomped on in the garbage beneath someone's lunch.

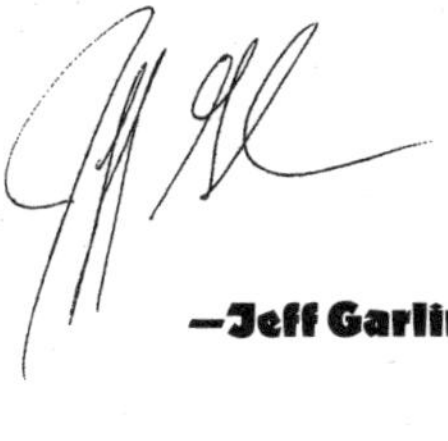

—Jeff Garlin

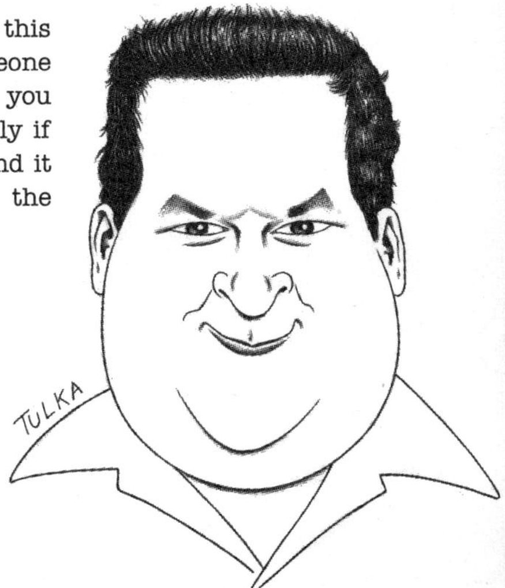
TULKA

ILLUSTRATION BY RICK TULKA

SERGIO ARAGONES DEPT.

A MAD LOOK AT THE.. DISNEY

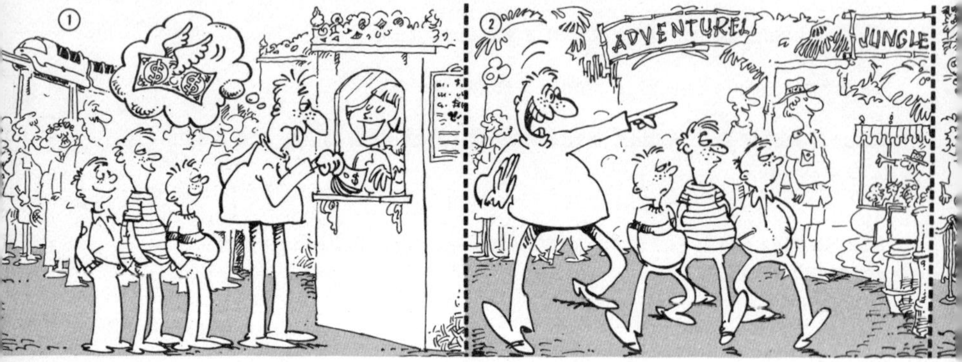
1
2
ADVENTUREL
JUNGLE

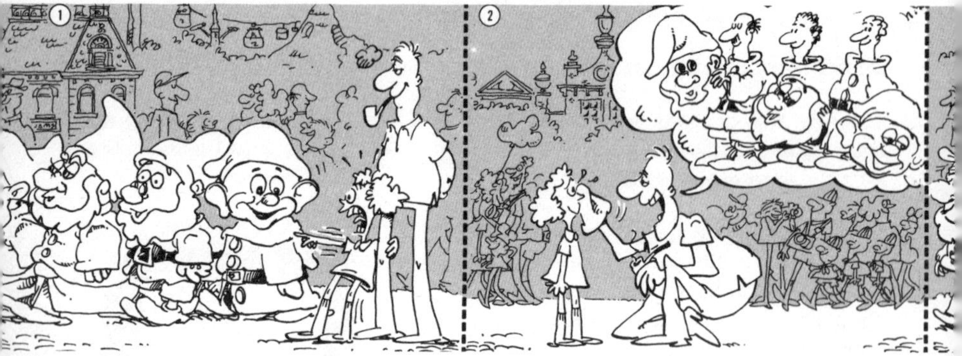
1
2

ARTIST AND WRITER

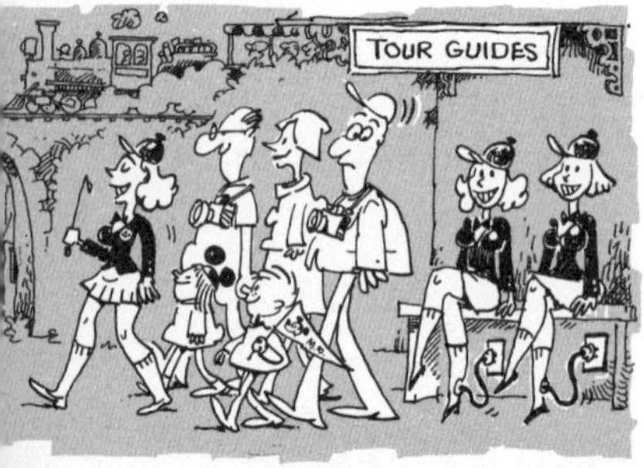
TOUR GUIDES

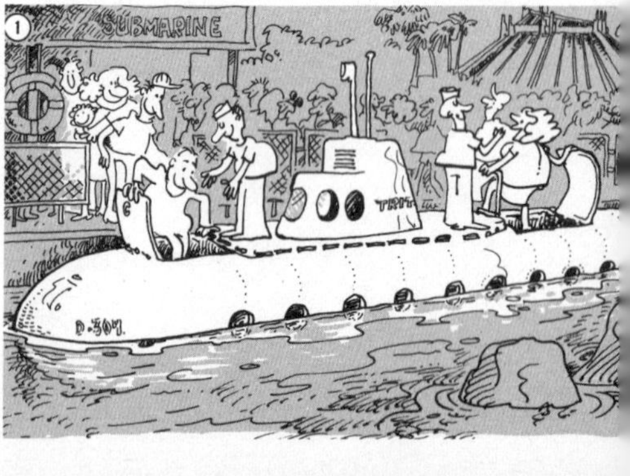
1
SUBMARINE

WORLDS

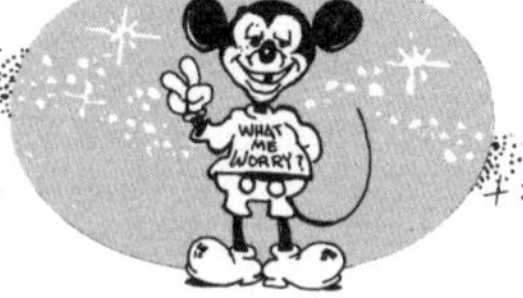
WHAT ME WORRY?

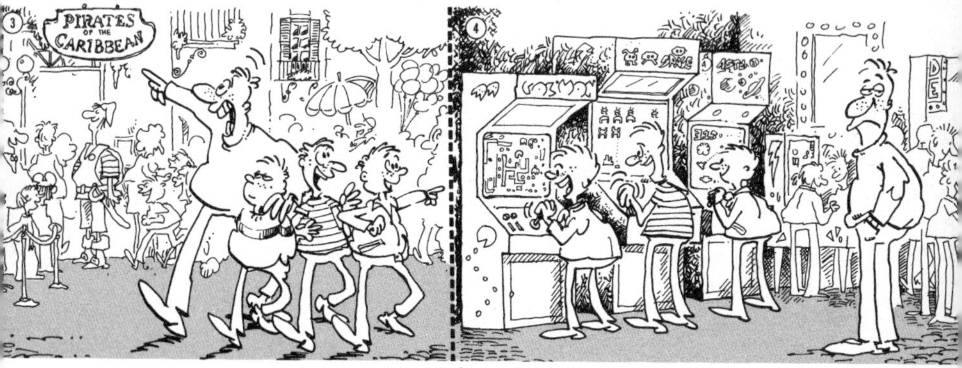
PIRATES OF THE CARIBBEAN

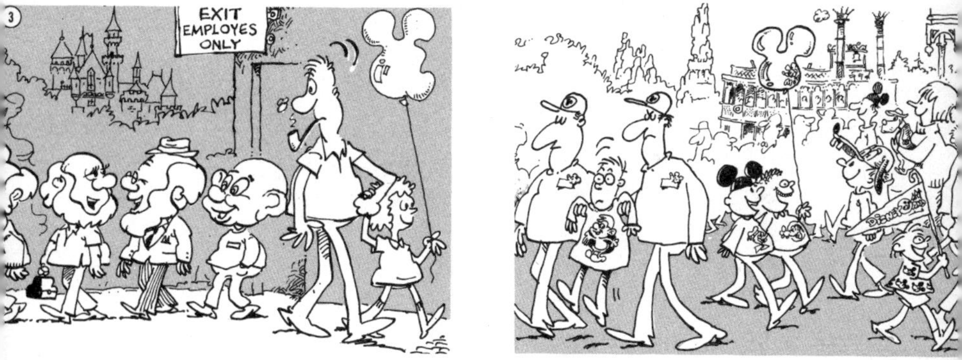
EXIT EMPLOYES ONLY

SERGIO ARAGONES

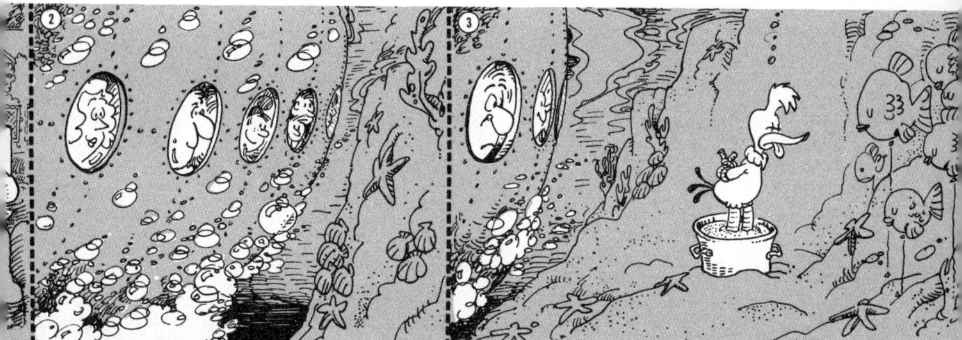

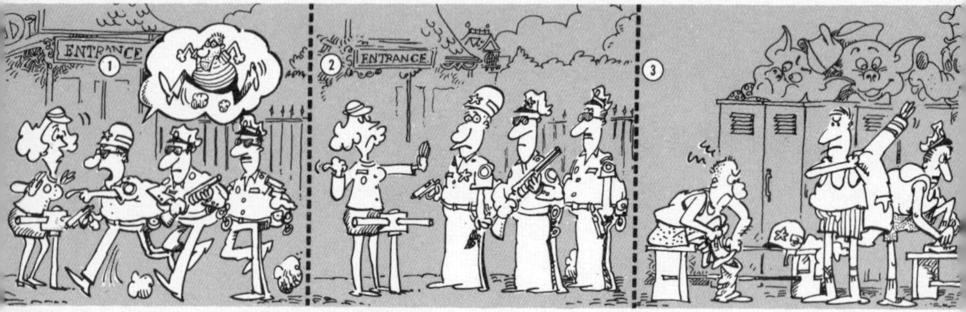
ENTRANCE
ENTRANCE

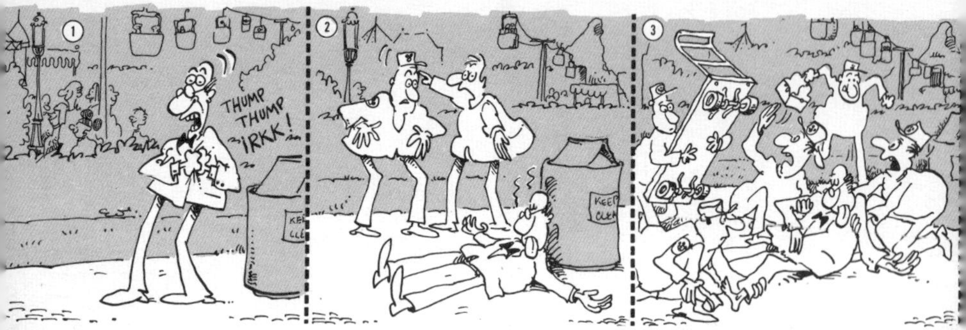
THUMP
THUMP
IRKK!
KEEP CLEAN

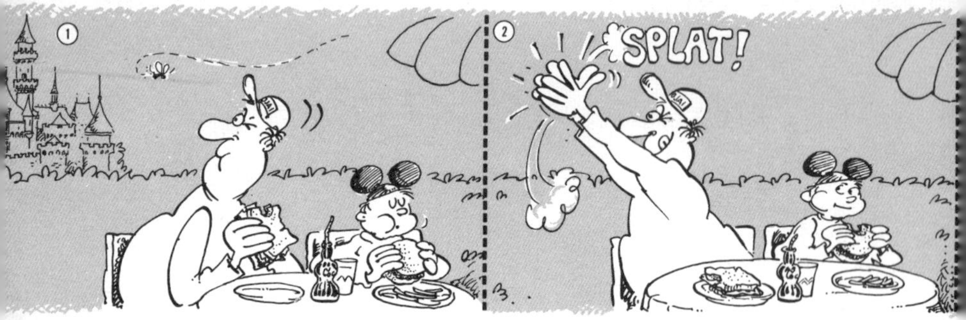
SPLAT!

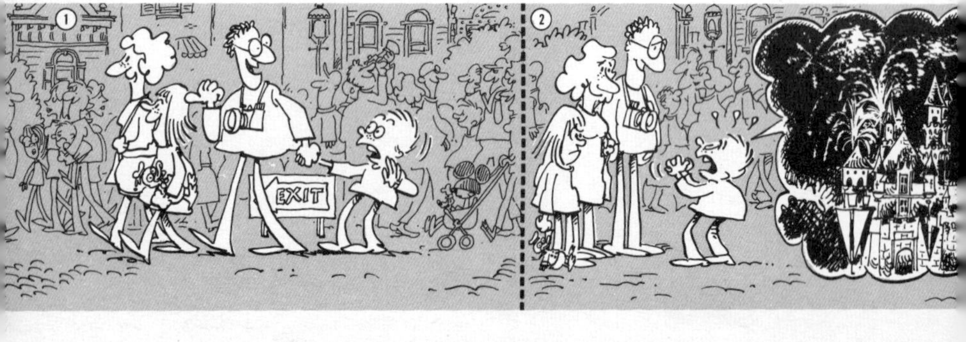
EXIT

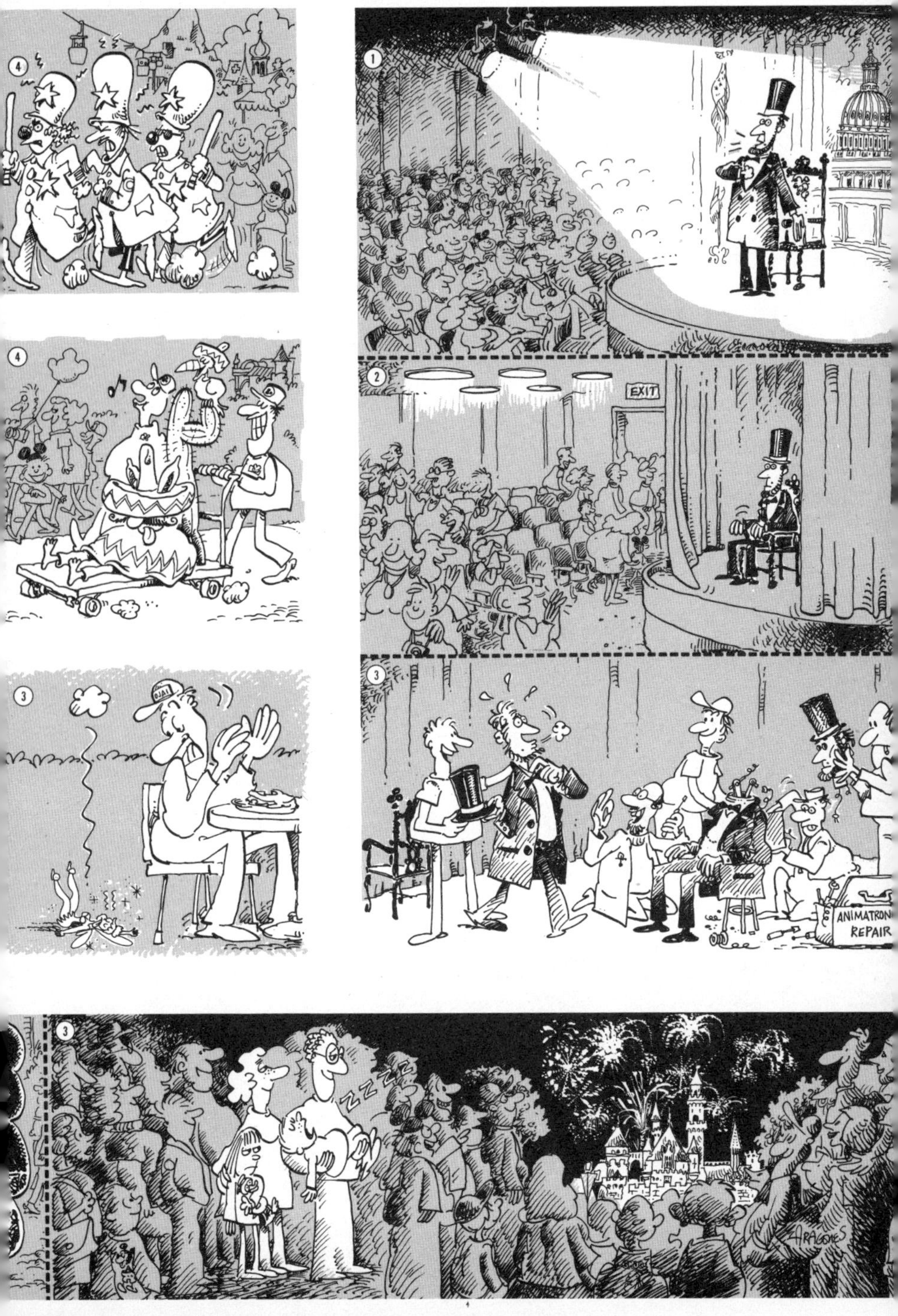
EXIT
OJAI
ANIMATRON
REPAIR
ARAGONES

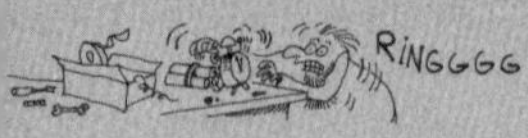
RINGGGG

WEARY OF RELATIVITY DEPT.

As Albert Einstein explained, Time is relative. Which means that, sometimes, Time passes faster or slower than other times. You find that hard to believe?

TIME DRAGS...

TIME DRAGS...

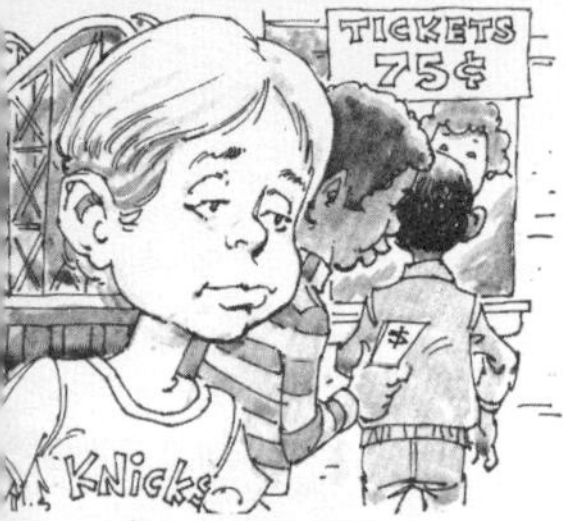
TICKETS
75¢
$
Knicks

...when you're waiting your turn on the roller coaster.

TIME FLIES...

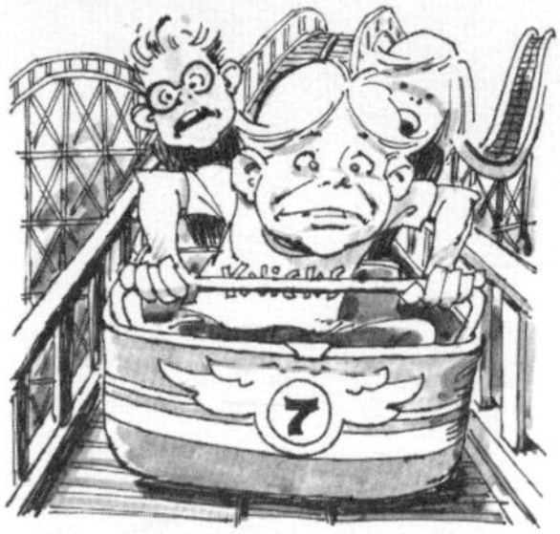
7

...when you're on the ride.

TIME DRAGS...

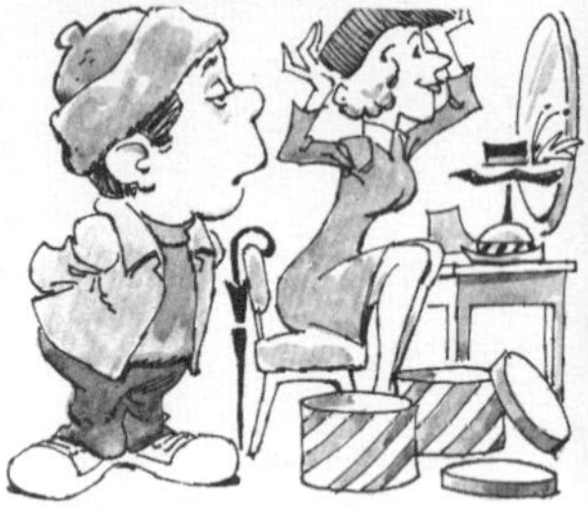

...when you're waiting for your Mother in the Hat Department.

TIME DRAGS...

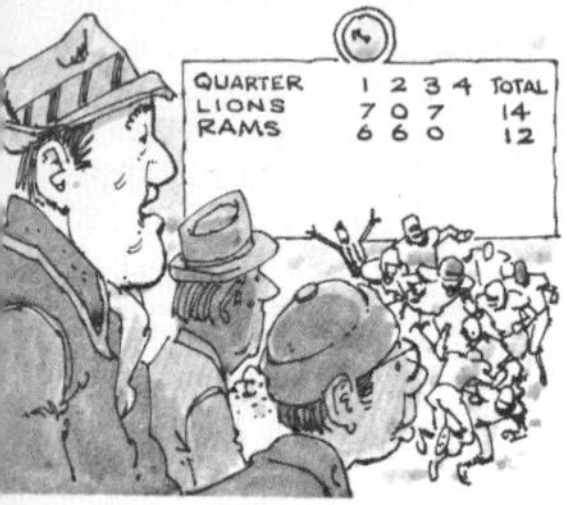
QUARTER 1 2 3 4 TOTAL
LIONS 7 0 7 14
RAMS 6 6 0 12

...when your football team is winning by only 2 points.

TIME FLIES...

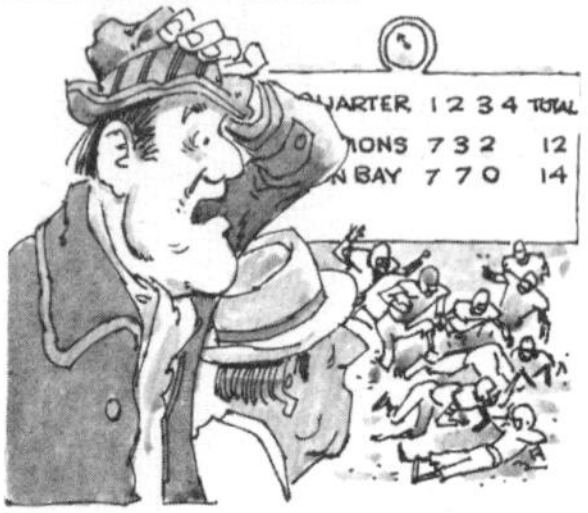
UARTER 1 2 3 4 TOTAL
IONS 7 3 2 12
N BAY 7 7 0 14

...when your football team is losing by only 2 points.

TIME DRAGS...

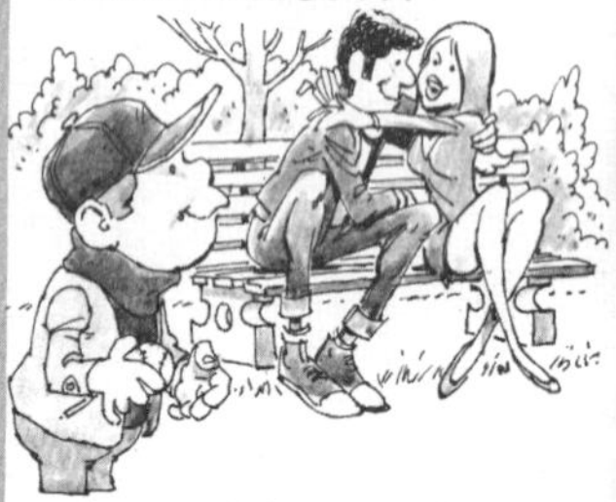

...between being a child... and becoming a young adult.

TIME DRAGS...

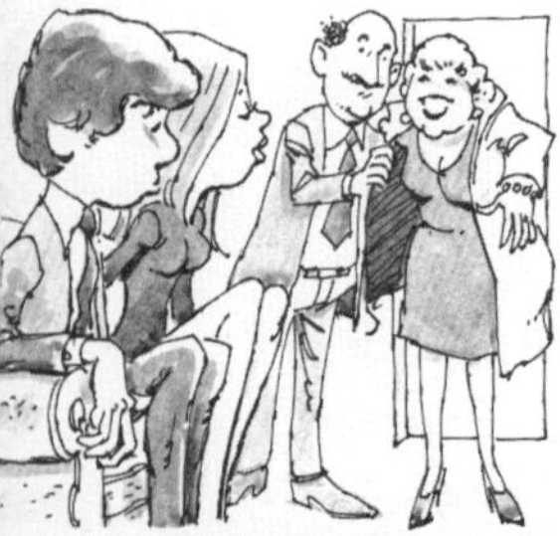

...till her parents go out.

TIME FLIES...

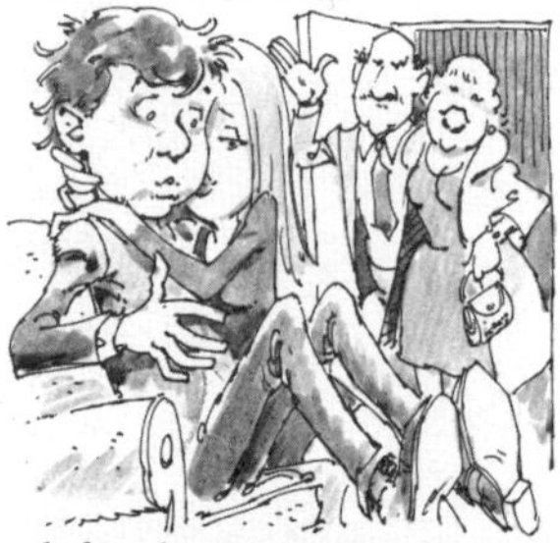

...before they come back.

TIME DRAGS...

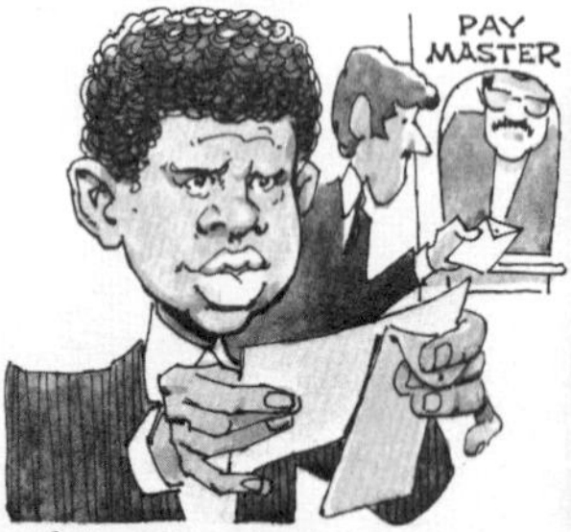
PAY
MASTER

...between paychecks.

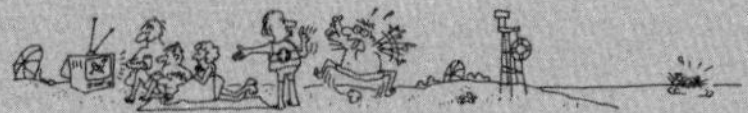

Well, notice how fast Time goes when you're enjoying yourself, as compared to how slow it passes when you're reading a dull article like this one, called . . .

TIME FLIES...

ARTIST:
JACK RICKARD

WRITER:
STAN HART

TIME FLIES...

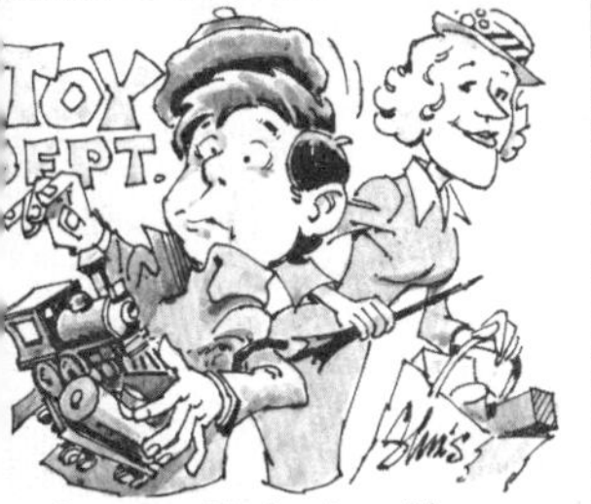

. . when your Mother is waiting for you in the Toy Department.

TIME DRAGS...

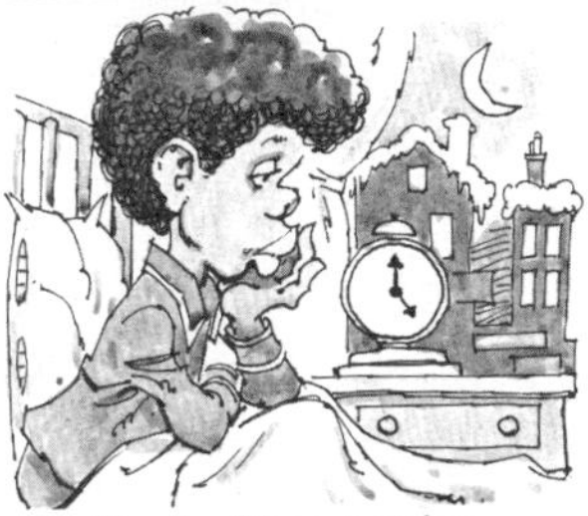

. . . waiting for Xmas morning, so you can open your presents.

TIME FLIES...

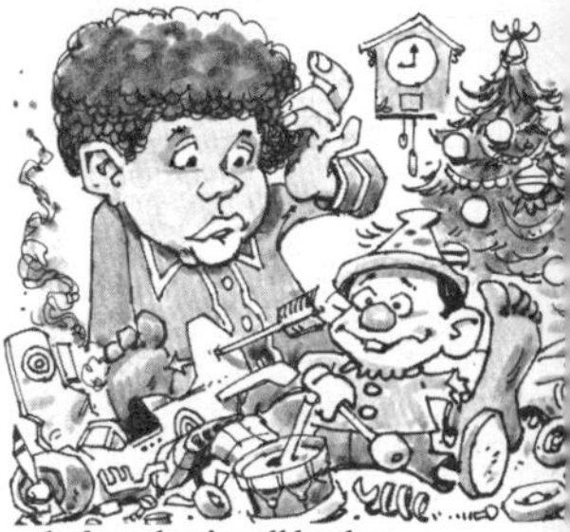

. . . before they're all broken.

TIME FLIES...

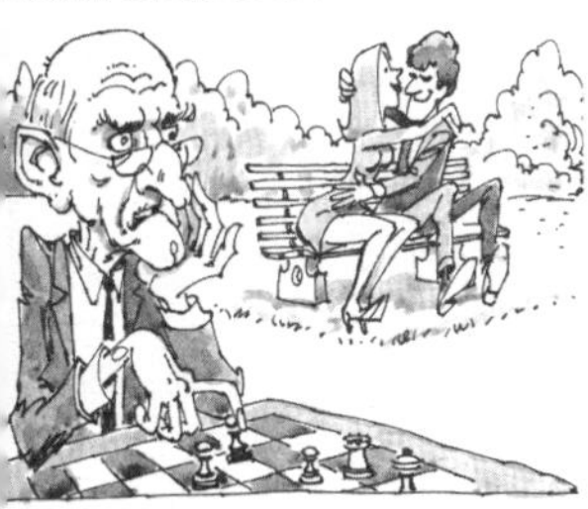

. . between being a young adult
. . and becoming an old adult.

TIME DRAGS . . .

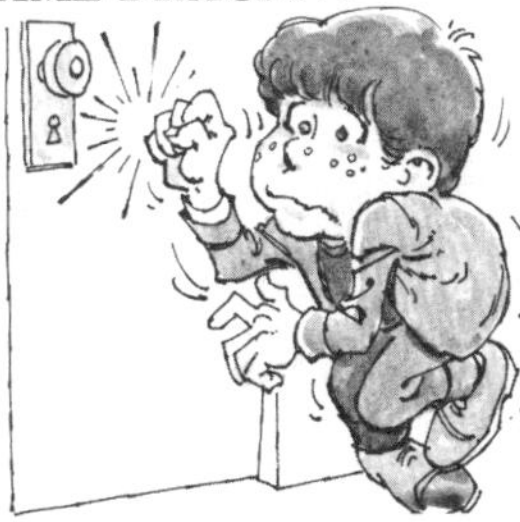

. . . waiting for someone to get out of the bathroom.

TIME FLIES...

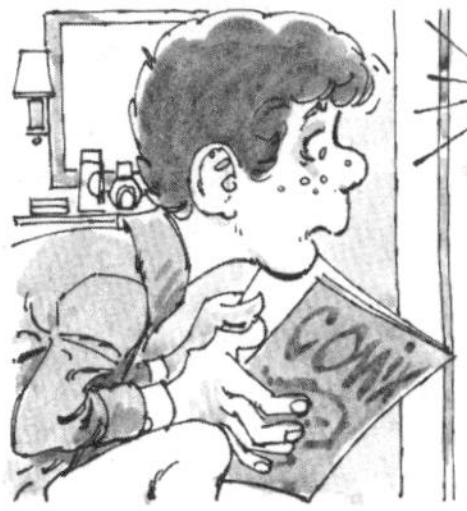

. . . before someone wants you to get out of the bathroom.

TIME FLIES...

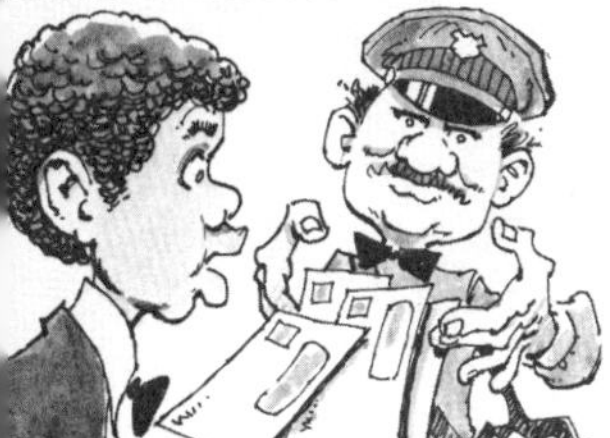

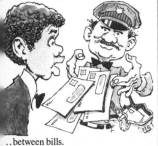

. . between bills.

TIME FLIES . . .

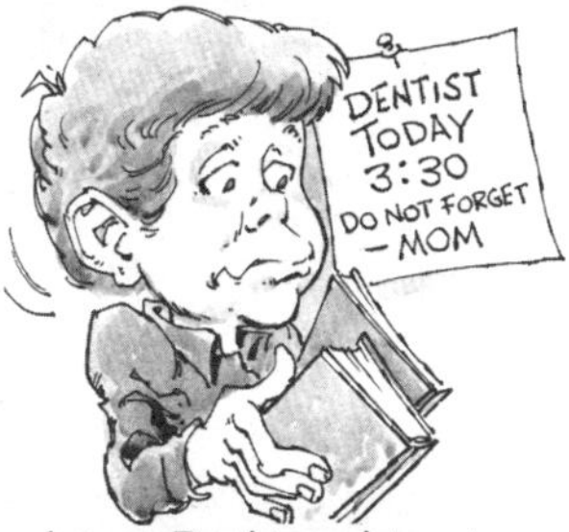
DENTIST
TODAY
3:30
DO NOT FORGET
-MOM

. . . between Dentist appointments.

TIME DRAGS . . .

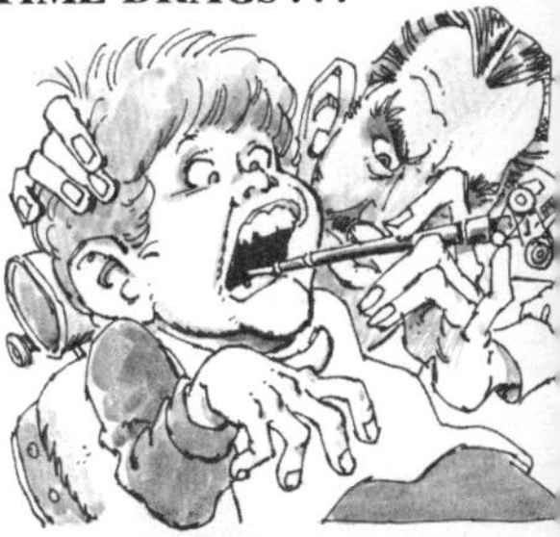

. . . when he's drilling your tooth.

IF YOU THINK WE HUMANS ARE THE ONLY ONES WHO

HEADLINES OF TH

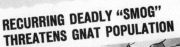

RECURRING DEADLY "SMOG" THREATENS GNAT POPULATION

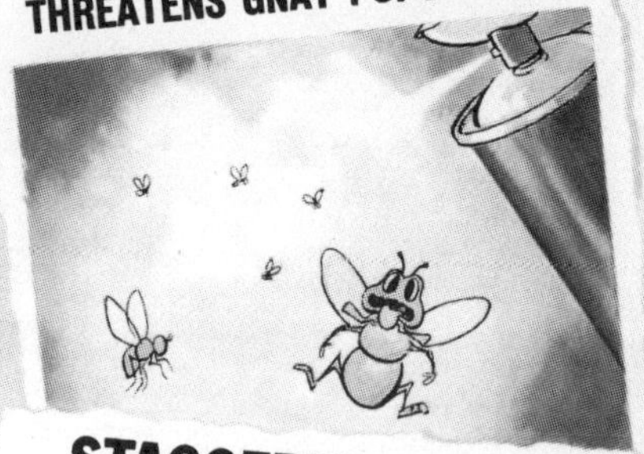

SURPRISE TERMITE DEMOLITION ACTIVATES URBAN RENEWAL PROGRAM

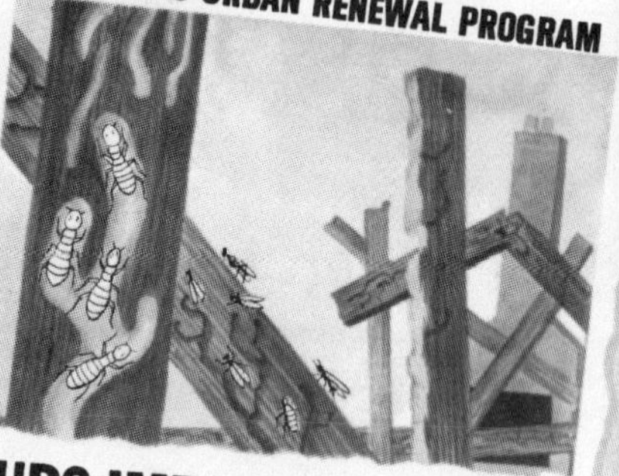

STAGGERED LUNCH HOURS IMPLEMENTED AT LEADING INDUSTRIAL BEEHIVE COMPLEXES

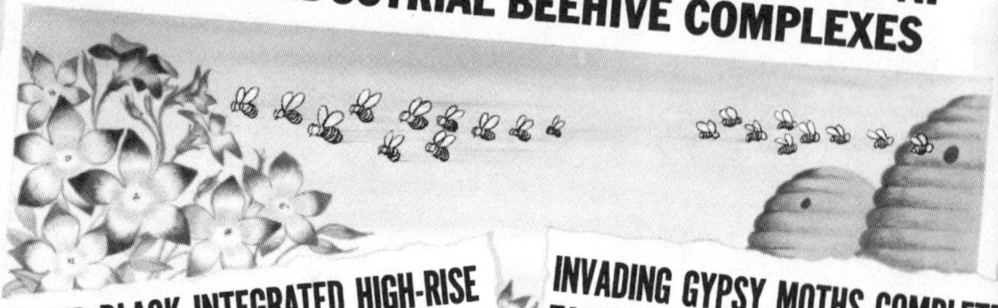

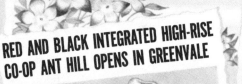

RED AND BLACK INTEGRATED HIGH-RISE CO-OP ANT HILL OPENS IN GREENVALE

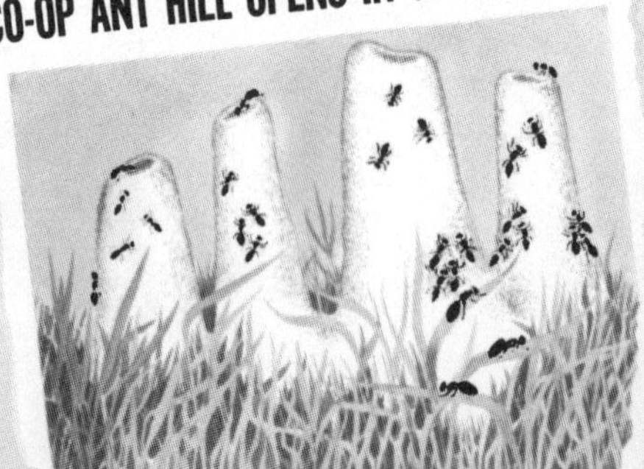

INVADING GYPSY MOTHS COMPLETE TACTICAL DEFOLIATION OPERATION

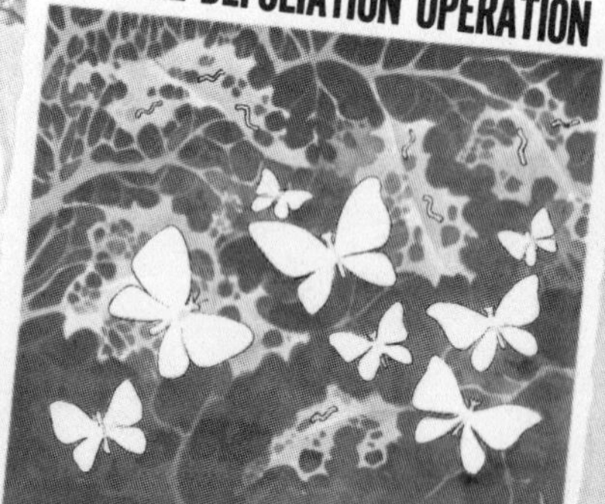

UFFER FROM THE PROBLEMS OF TODAY, DIG THESE…

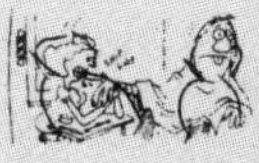

E INSECT WORLD

ARTIST: BOB CLARKE WRITER: PAUL PETER PORGES

DECOY FLY NABS KILLER OF HUNDREDS IN HIGH-CRIME-POND-AREA

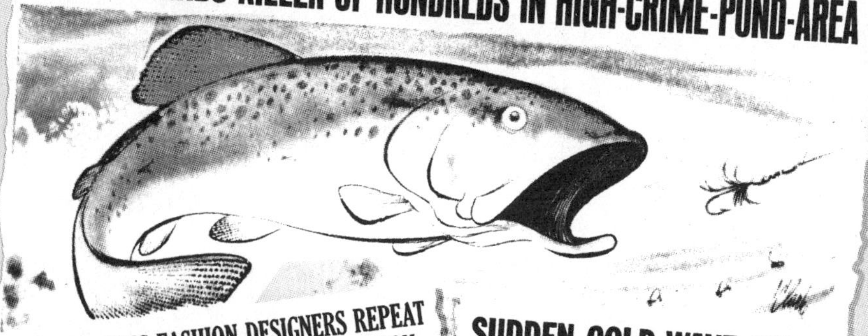

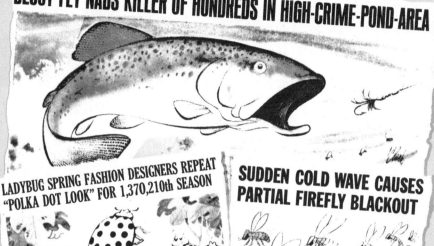

LADYBUG SPRING FASHION DESIGNERS REPEAT "POLKA DOT LOOK" FOR 1,370,210th SEASON

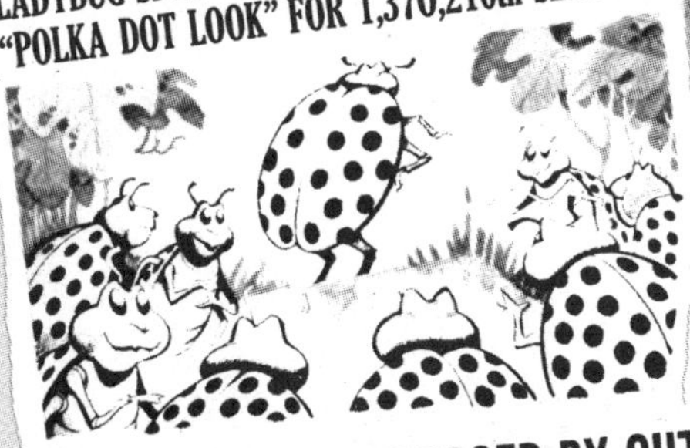

SUDDEN COLD WAVE CAUSES PARTIAL FIREFLY BLACKOUT

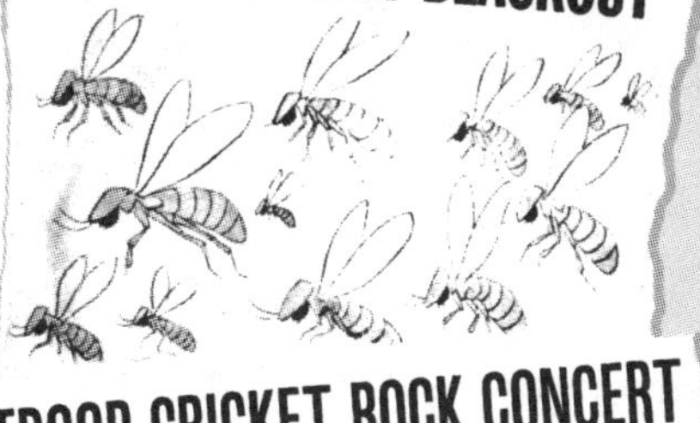

LOCAL CITIZENS OUTRAGED BY OUTDOOR CRICKET ROCK CONCERT

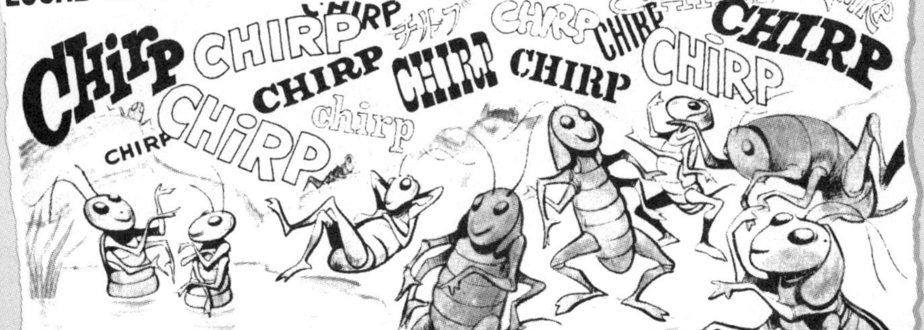
CHIRP
CHIRP
CHIRP
CHIRP
CHIRP
CHIRP
CHIRP
CHIRP
CHIRP
CHIRP
CHIRP
chirp
CHIRP

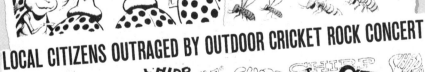

ONE-CENTIPEDE-CHORUS LINE OPENS IN FOREST HILLS TO RAVE REVIEWS

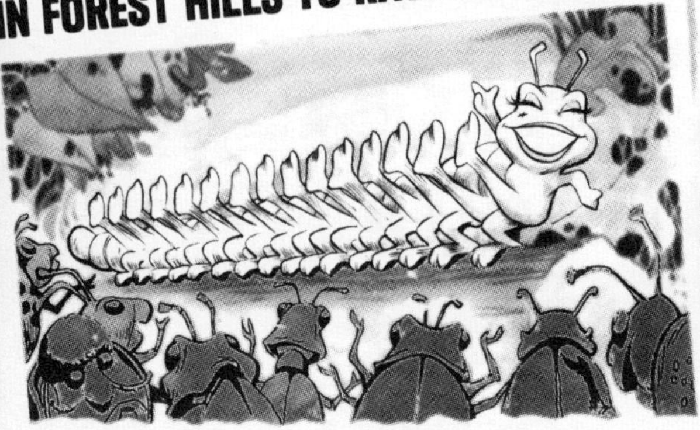

LOCAL BUGS WARNED OF UNMARKED SPEED TRAPS

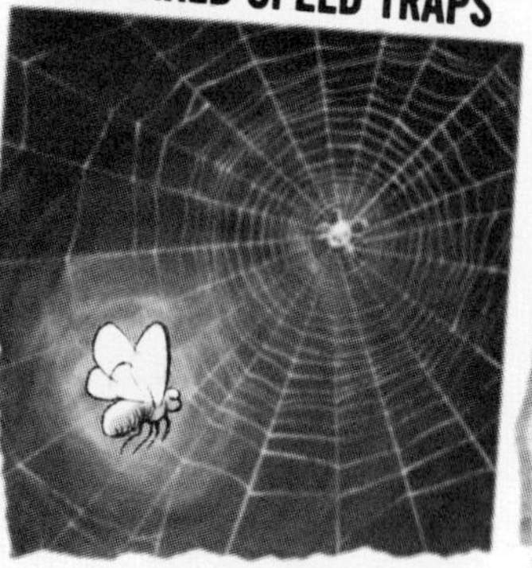

INCHWORM SETS NEW WORLD'S RECORD FOR OUTDOOR MILE: 5 MONTHS, 3 DAYS, 8 HOURS, 12 MINUTES, 45 SECONDS

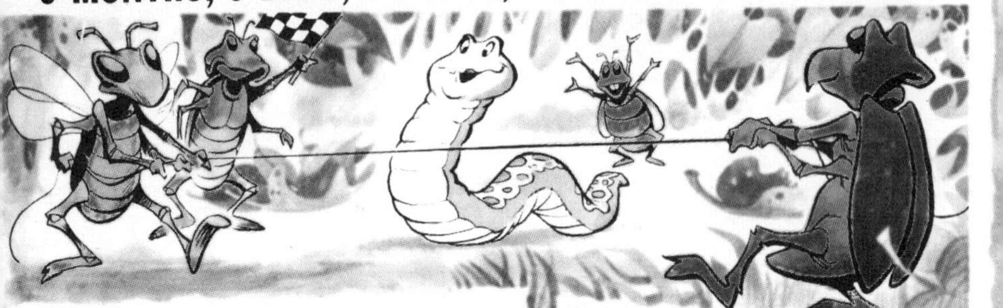

GROUND SMOG CAUSES DRAGON FLY STACK-UP AND TAKE-OFF DELAYS

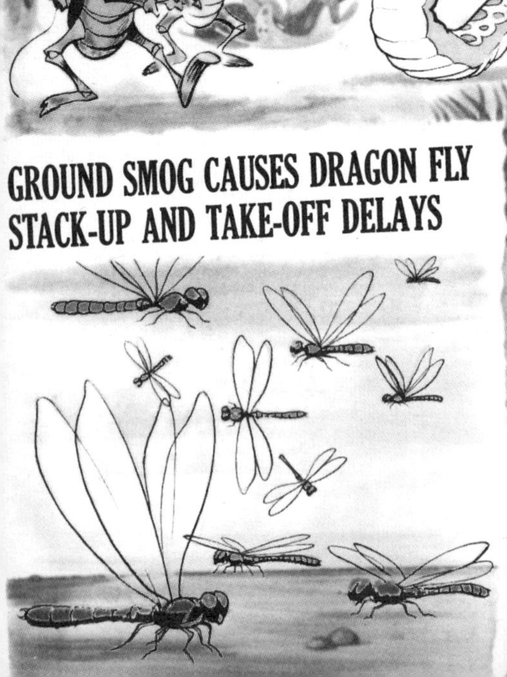

GARDEN APARTMENT RESTRICTED TO WASPS IS CITED BY INSECT RIGHTS COMMISSION

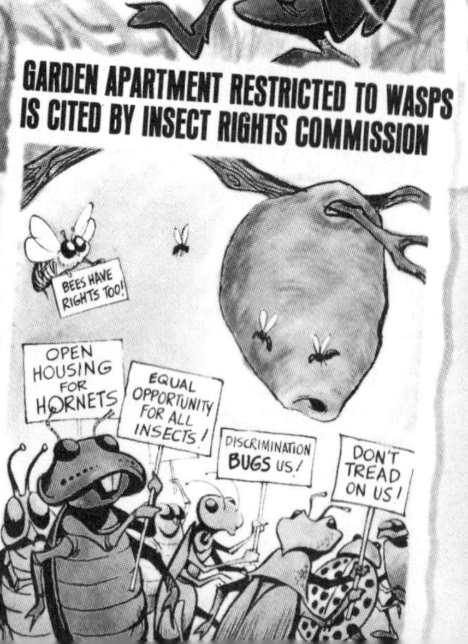

BEES HAVE RIGHTS TOO!
OPEN HOUSING FOR HORNETS
EQUAL OPPORTUNITY FOR ALL INSECTS!
DISCRIMINATION BUGS US!
DON'T TREAD ON US!

BS.A.T. DEPT.

ARTIST: GEORGE WOODBRIDGE WRITER: FRANK JACOBS

Thinking about what career to get into? Wondering whether or not you'll fit in? Well, here's the second in a series of tests designed to help you choose your future line of work. Mainly, discover your true abilities by taking...

MAD'S APTITUDE TEST NUMBER TWO

WILL YOU MAKE A GOOD TEACHER?

1. You wish to become a teacher. This requires a fierce desire to:
   - A. Learn first-hand what it's like to live at the poverty level.
   - B. Discover how much abuse a human being is able to withstand.
   - C. Somehow survive until you're able to retire and draw your pension.
   - D. All of the above.

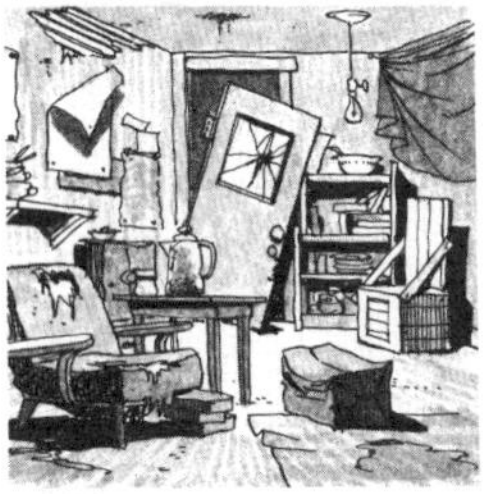

2. Looking at the above, you should be able to tell that it is:
   - A. The Faculty Lounge at a typical junior high school.
   - B. A teacher's version of a luxury apartment.
   - C. The set for a Senior Class play.
   - D. Any of the above.

3. As a high-school teacher, your class is disrupted by three unruly students playing a "boom box" at peak volume. What should you do *before* trying to take away the radio?
   - A. Make sure that your medical insurance is paid up.
   - B. Find out if injuries such as concussion and broken ribs will interfere with your teaching duties the rest of the term.
   - C. Have yourself examined by a qualified psychiatrist.
   - D. All of the above.

4. The three students punch you out. After you regain consciousness, you complain to the principal. You can count on him to tell you:
   - A. "Forget it. Boys will be boys."
   - B. "Forget it. Girls will be girls."
   - C. "It's obvious you're not getting through to them."
   - D. Any of the above.

5. Complete the following. In prestige, salary and respect in the community, a teacher's job compares favorably with that of ______________ .
   - A. A busboy.
   - B. A Haitian refugee.
   - C. A migrant worker.
   - D. All of the above.

6. For homework, you assign your class a difficult problem to solve. The next day you call on one student to give the answer. Which one?
   - A. The dumbest in the class so you can be entertained by his fumbling, bumbling attempts at an answer.
   - B. The worst behaved in the class so you can get some revenge for his turning your classroom into a shambles.
   - C. The smartest in the class so that *you* can find out what the answer is.
   - D. Any of the above.

7. As a teacher, you discover several students getting high on grass. Your proper response is to:
   - A. Be glad it's only grass.
   - B. Confiscate it, then take it home to compare it with your own.
   - C. Let them get stoned since they sleep through your classes anyway.
   - D. Any of the above.

27,932

8. A look at the numbers above should tell you that this teacher is:
   - A. Figuring out how many hours of moonlighting it will take for her income to equal that of a street-cleaner.
   - B. Calculating how many more days of hell she'll have to face until Christmas Vacation.
   - C. Figuring how much in debt she'll be if she has steak *twice* a month.
   - D. Any of the above.

9. As a teacher, your summer vacation can prove of value, because:
   - A. You can make more in three months as a fill-in factory worker than in the nine you spend teaching.
   - B. It takes that long for the welts and bruises to completely disappear.
   - C. You can relax, mull over your life, and decide whether you might want to go into a less hectic, stress-ridden career, such as air traffic controller.
   - D. Any of the above.

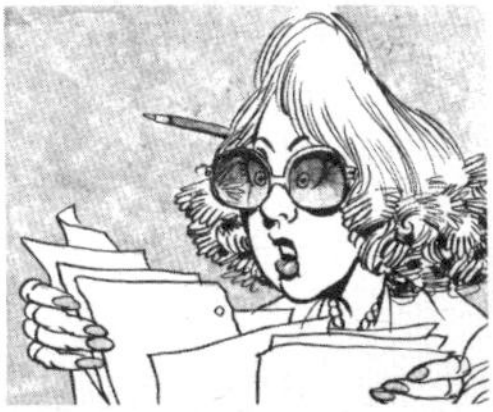

10. You discover that one-fourth of your class is failing a required subject. What should you do?
    - A. Pass them anyway so you won't have to put up with them next year.
    - B. Transfer to another school where they don't know what a dud you are.
    - C. Realize at last that you are in the wrong profession.
    - D. Any of the above.

SCORING

If you answered "D" to all of the questions, you have the ability to make a swell Teacher.

NOMENCULTURE DEPT.

BOYS JUST WAN

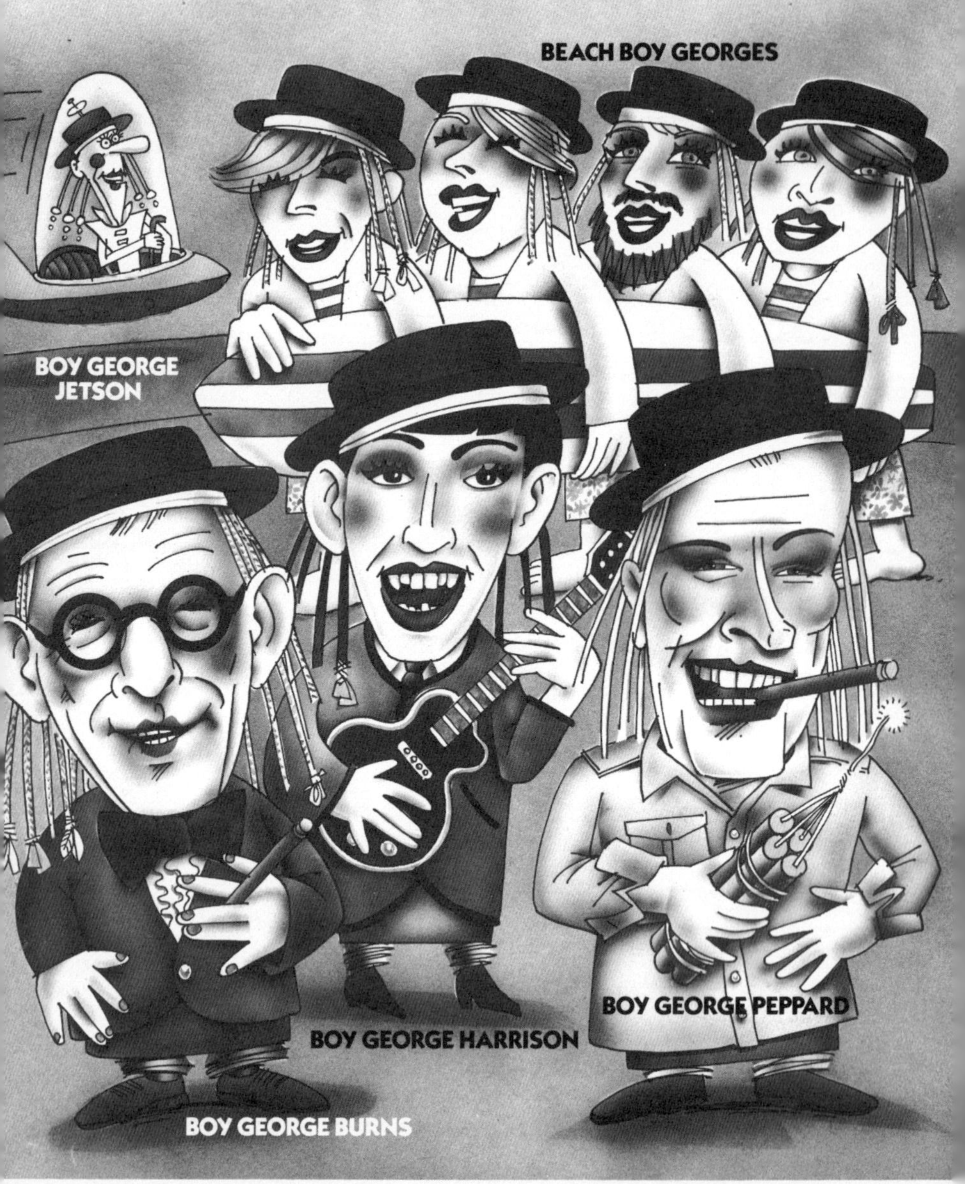
BEACH BOY GEORGES
BOY GEORGE JETSON
BOY GEORGE PEPPARD
BOY GEORGE HARRISON
BOY GEORGE BURNS

NA BE GEORGE

ARTIST AND WRITER: TOM HACHTMAN

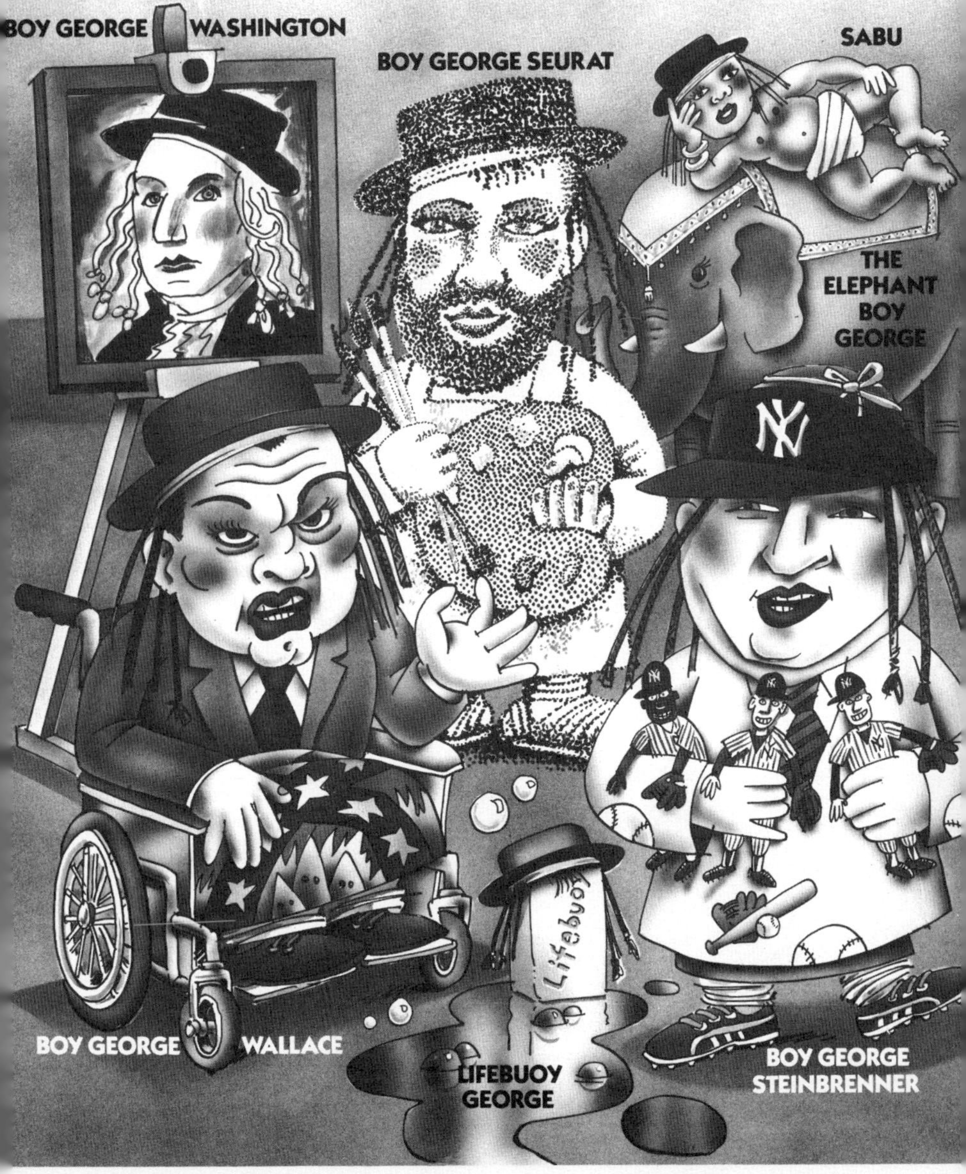

BOY GEORGE WASHINGTON
BOY GEORGE SEURAT
SABU
THE ELEPHANT BOY GEORGE
NY
Lifebuoy
BOY GEORGE WALLACE
LIFEBUOY GEORGE
BOY GEORGE STEINBRENNER

Ever wonder why hospital nurses are late with bedpans, why doctors and internes can't be located and hav

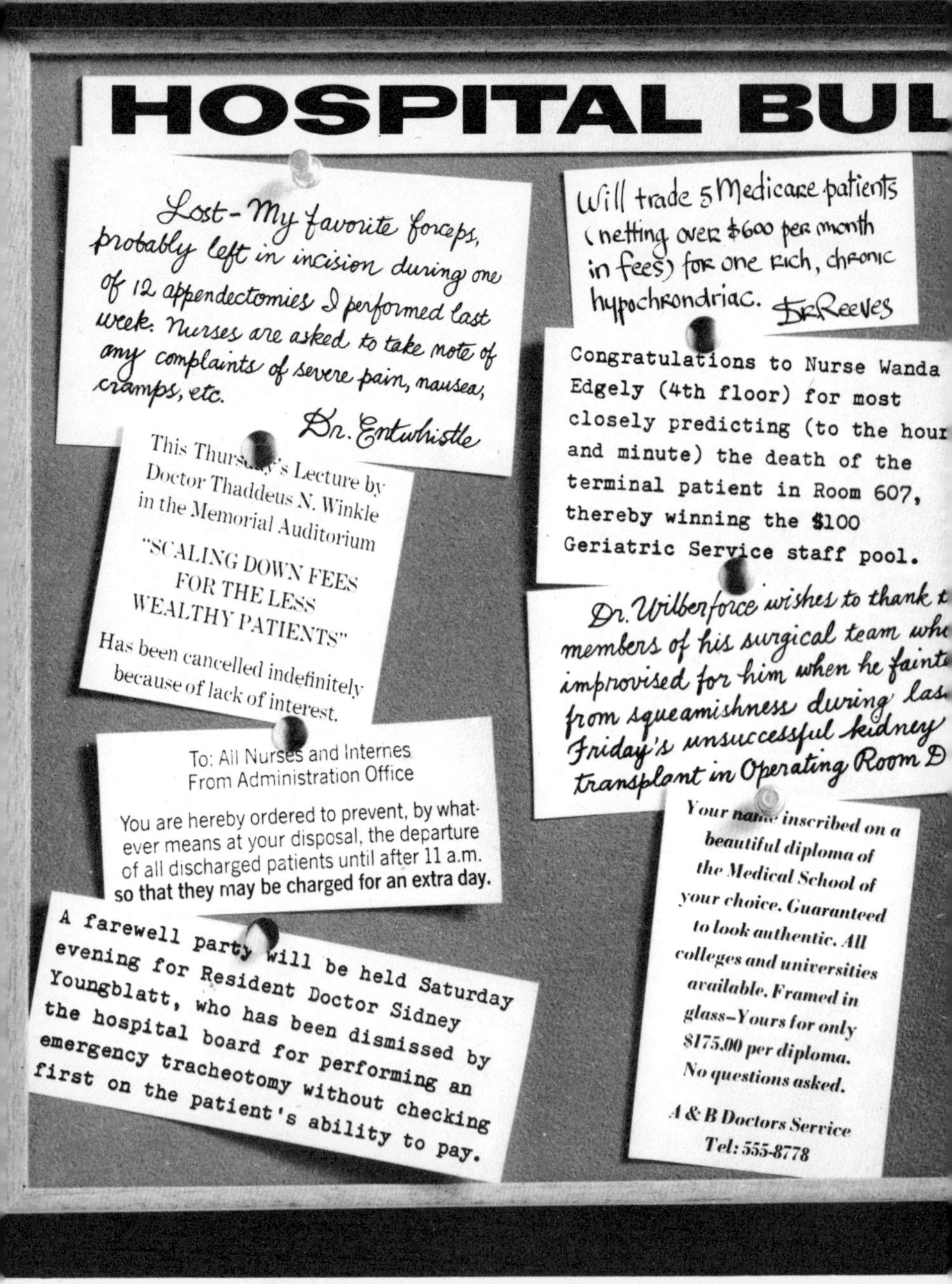
HOSPITAL BUL
Lost - My favorite forceps, probably left in incision during one of 12 appendectomies I performed last week. Nurses are asked to take note of any complaints of severe pain, nausea, cramps, etc.
Dr. Entwhistle
Will trade 5 Medicare patients (netting over $600 per month in fees) for one rich, chronic hypochrondriac. Dr Reeves
Congratulations to Nurse Wanda Edgely (4th floor) for most closely predicting (to the hour and minute) the death of the terminal patient in Room 607, thereby winning the $100 Geriatric Service staff pool.
This Thurs 's Lecture by Doctor Thaddeus N. Winkle in the Memorial Auditorium
"SCALING DOWN FEES FOR THE LESS WEALTHY PATIENTS"
Has been cancelled indefinitely because of lack of interest.
Dr. Wilberforce wishes to thank t members of his surgical team whe improvised for him when he faint from squeamishness during las Friday's unsuccessful kidney transplant in Operating Room D
To: All Nurses and Internes
From Administration Office
You are hereby ordered to prevent, by whatever means at your disposal, the departure of all discharged patients until after 11 a.m. so that they may be charged for an extra day.
Your na inscribed on a beautiful diploma of the Medical School of your choice. Guaranteed to look authentic. All colleges and universities available. Framed in glass–Yours for only $175.00 per diploma. No questions asked.
A & B Doctors Service
Tel: 555-8778
A farewell party will be held Saturday evening for Resident Doctor Sidney Youngblatt, who has been dismissed by the hospital board for performing an emergency tracheotomy without checking first on the patient's ability to pay.

be paged? Most likely because they're checking out the latest offers, announcements, etc. on their . . .

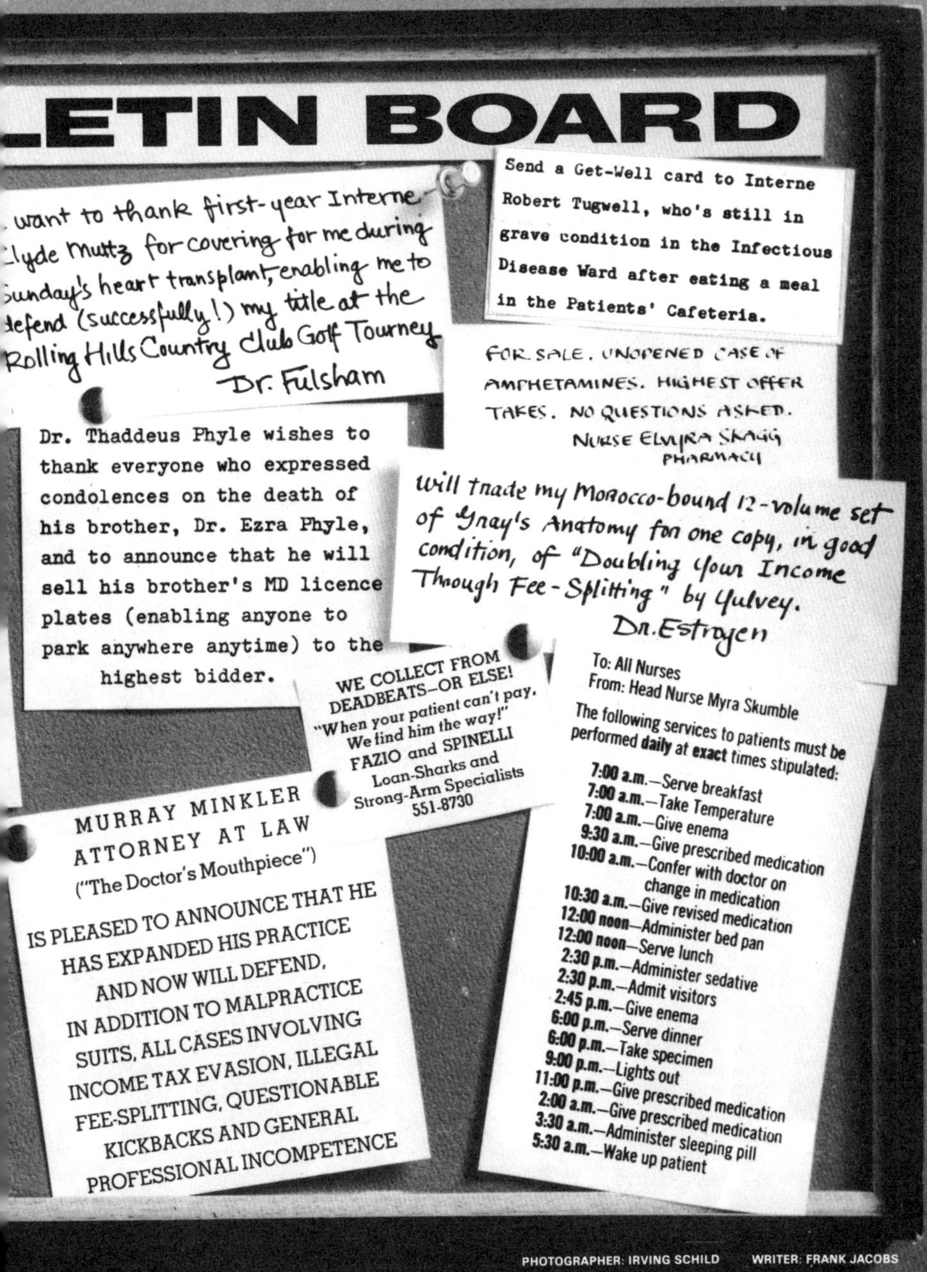

LETIN BOARD
want to thank first-year Interne Clyde Mutz for covering for me during Sunday's heart transplant, enabling me to defend (successfully!) my title at the Rolling Hills Country Club Golf Tourney
Dr. Fulsham
Send a Get-Well card to Interne Robert Tugwell, who's still in grave condition in the Infectious Disease Ward after eating a meal in the Patients' Cafeteria.
FOR SALE. UNOPENED CASE OF AMPHETAMINES. HIGHEST OFFER TAKES. NO QUESTIONS ASKED.
NURSE ELVIRA SKAGG
PHARMACY
Dr. Thaddeus Phyle wishes to thank everyone who expressed condolences on the death of his brother, Dr. Ezra Phyle, and to announce that he will sell his brother's MD licence plates (enabling anyone to park anywhere anytime) to the highest bidder.
Will trade my Morocco-bound 12-volume set of Gray's Anatomy for one copy, in good condition, of "Doubling Your Income Through Fee-Splitting" by Yulvey.
Dr. Estrogen
WE COLLECT FROM DEADBEATS—OR ELSE!
"When your patient can't pay, We find him the way!"
FAZIO and SPINELLI
Loan-Sharks and Strong-Arm Specialists
551-8730
To: All Nurses
From: Head Nurse Myra Skumble
The following services to patients must be performed daily at exact times stipulated:
7:00 a.m.—Serve breakfast
7:00 a.m.—Take Temperature
7:00 a.m.—Give enema
9:30 a.m.—Give prescribed medication
10:00 a.m.—Confer with doctor on change in medication
10:30 a.m.—Give revised medication
12:00 noon—Administer bed pan
12:00 noon—Serve lunch
2:30 p.m.—Administer sedative
2:30 p.m.—Admit visitors
2:45 p.m.—Give enema
6:00 p.m.—Serve dinner
6:00 p.m.—Take specimen
9:00 p.m.—Lights out
11:00 p.m.—Give prescribed medication
2:00 a.m.—Give prescribed medication
3:30 a.m.—Administer sleeping pill
5:30 a.m.—Wake up patient
MURRAY MINKLER
ATTORNEY AT LAW
("The Doctor's Mouthpiece")
IS PLEASED TO ANNOUNCE THAT HE HAS EXPANDED HIS PRACTICE AND NOW WILL DEFEND, IN ADDITION TO MALPRACTICE SUITS, ALL CASES INVOLVING INCOME TAX EVASION, ILLEGAL FEE-SPLITTING, QUESTIONABLE KICKBACKS AND GENERAL PROFESSIONAL INCOMPETENCE

PHOTOGRAPHER: IRVING SCHILD   WRITER: FRANK JACOBS

DON MARTIN DEPT.

IN THE ACME RITZ CENTRAL ARMS WALDORF PLAZA HOTEL

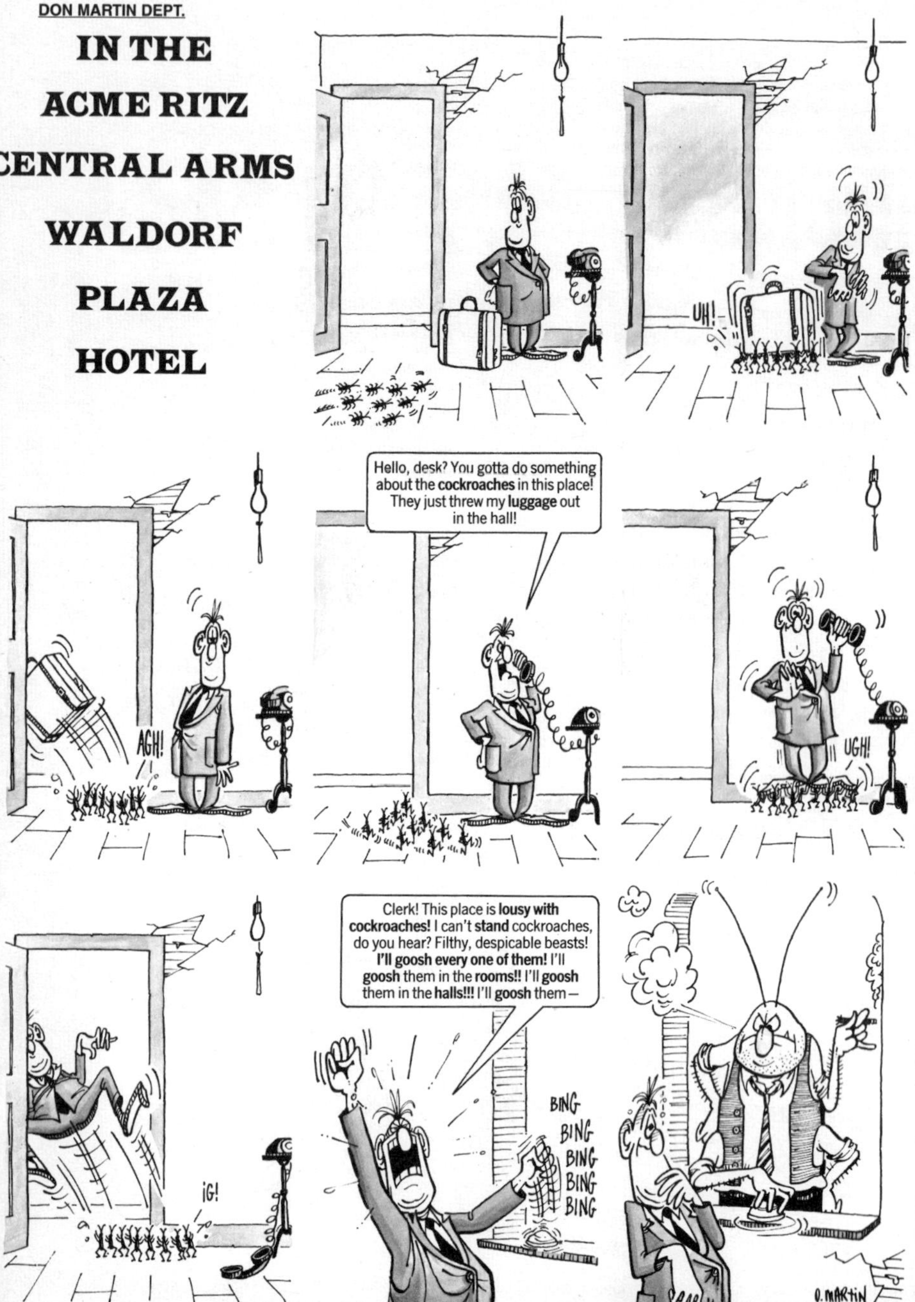
UH!
AGH!
Hello, desk? You gotta do something about the **cockroaches** in this place! They just threw my **luggage** out in the hall!
UGH!
¡G!
Clerk! This place is **lousy with cockroaches!** I can't **stand** cockroaches, do you hear? Filthy, despicable beasts! **I'll goosh every one of them!** I'll **goosh** them in the **rooms!!** I'll **goosh** them in the **halls!!!** I'll **goosh** them –
BING
BING
BING
BING
BING
D. MARTIN

GOONSTRUCK DEPT.

Everyone knows that the world's greatest actors are not in the movies! Nope, they're in arenas around the country! That's right, the world's greatest actors are professional wrestlers! After all, who but the very best of actors could make such a large percentage of the populace believe their preposterous routines are real? This got us to thinking. As long as Hollywood continually insists on redoing old film classics, why not hire these potential Academy Award winners for some honest work! So, join us now in a futuristic stroll down memory lane as MAD begins...

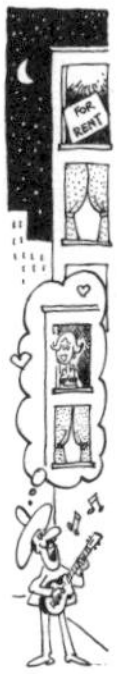
FOR RENT

Recasting Famous Old Movies With Today's Famous Wrestlers

ARTIST: SAM VIVIANO WRITER: J. PRETE

THE GODFATHER starring Bruno Sammartino

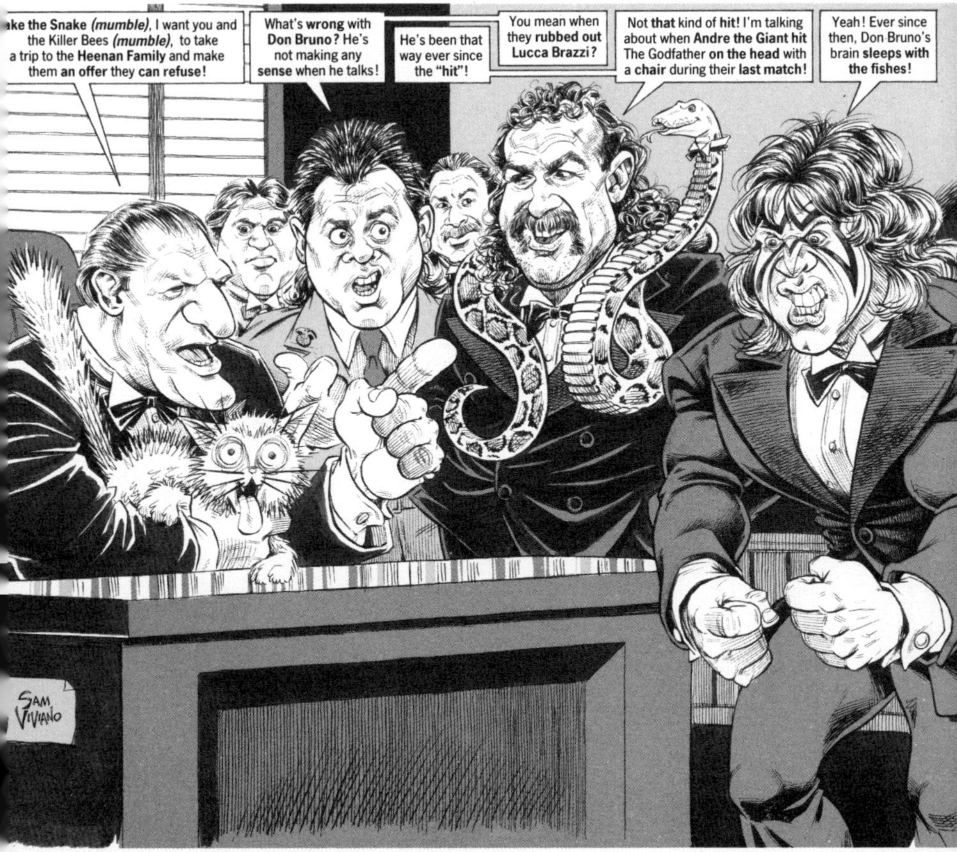
ake the Snake *(mumble)*, I want you and the Killer Bees *(mumble)*, to take a trip to the **Heenan Family** and make them **an offer** they **can refuse**!
What's **wrong** with **Don Bruno?** He's not making any **sense** when he talks!
He's been that way ever since the **"hit"**!
You mean when they **rubbed out Lucca Brazzi?**
Not **that** kind of **hit!** I'm talking about when **Andre the Giant hit** The Godfather **on the head** with a **chair** during their **last match!**
Yeah! Ever since then, Don Bruno's brain **sleeps with the fishes!**
SAM VIVIANO

THE UNTOUCHABLES

starring The Honky Tonk Man, The Hart Foundation, Jimmy "The Mouth of the South" Hart and the Rougeaus

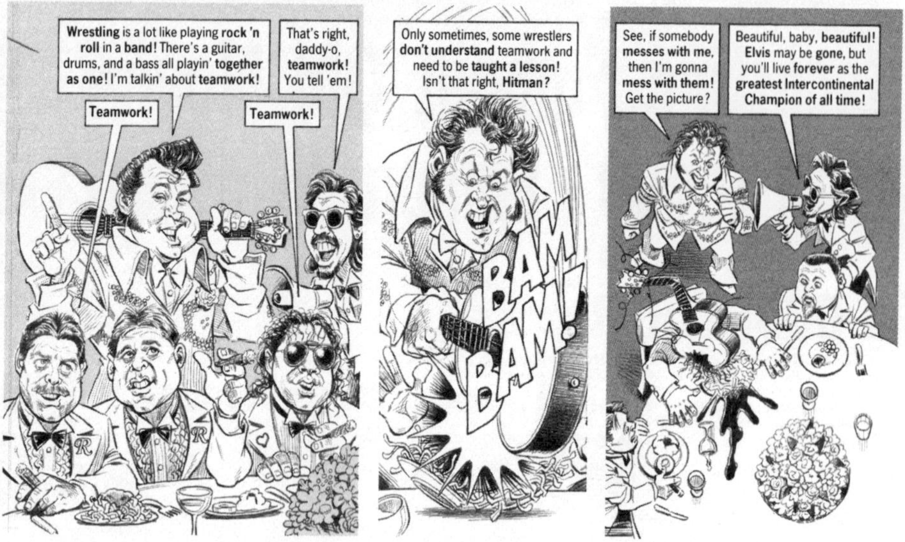

Wrestling is a lot like playing rock 'n roll in a band! There's a guitar, drums, and a bass all playin' together as one! I'm talkin' about teamwork!
That's right, daddy-o, teamwork! You tell 'em!
Teamwork!
Teamwork!
Only sometimes, some wrestlers don't understand teamwork and need to be taught a lesson! Isn't that right, Hitman?
BAM BAM BAM!
See, if somebody messes with me, then I'm gonna mess with them! Get the picture?
Beautiful, baby, beautiful! Elvis may be gone, but you'll live forever as the greatest Intercontinental Champion of all time!

GOOD MORNING, VIETNAM

starring Bobby "The Brain" Heenan

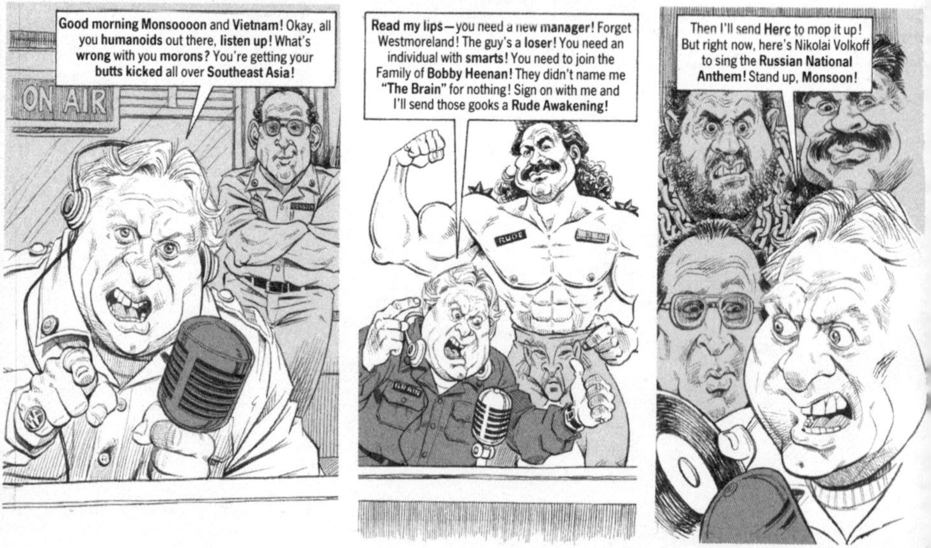

Good morning Monsoooon and Vietnam! Okay, all you humanoids out there, listen up! What's wrong with you morons? You're getting your butts kicked all over Southeast Asia!
ON AIR
Read my lips—you need a new manager! Forget Westmoreland! The guy's a loser! You need an individual with smarts! You need to join the Family of Bobby Heenan! They didn't name me "The Brain" for nothing! Sign on with me and I'll send those gooks a Rude Awakening!
RUDE
BRAIN
Then I'll send Herc to mop it up! But right now, here's Nikolai Volkoff to sing the Russian National Anthem! Stand up, Monsoon!

NO WAY OUT

STARRING Nikolai Volkoff AND Slick

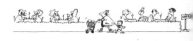

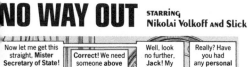

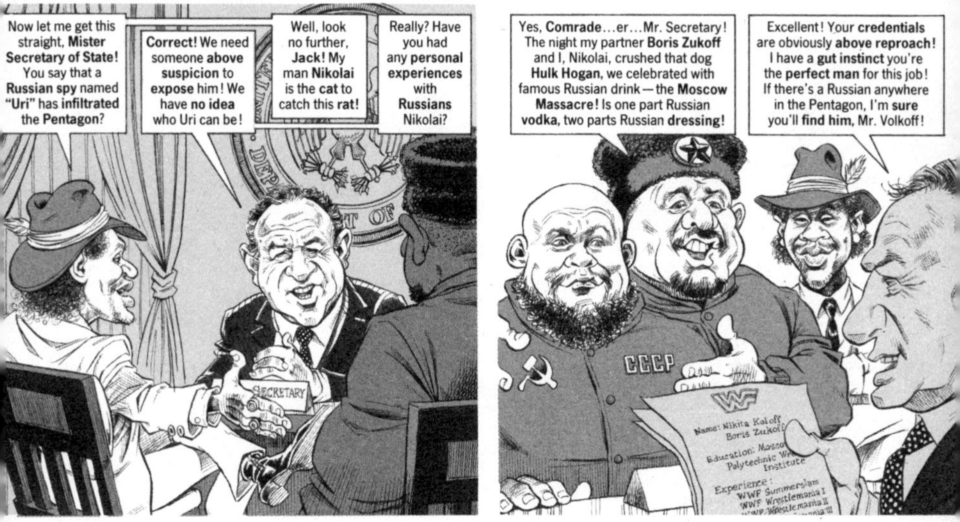

Now let me get this straight, **Mister Secretary of State**! You say that a **Russian spy** named **"Uri"** has **infiltrated** the **Pentagon**?
Correct! We need someone **above suspicion** to **expose** him! We have **no idea** who Uri can be!
Well, look no further, **Jack**! My man **Nikolai** is the **cat** to catch this **rat**!
Really? Have you had any **personal experiences** with **Russians** Nikolai?
SECRETARY
Yes, **Comrade**…er…Mr. Secretary! The night my partner **Boris Zukoff** and I, Nikolai, crushed that dog **Hulk Hogan**, we celebrated with famous Russian drink—the **Moscow Massacre**! Is one part Russian **vodka**, two parts Russian **dressing**!
Excellent! Your **credentials** are obviously **above reproach**! I have a **gut instinct** you're the **perfect man** for this job! If there's a Russian anywhere in the Pentagon, I'm **sure** you'll **find him**, Mr. Volkoff!
CCCP
WF
Name: Nikita Koloff
Boris Zukoff
Experience:
WWF Summerslam
WWF Wrestlemania I

TRADING PLACES

STARRING JESSE "THE BODY" VENTURA, VINCE McMAHON, TED "THE MILLION DOLLAR MAN" DIBIASE AND THE JUNK YARD DOG

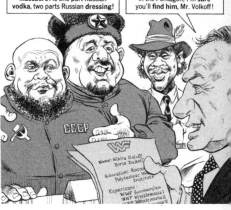

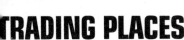

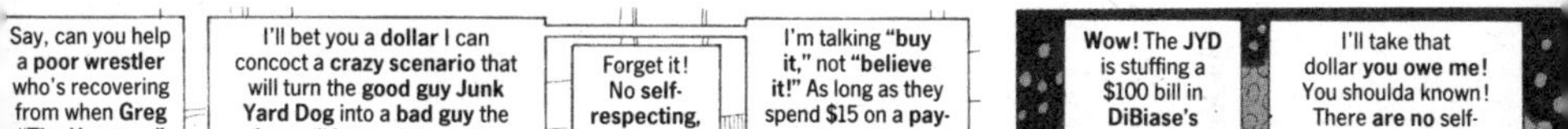

Say, can you help a **poor wrestler** who's recovering from when **Greg "The Hammer" Valentine** did him in with a **Figure Four Leglock**?
I'll bet you a **dollar** I can concoct a **crazy scenario** that will turn the **good guy Junk Yard Dog** into a **bad guy** the fans will **hate**, while, at the same time, turning the **hated Million Dollar Man** into a **good guy** fans **adore**! All in **one week**!
Forget it! No **self-respecting, intelligent** wrestling fan will **believe it**!
I'm talking **"buy it,"** not **"believe it!"** As long as they spend $15 on a **pay-per-view**, who cares **what** they believe!
It's a bet, McMahon!
Wow! The **JYD** is stuffing a **$100 bill** in **DiBiase's mouth** and the fans are **booing**! What a **turnabout**!
I'll take that dollar **you owe me**! You shoulda known! There **are no** self-respecting, **intelligent** wrestling fans—only **genetic mutants** who **swallow anything**!

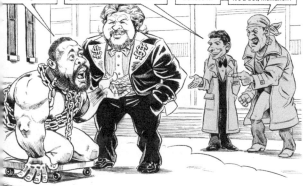

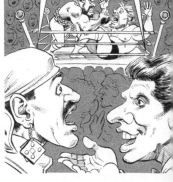

BIG

starring George "The Animal" Steele

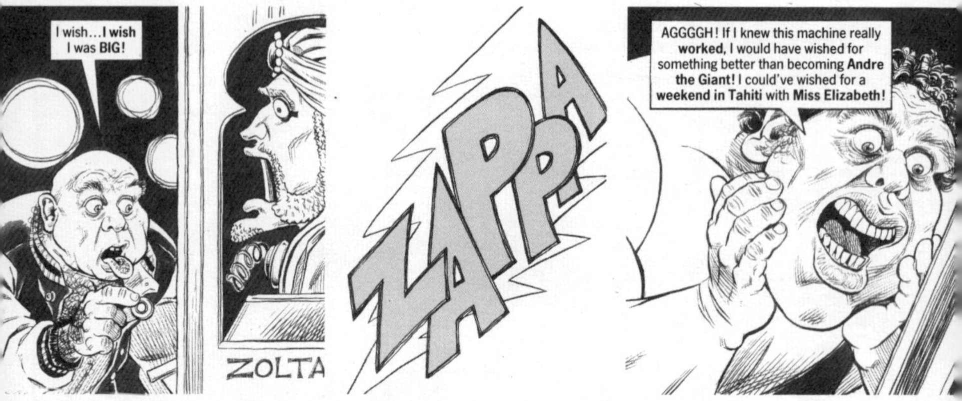
I wish...I wish I was BIG!
ZOLTA
ZAPPA
AGGGGH! If I knew this machine really worked, I would have wished for something better than becoming Andre the Giant! I could've wished for a weekend in Tahiti with Miss Elizabeth!

CASABLANCA

starring Hulk Hogan, Randy "Macho Man" Savage, Miss Elizabeth and Mr. Fuji

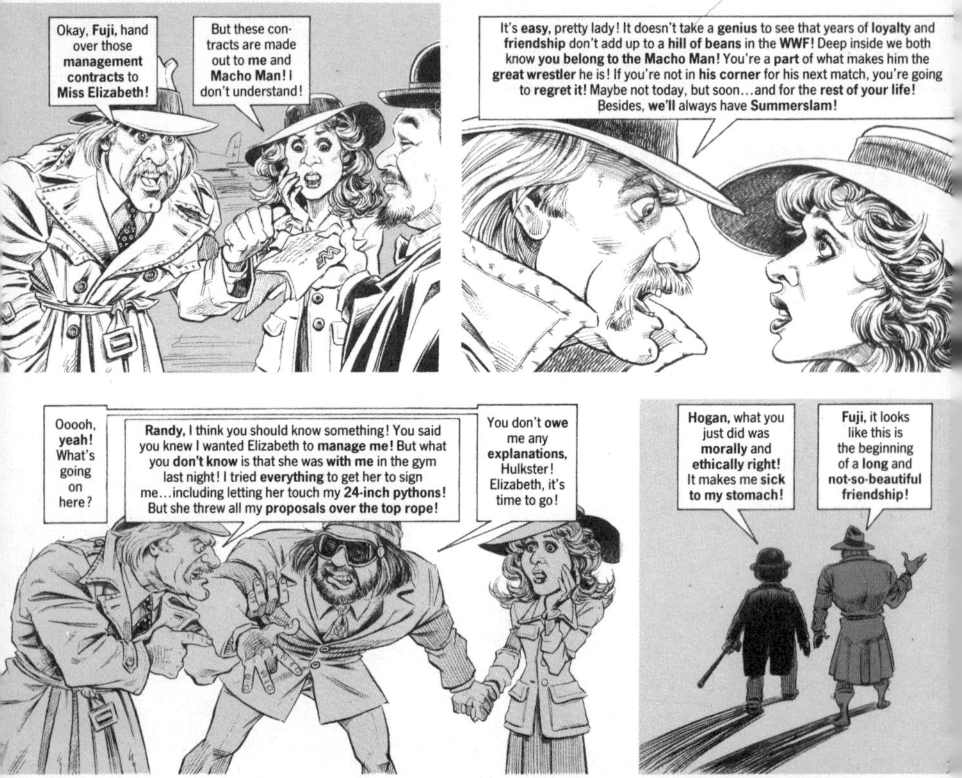
Okay, Fuji, hand over those management contracts to Miss Elizabeth!
But these contracts are made out to me and Macho Man! I don't understand!
It's easy, pretty lady! It doesn't take a genius to see that years of loyalty and friendship don't add up to a hill of beans in the WWF! Deep inside we both know you belong to the Macho Man! You're a part of what makes him the great wrestler he is! If you're not in his corner for his next match, you're going to regret it! Maybe not today, but soon...and for the rest of your life! Besides, we'll always have Summerslam!
Ooooh, yeah! What's going on here?
Randy, I think you should know something! You said you knew I wanted Elizabeth to manage me! But what you don't know is that she was with me in the gym last night! I tried everything to get her to sign me...including letting her touch my 24-inch pythons! But she threw all my proposals over the top rope!
You don't owe me any explanations, Hulkster! Elizabeth, it's time to go!
Hogan, what you just did was morally and ethically right! It makes me sick to my stomach!
Fuji, it looks like this is the beginning of a long and not-so-beautiful friendship!

A DRYER SENSE OF HUMOR DEPT.

DRAMA ON PAGE 29

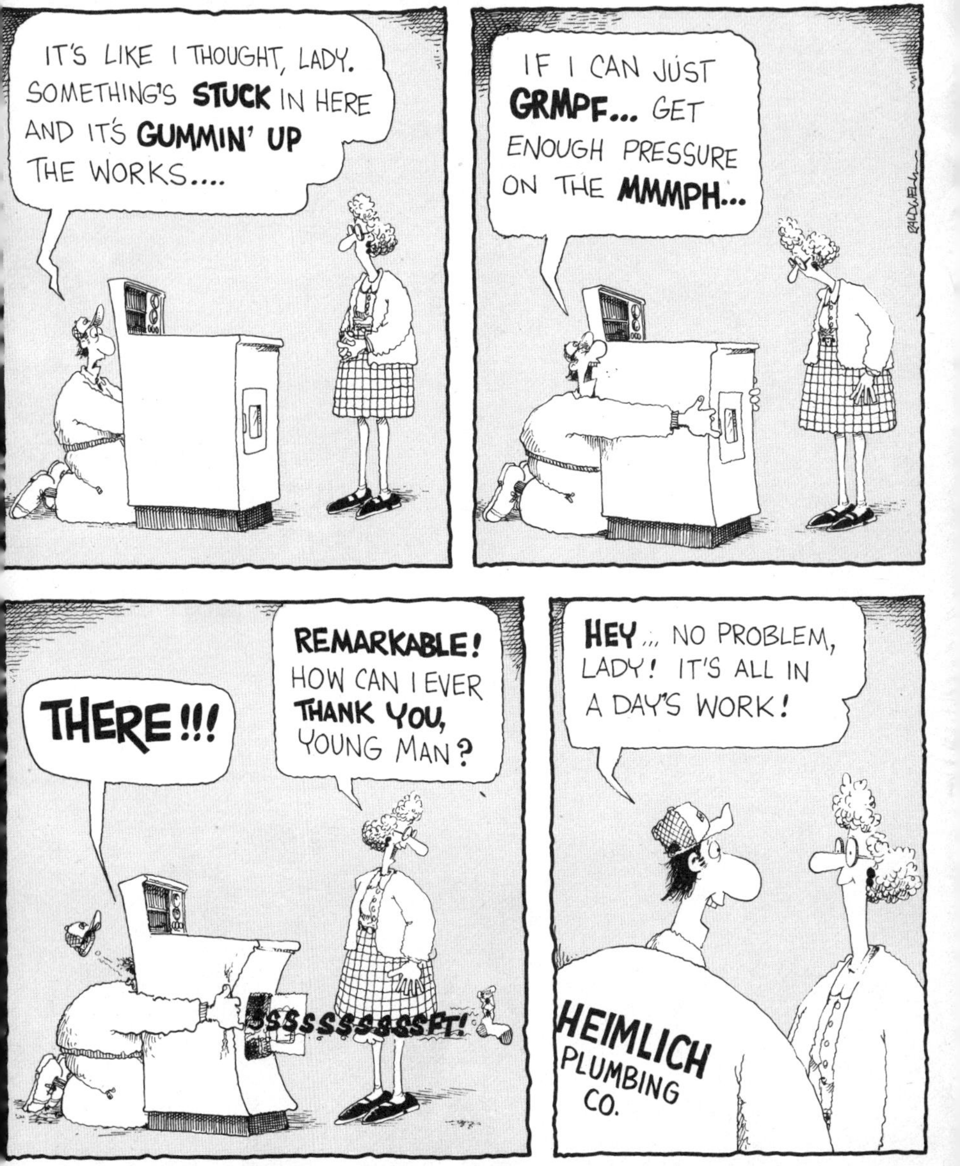
IT'S LIKE I THOUGHT, LADY. SOMETHING'S STUCK IN HERE AND IT'S GUMMIN' UP THE WORKS....
IF I CAN JUST GRMPF... GET ENOUGH PRESSURE ON THE MMMPH...
THERE!!!
REMARKABLE! HOW CAN I EVER THANK YOU, YOUNG MAN?
SSSSSSSSSSSPT!
HEY... NO PROBLEM, LADY! IT'S ALL IN A DAY'S WORK!
HEIMLICH PLUMBING CO.

PUT YOUR FUNNY WHERE YOUR MOUTH IS! DEPT.

Christmas Shopping Time, Christmas Gift-Giving Time and Christmas Vacatio Time are almost upon us . . . which means we're in for it! Namely, we're in f

MORE SNAPPY ANSWERS

ARTIST: PAUL COKER, J

AT A CHRISTMAS OFFICE PARTY...

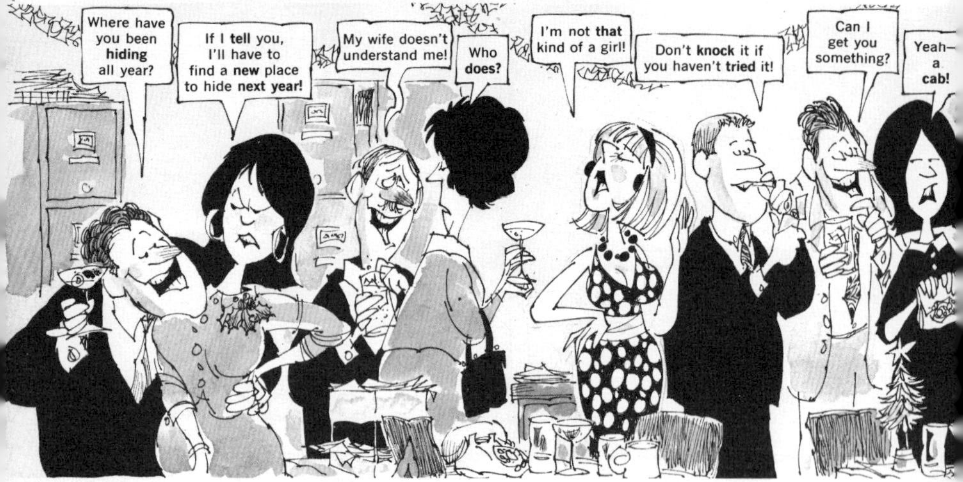

Where have you been hiding all year?
If I tell you, I'll have to find a new place to hide next year!
My wife doesn't understand me!
Who does?
I'm not that kind of a girl!
Don't knock it if you haven't tried it!
Can I get you something?
Yeah— a cab!

WHILE CHRISTMAS SHOPPING...

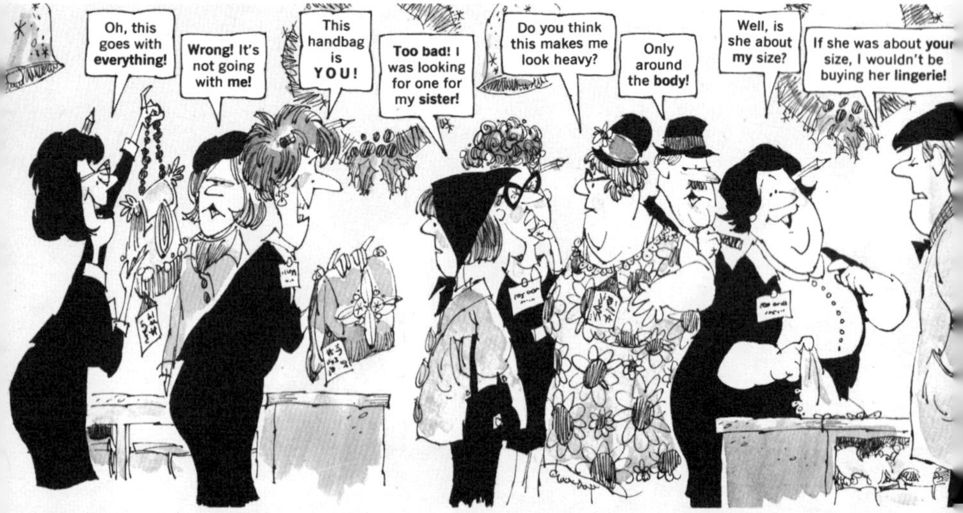

Oh, this goes with everything!
Wrong! It's not going with me!
This handbag is YOU!
Too bad! I was looking for one for my sister!
Do you think this makes me look heavy?
Only around the body!
Well, is she about my size?
If she was about your size, I wouldn't be buying her lingerie!

nother heaping helping of those sickening "Old Clichés," And so, once again, IAD comes to the rescue of cliché-sufferers. Now you can fight back with . . .

TO THOSE OLD CLICHES

RITER: STAN HART

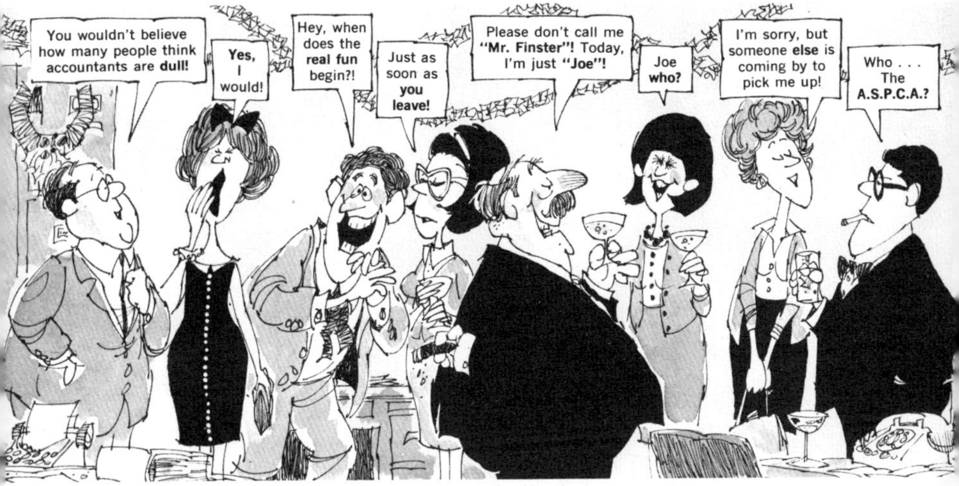

You wouldn't believe how many people think accountants are **dull!**
Yes, I would!
Hey, when does the **real fun** begin?!
Just as soon as **you leave!**
Please don't call me **"Mr. Finster"!** Today, I'm just **"Joe"!**
Joe **who?**
I'm sorry, but someone **else** is coming by to pick me up!
Who . . . The **A.S.P.C.A.?**

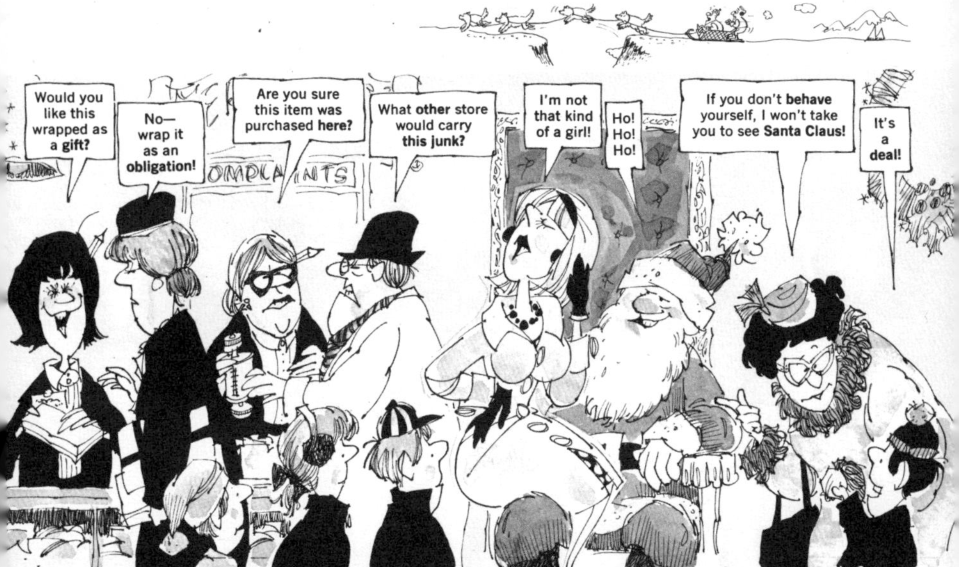

Would you like this wrapped as a **gift?**
No—wrap it as an **obligation!**
Are you sure this item was purchased **here?**
What **other** store would carry **this junk?**
COMPLAINTS
I'm not that kind of a girl!
Ho! Ho! Ho!
If you don't **behave** yourself, I won't take you to see **Santa Claus!**
It's a **deal!**

AT A CHRISTMAS VACATION HOMECOMING...

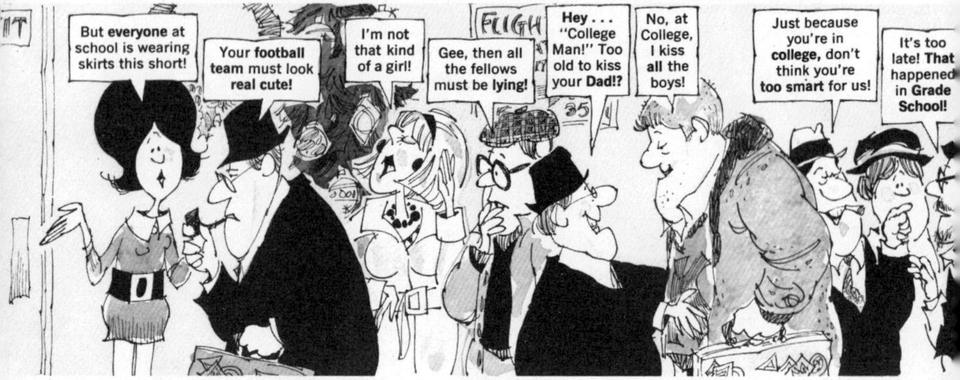

But everyone at school is wearing skirts this short!
Your football team must look real cute!
I'm not that kind of a girl!
Gee, then all the fellows must be lying!
Hey... "College Man!" Too old to kiss your Dad!?
No, at College, I kiss all the boys!
Just because you're in college, don't think you're too smart for us!
It's too late! That happened in Grade School!

AT A SOUTHERN RESORT...

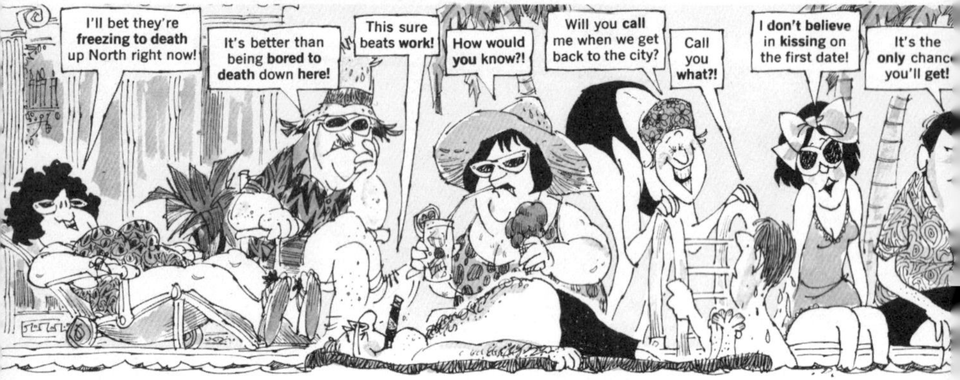

I'll bet they're freezing to death up North right now!
It's better than being bored to death down here!
This sure beats work!
How would you know?!
Will you call me when we get back to the city?
Call you what?!
I don't believe in kissing on the first date!
It's the only chanc you'll get!

WHILE OPENING CHRISTMAS GIFTS...

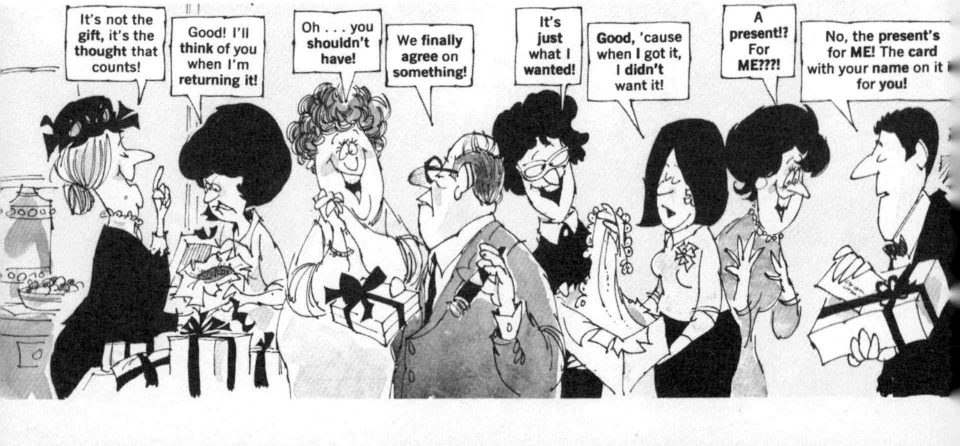

It's not the gift, it's the thought that counts!
Good! I'll think of you when I'm returning it!
Oh... you shouldn't have!
We finally agree on something!
It's just what I wanted!
Good, 'cause when I got it, I didn't want it!
A present!? For ME???!
No, the present's for ME! The card with your name on it i for you!

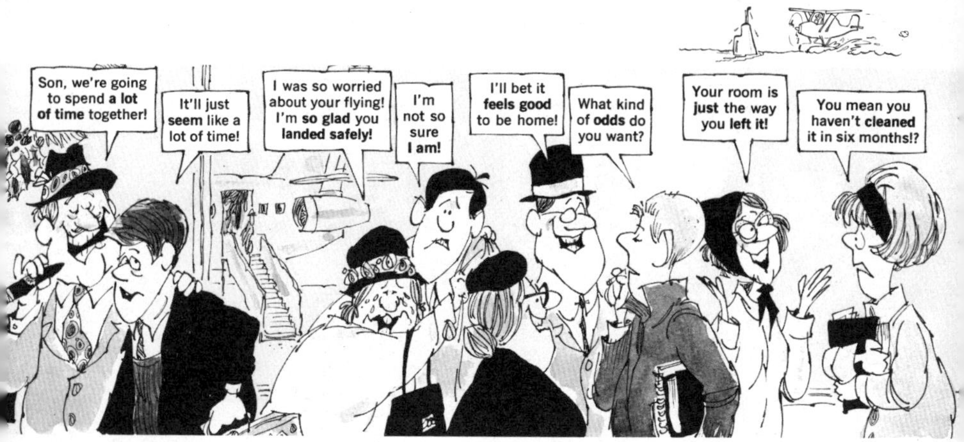
Son, we're going to spend **a lot of time** together!
It'll just **seem** like a lot of time!
I was so worried about your flying! I'm **so glad** you **landed safely!**
I'm not so sure **I am!**
I'll bet it **feels good** to be home!
What kind of **odds** do you want?
Your room is **just** the way you **left it!**
You mean you haven't **cleaned** it in six months!?

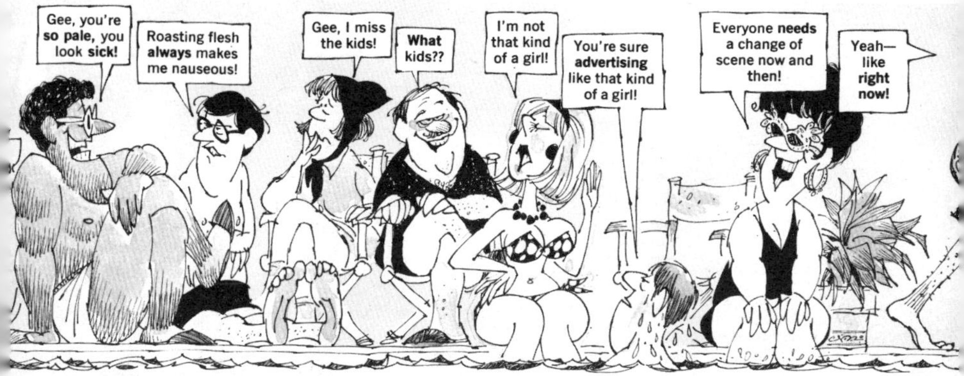
Gee, you're **so pale,** you look **sick!**
Roasting flesh **always** makes me nauseous!
Gee, I miss the kids!
What kids??
I'm not that kind of a girl!
You're sure **advertising** like that kind of a girl!
Everyone **needs** a change of scene now and then!
Yeah— like **right now!**

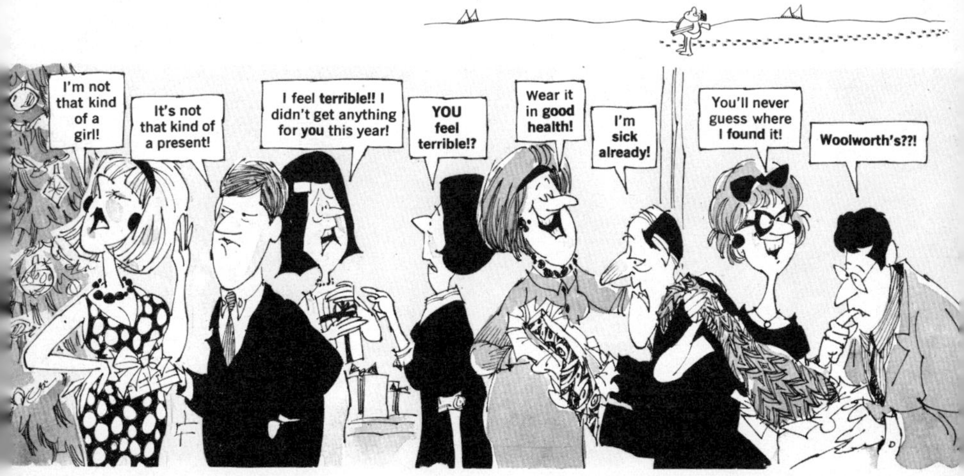
I'm not that kind of a girl!
It's not that kind of a present!
I feel **terrible!!** I didn't get anything for **you** this year!
YOU feel terrible!?
Wear it in **good health!**
I'm **sick already!**
You'll never guess where **I found it!**
Woolworth's??!

STIR CRAZIES DEPT.

A MAD Look At

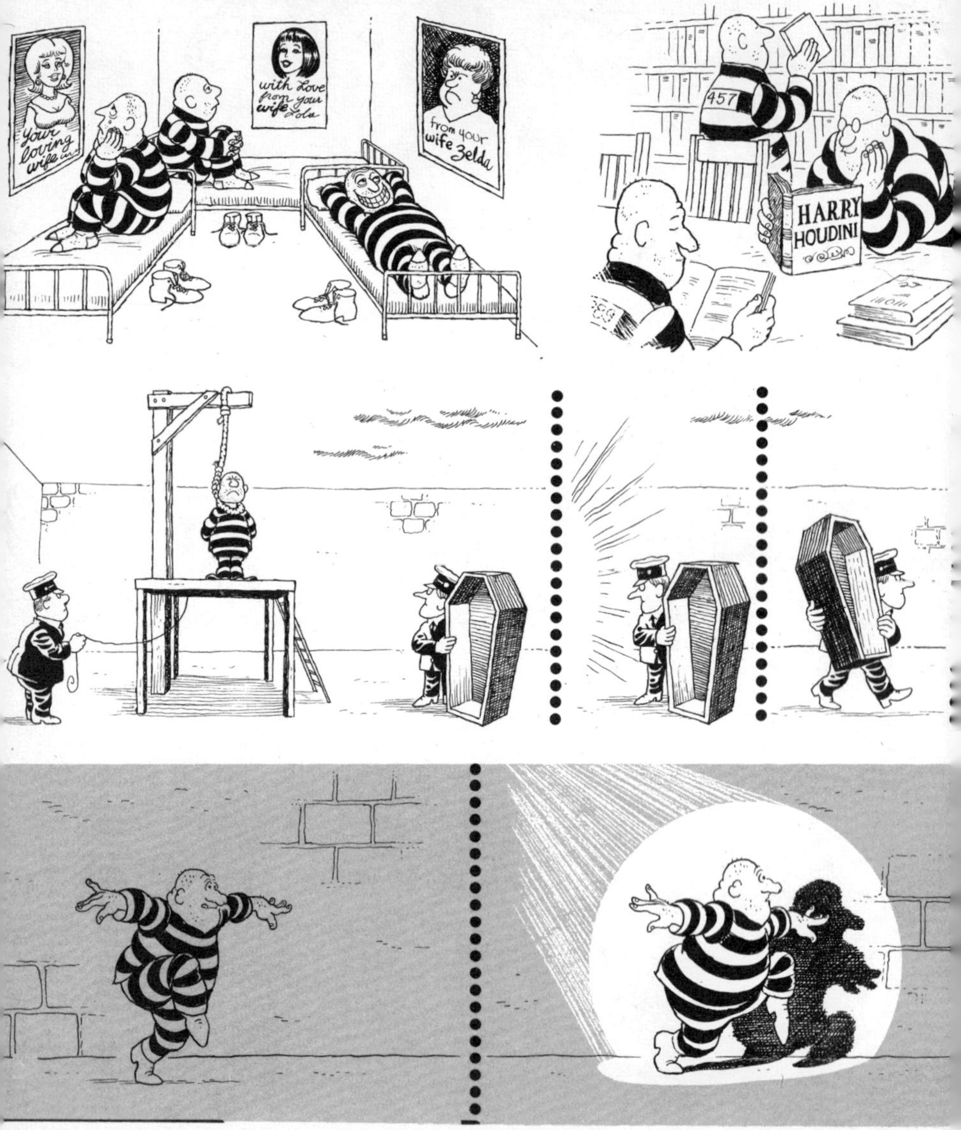

Your loving wife
with Love from your wife Lola
from your wife Zelda
457
HARRY HOUDINI

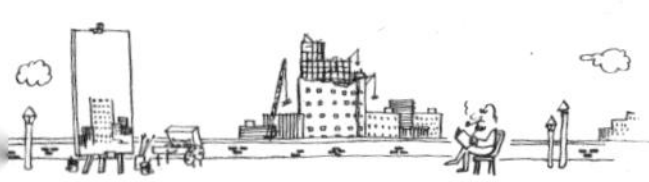

Shut-Ins

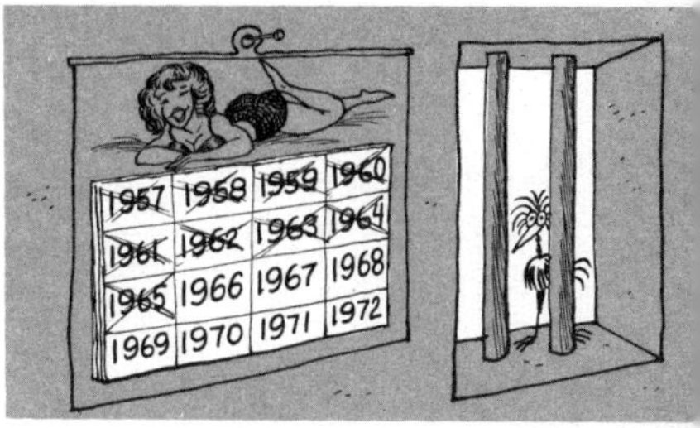

1957 1958 1959 1960
1961 1962 1963 1964
1965 1966 1967 1968
1969 1970 1971 1972

ARTIST & WRITER: AL JAFFEE

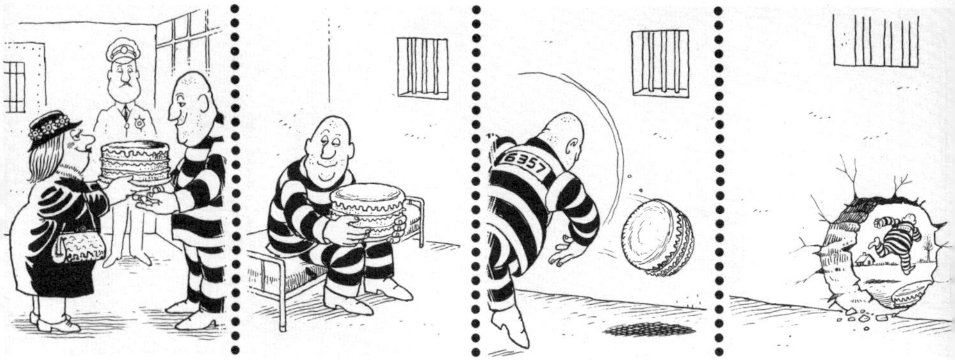

6357

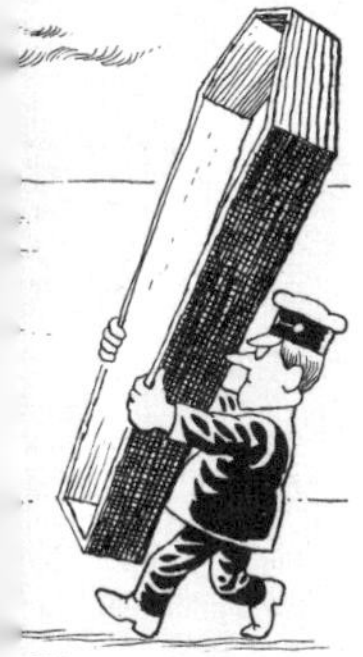

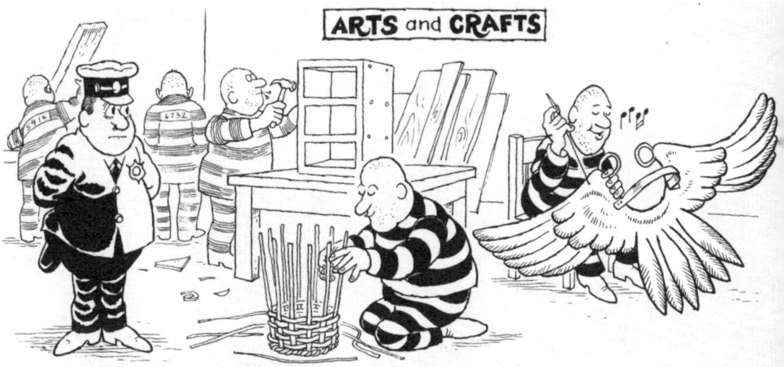

ARTS and CRAFTS
5416
6732

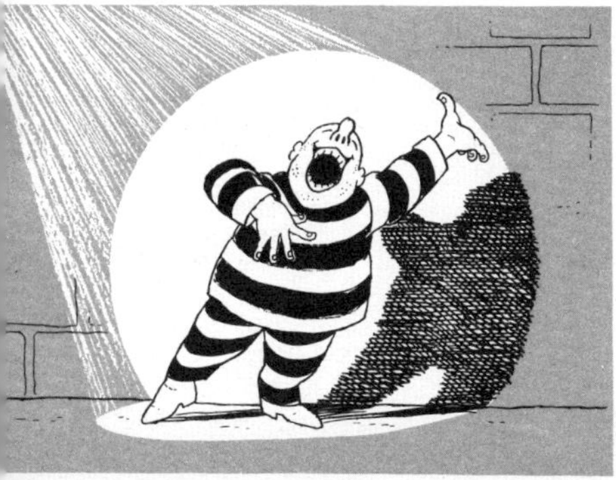

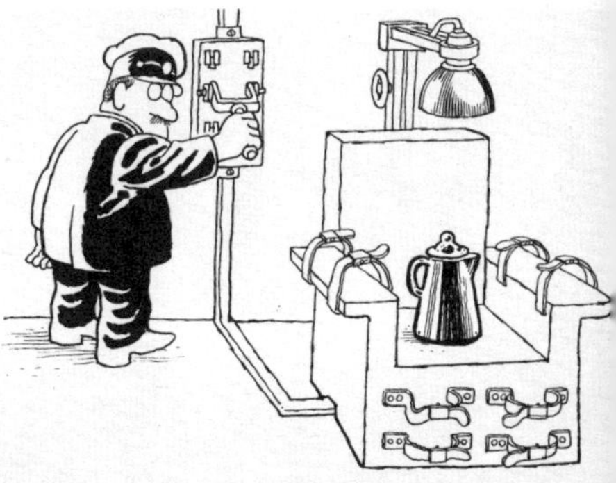

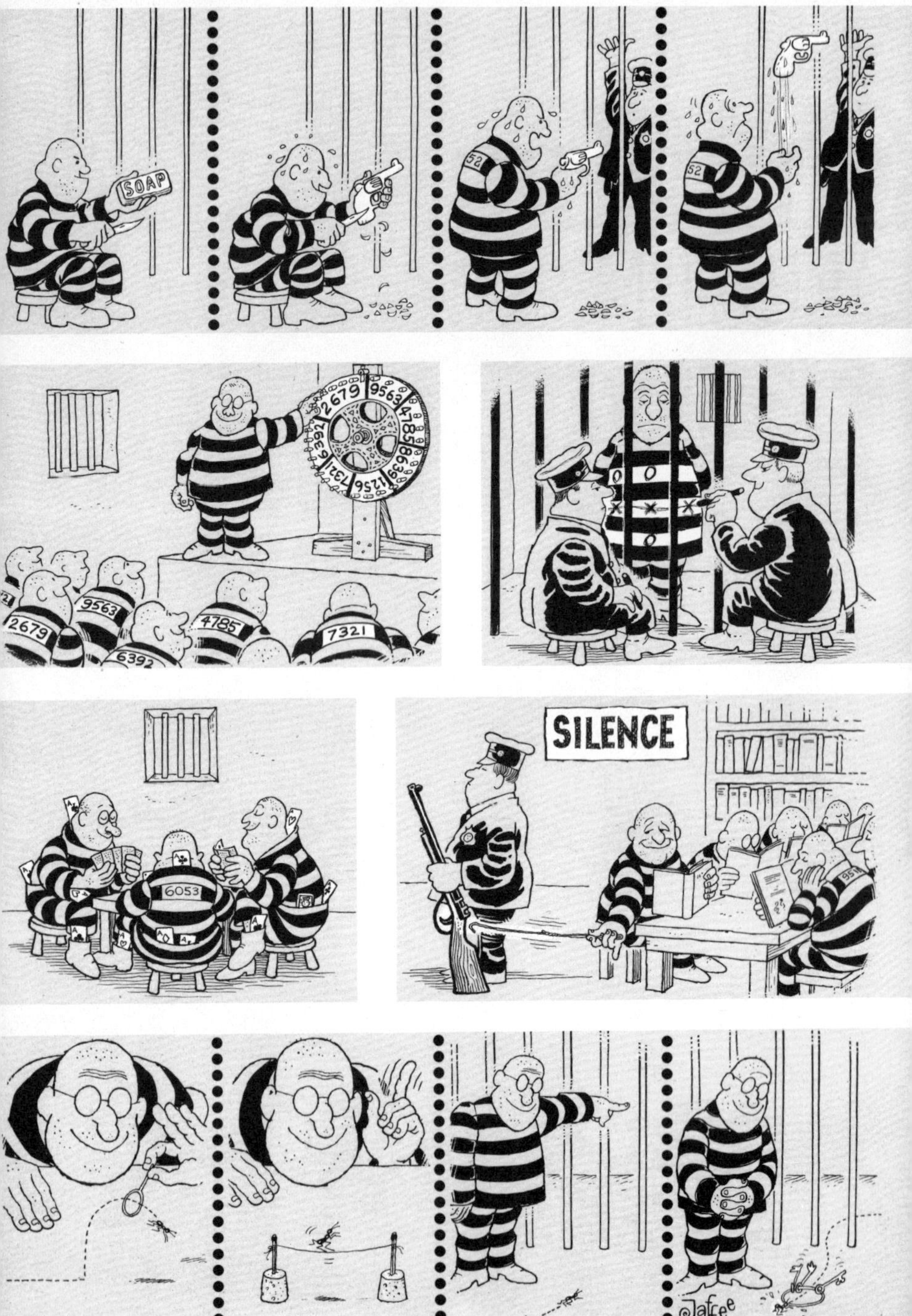
SOAP
52
52
2679
9563
4785
8639
1256
7321
6392
9563
2679
4785
7321
6392
6053
SILENCE
Jaffee

DON MARTIN DEPT.

IN A DEPARTMENT STORE

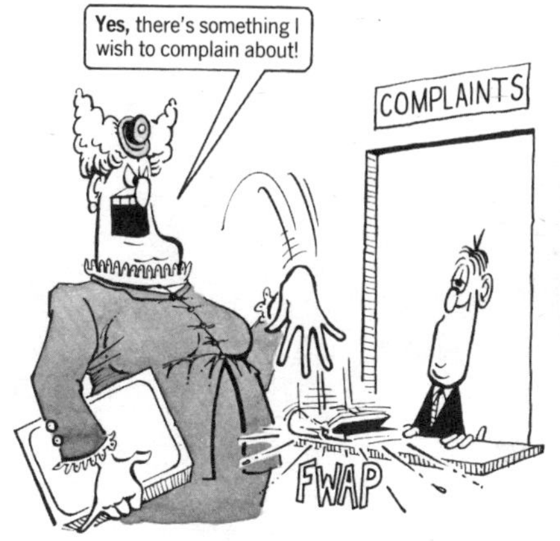
Yes, there's something I wish to complain about!
COMPLAINTS
FWAP

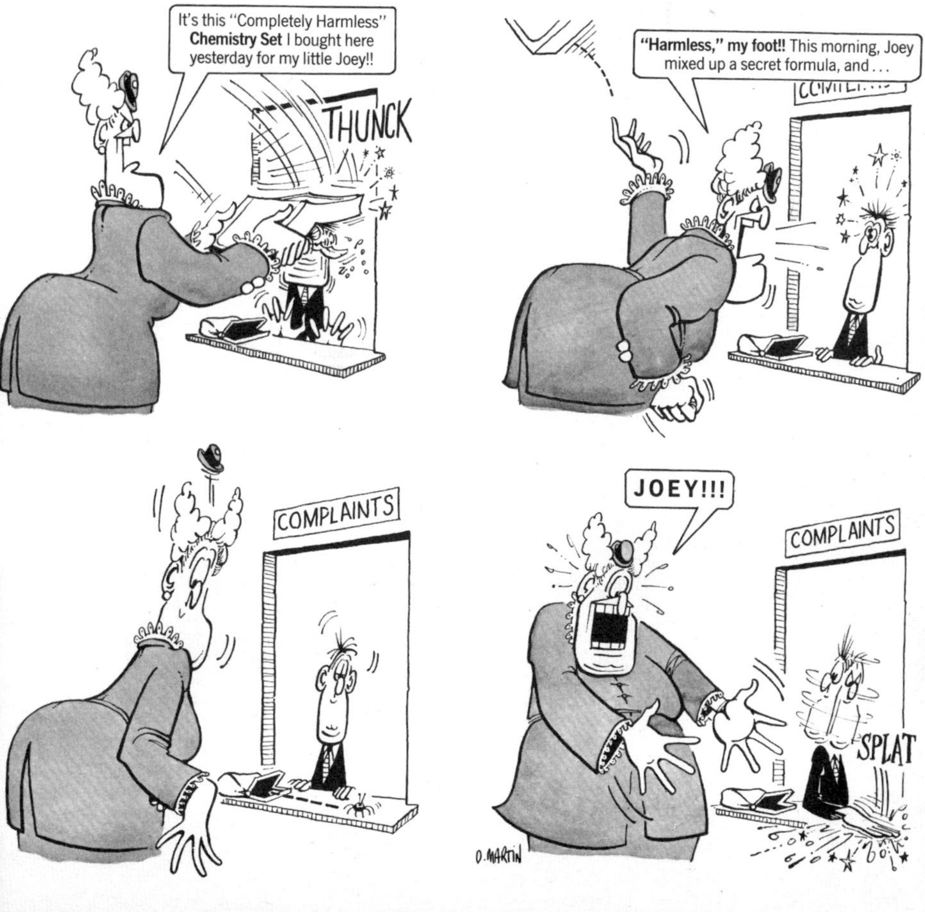
It's this "Completely Harmless" **Chemistry Set** I bought here yesterday for my little Joey!!
THUNCK
"Harmless," my foot!! This morning, Joey mixed up a secret formula, and . . .
COMPLAINTS
JOEY!!!
COMPLAINTS
SPLAT
D. MARTIN

HEAVY MENTAL DEPT.

MAD'S Sure Signs of INSANITY

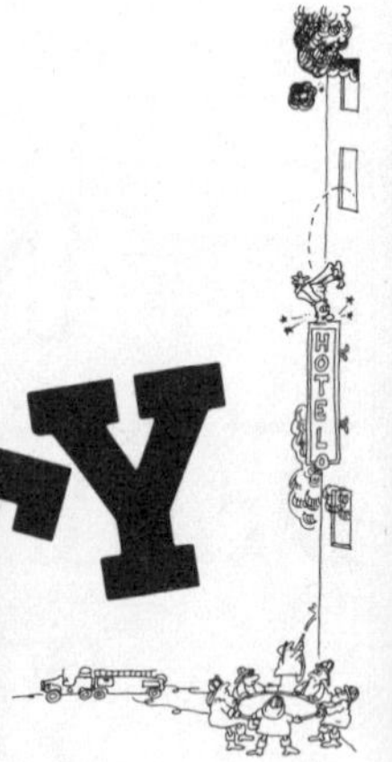

HOTEL

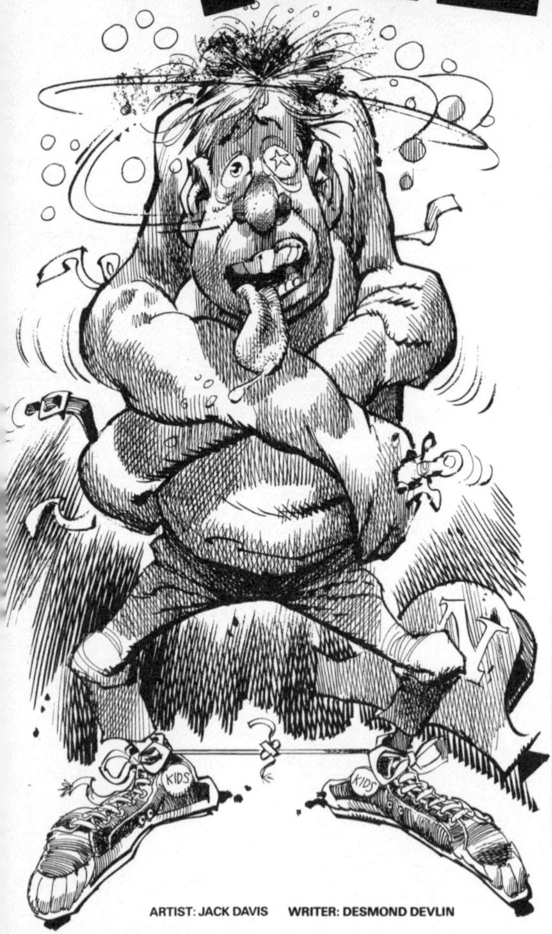

KIDS
KIDS

ARTIST: JACK DAVIS WRITER: DESMOND DEVLIN

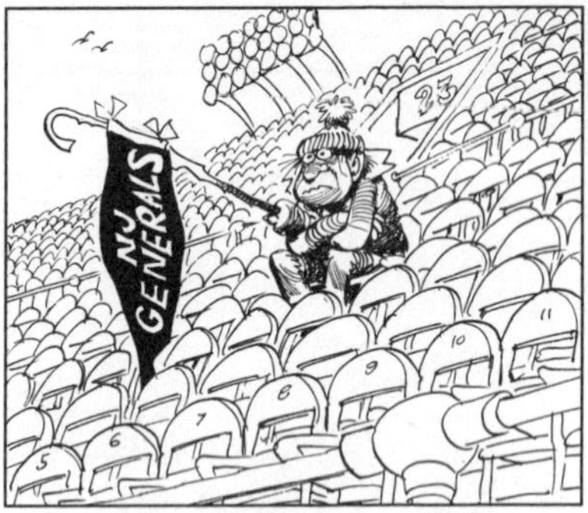

NJ GENERALS
23

...You have a special clause added to your will that leaves your USFL season tickets to your children for many years to come.

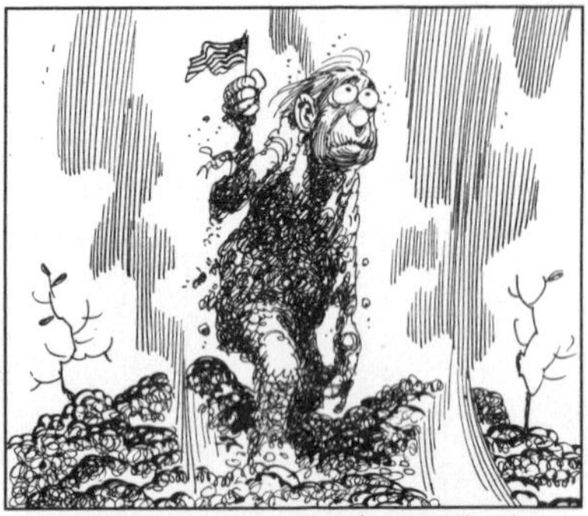

You think it's O.K. to sink $300 billion into a "Star Wars" system that will positively stop 9 out of every 10 nuclear missiles shot at us.

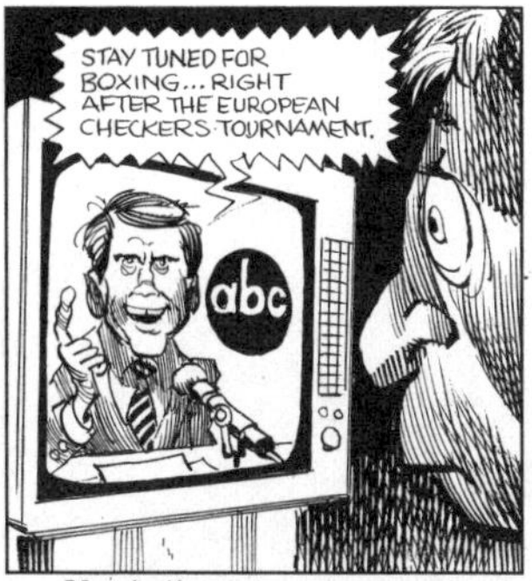
STAY TUNED FOR BOXING... RIGHT AFTER THE EUROPEAN CHECKERS TOURNAMENT.
abc

...You believe the announcers on ABC's "Wide World Of Sports" when they say that the headline boxing match is coming up "soon."

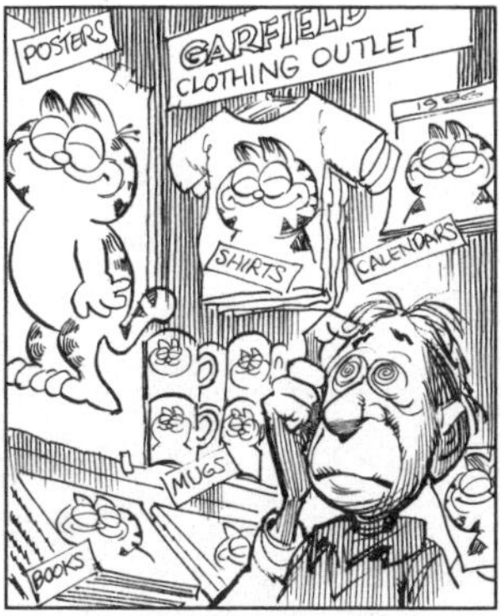
POSTERS
GARFIELD CLOTHING OUTLET
SHIRTS
CALENDARS
MUGS
BOOKS

You don't have any idea where you can find any "Garfield" merchandise.

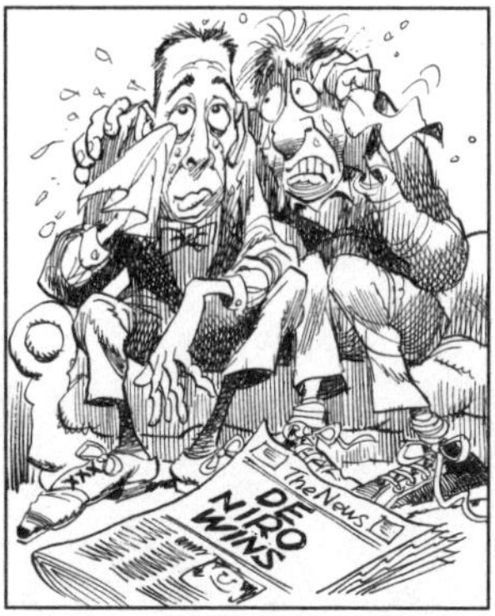
The News
DE NIRO WINS

You're just sick that Pee-Wee Herman was shafted out of an Oscar.

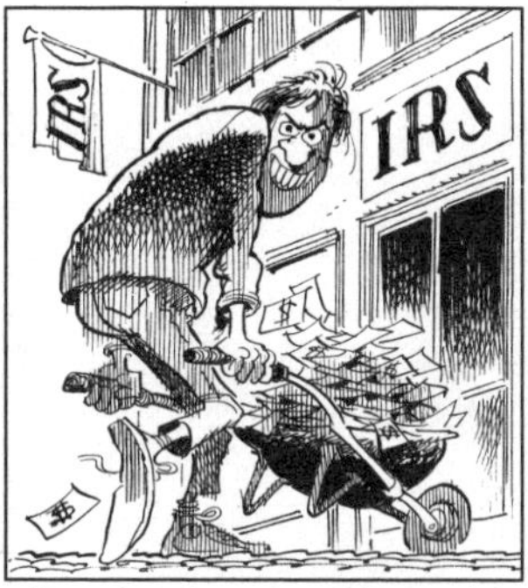
IRS
IRS

You take advantage of the special IRS program that offers to let *them* figure out your taxes for you.

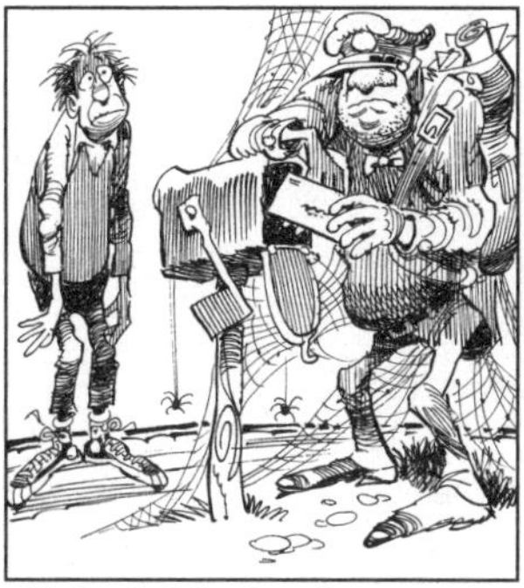

You're glad the zip codes went to 9 digits, because you know that now you'll get fast, efficient service.

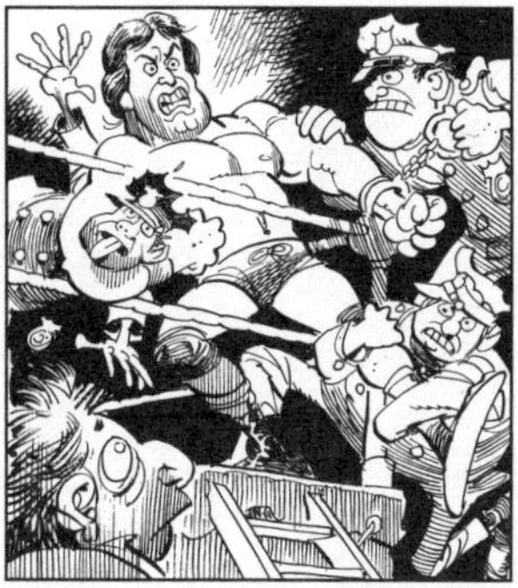

You think the pro-wrestling commission will really come down hard on those flagrant rule breakers.

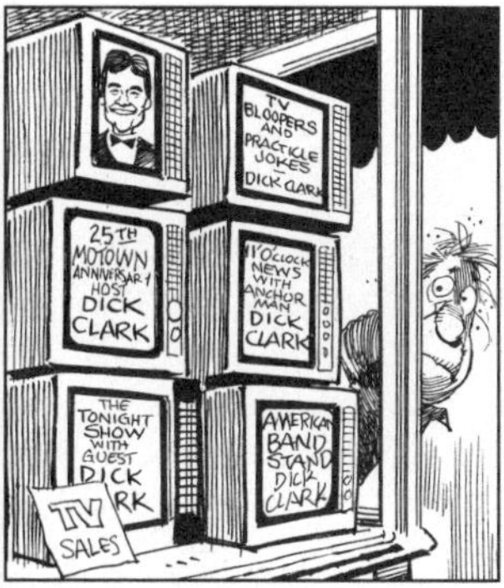
TV BLOOPERS AND PRACTICLE JOKES DICK CLARK
25TH MOTOWN ANNIVERSARY HOST DICK CLARK
11 O'CLOCK NEWS WITH ANCHOR MAN DICK CLARK
THE TONIGHT SHOW WITH GUEST
AMERICAN BANDSTAND DICK CLARK
TV SALES

You feel that Dick Clark doesn't get enough television exposure.

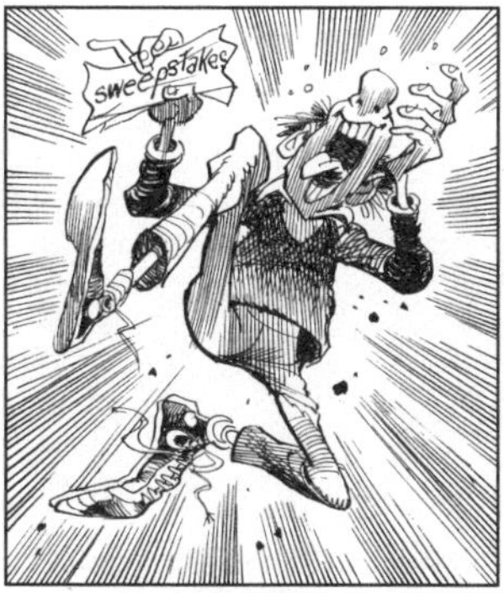
sweepstakes

You believe envelopes that claim; "You may already be a winner!"

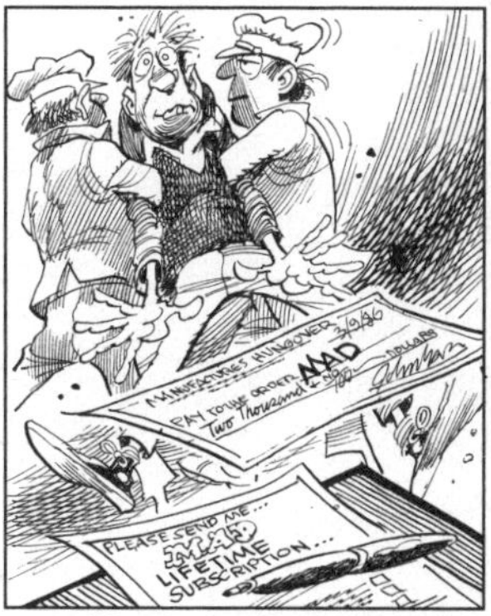
MAD
Two Thousand
PLEASE SEND ME... MAD LIFETIME SUBSCRIPTION...

You *re*-subscribe to MAD.

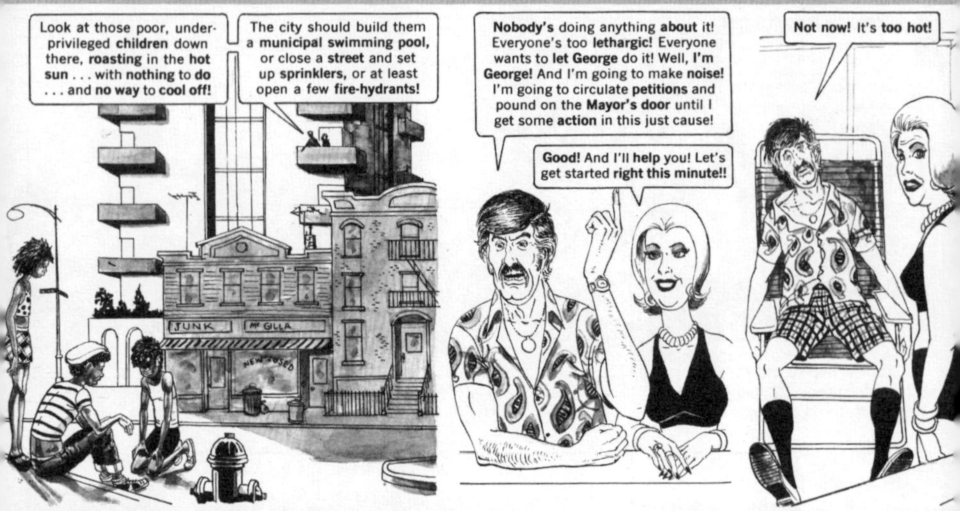
Look at those poor, under-privileged children down there, roasting in the hot sun . . . with nothing to do . . . and no way to cool off!
The city should build them a municipal swimming pool, or close a street and set up sprinklers, or at least open a few fire-hydrants!
JUNK
McGILLA
NEW-USED
Nobody's doing anything about it! Everyone's too lethargic! Everyone wants to let George do it! Well, I'm George! And I'm going to make noise! I'm going to circulate petitions and pound on the Mayor's door until I get some action in this just cause!
Good! And I'll help you! Let's get started right this minute!!
Not now! It's too hot!

BERG'S-EYE VIEW DEPT.

THE LIGHTER SIDE OF... HOT

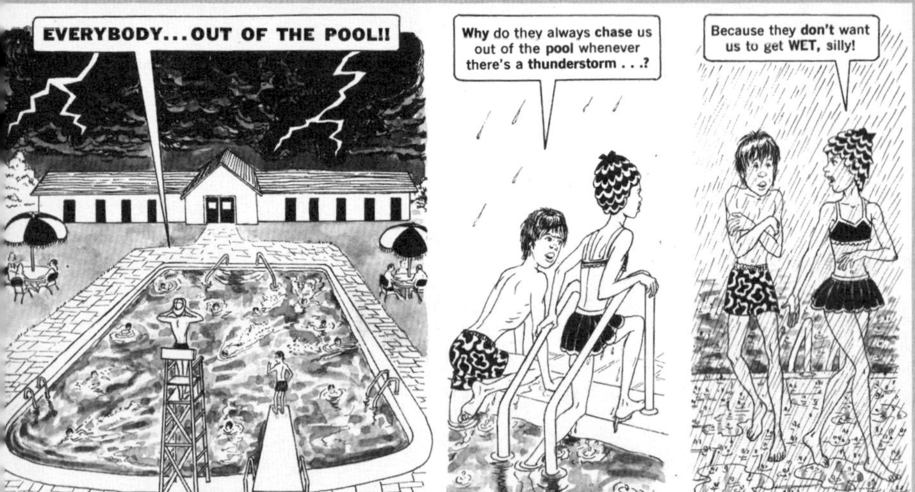
EVERYBODY... OUT OF THE POOL!!
Why do they always chase us out of the pool whenever there's a thunderstorm . . .?
Because they don't want us to get WET, silly!

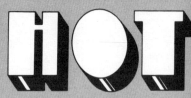

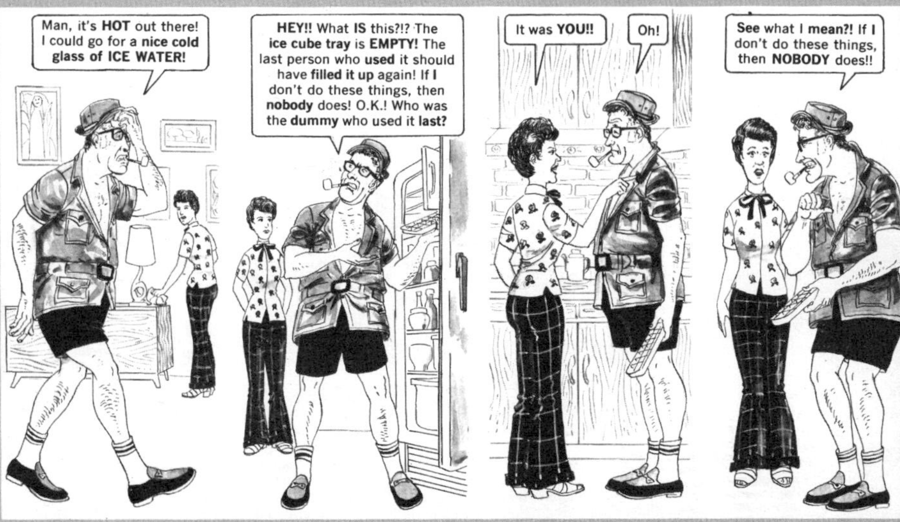

Man, it's HOT out there! I could go for a nice cold glass of ICE WATER!
HEY!! What IS this?!? The ice cube tray is EMPTY! The last person who used it should have filled it up again! If I don't do these things, then nobody does! O.K.! Who was the dummy who used it last?
It was YOU!!
Oh!
See what I mean?! If I don't do these things, then NOBODY does!!

WEATHER

ARTIST & WRITER: DAVE BERG

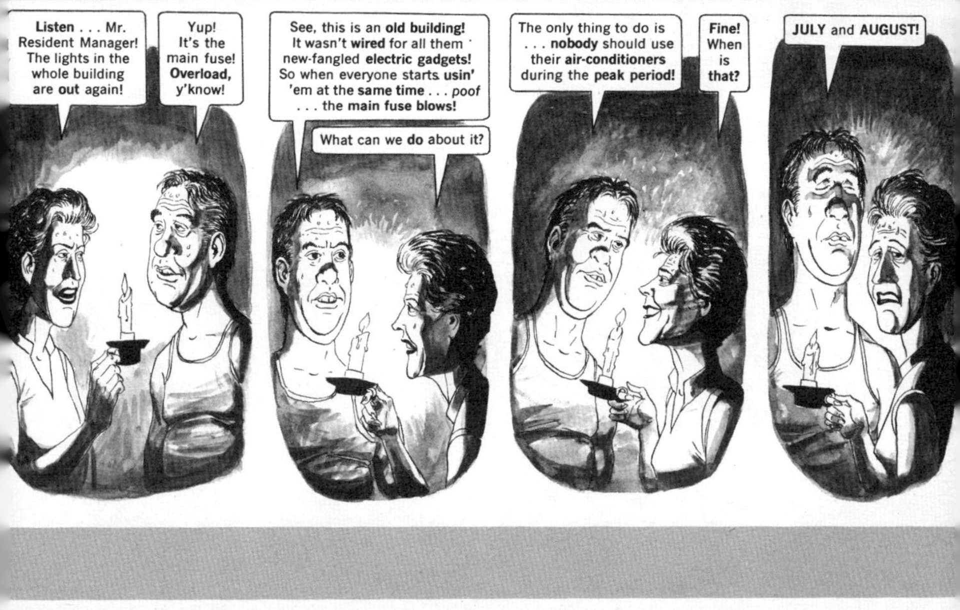

Listen . . . Mr. Resident Manager! The lights in the whole building are out again!
Yup! It's the main fuse! Overload, y'know!
See, this is an old building! It wasn't wired for all them new-fangled electric gadgets! So when everyone starts usin' 'em at the same time . . . poof . . . the main fuse blows!
What can we do about it?
The only thing to do is . . . nobody should use their air-conditioners during the peak period!
Fine! When is that?
JULY and AUGUST!

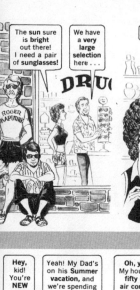

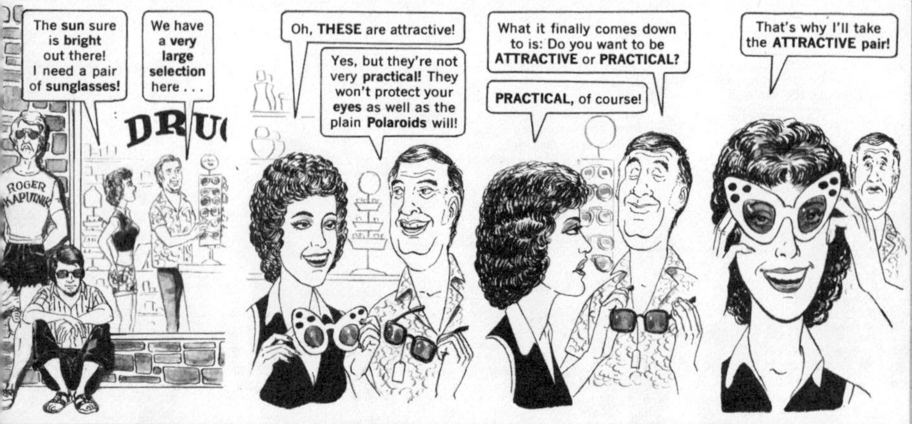
The sun sure is bright out there! I need a pair of sunglasses!
We have a very large selection here . . .
ROGER
Oh, THESE are attractive!
Yes, but they're not very practical! They won't protect your eyes as well as the plain Polaroids will!
What it finally comes down to is: Do you want to be ATTRACTIVE or PRACTICAL?
PRACTICAL, of course!
That's why I'll take the ATTRACTIVE pair!

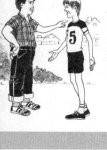

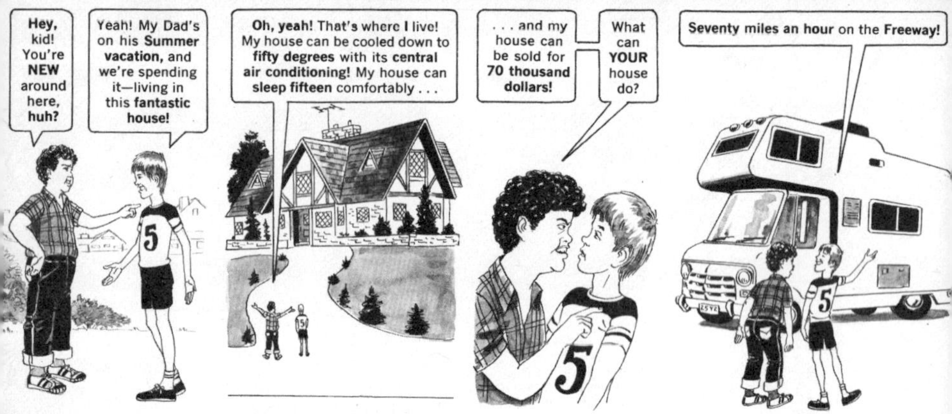
Hey, kid! You're NEW around here, huh?
Yeah! My Dad's on his Summer vacation, and we're spending it—living in this fantastic house!
Oh, yeah! That's where I live! My house can be cooled down to fifty degrees with its central air conditioning! My house can sleep fifteen comfortably . . .
. . . and my house can be sold for 70 thousand dollars!
What can YOUR house do?
Seventy miles an hour on the Freeway!

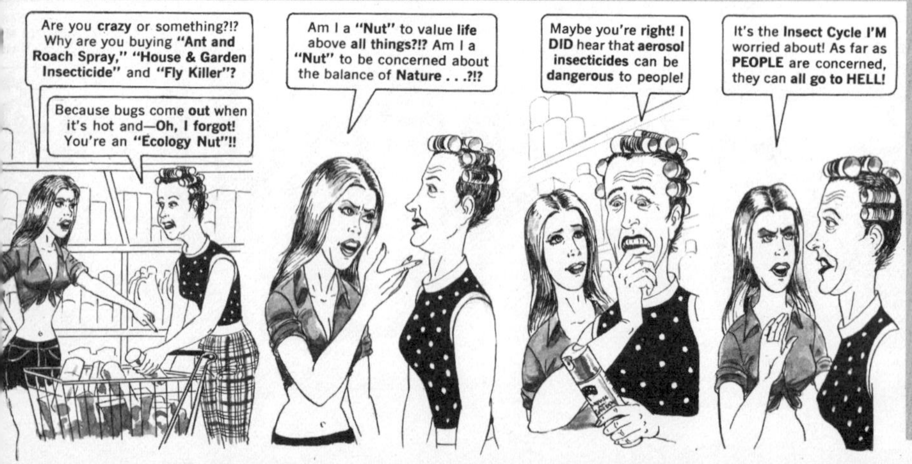
Are you crazy or something?!? Why are you buying "Ant and Roach Spray," "House & Garden Insecticide" and "Fly Killer"?
Because bugs come out when it's hot and—Oh, I forgot! You're an "Ecology Nut"!!
Am I a "Nut" to value life above all things?!? Am I a "Nut" to be concerned about the balance of Nature . . .?!?
Maybe you're right! I DID hear that aerosol insecticides can be dangerous to people!
It's the Insect Cycle I'M worried about! As far as PEOPLE are concerned, they can all go to HELL!

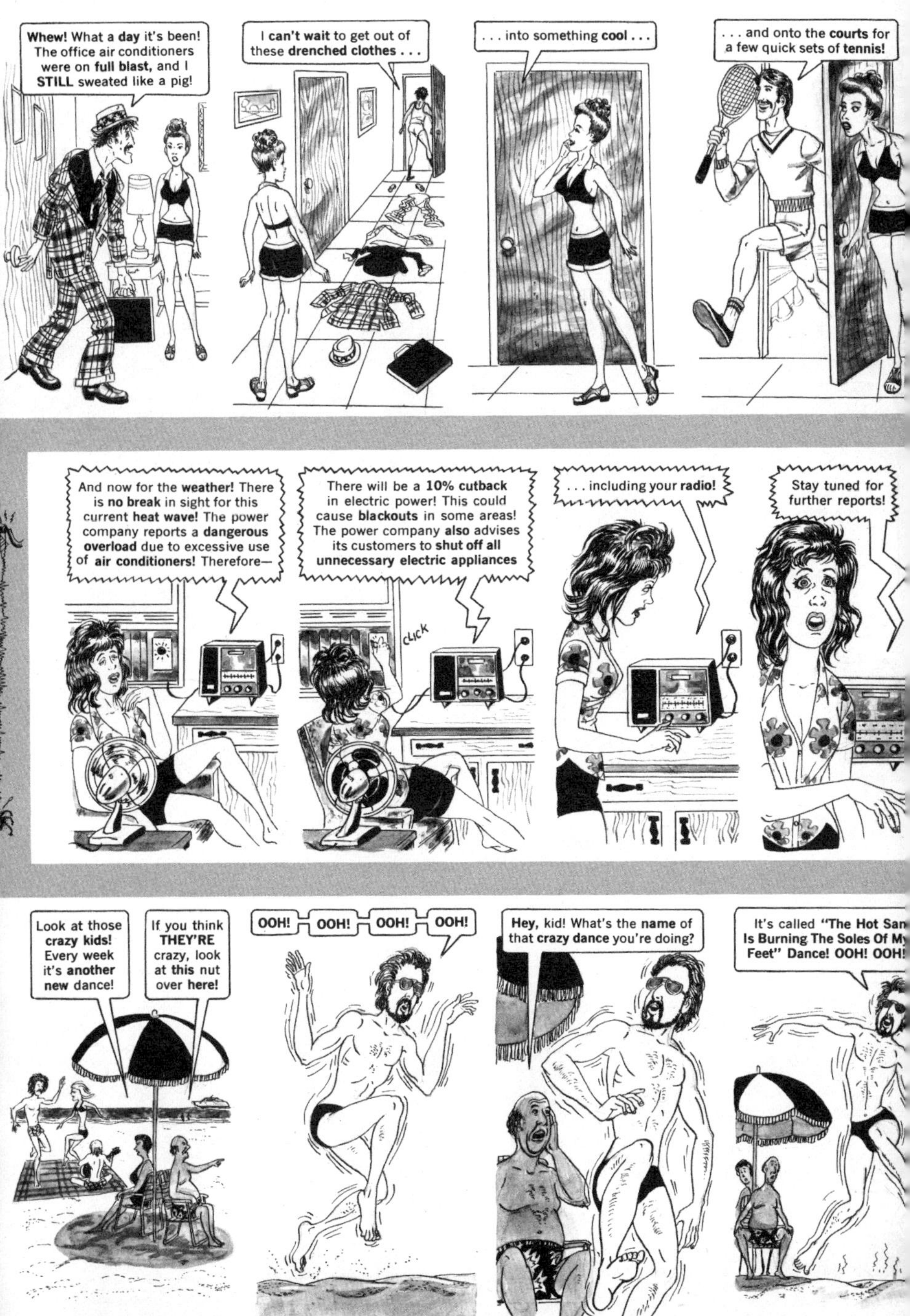

Whew! What a day it's been! The office air conditioners were on full blast, and I STILL sweated like a pig!
I can't wait to get out of these drenched clothes . . .
. . . into something cool . . .
. . . and onto the courts for a few quick sets of tennis!
And now for the weather! There is no break in sight for this current heat wave! The power company reports a dangerous overload due to excessive use of air conditioners! Therefore—
There will be a 10% cutback in electric power! This could cause blackouts in some areas! The power company also advises its customers to shut off all unnecessary electric appliances
CLICK
. . . including your radio!
Stay tuned for further reports!
Look at those crazy kids! Every week it's another new dance!
If you think THEY'RE crazy, look at this nut over here!
OOH! OOH! OOH! OOH!
Hey, kid! What's the name of that crazy dance you're doing?
It's called "The Hot San Is Burning The Soles Of M Feet" Dance! OOH! OOH!

That chintzy, cheap, paper decoration is hideous!

That is **not** a decoration! That **gets rid** of flies!

Actually, that **hideous paper decoration** is only a **cover** for the chemically-treated plastic strip inside!

Really? But, how does it work?

YOU'RE the Chemistry Major! **YOU** tell **ME!**

Okay . . . I WILL . . .
The fly takes **one look** at that hideous thing . . . and **LEAVES!!**

Oh, boy! What a **NIGHT!!**

It was **hot** and **muggy** . . . and the **bugs** were biting . . . and my **heat rash** was itching . . .

. . . and then this guy started **following me around**, telling me how **BEAUTIFUL** I was!

It was the **GREATEST NIGHT** of my **LIFE!!**

I don't know what's worse! This beastly hot weather, or the **constant repetition of—**

Don't say it! If I hear it one more time, I'll **SCREAM!!**

Hi! Isn't it just **awful?!** Y'know, it's **not** the **HEAT** . . . it's the **HUMIDITY!**

Y A A A A H H H H !

Y'know, it's **NOT** the heat! And it's **NOT** the humidity! It's all that **SCREAMING!!**

JOKE AND DAGGER DEPT.

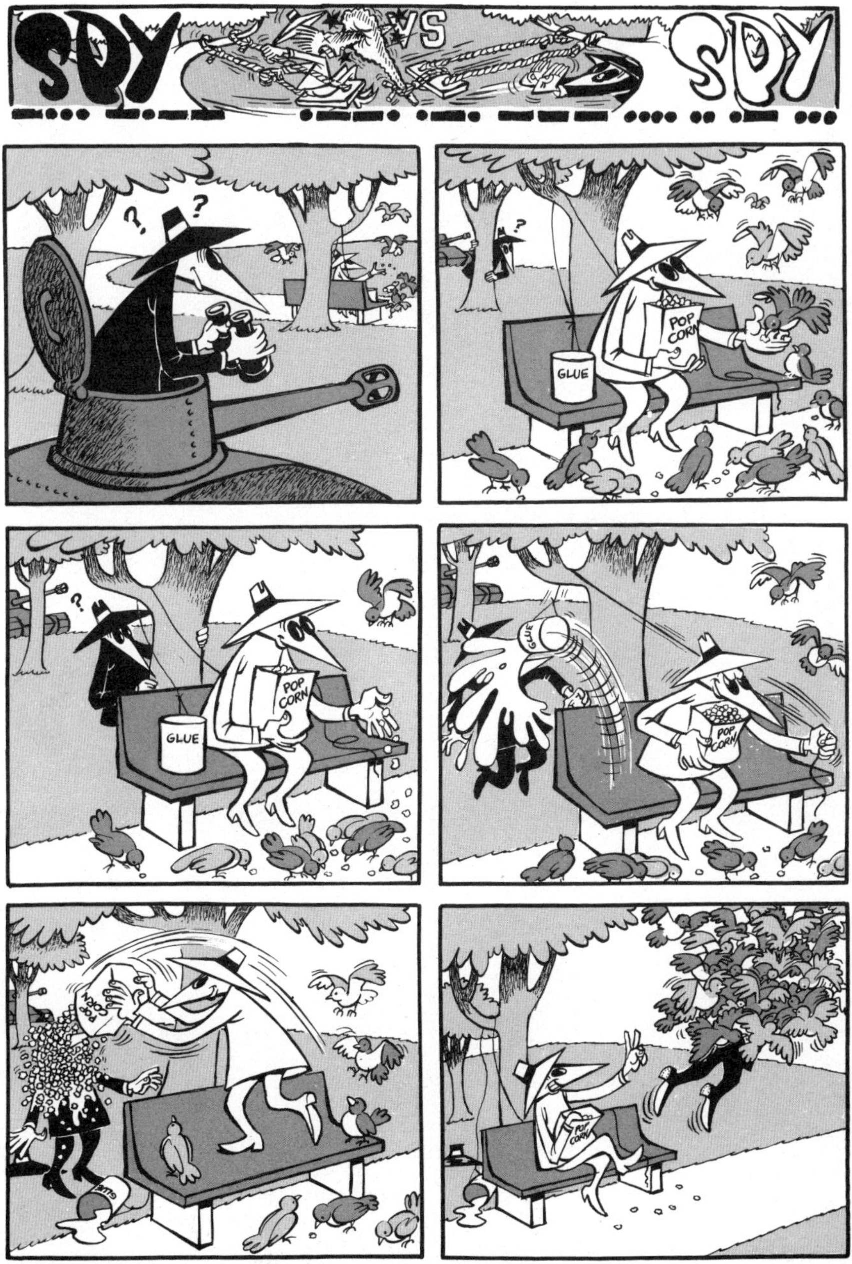
SPY
VS
SPY
?
?
?
GLUE
POP CORN
?
GLUE
POP CORN
GLUE
POP CORN
POP CORN
GLUE
POP CORN

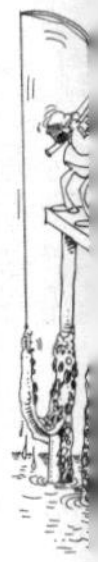

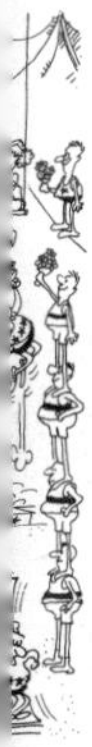

GRINDING THE ACTS DEPT.

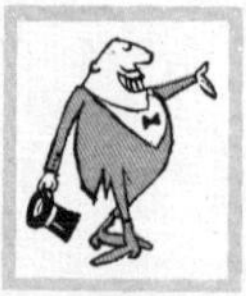

A MAD LOOK

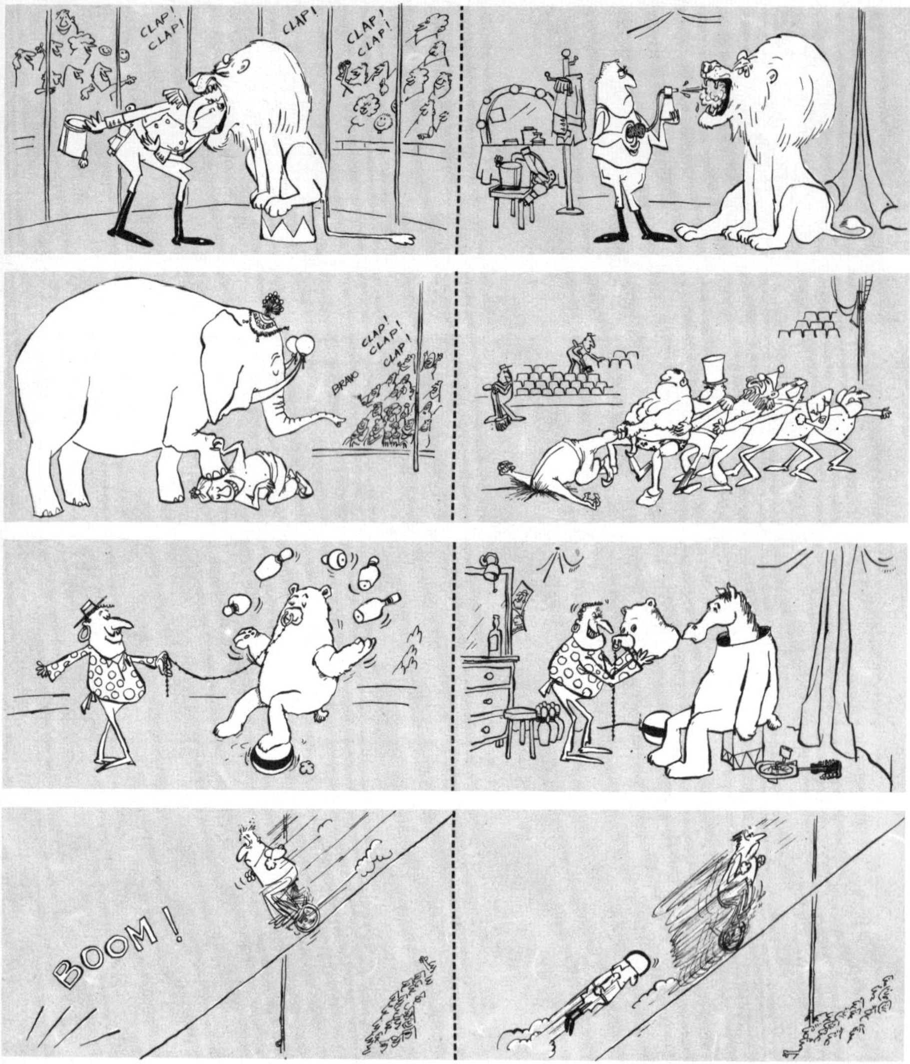
CLAP!
CLAP!
CLAP!
CLAP!
CLAP!
CLAP!
CLAP!
CLAP!
BRAVO
BOOM!

AT THE CIRCUS

ARTIST & WRITER: SERGIO ARAGONES

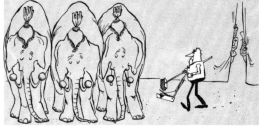

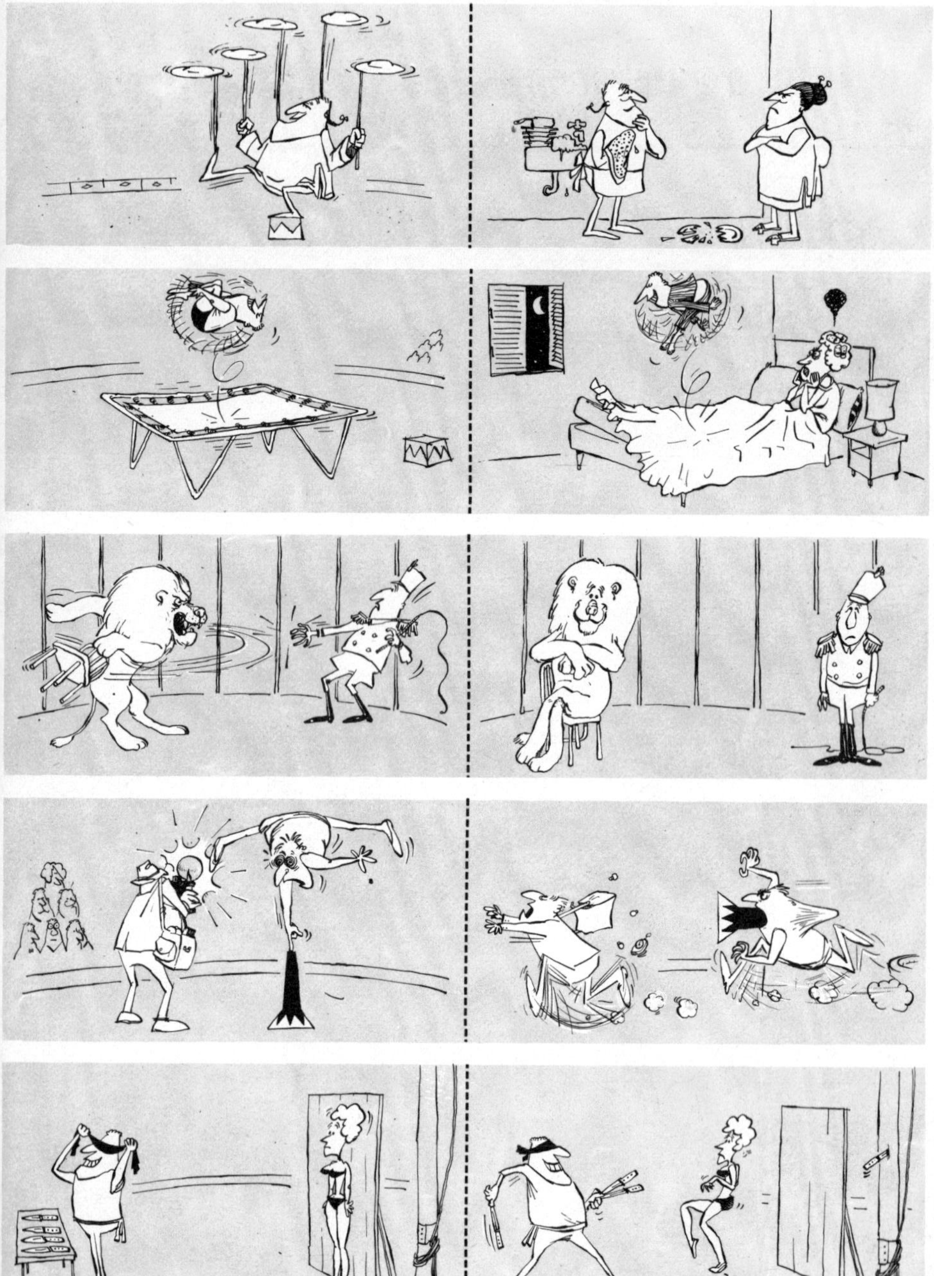

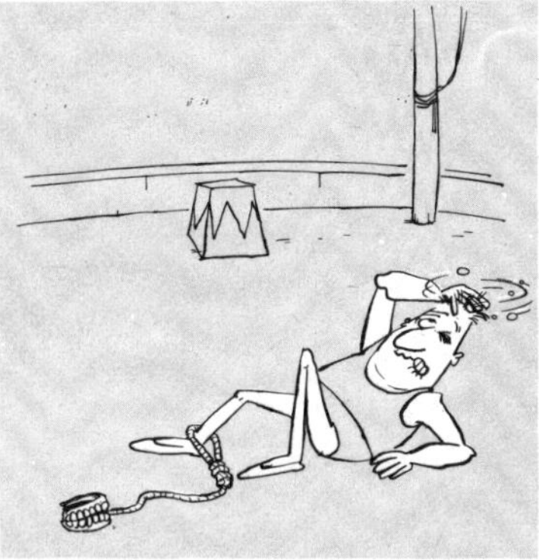

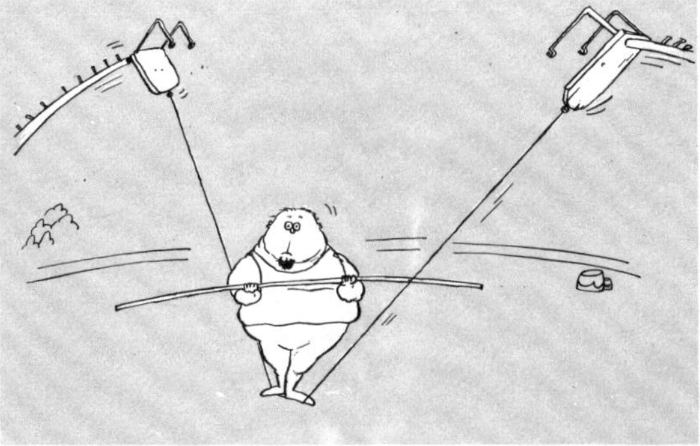

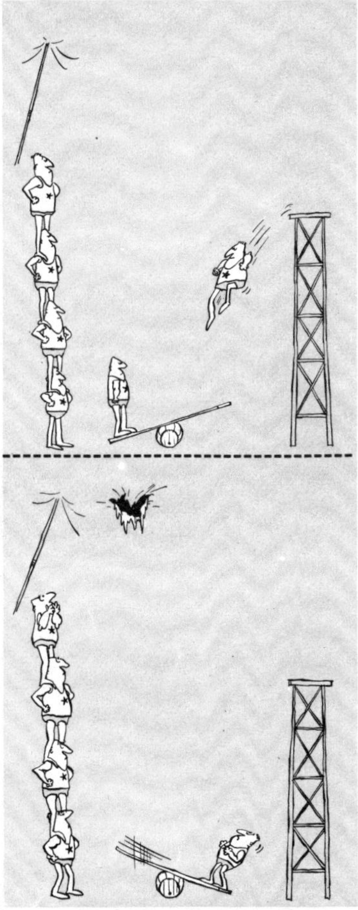

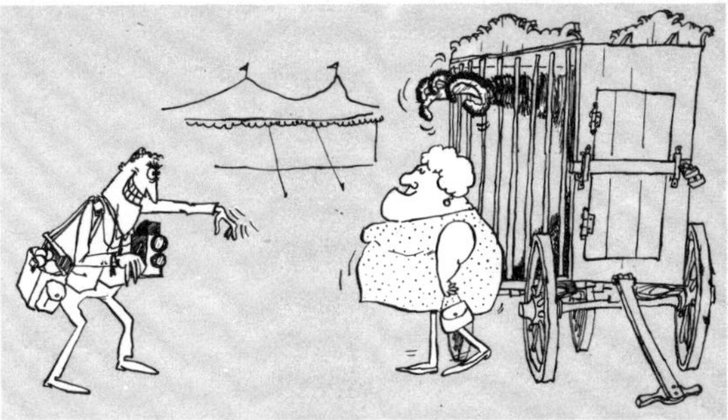

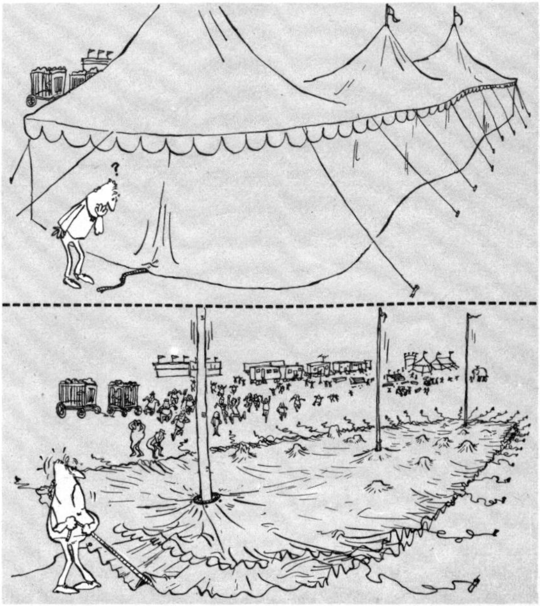

NURSERY WHINES DEPT.

BABY EXPO

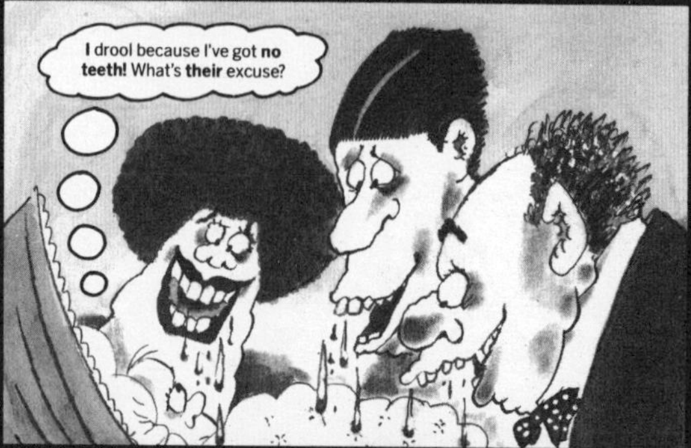
I drool because I've got **no teeth!** What's **their** excuse?

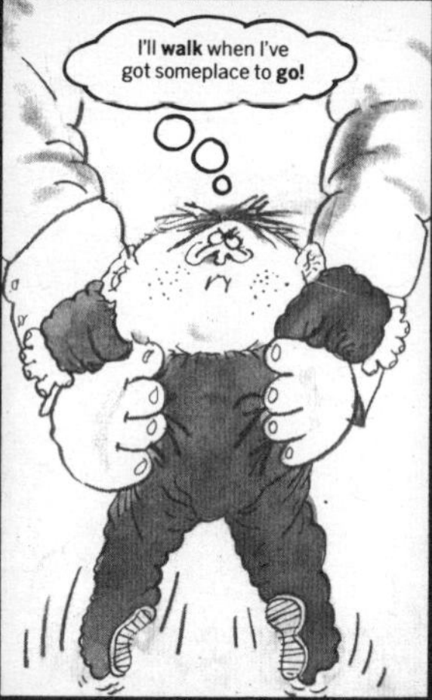
I'll **walk** when I've got someplace to **go!**

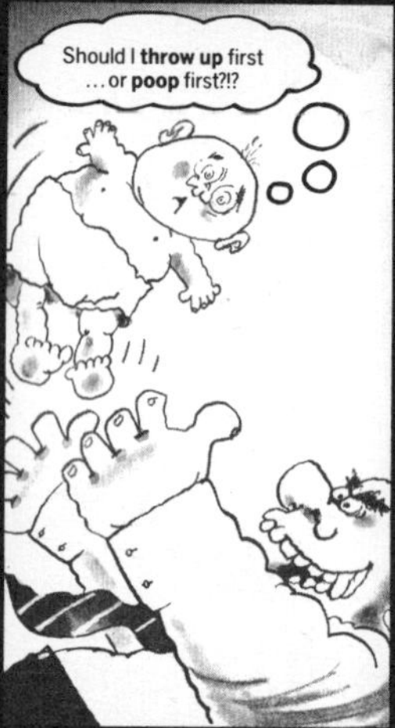
Should I **throw up** first ... or **poop** first?!?

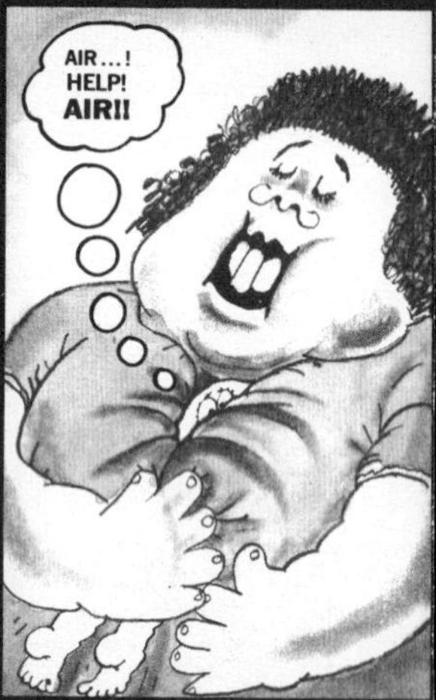
AIR ... !
HELP!
AIR!!

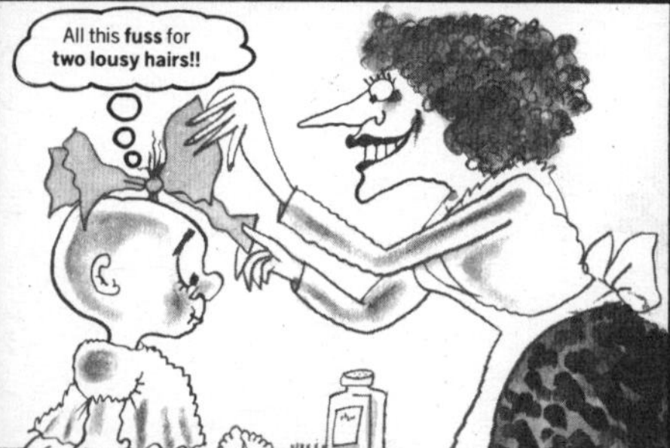
All this **fuss** for **two lousy hairs!!**

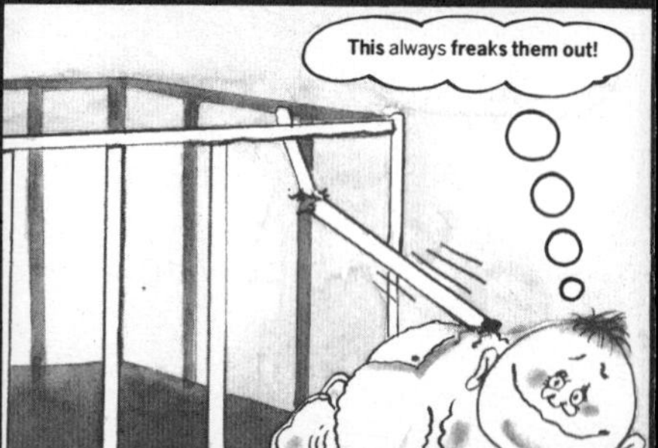
This always **freaks them out!**
PORGES

TALK
OSED

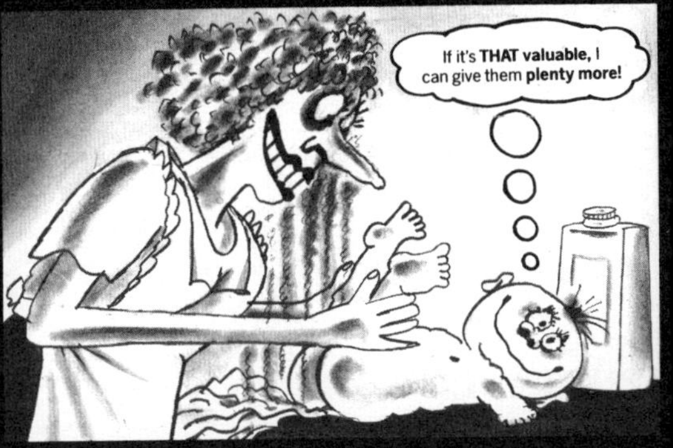

If it's **THAT valuable,** I can give them **plenty more!**

WRITER AND ARTIST: PAUL PETER PORGES

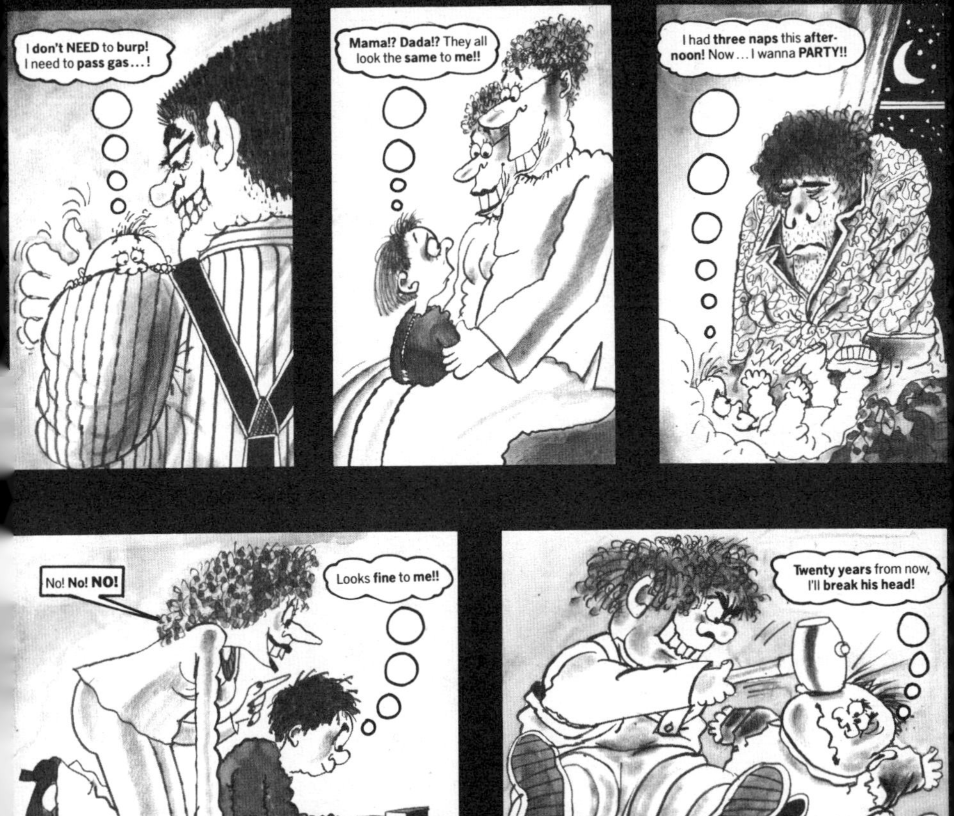

I **don't NEED** to **burp!** I need to **pass gas . . . !**
Mama!? Dada!? They all look the **same** to **me!!**
I had **three naps** this **after-noon!** Now . . . I wanna **PARTY!!**
No! **No! NO!**
Looks **fine** to **me!!**
Twenty years from now, I'll **break his head!**

UNFORKED TONGUE-IN-CHEEK DEPT.

In the past few years, there has been a trend toward honesty. Naturally, this has not been a voluntary trend, but one that has been legislated. We now have "Truth In Lending Laws" that alert the poor sap who's borrowing money just what he's in the bag for. Also, there's

IF THEY PASSED OTHER 'TRU

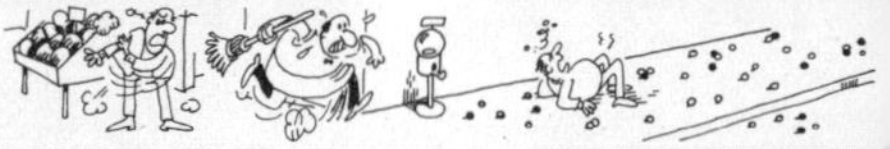

TRUTH IN CONFIRMATIONS

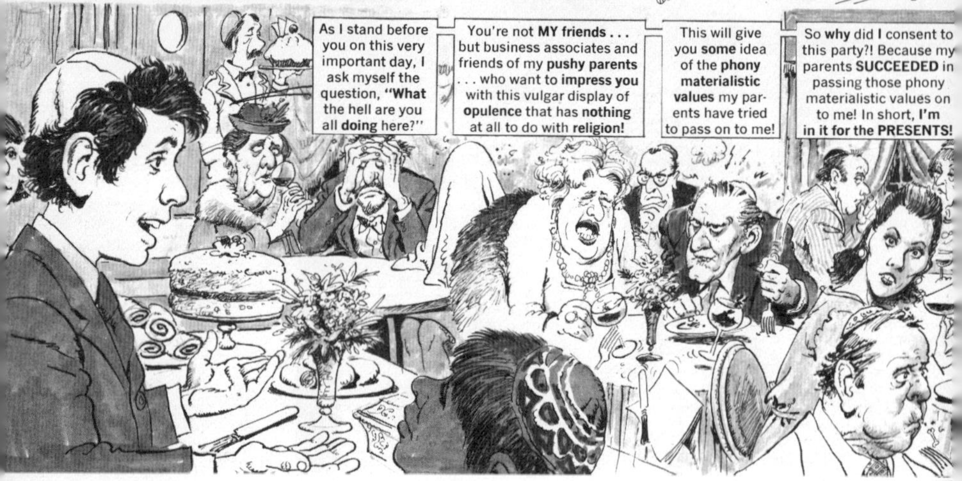
As I stand before you on this very important day, I ask myself the question, "What the hell are you all doing here?"
You're not MY friends . . . but business associates and friends of my pushy parents . . . who want to impress you with this vulgar display of opulence that has nothing at all to do with religion!
This will give you some idea of the phony materialistic values my parents have tried to pass on to me!
So why did I consent to this party?! Because my parents SUCCEEDED in passing those phony materialistic values on to me! In short, I'm in it for the PRESENTS!

TRUTH IN RETIREMENTS

ARTIST: HARRY NORTH

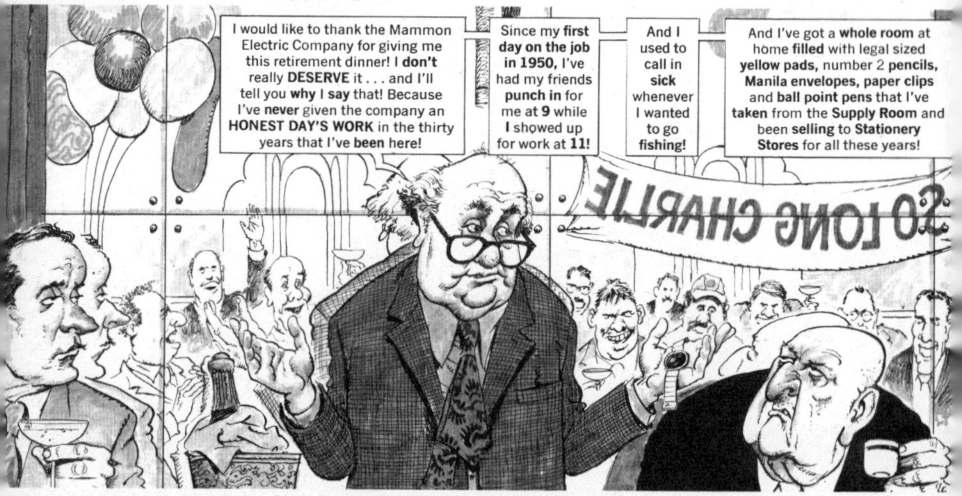
I would like to thank the Mammon Electric Company for giving me this retirement dinner! I don't really DESERVE it . . . and I'll tell you why I say that! Because I've never given the company an HONEST DAY'S WORK in the thirty years that I've been here!
Since my first day on the job in 1950, I've had my friends punch in for me at 9 while I showed up for work at 11!
And I used to call in sick whenever I wanted to go fishing!
And I've got a whole room at home filled with legal sized yellow pads, number 2 pencils, Manila envelopes, paper clips and ball point pens that I've taken from the Supply Room and been selling to Stationery Stores for all these years!

'Truth In Advertising Laws" and "Truth In Packaging Laws" to protect the unsuspecting consumer. What do you think might happen if these "Truth In . . . Laws" were extended to other areas? What areas, you ask? Glad you did—because here's how marvelous life will be . . .

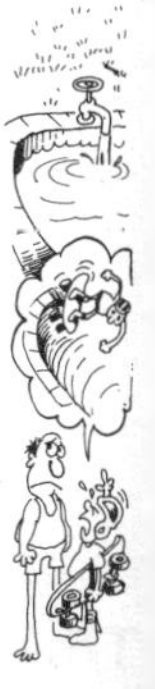

TH IN . . . LAWS'

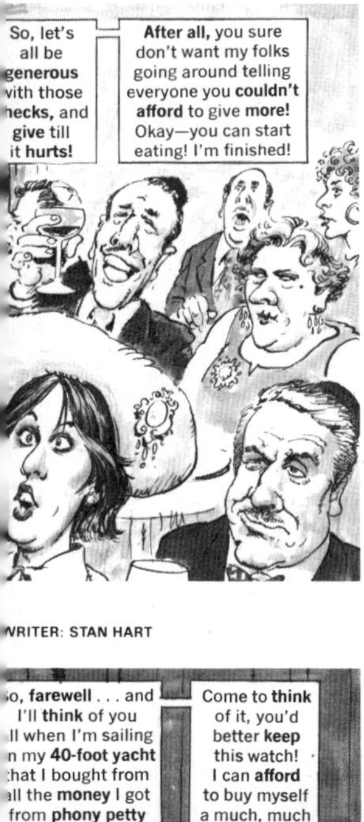

So, let's all be generous vith those hecks, and give till it hurts!
After all, you sure don't want my folks going around telling everyone you couldn't afford to give more! Okay—you can start eating! I'm finished!

TRUTH IN ACADEMY AWARDS

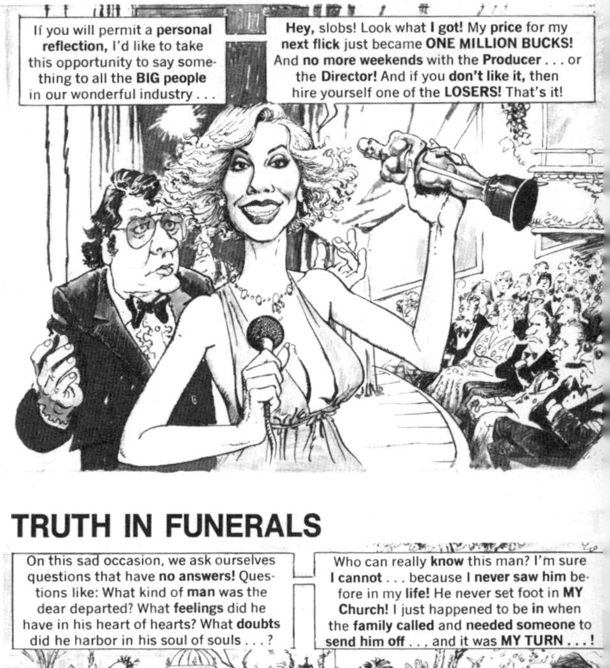

If you will permit a personal reflection, I'd like to take this opportunity to say something to all the BIG people in our wonderful industry . . .
Hey, slobs! Look what I got! My price for my next flick just became ONE MILLION BUCKS! And no more weekends with the Producer . . . or the Director! And if you don't like it, then hire yourself one of the LOSERS! That's it!

VRITER: STAN HART

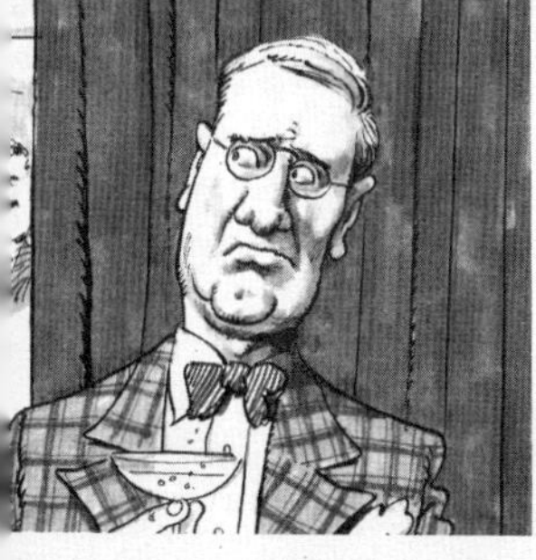

io, farewell . . . and I'll think of you ll when I'm sailing n my 40-foot yacht hat I bought from ll the money I got from phony petty cash vouchers!
Come to think of it, you'd better keep this watch! I can afford to buy myself a much, much better one!

TRUTH IN FUNERALS

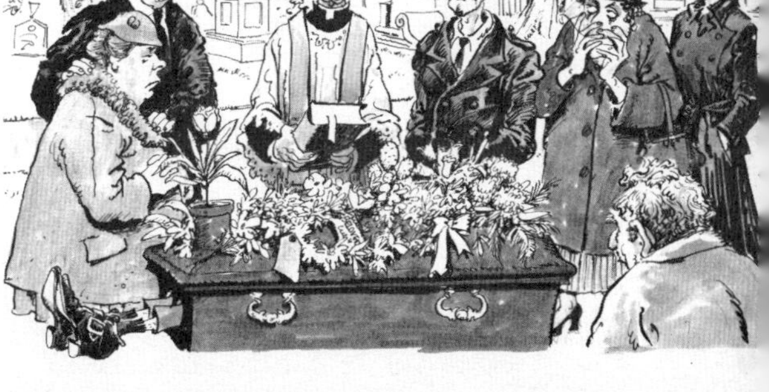

On this sad occasion, we ask ourselves questions that have no answers! Questions like: What kind of man was the dear departed? What feelings did he have in his heart of hearts? What doubts did he harbor in his soul of souls . . . ?
Who can really know this man? I'm sure I cannot . . . because I never saw him before in my life! He never set foot in MY Church! I just happened to be in when the family called and needed someone to send him off . . . and it was MY TURN . . . !

TRUTH IN GRADUATIONS

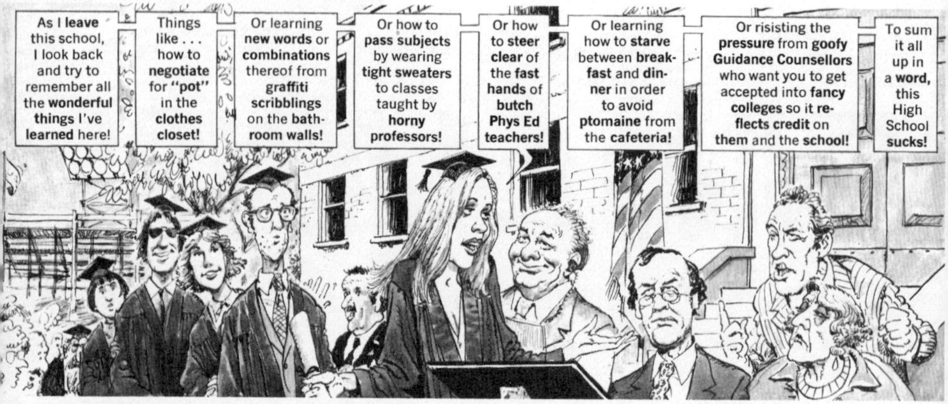
As I **leave** this school, I look back and try to remember all the **wonderful things** I've **learned** here!
Things like . . . how to **negotiate** for **"pot"** in the **clothes closet!**
Or learning **new words** or **combinations** thereof from **graffiti scribblings** on the **bathroom walls!**
Or how to **pass subjects** by wearing **tight sweaters** to classes taught by **horny professors!**
Or how to **steer clear** of the **fast hands** of **butch Phys Ed teachers!**
Or learning how to **starve** between **breakfast** and **dinner** in order to avoid **ptomaine** from the **cafeteria!**
Or risisting the **pressure** from **goofy Guidance Counsellors** who want you to get accepted into **fancy colleges** so it **reflects credit** on **them** and the **school!**
To sum it all up in a **word,** this High School **sucks!**

TRUTH IN CAMPAIGNING

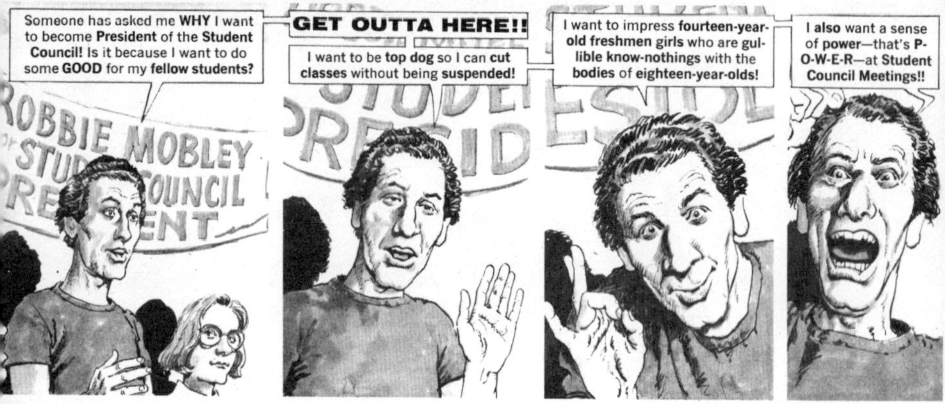
Someone has asked me **WHY** I want to become **President** of the **Student Council!** Is it because I want to do some **GOOD** for my **fellow students?**
GET OUTTA HERE!!
I want to be **top dog** so I can **cut classes** without being **suspended!**
I want to impress **fourteen-year-old freshmen girls** who are **gullible know-nothings** with the **bodies** of **eighteen-year-olds!**
I also want a sense of **power**—that's **P-O-W-E-R**—at **Student Council Meetings!!**

TRUTH IN BROTHERHOOD WEEK

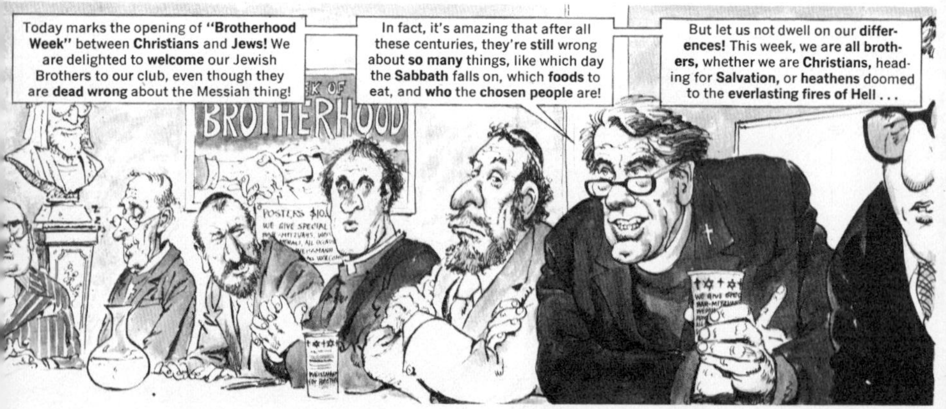
Today marks the opening of **"Brotherhood Week"** between **Christians** and **Jews!** We are delighted to **welcome** our Jewish Brothers to our club, even though they are **dead wrong** about the Messiah thing!
In fact, it's amazing that after all these centuries, they're **still** wrong about **so many** things, like which day the **Sabbath** falls on, which **foods** to eat, and **who** the **chosen people** are!
But let us not dwell on our **differences!** This week, we are **all brothers,** whether we are **Christians,** heading for **Salvation,** or **heathens** doomed to the **everlasting fires of Hell . . .**
BROTHERHOOD

TRUTH IN WEDDINGS

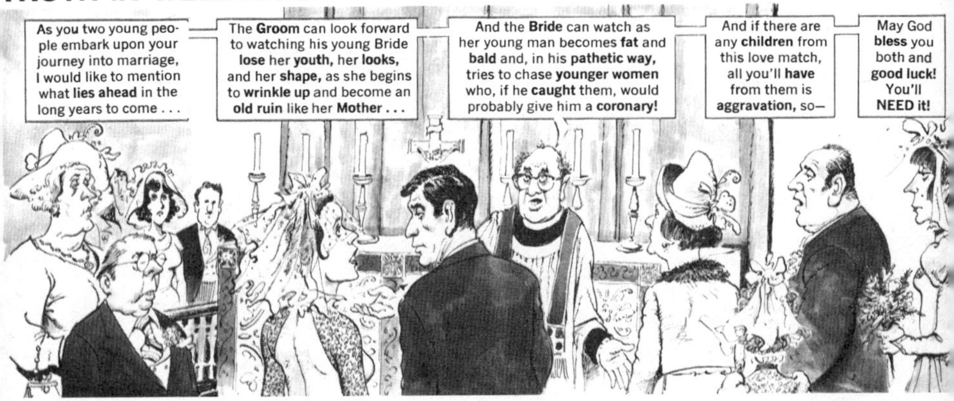
As you two young people embark upon your journey into marriage, I would like to mention what lies ahead in the long years to come . . .
The Groom can look forward to watching his young Bride lose her youth, her looks, and her shape, as she begins to wrinkle up and become an old ruin like her Mother . . .
And the Bride can watch as her young man becomes fat and bald and, in his pathetic way, tries to chase younger women who, if he caught them, would probably give him a coronary!
And if there are any children from this love match, all you'll have from them is aggravation, so—
May God bless you both and good luck! You'll NEED it!

TRUTH IN ORIENTATION

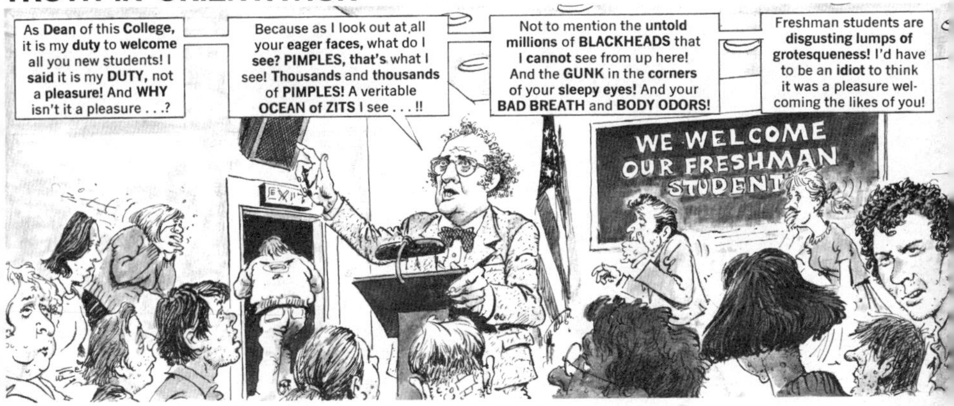
As Dean of this College, it is my duty to welcome all you new students! I said it is my DUTY, not a pleasure! And WHY isn't it a pleasure . . .?
Because as I look out at all your eager faces, what do I see? PIMPLES, that's what I see! Thousands and thousands of PIMPLES! A veritable OCEAN of ZITS I see . . . !!
Not to mention the untold millions of BLACKHEADS that I cannot see from up here! And the GUNK in the corners of your sleepy eyes! And your BAD BREATH and BODY ODORS!
Freshman students are disgusting lumps of grotesqueness! I'd have to be an idiot to think it was a pleasure welcoming the likes of you!
WE WELCOME OUR FRESHMAN STUDENT
EXIT

TRUTH IN HALFTIME

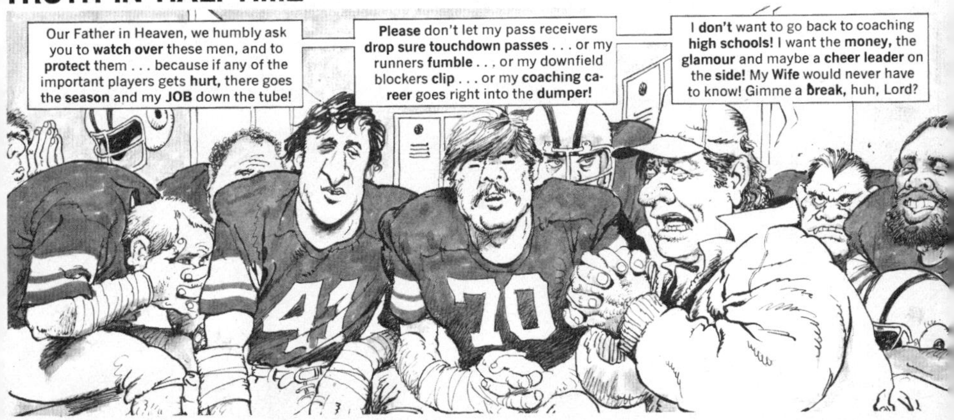
Our Father in Heaven, we humbly ask you to watch over these men, and to protect them . . . because if any of the important players gets hurt, there goes the season and my JOB down the tube!
Please don't let my pass receivers drop sure touchdown passes . . . or my runners fumble . . . or my downfield blockers clip . . . or my coaching career goes right into the dumper!
I don't want to go back to coaching high schools! I want the money, the glamour and maybe a cheer leader on the side! My Wife would never have to know! Gimme a break, huh, Lord?
41
70

FOR WHOM THE BELCH TOLLS DEPT.

A MAD LOOK AT... BURPS

ADAM AND EVE

Burp
TO THE EGRESS

SIR ISAAC NEWTON

ZZZZZZZZ
BURP
BLOINNK!

ARTIST: BOB CLARK

LUCREZIA BORGIA

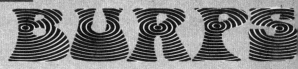

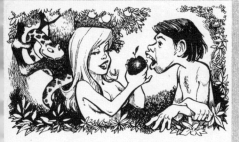

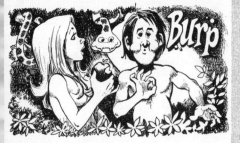

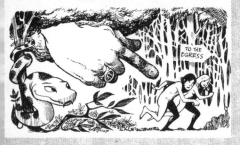

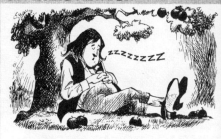

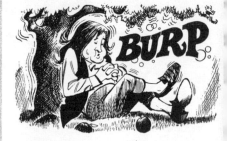

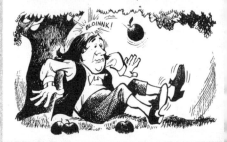

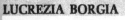

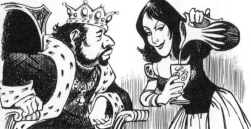

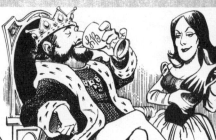

THROUGH HISTORY

GEORGE WASHINGTON

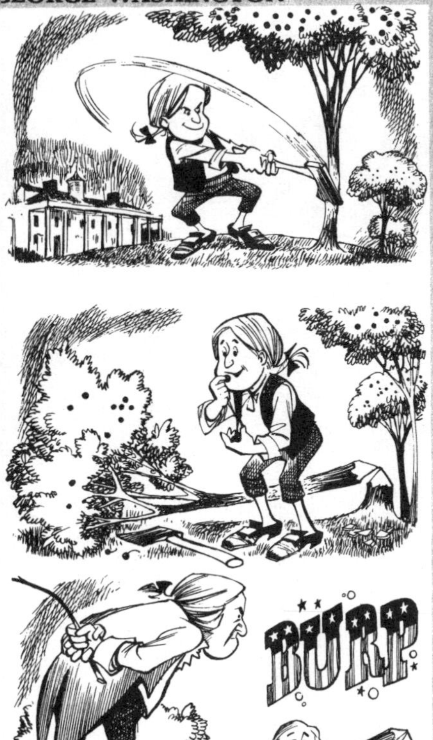
BURP

HENRY VIII

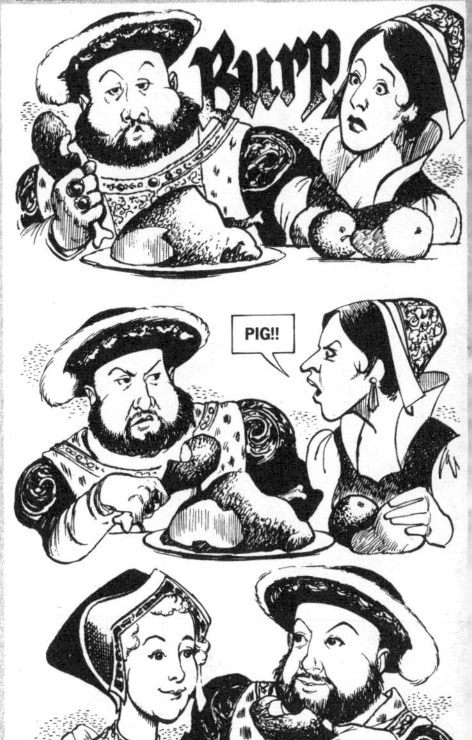
BURP
PIG!!

RITER: PAUL PETER PORGES

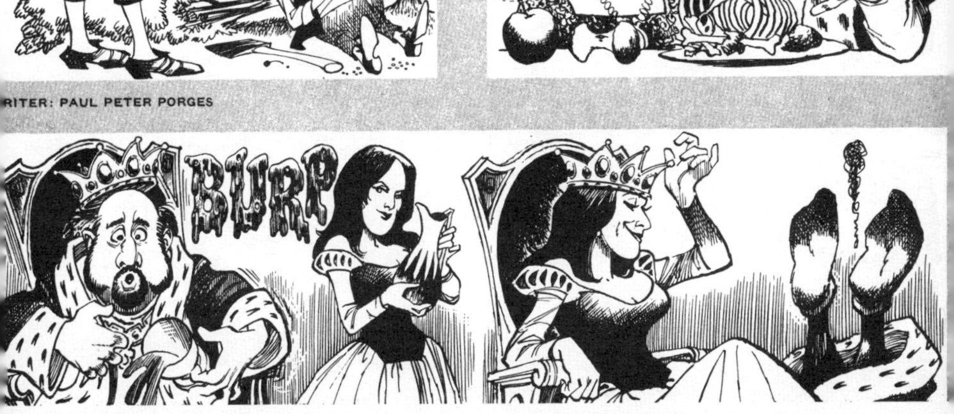
BURP

NAPOLEON

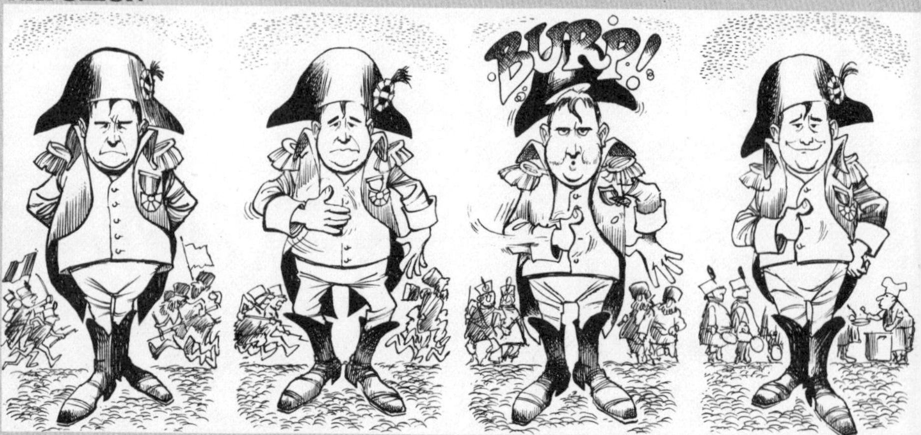
BURP!

ALEXANDER GRAHAM BELL

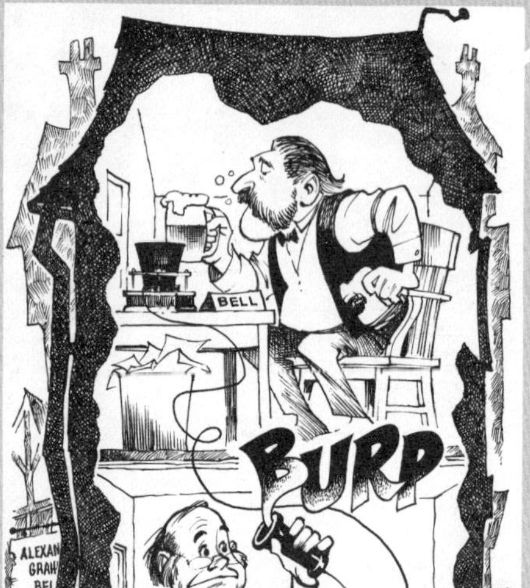
BELL
BURP
WATSON

ANCIENT POMPEII

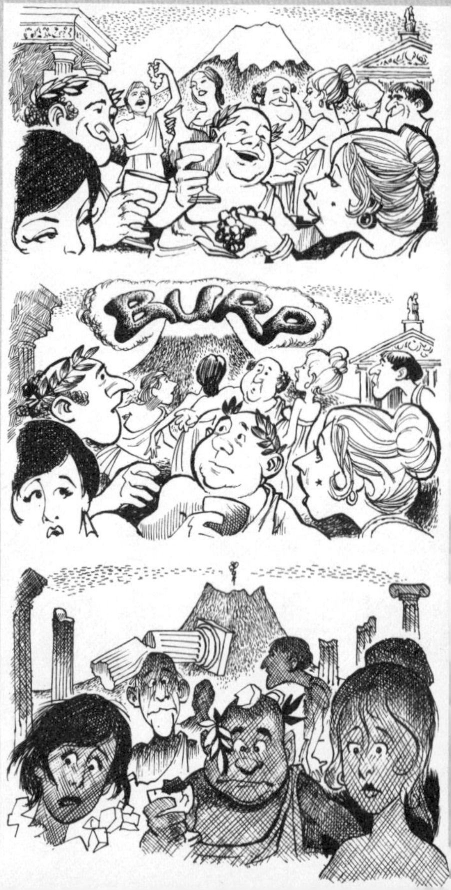
BURP

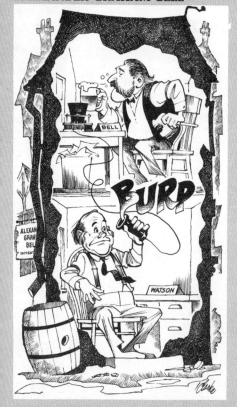

DON MARTIN DEPT.

A VISIT TO THE COUNTRY

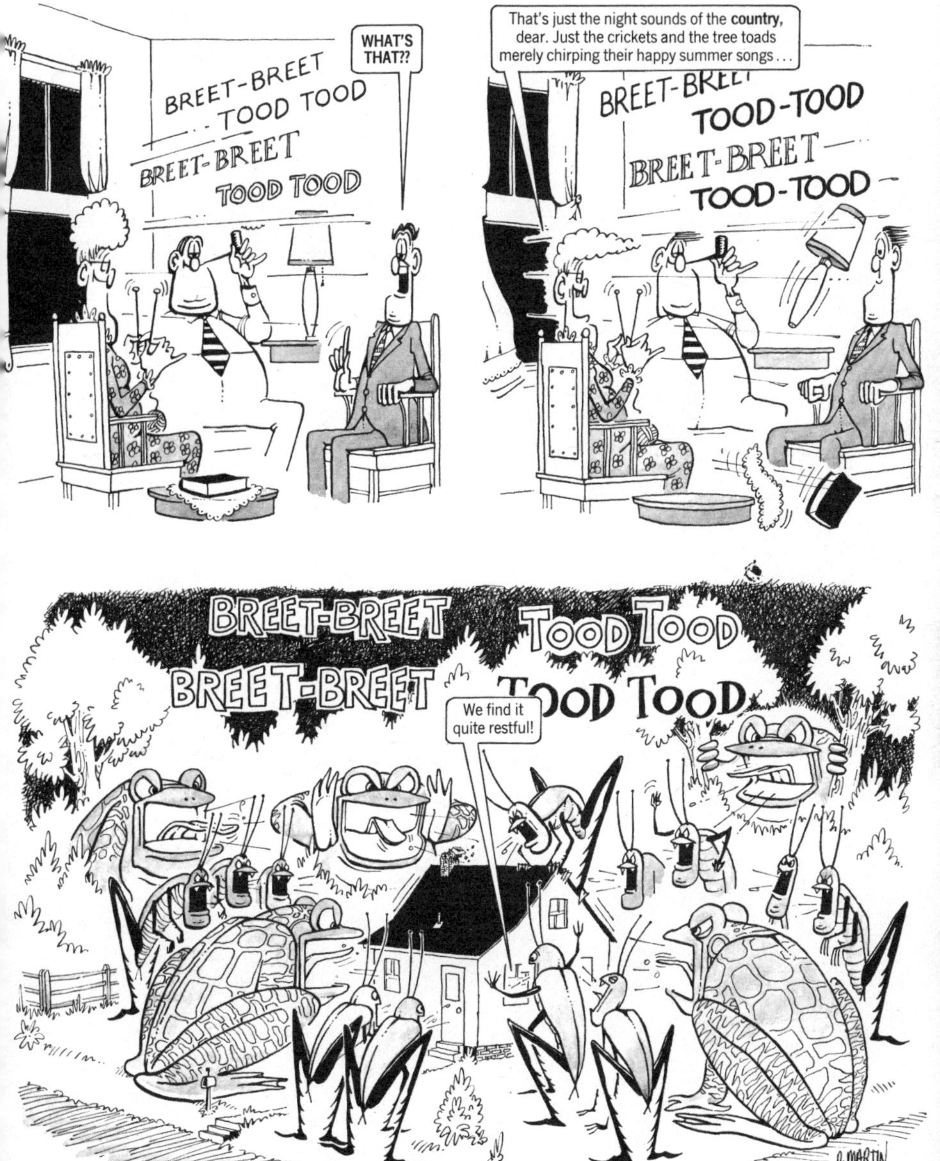

BREET-BREET
TOOD TOOD
BREET-BREET
TOOD TOOD
WHAT'S THAT??
That's just the night sounds of the **country**, dear. Just the crickets and the tree toads merely chirping their happy summer songs . . .
TOOD-TOOD
BREET-BREET
TOOD-TOOD
BREET-BREET
TOOD TOOD
BREET-BREET
TOOD TOOD
We find it quite restful!
D. MARTIN

DICK DePT.

A MAD PEEK BEHIND THE SCENES AT A HEALTH SPA

ARTIST: AL JAFFEE WRITER: DICK DE BARTOLO

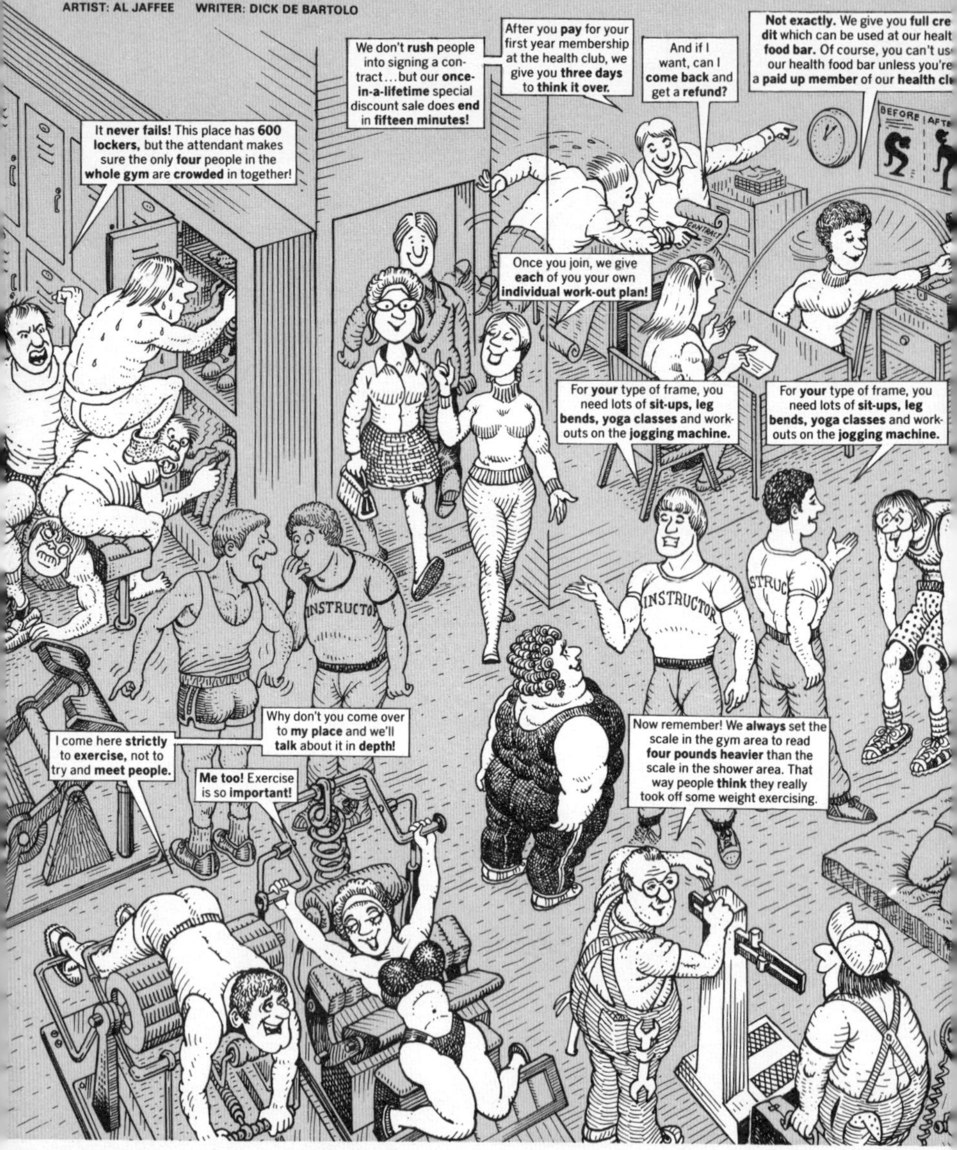

We don't rush people into signing a contract...but our once-in-a-lifetime special discount sale does end in fifteen minutes!
After you pay for your first year membership at the health club, we give you three days to think it over.
And if I want, can I come back and get a refund?
Not exactly. We give you full cre dit which can be used at our healt food bar. Of course, you can't us our health food bar unless you're a paid up member of our health cl
BEFORE AFTE
CONTRACT
It never fails! This place has 600 lockers, but the attendant makes sure the only four people in the whole gym are crowded in together!
Once you join, we give each of you your own individual work-out plan!
For your type of frame, you need lots of sit-ups, leg bends, yoga classes and work-outs on the jogging machine.
For your type of frame, you need lots of sit-ups, leg bends, yoga classes and work-outs on the jogging machine.
INSTRUCTOR
INSTRUCTOR
STRUC
I come here strictly to exercise, not to try and meet people.
Why don't you come over to my place and we'll talk about it in depth!
Me too! Exercise is so important!
Now remember! We always set the scale in the gym area to read four pounds heavier than the scale in the shower area. That way people think they really took off some weight exercising.

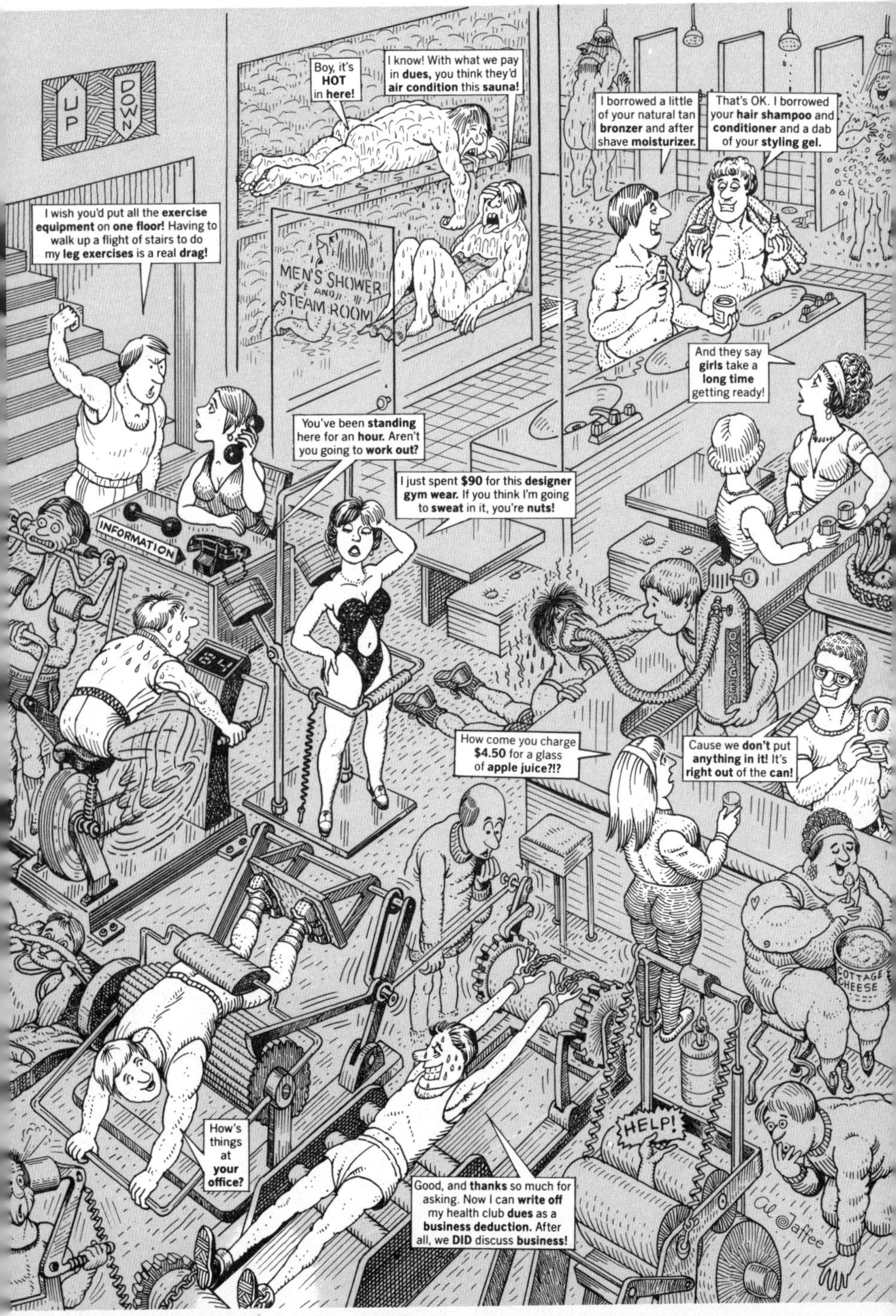
UP
DOWN
Boy, it's HOT in here!
I know! With what we pay in dues, you think they'd air condition this sauna!
I borrowed a little of your natural tan bronzer and after shave moisturizer.
That's OK. I borrowed your hair shampoo and conditioner and a dab of your styling gel.
I wish you'd put all the exercise equipment on one floor! Having to walk up a flight of stairs to do my leg exercises is a real drag!
MEN'S SHOWER AND STEAM ROOM
And they say girls take a long time getting ready!
You've been standing here for an hour. Aren't you going to work out?
I just spent $90 for this designer gym wear. If you think I'm going to sweat in it, you're nuts!
INFORMATION
84
OXYGEN
How come you charge $4.50 for a glass of apple juice?!?
Cause we don't put anything in it! It's right out of the can!
COTTAGE CHEESE
HELP!
How's things at your office?
Good, and thanks so much for asking. Now I can write off my health club dues as a business deduction. After all, we DID discuss business!
Al Jaffee

ODDS FOR THE LOVE OF MOOLA DEPT.

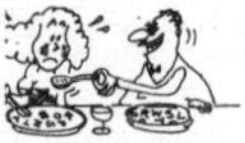

It's a national craze! Everybody, into the pool! No, not the swimming pool, clod! The "Baseball High Inning" pool, the "Biggest Fish" pool, the "What Time Will The Ship Drop Anchor?" pool, the "In What Round Will The Fight End?" pool, and whatever other pool is being organized this week! How far will this new compulsion go? It's just getting started! And so, to add to the list, MAD now suggests . . .

OTHE

THE "FAMILY VACATION TRIP CAR-SICK" POOL

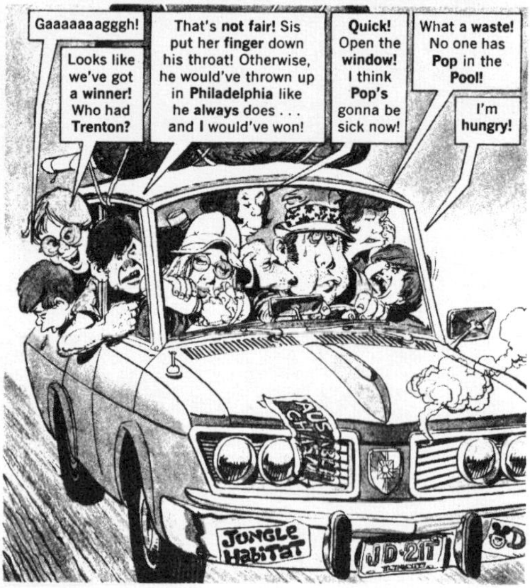
Gaaaaaaagggh!
Looks like we've got a winner! Who had Trenton?
That's not fair! Sis put her finger down his throat! Otherwise, he would've thrown up in Philadelphia like he always does . . . and I would've won!
Quick! Open the window! I think Pop's gonna be sick now!
What a waste! No one has Pop in the Pool!
I'm hungry!
JUNGLE HABITAT
JD·21T

THE "WHAT INNING WILL THE FIRST SPECTA FALL ASLEEP AT THE BASEBALL GAME?" P

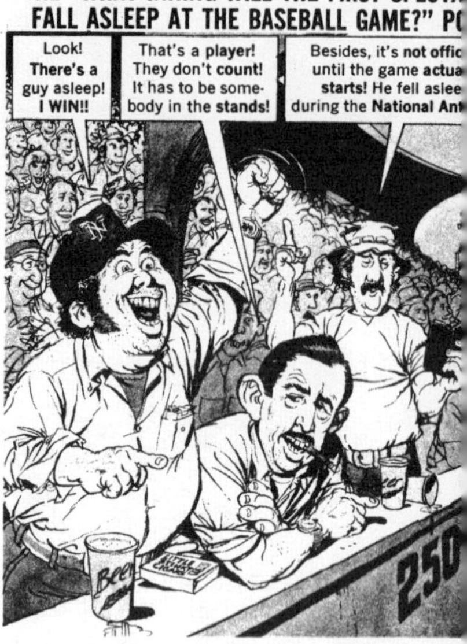
Look! There's a guy asleep! I WIN!!
That's a player! They don't count! It has to be somebody in the stands!
Besides, it's not offic until the game actua starts! He fell aslee during the National An
250

THE "WHAT TIME WILL THE NEXT OFFICE COLLECTION BE TAKEN?" POOL

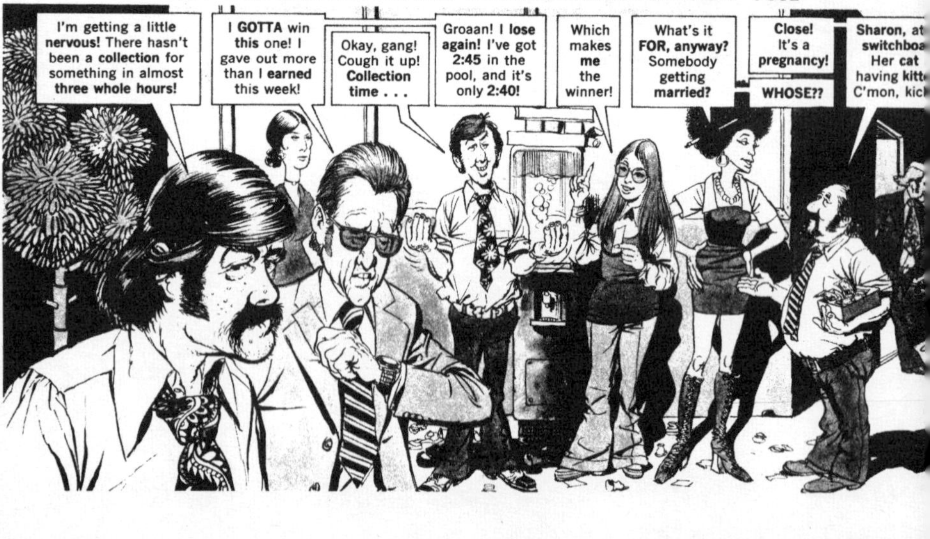
I'm getting a little nervous! There hasn't been a collection for something in almost three whole hours!
I GOTTA win this one! I gave out more than I earned this week!
Okay, gang! Cough it up! Collection time . . .
Groaan! I lose again! I've got 2:45 in the pool, and it's only 2:40!
Which makes me the winner!
What's it FOR, anyway? Somebody getting married?
Close! It's a pregnancy!
WHOSE??
Sharon, at switchboa Her cat having kitt C'mon, kick

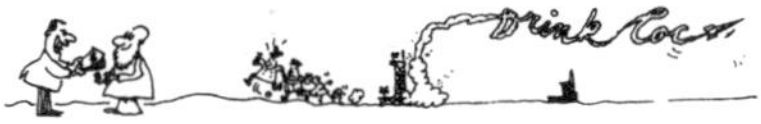

BETTING POOLS

ARTIST: GEORGE WOODBRIDGE WRITER: LOU SILVERSTONE

THE "WHAT TIME DOES THE SCHOOL BUS DRIVER BLOW HIS TOP?" POOL

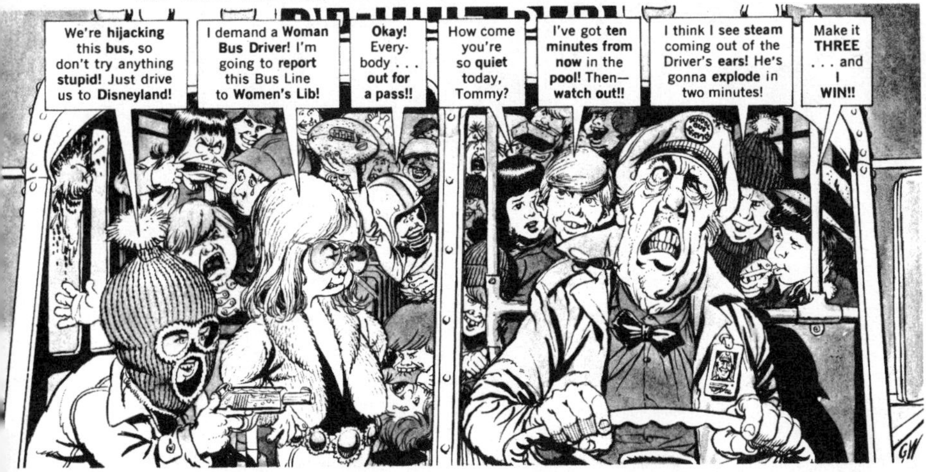
We're hijacking this bus, so don't try anything stupid! Just drive us to Disneyland!
I demand a Woman Bus Driver! I'm going to report this Bus Line to Women's Lib!
Okay! Every- body . . . out for a pass!!
How come you're so quiet today, Tommy?
I've got ten minutes from now in the pool! Then— watch out!!
I think I see steam coming out of the Driver's ears! He's gonna explode in two minutes!
Make it THREE . . . and I WIN!!
GW

HE "HOW LONG AFTER A GUY FINALLY QUITS SMOKING WILL HE LIGHT UP AGAIN?" POOL

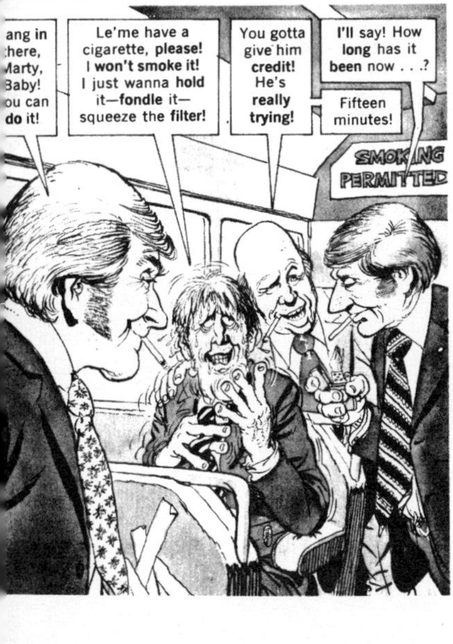
ang in there, Marty, Baby! ou can do it!
Le'me have a cigarette, please! I won't smoke it! I just wanna hold it—fondle it— squeeze the filter!
You gotta give him credit! He's really trying!
I'll say! How long has it been now . . .?
Fifteen minutes!
SMOKING PERMITTED

THE "WHO'LL BE FIRST ON THE BLOCK TO NEED FIRST AID AFTER SHOVELING HIS WALK?" POOL

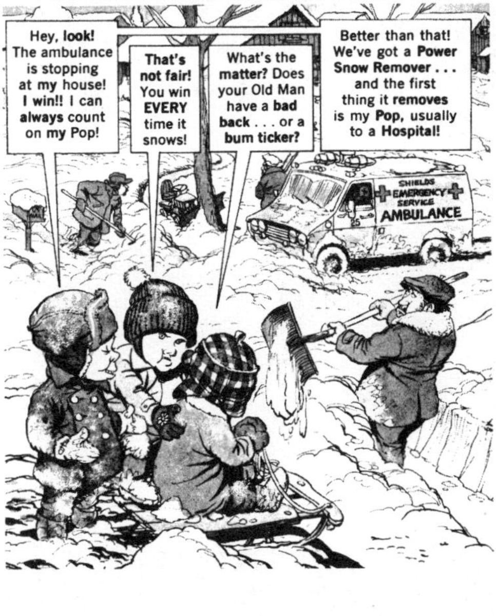
Hey, look! The ambulance is stopping at my house! I win!! I can always count on my Pop!
That's not fair! You win EVERY time it snows!
What's the matter? Does your Old Man have a bad back . . . or a bum ticker?
Better than that! We've got a Power Snow Remover . . . and the first thing it removes is my Pop, usually to a Hospital!
SHIELDS EMERGENCY SERVICE AMBULANCE

POINT OF YOU DEPT.

A MAD GUIDE TO... WHAT'S CUTE...

ARTIST: PAUL

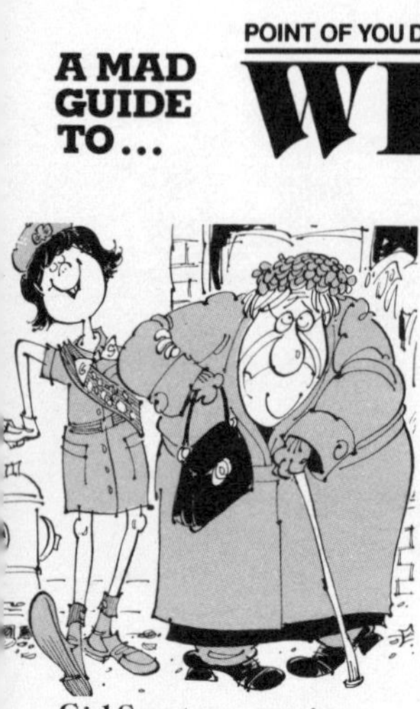

Girl Scouts are cute!

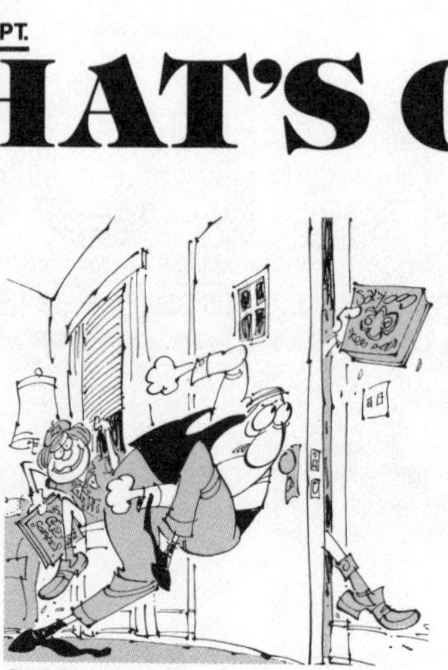

Girl Scouts selling cookies are not!

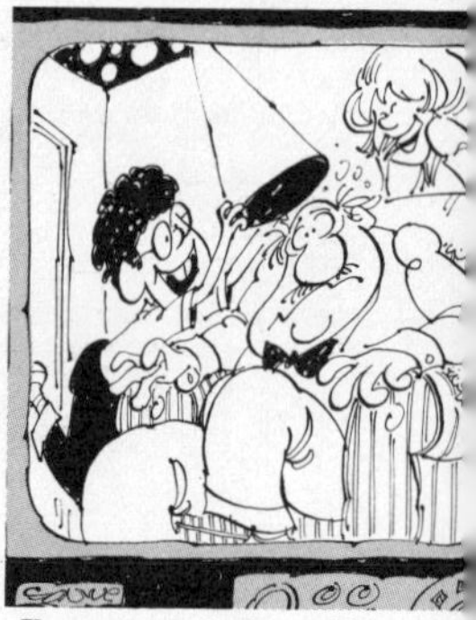

Precocious kids on TV are c

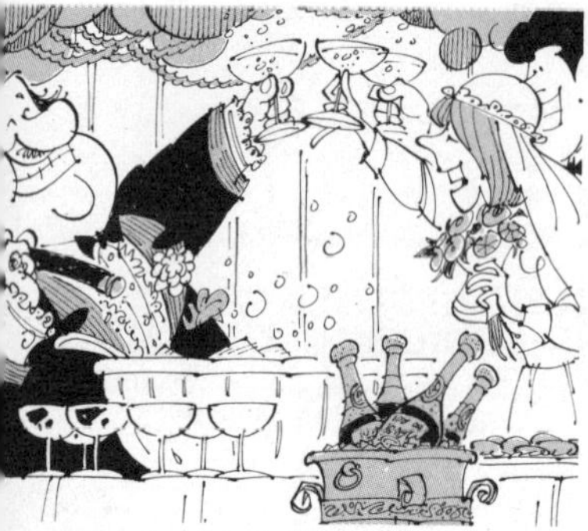

Your daughter's first wedding is cute!

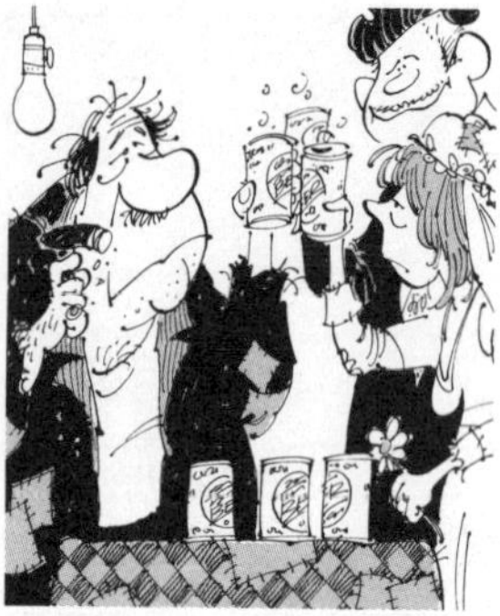

Her fourth wedding is not!

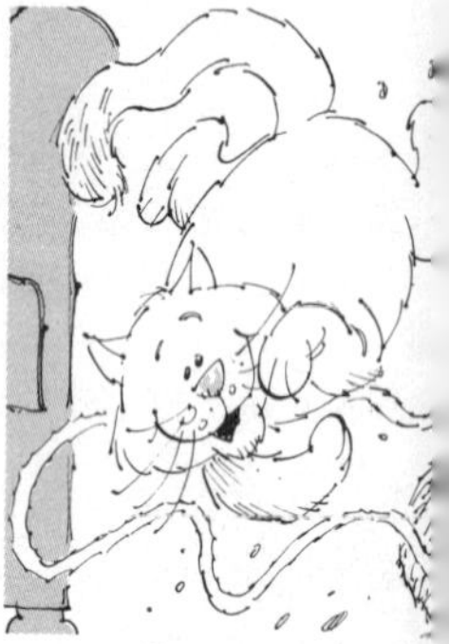

Cats are cute!

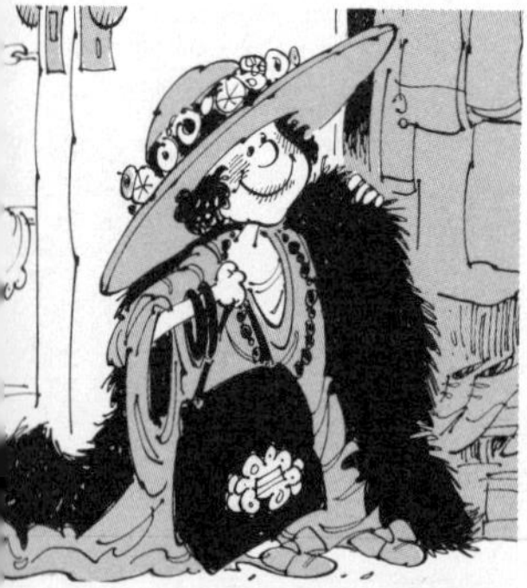

Your little daughter dressing up in Mom's clothes is cute!

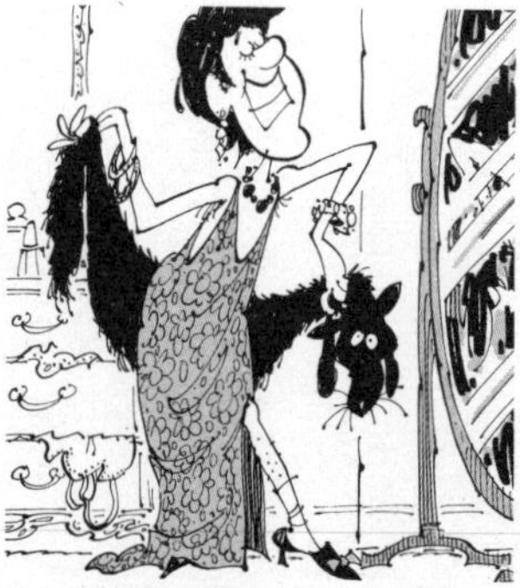

Your grown-up son dressing up in Mom's clothes is not!

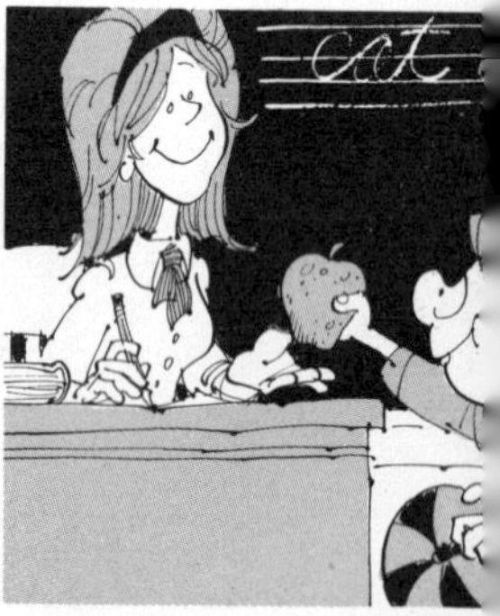
cat

Your son's crush on his second grade teacher is cute!

AND WHAT'S NOT

TER: MARK DRESSLER

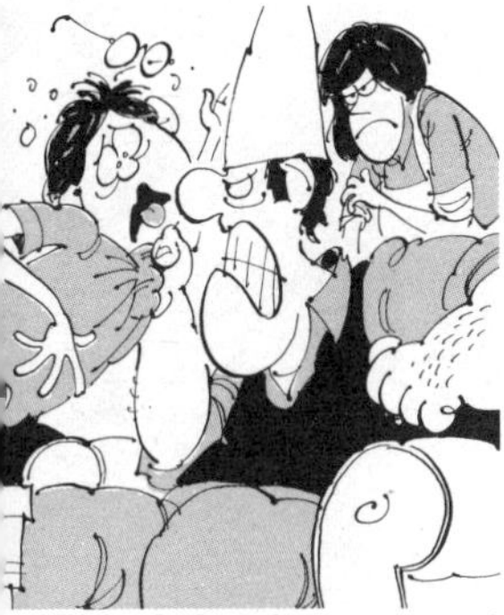

ecocious kids at home are not!

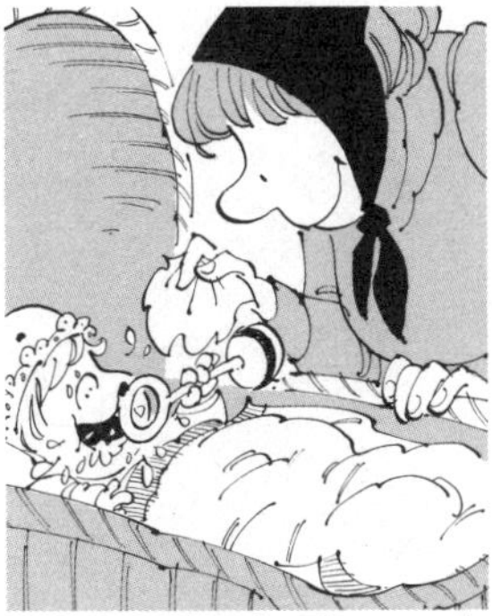

Babies that drool are cute!

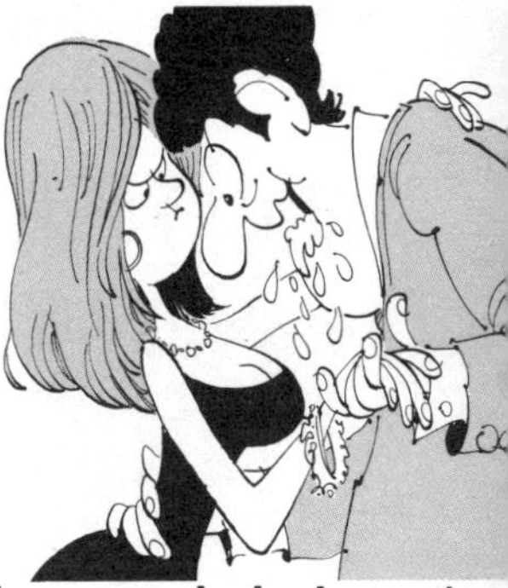

Grown men who drool are not!

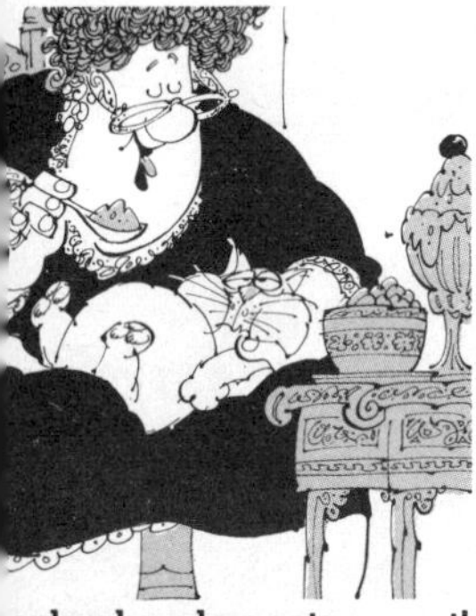

ople who adore cats are not!

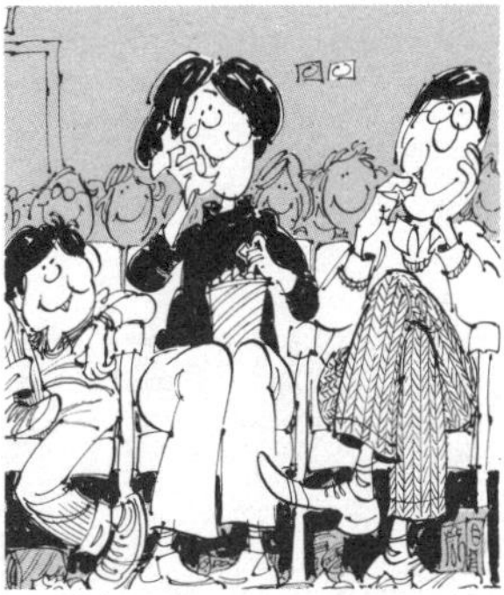

E.T. in the movie was cute!

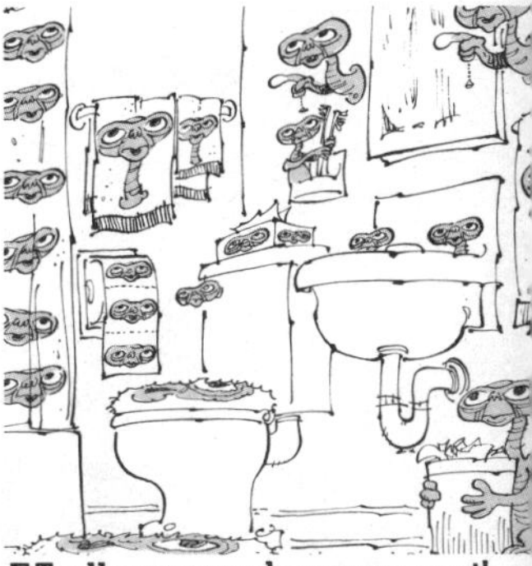

E.T. all over your house was not!

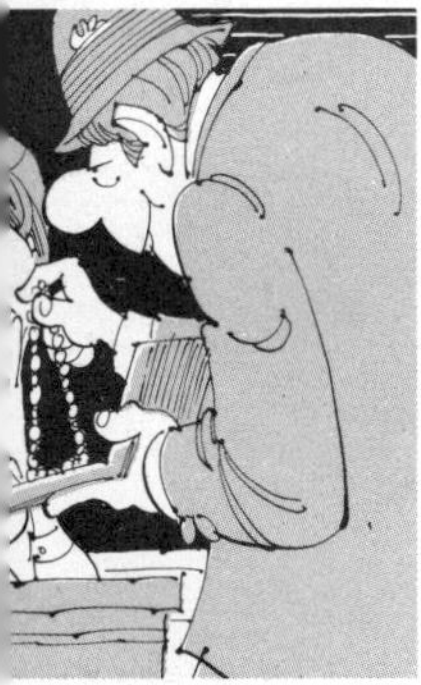

ur husband's crush on
e same teacher is not!

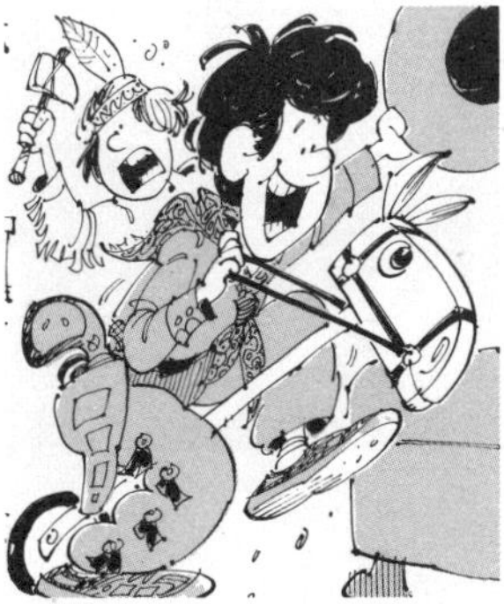

Playing "Cowboys and Indians"
when you're a kid is cute...!

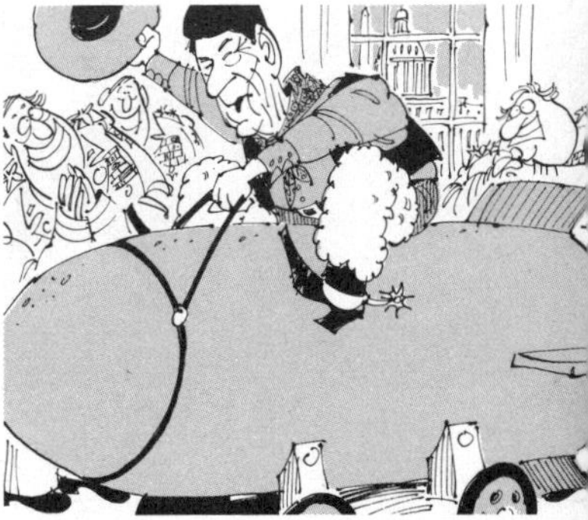

Playing "Cowboys and Indians" when
you're President of the U.S. is not!

DICK DePT.

They sounded great at first, but upon reflection they really didn't turn out right. Here's our latest collection of....

ADS

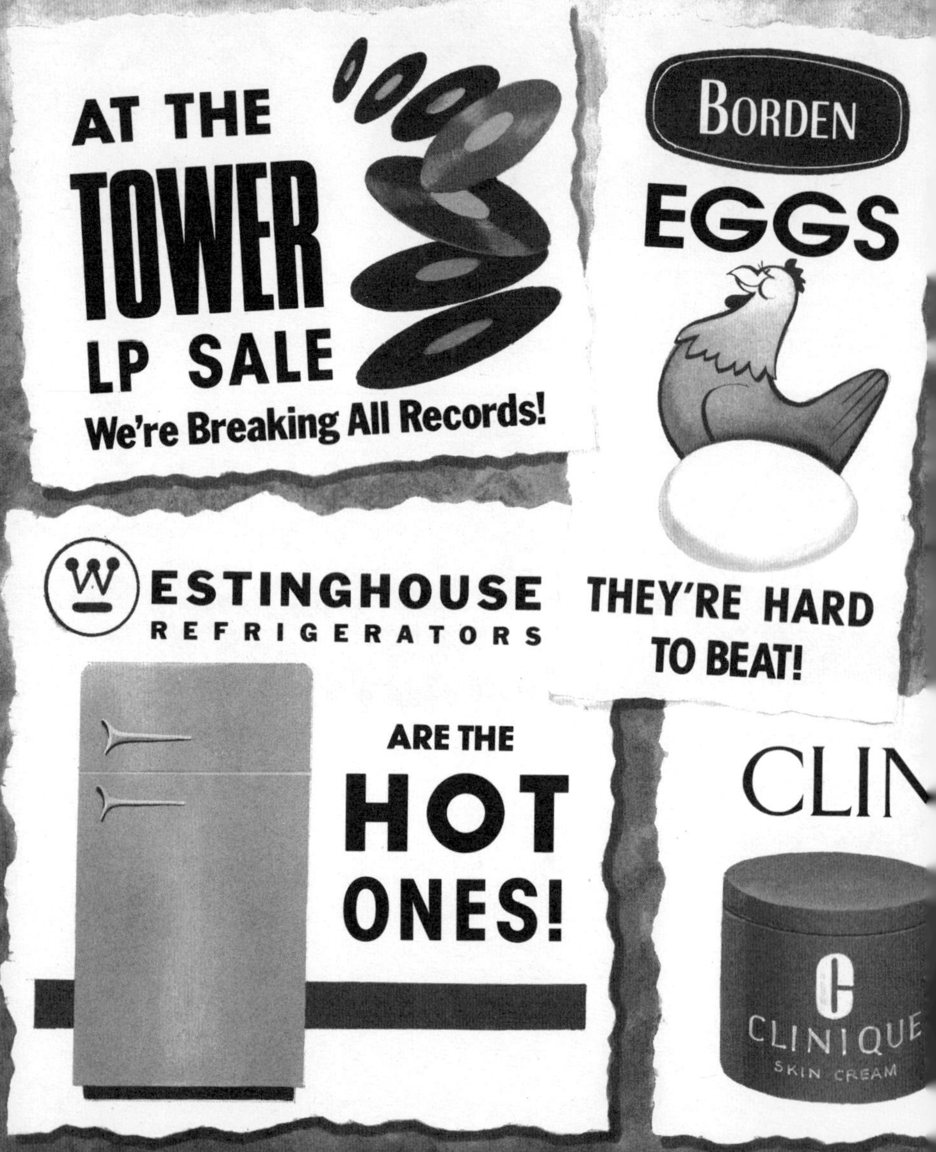
AT THE
TOWER
LP SALE
We're Breaking All Records!
BORDEN
EGGS
THEY'RE HARD
TO BEAT!
W
ESTINGHOUSE
REFRIGERATORS
ARE THE
HOT
ONES!
CLIN
C
CLINIQUE
SKIN CREAM

we never got to see!

ARTIST: BOB CLARKE WRITER: DICK DE BARTOLO

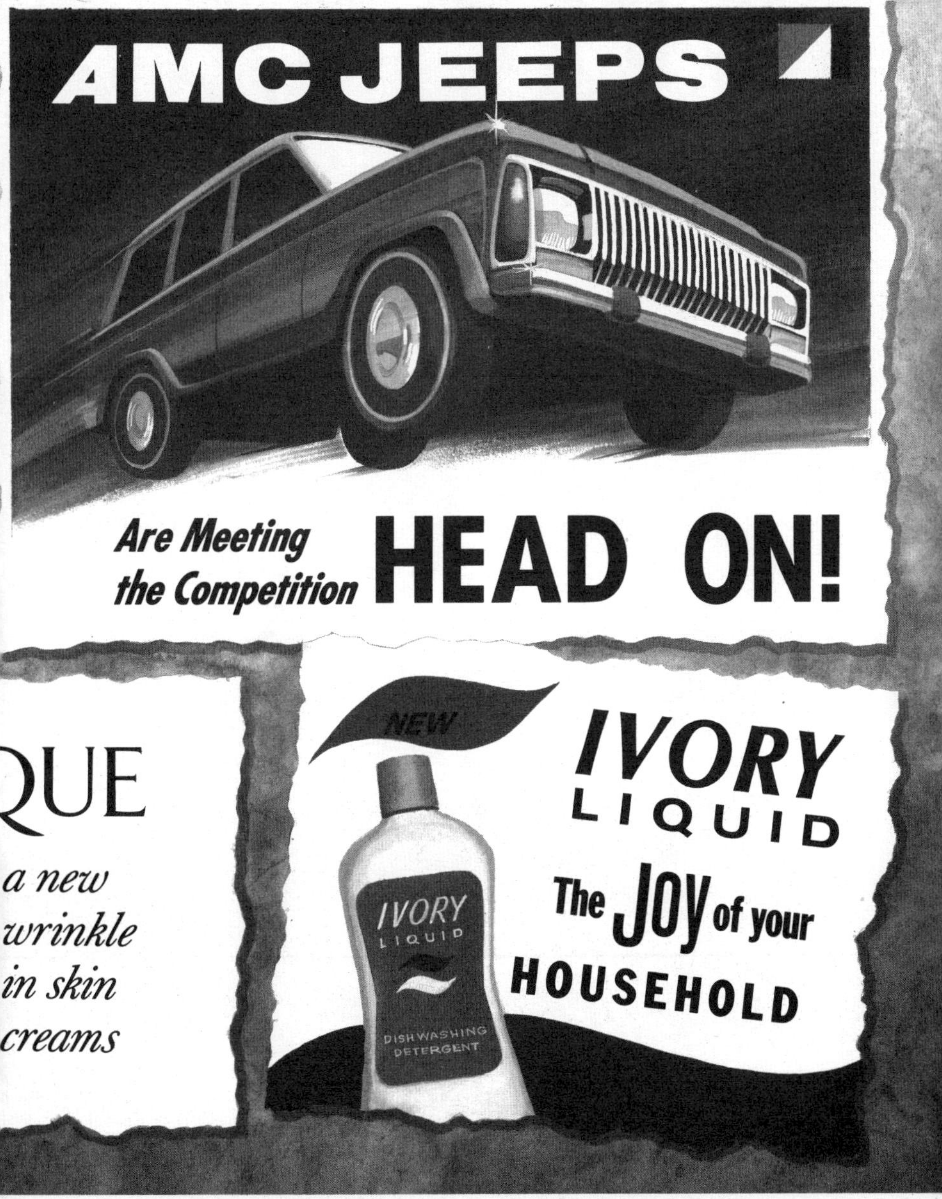

AMC JEEPS
Are Meeting the Competition
HEAD ON!
QUE
a new wrinkle in skin creams
NEW
IVORY
LIQUID
IVORY LIQUID
DISHWASHING DETERGENT
The JOY of your
HOUSEHOLD

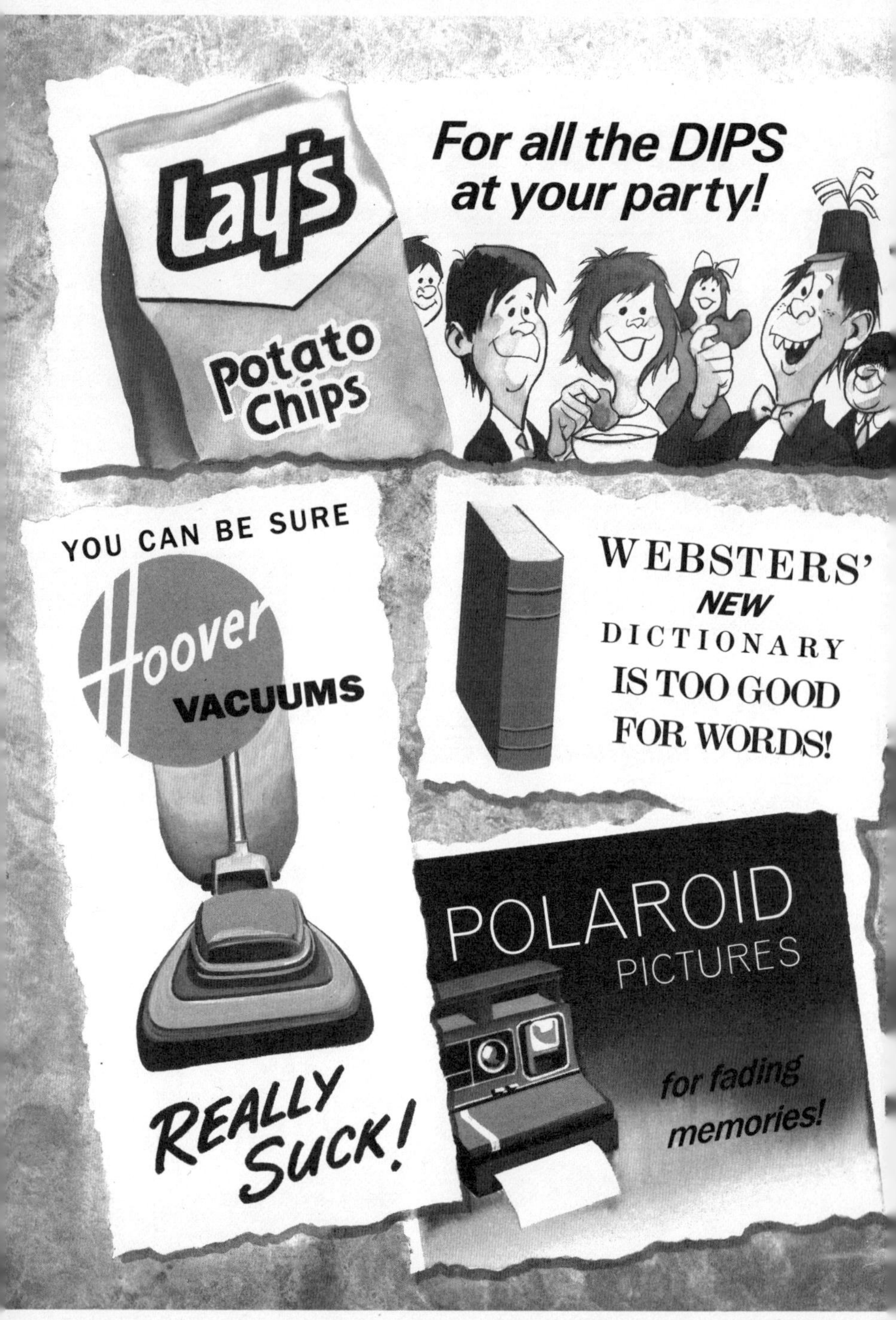

Lay's
Potato Chips
For all the DIPS at your party!
YOU CAN BE SURE
Hoover
VACUUMS
REALLY SUCK!
WEBSTERS'
NEW
DICTIONARY
IS TOO GOOD FOR WORDS!
POLAROID
PICTURES
for fading memories!

DON MARTIN DEPT.

A FINE DAY IN THE CITY

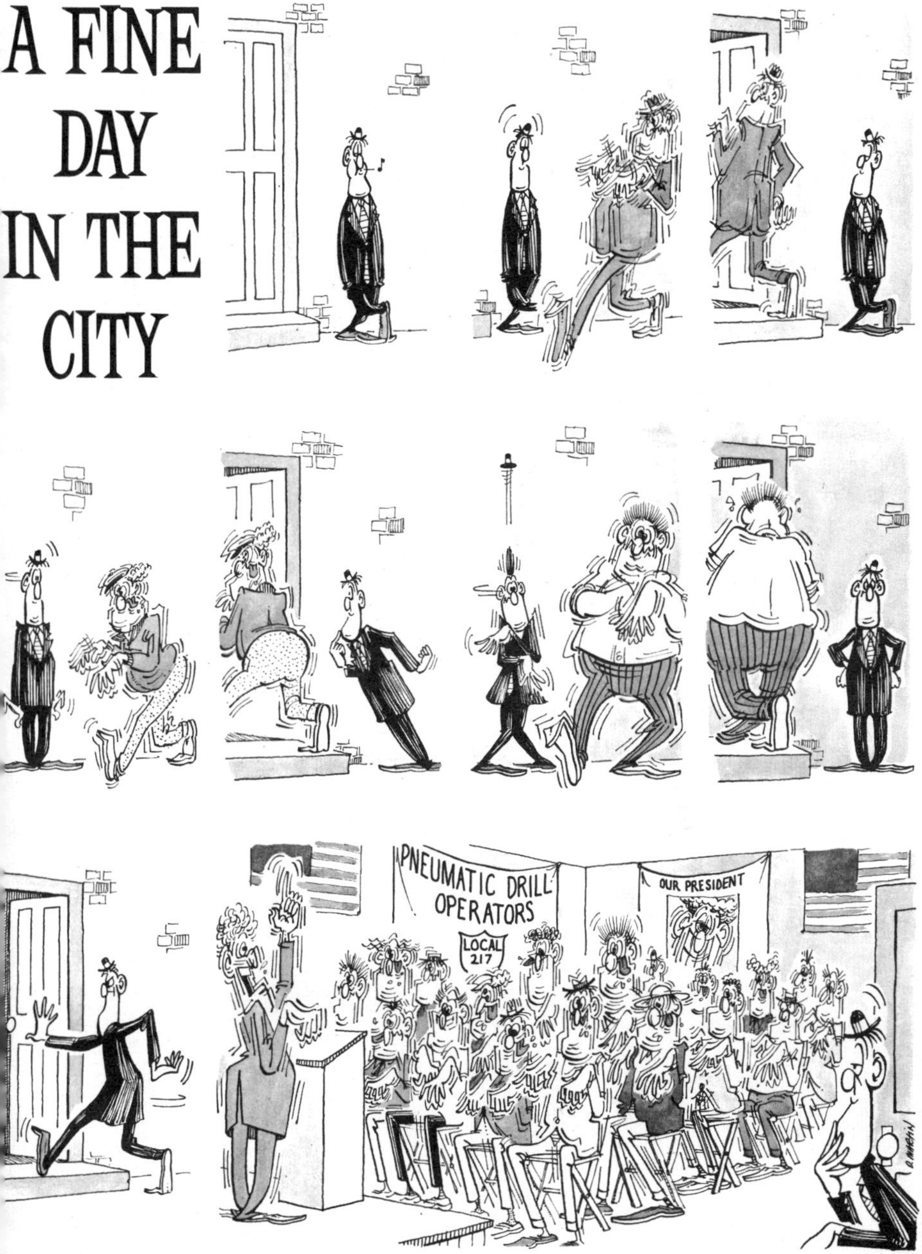
PNEUMATIC DRILL OPERATORS
LOCAL 217
OUR PRESIDENT
D. MARTIN

CASSETTING NEW LOWS DEPT.

If you've been in a video store lately you've probably seen "gems" like old TV shows and ads repackaged into "Special Collections." The same junk you got over the air for free, people are now trying to rent or sell to you! With a video industry *that* greedy it's obvious where all this is leading! So, let's preview some...

Junky Vide

ARTIST: ANGELO TORR

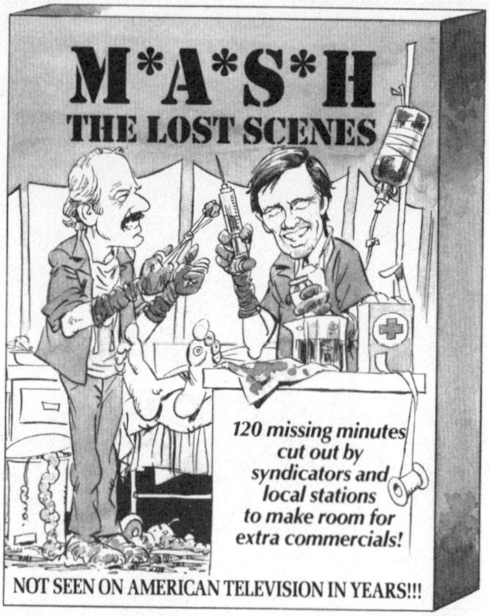

M*A*S*H
THE LOST SCENES
120 missing minutes cut out by syndicators and local stations to make room for extra commercials!
NOT SEEN ON AMERICAN TELEVISION IN YEARS!!!

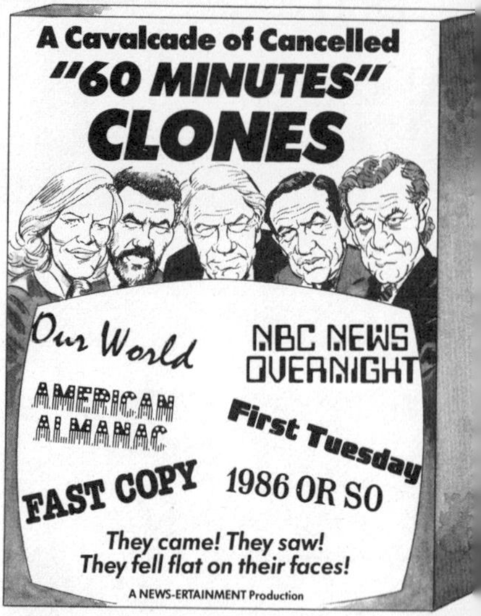

A Cavalcade of Cancelled
"60 MINUTES"
CLONES
Our World
NBC NEWS OVERNIGHT
AMERICAN ALMANAC
First Tuesday
FAST COPY
1986 OR SO
They came! They saw! They fell flat on their faces!
A NEWS-ERTAINMENT Production

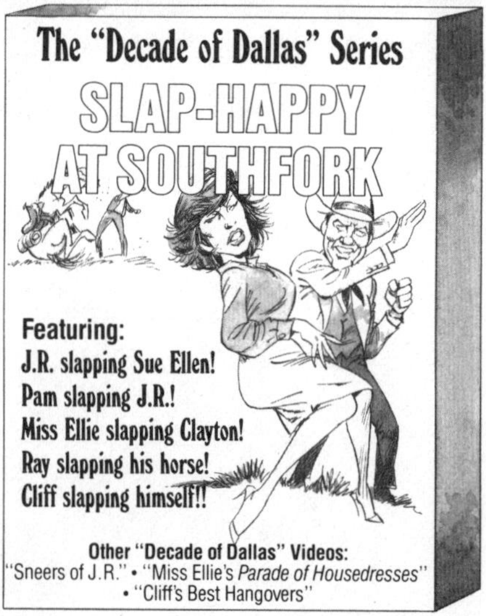

The "Decade of Dallas" Series
SLAP-HAPPY AT SOUTHFORK
Featuring:
J.R. slapping Sue Ellen!
Pam slapping J.R.!
Miss Ellie slapping Clayton!
Ray slapping his horse!
Cliff slapping himself!!
Other "Decade of Dallas" Videos:
"Sneers of J.R." • "Miss Ellie's Parade of Housedresses" • "Cliff's Best Hangovers"

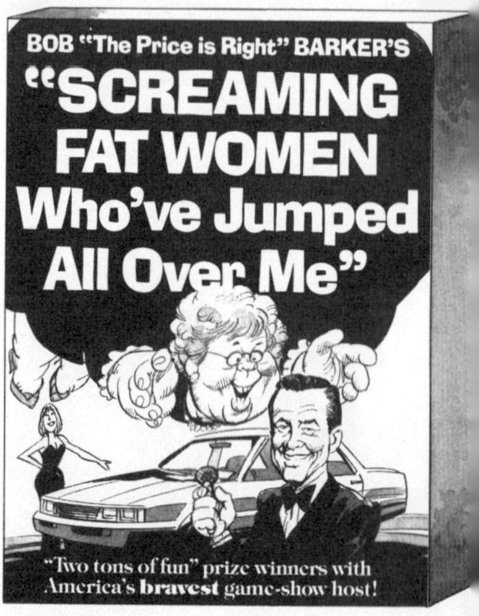

BOB "The Price is Right" BARKER'S
"SCREAMING FAT WOMEN Who've Jumped All Over Me"
"Two tons of fun" prize winners with America's bravest game-show host!

Collections WE'RE SURE TO SEE

ER: MIKE SNIDER

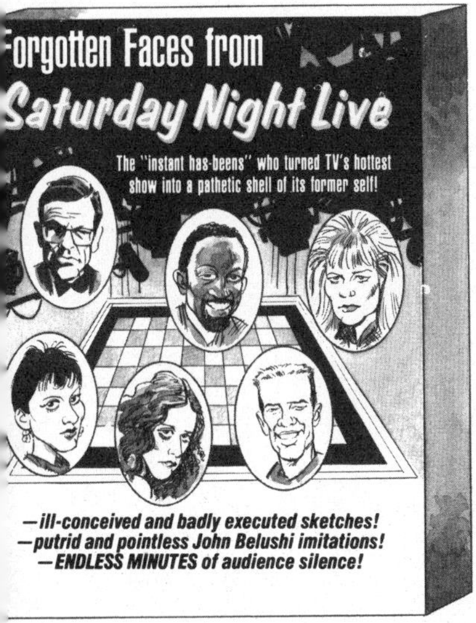

orgotten Faces from
Saturday Night Live
The "instant has-beens" who turned TV's hottest show into a pathetic shell of its former self!
—ill-conceived and badly executed sketches!
—putrid and pointless John Belushi imitations!
—ENDLESS MINUTES of audience silence!

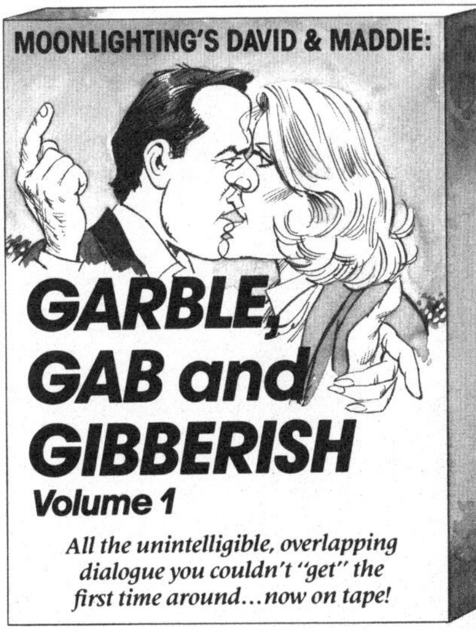

MOONLIGHTING'S DAVID & MADDIE:
GARBLE, GAB and GIBBERISH
Volume 1
All the unintelligible, overlapping dialogue you couldn't "get" the first time around...now on tape!

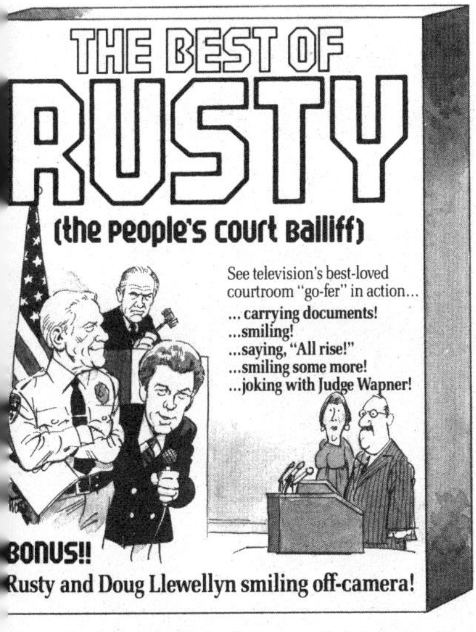

THE BEST OF
RUSTY
(the people's court bailiff)
See television's best-loved courtroom "go-fer" in action...
... carrying documents!
...smiling!
...saying, "All rise!"
...smiling some more!
...joking with Judge Wapner!
BONUS!!
Rusty and Doug Llewellyn smiling off-camera!

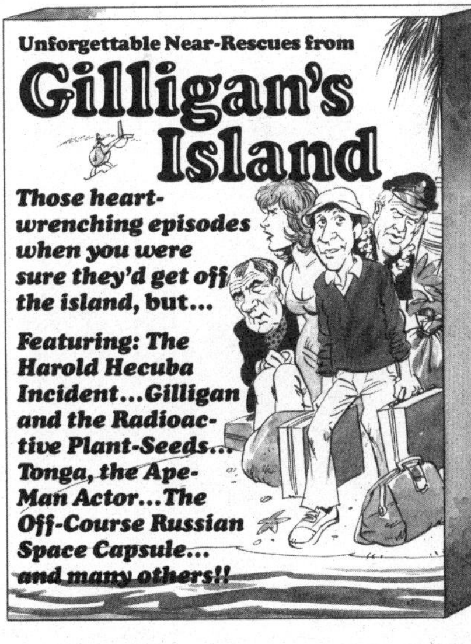

Unforgettable Near-Rescues from
Gilligan's Island
Those heart-wrenching episodes when you were sure they'd get off the island, but...
Featuring: The Harold Hecuba Incident...Gilligan and the Radioactive Plant-Seeds...Tonga, the Ape-Man Actor...The Off-Course Russian Space Capsule...and many others!!

IT'S WANING CATS AND DOGS AND... DEPT.

Your Pet Has Reached

...your parrot makes special menu requests...
AND SOME LUKEWARM MILK
...your dachshund's middle is lower than its ends...
...your angora runs out of angora...
...your doberman gives limp handshakes...
...your schnauzer doesn't recognize his old friends...
PORGES

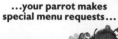

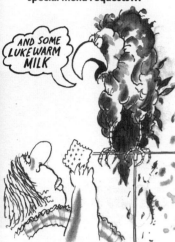

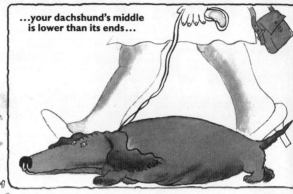

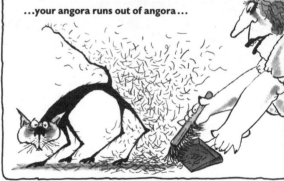

ARTIST & WRITER: PAUL PETER PORGES

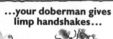

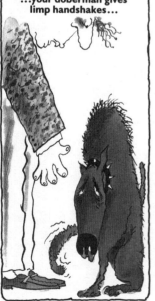

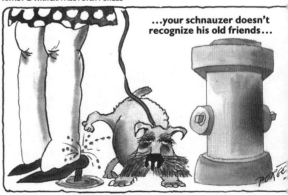

Blissful Retirement When

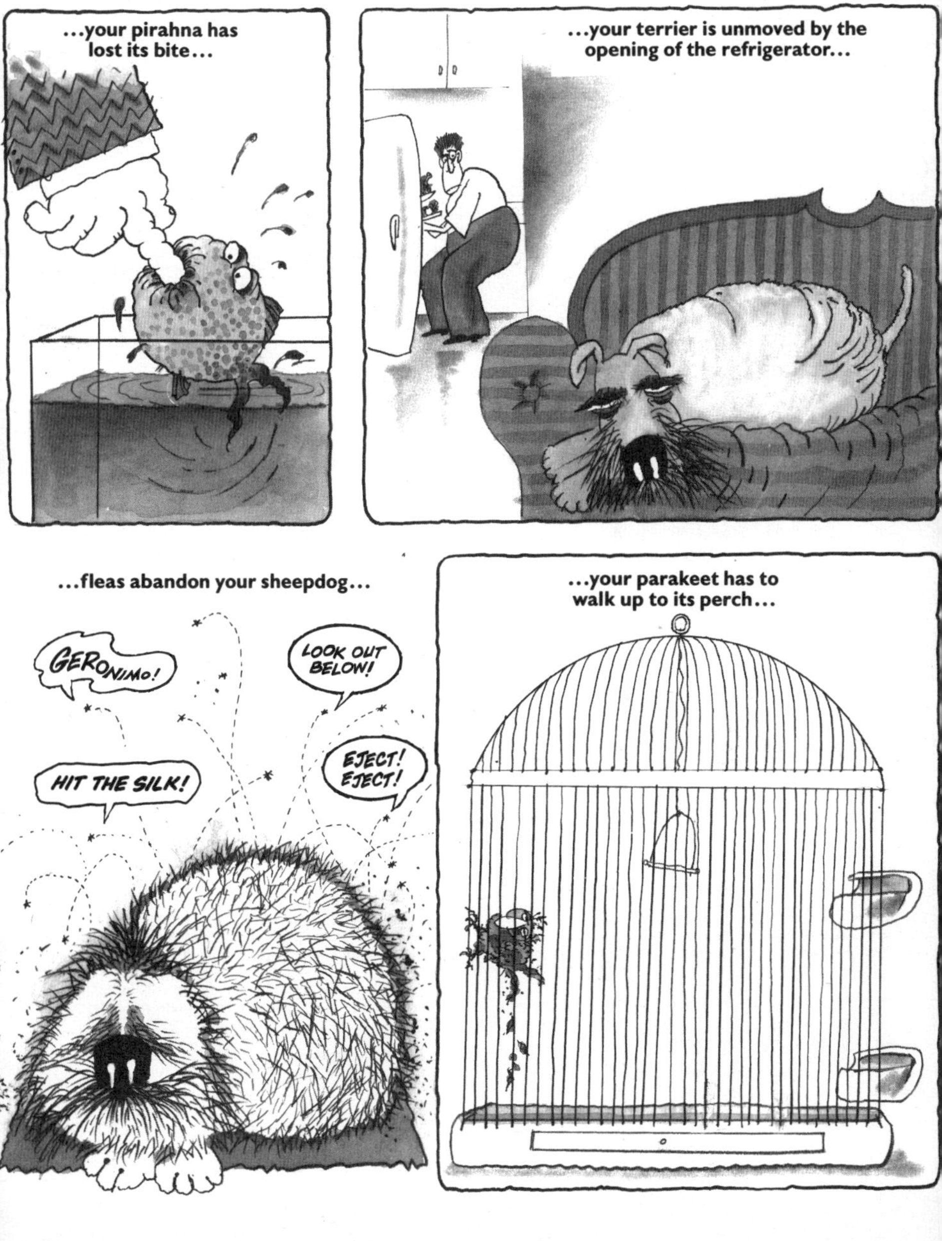

...your pirahna has lost its bite...
...your terrier is unmoved by the opening of the refrigerator...
...fleas abandon your sheepdog...
GERONIMO!
LOOK OUT BELOW!
HIT THE SILK!
EJECT! EJECT!
...your parakeet has to walk up to its perch...

ASK KICKERS DEPT.

Have you ever stopped to think of how many forms you fill out in the course of a year while applying for such varied things as charge accounts and medical care and school admissions? More important, have you ever stopped to think that most of the people asking the questions are the same ones who are also asking you t

IF "THEY" HAD TO FILL OU

ARTIST: HARRY NORT

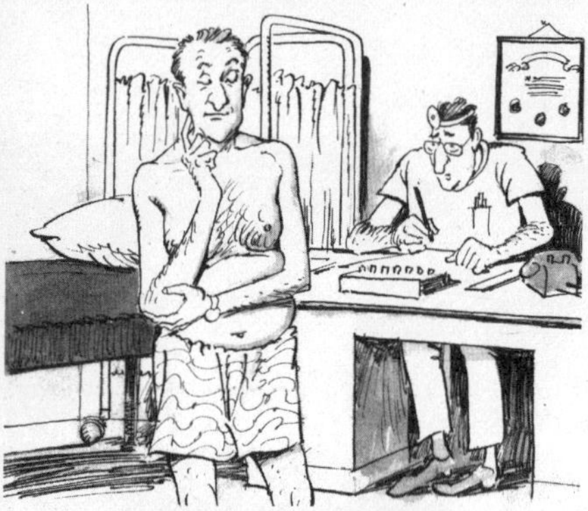

NEW PATIENT'S QUESTIONNAIRE FOR AN UNFAMILIAR DOCTOR

Please cooperate by answering all of the following questions completely. Your assistance will better enable the new patient now awaiting treatment to diagnose your qualifications for messing around with the only body that he (or she) will ever have.
(P.S. Just this once, try writing legibly, as there is no pharmacist on hand to attempt to decipher your usual childish scrawl.)

1. Do you plan to show off by describing my condition to me in complicated medical jargon that you know I can't understand? ____________

2. Do you plan to ask for a specimen, and then just stand there and wait, thus making me too nervous to give you one? ____________

3. Is your examining table covered with that hard, slick paper that sticks to a person's sweaty body on hot days? ____________

4. Do you customarily stick a tongue depressor so far back in a patient's throat that he tends to lose his cookies? ____________

5. Will you look in my ear with a flashlight, just so you can get close enough to breathe germs on me that you picked up from your previous patient? ____________

6. When giving injections, how many stabs must you usually make before finding a vein? ____________

7. Give a phone number where I can reach you tonight after the treatment you provide this afternoon fails to work. ____________

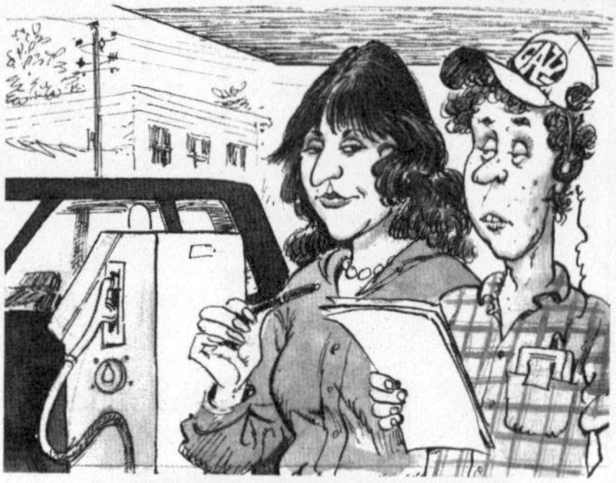

OIL COMPANY'S APPLICATION TO BECOME A CREDIT CARD APPLICANT'S OIL COMPANY

Since the motorist presenting this questionnaire has just been required to fill out a long, probing form in order to buy gas and service from your company on credit, it seems only fair that you should reveal a few of your deepest secrets, too. Therefore, please find an employee who can read and write, and instruct him to answer the following. Also, instruct him not to leave dirty smudges on the paper, like those he usually leaves on everything he touches.

1. Please explain why "Full Service" costs 12-cents a gallon more, when all I get for it is a dirty rag rubbed over my windshield. ____________

2. Are credit card holders entitled to such preferential treatment as actually getting new spark plugs when they are charged for them? ____________

3. How high must your prices go before you can afford to hire someone to mop your rest room floor once a month? ____________

4. Do you plan to raise gas prices again next summer, solely because you know motorists will buy more then, no matter how much it costs? ____________

5. Will you continue to lower the octane rating on your unleaded gas until every car requires the premium grade costing 20-cents a gallon more? ____________

6. Why does your dealer in my neighborhood insist that I need eight quarts of oil to fill a five-quart crankcase? ____________

7. Once I have my credit card, can I be waited on by that cheerful guy who does your TV commercials, rather than the grouch I presently get? ____________

give them your money, your time or your trust? Well, now that you've stopped to think about it, don't you also think that matters should really be reversed, and you are the one who's entitled to do the questioning? MAD certainly thinks so! That's why we've prepared these nosy, fact-finding forms you'd sure enjoy using

"YOUR" QUESTIONNAIRES

WRITER: TOM KOCH

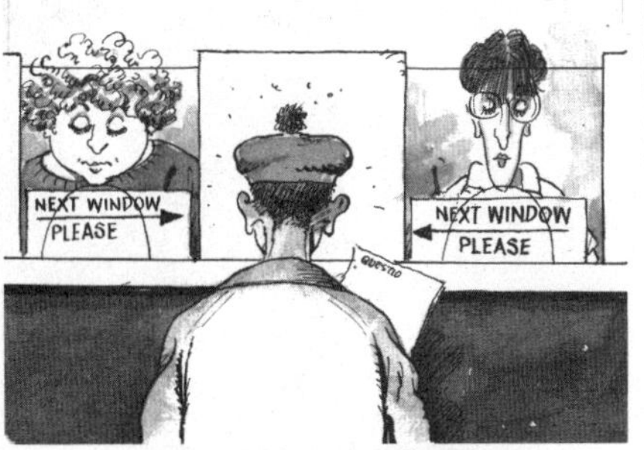
NEXT WINDOW PLEASE
NEXT WINDOW PLEASE

POTENTIAL DEPOSITOR'S REQUEST FOR FULL DISCLOSURE OF BANKING COMPETENCE

This questionnaire is being presented to you by an ordinary working stiff who contemplates entrusting his life savings to your financial institution. Please take a moment to glance around at your employees, and imagine how nervous you would feel giving money to any of them. Then fill out this form in full.
(Note: Your answers to these questions will not be kept any more confidential than you keep the deposit figures of your customers when credit agencies come snooping around.)

1. If I have $10,000 in my account, and try to withdraw $50, how many of your people must vouch for my honesty before I get it? ____________

2. Are your tellers specifically instructed to go on their coffee breaks whenever there are more than four people waiting in line? ____________

3. Do you have one of those drive-in windows where the girl behind the glass can hear everything I say, but I can't hear her at all? ____________

4. Why am I allowed only 20 minutes of free parking in your lot when you know that the simplest transaction will take twice that long? ____________

5. If you really have $500-million in assets, why can't you afford one workable ball point pen for use in filling out deposit slips? ____________

6. Describe how your 73-year-old security guard with the thick glasses and the hearing aid plans to protect my money. ____________

7. How many years must I have an account here before at least one of your tellers remembers having seen me before? ____________

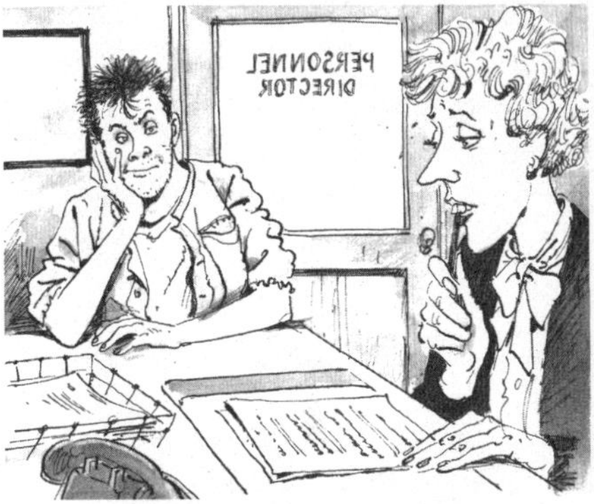
PERSONNEL DIRECTOR

PROSPECTIVE EMPLOYER'S APPLICATION FOR JOB APPLICANT'S ACCEPTANCE

This vital form is presented by a potential employee who may soon have to start making changes in his leisurely life-style to go to work for your outfit. Naturally, this raises a lot of questions about your company's worthiness to ask for such a drastic personal sacrifice. Please take ample time to answer all of the following questions fully and truthfully. Failure to do so could result in my missing a chance to go to work somewhere else that has a better deal to offer.

1. How many weeks of paid vacation will I get the first year? ____________

2. Can I take this vacation time before starting work, and if so, who do I see about getting paid for it in advance? ____________

3. Must I actually show up for work at least once before phoning in sick, and starting to collect disability insurance? ____________

4. Give names and department locations of three attractive members of the opposite sex who are currently hot to start a new relationship. ____________

5. Will someone be assigned to punch my time card for me on days when I am late, or must I make my own arrangements for that? ____________

6. List some items of value that employees can safely carry out of the building without being stopped by the guard at the front gate. ____________

7. If I start next Monday, how soon can I retire with full benefits? ____________

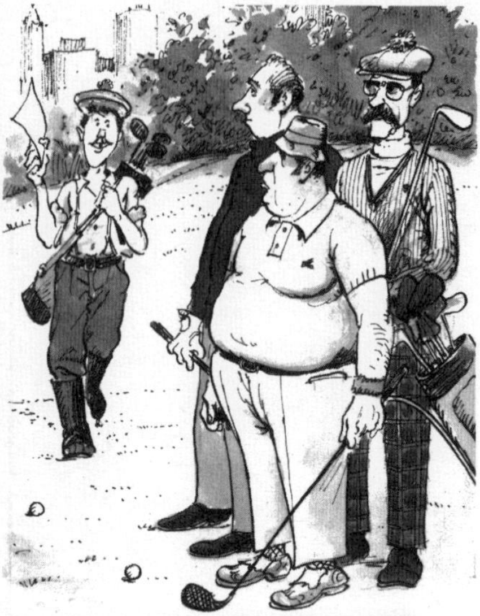

POTENTIAL COUNTRY CLUB JOINER'S REQUEST FOR MUTUAL DISCLOSURE OF INFORMATION

While your Membership Screening Committee is naturally concerned about admitting an applicant whose character, morality and community standing may not measure up to your standards, it is equally true that the applicant presenting this questionnaire isn't sure he wants to associate with you either. Therefore, please be advised that said applicant doesn't intend to write his check for membership fees until your club officials have written their answers to the questions on this form.

1. Can I assume that you asked all those personal things about my religion because you want to be sure I don't have any, and will thus be available to play golf with you on Sunday? ______

2. I notice that you've had trouble finding black people who want to join your club. Would you like my help in finding some for you? ______

3. As community leaders, don't you feel obligated to tell the police that club members gamble for real money on your golf course? ______

4. In reference to Question Number 3, shouldn't your police report also mention the gambling in your card room? ______

5. Is that guard at the gate supposed to keep non-members from entering, or to keep members from leaving when they're too drunk to drive home? ______

6. What does your Pro Shop do with all the money it makes selling 75-cent golf balls for three-dollars apiece?

7. Did you eyer stop to figure that I could play 800 rounds of golf a year at a public course for less than you charge in annual dues? ______

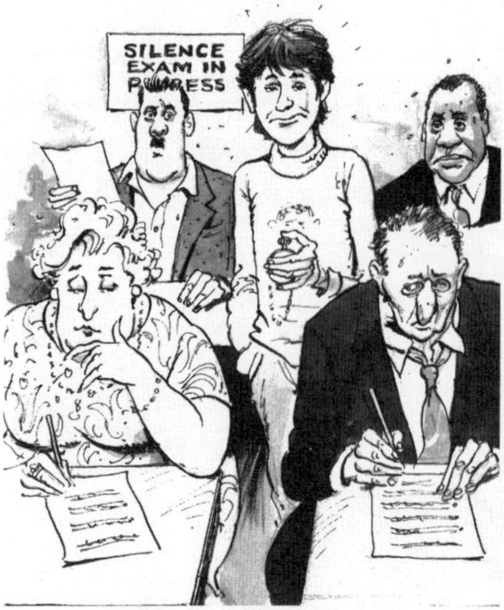
SILENCE
EXAM IN
P[?]GRESS

CAMPUS ADMINISTRATORS' STUDENT ACCOMMODATIONS TEST

READ ALL INSTRUCTIONS BEFORE ATTEMPTING TO ANSWER QUESTIONS!

This S.A.T. Exam is being given to selected college administrative personnel and professors by a recent high school graduate who has the tuition money your school needs. Therefore, acceptable answers to all questions are of utmost importance if you hope to enroll this desirable young person. This S.A.T. may determine the whole future course of your life. So don't get nervous and blow it all by choking up.

1. Do your dormitories have any Freshman Restrictions, such as a curfew requiring me to be in by breakfast time? ______

2. Is there an adequate number of students of the opposite sex on campus, and, if not, what steps are being taken to correct this? ______

3. Does your library have plenty of dimly lit, secluded corners where I can take a date on occasions when I can't afford a motel room? ______

4. How far off campus (plus or minus one block) is the nearest tavern employing a bartender who never checks I.D.s? ______

5. Name at least three potential All-American football players who have signed letters of intent to enroll at your school next fall. ______

6. Are your faculty members specifically instructed not to give hard homework assignments that might interfere with my social life? ______

7. Use this space to give your sworn assurance that you can get me a job paying at least $30,000 a year following my graduation. ______

JOKE AND DAGGER DEPT.

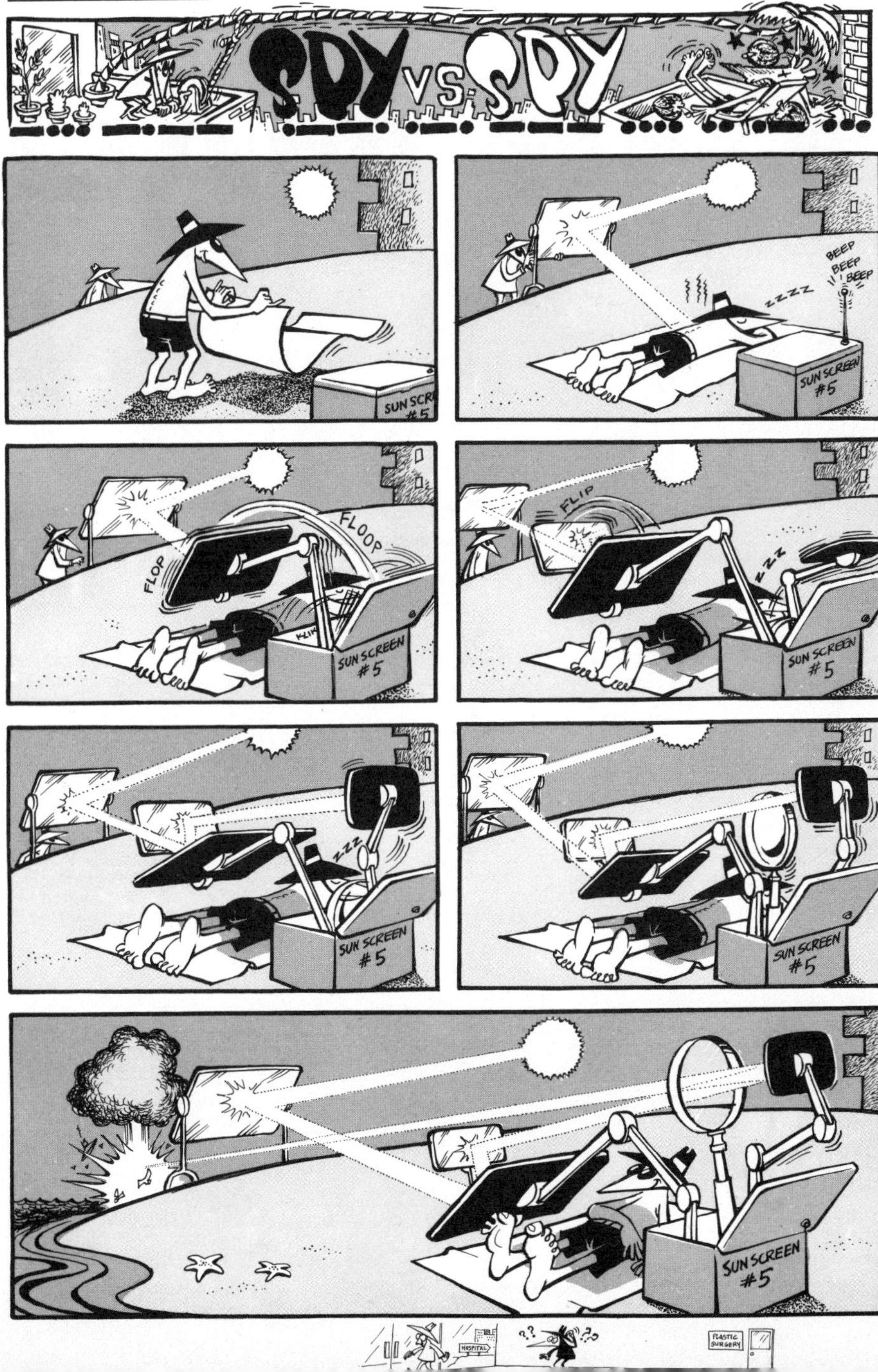
SPY VS SPY
SUN SCR
#5
BEEP
BEEP
BEEP
ZZZZ
SUN SCREEN
#5
FLOP
FLOOP
KLIK
SUN SCREEN
#5
FLIP
ZZZ
SUN SCREEN
#5
ZZZ
SUN SCREEN
#5
SUN SCREEN
#5
SUN SCREEN
#5
HOSPITAL
PLASTIC SURGERY

VEX EDUCATION DEPT.

Everyone has his "Pet Hate"—and that's good. Blowing off steam about your pet hate makes you feel better. And since MAD's purpose is to make everyone feel

THE MAD

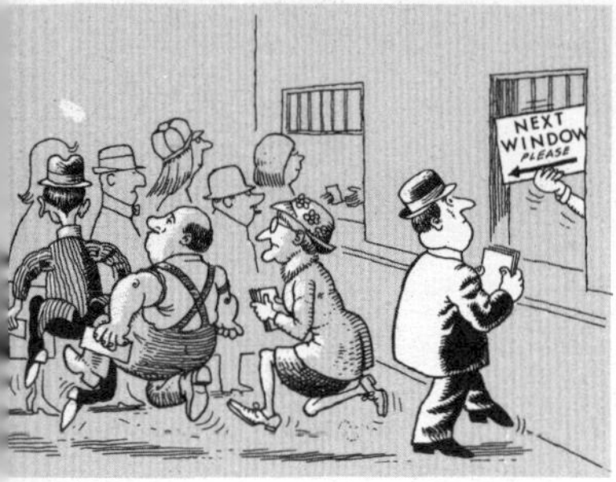
NEXT WINDOW PLEASE

Don't You Hate . . . clerks who go to lunch just as you reach their window!

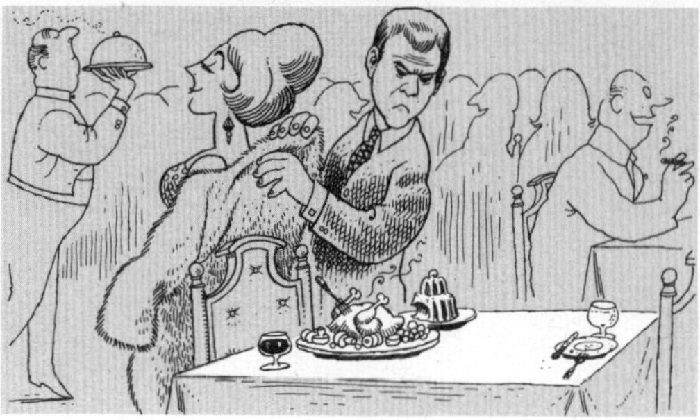

Don't You Hate . . . a date who orders the most expensive items on the menu, and then hardly eats anything!

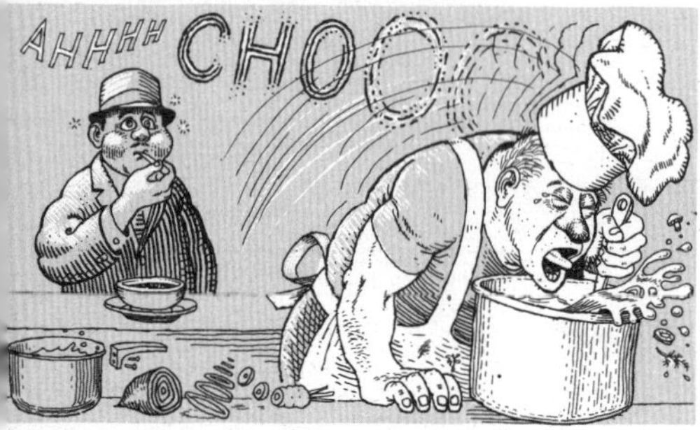
AHHHH CHOO

Don't You Hate . . . restaurant workers who are so dedicated to their jobs they even come in when they're sick!

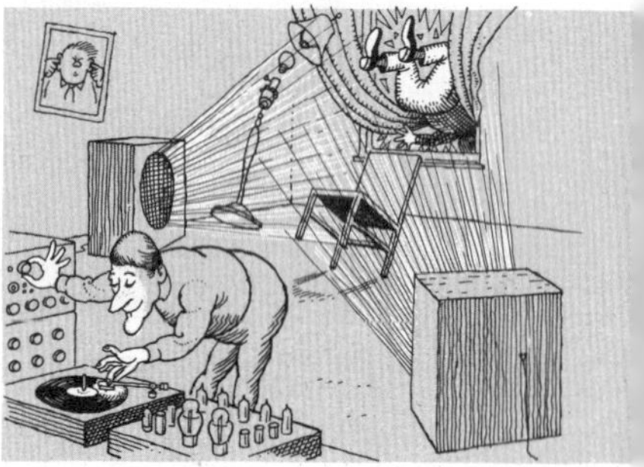

Don't You Hate . . . retards who play their Hi-Fi sets at concert hall pitch!

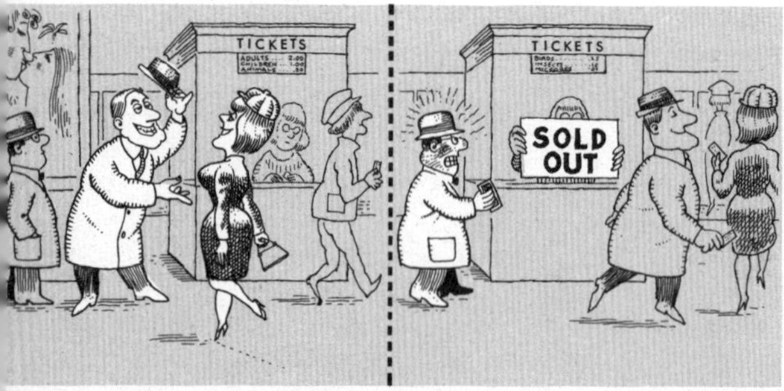
TICKETS
TICKETS
SOLD OUT

Don't You Hate . . . meatheads who let other people in ahead of them on a line!

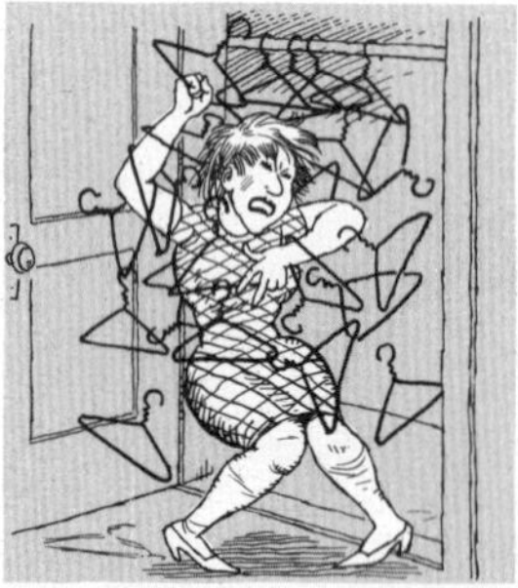

Don't You Hate . . . wire hangers!

wonderful, we've decided to present a *whole collection* of pet hates. Now you can blow off steam about more than one, namely any that strike your fancy from . . .

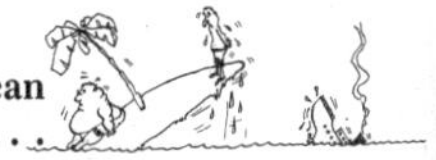

HATE BOOK

ARTIST & WRITER: AL JAFFEE

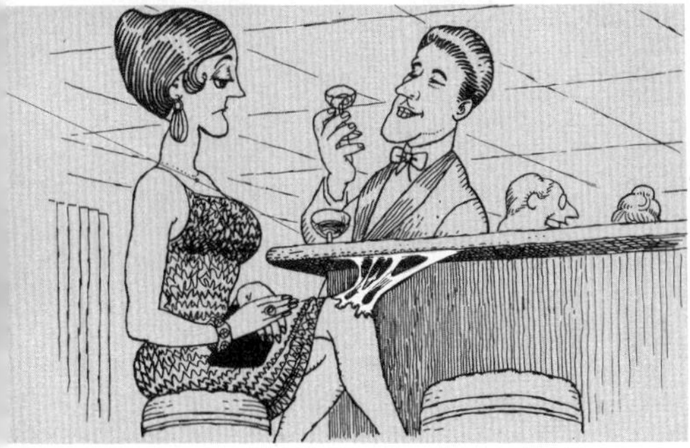

Don't You Hate . . . finding carefully hidden chewing gum!

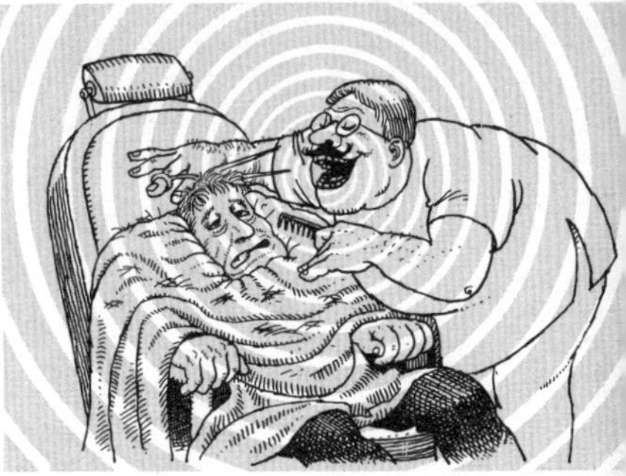

Don't You Hate . . . talkative barbers with bad breath!

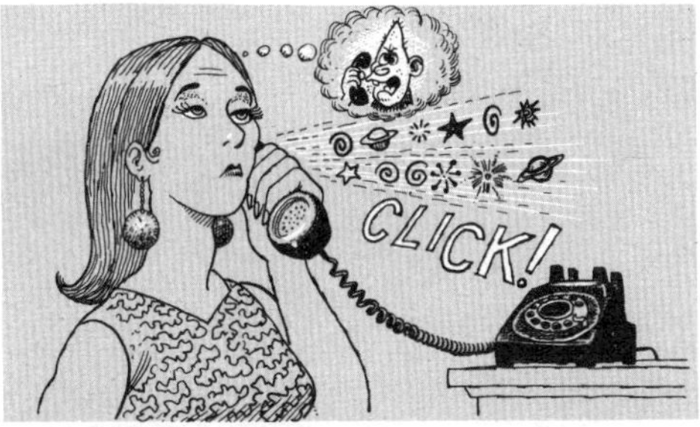
CLICK!

Don't You Hate . . . cretins who play brilliant phone games like talking dirty, or asking stupid questions, or laughing, or screaming, etc., and then hanging up!

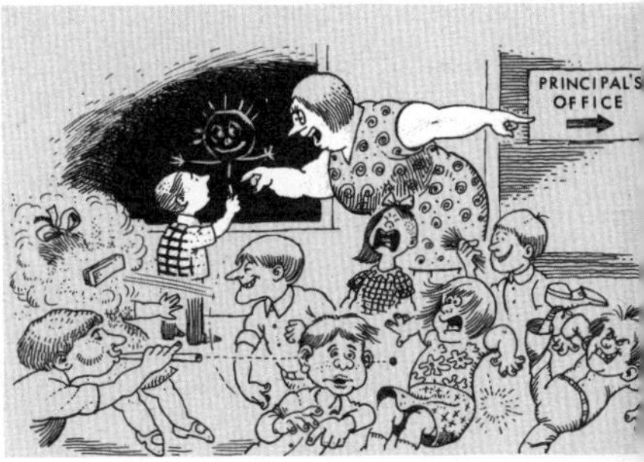
PRINCIPAL'S OFFICE

Don't You Hate . . . teachers who catch only you . . . when everyone else is misbehaving!

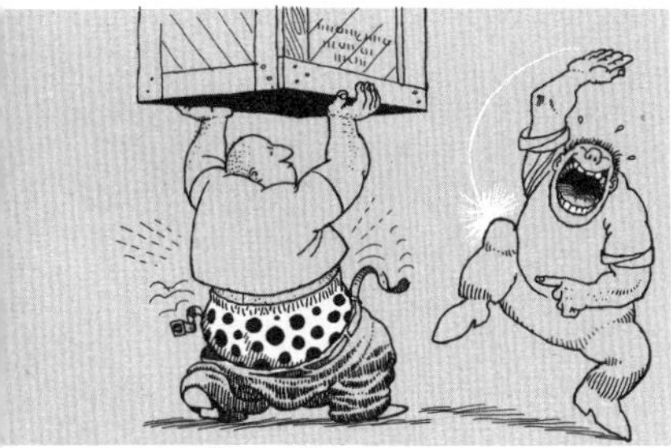

Don't You Hate . . . people who find humor in the misfortunes of others!

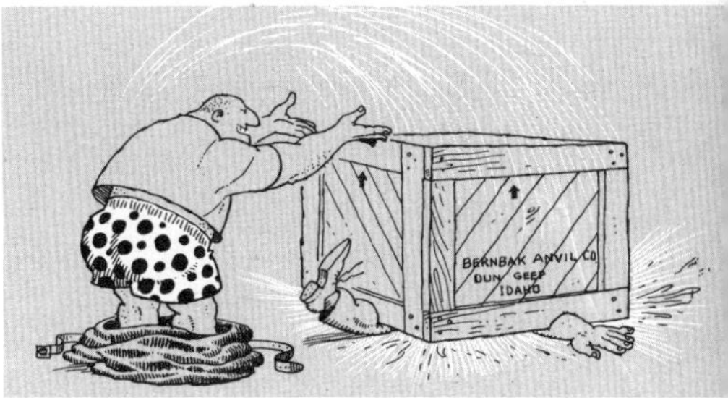
BERNBAK ANVIL CO
DUN GEEP
IDAHO

Don't You Hate . . . people who can't see the humor of finding humor in the misfortunes of others!

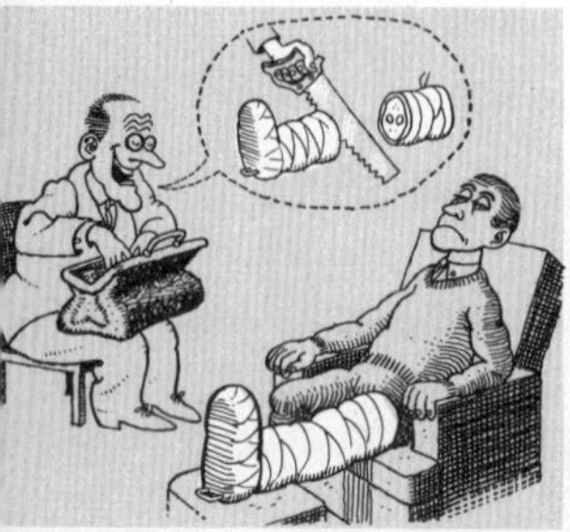

Don't You Hate... "funny" doctors!

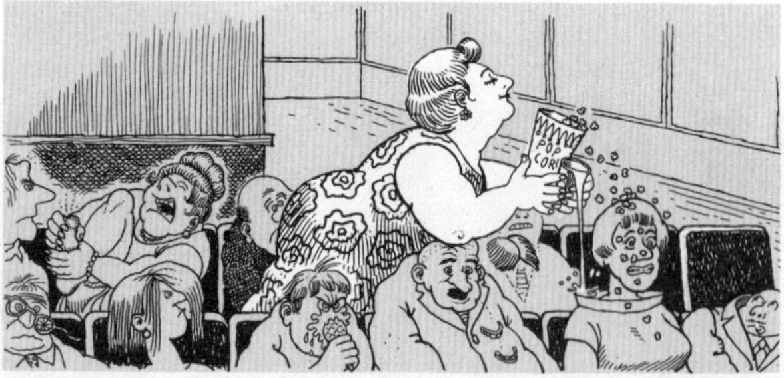
POP

Don't You Hate... fat slobs who go back and forth to their theatre seats!

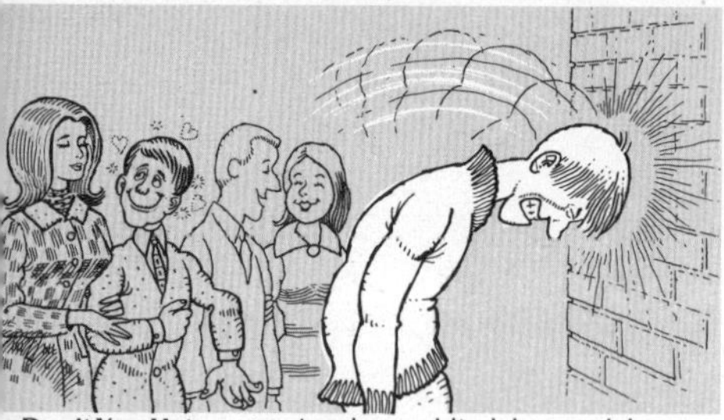

Don't You Hate... turning down a blind date, and then finding out she looked like Ursula Andress!

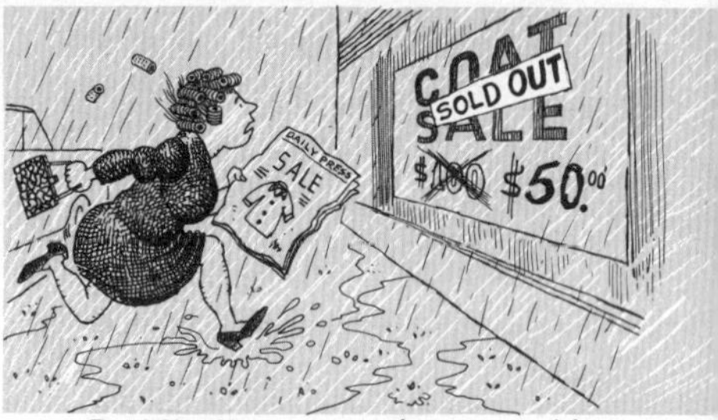
COAT
SOLD OUT
SALE
$100 $50.00
DAILY PRESS
SALE

Don't You Hate... stores that are out of the one thing you drove 20 miles to get!

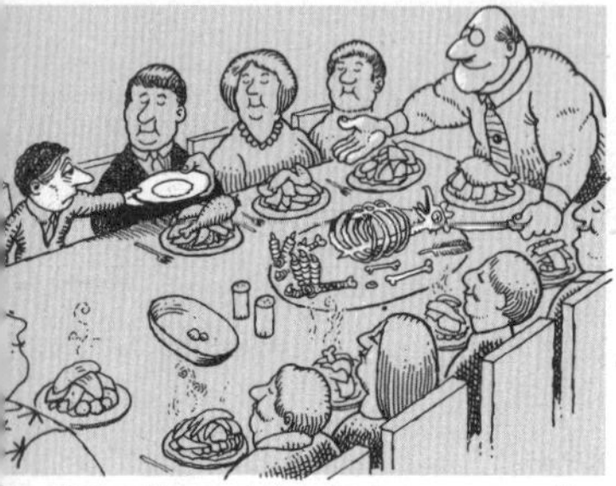

Don't You Hate... being the last one served!

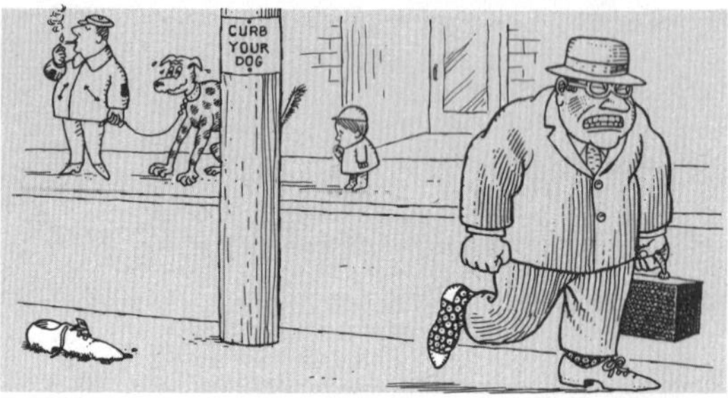
CURB YOUR DOG

Don't You Hate... people who keep enormous dogs in the city!

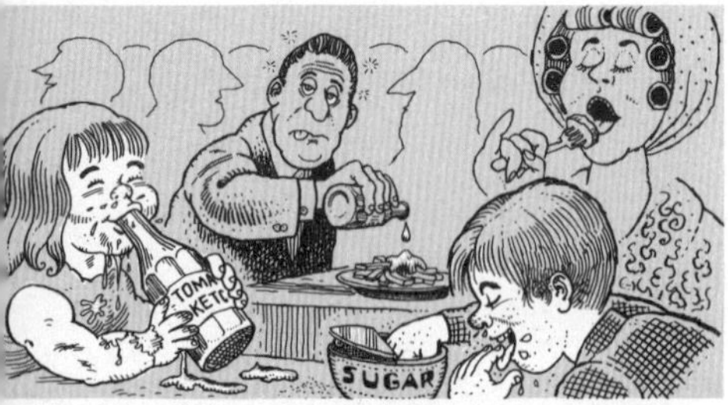
SUGAR

Don't You Hate... parents who don't supervise their ill-mannered brats in restaurants!

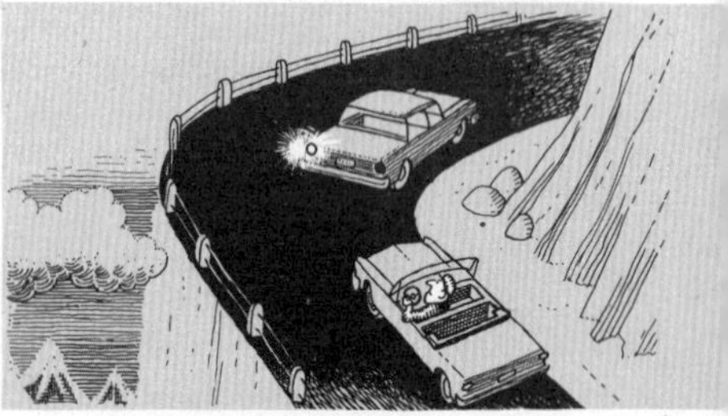

Don't You Hate... idiots who signal a left... and then make a right turn!

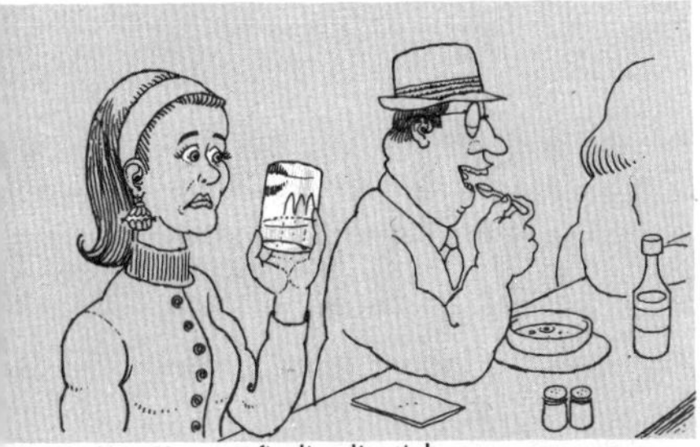

Don't You Hate . . . finding lipstick smears on your glass, and it's not your color!

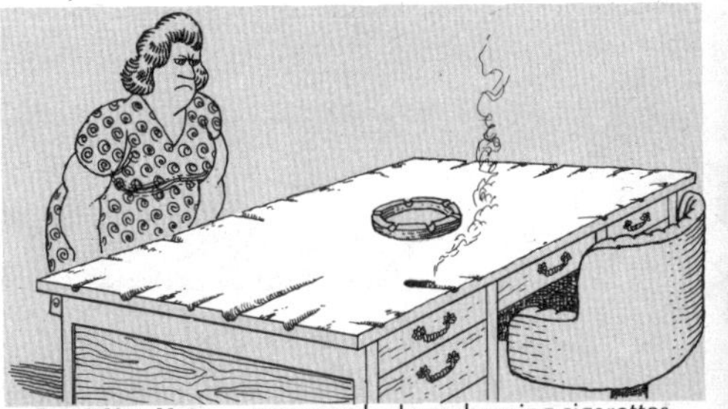

Don't You Hate . . . morons who leave burning cigarettes on the edges of tables and desks!

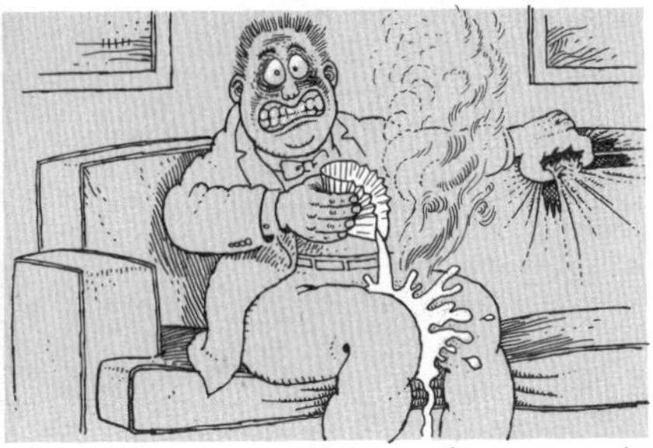

Don't You Hate . . . hot drinks served in paper cups!

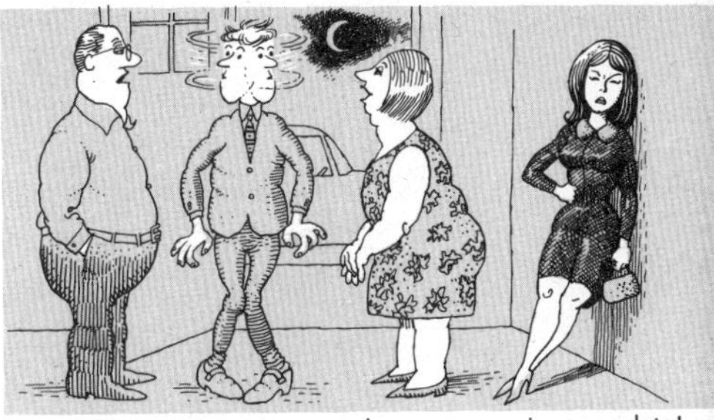

Don't You Hate . . . parents who cross-examine your date!

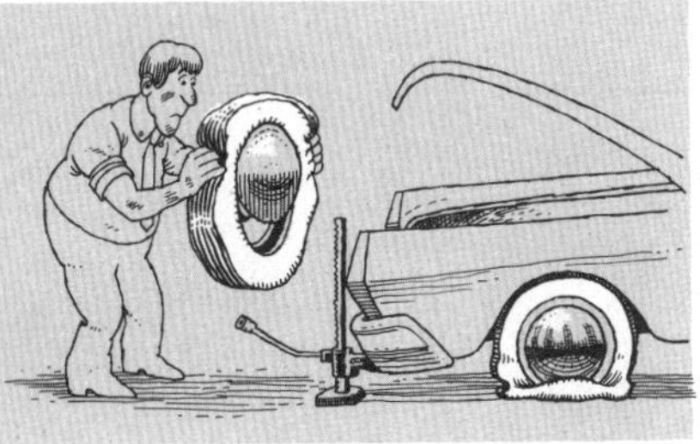

Don't You Hate . . . spare tires that are flatter than the one you're changing!

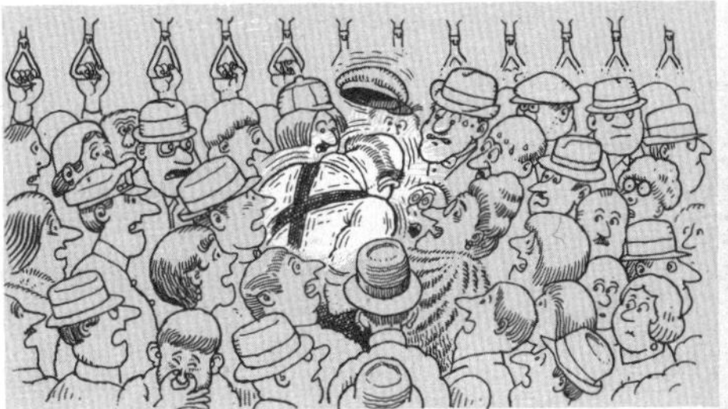

Don't You Hate . . . people who get sick to their stomach in crowded places!

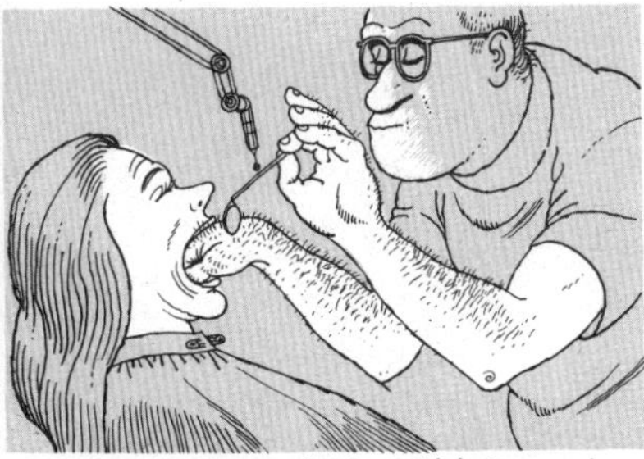

Don't You Hate . . . dentists with hairy arms!

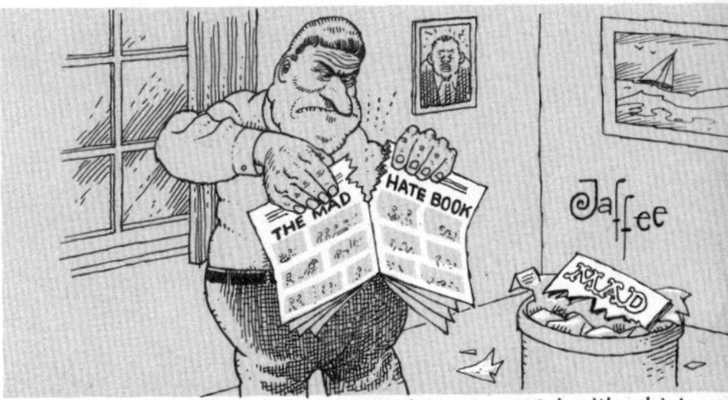
THE MAD
HATE BOOK
Jaffee
MAD

Don't You Hate . . . magazines that print articles like this!

STRONG GUESTS OF WIND DEPT.

FIRST ANNUA
GUESTS OF THE PI

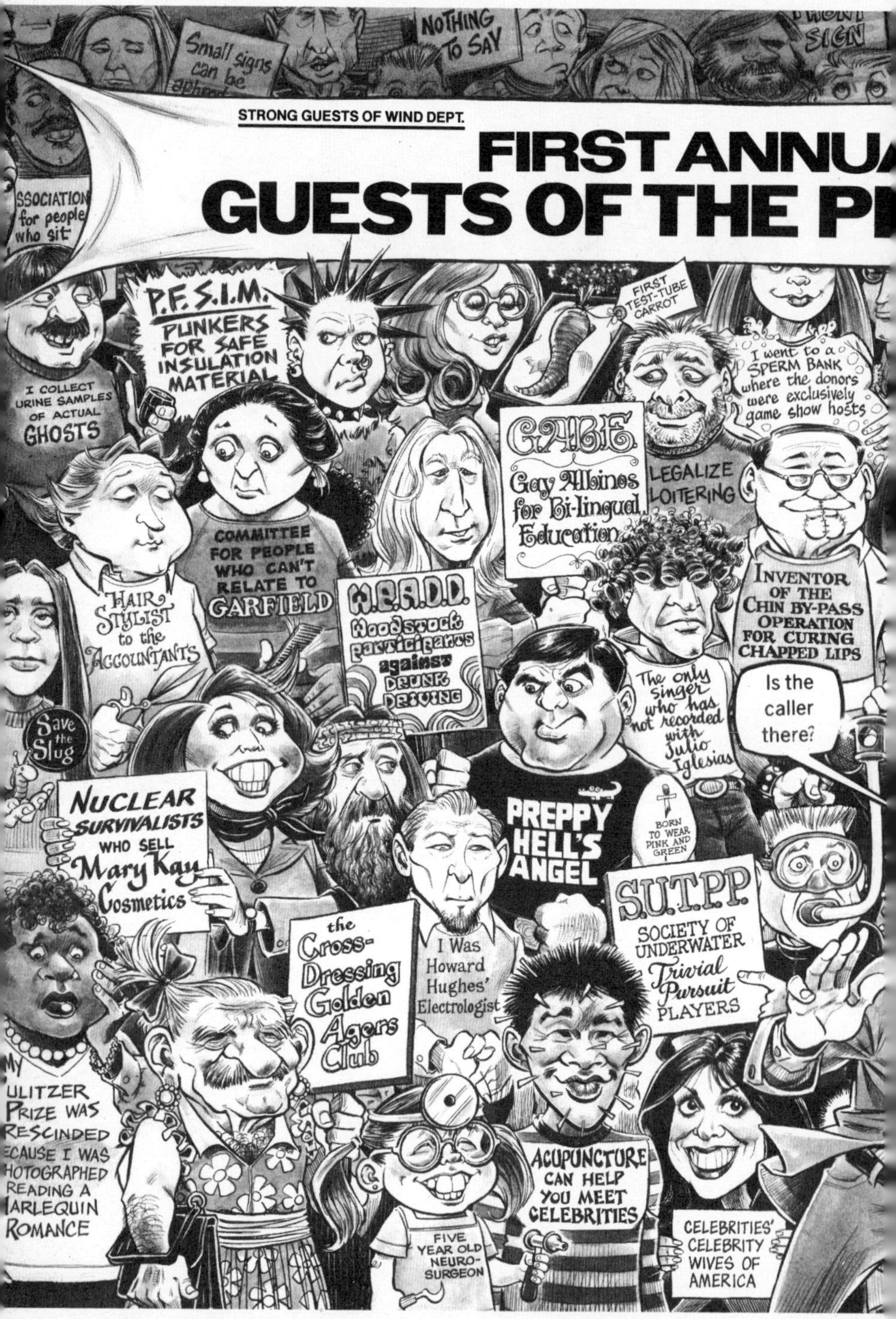

Small signs can be
NOTHING TO SAY
SIGN
SSOCIATION for people who sit
P.F.S.I.M. PUNKERS FOR SAFE INSULATION MATERIAL
FIRST TEST-TUBE CARROT
I went to a SPERM BANK where the donors were exclusively game show hosts
I COLLECT URINE SAMPLES OF ACTUAL GHOSTS
G.A.B.E. Gay Albinos for Bi-lingual Education
LEGALIZE LOITERING
COMMITTEE FOR PEOPLE WHO CAN'T RELATE TO GARFIELD
HAIR STYLIST to the ACCOUNTANTS
W.P.A.D.D. Woodstock participants against DRUNK DRIVING
INVENTOR OF THE CHIN BY-PASS OPERATION FOR CURING CHAPPED LIPS
The only singer who has not recorded with Julio Iglesias
Is the caller there?
Save the Slug
NUCLEAR SURVIVALISTS WHO SELL Mary Kay Cosmetics
PREPPY HELL'S ANGEL
BORN TO WEAR PINK AND GREEN
S.U.T.P.P. SOCIETY OF UNDERWATER Trivial Pursuit PLAYERS
the Cross-Dressing Golden Agers Club
I Was Howard Hughes' Electrologist
MY ULITZER PRIZE WAS RESCINDED ECAUSE I WAS HOTOGRAPHED READING A ARLEQUIN ROMANCE
ACUPUNCTURE CAN HELP YOU MEET CELEBRITIES
FIVE YEAR OLD NEURO-SURGEON
CELEBRITIES' CELEBRITY WIVES OF AMERICA

. REUNION
L DONAHUE SHOW

ARTIST: SAM VIVIANO WRITER: ELIZABETH WHITE

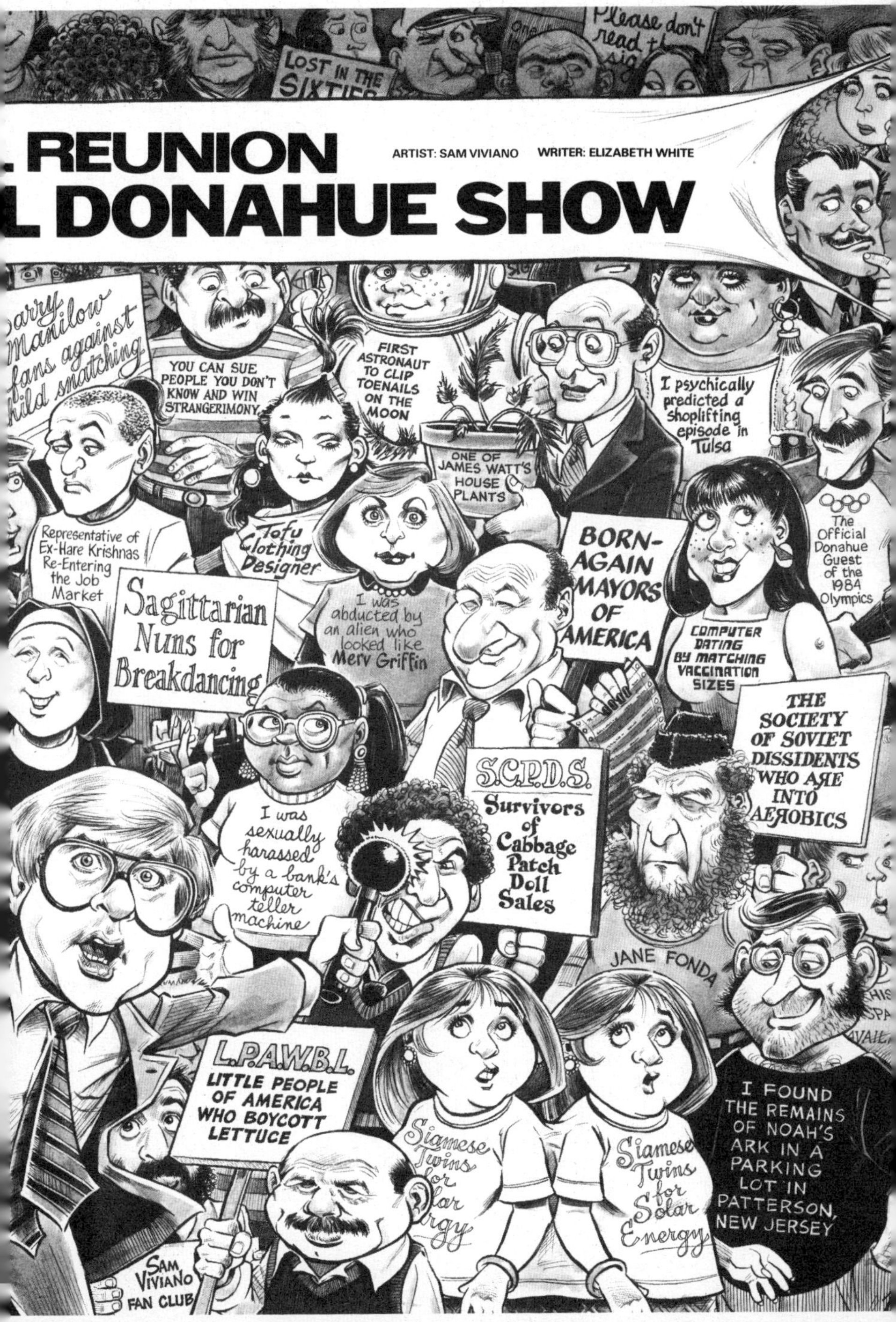
LOST IN THE
Please don't
read
arry Manilow fans against hild snatching
YOU CAN SUE PEOPLE YOU DON'T KNOW AND WIN STRANGERIMONY
FIRST ASTRONAUT TO CLIP TOENAILS ON THE MOON
ONE OF JAMES WATT'S HOUSE PLANTS
I psychically predicted a shoplifting episode in Tulsa
Representative of Ex-Hare Krishnas Re-Entering the Job Market
Tofu Clothing Designer
BORN-AGAIN MAYORS OF AMERICA
The Official Donahue Guest of the 1984 Olympics
Sagittarian Nuns for Breakdancing
I was abducted by an alien who looked like Merv Griffin
COMPUTER DATING BY MATCHING VACCINATION SIZES
THE SOCIETY OF SOVIET DISSIDENTS WHO ARE INTO AEROBICS
S.C.P.D.S. Survivors of Cabbage Patch Doll Sales
I was sexually harassed by a bank's computer teller machine
JANE FONDA
L.P.A.W.B.L. LITTLE PEOPLE OF AMERICA WHO BOYCOTT LETTUCE
Siamese Twins for Solar Energy
Siamese Twins for Solar Energy
I FOUND THE REMAINS OF NOAH'S ARK IN A PARKING LOT IN PATTERSON, NEW JERSEY
SAM VIVIANO FAN CLUB

I'm **not satisfied!** The kids are **spoiled!** They should be **sharing** in the **family chores,** even though we can **probably** do the jobs **much better!** And **I'm starting** as of **right now!**
Listen, you two . . . and **no back talk!** I'm **not satisfied** with your **contributions** around this house! So I'm **telling** you . . . **go out there and WAX THE CAR!**
Okay, Pop! **Sure!** Don't get yourself **worked up!**
5
We **did** it! Are you **satisfied?**
Yes . . . I'm **satisfied!**
NOW what are you doing?!?
I was satisfi
89 WA

BERG'S-EYE VIEW DEPT.

THE LIGHTER SIDE OF... CH

Did you turn off the **light** in the **kitchen!**
Yes, dear!
Are you **sure?** That's what you said **LAST** night, but you'd left it on **anyway!**
I'm **pretty sure . . .**
Now you're only **"pretty sure"!** That's not very **definite!** You probably **forgot** to turn it off!
Dammit! Now you've got **me** wondering! I won't be able to **fall asleep** until I get up and check if I **did** or **not!**
While you're **down** in the **kitchen,** dear, will you bring me a **glass of milk?**

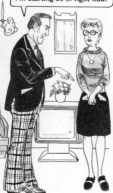

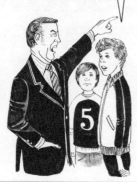

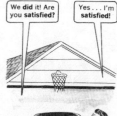

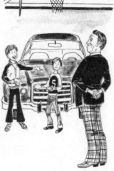

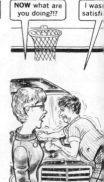

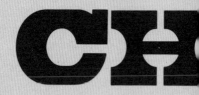

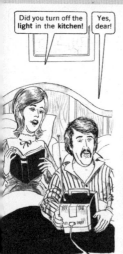

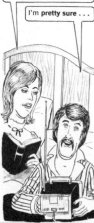

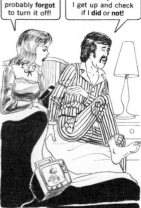

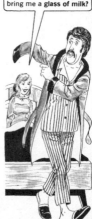

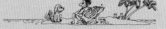

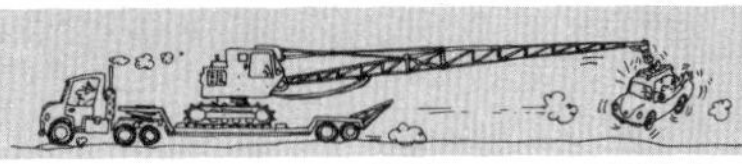

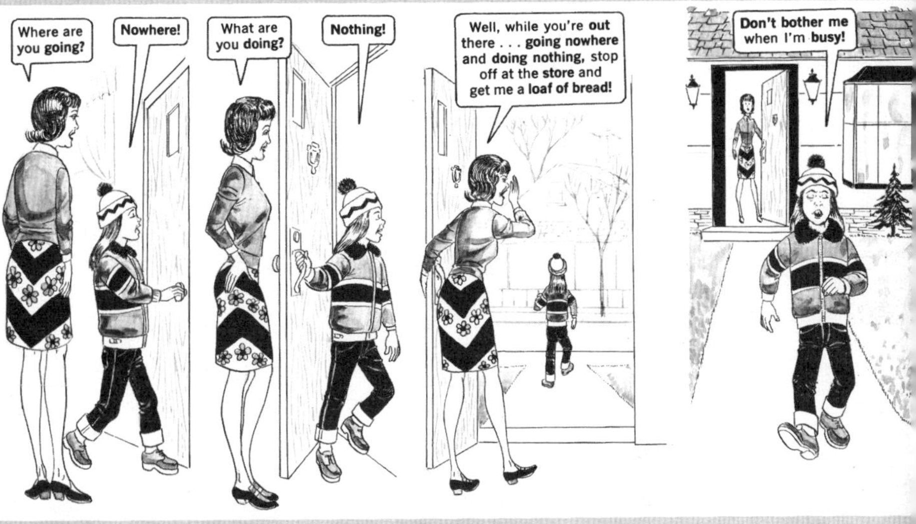

Where are you going?
Nowhere!
What are you doing?
Nothing!
Well, while you're out there . . . going nowhere and doing nothing, stop off at the store and get me a loaf of bread!
Don't bother me when I'm busy!

ORES

ARTIST & WRITER:
DAVE BERG

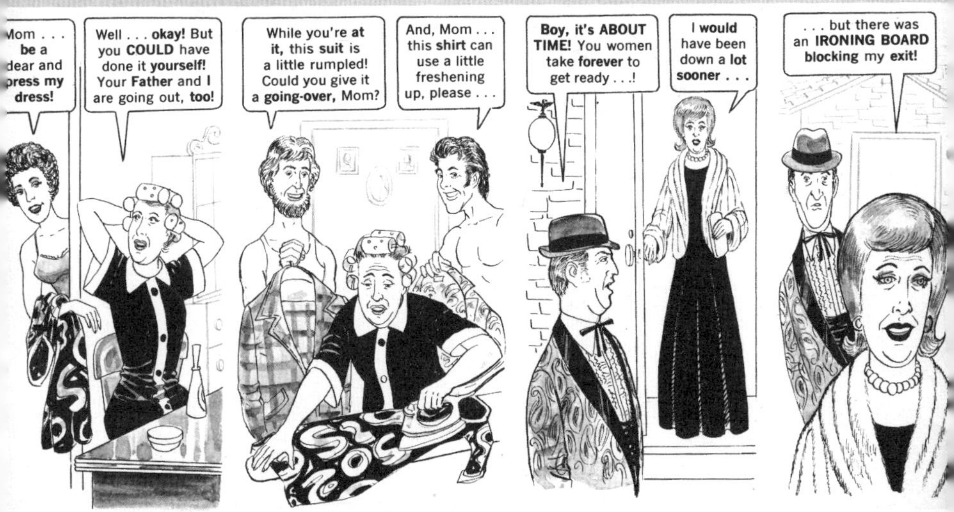

Mom . . . be a dear and press my dress!
Well . . . okay! But you COULD have done it yourself! Your Father and I are going out, too!
While you're at it, this suit is a little rumpled! Could you give it a going-over, Mom?
And, Mom . . . this shirt can use a little freshening up, please . . .
Boy, it's ABOUT TIME! You women take forever to get ready . . .!
I would have been down a lot sooner . . .
. . . but there was an IRONING BOARD blocking my exit!

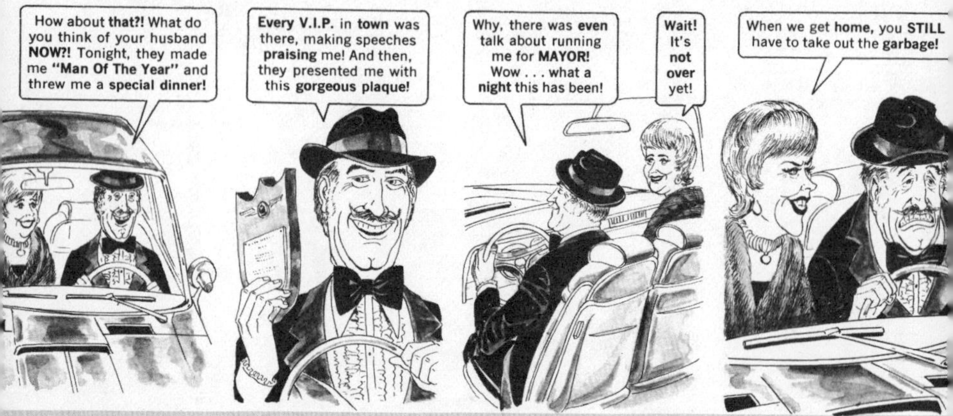
How about that?! What do you think of your husband NOW?! Tonight, they made me "Man Of The Year" and threw me a special dinner!
Every V.I.P. in town was there, making speeches praising me! And then, they presented me with this gorgeous plaque!
Why, there was even talk about running me for MAYOR! Wow . . . what a night this has been!
Wait! It's not over yet!
When we get home, you STILL have to take out the garbage!

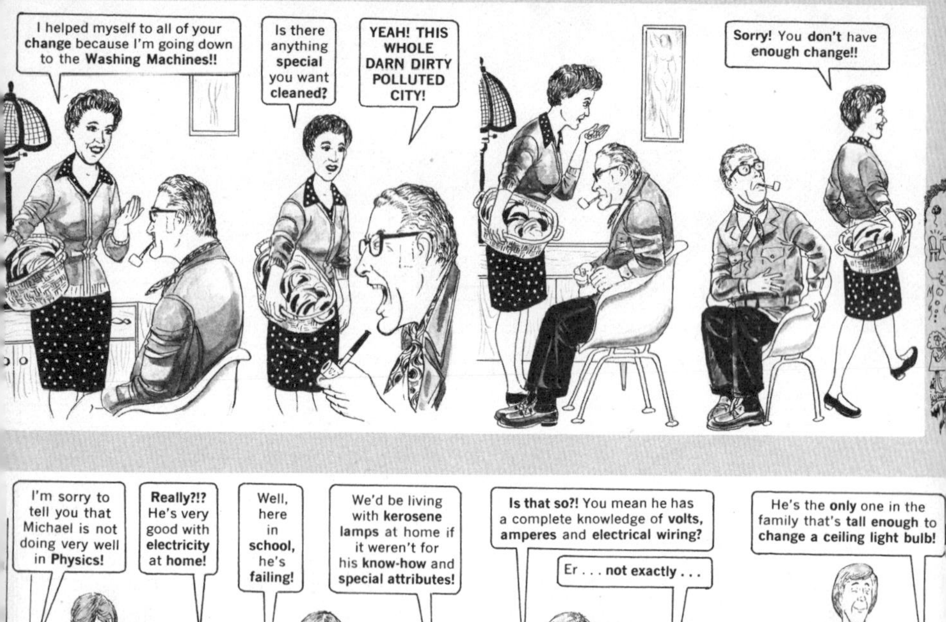
I helped myself to all of your change because I'm going down to the Washing Machines!!
Is there anything special you want cleaned?
YEAH! THIS WHOLE DARN DIRTY POLLUTED CITY!
Sorry! You don't have enough change!!

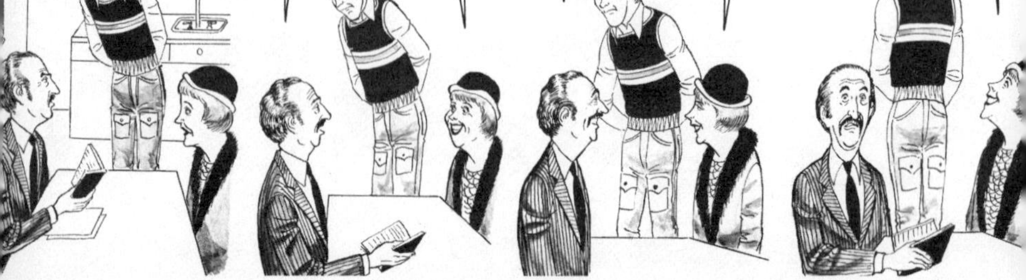
I'm sorry to tell you that Michael is not doing very well in Physics!
Really?!? He's very good with electricity at home!
Well, here in school, he's failing!
We'd be living with kerosene lamps at home if it weren't for his know-how and special attributes!
Is that so?! You mean he has a complete knowledge of volts, amperes and electrical wiring?
Er . . . not exactly . . .
He's the only one in the family that's tall enough to change a ceiling light bulb!

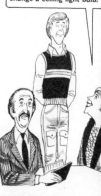

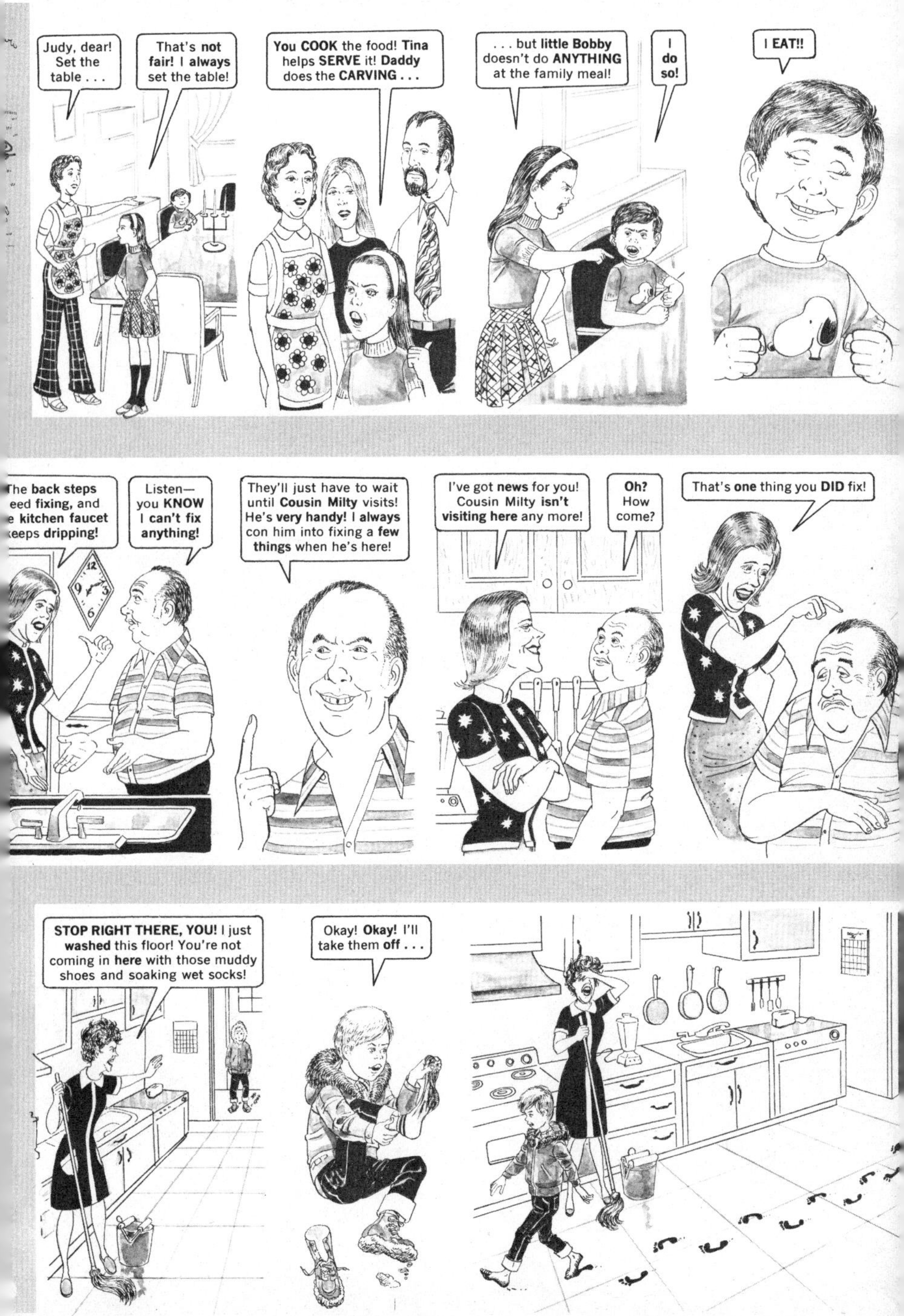
Judy, dear! Set the table . . .
That's not fair! I always set the table!
You COOK the food! Tina helps SERVE it! Daddy does the CARVING . . .
. . . but little Bobby doesn't do ANYTHING at the family meal!
I do so!
I EAT!!
The back steps eed fixing, and e kitchen faucet eeps dripping!
Listen— you KNOW I can't fix anything!
They'll just have to wait until Cousin Milty visits! He's very handy! I always con him into fixing a few things when he's here!
I've got news for you! Cousin Milty isn't visiting here any more!
Oh? How come?
That's one thing you DID fix!
STOP RIGHT THERE, YOU! I just washed this floor! You're not coming in here with those muddy shoes and soaking wet socks!
Okay! Okay! I'll take them off . . .
12
3
6

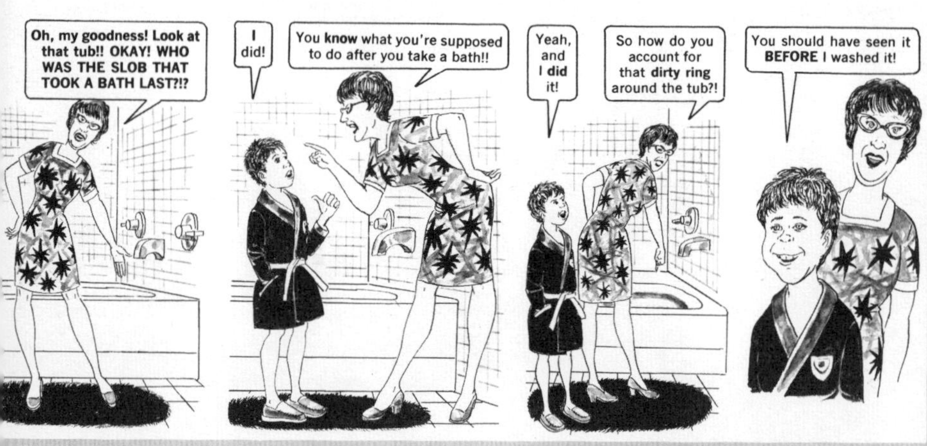
Oh, my goodness! Look at that tub!! OKAY! WHO WAS THE SLOB THAT TOOK A BATH LAST?!?
I did!
You know what you're supposed to do after you take a bath!!
Yeah, and I did it!
So how do you account for that dirty ring around the tub?!
You should have seen it BEFORE I washed it!

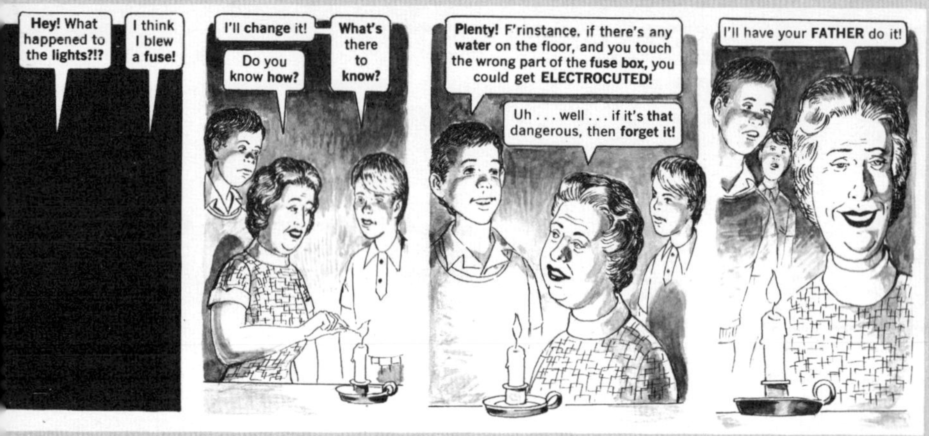
Hey! What happened to the lights?!?
I think I blew a fuse!
I'll change it!
Do you know how?
What's there to know?
Plenty! F'rinstance, if there's any water on the floor, and you touch the wrong part of the fuse box, you could get ELECTROCUTED!
Uh . . . well . . . if it's that dangerous, then forget it!
I'll have your FATHER do it!

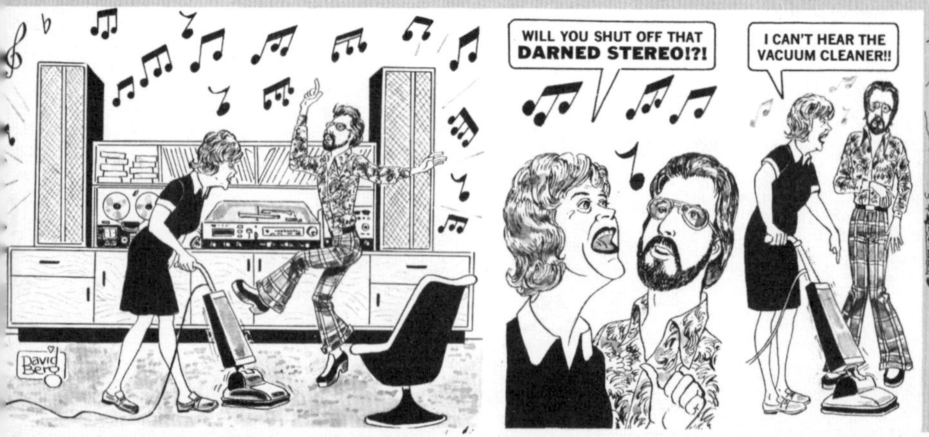
David Berg
WILL YOU SHUT OFF THAT DARNED STEREO!?!
I CAN'T HEAR THE VACUUM CLEANER!!

DON MARTIN DEPT.

IN AN ALLEY

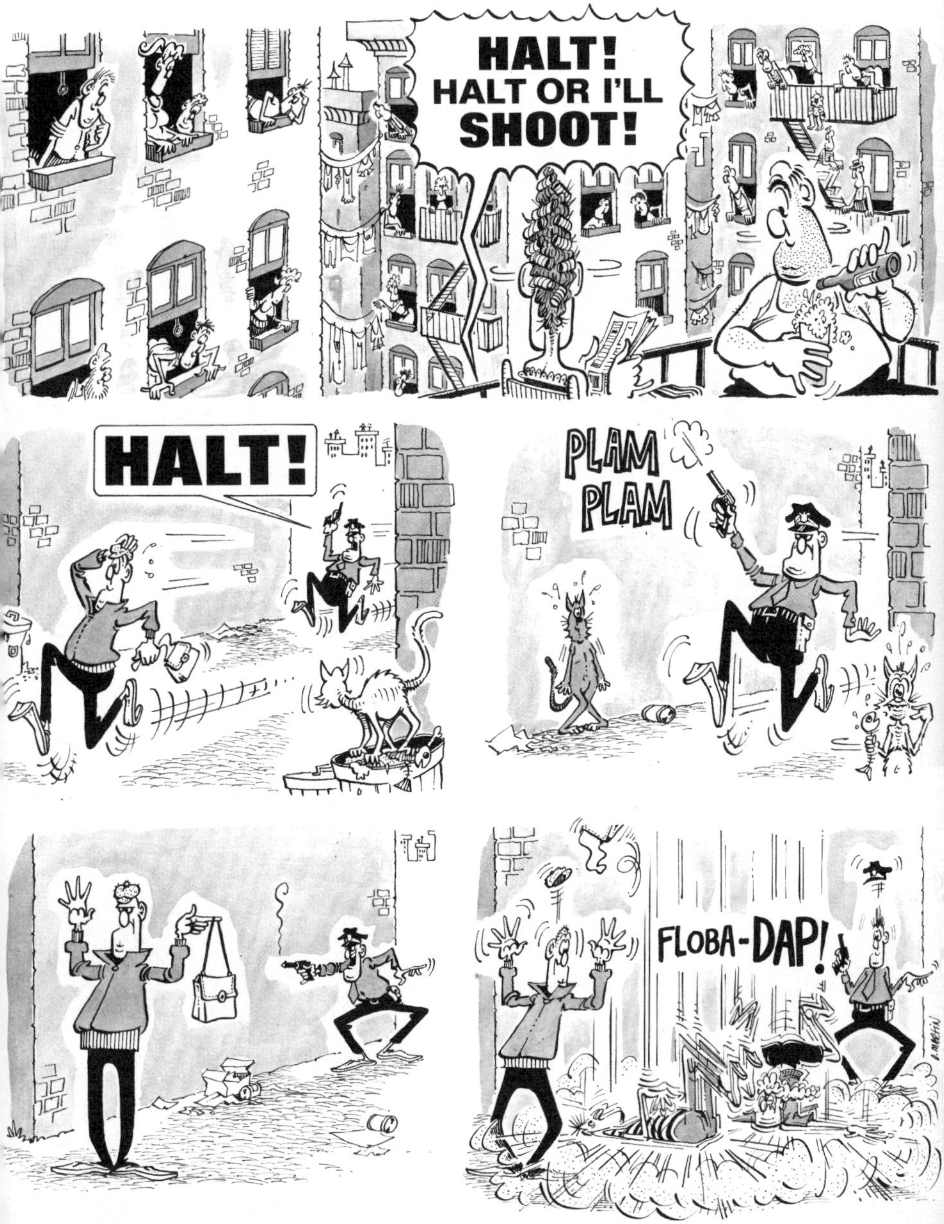
HALT!
HALT OR I'LL
SHOOT!
HALT!
PLAM
PLAM
FLOBA-DAP!

JOY-SCHTICK DEPT.

Were you one of the unlucky ones who got a Nintendo or a Sega or some other video game system over the holidays? You say you can never play with it because you just can't figure out the cockeyed and confusing game cartridge instructions? We're not surprised! You'd probably have more fun and get higher scores if you created your own rules by filling in the blanks below with the words and phrases on the corresponding lists. At least that's what one MAD writer told us when he conned us into buying MAD's...

ALL-PURPOSE VIDEO GAME INSTRUCTIONS KIT

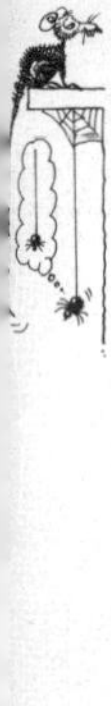

HOW TO PLAY

Save ______ (1) ______ **from being** ______ (2) ______ **by** ______ (3) ______ ______ (4) ______ ______ (5) ______ **. Using** ______ (6) ______ **, destroy their** ______ (7) ______ **with** ______ (8) ______ **while avoiding the** ______ (9) ______ **of their** ______ (10) ______ **.**

SCORING

______ (11) ______ ______ (12) ______

ARTIST: HARVEY KURTZMAN WRITER: FRANK JACOBS

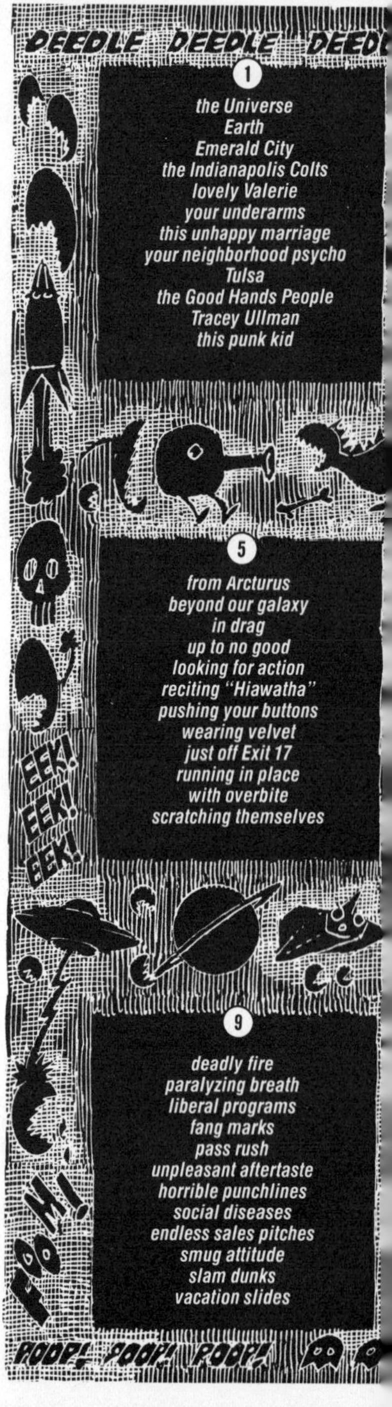

DEEDLE DEEDLE DEEDL
EEK! EEK! EEK!
FOOM!
POOP! POOP! POOP!

1

the Universe
Earth
Emerald City
the Indianapolis Colts
lovely Valerie
your underarms
this unhappy marriage
your neighborhood psycho
Tulsa
the Good Hands People
Tracey Ullman
this punk kid

5

from Arcturus
beyond our galaxy
in drag
up to no good
looking for action
reciting "Hiawatha"
pushing your buttons
wearing velvet
just off Exit 17
running in place
with overbite
scratching themselves

9

deadly fire
paralyzing breath
liberal programs
fang marks
pass rush
unpleasant aftertaste
horrible punchlines
social diseases
endless sales pitches
smug attitude
slam dunks
vacation slides

EEDLE! *YO YO* 👾👾👾 💥 *TAK!* IN ⬛⬛⬛ OUT *MEEP!*

2
wiped out
overrun
taxed to death
bench-pressed
baked at 350°
humiliated
slobbered over
sweet-talked
tail-piped
reincarnated
spindled and mutilated
Sanforized

3
invading
alien
whining
bleeding-heart
rush-hour
lead-free
guilt-ridden
sleazy
unabridged
nerdlike
low-calorie
Methodist

ZAP!

4
spacemen
mutants
Hukons
Zarks
flashers
summer replacements
wimps
saxophonists
break-dancers
zinc worshipers
Cornhuskers
Peruvian Jaycees

YOING! YOING! YOING!

6
the Blast Button
the joystick
lies and deceit
your toes
the bump-and-run
Herbalife
Bob's lawn mower
limp pizza
the handy twist-top lid
the gifts God gave you
hired gnomes
all Utica has to offer

7
armies
missiles
"nice guy" image
moments of intimacy
Roach Motels
hopes of citizenship
singles bars
dream kitchens
retirement villages
Olympic pin collections
memories of Duluth
pockets of cellulite

FROOSH!

8
atomic torpedoes
rockets
killer minnows
spit
a dash of tabasco
a knee in the groin
a belt-high fastball
stoned droids
attack poodles
raw sewage
Pia Zadora films
fur-bearing mercenaries

WIBBLE! WIBBLE! WIBBLE!

10
phasers
space cannon
trained gnats
Alf look-alikes
in-laws
trivia freaks
few remaining virgins
all-Capricorn army
fiddlers three
late-night talk shows
vegetarian death squads
anti-abortionists

11
Every 100 ships destroyed
Every 1000 Fleegs vaporized
A score of 600 zillion
Landing on Baltic Avenue
Tipping the maitre d'
Bathing regularly
Punching yourself in the face
Rolling a hard six
Saying you're a friend of Sid's
Getting it on with a Martian
Raising with a pair of kings
Draining your sinuses

EEK!

12
extends your playing time
wins a free game patch
looks good on your resumé
brings on rigor mortis
means oh so very much
helps control psoriasis
brings grief and suffering
feeds an Albanian
provides a cheap thrill
sucks
won't help James Caan's career
means absolutely nothing

ZAK! *SHIM! SHIM!* GAME OVER √67•4•3

EVERYTHING'S COMING UP SUB ROSA DEPT.

A COLLECTION OF MAD

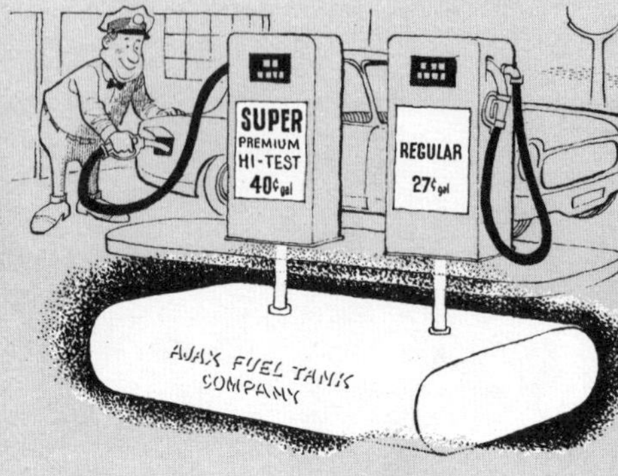
SUPER
PREMIUM
HI-TEST
40¢ gal
REGULAR
27¢ gal
AJAX FUEL TANK
COMPANY

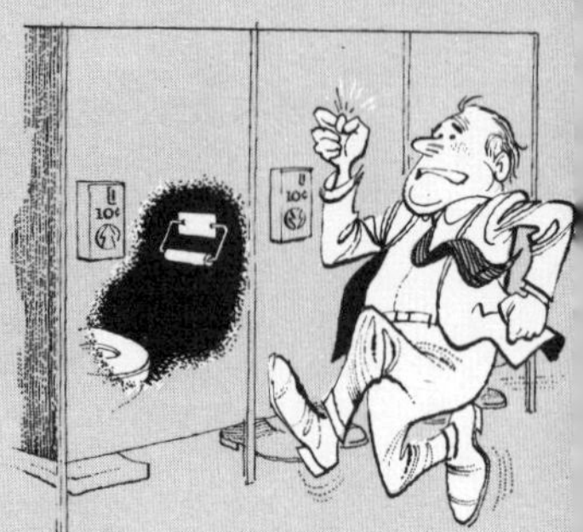
10¢
10¢

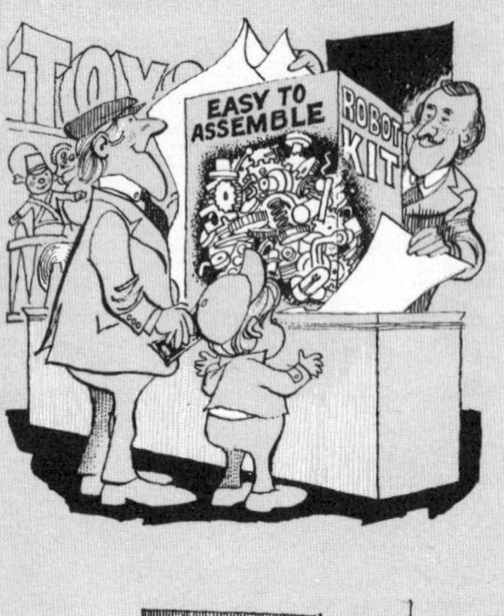
EASY TO
ASSEMBLE
ROBOT
KIT

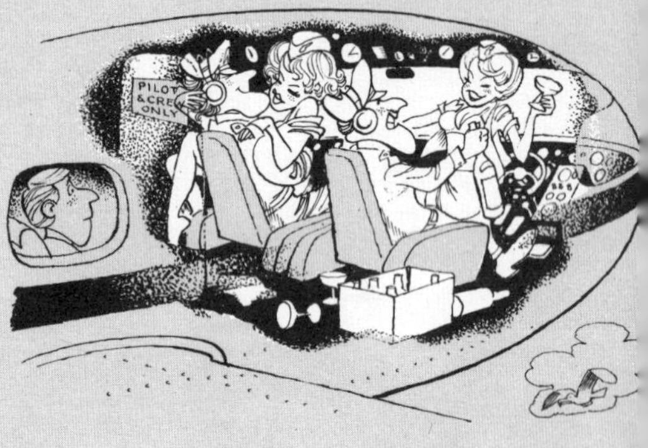
PILO
&CRE
ONLY

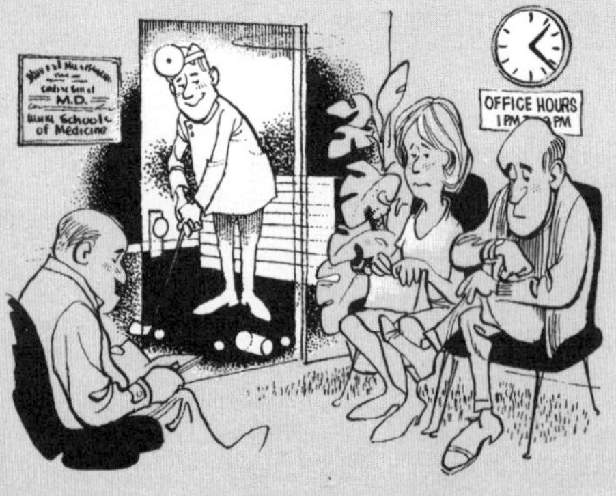
M.D.
School of Medicine
OFFICE HOURS

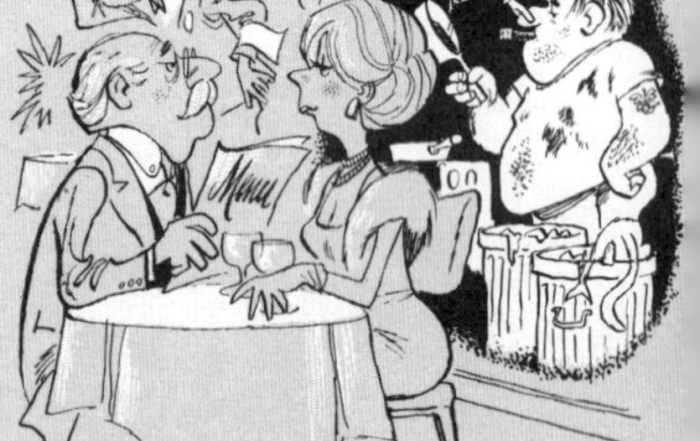
IN
OUT
Menu

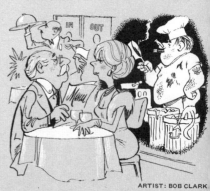

ARTIST: BOB CLARK

X-RAYVINGS

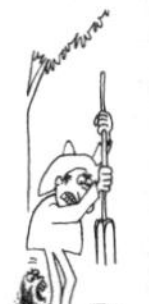

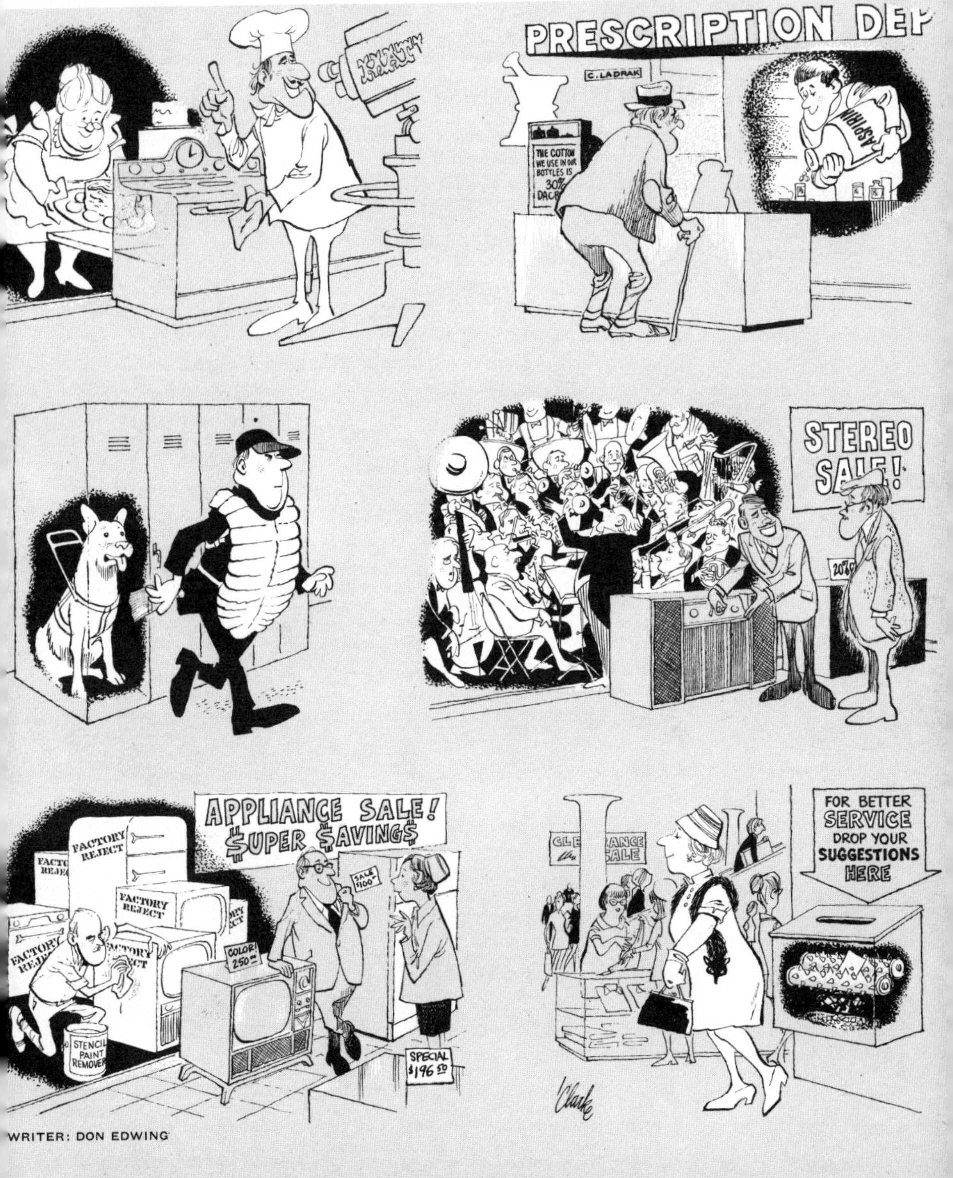
PRESCRIPTION DEP
C. LADRAK
THE COTTON WE USE IN OUR BOTTLES IS 30% DACR
ASPIRIN
STEREO SALE!
APPLIANCE SALE! $UPER $AVING$
FACTORY REJECT
FACTORY REJECT
FACTORY REJECT
FACTORY REJECT
SALE $100
COLOR! 250
STENCIL PAINT REMOVER
SPECIAL $196.50
CLEARANCE SALE
FOR BETTER SERVICE DROP YOUR SUGGESTIONS HERE
Clarke

WRITER: DON EDWING

GIVIN' 'EM A RIBBIN' DEPT.

Why restrict the awarding of medals to the military? After all, Civilians perform heroic acts while fighting life's daily battles as well! Let's recognize them with

THIS ISSUE'S PROPOSED MAD MEDALS

. . . TO BE PRESENTED TO DESERVING MEDICAL WORKERS

THE FETID FOOD CITATION

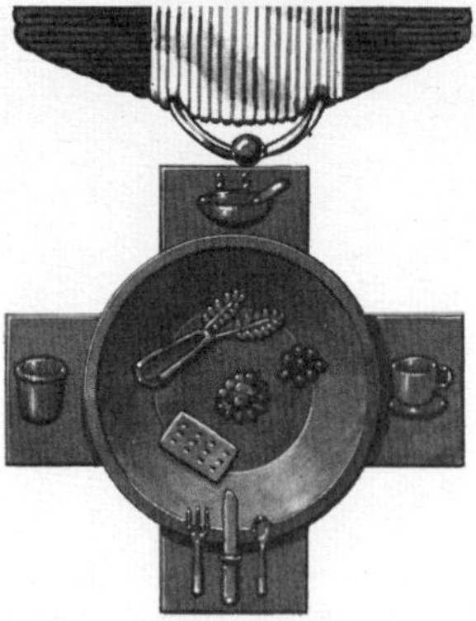

For bravely facing without fear the verbal wrath and physical abuse of hospital patients while courageously producing inedible food so patients won't over-eat and get tummy aches.

THE WINGED BILL MEDAL

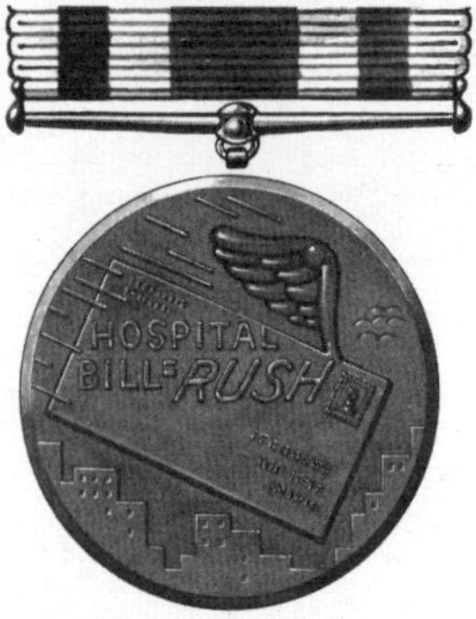
HOSPITAL
BILLS RUSH

For promptness above and beyond belief in sending out bills so that patients need not suffer the agony of delay in arranging loans, or selling their cars or homes to raise money to pay them.

THE STONE HEART AWARD

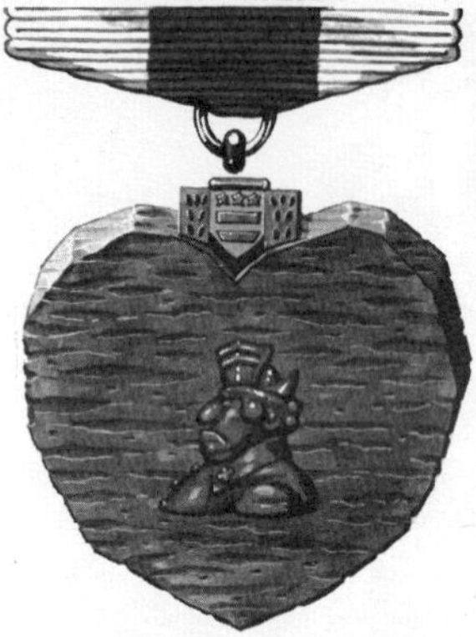

For gallantly treating all patients—regardless of race, color or creed—with equality . . . which means never ever showing favoritism such as being sweet, considerate and understanding.

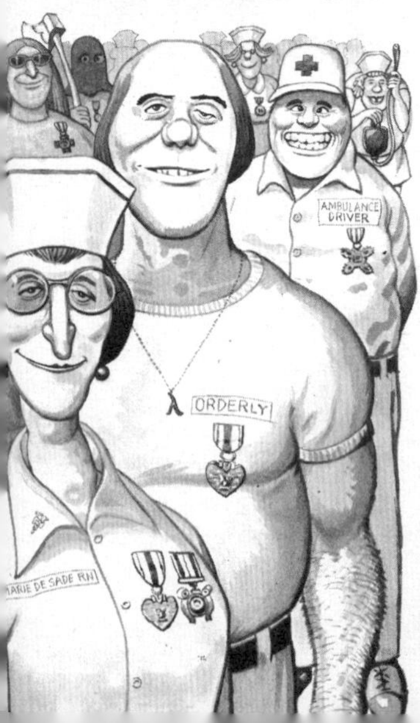
AMBULANCE DRIVER
ORDERLY
ARIE DE SADE RN

THE SCREAMING SIREN MEDAL

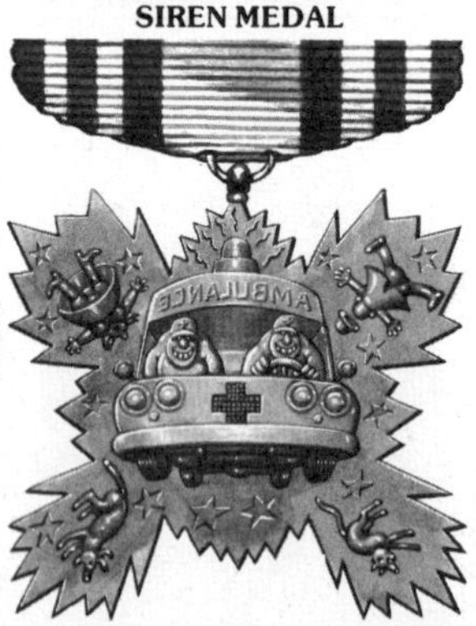
AMBULANCE

For heroically risking life and limb in order to race patients to the hospital emergency room, even though the place is hopelessly overcrowded and the patients won't even be looked at for eight or nine hours at the least.

THE SILVER BEDPAN AWARD

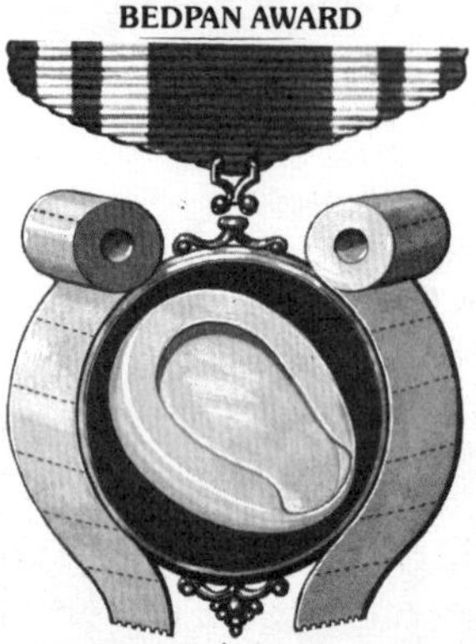

For ignoring the selfish screams of emergency patients while faithfully carrying out the vital job of filling out Blue Cross forms. As many of the patients will die, catering to their whims would be a waste of time anyway.

ARTIST & WRITER: AL JAFFEE

CLAUSE AND DEFECT DEPT.

Everybody has seen television commercials promoting some sort of "special offer"...

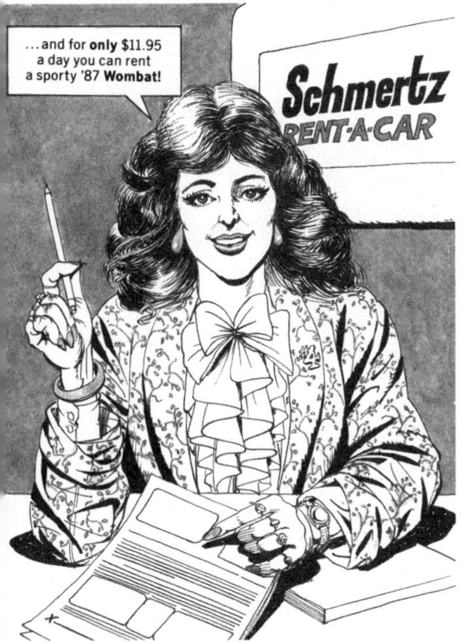
...and for **only** $11.95 a day you can rent a sporty '87 **Wombat!**
Schmertz RENT-A-CAR

...and then heard the fast-spoken voice-over disclaimer at the tail end of the commercial.

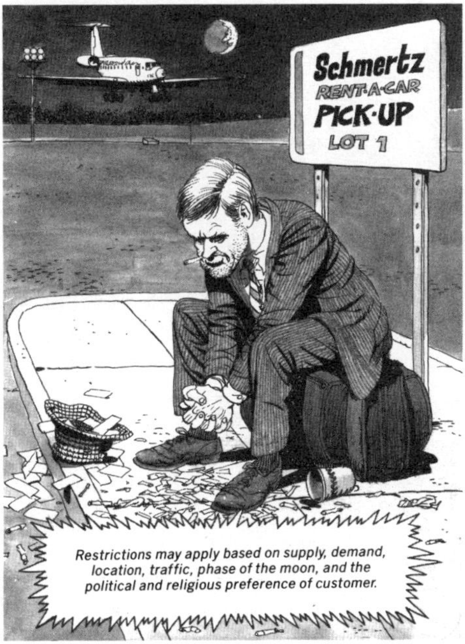
Schmertz RENT-A-CAR PICK-UP LOT 1
Restrictions may apply based on supply, demand, location, traffic, phase of the moon, and the political and religious preference of customer.

nfortunately, not all commercials have disclaimers, which is why consumers so often end up pped-off and disgusted. And which is why MAD, ever eager to improve the world, presents...

DISCLAIMERS FOR TV COMMERCIALS THAT DON'T HAVE DISCLAIMERS

ARTIST: GEORGE WOODBRIDGE WRITER: FRANK JACOBS

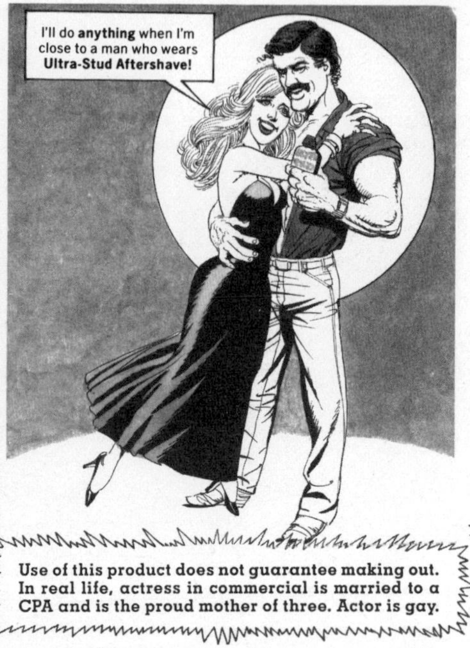
I'll do **anything** when I'm close to a man who wears **Ultra-Stud Aftershave!**
Use of this product does not guarantee making out. In real life, actress in commercial is married to a CPA and is the proud mother of three. Actor is gay.

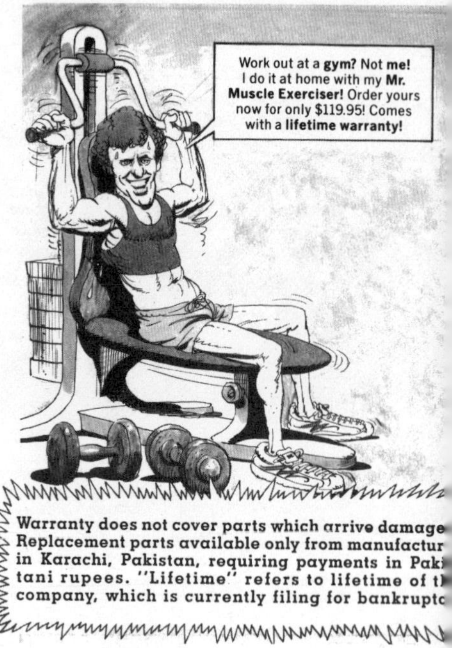
Work out at a **gym?** Not **me!** I do it at home with my **Mr. Muscle Exerciser!** Order yours now for only $119.95! Comes with a **lifetime warranty!**
Warranty does not cover parts which arrive damage
Replacement parts available only from manufactur
in Karachi, Pakistan, requiring payments in Paki
tani rupees. "Lifetime" refers to lifetime of t
company, which is currently filing for bankrupto

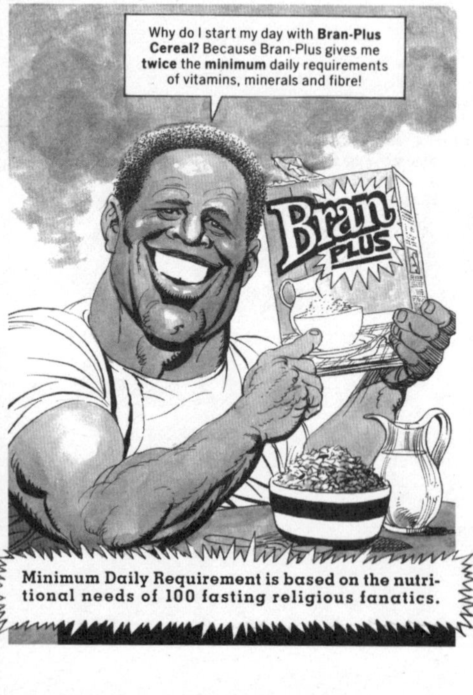
Why do I start my day with **Bran-Plus Cereal?** Because Bran-Plus gives me **twice** the **minimum** daily requirements of vitamins, minerals and fibre!
Bran PLUS
Minimum Daily Requirement is based on the nutritional needs of 100 fasting religious fanatics.

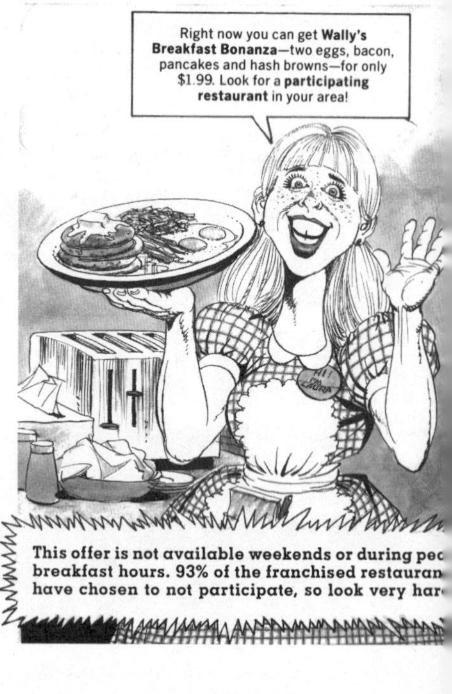
Right now you can get **Wally's Breakfast Bonanza**—two eggs, bacon, pancakes and hash browns—for only $1.99. Look for a **participating restaurant** in your area!
This offer is not available weekends or during pea
breakfast hours. 93% of the franchised restauran
have chosen to not participate, so look very har

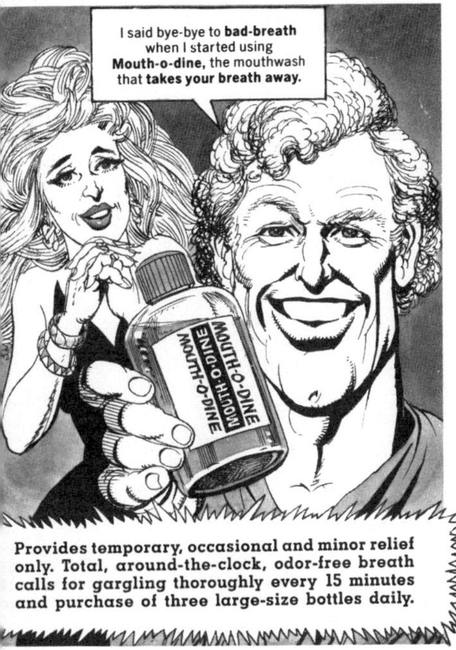
I said bye-bye to **bad-breath** when I started using **Mouth-o-dine,** the mouthwash that **takes your breath away.**
MOUTH-O-DINE
MOUTH-O-DINE
Provides temporary, occasional and minor relief only. Total, around-the-clock, odor-free breath calls for gargling thoroughly every 15 minutes and purchase of three large-size bottles daily.

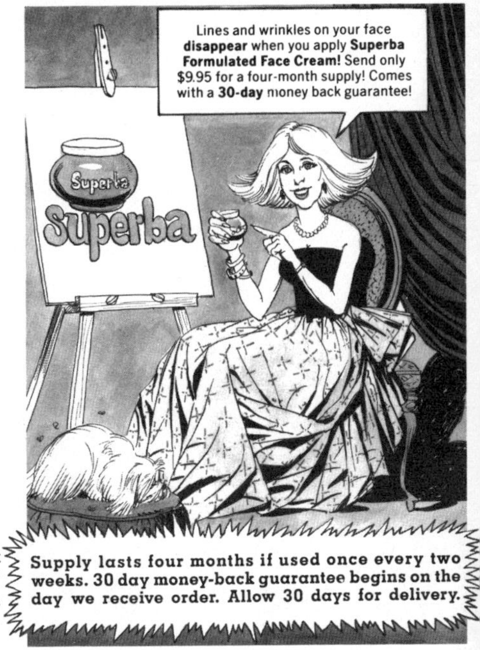
Lines and wrinkles on your face **disappear** when you apply **Superba Formulated Face Cream!** Send only $9.95 for a four-month supply! Comes with a **30-day** money back guarantee!
Superba
Superba
Supply lasts four months if used once every two weeks. 30 day money-back guarantee begins on the day we receive order. Allow 30 days for delivery.

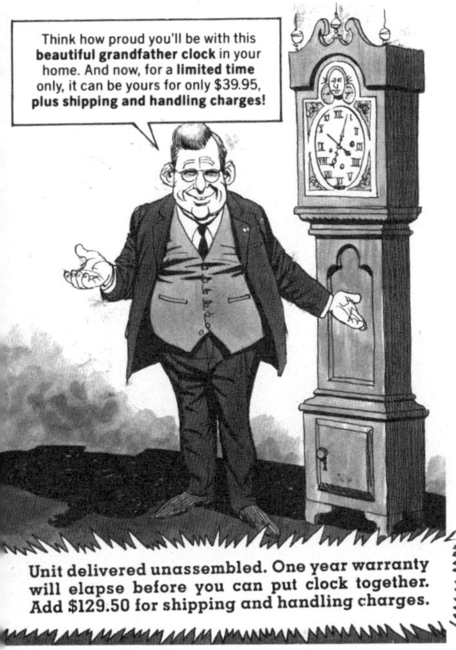
Think how proud you'll be with this **beautiful grandfather clock** in your home. And now, for a **limited time** only, it can be yours for only $39.95, **plus shipping and handling charges!**
Unit delivered unassembled. One year warranty will elapse before you can put clock together. Add $129.50 for shipping and handling charges.

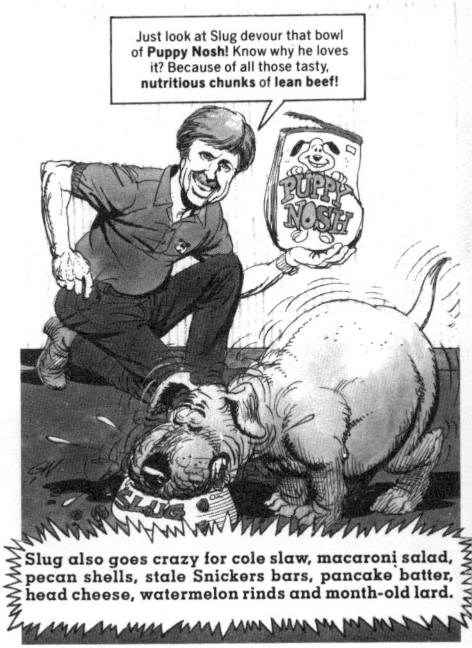
Just look at Slug devour that bowl of **Puppy Nosh!** Know why he loves it? Because of all those tasty, **nutritious chunks** of **lean beef!**
PUPPY NOSH
SLUG
Slug also goes crazy for cole slaw, macaroni salad, pecan shells, stale Snickers bars, pancake batter, head cheese, watermelon rinds and month-old lard.

WORD GAME PRESERVE DEPT.

Here we go again with the game in which we take ordinary Dictionary words, and dream up some kookie animals that these words suggest. Mainly, here we go with

THE RETURN OF THE MAD

superficial

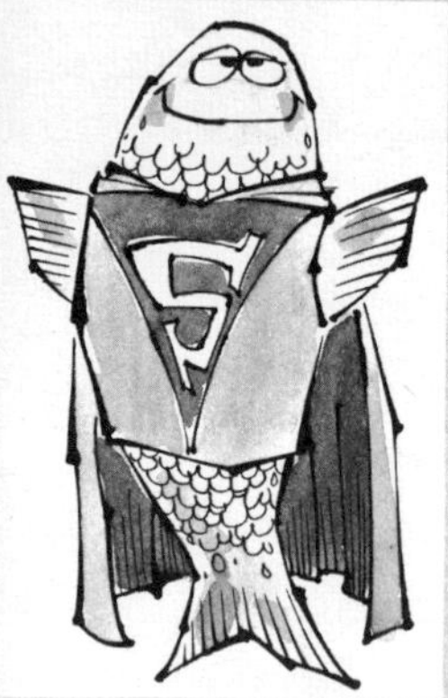

Araby

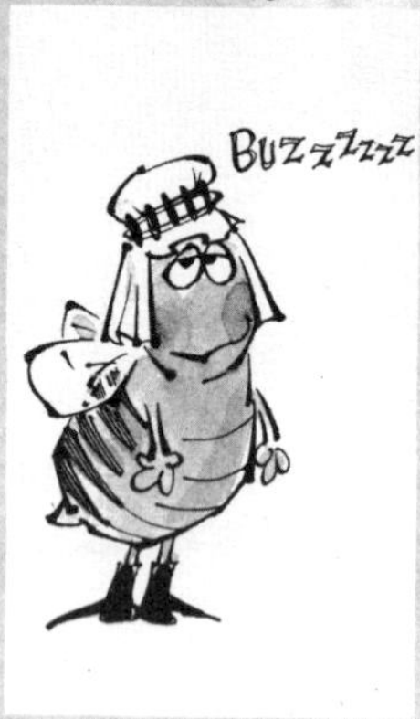
BUZZZZZZZ

billy club

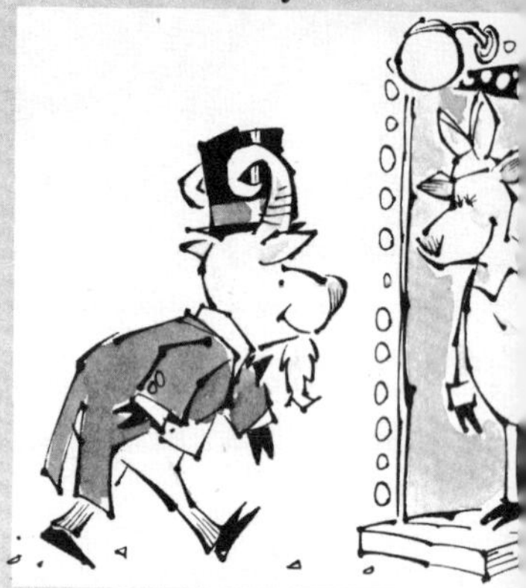

ordain

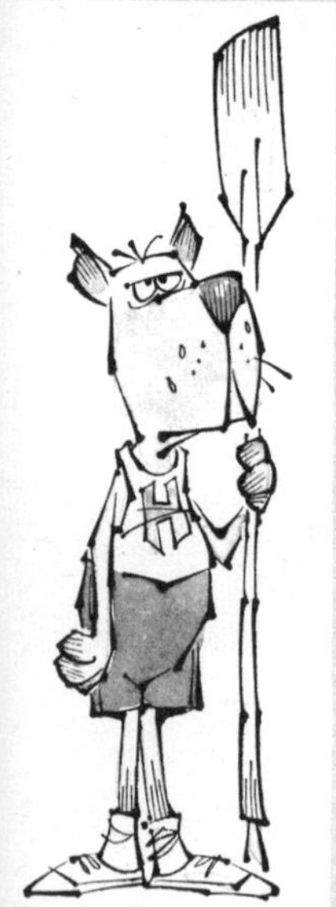

threadbare

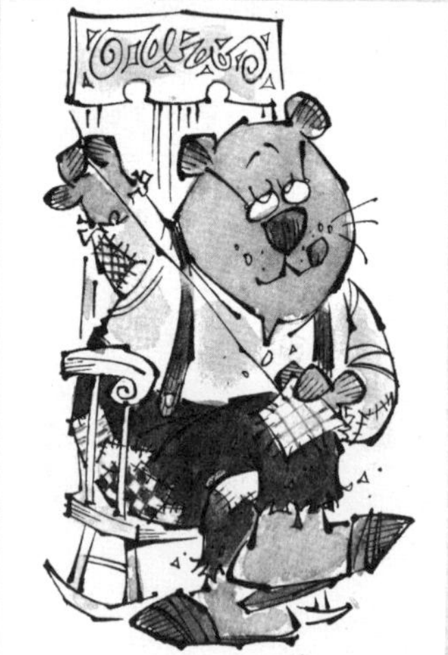

humdinger

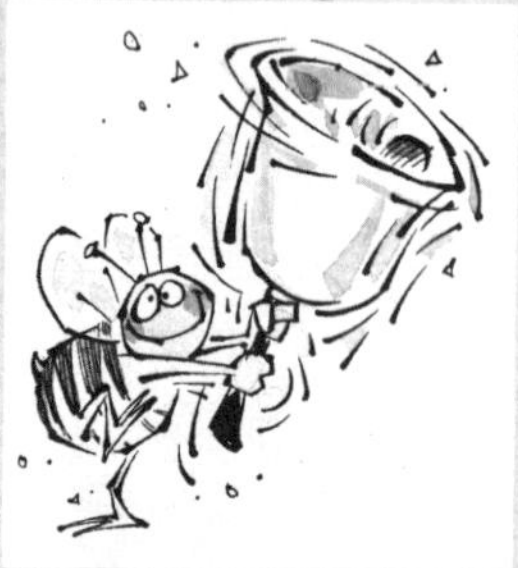

romantic

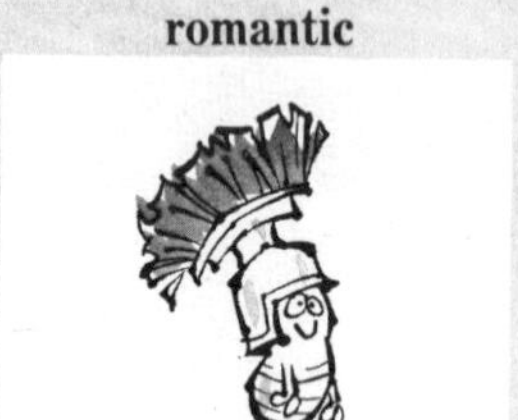

BEASTLIES

ARTIST: PAUL COKER JR. WRITER: PHIL HAHN

first aid kit

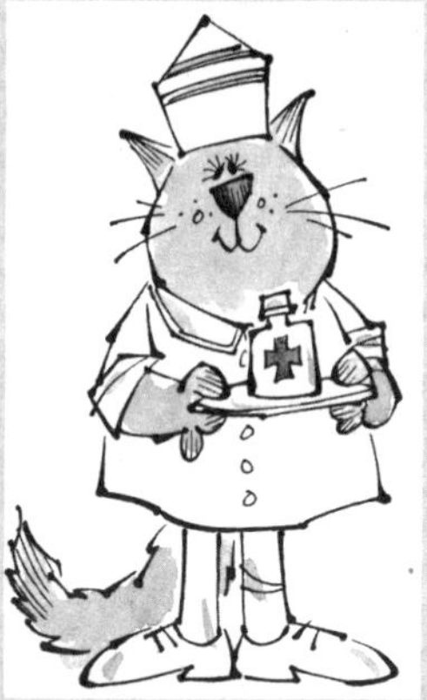

Good Housekeeping Seal

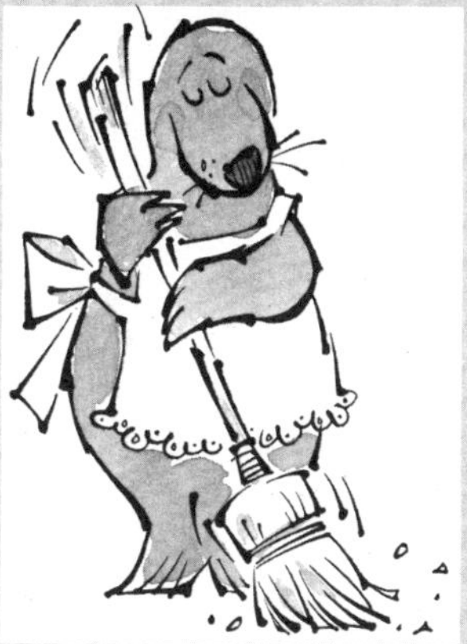

Balboa

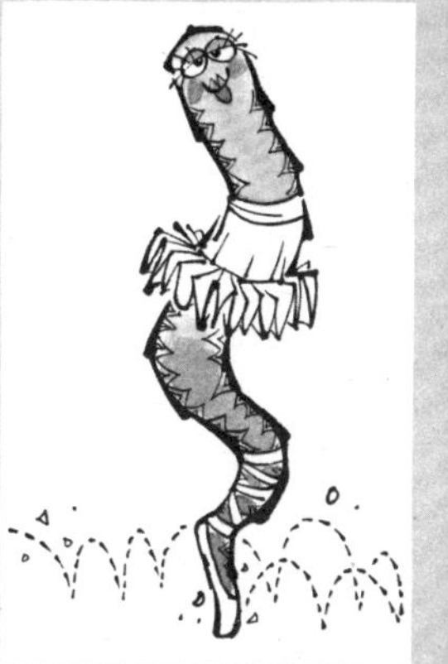

bum steer

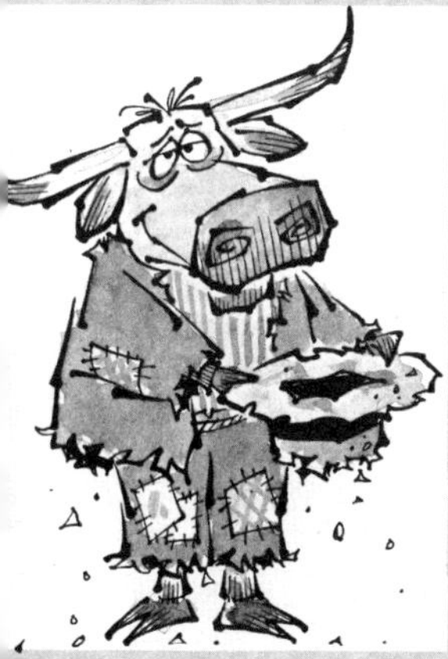

Bangkok

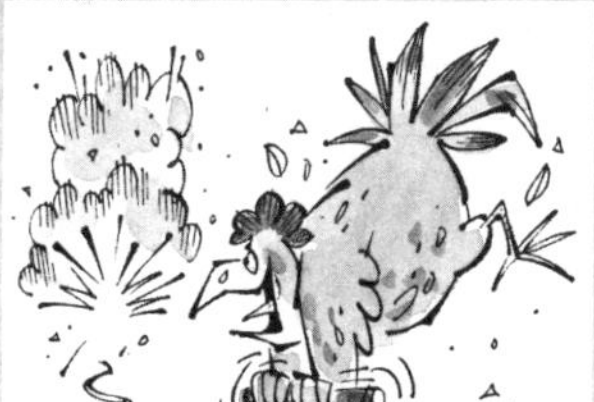

sourdough

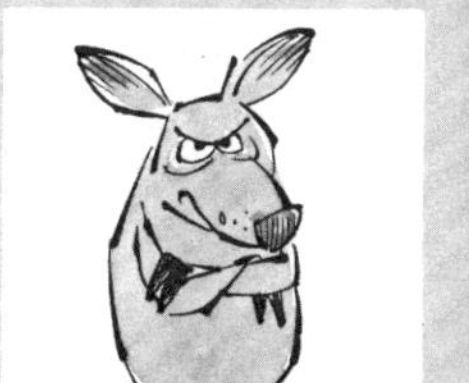

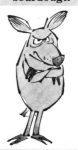

crochet

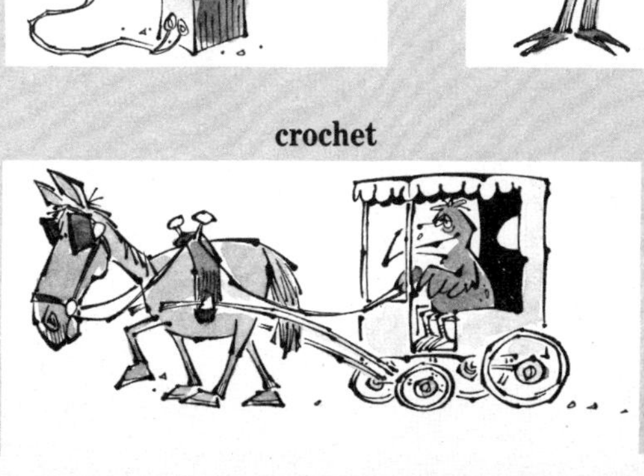

DON MARTIN DEPT.

One Day In The Pasture

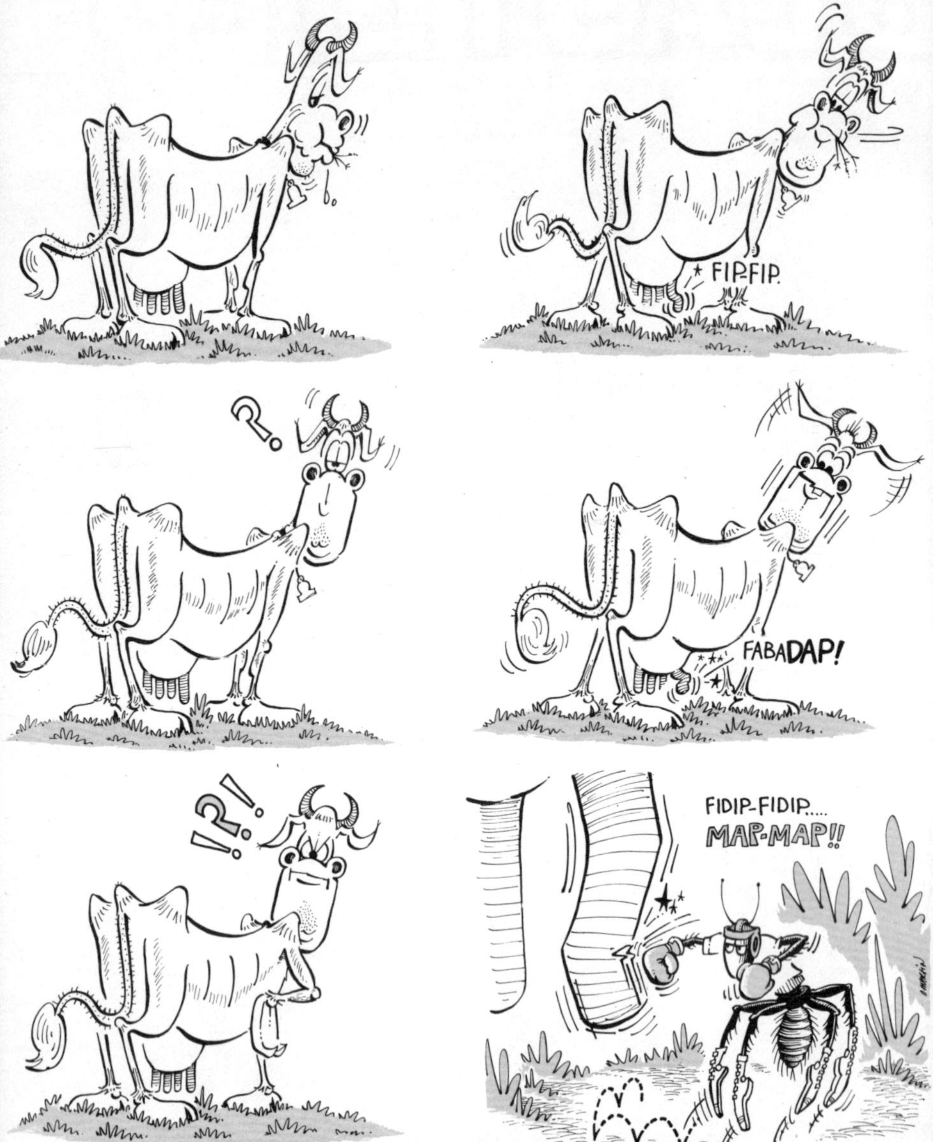
FIP-FIP
?
FABADAP!
!?!
FIDIP-FIDIP.....
MAP-MAP!!

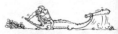

DISC-CLAIMERS DEPT.

Recently, there's been a lot of hullabaloo about whether or not there should be warning labels on record albums. After seconds of soul searching and carelessly weighing both sides of this important issue, we at MAD dare to say YES!! There should definitely be warning labels on selected discs!

So without any further ado (except for the rest of this intro!), here are some...

Badly Needed WARNING LABELS for ROCK ALBUMS

WRITER: DESMOND DEVLIN

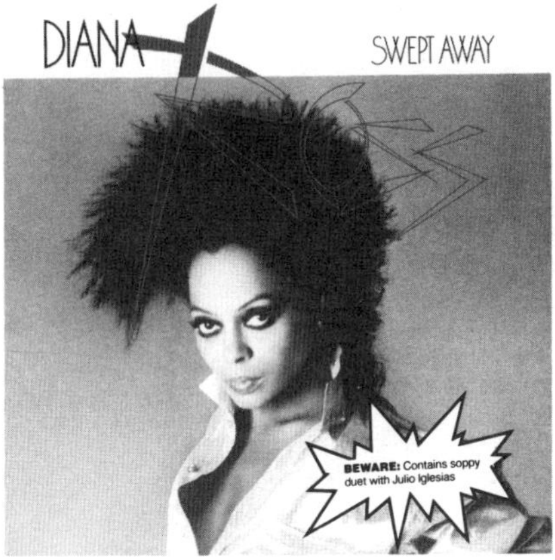
DIANA
SWEPT AWAY
BEWARE: Contains soppy duet with Julio Iglesias

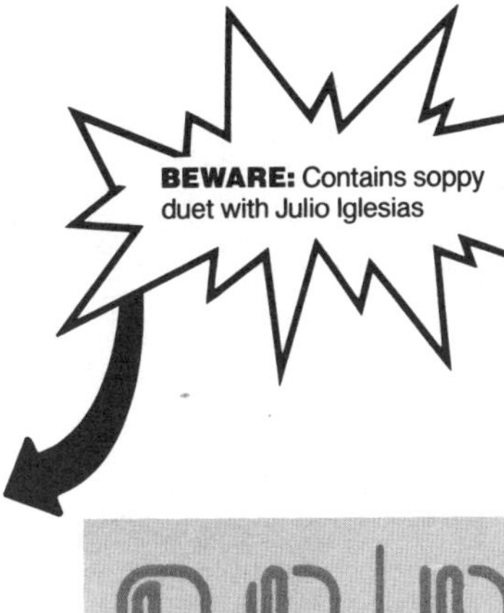
BEWARE: Contains soppy duet with Julio Iglesias

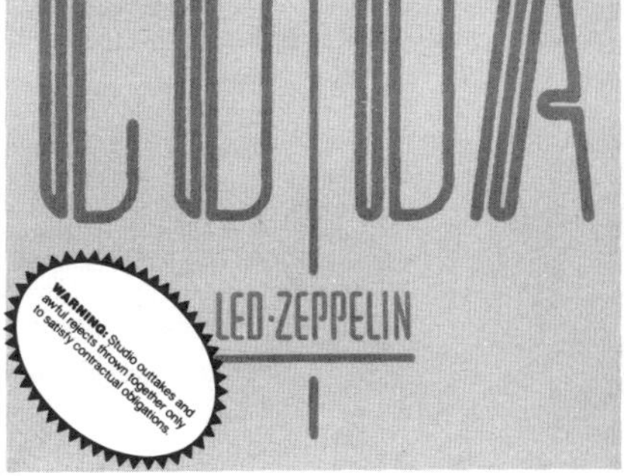
CODA
LED-ZEPPELIN
WARNING: Studio outtakes and awful rejects thrown together only to satisfy contractual obligations.

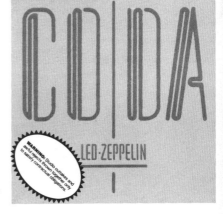

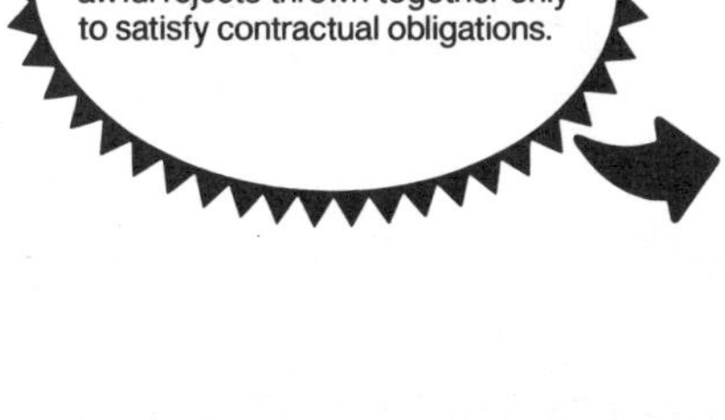
WARNING: Studio outtakes and awful rejects thrown together only to satisfy contractual obligations.

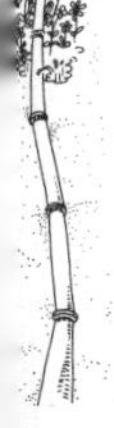

BILLY JOEL
GREATEST HITS

Paul Simon Greatest Hits, Etc.

STEVIE WONDER'S
Original Musiquarium I

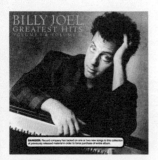

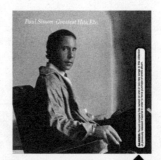

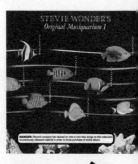

DANGER: Record company has tacked on one or two new songs to this collection of previously released material in order to force purchase of entire album.

Tina
TURNER
CAUTION: This woman may be as old as your mother.
Private Dancer

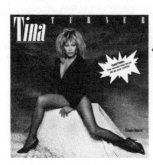

CAUTION:
This woman may be as old as your mother.

EAT AT AL'S
EAT AT JOE'S
EAT AT JOE'S

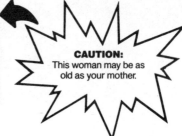

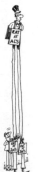

DANGER:
Take ONLY in small doses. One song provides the daily adult requirement of pretentiousness.

Neil Diamond
I'm Glad You're Here With Me Tonight

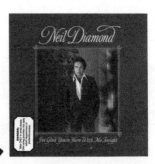

WARNING: Contains good music and intelligent lyrics. As such, it may be unsuitable for today's listeners.

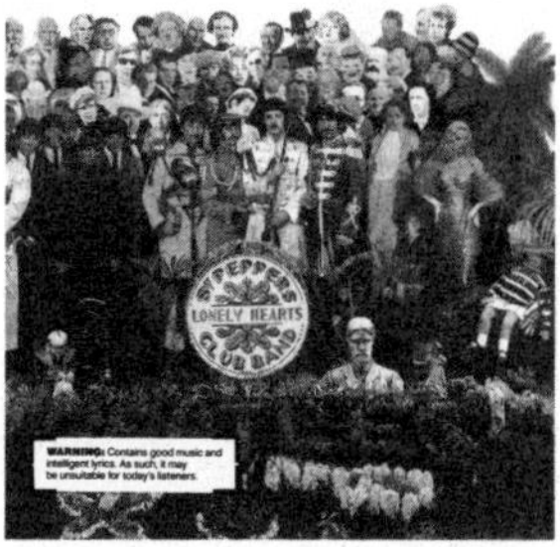

LONELY HEARTS
CLUB BAND
WARNING: Contains good music and intelligent lyrics. As such, it may be unsuitable for today's listeners.

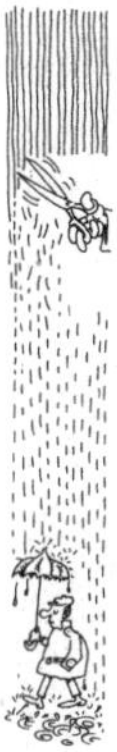

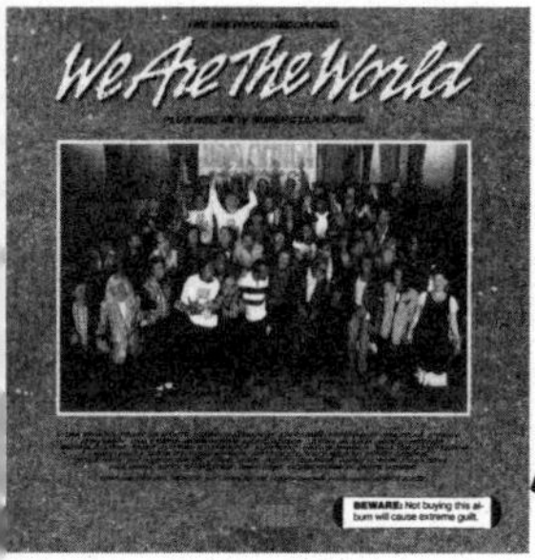

We Are The World
BEWARE: Not buying this album will cause extreme guilt.

BEWARE: Not buying this album will cause extreme guilt.

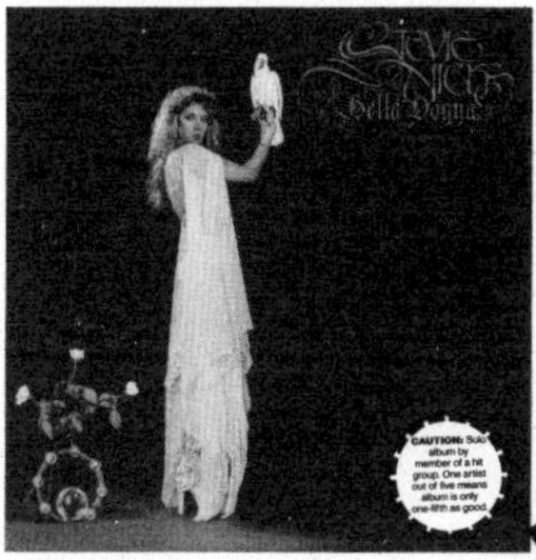

Stevie Nicks
Bella Donna
CAUTION: Solo album by member of a hit group. One artist out of five means album is only one-fifth as good.

CAUTION: Solo album by member of a hit group. One artist out of five means album is only one-fifth as good.

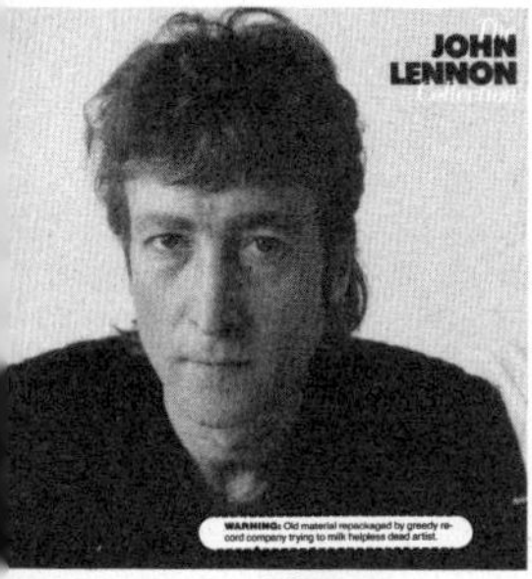

JOHN
LENNON
WARNING: Old material repackaged by greedy record company trying to milk helpless dead artist.

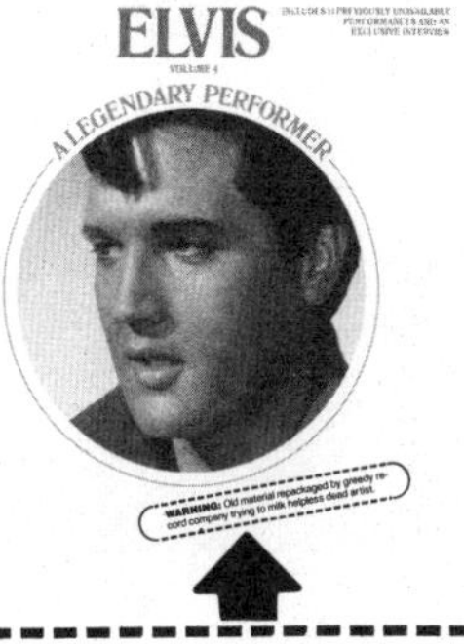

ELVIS
A LEGENDARY PERFORMER
WARNING: Old material repackaged by greedy record company trying to milk helpless dead artist.

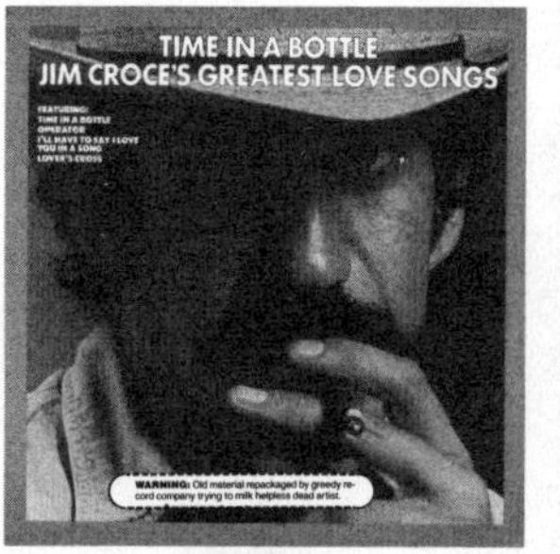

TIME IN A BOTTLE
JIM CROCE'S GREATEST LOVE SONGS
WARNING: Old material repackaged by greedy record company trying to milk helpless dead artist.

WARNING: Old material repackaged by greedy record company trying to milk helpless dead artist.

THE QUEST IS YET TO COME DEPARTMENT

How Many Of These Hard-To-Fin

MAD'S GREAT AMERI

1 A needlepoint sampler in an Iowa Grand-mother's kitchen that reads "Use it or lose it!"

2 A swizzle-stick or napkin from a straight bar in San Francisco.

3 A Utility Executive who lives within 50 miles of his company's nuclear power plant.

4 A horse in the Kentucky Derby named "Frank" o "Charlie."

5 A car salesman who did get the word that plaid pants and white buck shoes are "out."

7 A U.P.I. newspaper story in which Margaret Thatcher, rhubarb and the Andromeda Galaxy are all mentioned.

8 An exact replica of the Statute Of Liberty, only bigger!

9 A TV Guide listing for new network sitcom th does not contain t words "riotous," "za or "madcap."

10 A wa

12 Arm-warm

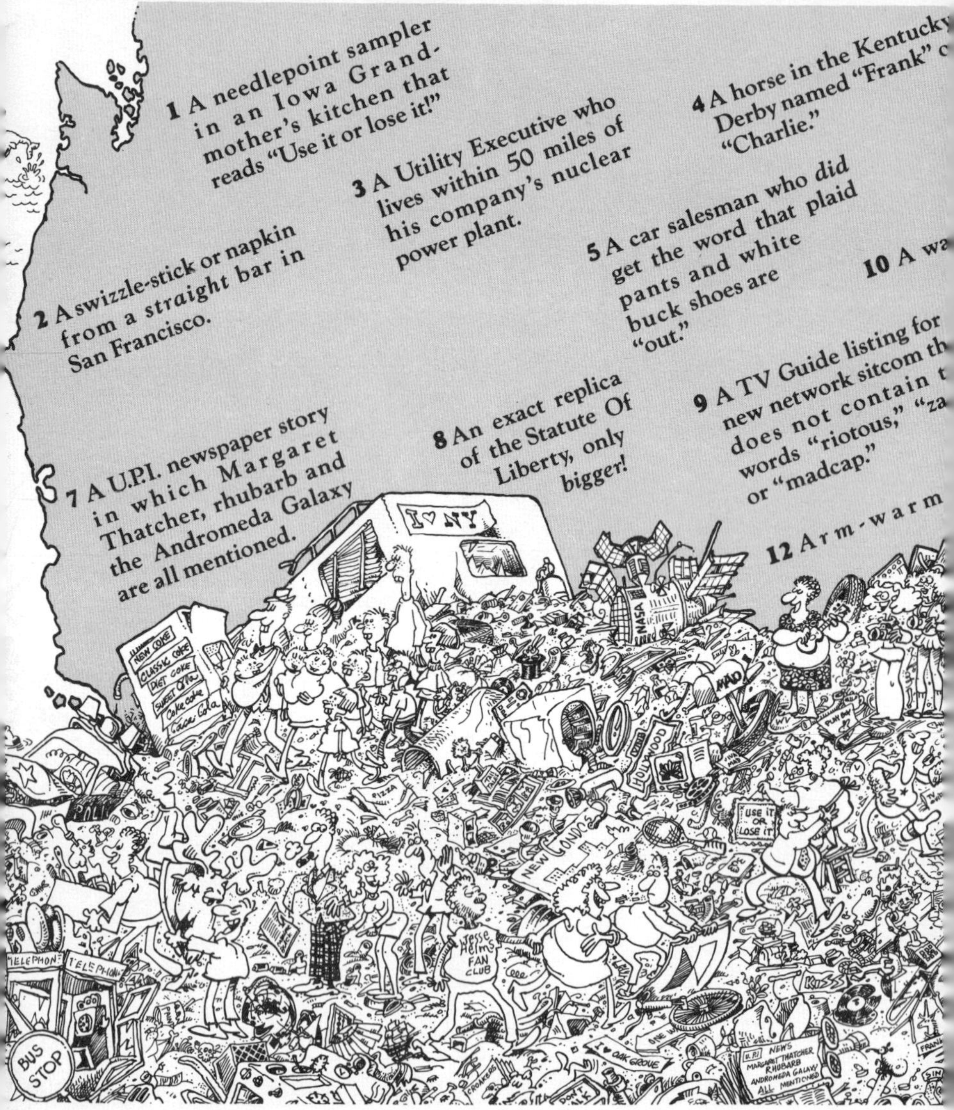

I ♥ NY
NEW COKE
CLASSIC COKE
DIET COKE
Coca-Cola
NASA
MAD
HOLLYWOOD
USE IT OR LOSE IT
Jesse Helms FAN CLUB
TELEPHONE
BUS STOP
I ♥ OAK GROVE
U.P.I. NEWS MARGARET THATCHER RHUBARB ANDROMEDA GALAXY ALL MENTIONED

...tems Can You Come Up With In...
...AN SCAVENGER HUNT

ARTIST: SERGIO ARAGONES WRITER: MIKE SNIDER

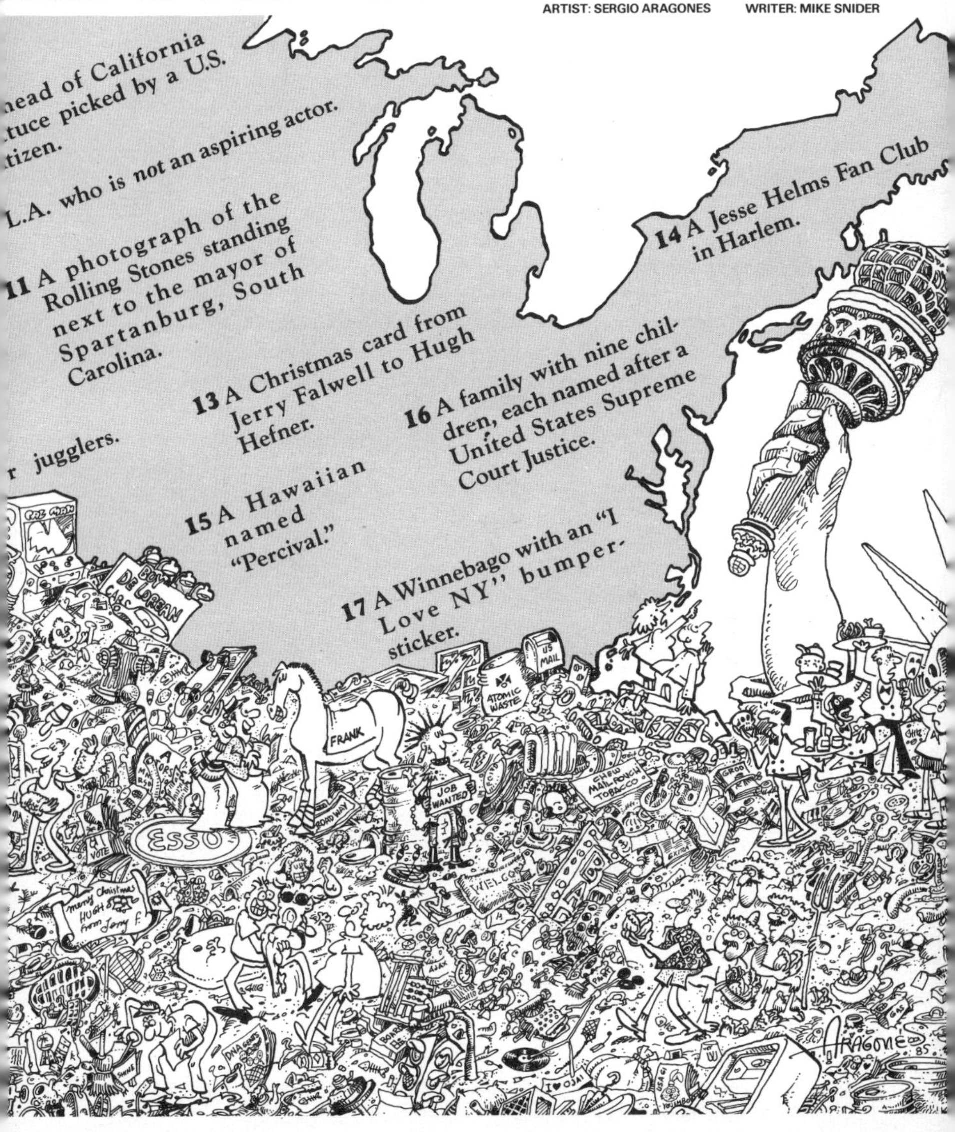
...head of California
...tuce picked by a U.S.
...tizen.
...L.A. who is *not* an aspiring actor.
11 A photograph of the Rolling Stones standing next to the mayor of Spartanburg, South Carolina.
...r jugglers.
13 A Christmas card from Jerry Falwell to Hugh Hefner.
14 A Jesse Helms Fan Club in Harlem.
15 A Hawaiian named "Percival."
16 A family with nine children, each named after a United States Supreme Court Justice.
17 A Winnebago with an "I Love NY" bumper sticker.
DE LOREAN
US MAIL
ATOMIC WASTE
FRANK
JOB WANTED
CHEW MAIL POUCH TOBACCO
ESSO
VOTE
Merry Christmas HUGH from Jerry F.
AJAX
I ♥ OJAI
ARAGONES '85

HARPER'S BIZARRE DEPT.

MAD'S INDEX

WRITERS: MIKE SNIDER AND FRANK JACOBS

A potpourri of unrelated, page filling facts 'n figures bearing no resemblance to the sort of similar index in Harper's (the magazine we ripped-off this idea from)!

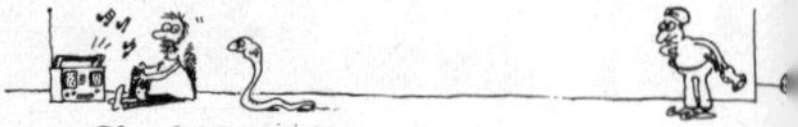

Average life expectancy (in seconds) of an enemy soldier in a Chuck Norris film : 4
Number of men who have written letters proposing marriage to Vanna White : 3,506
To Pat Sajak : 244
Difference, in laughs-per-minute, between NBC's "227" and the Iran-Iraq War : 0
Age most people stop believing in Santa Claus : 8
In politicians : 7
In Geraldo Rivera : 5
Number of chemical elements in the universe : 104
In a glass of New Jersey tap water : 98
Chance average male has of picking up hot-to-trot bimbo in singles bar : 1 in 14
Of picking up disturbing rash : 1 in 6
Number of "Yuppie-dramas" now being developed by the 3 major networks : thirtysomething
Number of days into baseball season before Cleveland Indians are written off as pennant contenders : 5
Average powder base (in inches) on Aspen ski slope : 17
On Tammy Bakker : ¼
Percentage of insomniacs who nightly fall asleep by taking sleeping pills : 31
By watching Fox Network shows : 47
Number of months in the year 1987 : 12
In 1988 : 12
Number of "w"s in the word "Israeli" : 0
When Tom Brokaw pronounces it : 2
Salary of the average Pro Wrestler : $47,500/yr.
If Pro Wrestling didn't exist : $3.35/hr.
Number of Monopoly games started in 1987 but never played to completion : 1,852,799
Number of things that annoy Andy Rooney : 2,000,000
Number of people annoyed by Andy Rooney : 23,000,000
Average miles per gallon you can expect if a car maker's ad says "39 mph, city" : 23
Number of people who aren't doctors, but play them on TV : 57
Who aren't doctors, but play them in our nation's hospitals : 5,820
Number of Supreme Court Justices who wear nothing under their robes : 4
Water content of average "all natural" citrus fruit drink : 89%
Of average cup of beer sold at any baseball stadium : 89%
Number of people in the history of air travel who have been able to get a $99 Maxsaver fare to the coast : 2
Restrictions for that fare : 237
Percentage of the public who understand the new tax code : 11%
Percentage of accountants who understand it : 9%
Percentage of IRS employees who understand it : 6%
Number of people who work for the government : about half
Number of Americans who believe any of the statistics on this page are accurate : 2,487,644
Who believe TV Evangelists are trustworthy : 2,487,644

Note: It will be necessary to adjust your "horizontal hold" for the following article!

VC℞ DEPT.

For the past couple of years, a new illness has been sweeping America. Its symptoms are painful, its effects debilitating, and no one ever really recovers from it. We at MAD wanted to alert our readers to this scourge and assigned one of our top investigative reporters the task of researching and reporting on it. Unfortunately, he died! So we're going to have to fill the next three pages with the following diseased article called...

VIDEO MALADIES

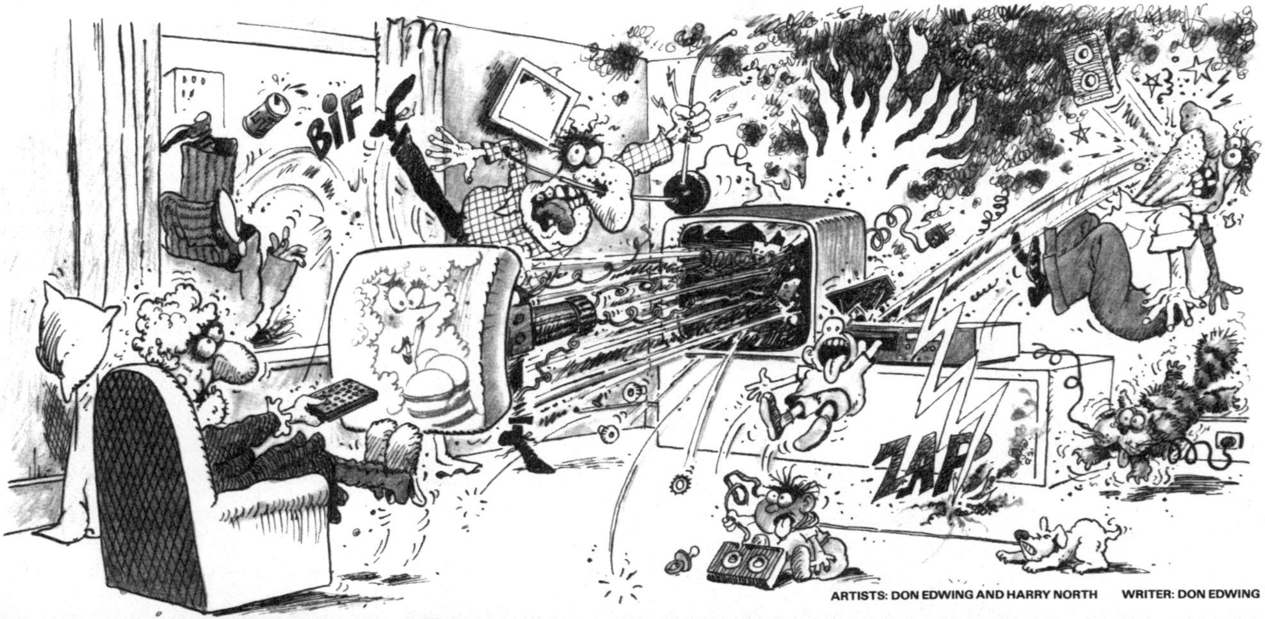
BIF
ZAP

ARTISTS: DON EDWING AND HARRY NORTH WRITER: DON EDWING

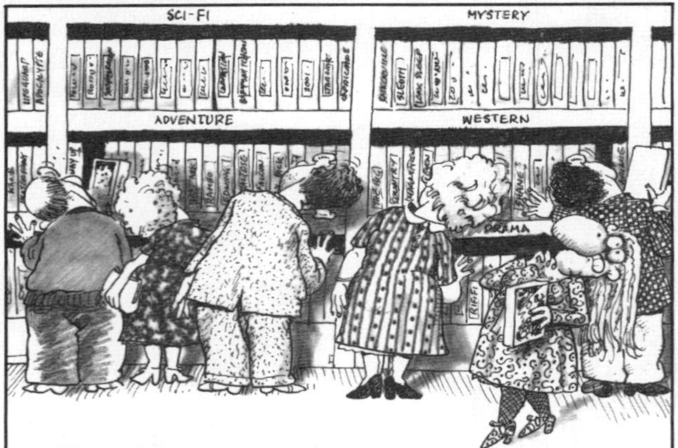
SCI-FI
MYSTERY
ADVENTURE
WESTERN
DRAMA

The "Video Store Tape Reading" Neck Strain

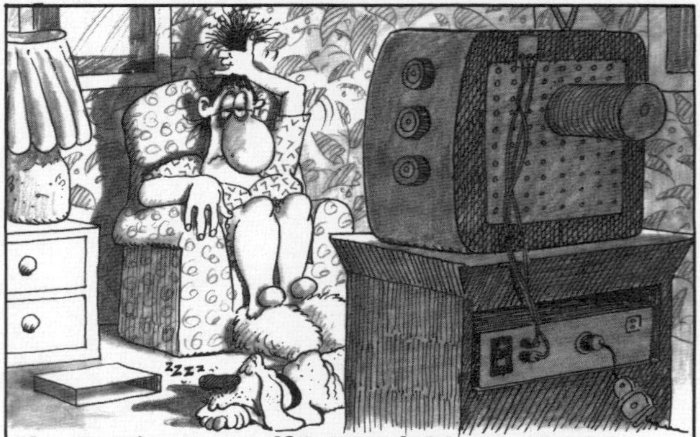
ZZZZ

The "Forcing Yourself To Watch A Lousy Movie Just Because You're Paying Rent On It" Narcolepsy

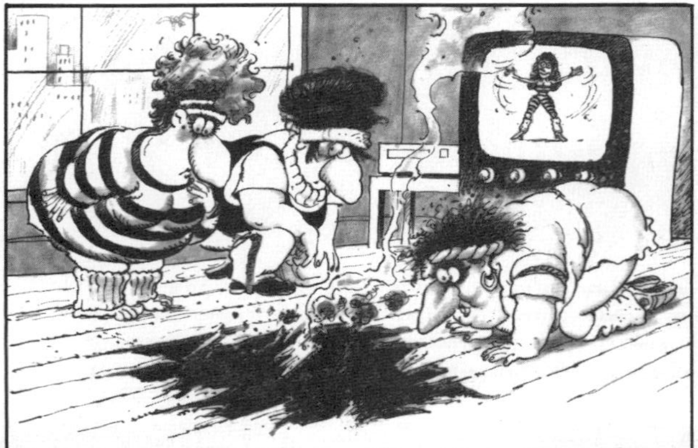

The "Jane Fonda Workout Floor Cave-In" Bruises

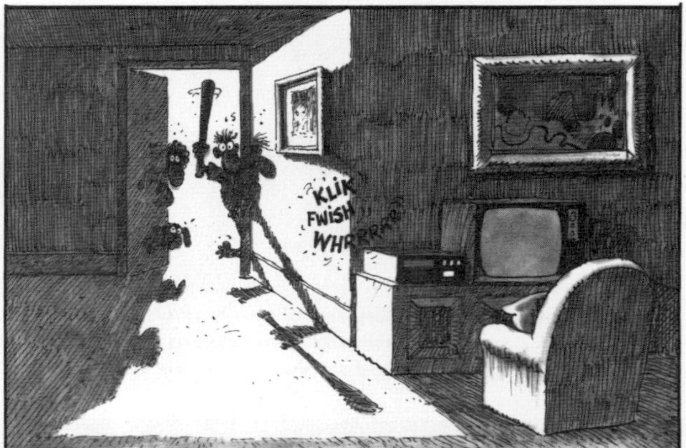
KLIK
FWISH
WHRRRRR

The "Forgotten VCR Pre-Set Night Noise" Nerves

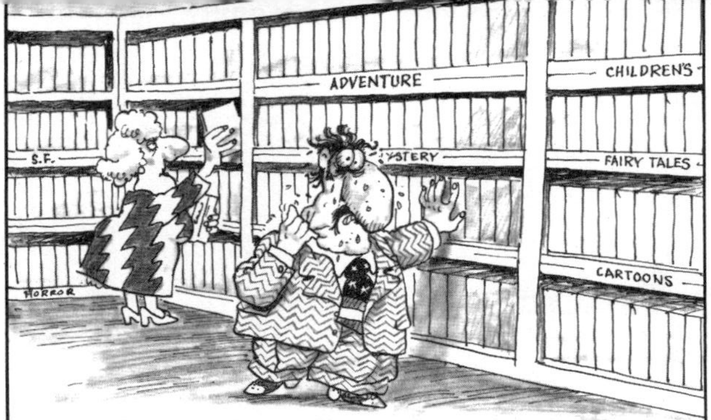
ADVENTURE
CHILDREN'S
S.F.
MYSTERY
FAIRY TALES
HORROR
CARTOONS
The "I've Already Seen Every Cassette In The Store" Sweats And Jitters

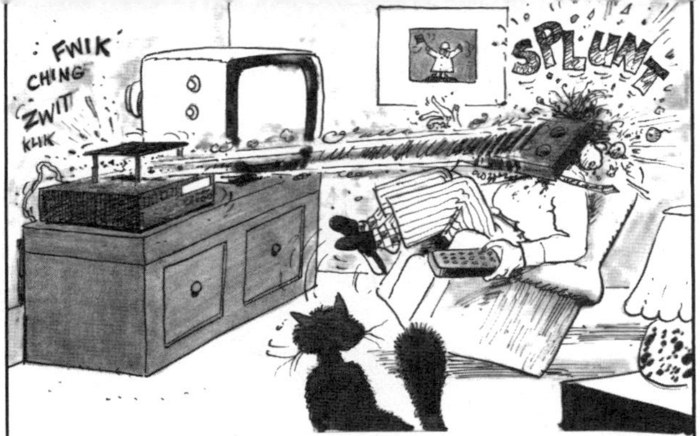
FWIK
CHING
ZWITT
KLIK
SPLUNT
The "Over-Active VCR Tape Ejector" Face Injury

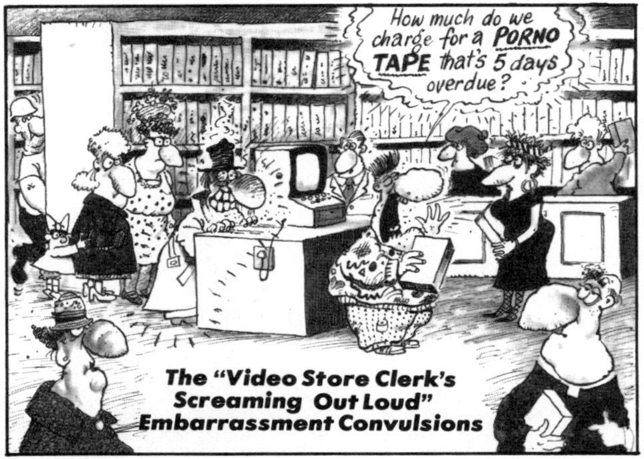
How much do we charge for a PORNO TAPE that's 5 days overdue?
The "Video Store Clerk's Screaming Out Loud" Embarrassment Convulsions

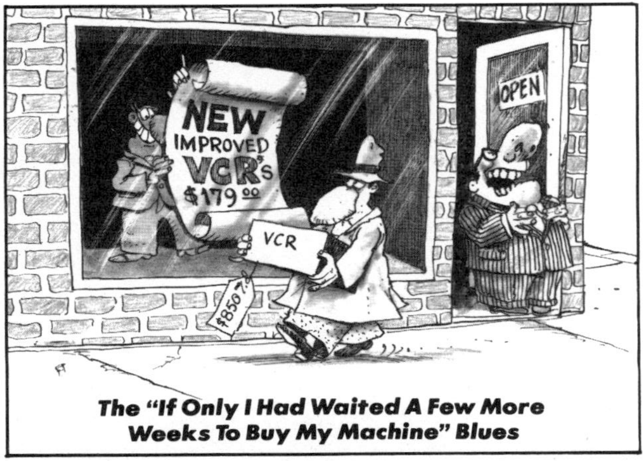
NEW IMPROVED VCR's $179.00
VCR
$850
OPEN
The "If Only I Had Waited A Few More Weeks To Buy My Machine" Blues

CHARGE OF THE TIGHT BRIGADE DEPT.

TALK ABO

Tips from the Experts in t

ARTIST & WRI

Ride your car as much as possible in neutral!

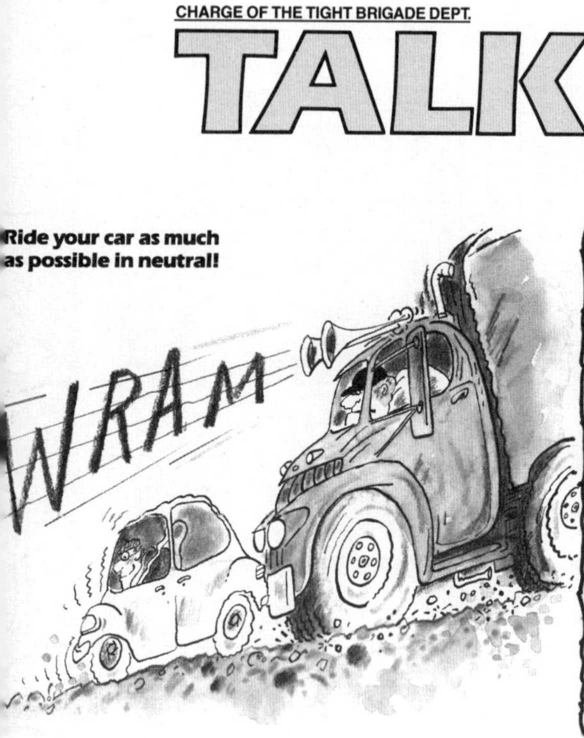
WRAM

Read by public lighting!

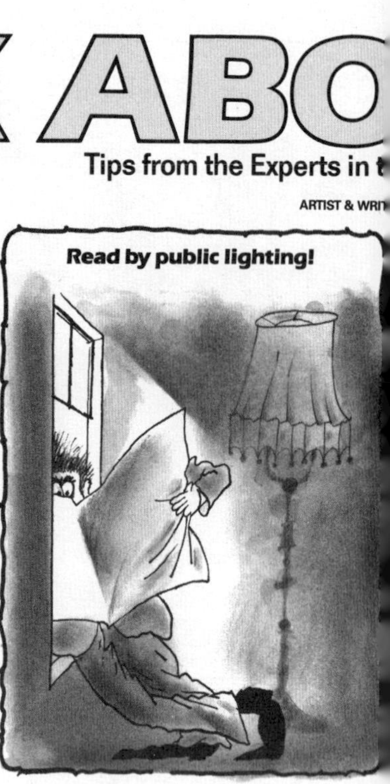

Save on doormats by using your neighbor's!

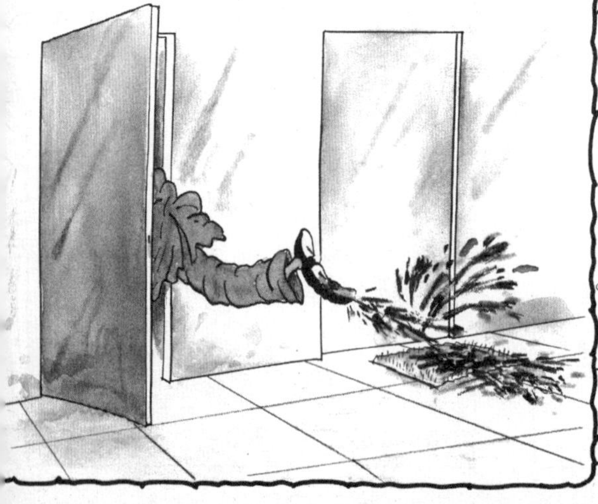

Use airline and motel soap exclusively!

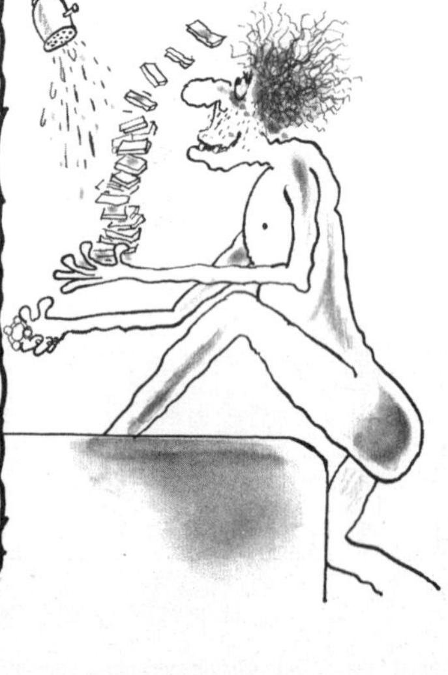

UT CHEAP!

ight-fisted Game of Stinginess

AUL PETER PORGES

Pay your check under someone else's tip!

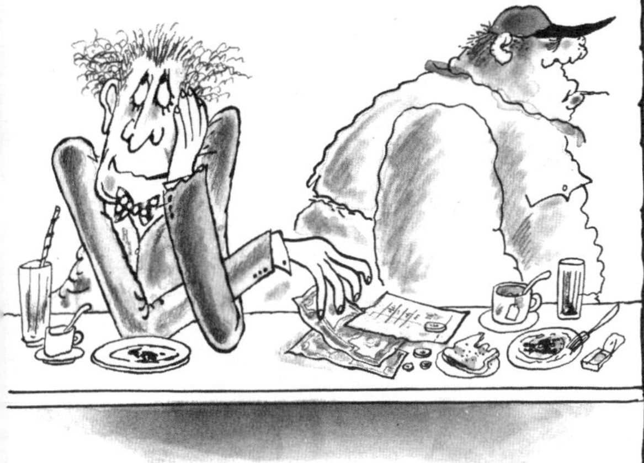

Recycle old laces from discarded shoes!

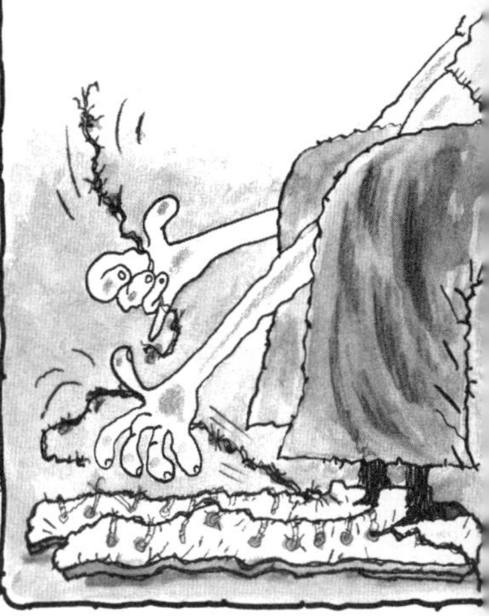

Reduce hot water costs by washing everything in the same load!

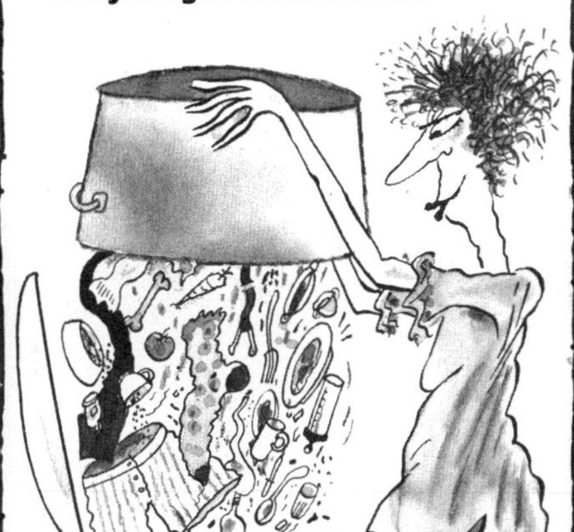

Use your neighbor's barbecu

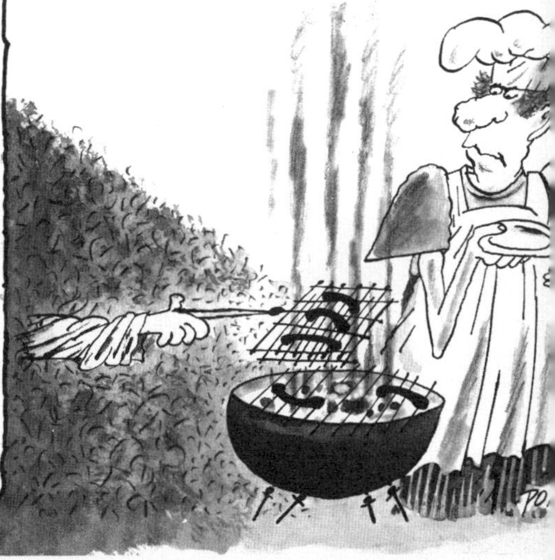

THINGS THAT GO BUMP IN THE TRITE DEPT.

Hey, gang! It's time once again for MAD's nutty old "Cliché Monster" game. Here's how it works: Take any familiar phrase or colloquial expression, give it an eerie setting so you create a new-type monster, and you're playing it. Mainly, you're—

HORRIFYING CLICHÉS

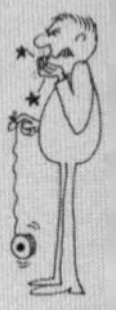

ARTIST: PAUL COKER, JR. WRITER: MAY SAKAMI

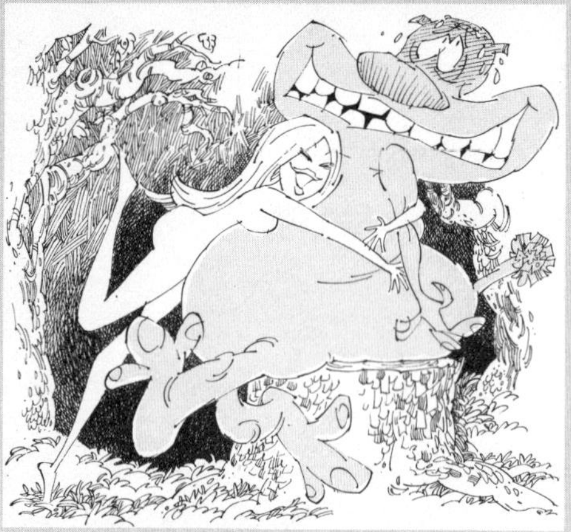

Embracing A BELIEF

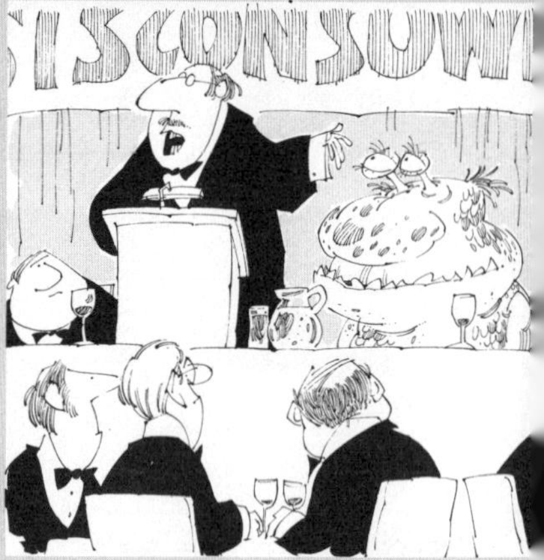

Introducing A RESOLUTION

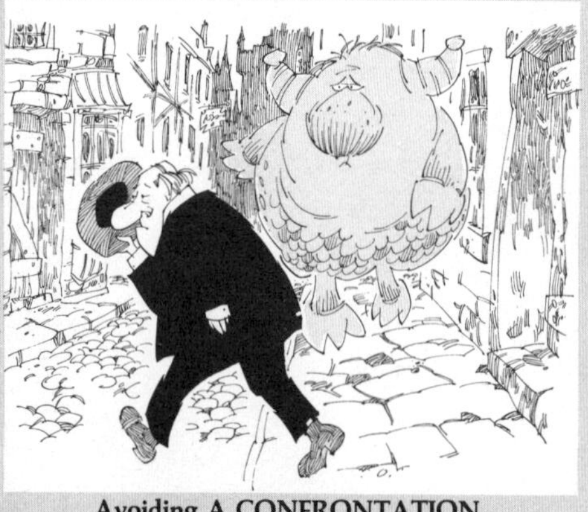

Avoiding A CONFRONTATION

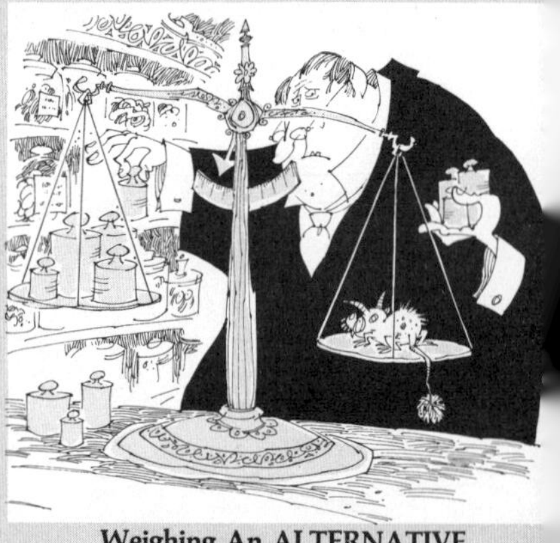

Weighing An ALTERNATIVE

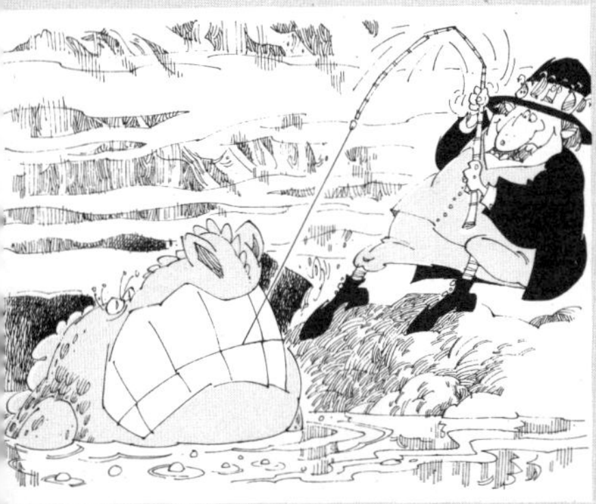

Fishing For A COMPLIMENT

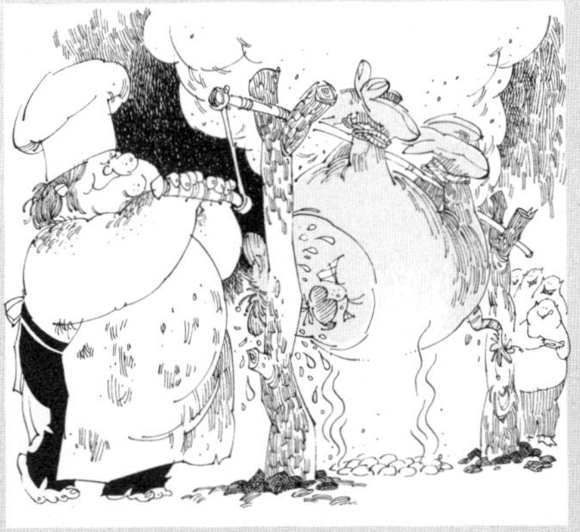

Grilling A SUSPECT

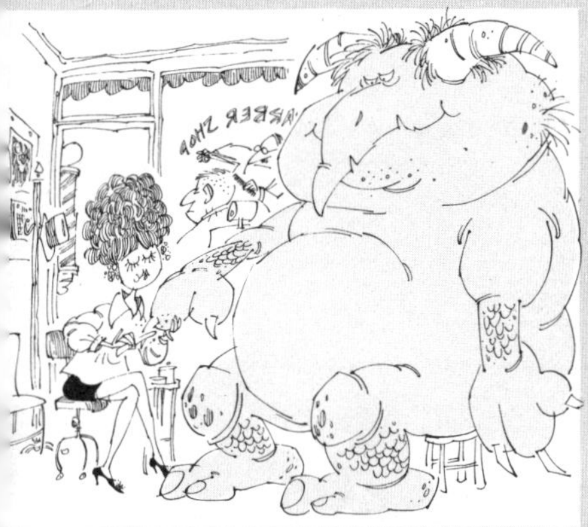

Filing A RETURN

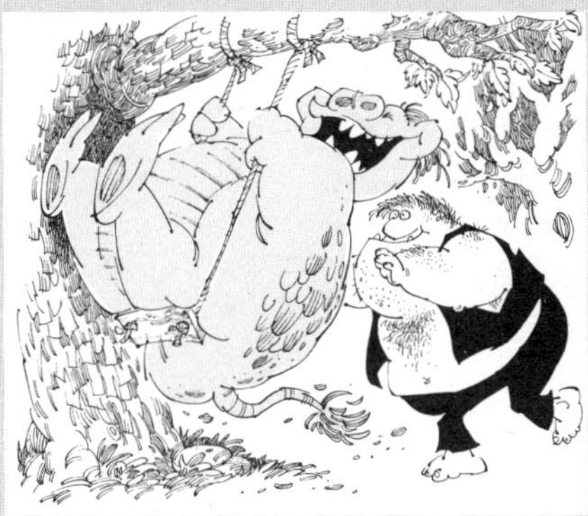

Swinging A DEAL

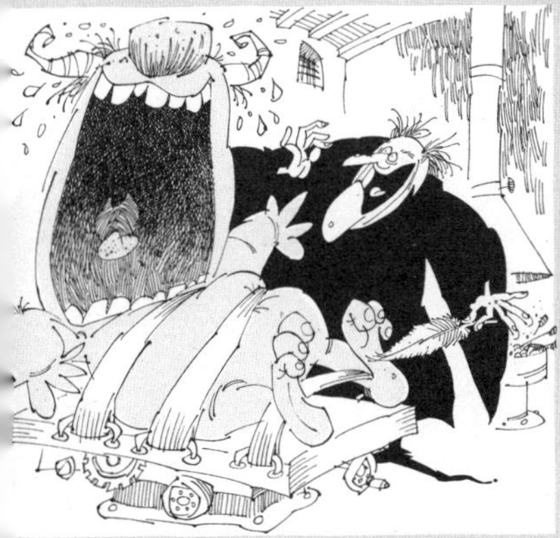

Tickling A FANCY

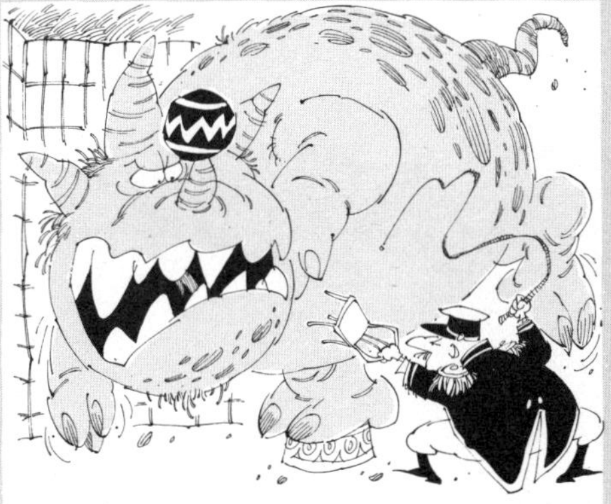

Controlling An IMPULSE

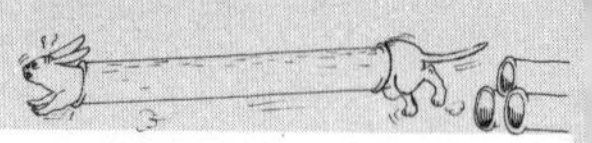

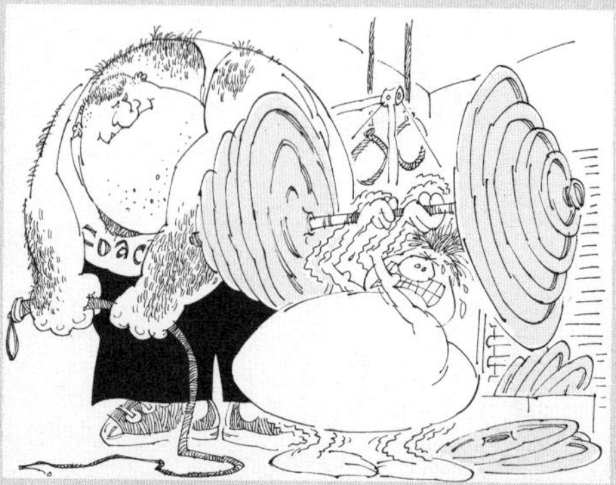

Developing A TECHNIQUE

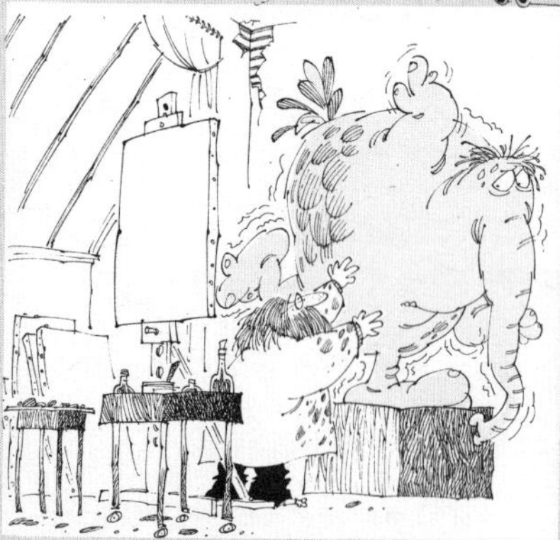

Posing A PROBLEM

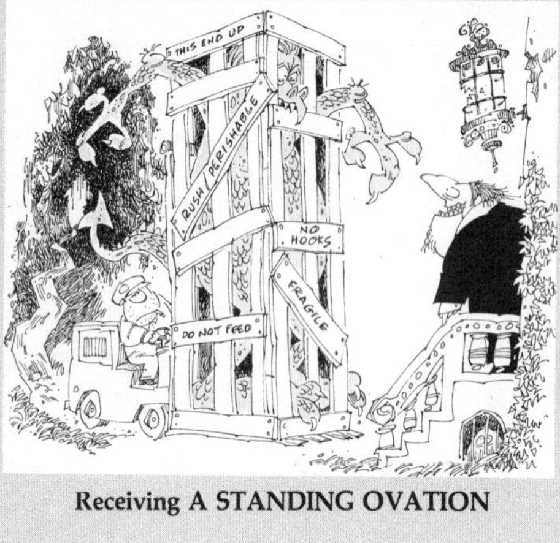
THIS END UP
RUSH / PERISHABLE
NO HOOKS
FRAGILE
DO NOT FEED

Receiving A STANDING OVATION

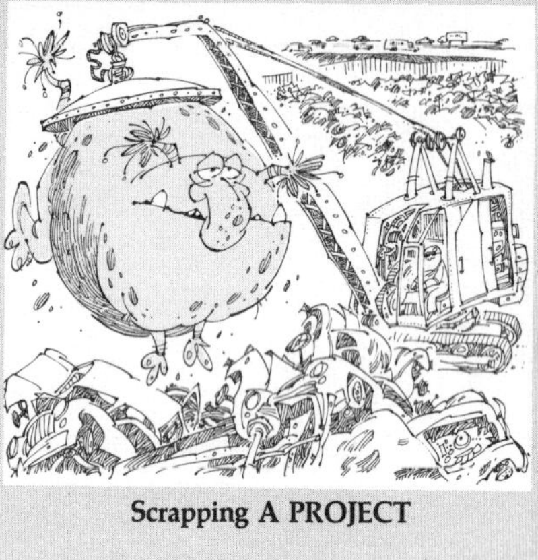

Scrapping A PROJECT

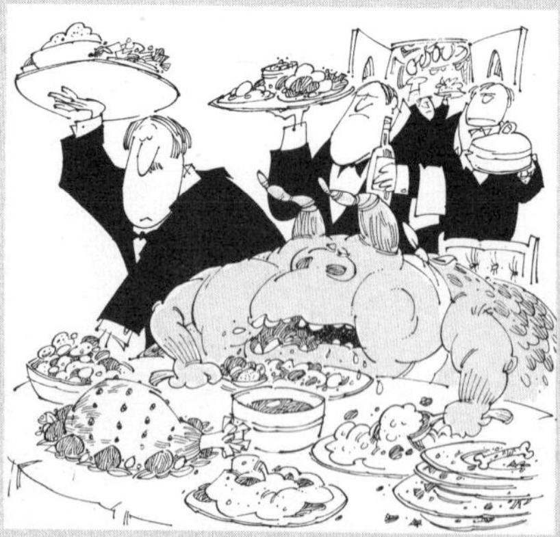

Serving A SUMMONS

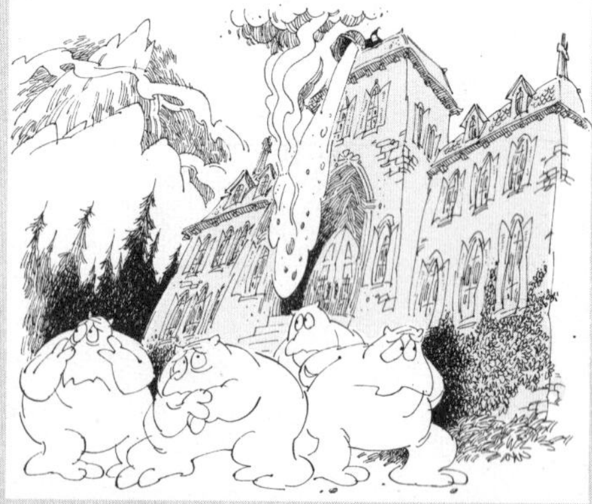

Pouring Oil On TROUBLED WATERS

DON MARTIN DEPT.

IN THE HOSPITAL

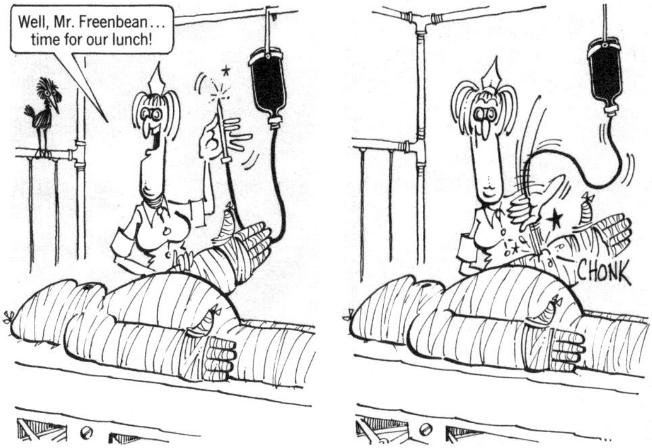
Well, Mr. Freenbean... time for our lunch!
CHONK

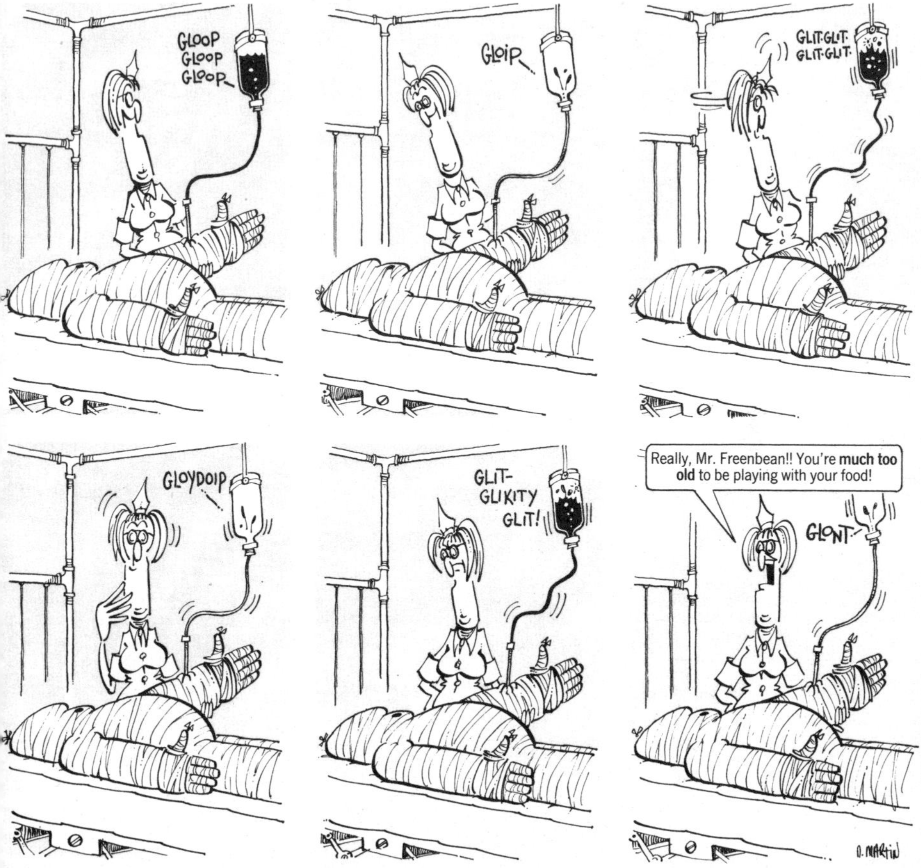
GLOOP GLOOP GLOOP
GLOIP
GLIT·GLIT· GLIT·GLIT·
GLOYDOIP
GLIT- GLIKITY GLIT!
Really, Mr. Freenbean!! You're **much too old** to be playing with your food!
GLONT
D. MARTIN

STATISTICKLE DEPT.

FURTHER ADDITIONS TO... MAD'S TABLE OF L USELESS WEIGHTS

7.9 YARDS

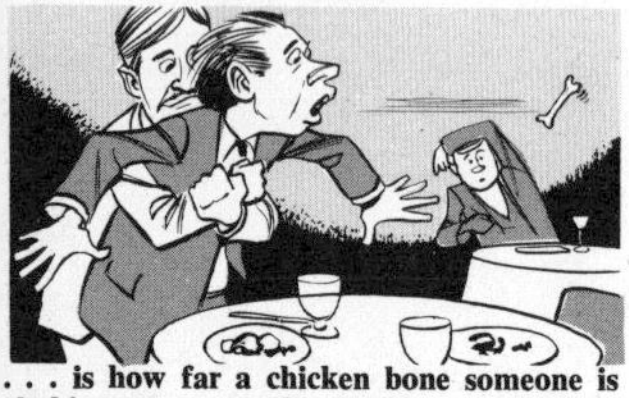

. . . is how far a chicken bone someone is choking on catapults across a restaurant when you perform the "Heimlich Maneuver."

.0005 LITERS

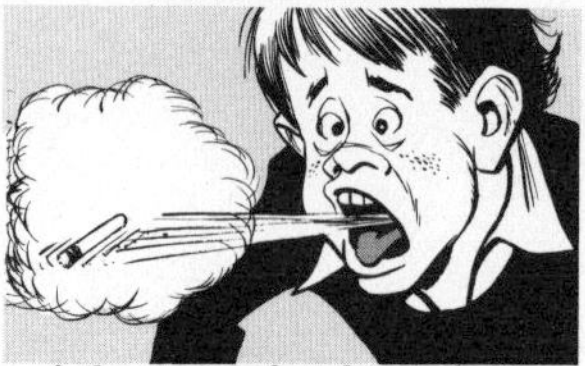

. . . is the amount of smoke a typical teen-ager "inhales" when he lights up his very first cigarette before he starts coughing.

6.9 INCHES

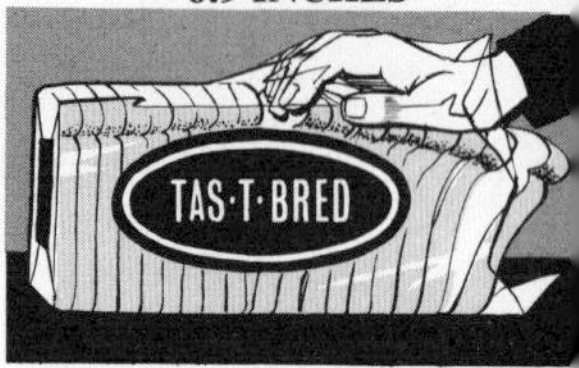
TAS·T·BRED

. . . is how far a person shoves his finger into a freshly-opened loaf of bread to pu out a slice without removing the end piec

19.5 INCHES

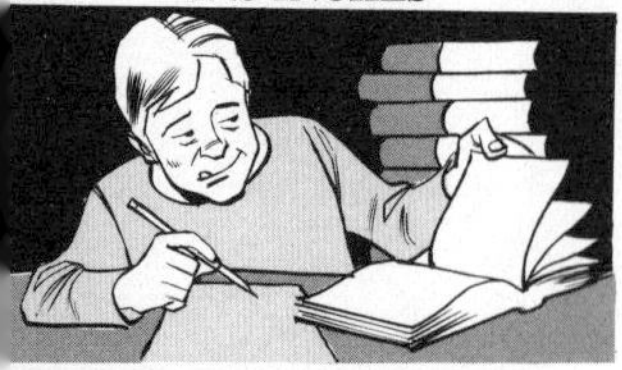

. . . is the total depth of lines that are plagiarized for the average term paper.

3.3 OUNCES

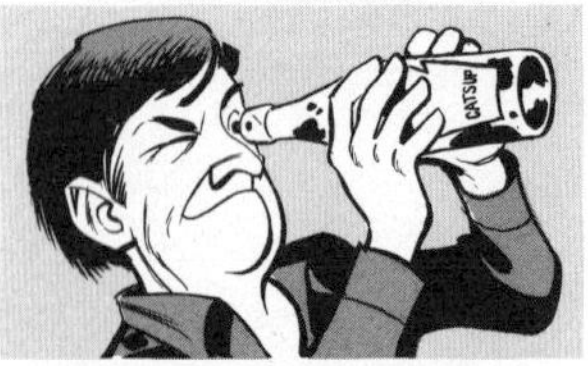
CATSUP

. . . is the amount of ketchup on the sides of the bottle that you'll never get out.

9.8 YARDS

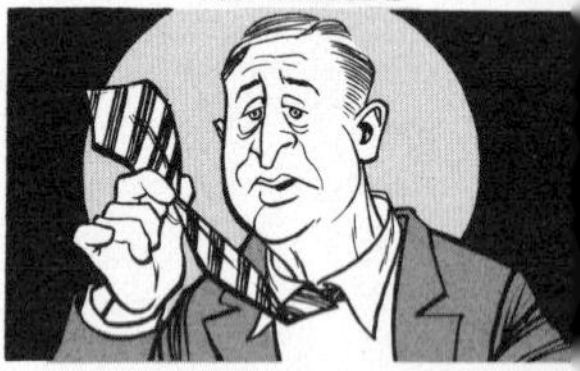

. . . is the total distance Rodney Danger field yanks his tie during one monologue

6.8 OUNCES

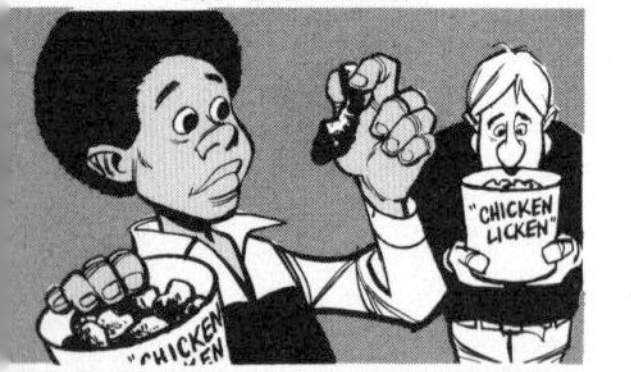
"CHICKEN LICKEN"

. . . is the total amount of Fried Chicken-In-A-Bucket that's a complete "mystery."

284 POUNDS

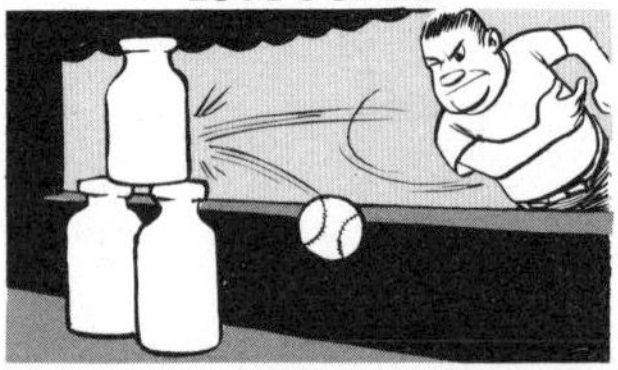

. . . is the total weight of the three Knock 'Em Down pins in an average carnival booth.

8.7 GALLONS

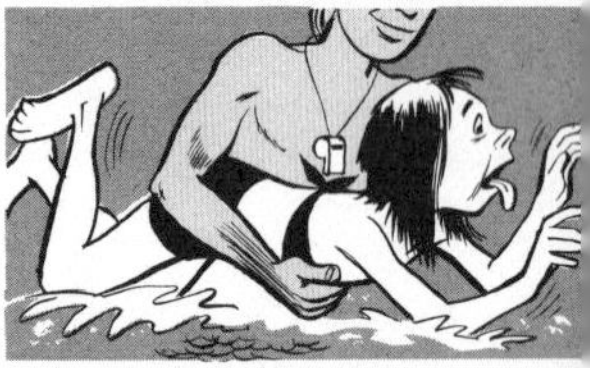

. . . is the amount of water you swallowe when you were first learning how to swim

1.2 OUNCES

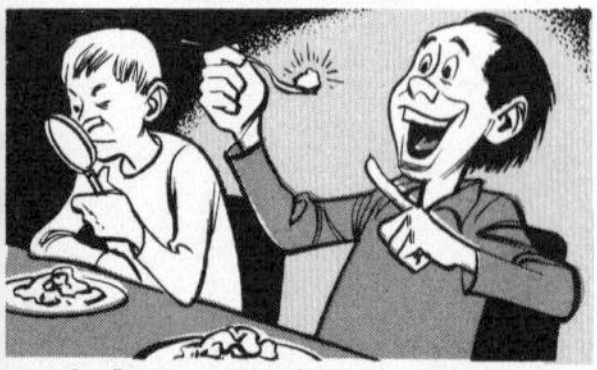

. . . is the amount of food per serving in a school's hot lunch program that's edible.

2.7 FEET

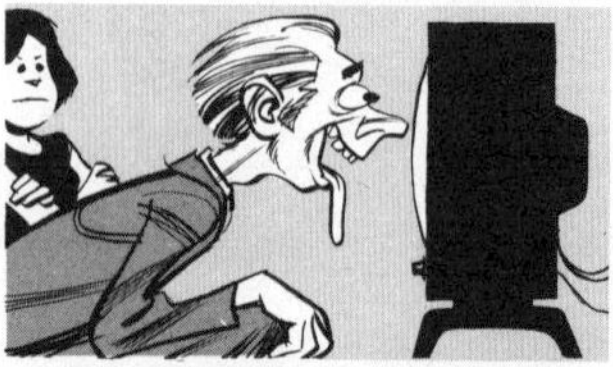

. . . is how much closer a horny guy sits to the TV set when watching a "jiggle" show.

4.6 OUNCES

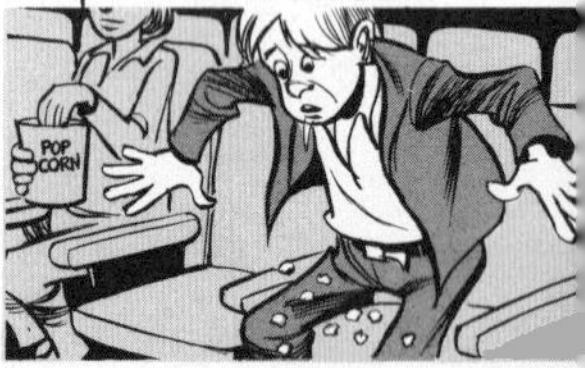
POP CORN

. . . is the amount of popcorn on your la when you get up at the end of the movie

ARTIST: BOB CLARKE WRITER: JOHN FICARRA

TLE-KNOWN AND VERY MEASURES & DISTANCES

827 YARDS

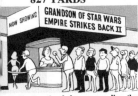

NOW SHOWING
GRANDSON OF STAR WARS
EMPIRE STRIKES BACK II

. is the length of the average line that rm all around a movie theater during the st week that a 'Star Wars' sequel opens.

11.3 FEET

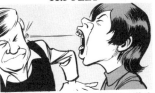

. . . is the distance that the tiny little rubber band from your braces shoots from your mouth across the room when you yawn.

8.5 INCHES

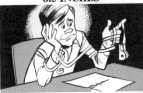

. . . is the amount of Scotch Tape you can pull off a roll before it starts getting twisted and mangled all over your hands.

137 POUNDS

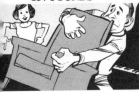

. is the minimum weight of any piece of rniture your wife wants moved . . . again!

.004 CENTIMETERS

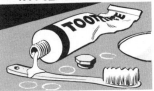

. . . is the diameter of the circle that a toothpaste cap leaves on a bathroom sink.

1.9 MILES

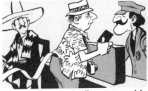

. . . is the length of toilet paper used by a typical American vacationing in Mexico.

5.7 MILES

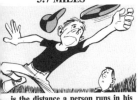

. . is the distance a person runs in his etime chasing poorly-thrown Frizbees.

9.7 INCHES

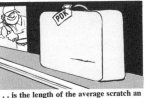

PDK

. . . is the length of the average scratch an airline will put on your brand new luggage.

2.7 YARDS

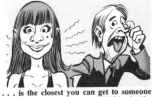

. . . is the closest you can get to someone who buys cologne for under $1.99 a bottle.

18.4 INCHES

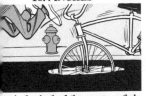

. . is the depth of the average pothole ou'll find on any street in New York City.

1.2 INCHES

National Enquirer

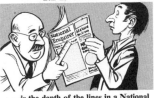

. . . is the depth of the lines in a National Enquirer story that is actually the truth.

6.5 GALLONS

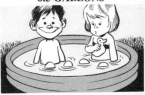

. . . is the amount of liquid in a kiddie pool that's neither water nor chlorine.

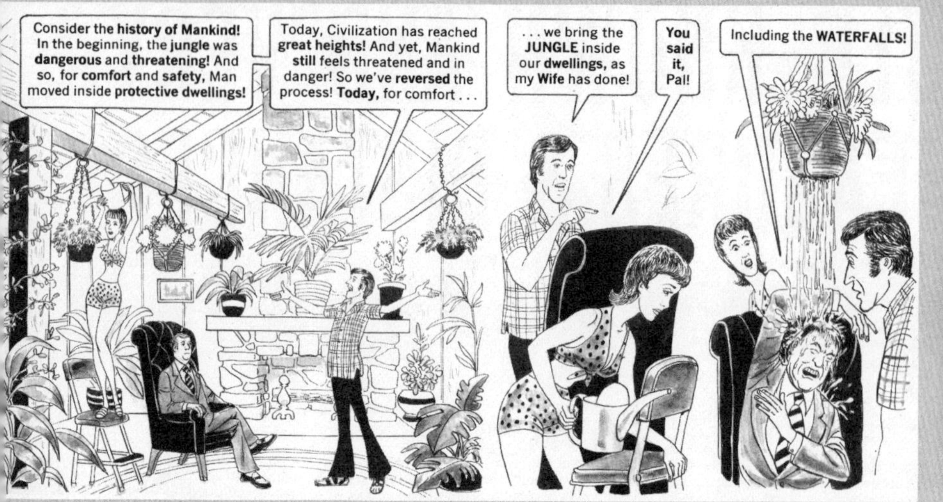

Consider the history of Mankind! In the beginning, the jungle was dangerous and threatening! And so, for comfort and safety, Man moved inside protective dwellings!
Today, Civilization has reached great heights! And yet, Mankind still feels threatened and in danger! So we've reversed the process! Today, for comfort . . .
. . . we bring the JUNGLE inside our dwellings, as my Wife has done!
You said it, Pal!
Including the WATERFALLS!

BERG'S-EYE VIEW DEPT.

THE LIGHTER SIDE OF...

INDOOR GAR

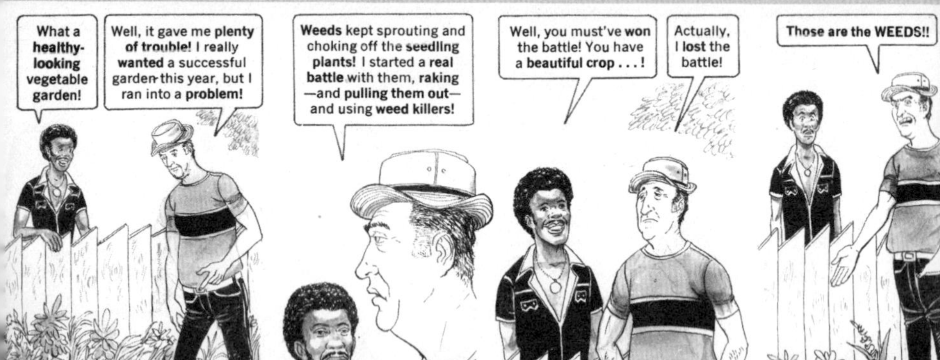

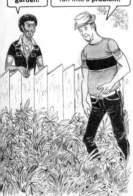

What a healthy-looking vegetable garden!
Well, it gave me plenty of trouble! I really wanted a successful garden this year, but I ran into a problem!
Weeds kept sprouting and choking off the seedling plants! I started a real battle with them, raking—and pulling them out—and using weed killers!
Well, you must've won the battle! You have a beautiful crop . . . !
Actually, I lost the battle!
Those are the WEEDS!!

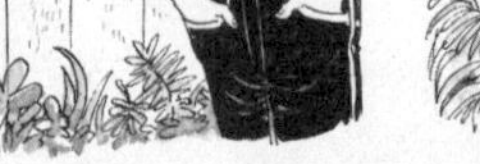

PSTTT

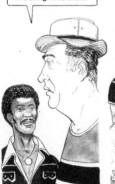

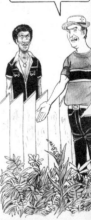

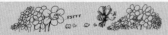

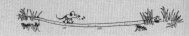

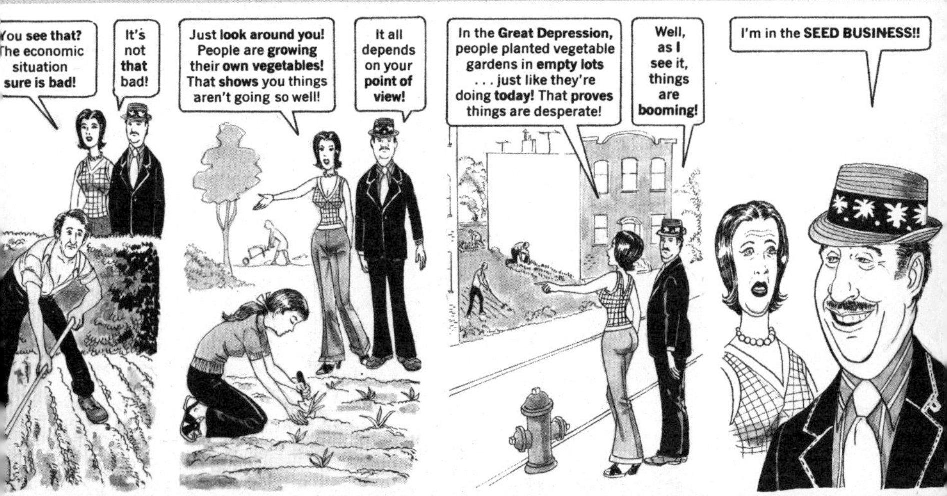
You see that? The economic situation sure is bad!
It's not that bad!
Just look around you! People are growing their own vegetables! That shows you things aren't going so well!
It all depends on your point of view!
In the Great Depression, people planted vegetable gardens in empty lots . . . just like they're doing today! That proves things are desperate!
Well, as I see it, things are booming!
I'm in the SEED BUSINESS!!

AND OUTDOOR DENING

ARTIST & WRITER: DAVE BERG

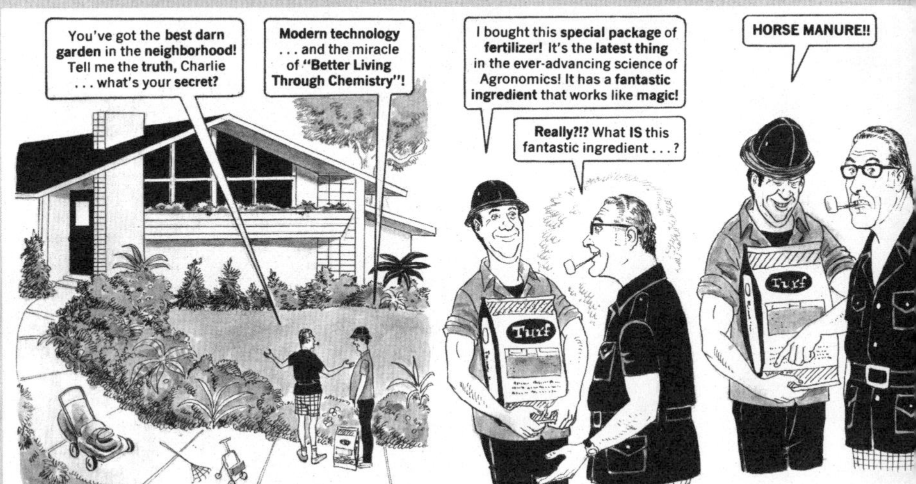
You've got the best darn garden in the neighborhood! Tell me the truth, Charlie . . . what's your secret?
Modern technology . . . and the miracle of "Better Living Through Chemistry"!
I bought this special package of fertilizer! It's the latest thing in the ever-advancing science of Agronomics! It has a fantastic ingredient that works like magic!
Really?!? What IS this fantastic ingredient . . . ?
HORSE MANURE!!
Turf
Turf

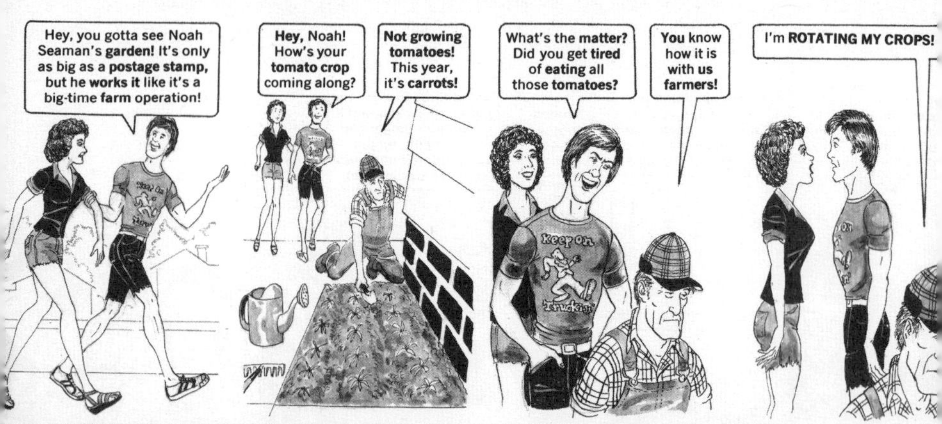
Hey, you gotta see Noah Seaman's garden! It's only as big as a postage stamp, but he works it like it's a big-time farm operation!
Hey, Noah! How's your tomato crop coming along?
Not growing tomatoes! This year, it's carrots!
What's the matter? Did you get tired of eating all those tomatoes?
Keep on Truckin'
You know how it is with us farmers!
I'm ROTATING MY CROPS!

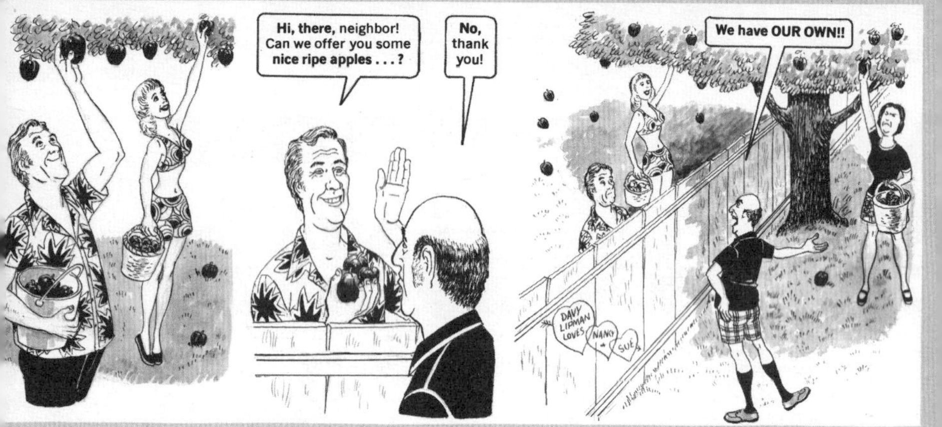
Hi, there, neighbor! Can we offer you some nice ripe apples . . . ?
No, thank you!
We have OUR OWN!!
DAVY LIPMAN LOVES
NANCY
SUE

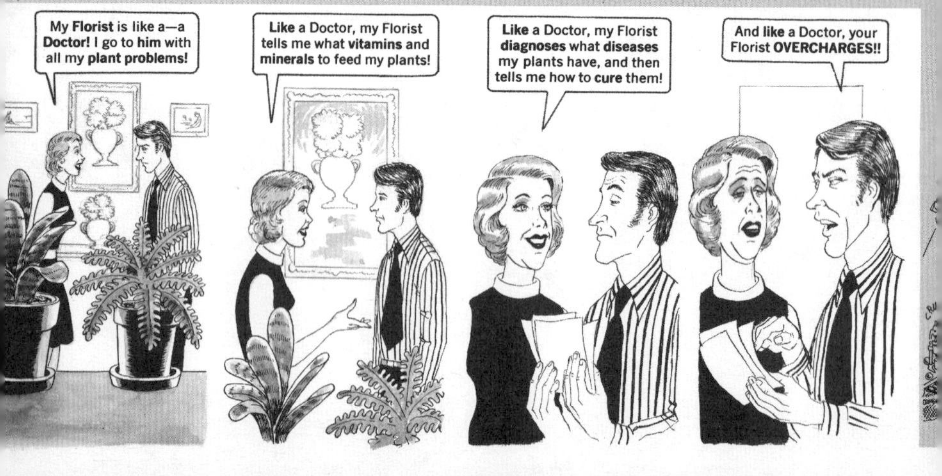
My Florist is like a—a Doctor! I go to him with all my plant problems!
Like a Doctor, my Florist tells me what vitamins and minerals to feed my plants!
Like a Doctor, my Florist diagnoses what diseases my plants have, and then tells me how to cure them!
And like a Doctor, your Florist OVERCHARGES!!

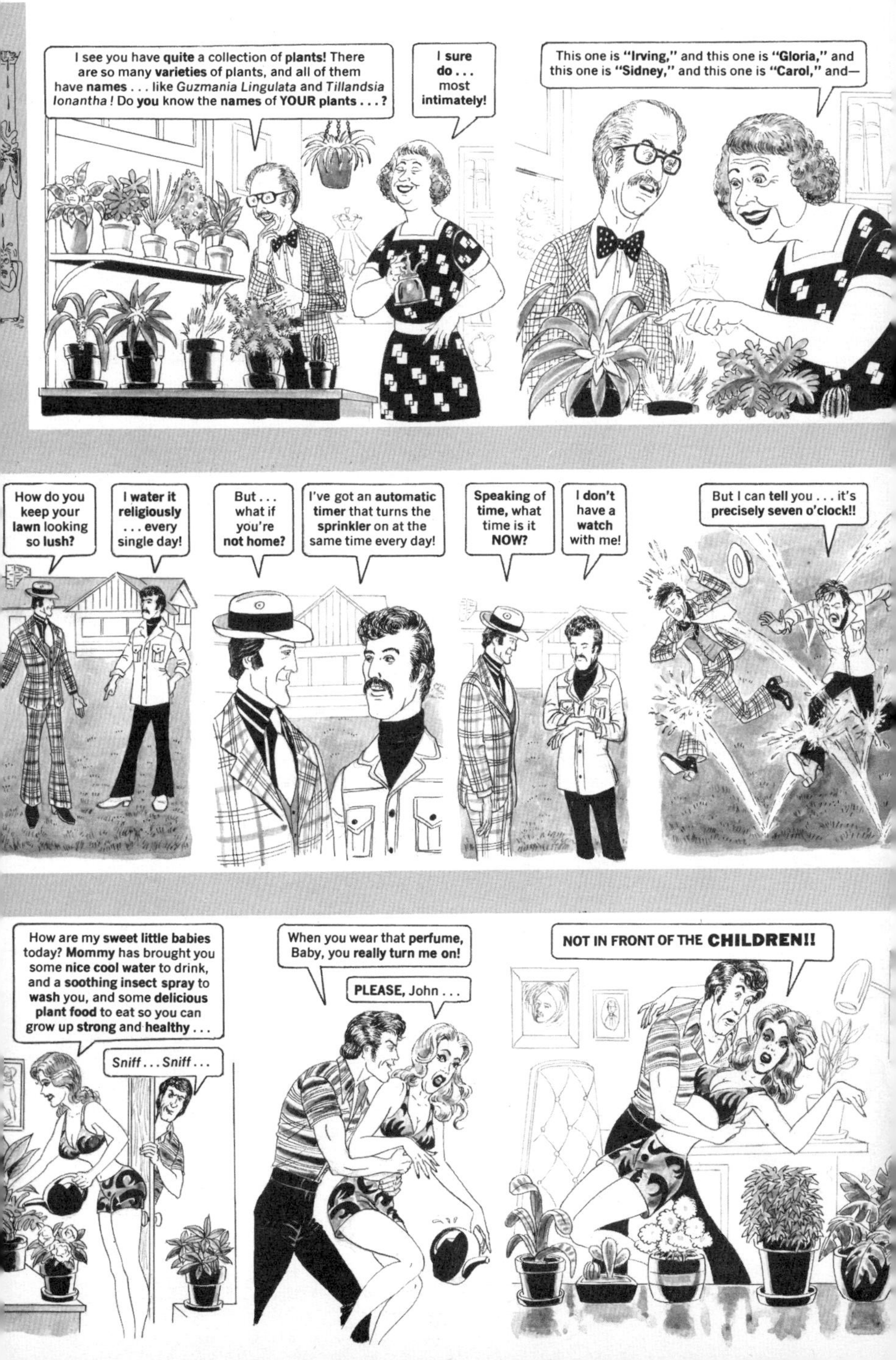
I see you have quite a collection of plants! There are so many varieties of plants, and all of them have names . . . like Guzmania Lingulata and Tillandsia Ionantha ! Do you know the names of YOUR plants . . . ?
I sure do . . . most intimately!
This one is "Irving," and this one is "Gloria," and this one is "Sidney," and this one is "Carol," and—
How do you keep your lawn looking so lush?
I water it religiously . . . every single day!
But . . . what if you're not home?
I've got an automatic timer that turns the sprinkler on at the same time every day!
Speaking of time, what time is it NOW?
I don't have a watch with me!
But I can tell you . . . it's precisely seven o'clock!!
How are my sweet little babies today? Mommy has brought you some nice cool water to drink, and a soothing insect spray to wash you, and some delicious plant food to eat so you can grow up strong and healthy . . .
Sniff . . . Sniff . . .
When you wear that perfume, Baby, you really turn me on!
PLEASE, John . . .
NOT IN FRONT OF THE CHILDREN!!

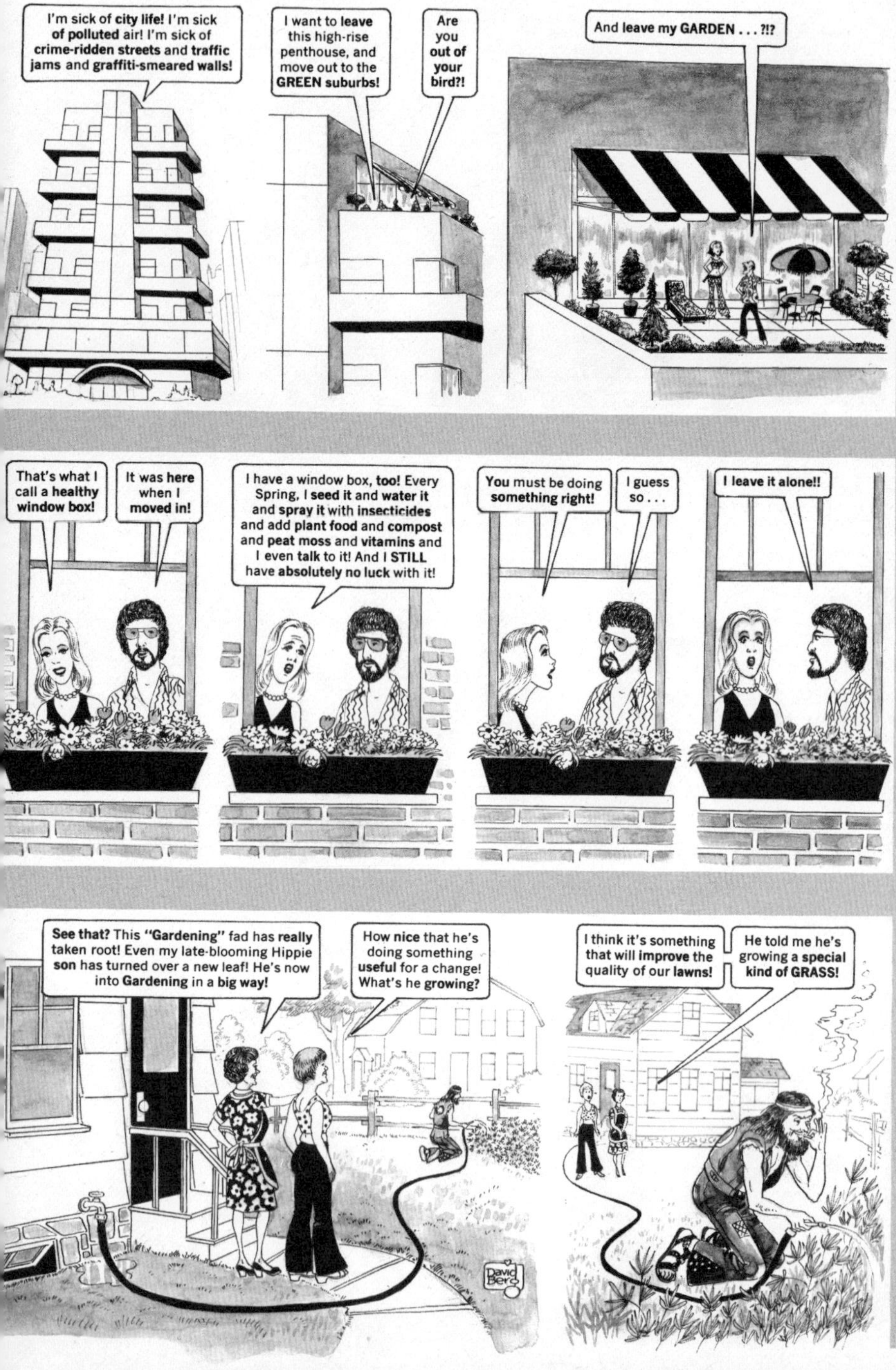
I'm sick of city life! I'm sick of polluted air! I'm sick of crime-ridden streets and traffic jams and graffiti-smeared walls!
I want to leave this high-rise penthouse, and move out to the GREEN suburbs!
Are you out of your bird?!
And leave my GARDEN . . . ?!?
That's what I call a healthy window box!
It was here when I moved in!
I have a window box, too! Every Spring, I seed it and water it and spray it with insecticides and add plant food and compost and peat moss and vitamins and I even talk to it! And I STILL have absolutely no luck with it!
You must be doing something right!
I guess so . . .
I leave it alone!!
See that? This "Gardening" fad has really taken root! Even my late-blooming Hippie son has turned over a new leaf! He's now into Gardening in a big way!
How nice that he's doing something useful for a change! What's he growing?
David Berg
I think it's something that will improve the quality of our lawns!
He told me he's growing a special kind of GRASS!

GIVIN' 'EM A RIBBIN' DEPT.

Why restrict the awarding of medals to the military? After all, Civilians perform heroic acts while fighting life's daily battles as well! Let's recognize them with

THIS ISSUE'S PROPOSED MAD MEDALS

. . . TO BE PRESENTED TO DESERVING WORKING PEOPLE

ARTIST & WRITER: AL JAFFEE

THE JOB-EFFICIENCY MEDAL

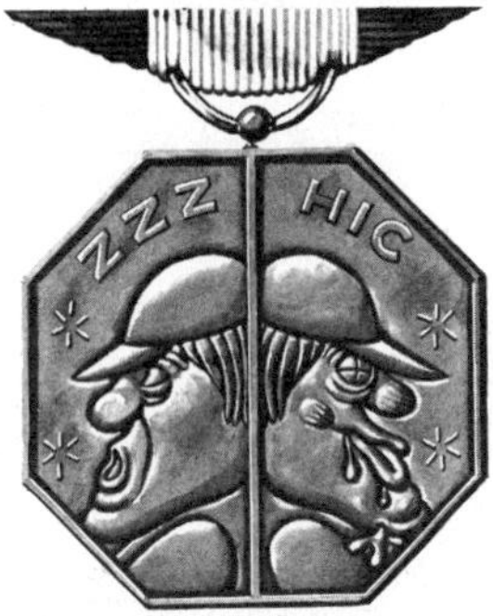
ZZZ
HIC

Presented to blue collar workers who manage to remain on the job without getting fired while half asleep (on Fridays) and hung over (on Mondays), even though the quality of work produced is disgraceful and dangerous.

THE PIGGY-BACK PARTS AWARD

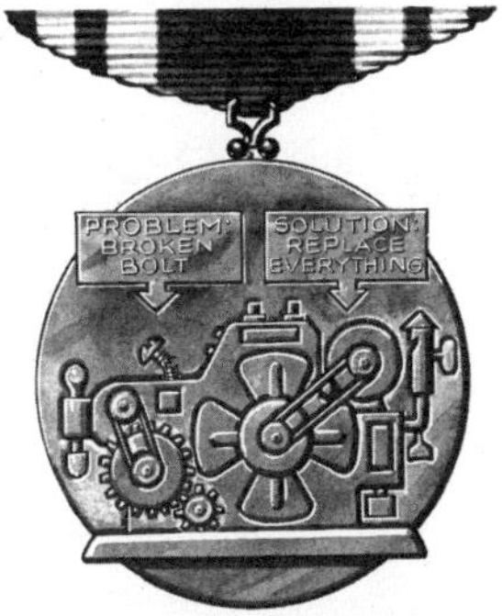
PROBLEM: BROKEN BOLT
SOLUTION: REPLACE EVERYTHING

Goes to repairmen who courageously replace an entire mechanical system in a car or an appliance, even though only a tiny part of it is malfunctioning . . . thus protecting thousands of jobs in the "Parts Manufacturing" industries.

THE PURLOINED PAPER CLIP MEDAL

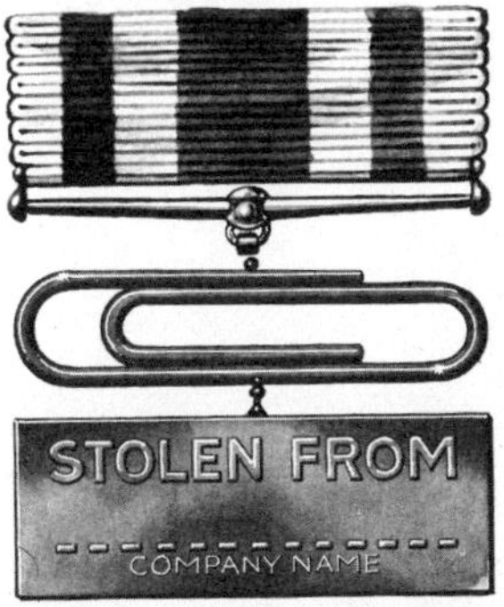
STOLEN FROM
COMPANY NAME

Goes to white collar workers who create fringe benefits by using company supplies and services, and by taking home anything that isn't nailed down. These are lots better than pay raises, since no taxes are collected on them.

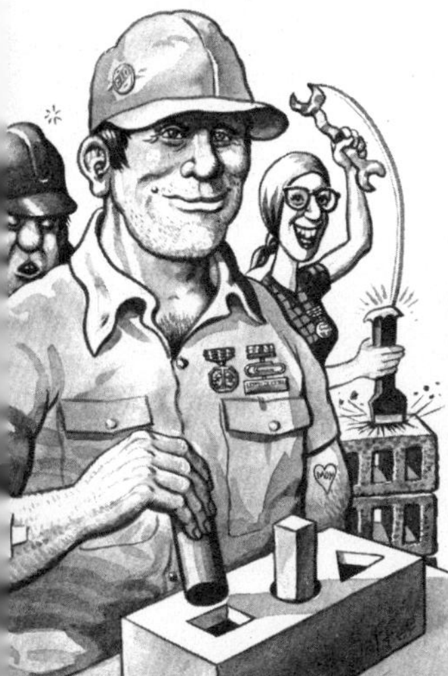

THE SILVER TONGUE AWARD

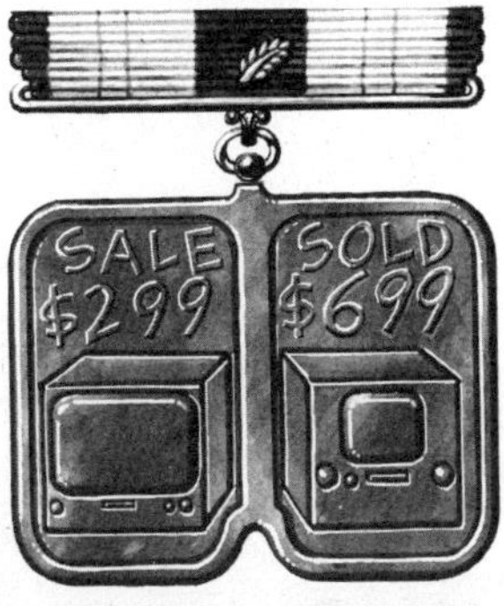
SALE $299
SOLD $699

Awarded to salespersons who bravely face suckers who come into the store for advertised bargains that do not exist, and manage to switch them into buying costlier but inferior products, thereby boosting our entire economy.

THE UNION MEDAL OF HONOR

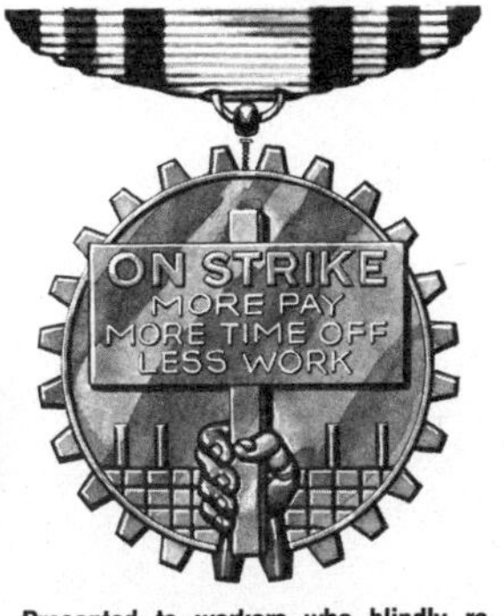
ON STRIKE
MORE PAY
MORE TIME OFF
LESS WORK

Presented to workers who blindly respond and heroically serve on picket lines without questioning the issues, the motives or anything else involved in strike situations, just as long as it means more money in their pockets.

TOONSTRUCK DEPT.

Don't you get the uncomfortable feeling that the brainstormers in Hollywood are busy thinking up ways to cash in on the great success of "Who Framed Roger Rabbit"? How will they do this? They will make lots and lots of sequels to films, mixing Toons along with the original live actors! Daffy and Dustin? Streep and Sylvester? Yup, we can envision the fast-approaching day

ARTIST: BOB CLARKE

WRITER: STAN HART

When ROGER RABBIT Technology Takes Over All Of Hollywood's Films

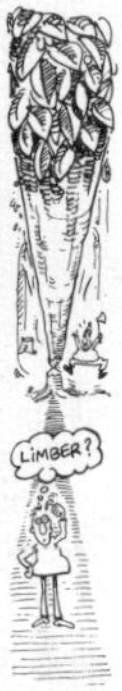
LIMBER?

ROXANNE TWO—NOSEY PEOPLE

In this sequel to "Roxanne," Martin's nose isn't even in the running as he goes face to face with the all-time schnoz champ, Pinocchio. Once again, Daryl Hannah opts for size—leaving Martin in the cold. Steve's only recourse is to ask Pinocchio's father to burn the boy as kindling. In a truly touching finale, the father refuses. Karl Malden should win a "Best Supporting Nose" Oscar for his role as Pinocchio's father.

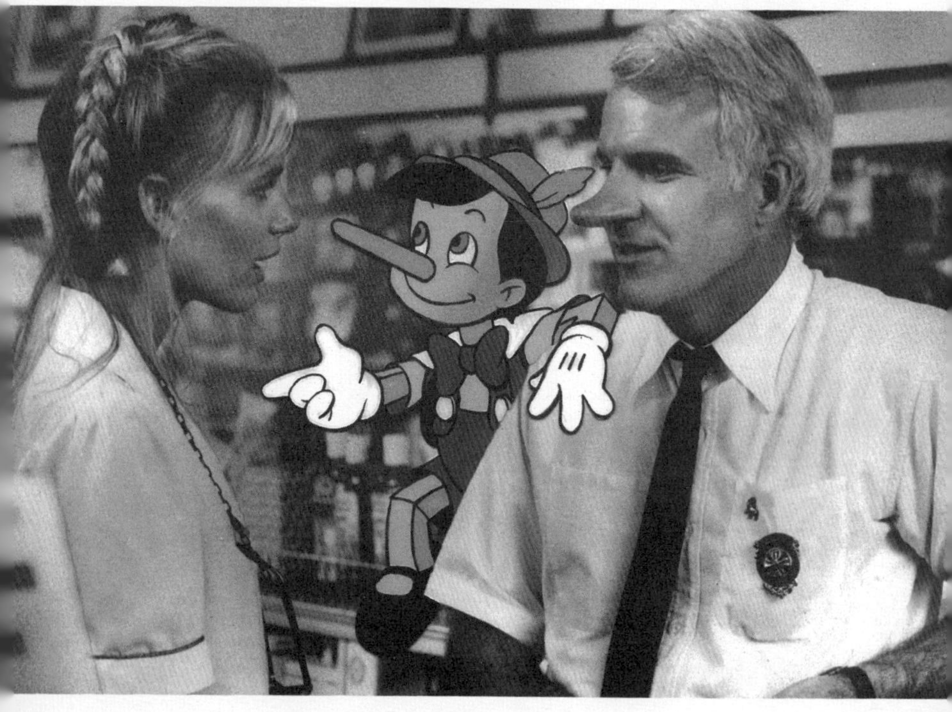

PRINCE *IS* PETER PAN

In a daring reversal of the trend of putting animated characters into live films, Prince has inserted himself into an animated film as Peter Pan. Prince engages the evil Captain Hook in an action-packed duel: it's Hook's razor-sharp sword against Prince's purse! But the agile Prince prevails and frees the Lost Boys, who he turns into a group of interior decorators and beauticians. During the course of the film, Prince also teaches Tinker Bell how to pout and mince, as well as what it means to be a woman.

BULL DURHAM AND THE SEVEN DWARFS ▶

Minor League catcher Kevin Costner and Pitcher Tim Robbins sense that the Durham Bulls' chances for a championship are slim after they meet their new team mates: Sneezy on first, Dopey on second, Grumpy at short, Doc on third, and Sleepy, Happy, and Bashful in the outfield. Susan Sarandon continues her custom of having an affair with a new player each year. This year, she chooses Sneezy in a mind and nose-blowing finale!

◀ THREE MEN AND A BABY HERMAN

The swinging bachelors who proved to be such schmucks when dealing with an infant girl really have their hands full with Baby Herman. At first the little tyke amuses the three oafs when he uses their after shave lotion and smokes big cigars. He soon becomes a lot less adorable when he jimmies the lock on their liquor cabinet, makes obscene phone calls and gets Steve Guttenberg's girlfriend "in trouble." But the three goofballs get their revenge when they change Baby Herman's diaper! Instead of using baby talcum powder, they substitute itching powder!

ROCKY *AND* BULLWINKLE *AND* ROCKY VI ▶

The Italian Stallion hires Bullwinkle T. Moose as his new sparring partner and Rocky J. Squirrel as his new trainer. Everything goes along just fine until the night Balboa's wife, Adrian, gets drunk and goes to bed with the wrong Rocky. It isn't Adrian's infidelity that upsets Balboa; he's infuriated because she couldn't tell the difference! In a dream sequence, the late, great Apollo Creed advises Balboa to fill the spit bucket with the dreaded Toon-destroying "Dip" next time he fights Bullwinkle. Balboa does and douses Rocky J. Squirrel in Bullwinkle's corner, thereby TKO-ing his domestic conflict.

STAR TREK 12— ►
THE SEARCH FOR GEORGE AND JUDY

The Starship Enterprise picks up The Jetsons, who have been wandering through space after losing their home due to the business failure of Spacely Sprockets. While William Shatner tries to help George fight his arch competitor, Cogswell's Cogs, Leonard Nimoy has other problems—the Vulcan has fallen in love. Unfortunately it's with Rosie, the Jetson's robot maid, whose lovemaking is, at best, mechanical.

◄ ARTHUR III & DUMBO

After appearing in such box office disasters as "Miki and Maude" and "Santa Claus, the Movie," Deadly Dudley Moore gets some much needed help from the lovable flying pachyderm in his late film. Dudley still thinks the serious illness of alcoholism is a gold mine of cheap jokes. As a booze (and cliché) ridden drunk, he about to lose Liza Minelli (who would be no great loss to anyon sober). Suddenly he sees a pink Dumbo circling over head! Fearing that the Elephant is not house-broken, Moore pledges to sto drinking and swears off any more sequels to the dreary "Arthu.

TUCKER—A MAN AND HIS CAB ►

Jeff Bridges reprises his role as the hard-luck auto innovato Preston Tucker. This time, he devises a car that stands on its re wheels, bends around corners, makes wisecracks, shivers an sweats. But Tucker's ambitious plans to produce such a car a foiled by the Big Three—not Ford, Chrysler, and G.M.—Disne Warner Bros. and Hanna-Barbera!

RETURN OF ALIEN 6 ►

In this version of "Alien," Sigourney Weaver and the spaceship crew have their hands full as they try to capture a new alien, played by the Road Runner. They can't grab the slippery invader and the spaceship starts to fall out of control because the Road Runner's speed lines are screwing up the ship's computer readout. Sigourney finally corners Road Runner, but her attempt to talk to him is drowned out by his incessant and extremely irritating "Beep Beep!" Then she gets the brilliant idea of bringing in Wile E. Coyote and letting him and Road Runner drive themselves crazy, chasing each other through the spacecraft as it heads for home.

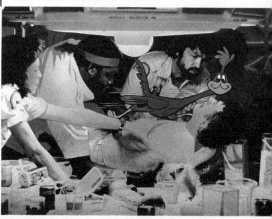

RE-BROADCAST NEWS ➤

Holly Hunter and William Hurt are paired again, but this time they work for competing networks. Because her company is an equal-opportunity employer, Holly is forced to hire Sylvester the Cat as her news anchorman, even though he sprays the camera with saliva whenever he speaks. Thinking that Holly has hired Sylvester to boost her network's ratings, Hurt tries to do her one better by employing Porky Pig. But Hurt gets into deep trouble when his new protégé makes the half-hour news run two hours and forty-five minutes because of his stuttering.

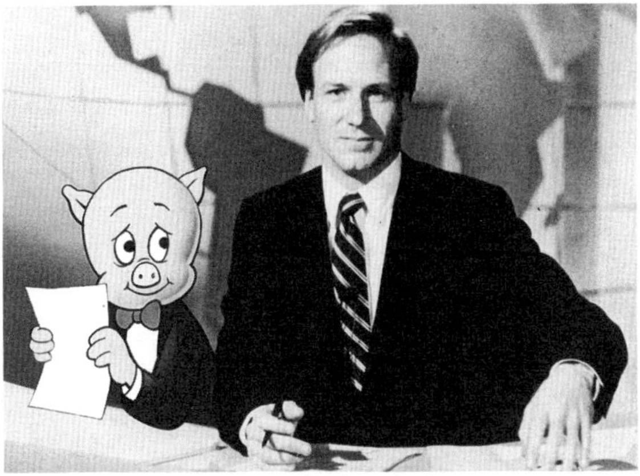

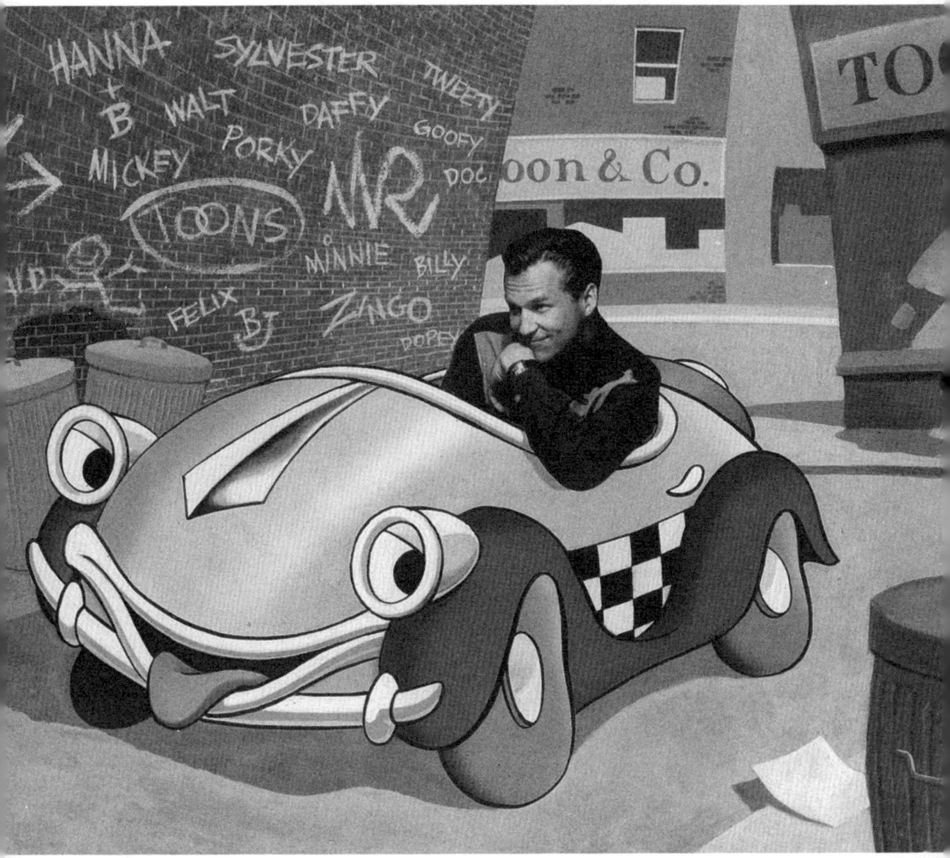
HANNA
+
B
SYLVESTER
TWEETY
WALT
DAFFY
GOOFY
PORKY
MICKEY
DOC
TOONS
MINNIE
BILLY
FELIX
BJ
ZINGO
DOPEY
oon & Co.

LOCALE COLOR DEPT.

A PORTFOLIO OF MAD

BRITAIN

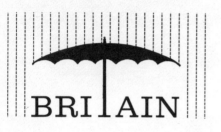

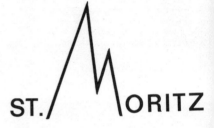

ST. MORITZ

SAN FRANCISCO

MIDDLE EAST

ROME

SPAIN

ATHENS

HOLLAND

PISA

TEXAS

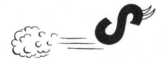

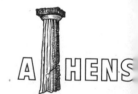

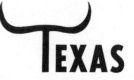

PLACELIES

WRITTEN AND DESIGNED BY: MAX BRANDEL

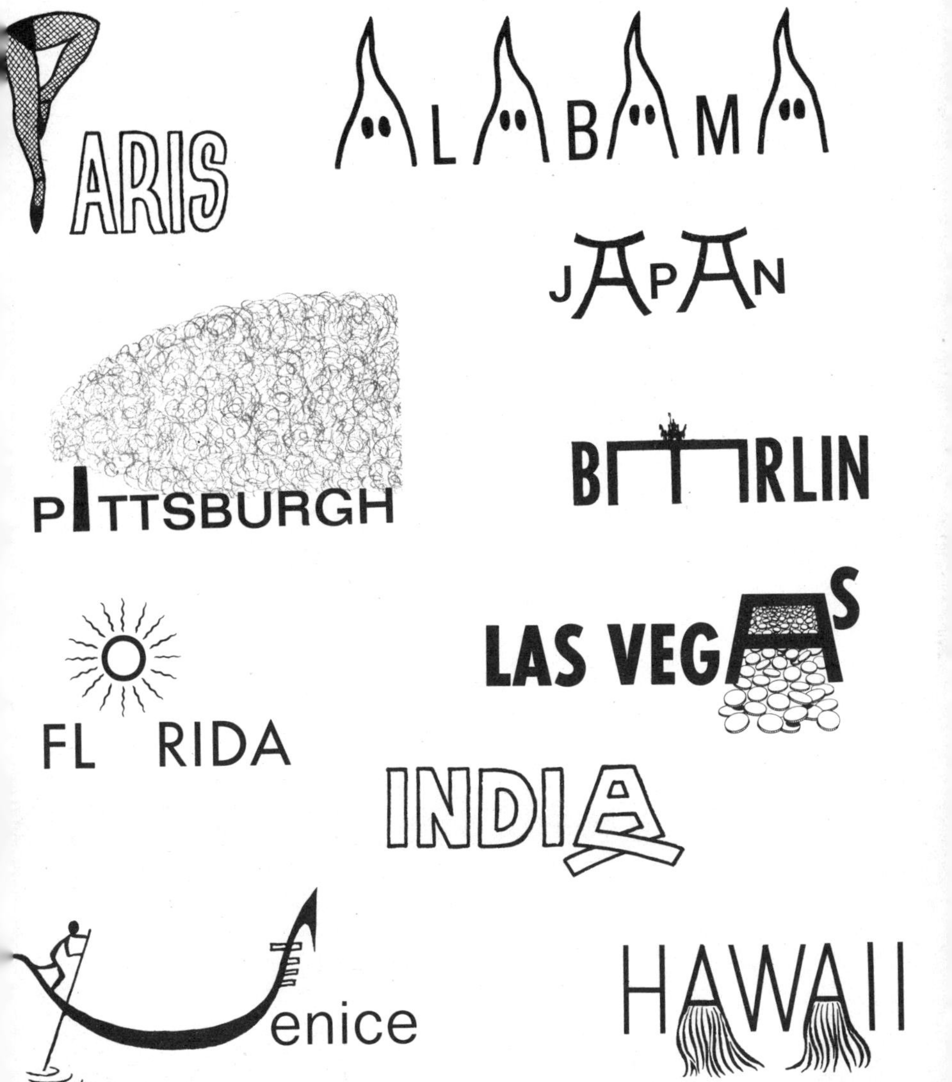
PARIS
ALABAMA
JAPAN
PITTSBURGH
BERLIN
FLORIDA
LAS VEGAS
INDIA
Venice
HAWAII

DO RE ME FA SO LA TEE-HEE DEPT.

A MAD LOOK AT

ARTIST & WRITER

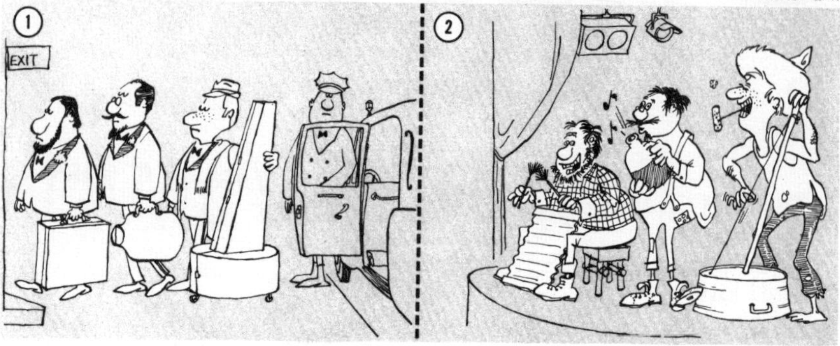
1
2
EXIT

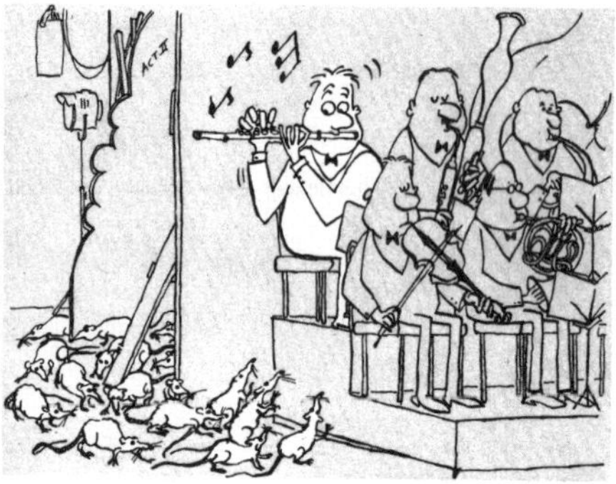

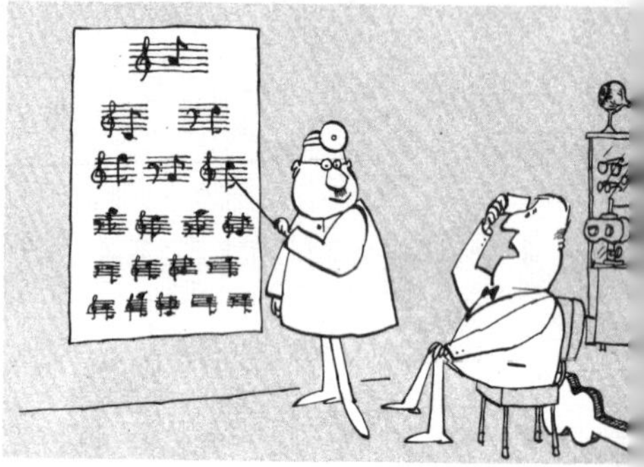

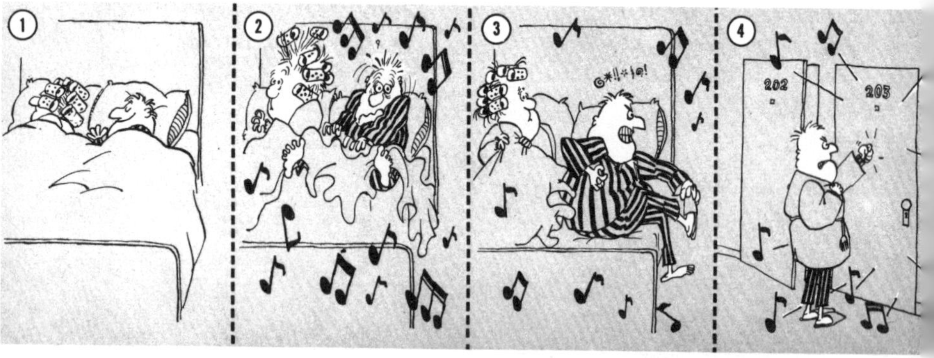
1
2
3
4
202
203

MUSICIANS

ERGIO ARAGONES

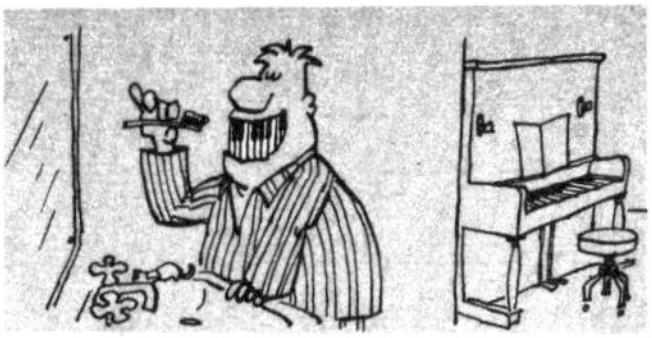

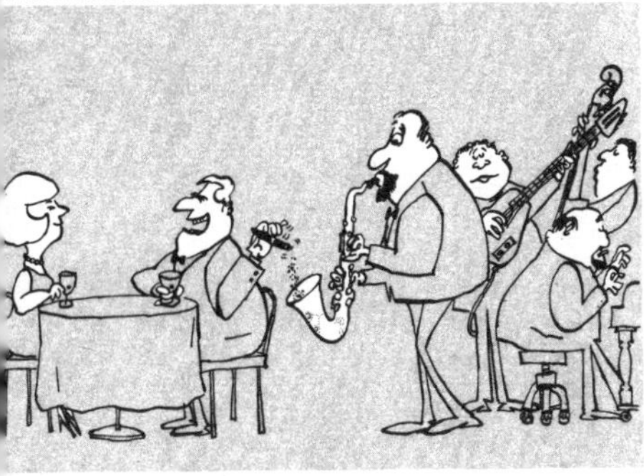

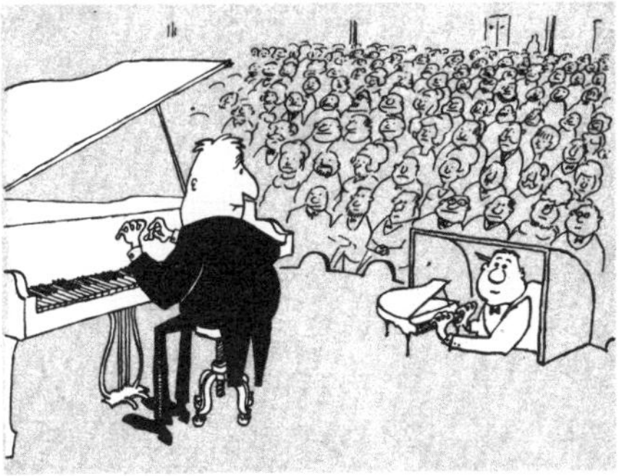

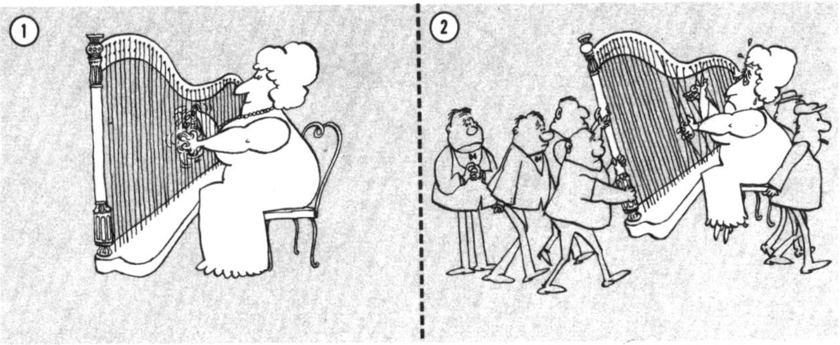
1
2

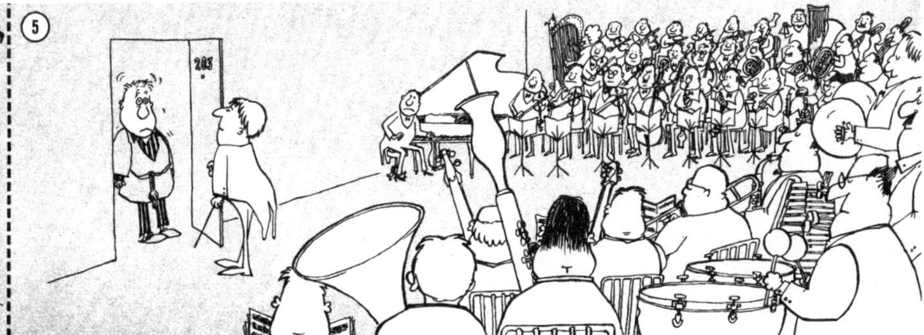
5

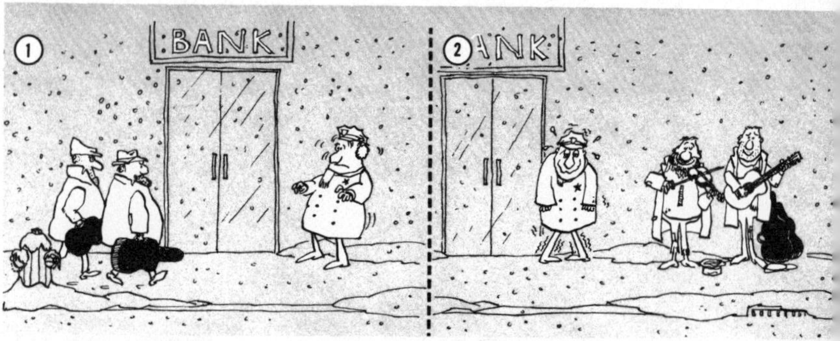
BANK
ANK

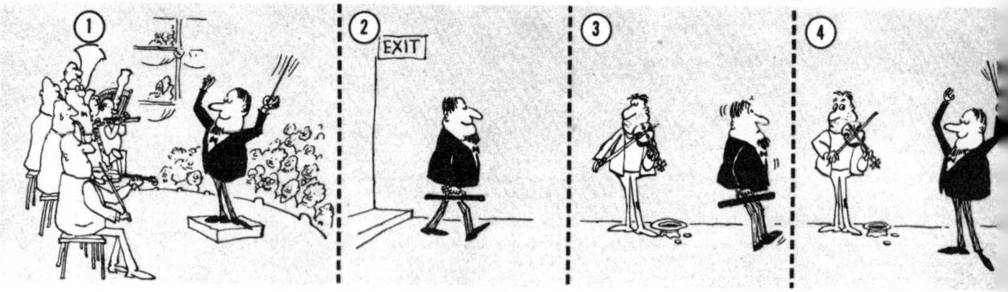
EXIT

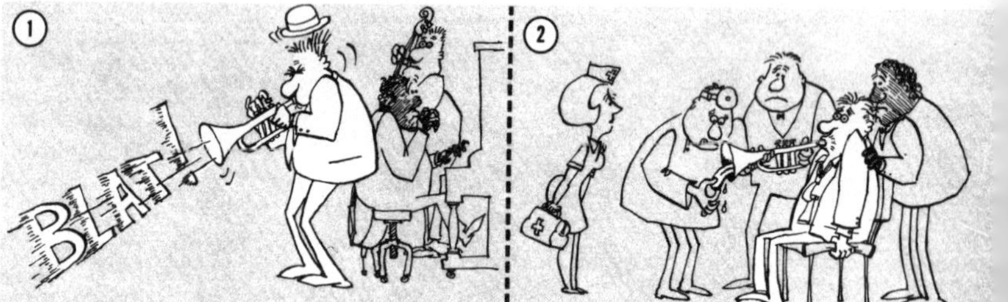
BLAT

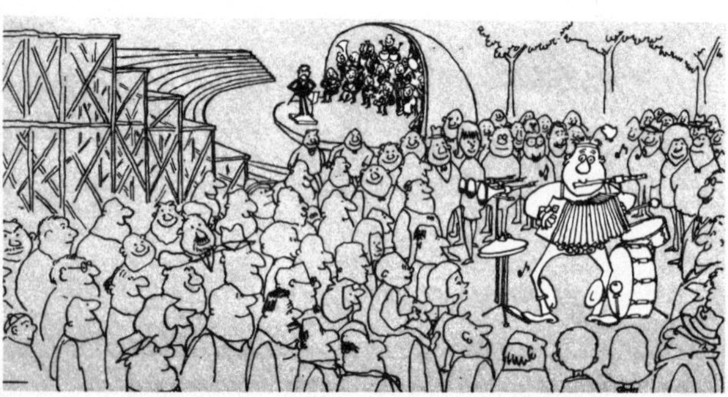

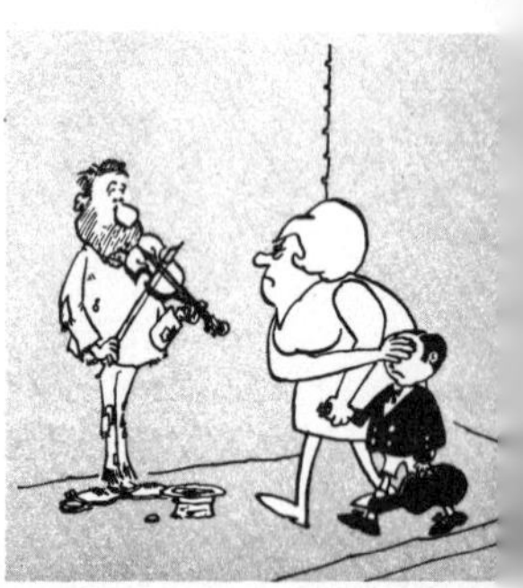

DON MARTIN DEPT.

LATER ON IN THE HOSPITAL

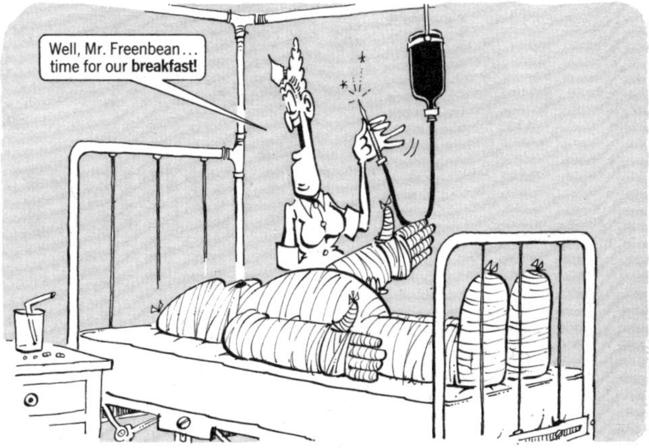

Well, Mr. Freenbean… time for our **breakfast!**

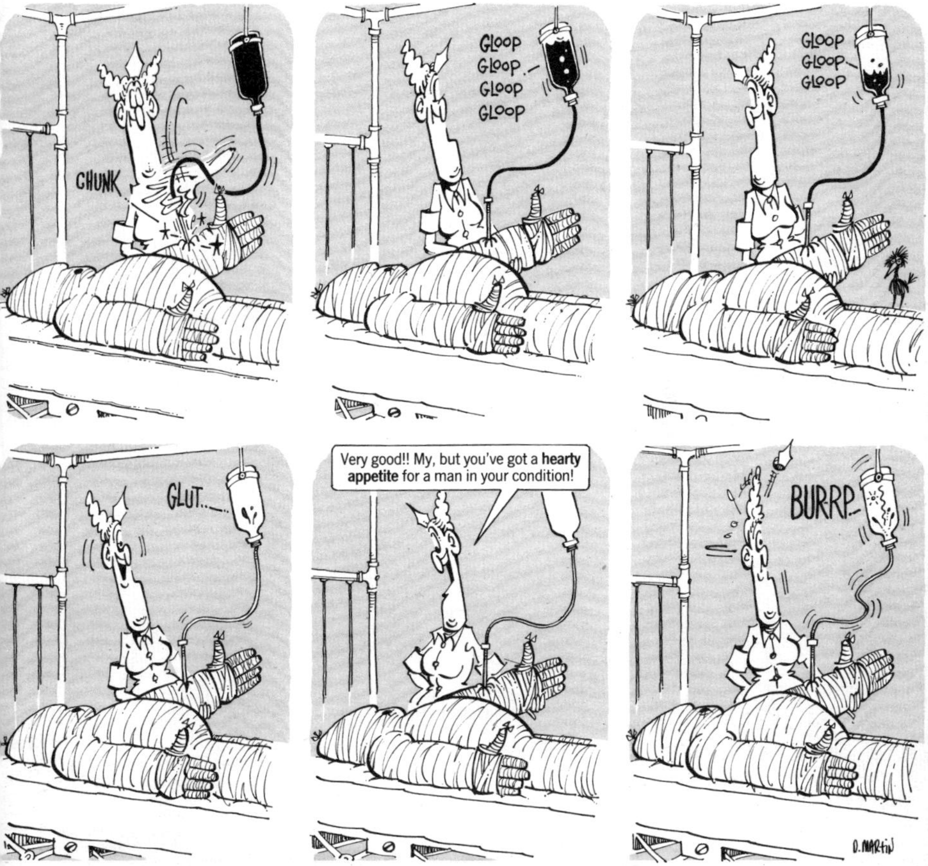

CHUNK
GLOOP
GLOOP
GLOOP
GLOOP
GLOOP
GLOOP
GLOOP
GLUT…
Very good!! My, but you've got a **hearty appetite** for a man in your condition!
BURRP
D. MARTIN

UNITED STATUS OF AMERICA DEPT.

THE MAD GUIDE TO...

ARTIST: GEORGE WOODBRIDGE WRITER: FRANK JACOB

YUPPIES

(Young Urban Professionals)

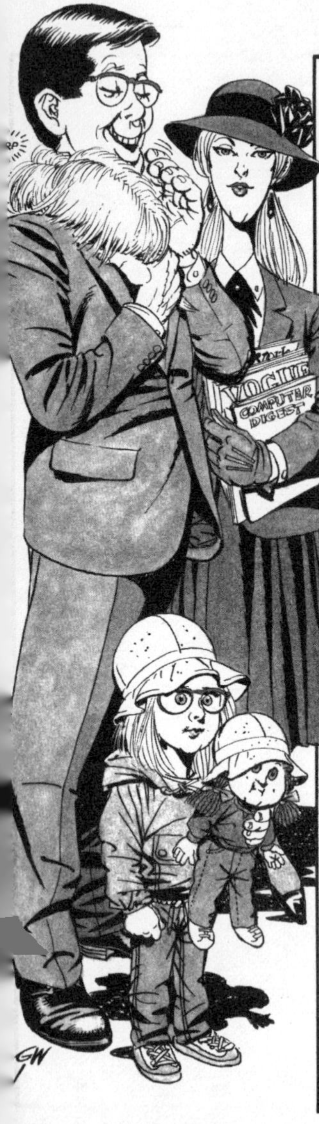
VOGUE
COMPUTER DIGEST
GW

Buy designer clothes for their kid's Cabbage Patch Dolls.

Feed their babies strained quiche.

Hire seasonal domestics to trim their Christmas trees.

Pass neighborhood zoning laws against fat people.

Burp their Lhasa apsos.

Own "his-and-her" satellite dishes.

Back trendy causes, such as Eskimo Gay Rights.

Buy Nautilus machines in decorator colors.

Commission oil paintings of their Porsches.

Install personal computers in their Jacuzzis.

Get suicidal when their yearly income drops below the $50,000 poverty level.

Chlorinate their bird-baths.

Have their toddlers checked out for "pre-school burn-out."

Drop from their party list anyone who visibly sweats.

Are called "sir" and "ma'am" by Yullies.

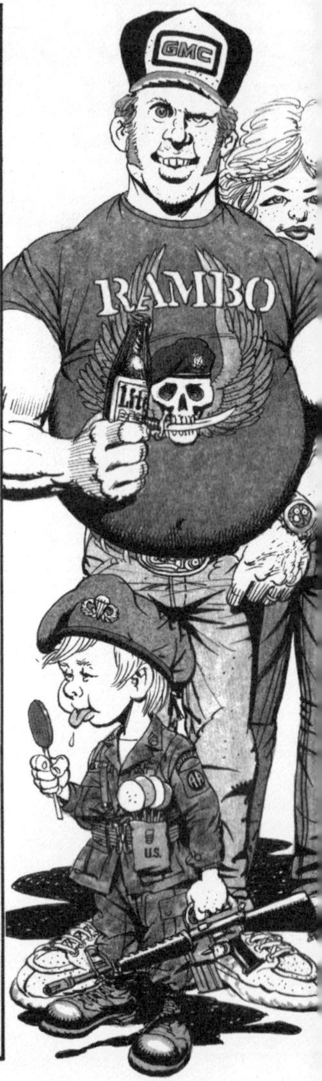
GMC
RAMBO
Lite
U.S.

ʃULLIES
(Young Urban Laborers)

YUFFIES
(Young Urban Failures)

Regard "Rambo" as an art film.

Entertain friends with "Championship Bowling" tapes from their VCR library.

Collect commemorative coins of pro wrestling stars.

Take sides watching Miller Lite commercials.

Demand absolute silence while watching "Wheel of Fortune."

Save Gallo wine labels in scrapbooks.

Regard finishing the TV Guide crossword as "bragging rights."

Have recurring dreams about rack-and-pinion steering.

Send away for the two-record collection of "Pat Boone's Greatest Hits."

Bargain-shop for lube jobs.

Consider "Doonesbury" heavy reading.

Regard owning a Sears charge card as "living in the fast lane."

Wear only their most expensive polyester leisure suit at weddings and funerals.

Are called "sir" and "ma'am" by Yuffies.

Socialize at Greyhound bus depots.

Look at lottery tickets as a sound investment.

Keep warm in winter by burning down their tenements.

Burglarize thrift shops.

Consider a Roach Motel an appropriate housewarming gift.

Read the "Enquirer" as a source of "news in depth."

Aren't sure if Halley's Comet is a car or a laxative.

Wear hand-me-down dentures.

Punch themselves in the head when they sleep through April.

List their street-gang membership as "Job Experience."

Regard Egg McMuffins as "nouvelle cuisine."

Take Rodney Dangerfield seriously.

Tattoo their children for identification purposes.

Are on a first-name basis with their local hospital blood-buyer.

Perform taste tests with Mennen Skin Bracer and Aqua Velva.

SHOE BIZ DEPT.

FOOTNOTES* TO

ARTIST: PAUL COKER, JR.

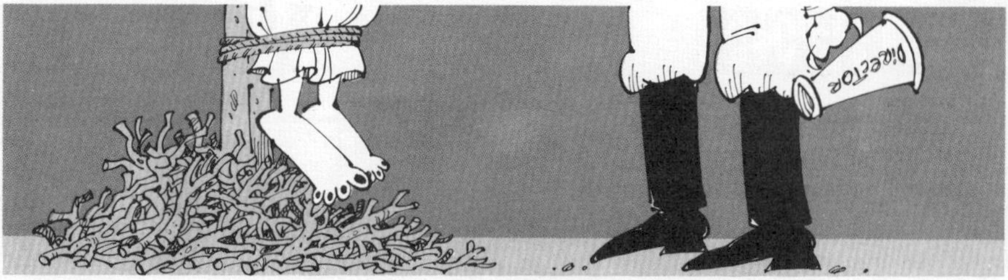
DIRECTOR

*"Sorry, but our Research Department insists that Joan of Arc did not wear nail polish!"

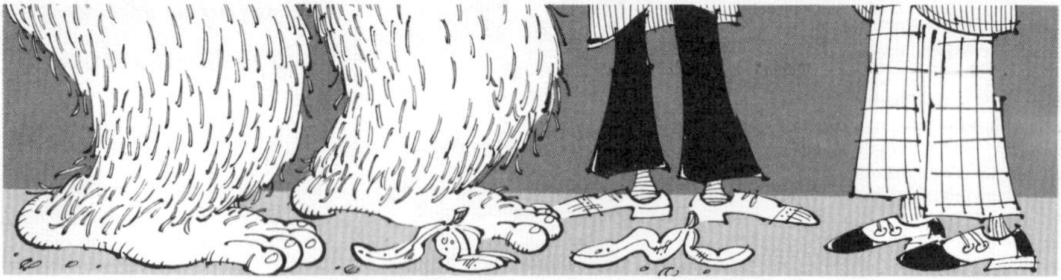

*"Okay! So he's got a great monster personality! But, can he act?"

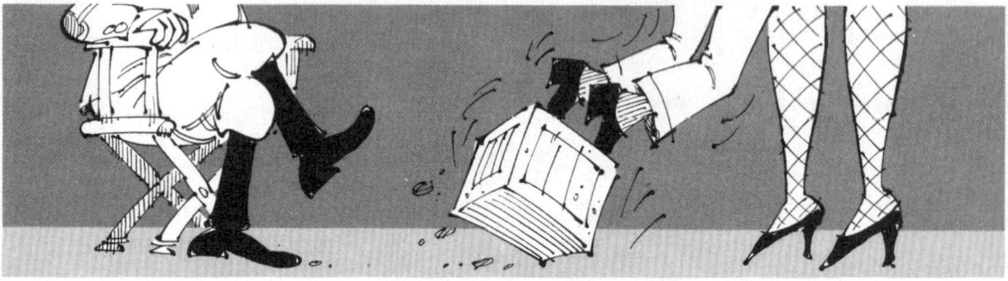

*"Either we get ourselves a taller leading man, or this one learns how to balance!"

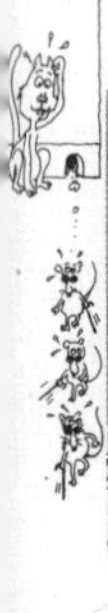

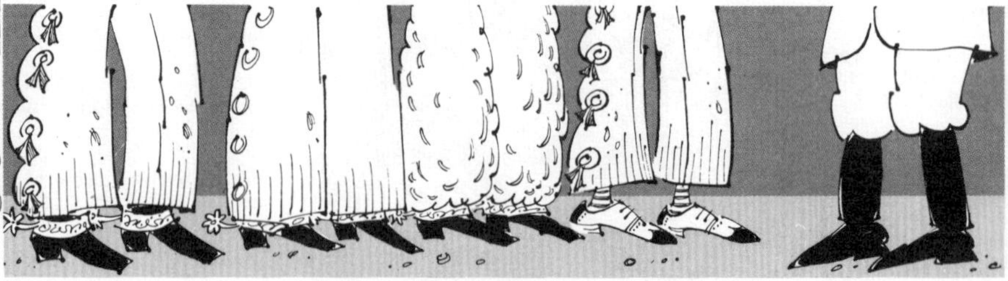

*"Get me the Wardrobe Department!"

HOLLYWOOD

ER: PAUL PETER PORGES

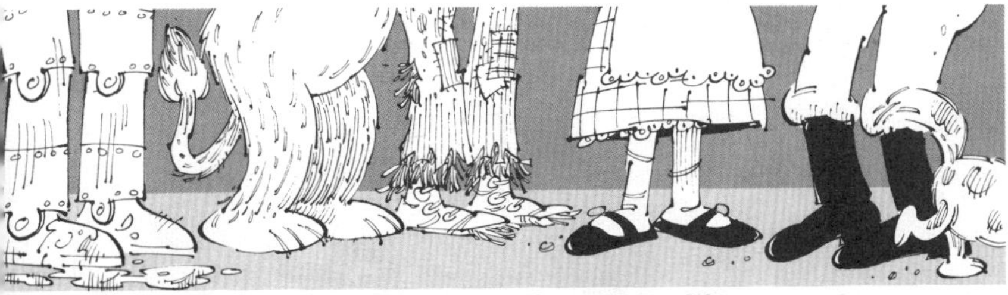

*"Toto did WHAT on the Tin Man...?!?"

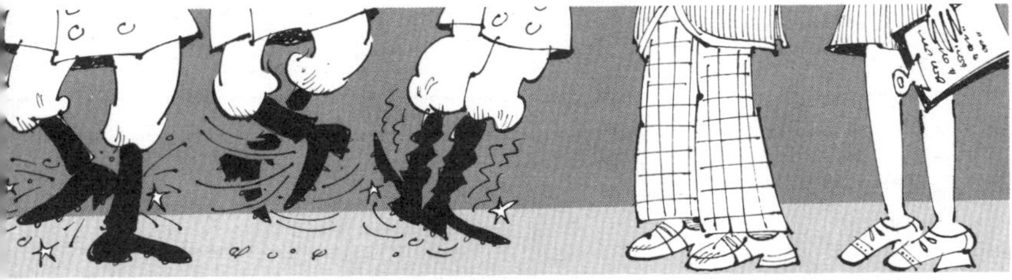

*"Uh—let's have some Nazi extras out here that know how to click their heels!"

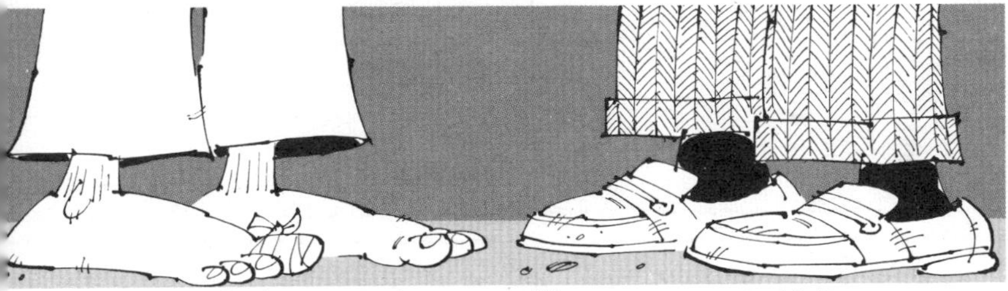

*"... but for the Kung Fu close-ups, we'll have to use your stand-in!"

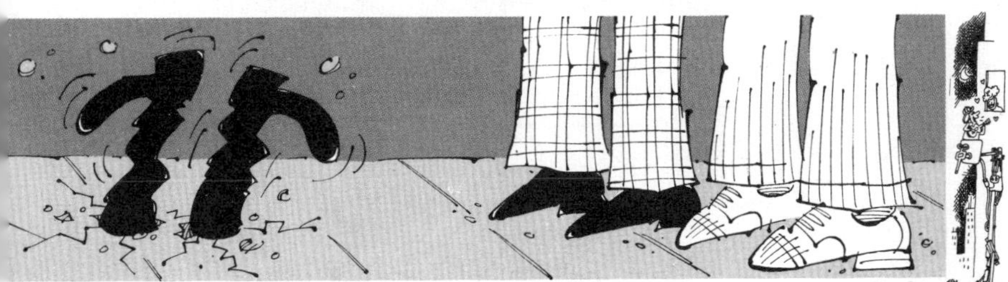

*"Meet the greatest stuntman in the business..."

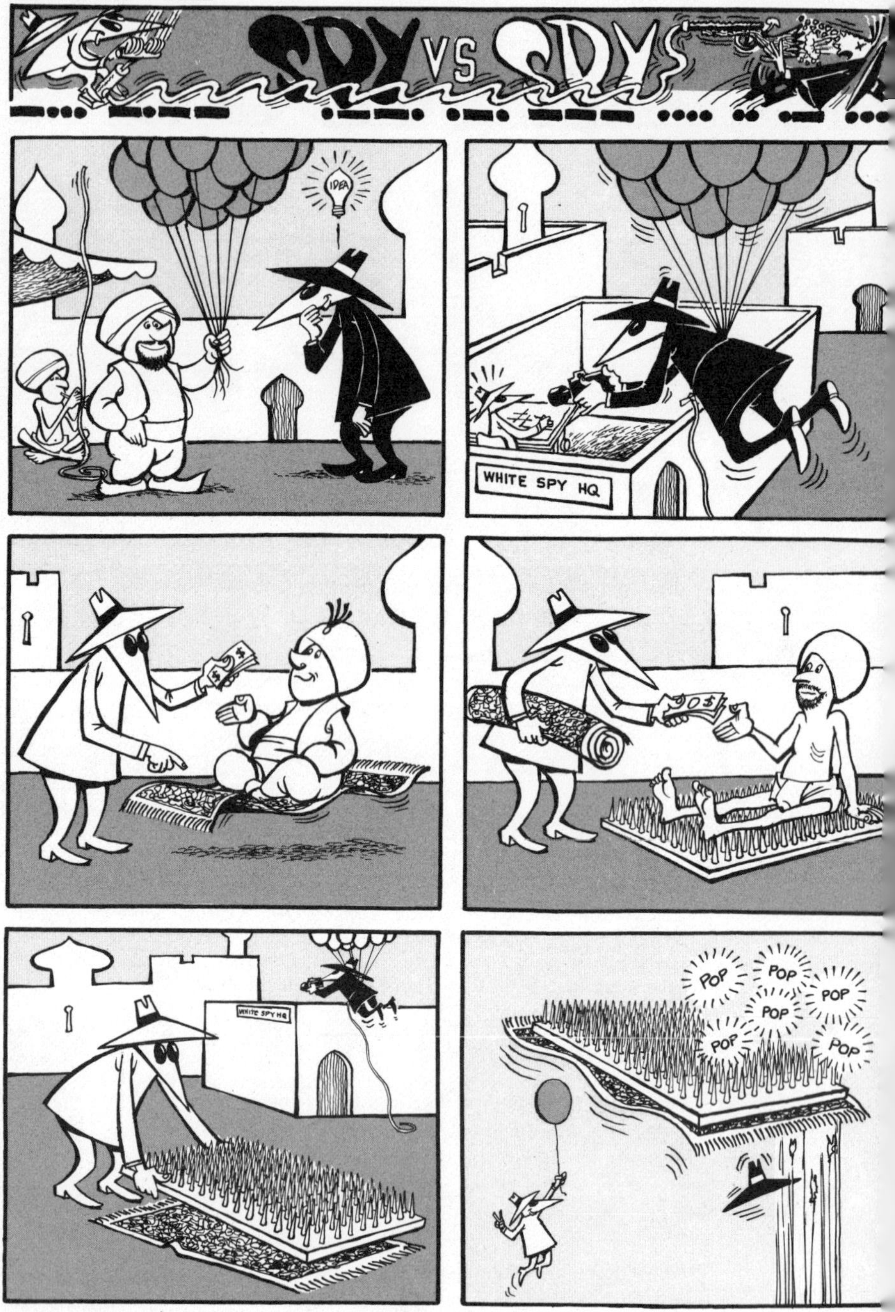
SPY VS SPY
IDEA
WHITE SPY HQ
WHITE SPY HQ
POP
POP
POP
POP
POP
POP

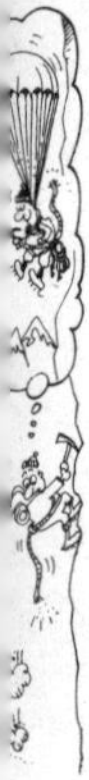

BLAST LAUGH DEPT.

Everyone knows that the best thing to do in difficult times is to keep busy! Keeping busy occupies your mind and prevents you from going into deep depression. So, just to be safe, here are some MAD suggestions for keeping busy during the difficult time ahead. Mainly, here are some

WARNING: THE SURGEON GENERAL HAS DETERMINED THAT EXPOSURE TO NUCLEAR RADIATION MAY BE HAZARDOUS TO YOUR HEALTH

THINGS TO DO ON THE DAY AFTER

WRITER AND ARTIST: AL JAFFEE

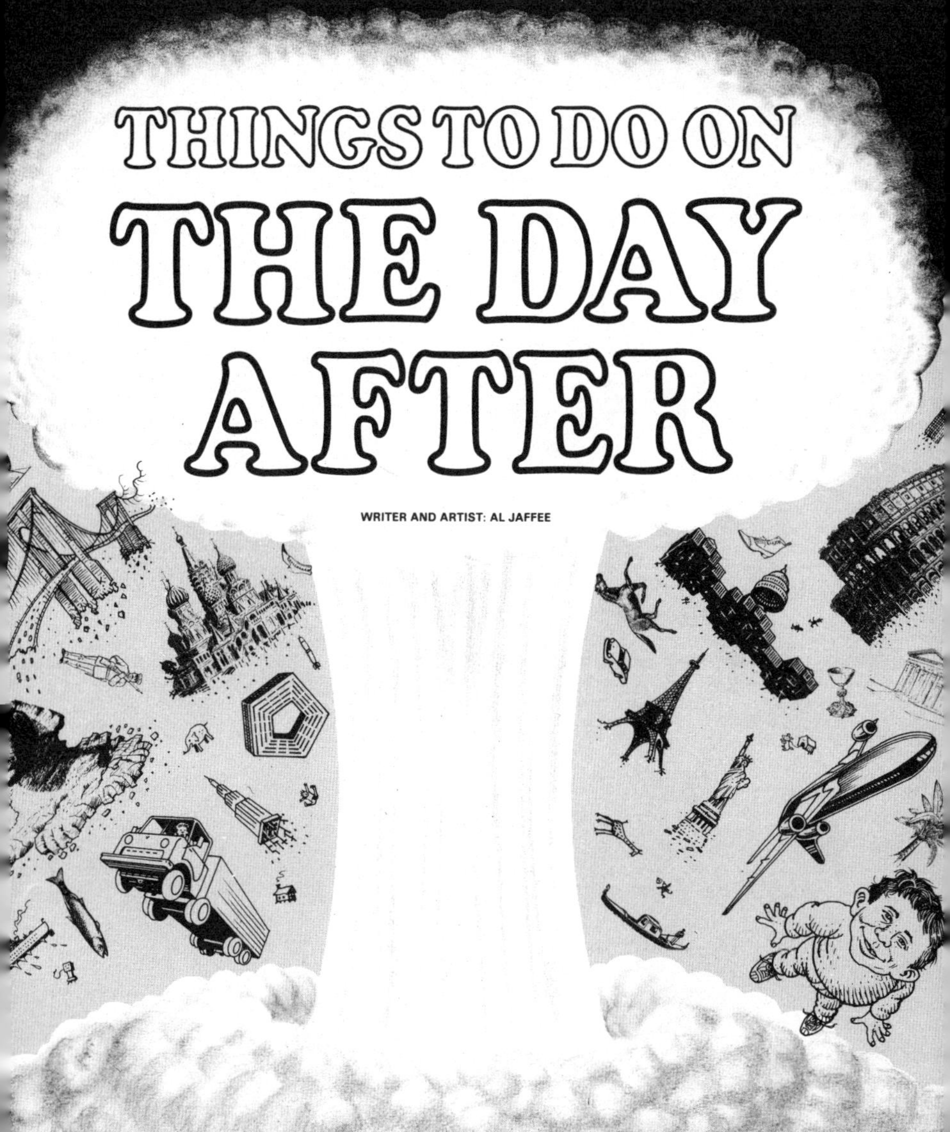

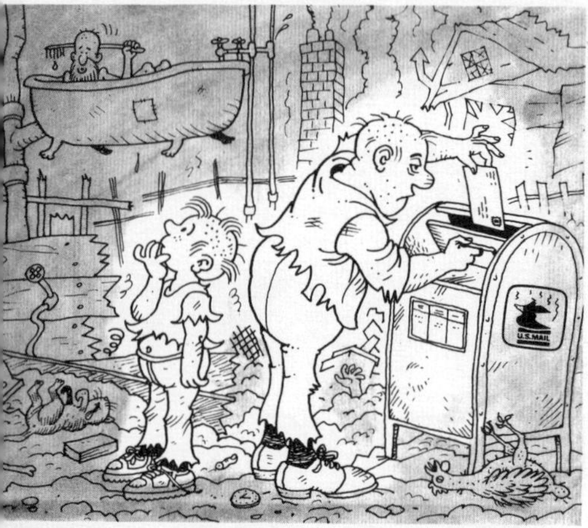
U.S. MAIL

Cancel your subscription to "House Beautiful" magazine.

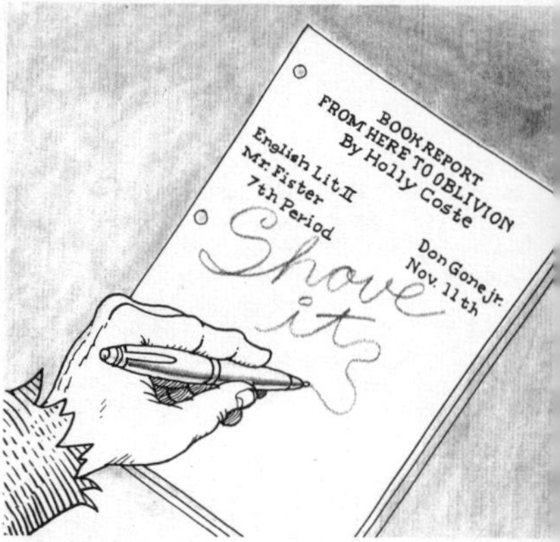
BOOK REPORT
FROM HERE TO OBLIVION
By Holly Coste
English Lit II
Mr. Fister
7th Period
Don Gone jr.
Nov. 11th
Shove it

Write a tender message on your overdue term pap

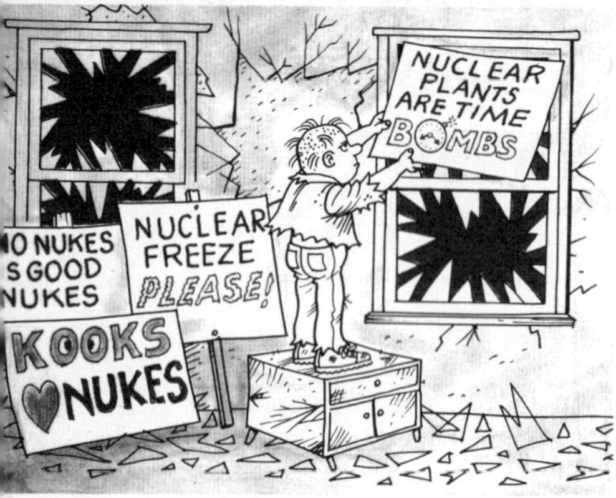
NUCLEAR PLANTS ARE TIME BOMBS
NUCLEAR FREEZE PLEASE!
O NUKES S GOOD NUKES
KOOKS ♥ NUKES

Use old "Nuclear Protest Signs" to close broken windows.

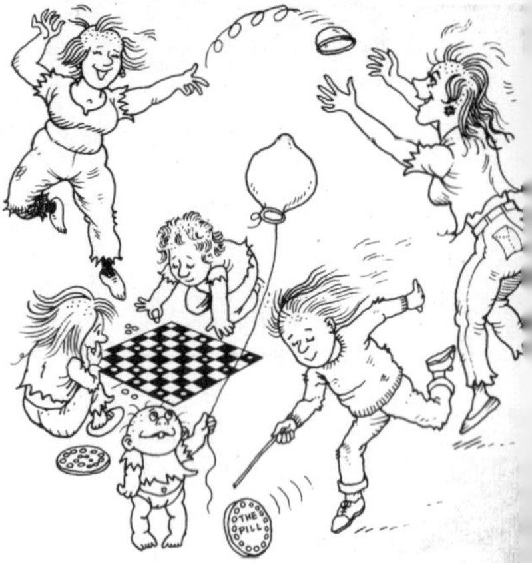
THE PILL

Use birth control devices for other recreational activities... now that everyone's sterile anyway.

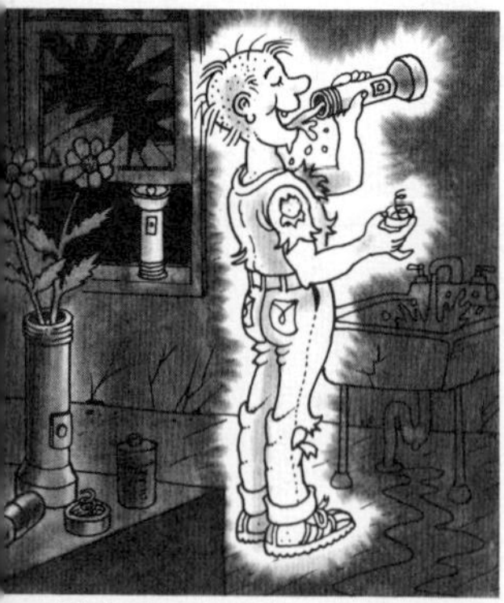

Find other uses for flashlights, now that you glow in the dark.

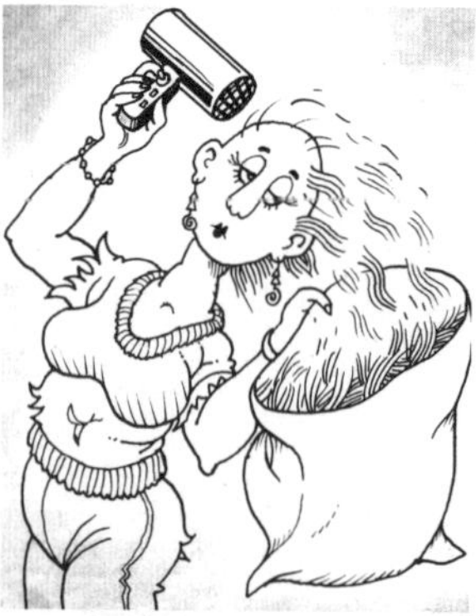

Stuff a pillow with your falling-out hair, and...

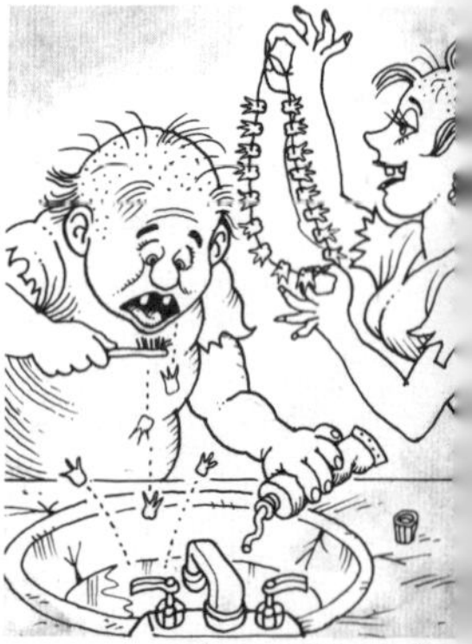

...make a necklace with your falling-out teeth.

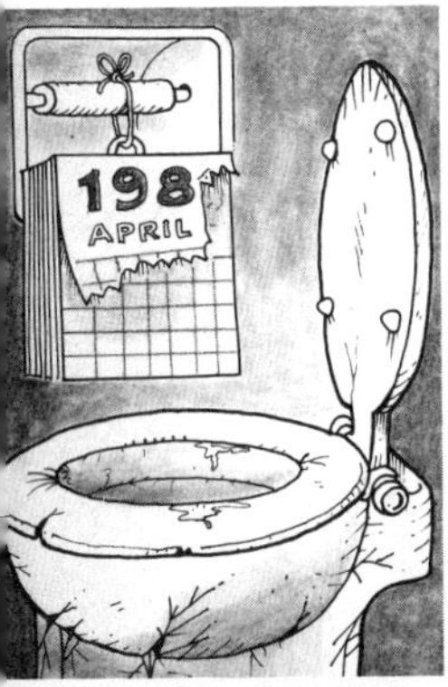
198
APRIL

ıt your Ten-Year-Calendar to
ore immediate practical use.

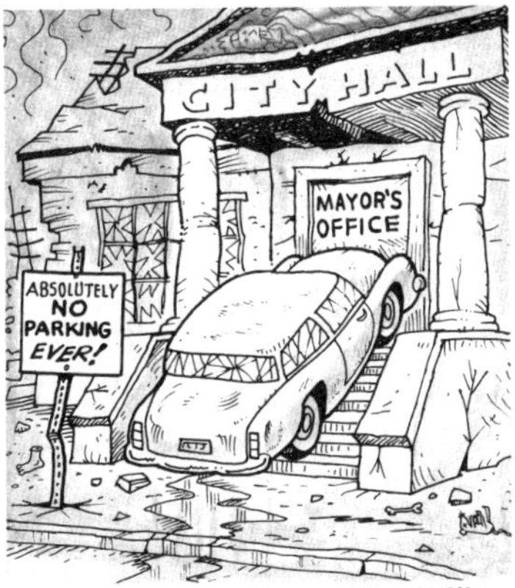
CITY HALL
MAYOR'S OFFICE
ABSOLUTELY NO PARKING EVER!

Park anywhere you like any time you like.

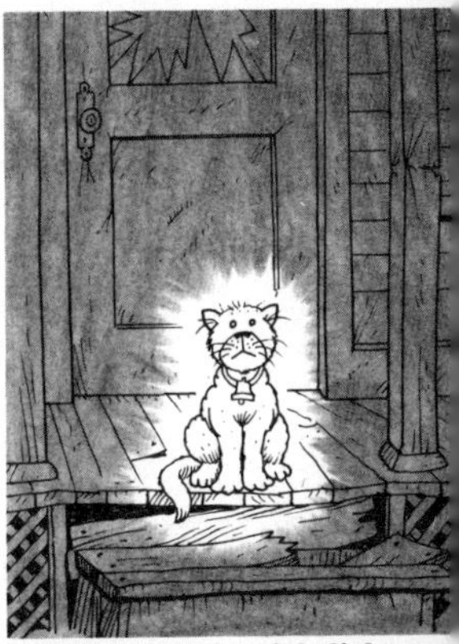

Put the cat out as a night light.

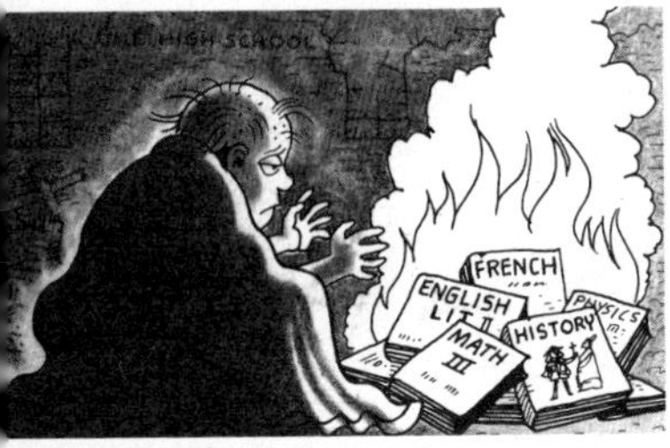
HIGH SCHOOL
FRENCH
ENGLISH LIT II
PHYSICS
HISTORY
MATH III

Use your school textbooks to keep warm.

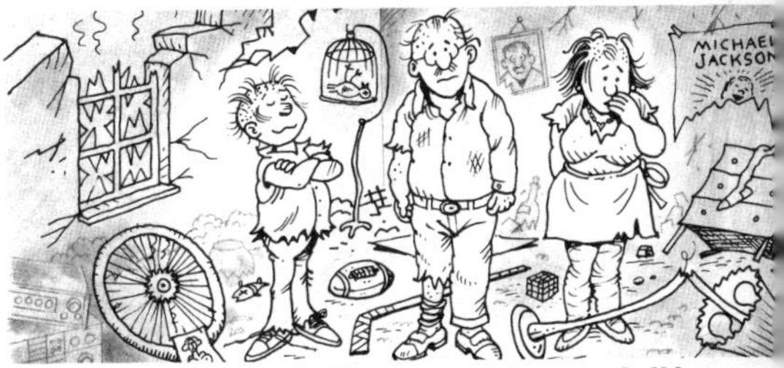
MICHAE
JACKSON

Promise to clean your room if your parents buy you a bulldozer.

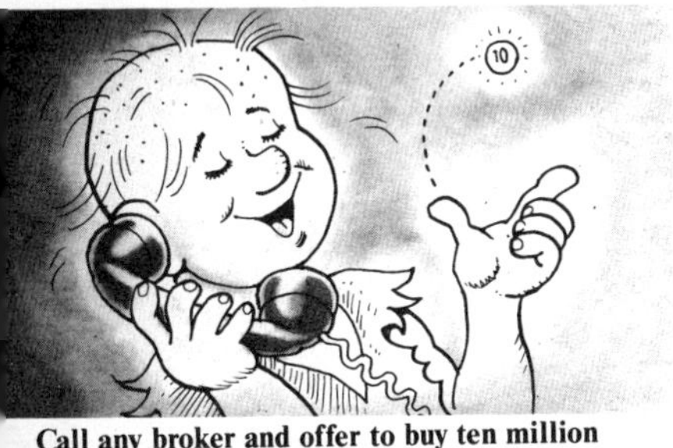
10

Call any broker and offer to buy ten million
shares of General Motors Corp. for ten cents.

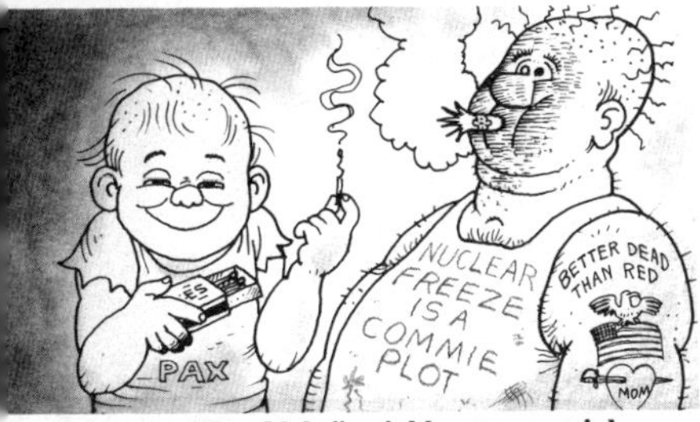
NUCLEAR FREEZE IS A COMMIE PLOT
BETTER DEAD THAN RED
PAX
MOM

Treat your "Pro-Nuke" neighbor to a special
cigar you've saved for just such an occasion.

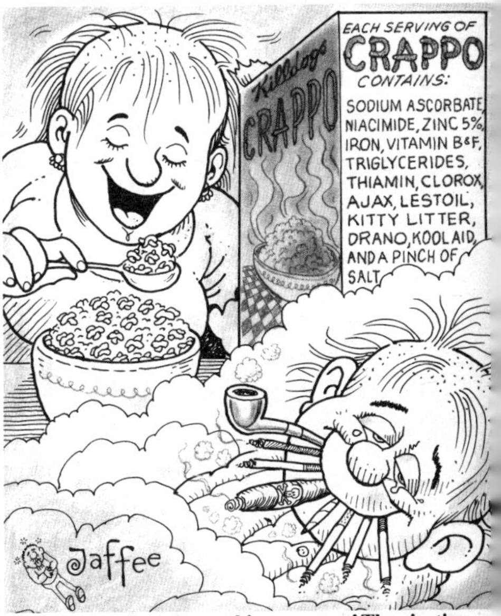
EACH SERVING OF
CRAPPO
CONTAINS:
SODIUM ASCORBATE, NIACIMIDE, ZINC 5%, IRON, VITAMIN B&F, TRIGLYCERIDES, THIAMIN, CLOROX, AJAX, LESTOIL, KITTY LITTER, DRANO, KOOL AID, AND A PINCH OF SALT
Killdogs
CRAPPO
Jaffee

Eat, drink and smoke anything you want! The nicotine,
tars and additives are the least of your problems now.

As you tear down the road of life in your everlasting pursuit of happiness, wha would you say is the most difficult goal to achieve? Finding the right girl, huh Wrong!! There's one thing tougher than finding the right girl, and that's gettin

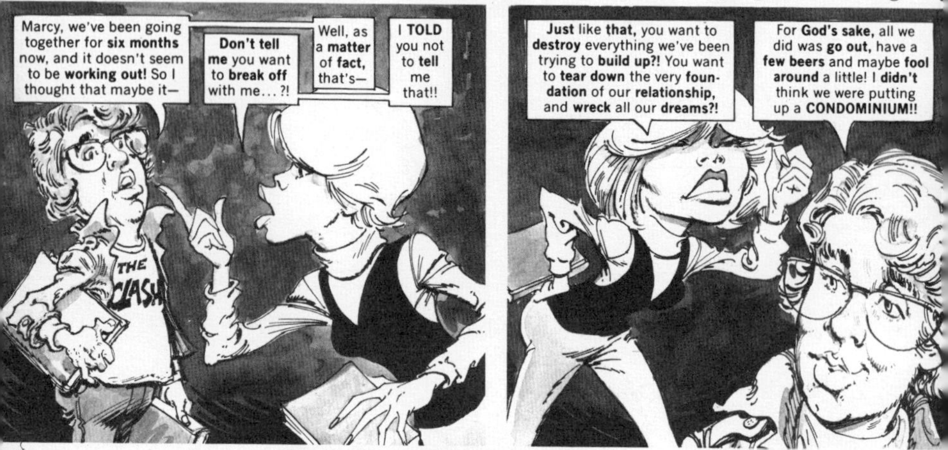
Marcy, we've been going together for six months now, and it doesn't seem to be working out! So I thought that maybe it—
Don't tell me you want to break off with me...?!
Well, as a matter of fact, that's—
I TOLD you not to tell me that!!
THE CLASH
Just like that, you want to destroy everything we've been trying to build up?! You want to tear down the very foundation of our relationship, and wreck all our dreams?!
For God's sake, all we did was go out, have a few beers and maybe fool around a little! I didn't think we were putting up a CONDOMINIUM!!

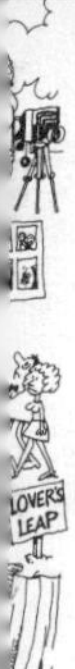
LOVER'S LEAP

That's what could happen to you unless you know how to handle things properly! Which brings us to the main reason we're running this dumb article. Mainly—your life could be saved if you merely follow...

CURING A SPLITTING HEADACHE DEPT.

MAD'S HEI
BREAKING

ARTIST: JACK RICKAF

THE SITUATION: You meet another girl who's more interesting, and you want to break off with the old one... THI

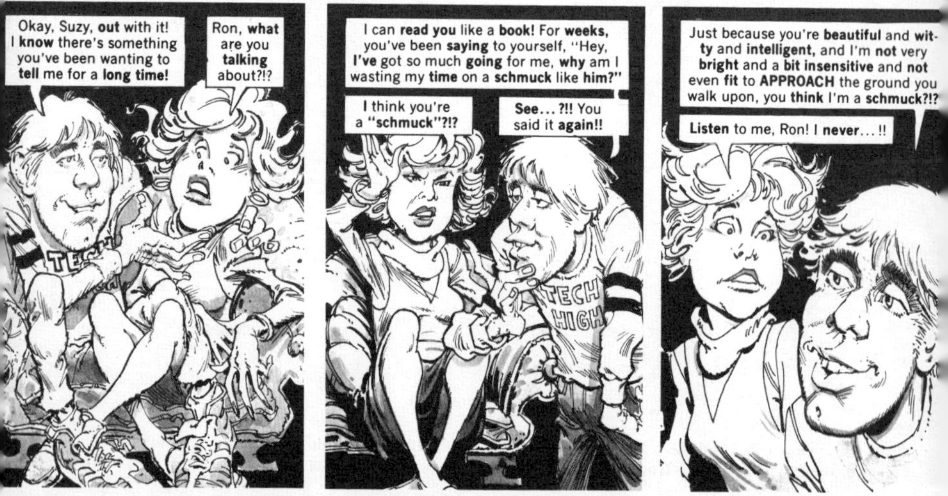
Okay, Suzy, out with it! I know there's something you've been wanting to tell me for a long time!
Ron, what are you talking about?!?
TECH
I can read you like a book! For weeks, you've been saying to yourself, "Hey, I've got so much going for me, why am I wasting my time on a schmuck like him?"
I think you're a "schmuck"?!?
See...?!! You said it again!!
TECH HIGH
Just because you're beautiful and witty and intelligent, and I'm not very bright and a bit insensitive and not even fit to APPROACH the ground you walk upon, you think I'm a schmuck?!?
Listen to me, Ron! I never...!!

rid of her! It's not as simple as it seems! F'rinstance, let's assume you're no longer interested in the girl you're going with, and you want to break it off. Here's what could happen if you commit the unpardonable sin of telling the truth:

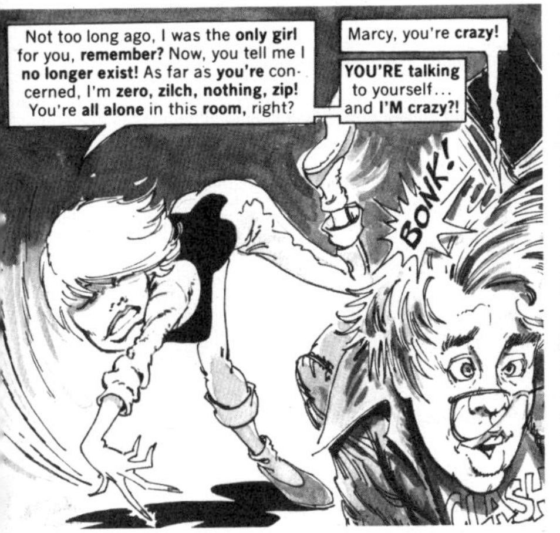

Not too long ago, I was the **only girl** for you, **remember?** Now, you tell me I **no longer exist!** As far as **you're** concerned, I'm **zero, zilch, nothing, zip!** You're **all alone** in this **room,** right?
Marcy, you're **crazy!**
YOU'RE talking to yourself... and **I'M crazy?!**
BONK!

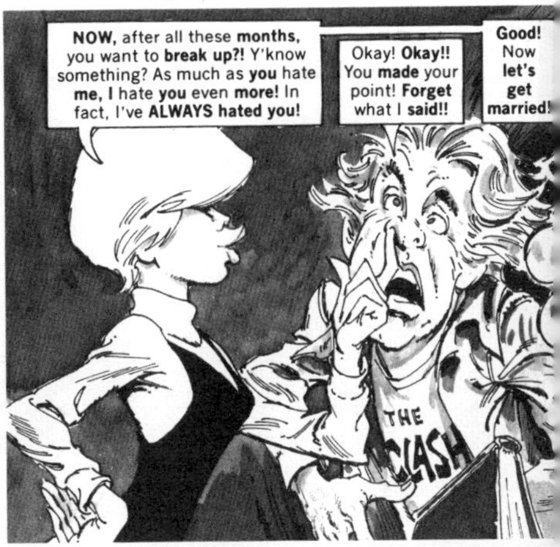

NOW, after all these **months,** you want to **break up?!** Y'know something? As much as **you** hate **me,** I hate **you** even **more!** In fact, I've **ALWAYS hated you!**
Okay! **Okay!!** You **made** your point! **Forget** what I **said!!**
Good! Now **let's get married!**
THE CLASH

PFUL HINTS ON
UP WITH A GIRL

WRITER: LARRY SIEGEL

WAY TO HANDLE IT: Make the old girl think that *she's* breaking off with *you!*

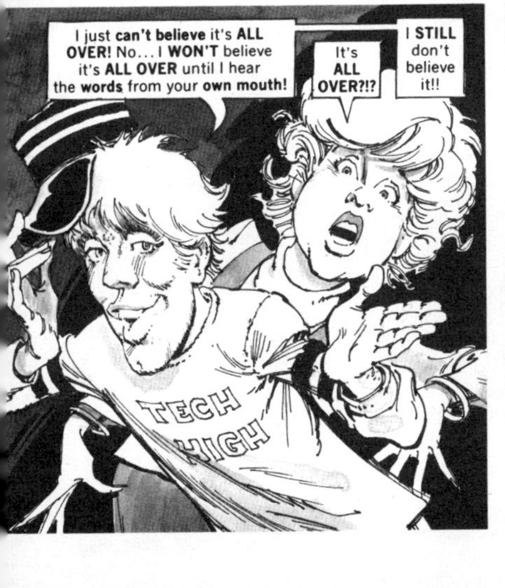

I just **can't believe** it's **ALL OVER!** No... I **WON'T** believe it's **ALL OVER** until I hear the **words** from your **own mouth!**
It's **ALL OVER?!?**
I **STILL** don't believe it!!
TECH HIGH

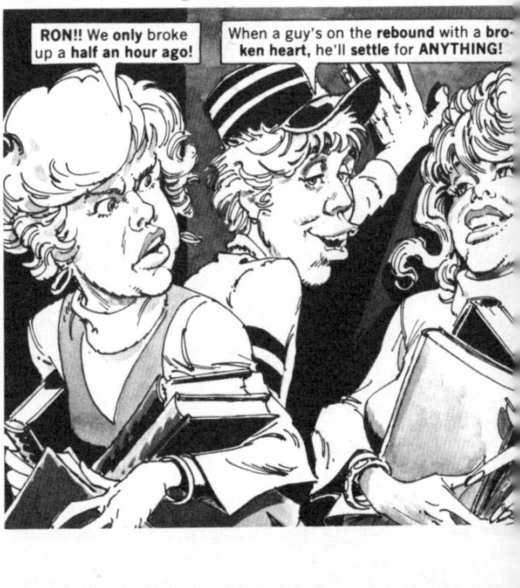

RON!! We **only** broke up a **half an hour ago!**
When a guy's on the **rebound** with a **broken heart,** he'll **settle** for **ANYTHING!**

THE SITUATION: You expected a little fun and a few laughs, but now the relationship is getting too serious...

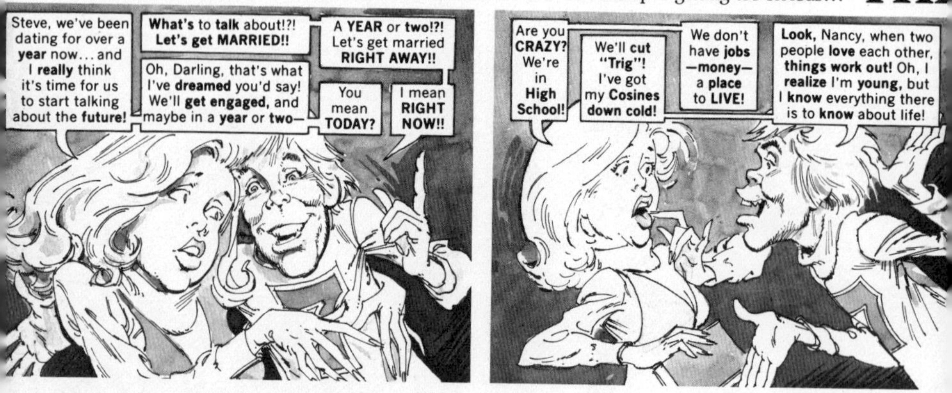
Steve, we've been dating for over a year now... and I really think it's time for us to start talking about the future!
What's to talk about!?! Let's get MARRIED!!
Oh, Darling, that's what I've dreamed you'd say! We'll get engaged, and maybe in a year or two—
A YEAR or two!?! Let's get married RIGHT AWAY!!
You mean TODAY?
I mean RIGHT NOW!!
Are you CRAZY? We're in High School!
We'll cut "Trig"! I've got my Cosines down cold!
We don't have jobs —money— a place to LIVE!
Look, Nancy, when two people love each other, things work out! Oh, I realize I'm young, but I know everything there is to know about life!

THE SITUATION: She's getting much too possessive, and it's time now to turn out the lights on the whole thing...

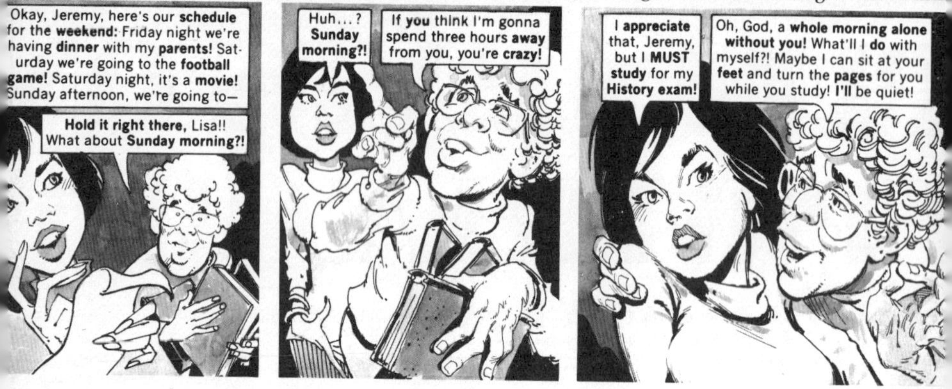
Okay, Jeremy, here's our schedule for the weekend: Friday night we're having dinner with my parents! Saturday we're going to the football game! Saturday night, it's a movie! Sunday afternoon, we're going to—
Hold it right there, Lisa!! What about Sunday morning?!
Huh...? Sunday morning?!
If you think I'm gonna spend three hours away from you, you're crazy!
I appreciate that, Jeremy, but I MUST study for my History exam!
Oh, God, a whole morning alone without you! What'll I do with myself?! Maybe I can sit at your feet and turn the pages for you while you study! I'll be quiet!

THE SITUATION: Your relationship has about as much fizz as an open bottle of Dr. Pepper and you want out...

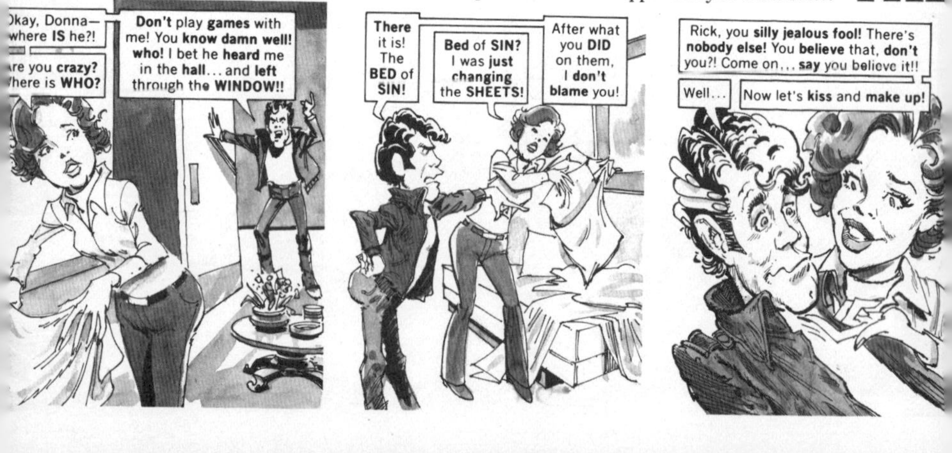
kay, Donna— where IS he?!
re you crazy? here is WHO?
Don't play games with me! You know damn well! who! I bet he heard me in the hall... and left through the WINDOW!!
There it is! The BED of SIN!
Bed of SIN? I was just changing the SHEETS!
After what you DID on them, I don't blame you!
Rick, you silly jealous fool! There's nobody else! You believe that, don't you?! Come on,,, say you believe it!!
Well...
Now let's kiss and make up!

VAY TO HANDLE IT: Scare the hell out of her!

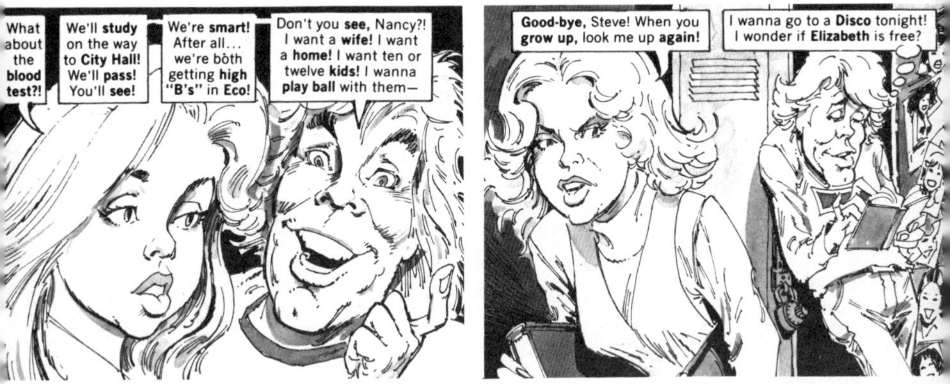
What about the blood test?!
We'll study on the way to City Hall! We'll pass! You'll see!
We're smart! After all... we're both getting high "B's" in Eco!
Don't you see, Nancy?! I want a wife! I want a home! I want ten or twelve kids! I wanna play ball with them—
Good-bye, Steve! When you grow up, look me up again!
I wanna go to a Disco tonight! I wonder if Elizabeth is free?

VAY TO HANDLE IT: Give her a taste of her own medicine!

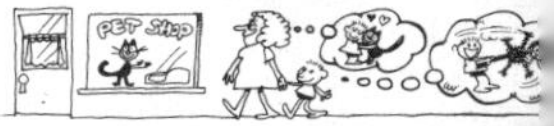
PET SHOP

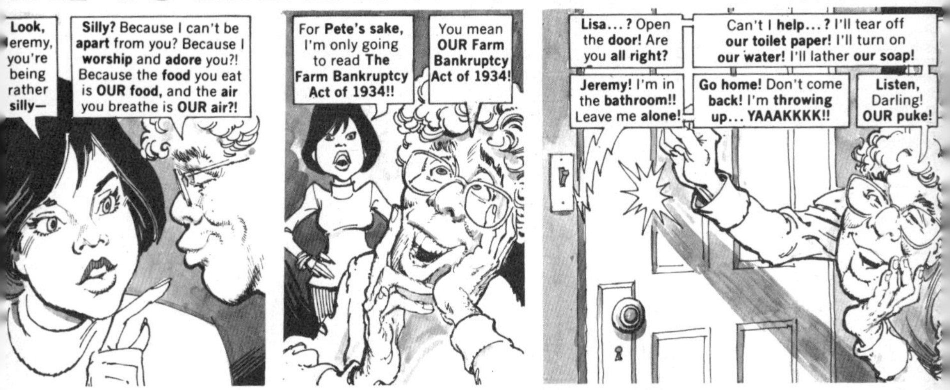
Look, Jeremy, you're being rather silly—
Silly? Because I can't be apart from you? Because I worship and adore you?! Because the food you eat is OUR food, and the air you breathe is OUR air?!
For Pete's sake, I'm only going to read The Farm Bankruptcy Act of 1934!!
You mean OUR Farm Bankruptcy Act of 1934!
Lisa...? Open the door! Are you all right?
Can't I help...? I'll tear off our toilet paper! I'll turn on our water! I'll lather our soap!
Jeremy! I'm in the bathroom!! Leave me alone!
Go home! Don't come back! I'm throwing up... YAAAKKKK!!
Listen, Darling! OUR puke!

VAY TO HANDLE IT: Drive her bananas with your jealousy!

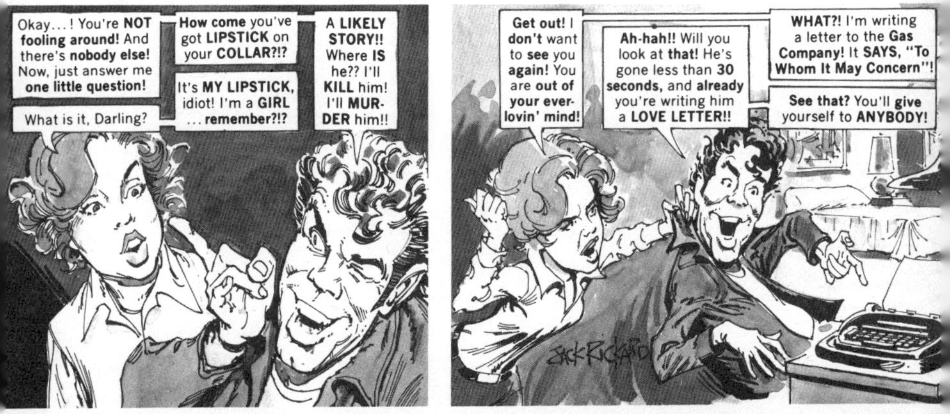
Okay...! You're NOT fooling around! And there's nobody else! Now, just answer me one little question!
What is it, Darling?
How come you've got LIPSTICK on your COLLAR?!?
It's MY LIPSTICK, idiot! I'm a GIRL ... remember?!?
A LIKELY STORY!! Where IS he?? I'll KILL him! I'll MURDER him!!
Get out! I don't want to see you again! You are out of your ever-lovin' mind!
Ah-hah!! Will you look at that! He's gone less than 30 seconds, and already you're writing him a LOVE LETTER!!
WHAT?! I'm writing a letter to the Gas Company! It SAYS, "To Whom It May Concern"!
See that? You'll give yourself to ANYBODY!
JACK RICKARD

SCOUTOLOGICAL DEPT.

For over seventy years, The Boy Scouts have awarded Merit Badges for accomplishments in various activities. Whoopie! But seventy years is a *long time.* How about *updating* some of the old badges to bring them into line with the *experiences* of The American Boy of the '80's? What do we mean by that? Well, stop being so argumentative and take a look at Mad's suggestions for...

MODER

SCORING MERIT BADGE

REPLACES:

NATURE STUDY MERIT BADGE

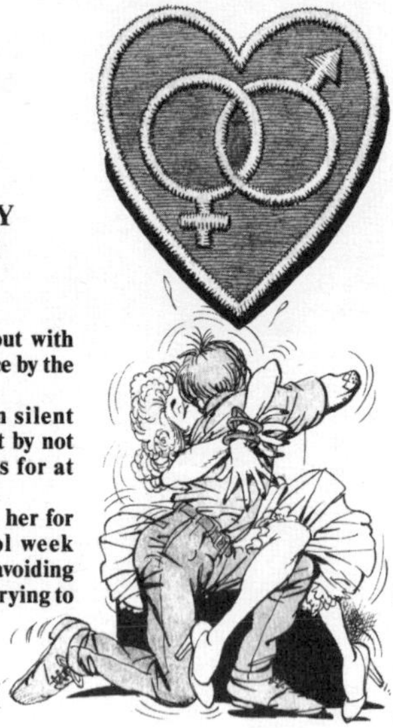

1. You must make out with the girl of your choice by the third date.
2. You must remain silent about your conquest by not telling your friends for at least one school day.
3. You must respect her for at least one school week while successfully avoiding the *guilt trip* she is trying to lay on you.

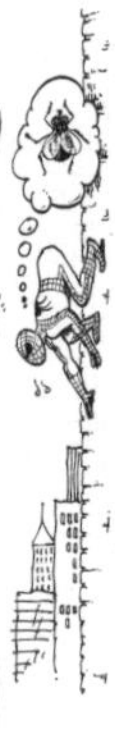

SURBURBAN SURVIVAL MERIT BADGE

REPLACES:

WILDERNESS SURVIVAL MERIT BADGE

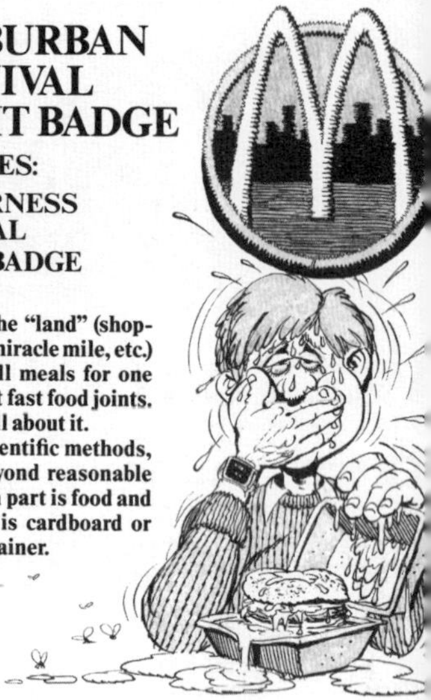

1. Live off the "land" (shopping mall, miracle mile, etc.) by eating all meals for one whole day at fast food joints.
2. Live to tell about it.
3. Using scientific methods, identify beyond reasonable doubt which part is food and which part is cardboard or plastic container.

DIVORCE SURVIVAL MERIT BADGE

REPLACES:

GENEOLOGY MERIT BADGE

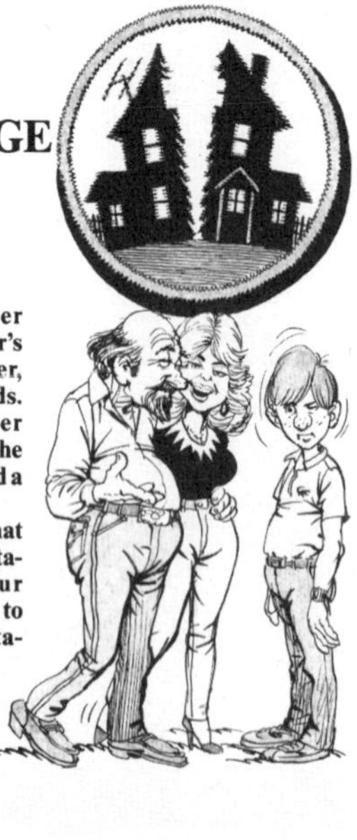

1. Do not tell your father which one of your mother's "friends" is sleeping over, even if it is one of *his* friends.
2. Agree with your father that the silly, young lady he is dating is "real swell, and a lot of fun."
3. Convince your *father* that you look forward to visitation day; convince your mother you look forward to coming home when visitation day is over.

ROAD MAP READING BADGE

REPLACES:

ORIENTEERING MERIT BADGE

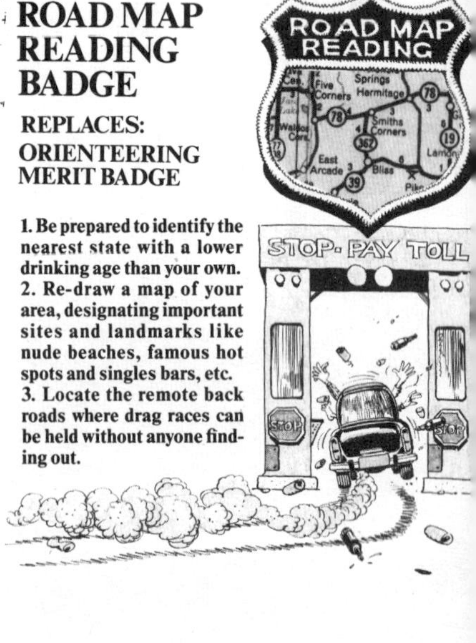
ROAD MAP READING
Five Corners
Springs
Hermitage
Smiths Corners
East Arcade
Bliss
STOP-PAY TOLL
STOP
STOP

1. Be prepared to identify the nearest state with a lower drinking age than your own.
2. Re-draw a map of your area, designating important sites and landmarks like nude beaches, famous hot spots and singles bars, etc.
3. Locate the remote back roads where drag races can be held without anyone finding out.

N MERIT BADGES

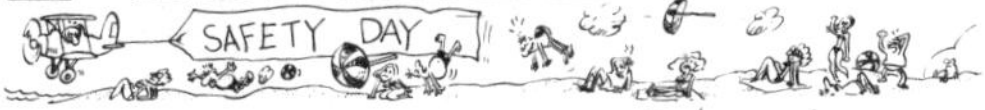
SAFETY DAY

ARTIST: GEORGE WOODBRIDGE WRITER: STAN HART

MEDICINAL PLANT GARDENING MERIT BADGE

REPLACES:

BOTANY MERIT BADGE

1. Grow the variety of "medicinal" plant your patrol leader suggests.
2. Engage your patrol to help you separate the seeds and stems from the leaves of the full grown plant.
3. Organize a sales drive to unload the produce, saving at least half the funds you collect for emergency bail.

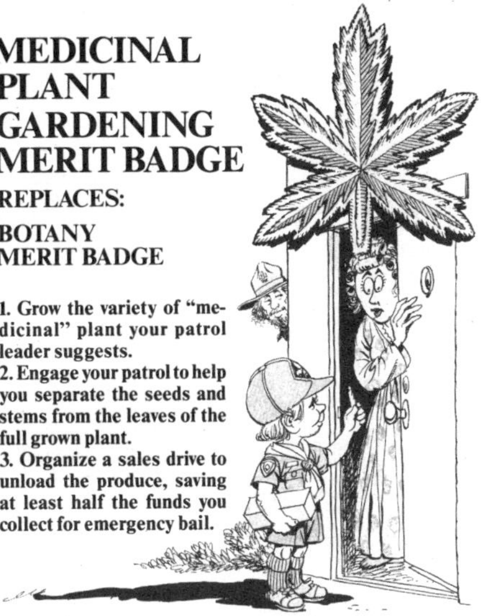

HEARING MERIT BADGE

REPLACES:

MUSIC MERIT BADGE

1. Use a boom box weighing up to but not exceeding 150 lbs. without suffering permanent hearing or brain damage.
2. Entertain people within a two mile radius with "your kind of music."
3. Master lip-reading or sign language so that you can communicate with others.

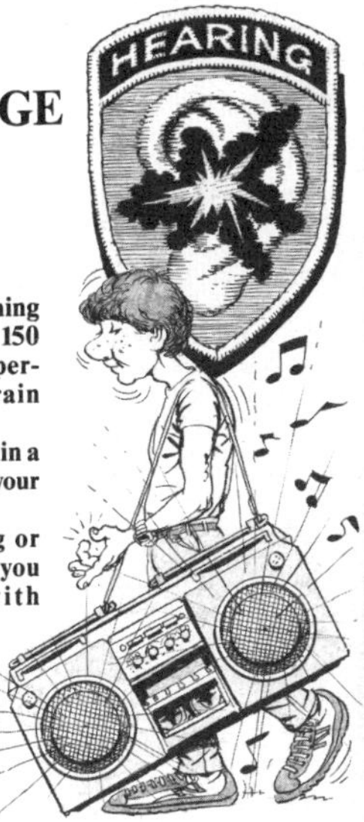
HEARING

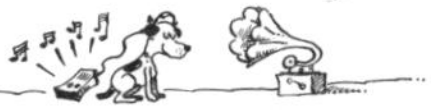

APRE SKI MERIT BADGE

REPLACES:

SKIING MERIT BADGE

1. Engage a pretty girl in a conversation about skiing without letting on that you've never been on the slopes in your life.
2. Help a pretty person get out of her wet ski clothes while preventing her from putting on dry clothes.
3. Avoid getting herpes for two consecutive skiing seasons.

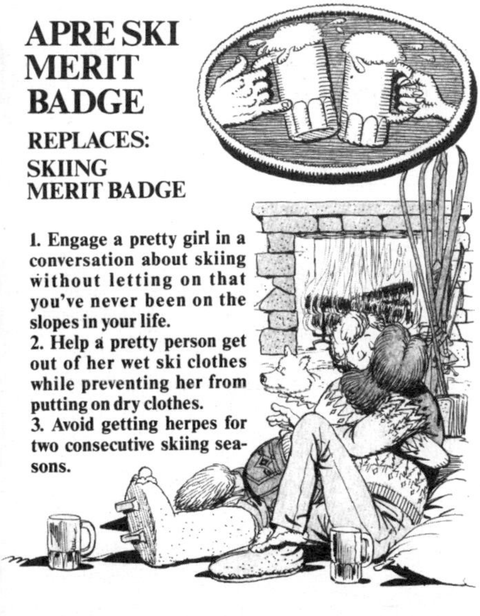

ELECTRONICS MERIT BADGE

REPLACES:

SPORTS MERIT BADGE

1. Resist the temptation to program the family computer so that it prints out dirty words and dopey jokes.
2. Demonstrate your computer and your skills to a friend without screwing up and looking like a complete jerk.
3. Break the code for your school's computerized record data bank so you can make a few bucks selling your friends the information.

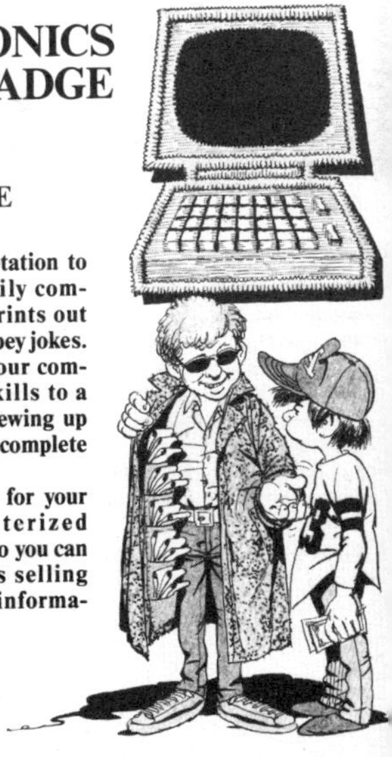

SCHOOL STUFF MERIT BADGE

DICK AND JANE
AT THE BEACH

REPLACES:

SCHOLARSHIP MERIT BADGE

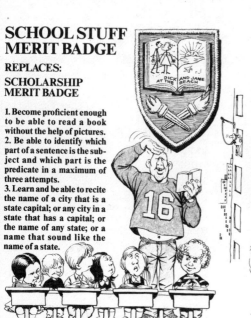

1. Become proficient enough to be able to read a book without the help of pictures.
2. Be able to identify which part of a sentence is the subject and which part is the predicate in a maximum of three attempts.
3. Learn and be able to recite the name of a city that is a state capital; or any city in a state that has a capital; or the name of any state; or a name that sound like the name of a state.

16

SLEEPING MERIT BADGE

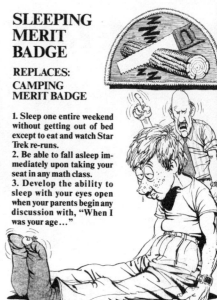

REPLACES:

CAMPING MERIT BADGE

1. Sleep one entire weekend without getting out of bed except to eat and watch Star Trek re-runs.
2. Be able to fall asleep immediately upon taking your seat in any math class.
3. Develop the ability to sleep with your eyes open when your parents begin any discussion with, "When I was your age…"

FREE ENTERPRISE MERIT BADGE

$

REPLACES:

AMERICAN BUSINESS MERIT BADGE

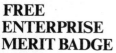

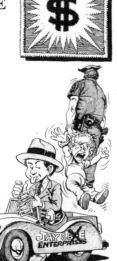

1. Learn the difference in insurance coverage between accidental fire and arson; and who to call to make the latter appear the former.
2. Go into a business venture with a partner and take advantage of him.
3. Compile a list of at least 25 tax loopholes that can be used in the business you are considering for the future.

JAY & BEE
ENTERPRISES

GROOMING MERIT BADGE

GROOMING
SHOE POLISH

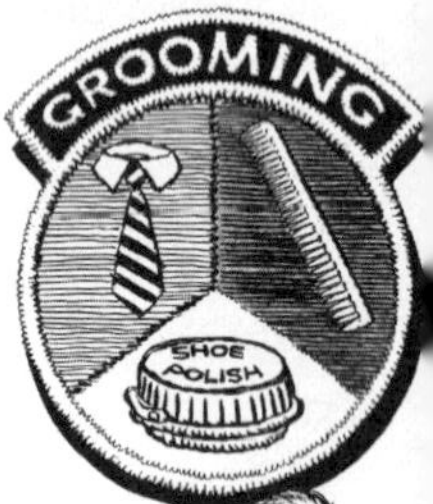

REPLACES:

PERSONAL APPEARANCE MERIT BADGE

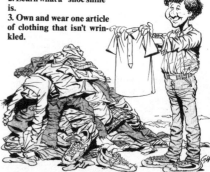

1. Learn what a "suit" is.
2. Learn what a "shoe shine" is.
3. Own and wear one article of clothing that isn't wrinkled.

GW

DON MARTIN DEPT.

STILL LATER ON IN THE HOSPITAL

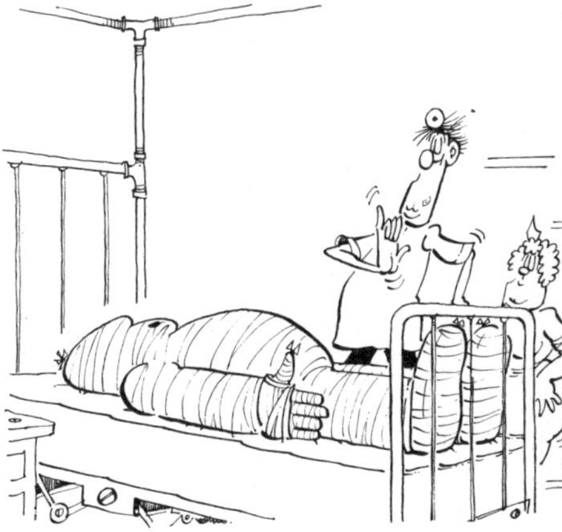

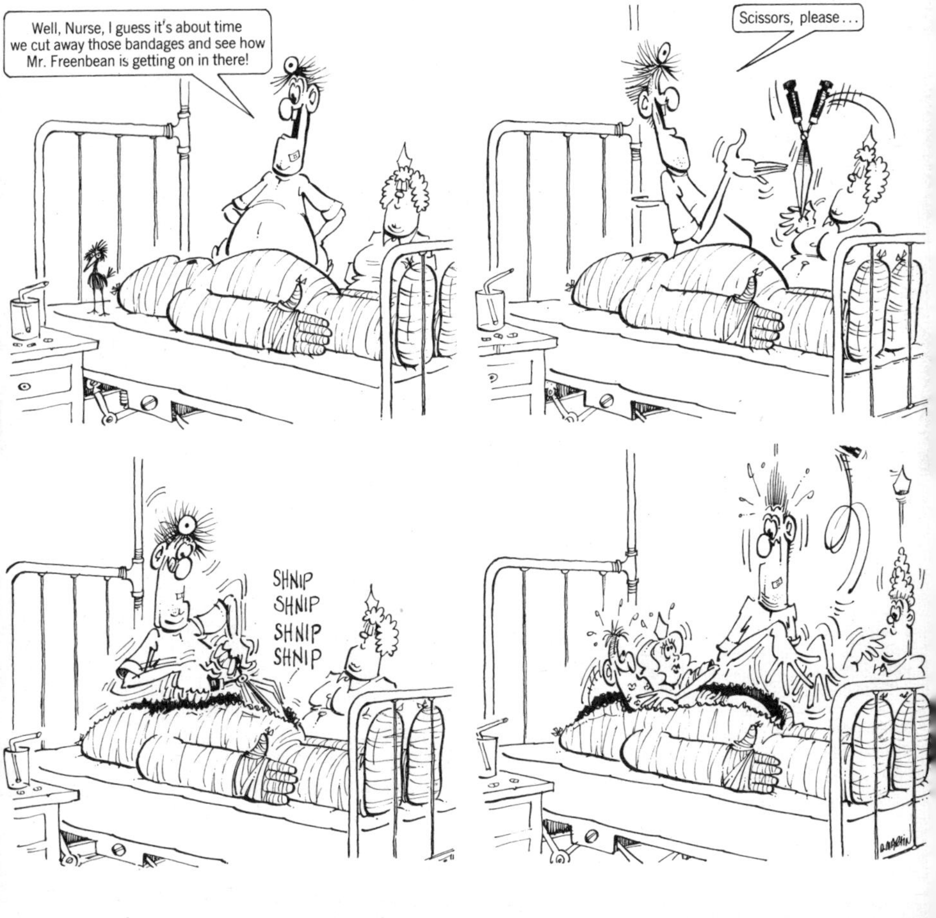
Well, Nurse, I guess it's about time we cut away those bandages and see how Mr. Freenbean is getting on in there!
Scissors, please...
SHNIP
SHNIP
SHNIP
SHNIP

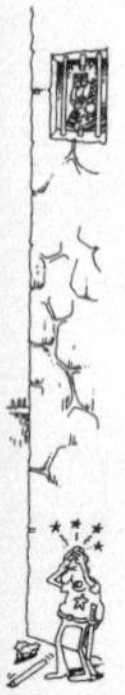

OSCAR-MIRED DEPT.

Every year Hollywood bestows Oscars on films of excellence. That's a fine idea. There's just one hitch. Hollywood stopped making films of excellence about 20 years ago! Anyone who goes to the movies knows that standards have dropped. Nowadays $5.00 buys a rehashed story line,

CUSTOMIZED AC
FOR CURRENT

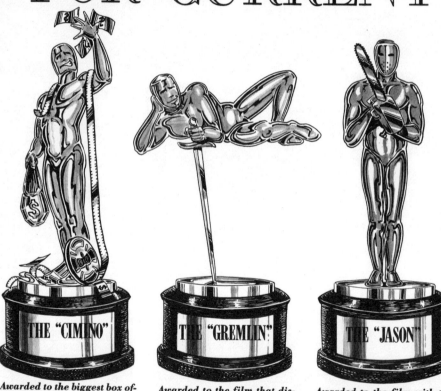

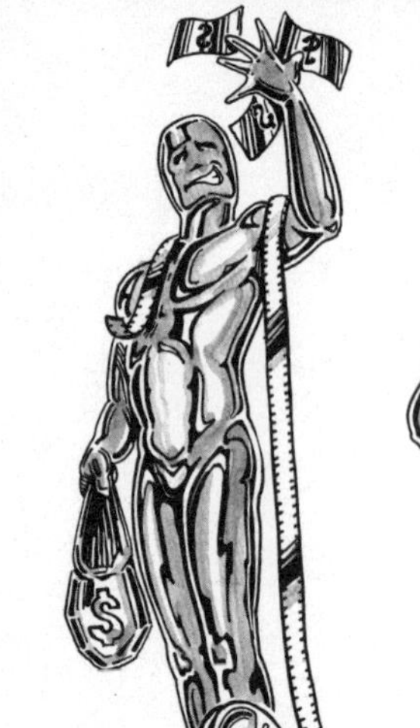
THE "CIMINO"

Awarded to the biggest box office bomb that was plagued by rumor and way over budget even before filming started.

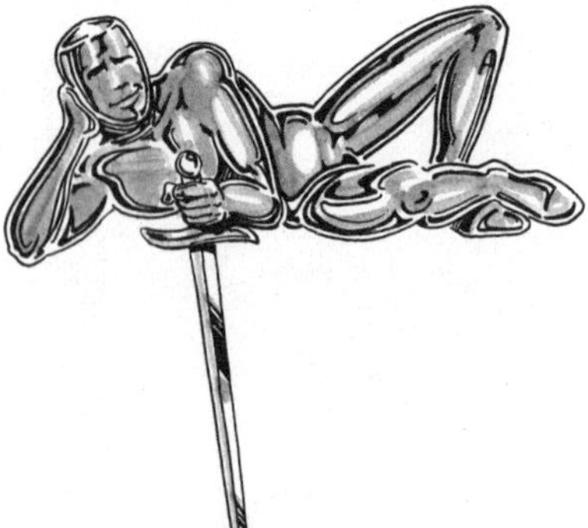
THE "GREMLIN"

Awarded to the film that displayed the flashiest special effects with the poorest acting and weakest story line.

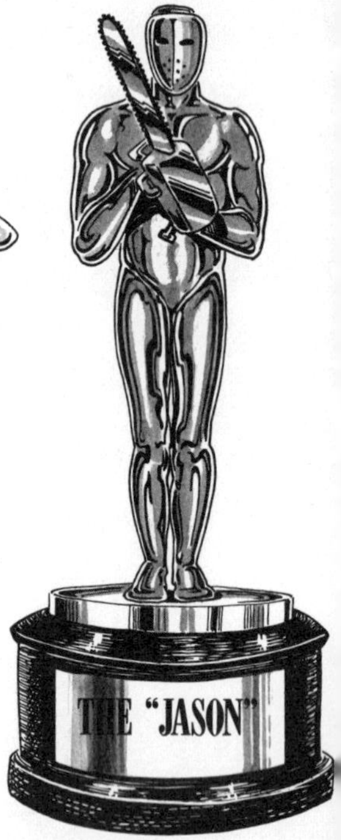
THE "JASON"

Awarded to the film with the most teenaged girls terrorized by a mentally disturbed homicidal maniac.

unintelligible dialogue, acting that makes TV look good and all the excitement of two used sparklers. That's not Oscar material! It's time for Hollywood to own up and start giving trophies that suit the films being made! But until they do, you'll have to put up with MAD's

ADEMY AWARDS
MOVIE TRENDS

ARTIST AND WRITER: MICHAEL MONTGOMERY

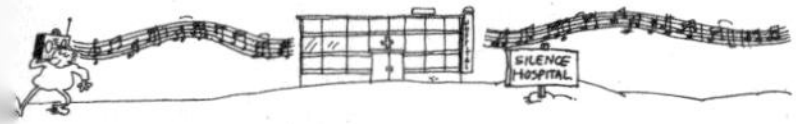
SILENCE HOSPITAL

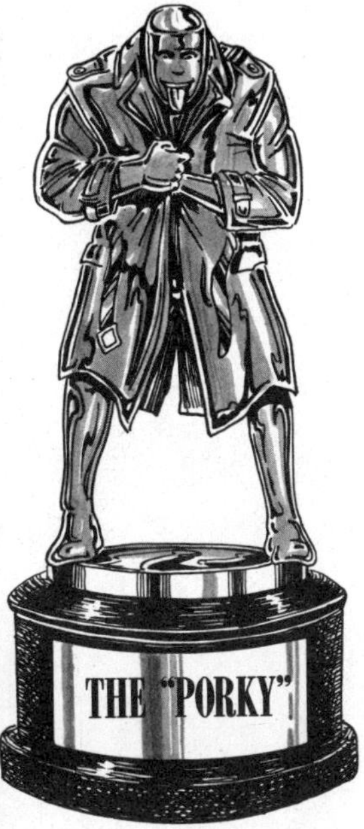
THE "PORKY"

Awarded to the film with the most unnecessary nudity and gratuitous sex, which had nothing whatsoever to do with the plot.

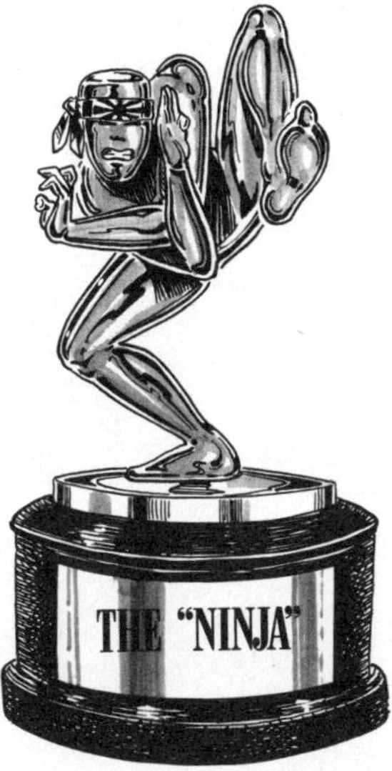
THE "NINJA"

Awarded to the martial arts movie with the most grunts and groans per minute, and the least coherent dialogue.

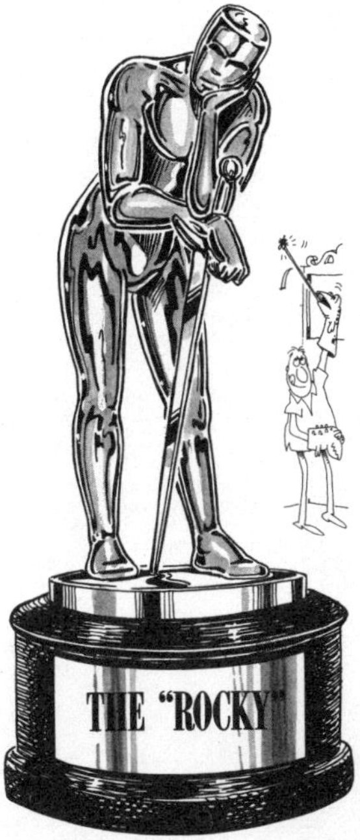
THE "ROCKY"

Awarded to the most boring and predictable sequel of a movie that wasn't very interesting to begin with.

AN EMBARRASSMENT OF RICHARD'S DEPT.

A Mad Peek Beh[...] RIPOFF MAIL[...]

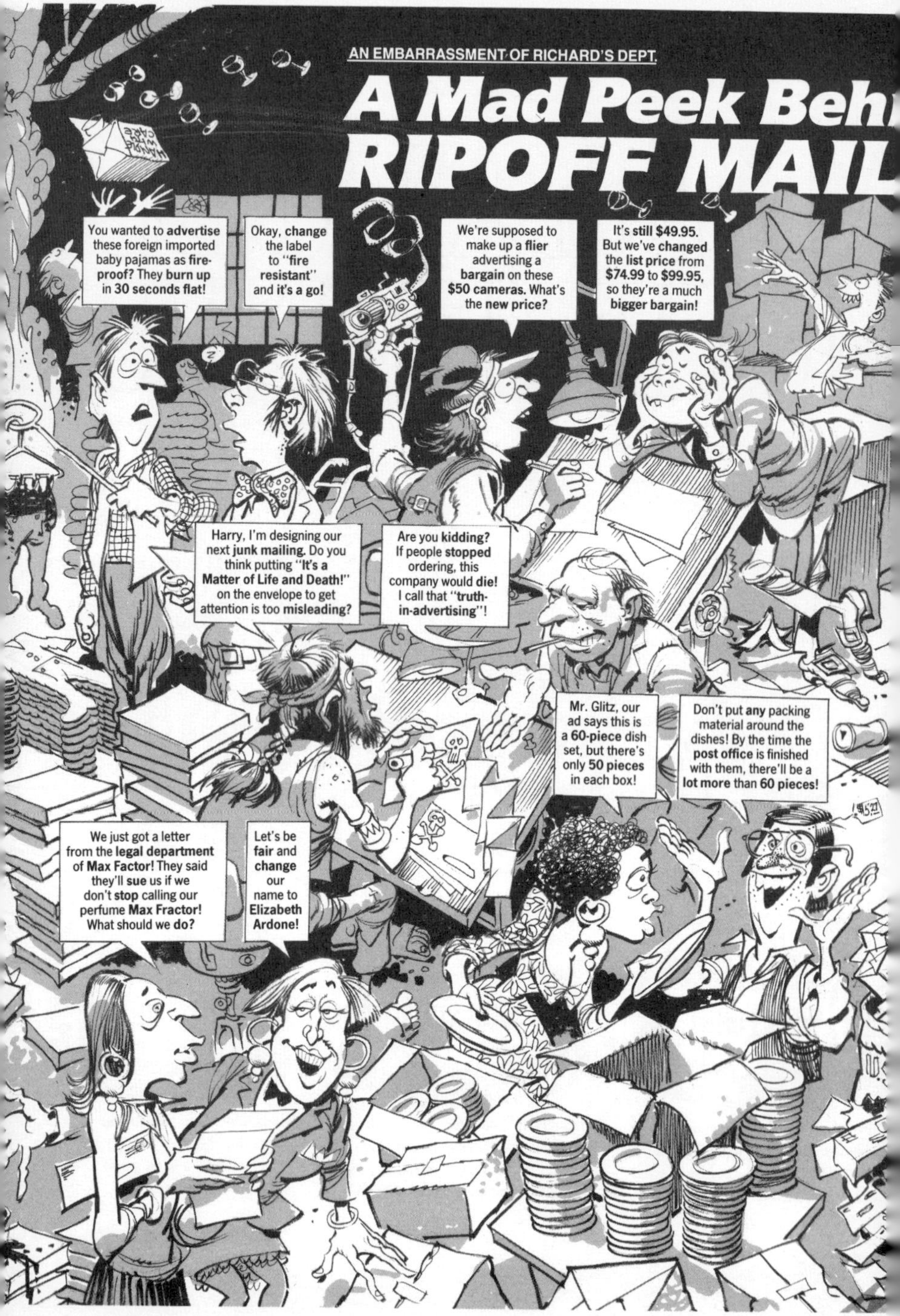
You wanted to **advertise** these foreign imported baby pajamas as **fire-proof?** They **burn up** in **30 seconds flat!**
Okay, **change** the label to "**fire resistant**" and **it's a go!**
We're supposed to make up a **flier** advertising a **bargain** on these **$50 cameras.** What's the **new price?**
It's **still $49.95.** But we've **changed** the **list price** from **$74.99** to **$99.95,** so they're a much **bigger bargain!**
Harry, I'm designing our next **junk mailing.** Do you think putting "**It's a Matter of Life and Death!**" on the envelope to get attention is too **misleading?**
Are you **kidding?** If people **stopped** ordering, this company would **die!** I call that "**truth-in-advertising**"!
Mr. Glitz, our ad says this is a **60-piece** dish set, but there's only **50 pieces** in each box!
Don't put **any** packing material around the dishes! By the time the **post office** is finished with them, there'll be a **lot more** than **60 pieces!**
We just got a letter from the **legal department** of **Max Factor!** They said they'll **sue** us if we don't **stop** calling our perfume **Max Fractor!** What should we **do?**
Let's be **fair** and **change** our name to **Elizabeth Ardone!**

ARTIST: JACK DAVIS WRITER: DICK DEBARTOLO

d The Scenes At A ORDER HOUSE

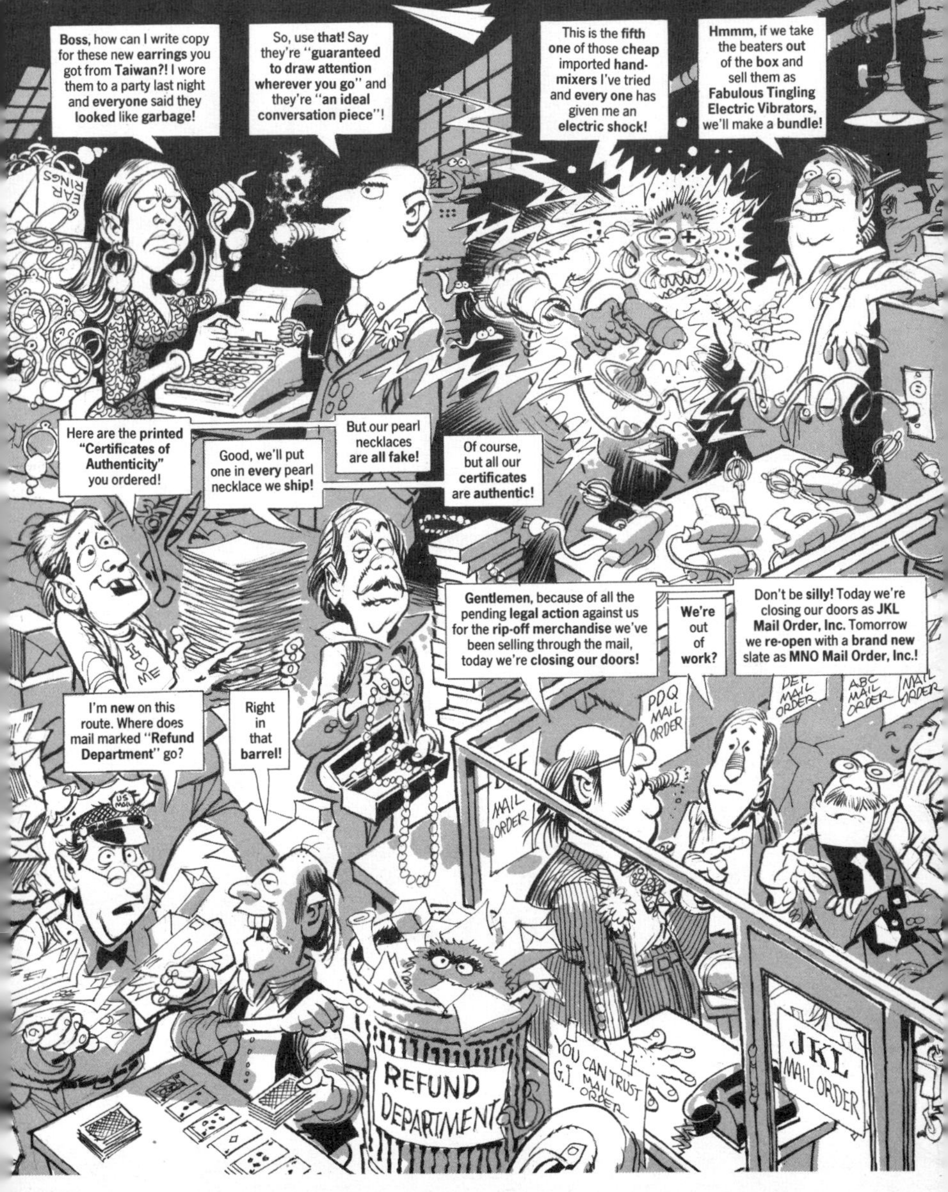

Boss, how can I write copy for these new earrings you got from Taiwan?! I wore them to a party last night and everyone said they looked like garbage!
So, use that! Say they're "guaranteed to draw attention wherever you go" and they're "an ideal conversation piece"!
This is the fifth one of those cheap imported hand-mixers I've tried and every one has given me an electric shock!
Hmmm, if we take the beaters out of the box and sell them as Fabulous Tingling Electric Vibrators, we'll make a bundle!
EAR RINGS
Here are the printed "Certificates of Authenticity" you ordered!
Good, we'll put one in every pearl necklace we ship!
But our pearl necklaces are all fake!
Of course, but all our certificates are authentic!
Gentlemen, because of all the pending legal action against us for the rip-off merchandise we've been selling through the mail, today we're closing our doors!
We're out of work?
Don't be silly! Today we're closing our doors as JKL Mail Order, Inc. Tomorrow we re-open with a brand new slate as MNO Mail Order, Inc.!
I ♥ ME
I'm new on this route. Where does mail marked "Refund Department" go?
Right in that barrel!
PDQ MAIL ORDER
DEF MAIL ORDER
ABC MAIL ORDER
MAIL ORDER
US MAIL
REFUND DEPARTMENT
YOU CAN TRUST G.I. MAIL ORDER
JKL MAIL ORDER

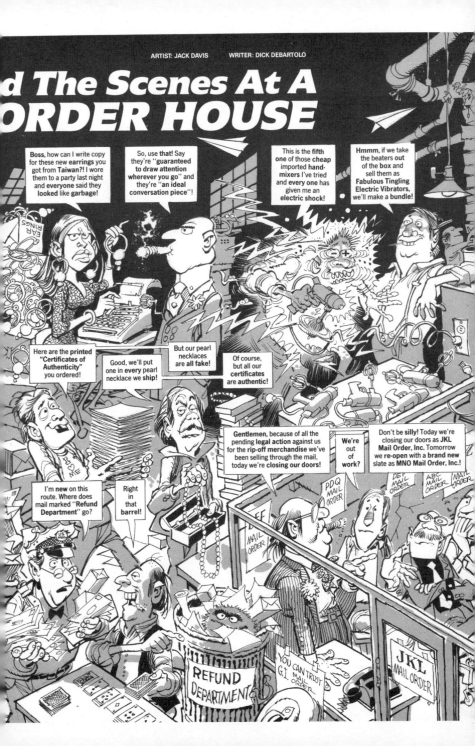

TAXI!!!

Where to, Mister?

Right to your **cash box**, buddy! This is a **STICK-UP!!**

Aw, c'mon! Gi'me a break! I'm only a part-time Cabby! I'm doin' this t' earn **extra dough!**

Is that so?!? Well, whadaya know!?! **We** got somethin' in **common!**

I'm doin' **THIS** t' earn extra dough, **TOO!** Now, fork it over . . . !!

THE LIGHTER SIDE OF...

MAKING

hese two young men offered to **clean out our basement** and take away **all our junk** for only **FIVE DOLLARS!**

Only **FIVE DOLLARS?!?** I would've paid them **three times** that much! **Boy**, are they **DUMB!!**

We're **all** finished, Ma'am

Well, **thank you!** And here's your five dollars!

Some haul, eh? Why, that **old frame** must be worth **eighty bucks** alone, and that **lamp** should bring at least **forty**—not counting the **other stuff!**

Yeah! **Boy**, are they **DUMB!**

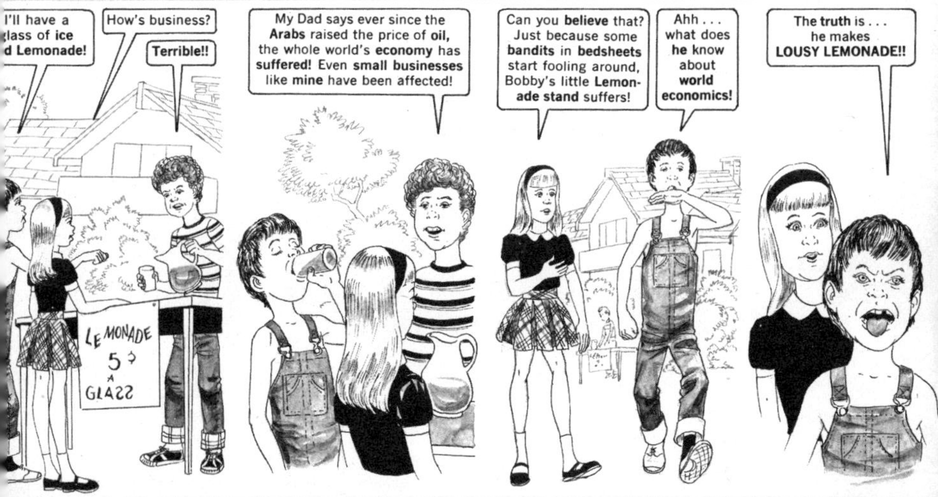
I'll have a glass of ice d Lemonade!
How's business?
Terrible!!
LEMONADE 5¢ A GLASS
My Dad says ever since the Arabs raised the price of oil, the whole world's economy has suffered! Even small businesses like mine have been affected!
Can you believe that? Just because some bandits in bedsheets start fooling around, Bobby's little Lemonade stand suffers!
Ahh . . . what does he know about world economics!
The truth is . . . he makes LOUSY LEMONADE!!

EXTRA MONEY

ARTIST & WRITER: DAVE BERG

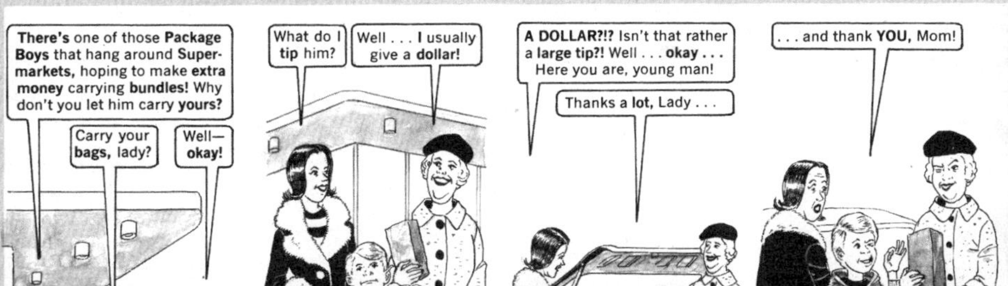
There's one of those Package Boys that hang around Supermarkets, hoping to make extra money carrying bundles! Why don't you let him carry yours?
Carry your bags, lady?
Well— okay!
What do I tip him?
Well . . . I usually give a dollar!
A DOLLAR?!? Isn't that rather a large tip?! Well . . . okay . . . Here you are, young man!
Thanks a lot, Lady . . .
M 85
. . . and thank YOU, Mom!

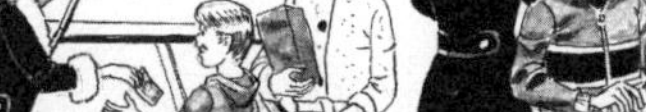

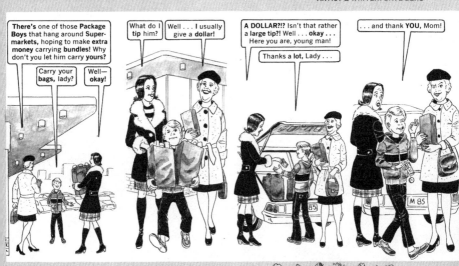

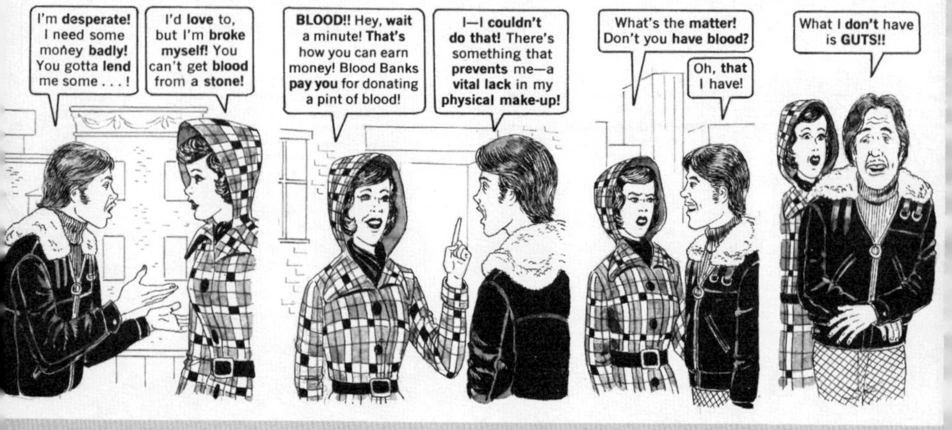

I'm desperate! I need some money badly! You gotta lend me some . . . !
I'd love to, but I'm broke myself! You can't get blood from a stone!
BLOOD!! Hey, wait a minute! That's how you can earn money! Blood Banks pay you for donating a pint of blood!
I—I couldn't do that! There's something that prevents me—a vital lack in my physical make-up!
What's the matter! Don't you have blood?
Oh, that I have!
What I don't have is GUTS!!

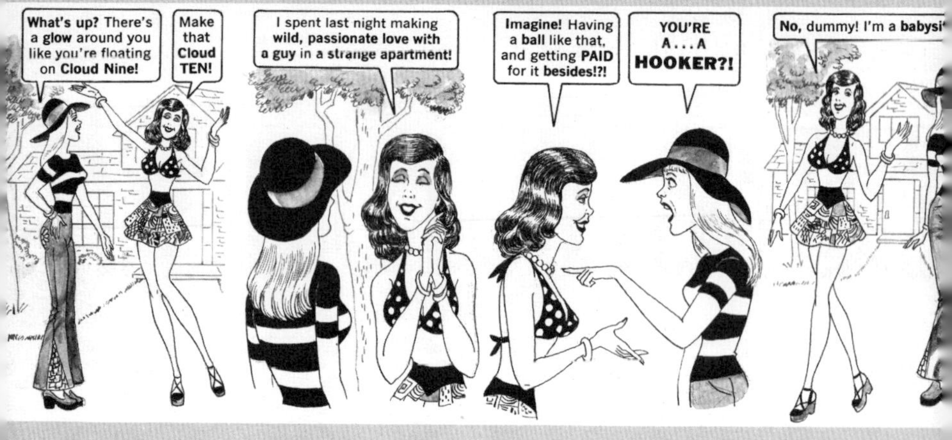

What's up? There's a glow around you like you're floating on Cloud Nine!
Make that Cloud TEN!
I spent last night making wild, passionate love with a guy in a strange apartment!
Imagine! Having a ball like that, and getting PAID for it besides!?!
YOU'RE A . . . A HOOKER?!
No, dummy! I'm a babysi

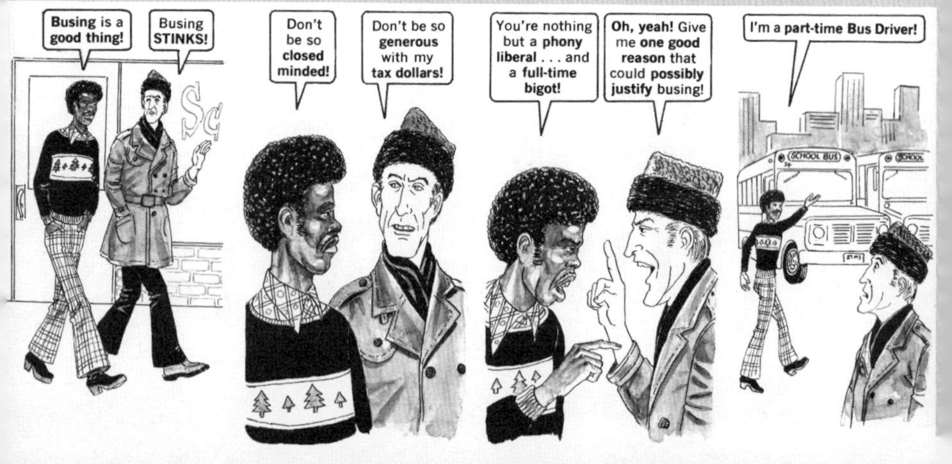

Busing is a good thing!
Busing STINKS!
Don't be so closed minded!
Don't be so generous with my tax dollars!
You're nothing but a phony liberal . . . and a full-time bigot!
Oh, yeah! Give me one good reason that could possibly justify busing!
I'm a part-time Bus Driver!
SCHOOL BUS

...nd this is my **Son** ... the **clever entrepreneur!** He collects **old comic books** and **carefully preserves** them in protective plastic bags! Go ahead, Son ... tell family what they're **worth!**

Well, these comic books are **Collectors' Items!** I can sell them for **big money** at Comic Book Conventions! F'rinstance, I could get **$300** for this old **"Superman"** comic ... and **$250** for this old **"Batman"** comic ...

... and **$500** for this **"Shock SuspenStories Number Three"** ... and **$1000** for this **"Panic"** ...

Wow! You certainly are an **enterprising young man!** You're going to be worth a **small fortune** when you sell them!

SELL them?!? Are you out of your **mind?!?** I wouldn't give up a **single one** of these books for the **world!**

Will you **look** at **that?!** What is he ... some kind of **NUT?!?**

No, he's a **Professional Dog-Walker!**

Isn't that a **dangerous job** ... being around all those **vicious dogs?**

It's about the **safest** job you can get nowadays!

What mugger would **dare** attack him with all that **protection?**

...Sir, I'll shovel the snow off your side walk for a reasonable price!

Son! You've got a **deal!**

I **can't believe** it! When I was a kid **we** made extra money by doing back-breaking work, but I thought kids of today were so **spoiled** and **soft**, they wouldn't ever **take on** manual labor jobs! Yet, **here's** a kid willing to work up a **sweat!**

You're **right!** He's working up a **sweat** all right ...

That's a pretty long walk from our **front door** to his **Father's** gas powered snow-blower!!

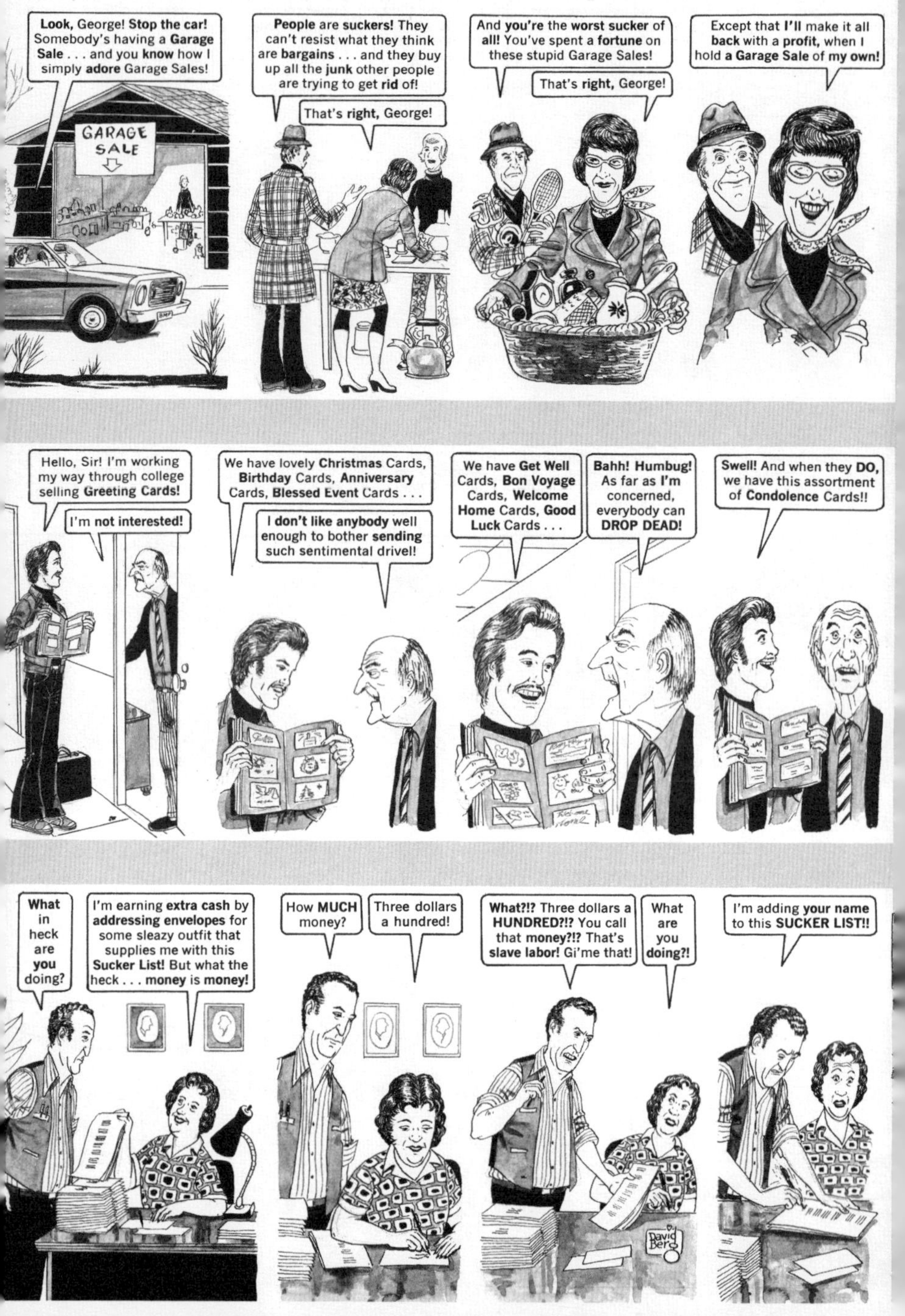

Look, George! Stop the car! Somebody's having a Garage Sale . . . and you know how I simply adore Garage Sales!
GARAGE SALE
People are suckers! They can't resist what they think are bargains . . . and they buy up all the junk other people are trying to get rid of!
That's right, George!
And you're the worst sucker of all! You've spent a fortune on these stupid Garage Sales!
That's right, George!
Except that I'll make it all back with a profit, when I hold a Garage Sale of my own!
Hello, Sir! I'm working my way through college selling Greeting Cards!
I'm not interested!
We have lovely Christmas Cards, Birthday Cards, Anniversary Cards, Blessed Event Cards . . .
I don't like anybody well enough to bother sending such sentimental drivel!
We have Get Well Cards, Bon Voyage Cards, Welcome Home Cards, Good Luck Cards . . .
Bahh! Humbug! As far as I'm concerned, everybody can DROP DEAD!
Swell! And when they DO, we have this assortment of Condolence Cards!!
What in heck are you doing?
I'm earning extra cash by addressing envelopes for some sleazy outfit that supplies me with this Sucker List! But what the heck . . . money is money!
How MUCH money?
Three dollars a hundred!
What?!? Three dollars a HUNDRED?!? You call that money?!? That's slave labor! Gi'me that!
What are you doing?!
I'm adding your name to this SUCKER LIST!!
David Berg

P, PLEASE! DEPT.

MAD'S Modern Believe It or Nuts!

ARTIST: BOB CLARKE

WRITER: FRANK JACOBS

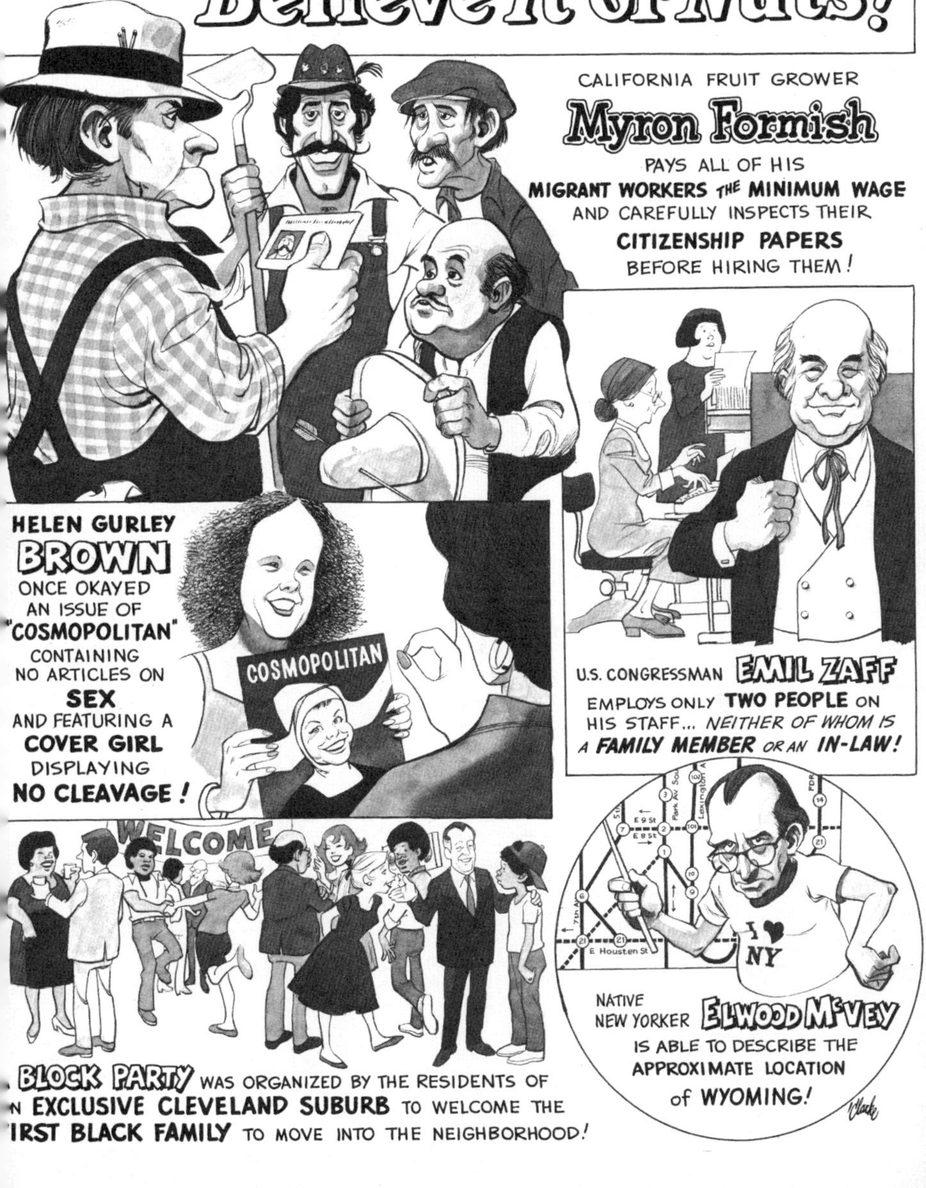

CALIFORNIA FRUIT GROWER
Myron Formish
PAYS ALL OF HIS MIGRANT WORKERS THE MINIMUM WAGE AND CAREFULLY INSPECTS THEIR CITIZENSHIP PAPERS BEFORE HIRING THEM!
U.S. CONGRESSMAN EMIL ZAFF
EMPLOYS ONLY TWO PEOPLE ON HIS STAFF... NEITHER OF WHOM IS A FAMILY MEMBER OR AN IN-LAW!
HELEN GURLEY BROWN
ONCE OKAYED AN ISSUE OF "COSMOPOLITAN" CONTAINING NO ARTICLES ON SEX AND FEATURING A COVER GIRL DISPLAYING NO CLEAVAGE!
COSMOPOLITAN
WELCOME
A BLOCK PARTY WAS ORGANIZED BY THE RESIDENTS OF AN EXCLUSIVE CLEVELAND SUBURB TO WELCOME THE FIRST BLACK FAMILY TO MOVE INTO THE NEIGHBORHOOD!
E 9 St
E 8 St
Park AV So
Lexington A
5th
7th A
FDR
E Housten St
I ♥ NY
NATIVE NEW YORKER ELWOOD McVEY
IS ABLE TO DESCRIBE THE APPROXIMATE LOCATION of WYOMING!
Clarke

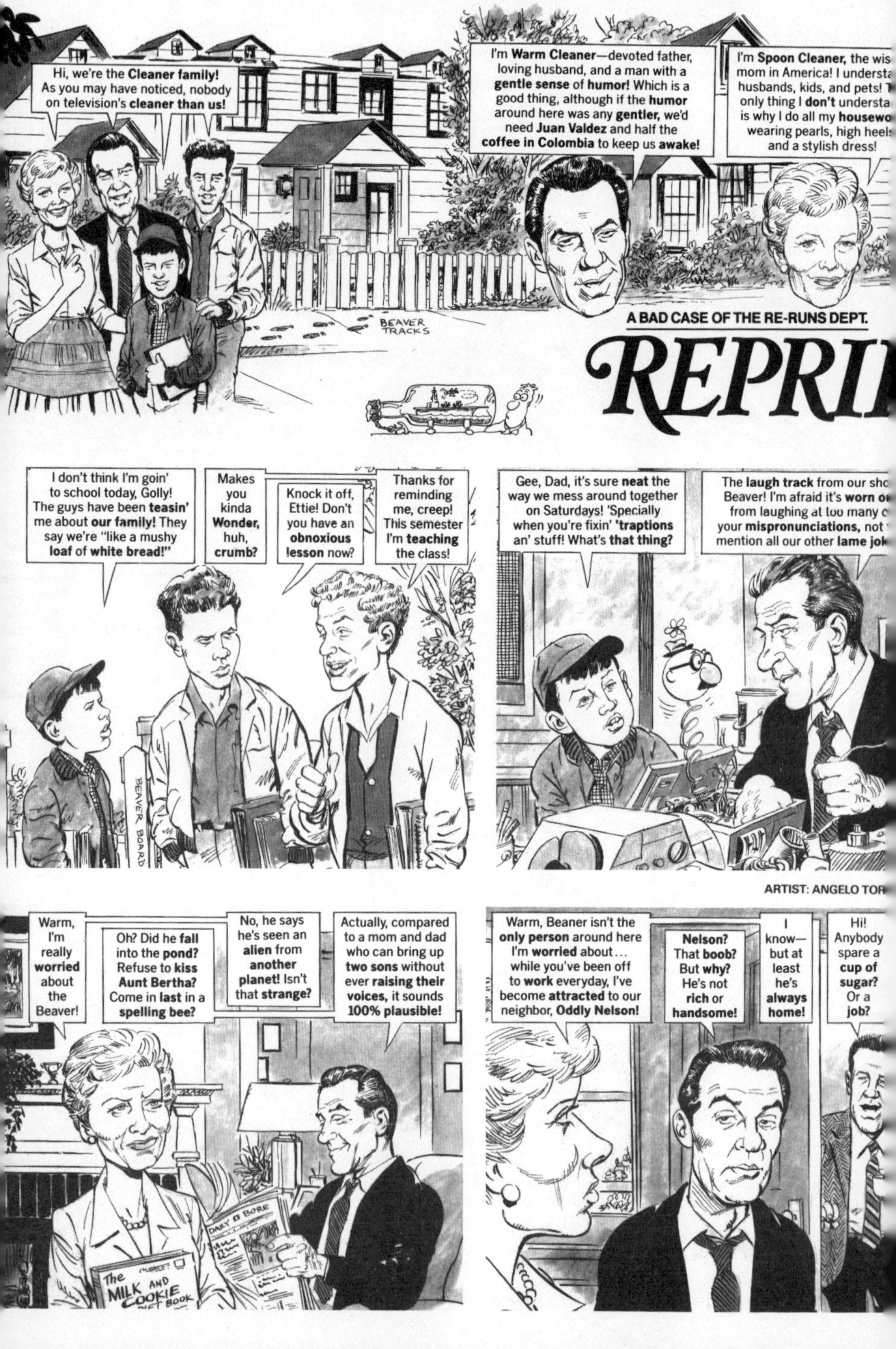

Hi, we're the **Cleaner family!** As you may have noticed, nobody on television's **cleaner than us!**
I'm **Warm Cleaner**—devoted father, loving husband, and a man with a **gentle sense** of **humor!** Which is a good thing, although if the **humor** around here was any **gentler,** we'd need **Juan Valdez** and half the **coffee in Colombia** to keep us **awake!**
I'm **Spoon Cleaner,** the wis mom in America! I understa husbands, kids, and pets! T only thing I **don't** understa is why I do all my **housewo** wearing pearls, high heel and a stylish dress!
BEAVER TRACKS
A BAD CASE OF THE RE-RUNS DEPT.
REPRI
I don't think I'm goin' to school today, Golly! The guys have been **teasin'** me about **our family!** They say we're "like a mushy **loaf** of **white bread!"**
Makes you kinda **Wonder,** huh, **crumb?**
Knock it off, Ettie! Don't you have an **obnoxious lesson** now?
Thanks for reminding me, creep! This semester I'm **teaching** the class!
BEAVER BOARD
Gee, Dad, it's sure **neat** the way we mess around together on Saturdays! 'Specially when you're fixin' **'traptions** an' stuff! What's **that thing?**
The **laugh track** from our sho Beaver! I'm afraid it's **worn o** from laughing at too many c your **mispronunciations,** not mention all our other **lame jok**
ARTIST: ANGELO TOR
Warm, I'm really **worried** about the Beaver!
Oh? Did he **fall** into the **pond?** Refuse to **kiss Aunt Bertha?** Come in **last** in a **spelling bee?**
No, he says he's seen an **alien** from **another planet!** Isn't that **strange?**
Actually, compared to a mom and dad who can bring up **two sons** without ever **raising their voices,** it sounds **100% plausible!**
DAILY BORE
The MILK AND COOKIE DIET BOOK
Warm, Beaner isn't the **only person** around here I'm **worried** about... while you've been off to **work** everyday, I've become **attracted** to our neighbor, **Oddly Nelson!**
Nelson? That **boob?** But **why?** He's not **rich** or **handsome!**
I know—but at least he's **always home!**
Hi! Anybody spare a **cup of sugar?** Or a **job?**

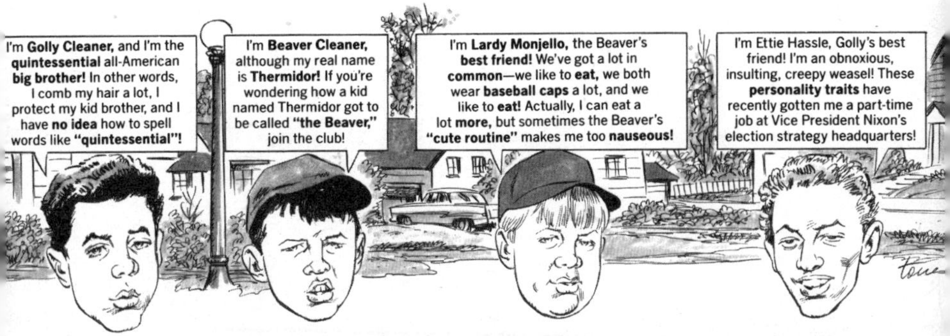
I'm **Golly Cleaner,** and I'm the **quintessential** all-American **big brother!** In other words, I comb my hair a lot, I protect my kid brother, and I have **no idea** how to spell words like **"quintessential"!**
I'm **Beaver Cleaner,** although my real name is **Thermidor!** If you're wondering how a kid named Thermidor got to be called **"the Beaver,"** join the club!
I'm **Lardy Monjello,** the Beaver's **best friend!** We've got a lot in **common**—we like to **eat,** we both wear **baseball caps** a lot, and we like to **eat!** Actually, I can eat a lot **more,** but sometimes the Beaver's **"cute routine"** makes me too **nauseous!**
I'm Ettie Hassle, Golly's best friend! I'm an obnoxious, insulting, creepy weasel! These **personality traits** have recently gotten me a part-time job at Vice President Nixon's election strategy headquarters!

E IT FOR BEAVER

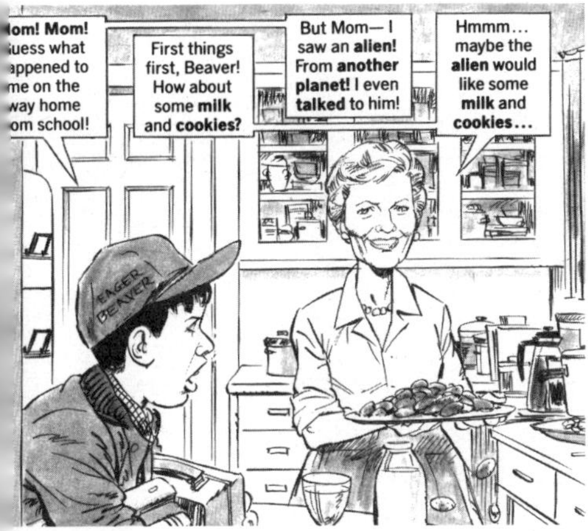
om! Mom! uess what appened to me on the way home om school!
First things first, Beaver! How about some **milk** and **cookies?**
But Mom— I saw an **alien!** From **another planet!** I even **talked** to him!
Hmmm… maybe the **alien** would like some **milk** and **cookies…**
EAGER BEAVER

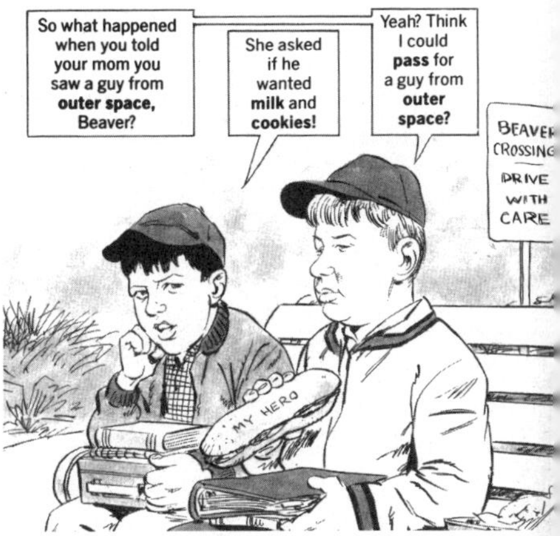
So what happened when you told your mom you saw a guy from **outer space,** Beaver?
She asked if he wanted **milk** and **cookies!**
Yeah? Think I could **pass** for a guy from **outer space?**
BEAVER CROSSING
DRIVE WITH CARE
MY HERO

ER: DENNIS SNEE

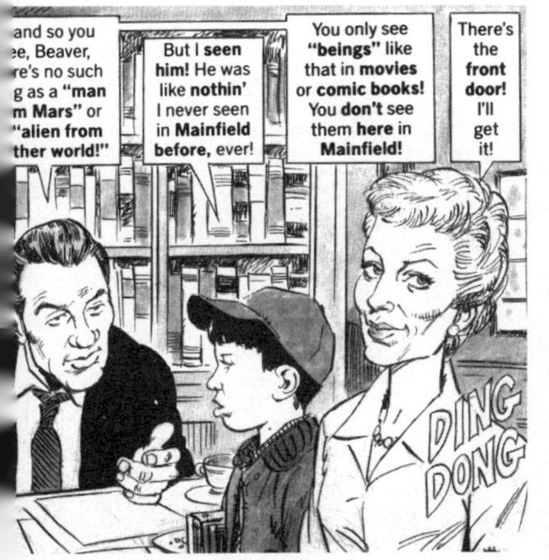
and so you ee, Beaver, re's no such g as a **"man m Mars"** or **"alien from ther world!"**
But I **seen him!** He was like **nothin'** I never seen in **Mainfield before,** ever!
You only see **"beings"** like that in **movies** or **comic books!** You **don't** see them **here** in **Mainfield!**
There's the **front door!** I'll get it!
DING DONG

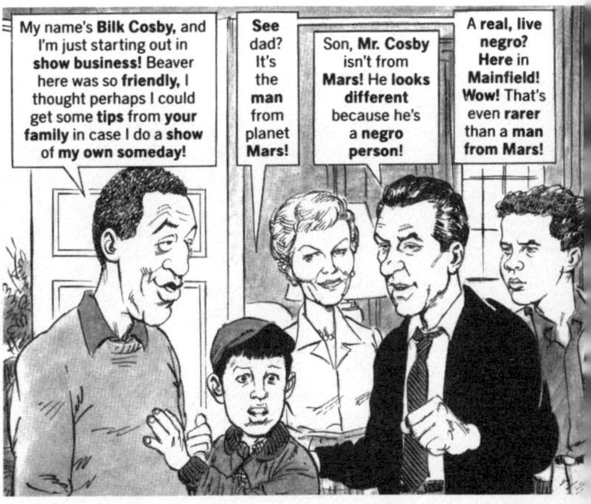
My name's **Bilk Cosby,** and I'm just starting out in **show business!** Beaver here was so **friendly,** I thought perhaps I could get some **tips** from **your family** in case I do a **show** of **my own someday!**
See dad? It's the **man** from planet **Mars!**
Son, **Mr. Cosby** isn't from **Mars!** He **looks different** because he's a **negro person!**
A **real, live negro? Here** in **Mainfield! Wow!** That's even **rarer** than a **man from Mars!**

SERGIO ARAGONES DEPT.

A MAD LOOK A

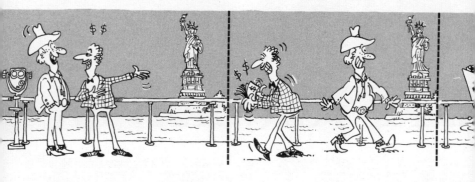

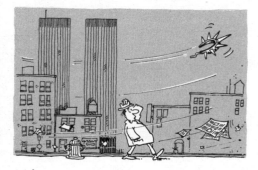

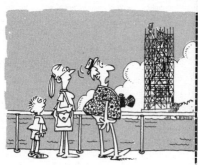

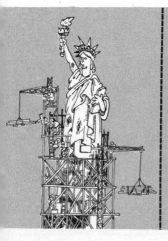

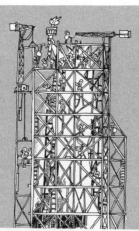

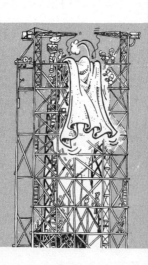

MS. LIBERTY

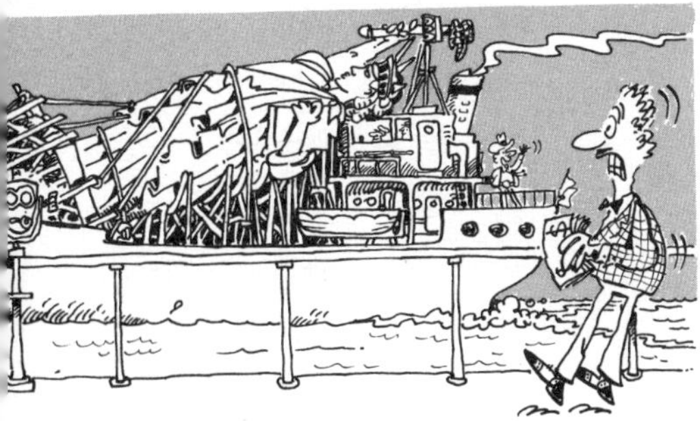

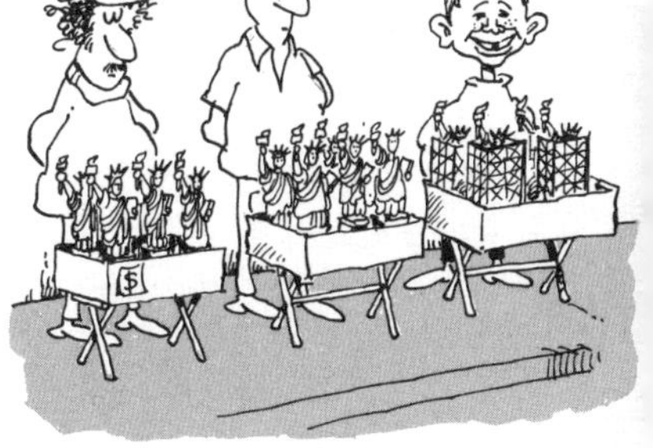

ARTIST AND WRITER: SERGIO ARAGONES

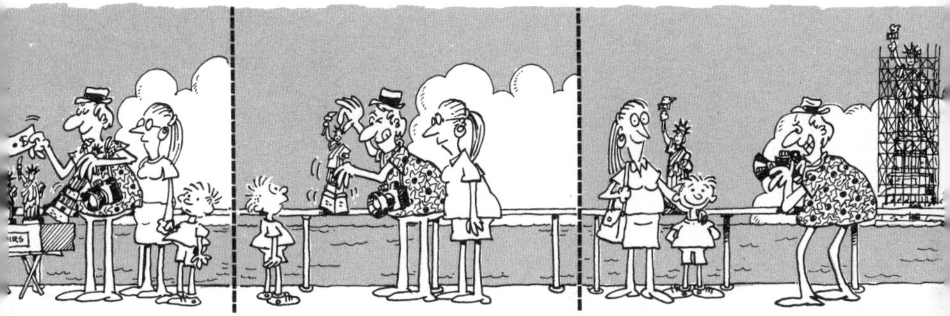

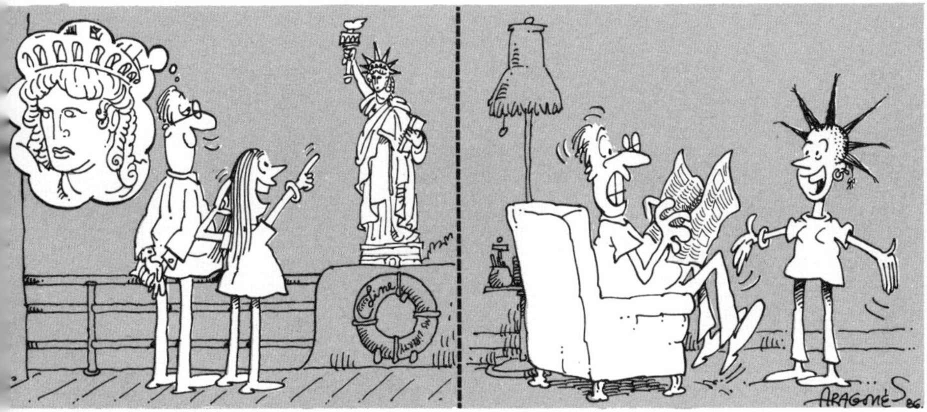
ARAGONÉS 86.

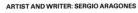

DON MARTIN DEPT.

MEANWHILE AT THE SCULPTOR'S STUDIO

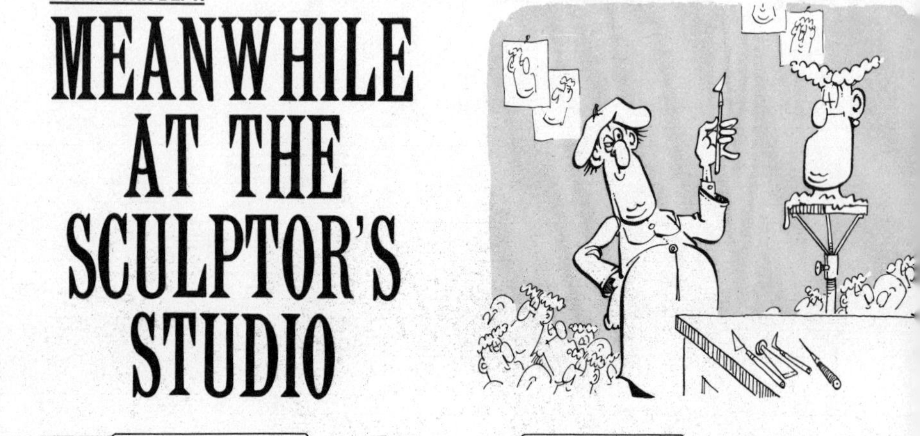

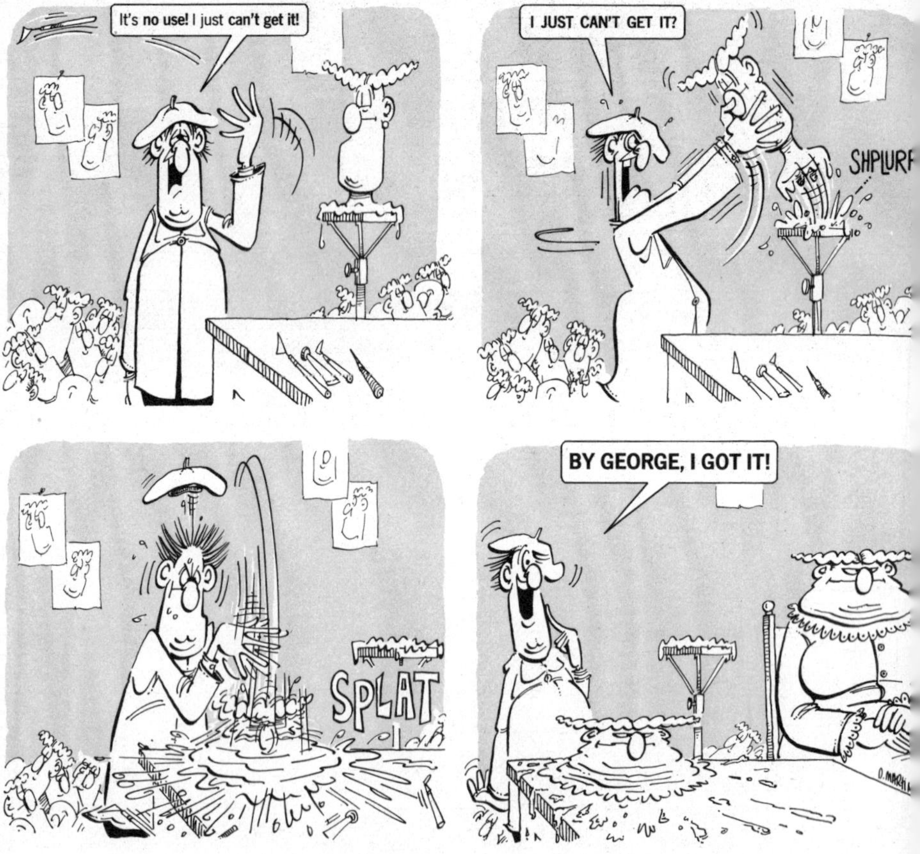
It's no use! I just can't get it!
I JUST CAN'T GET IT?
SHPLURF
SPLAT
BY GEORGE, I GOT IT!

CRASHING BORE DEPT.

If you've ever flown, you know that every airline passenger is provided with reading material to help while away the time and make you forget how boring and uncomfortable the trip really is. This reading material usually consists of three items: (1) A magazine that extols the virtues of the airline you're flying, (2) A mail order catalogue of products that are sold by the airline you're flying, and (3) A safety information guide that makes you wish you'd never heard of the airline you're flying. With this idiotic article, we take

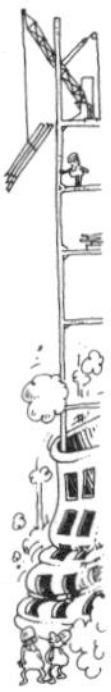

A MAD LOOK AT AIRLINE SAFETY INSTRUCTIONS

Airline emergency procedures look great...on paper!

SAFETY INFORMATION
INFORMATION DE SEGURIDAD
RENSIGNEMENTS POUR VOTRE SECURITÉ
ROTSA RUCK

BOING FATBELLY
727 FEET (AROUND THE MIDDLE)

WRITER AND ARTIST: AL JAFFEE

HOW TO LOCATE THIS CARD

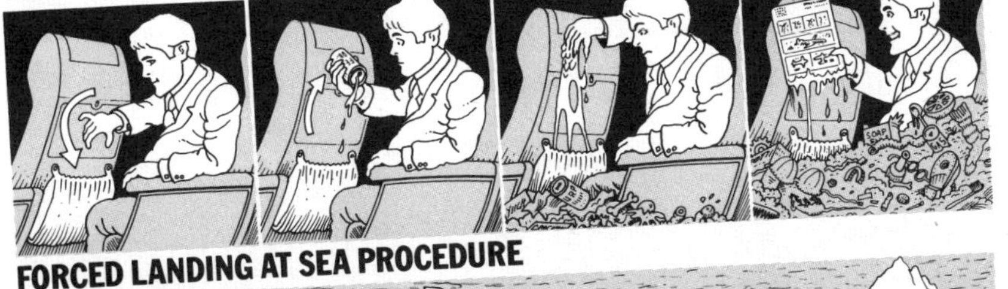
SOAP

FORCED LANDING AT SEA PROCEDURE

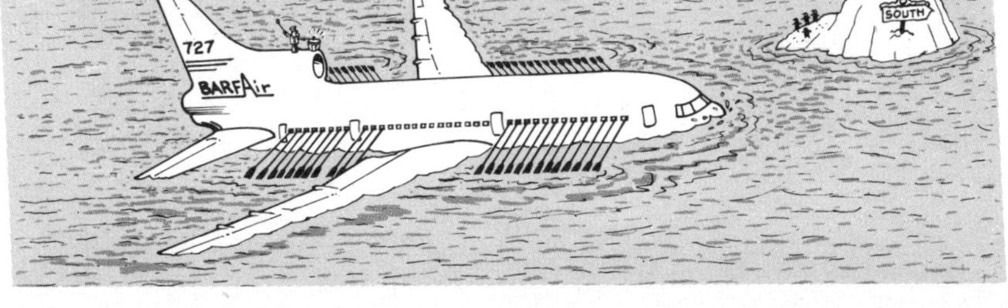
727
BARFAir
SOUTH

But in real life, they wouldn't quite work out that way...

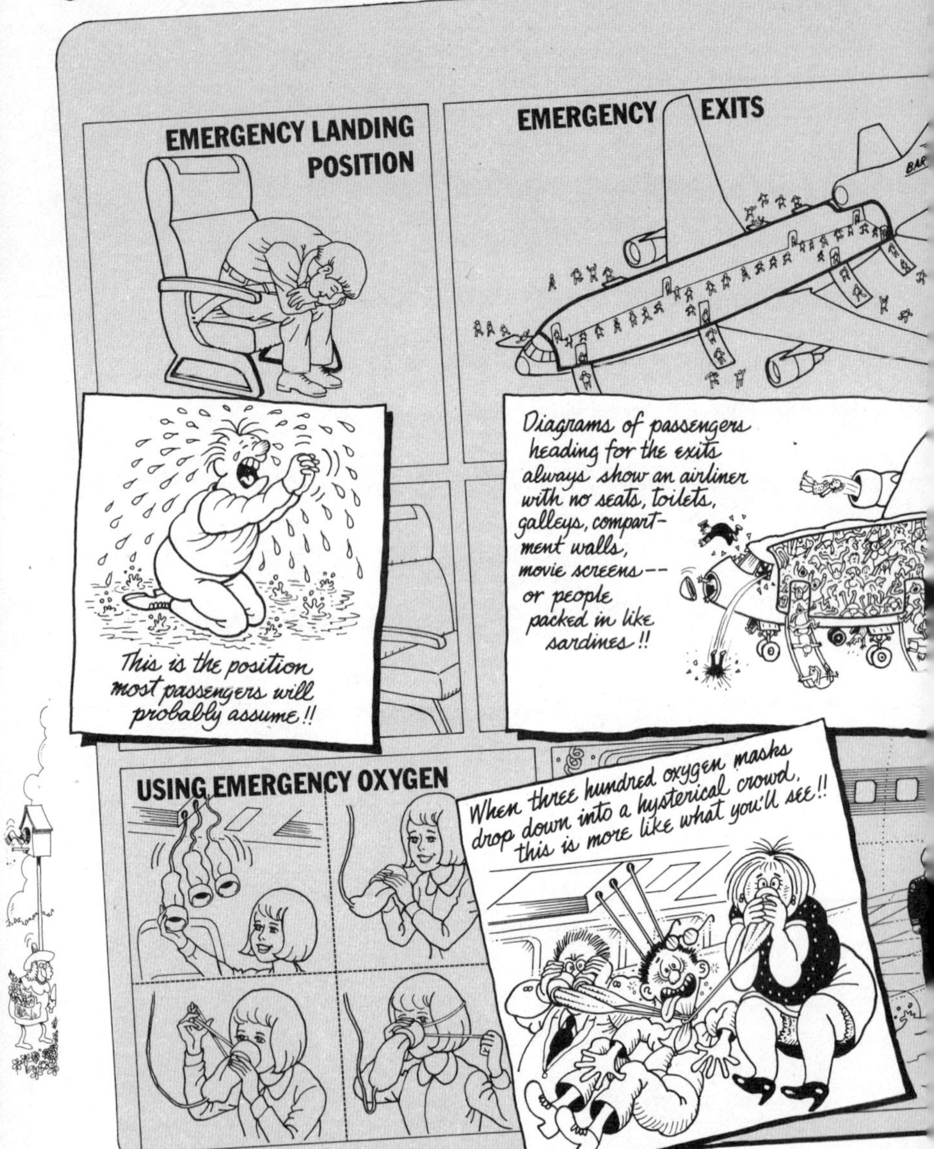

EMERGENCY LANDING POSITION
This is the position most passengers will probably assume!!
EMERGENCY EXITS
Diagrams of passengers heading for the exits always show an airliner with no seats, toilets, galleys, compartment walls, movie screens-- or people packed in like sardines!!
USING EMERGENCY OXYGEN
When three hundred oxygen masks drop down into a hysterical crowd, this is more like what you'll see!!

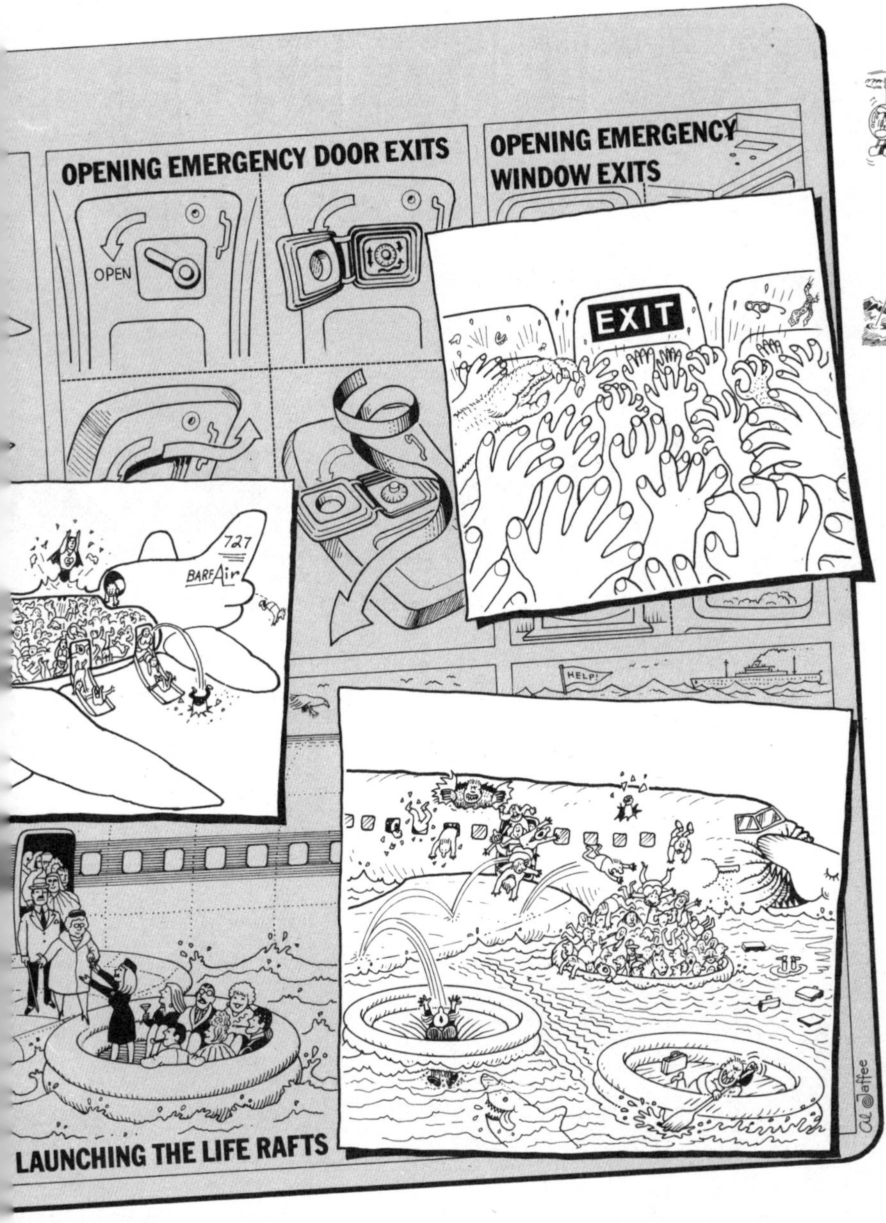

OPENING EMERGENCY DOOR EXITS
OPEN
OPENING EMERGENCY WINDOW EXITS
EXIT
727
BARF Air
HELP!
LAUNCHING THE LIFE RAFTS
Al Jaffee

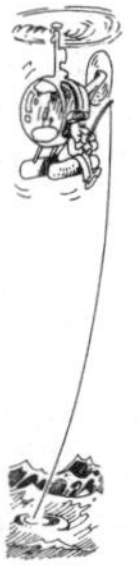

PRESSURE POINTS DEPT.

Nowadays, it seems like almost every Doctor or Psychiatrist has compiled "Stress Chart"... which is designed to measure the level of stress caused b certain events in our lives, like being imprisoned, or getting a divorc

THE MAD ST

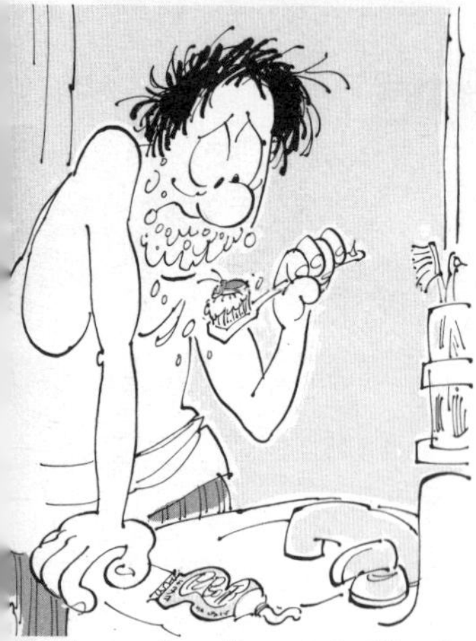

Finding a cockroach on your toothbrush.

20 units

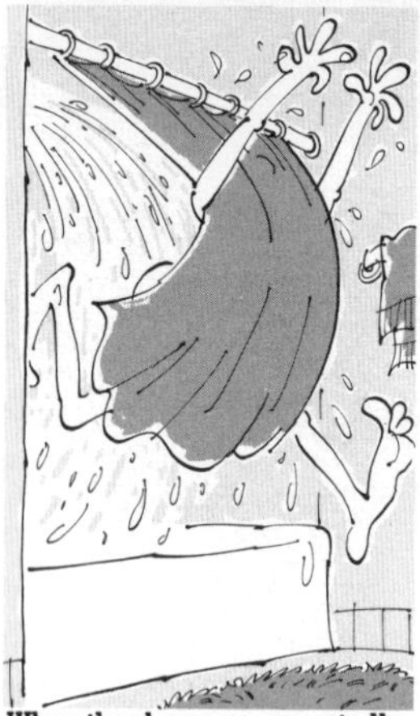

When the shower unexpectedly gets 50° hotter... or colder.

30 units

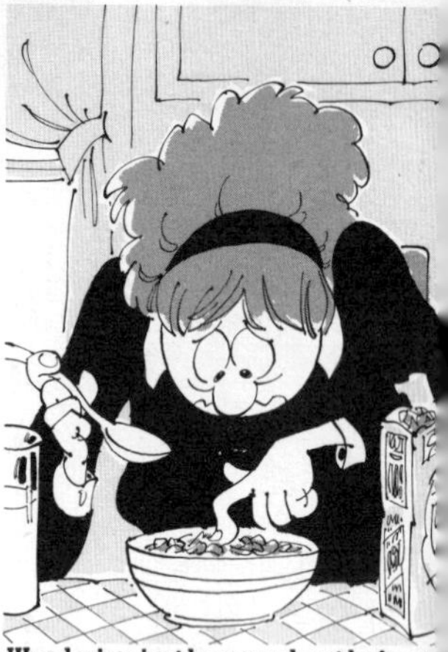

Wondering just how much rat hairs ar droppings in your food is "acceptable

15 units

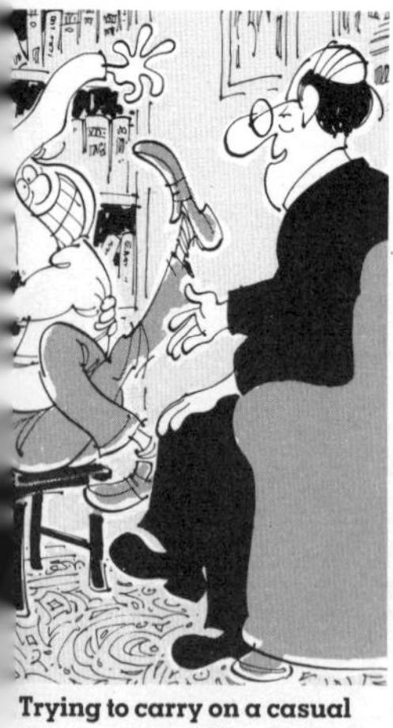

Trying to carry on a casual conversation with a Priest.

45 units

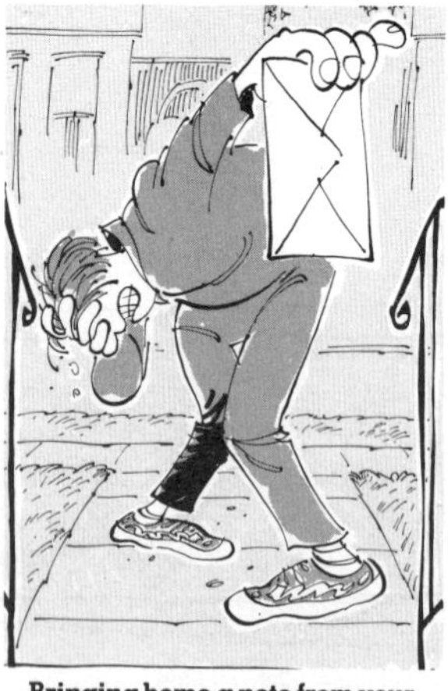

Bringing home a note from your teacher... in a sealed envelope.

40 units

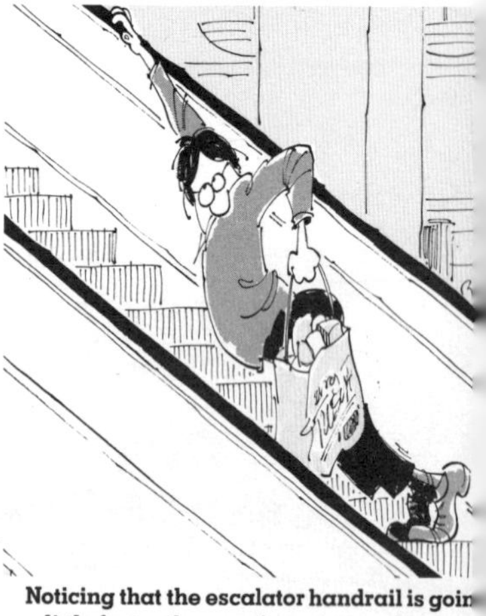

Noticing that the escalator handrail is goin a little faster than you're going on the step

15 units

or going to a hospital. This is a good idea...except that the events meas-
ured are usually big, major stuff! And MAD knows that it's really the little, everyday things that drive people crazy! Which is why it's time for...

RESS CHART

ARTIST: PAUL COKER WRITER: DESMOND DEVLIN

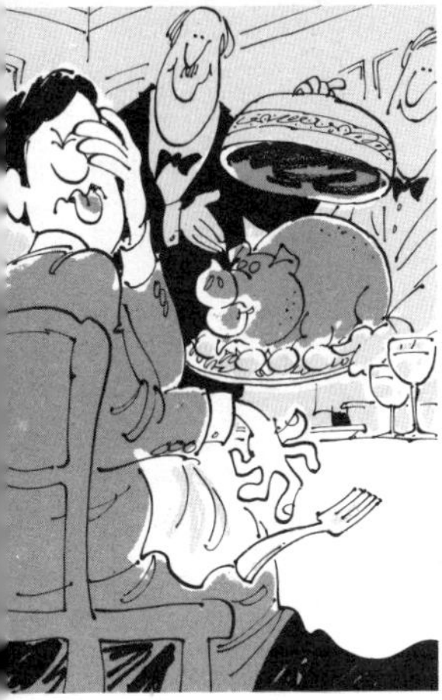

Eating food that looks back at you.

20 units

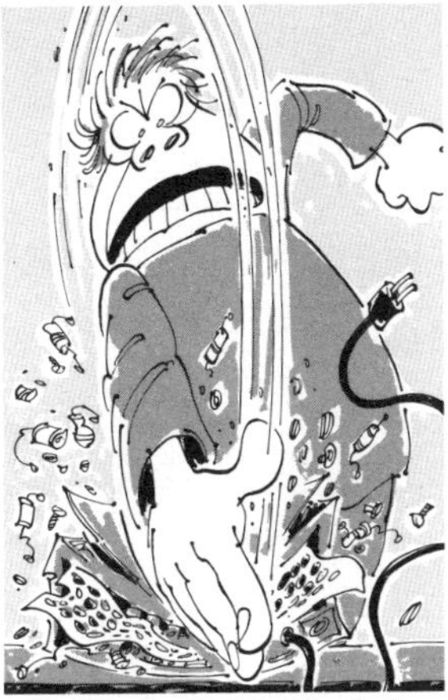

The D.J. who starts talking in the middle of your favorite record.

25 units

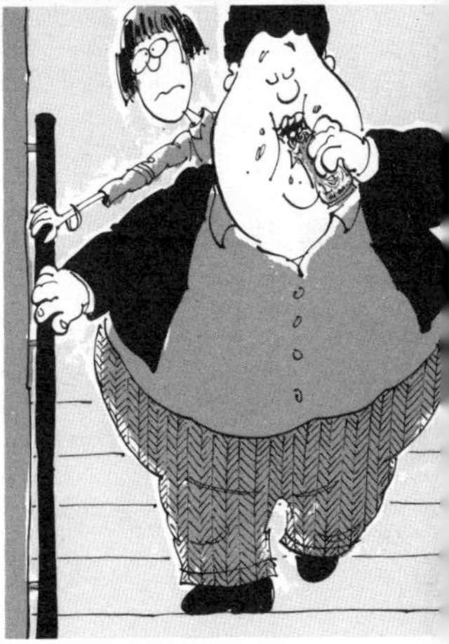

Fat people blocking you on stairways.

30 units

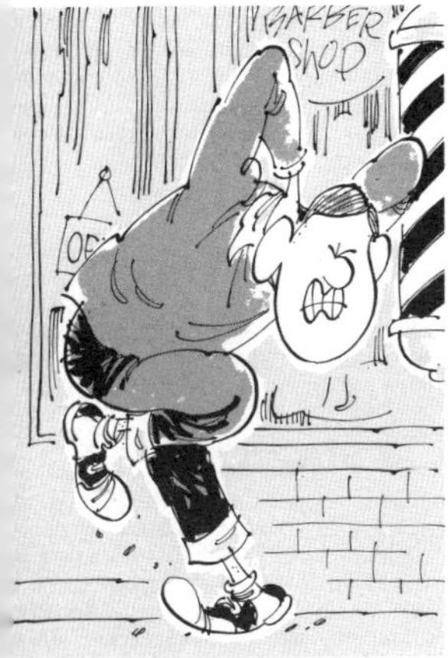
BARBER SHOP

Those irritating little hairs that are inside your shirt after your haircut.

1 unit per hair

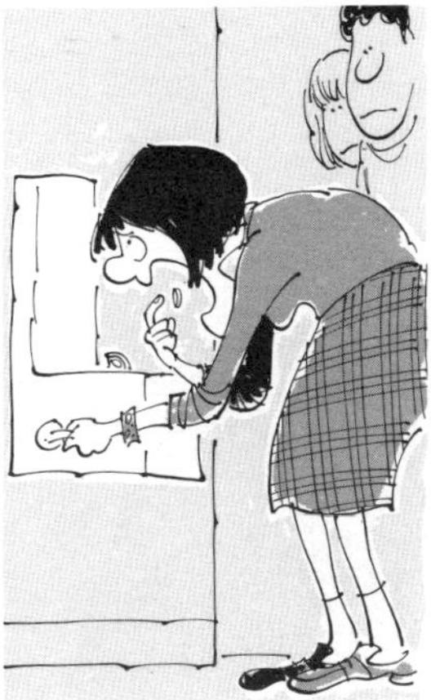

Trying to swallow an aspirin at a public water fountain.

20 units

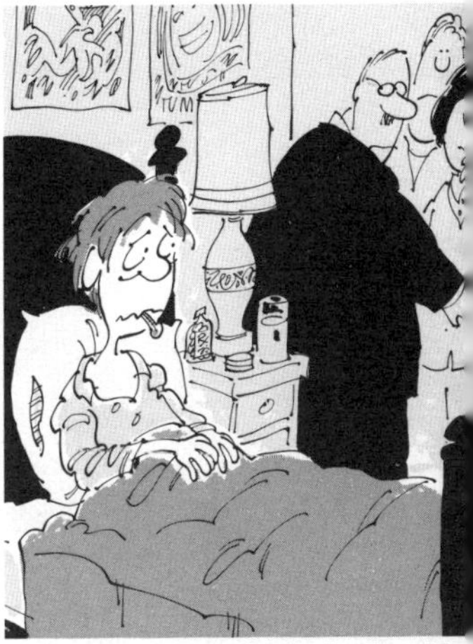

When your doctor takes the family aside.

40 units

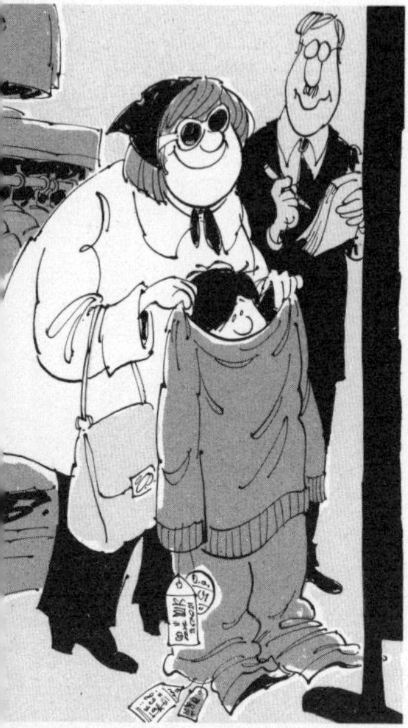

Getting clothes you have to grow into.

25 units

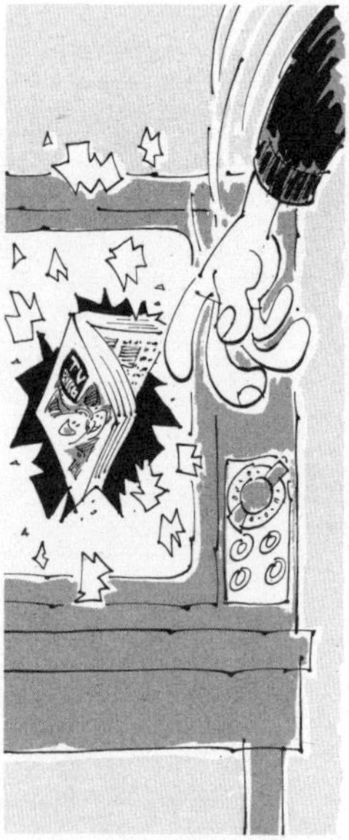

Your "TV Guide" arrives three or four days late.

15 units

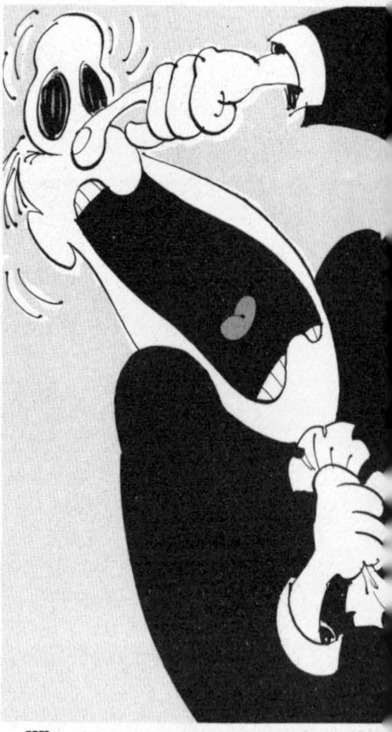

When you start to sneeze, and you don

15 units

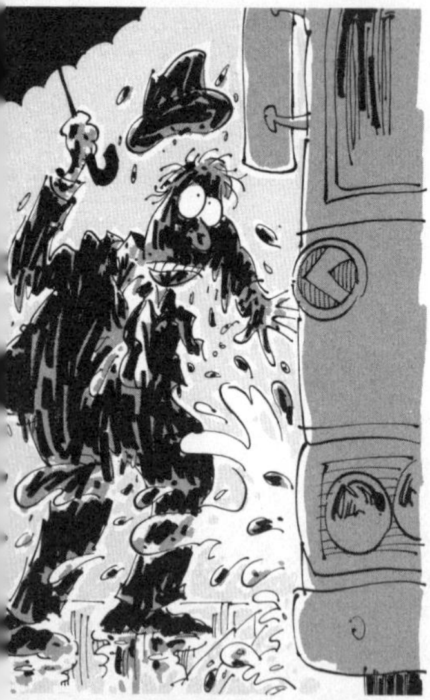

Getting splattered by a speeding bus.

30 units

While wearing a brand new suit.

40 units

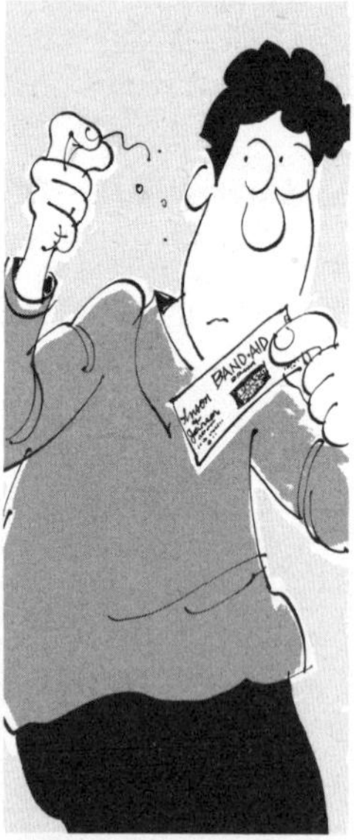
BAND-AID

When the little red string on the Band-Aid breaks.

10 units

SCORING

0-249

You're calmer than a cucumber, and a together as two peas in a pod. In oth er words, you're a vegetable! It would take something like THE DAY AFTER to faze you... maybe! Life doesn't bother you at all, and you don't let little things get to you... and with an atti tude like that, you're probably sicker than anybody else taking this test

149-299

You're the type who tends to get upset easily over certain things... things like gravity, the change of seasons, Tuesday, etc. We suggest that you do not seek employment near small child ren! Or even adults, for that matter!

OVER 300

You're under no more stress than the next guy (providing that the next guy is Charles Manson)! Frankly, you need a lot more help than you're gonna find here for a buck and change! In the meantime, why don't you stop by MAD's office next time you're in town! We're always on the lookout for fresh talent!

JOKE AND DAGGER DEPT.

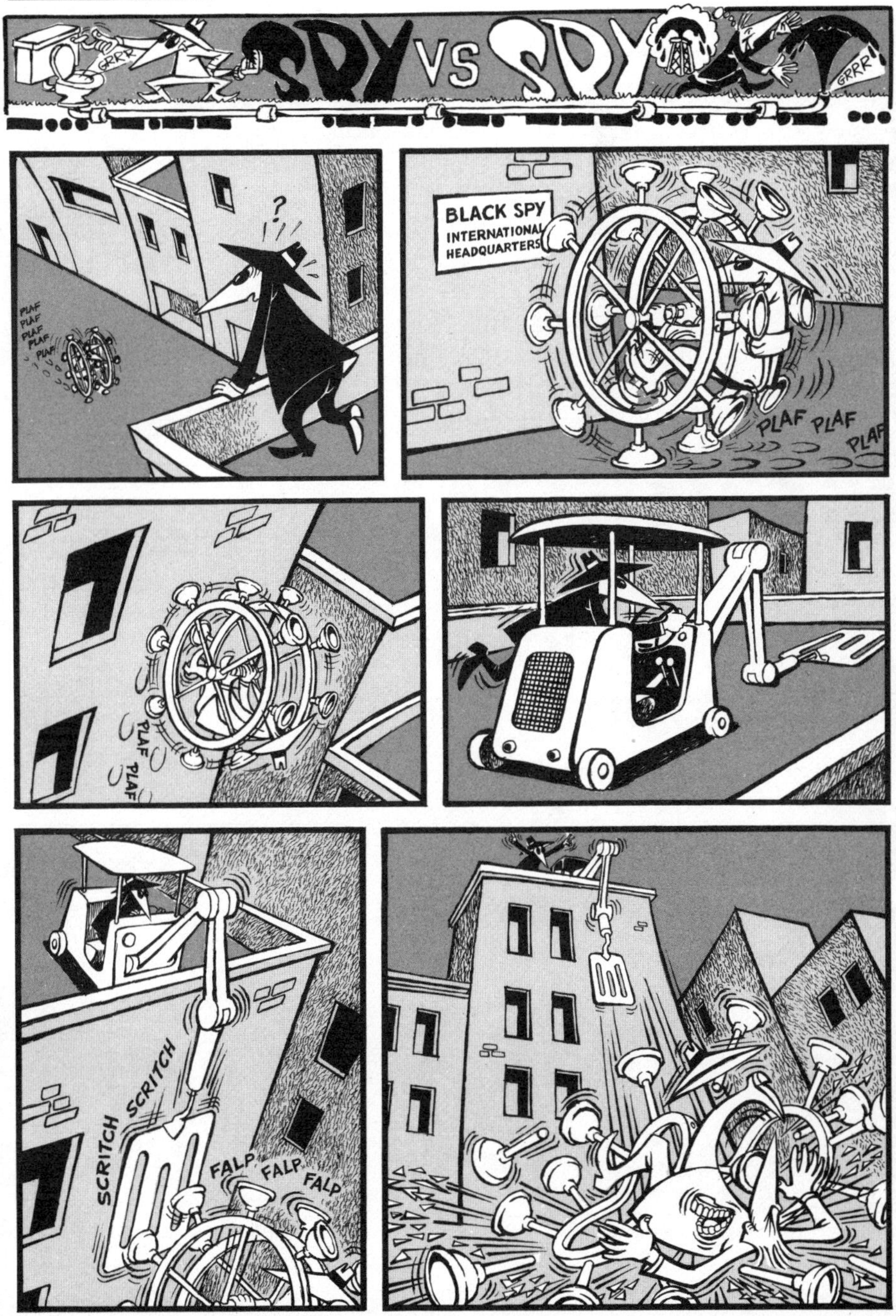
SPY VS SPY
GRRR
GRRR
?
PLAF
PLAF
PLAF
PLAF
PLAF
BLACK SPY
INTERNATIONAL
HEADQUARTERS
PLAF PLAF
PLAF
PLAF
PLAF
SCRITCH
SCRITCH
FALP
FALP
FALP

SOMEDAY SUPPLEMENT DEPT.

The other day, we came upon a small boy sitting on a curb, reading **The New York Times,** and crying. "Why are you crying, little boy?" we asked. "Because," he sobbed, "there ain't no comics in this newspaper!" This started us thinking. Practically everybody loves comics – and yet there are lots of publications that don't run them! How awful! How deplorable! But mainly, how wonderful! Because it gives us this opportunity to fill up four ridiculous pages with these:

COMICS FOR PUBLICATIONS THAT DON'T HAVE COMICS

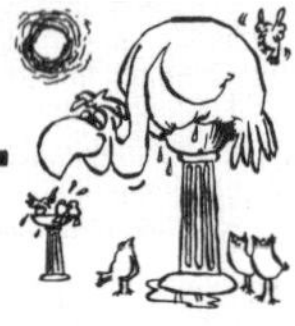

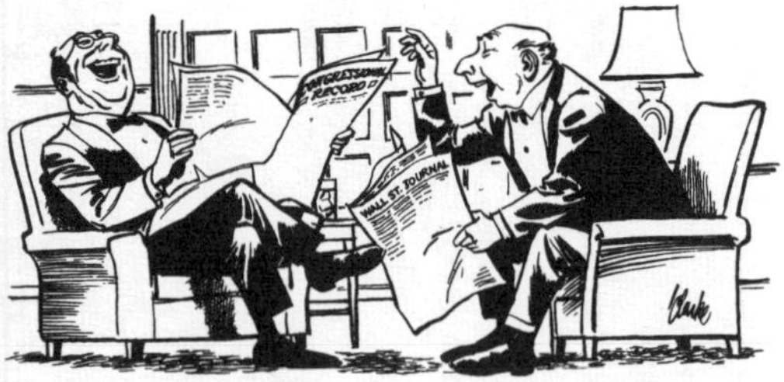
WALL ST. JOURNAL

ARTIST: BOB CLARKE WRITER: FRANK JACOBS

BRAINY

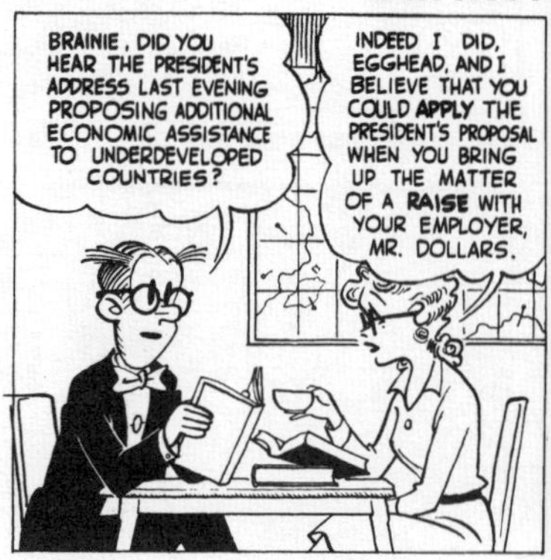
BRAINIE, DID YOU HEAR THE PRESIDENT'S ADDRESS LAST EVENING PROPOSING ADDITIONAL ECONOMIC ASSISTANCE TO UNDERDEVELOPED COUNTRIES?
INDEED I DID, EGGHEAD, AND I BELIEVE THAT YOU COULD **APPLY** THE PRESIDENT'S PROPOSAL WHEN YOU BRING UP THE MATTER OF A **RAISE** WITH YOUR EMPLOYER, MR. DOLLARS.

PITCHOUTS

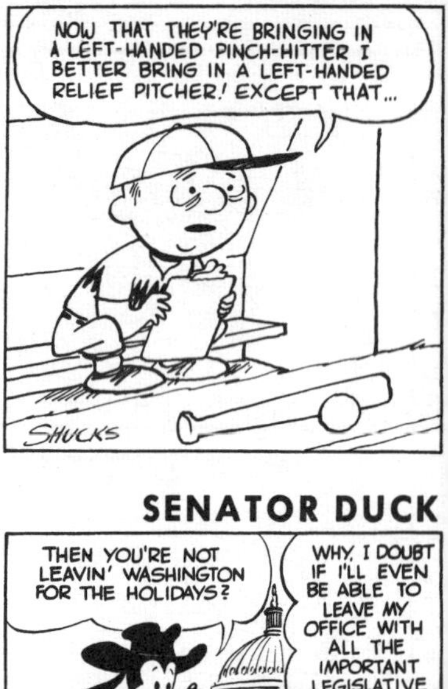
NOW THAT THEY'RE BRINGING IN A LEFT-HANDED PINCH-HITTER I BETTER BRING IN A LEFT-HANDED RELIEF PITCHER! EXCEPT THAT...
SHUCKS

SENATOR DUCK

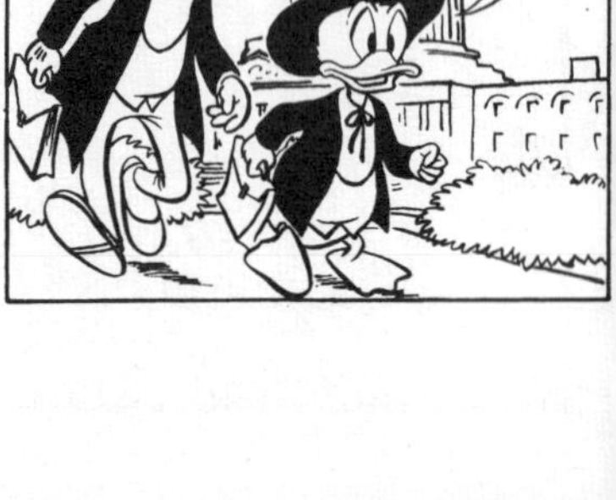
THEN YOU'RE NOT LEAVIN' WASHINGTON FOR THE HOLIDAYS?
WHY, I DOUBT IF I'LL EVEN BE ABLE TO LEAVE MY OFFICE WITH ALL THE IMPORTANT LEGISLATIVE WORK I HAVE TO DO!

—for The New York Times

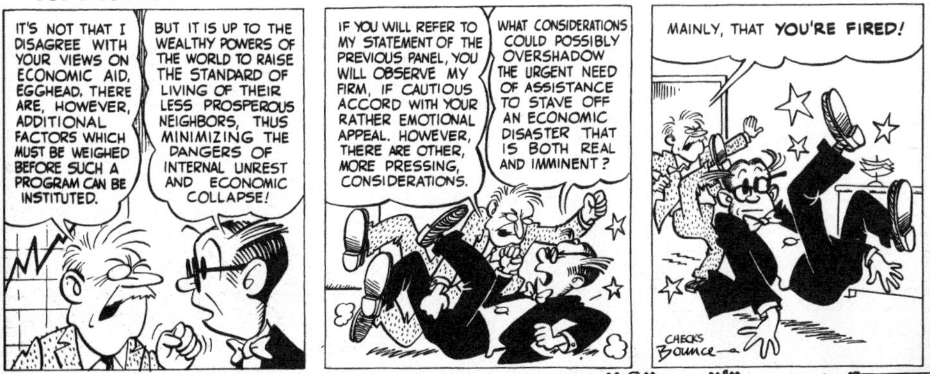
IT'S NOT THAT I DISAGREE WITH YOUR VIEWS ON ECONOMIC AID, EGGHEAD. THERE ARE, HOWEVER, ADDITIONAL FACTORS WHICH MUST BE WEIGHED BEFORE SUCH A PROGRAM CAN BE INSTITUTED.
BUT IT IS UP TO THE WEALTHY POWERS OF THE WORLD TO RAISE THE STANDARD OF LIVING OF THEIR LESS PROSPEROUS NEIGHBORS, THUS MINIMIZING THE DANGERS OF INTERNAL UNREST AND ECONOMIC COLLAPSE!
IF YOU WILL REFER TO MY STATEMENT OF THE PREVIOUS PANEL, YOU WILL OBSERVE MY FIRM, IF CAUTIOUS ACCORD WITH YOUR RATHER EMOTIONAL APPEAL. HOWEVER, THERE ARE OTHER, MORE PRESSING, CONSIDERATIONS.
WHAT CONSIDERATIONS COULD POSSIBLY OVERSHADOW THE URGENT NEED OF ASSISTANCE TO STAVE OFF AN ECONOMIC DISASTER THAT IS BOTH REAL AND IMMINENT?
MAINLY, THAT YOU'RE FIRED!
CHECKS Bounce

—for The Sporting News

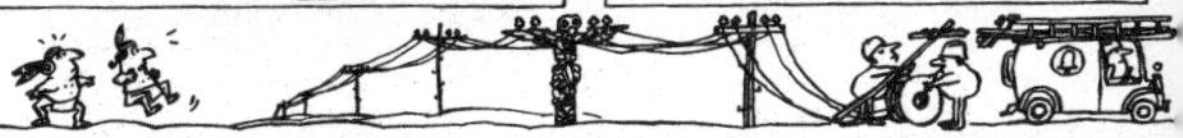

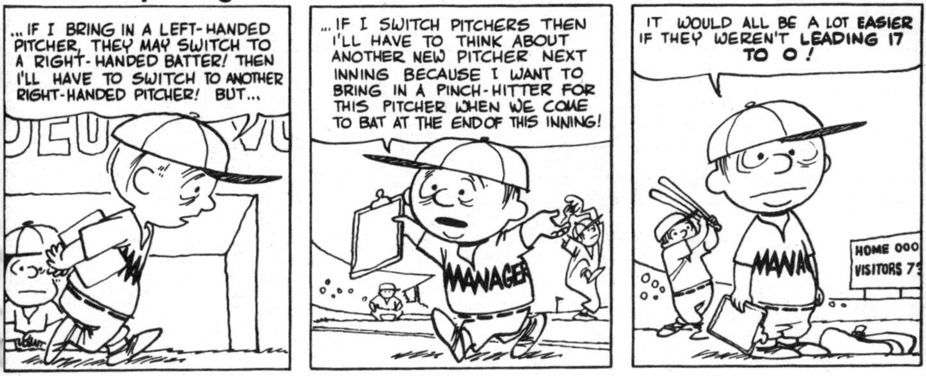
...IF I BRING IN A LEFT-HANDED PITCHER, THEY MAY SWITCH TO A RIGHT-HANDED BATTER! THEN I'LL HAVE TO SWITCH TO ANOTHER RIGHT-HANDED PITCHER! BUT...
...IF I SWITCH PITCHERS THEN I'LL HAVE TO THINK ABOUT ANOTHER NEW PITCHER NEXT INNING BECAUSE I WANT TO BRING IN A PINCH-HITTER FOR THIS PITCHER WHEN WE COME TO BAT AT THE END OF THIS INNING!
MANAGER
IT WOULD ALL BE A LOT EASIER IF THEY WEREN'T LEADING 17 TO 0!
HOME 000

—for The Congressional Record

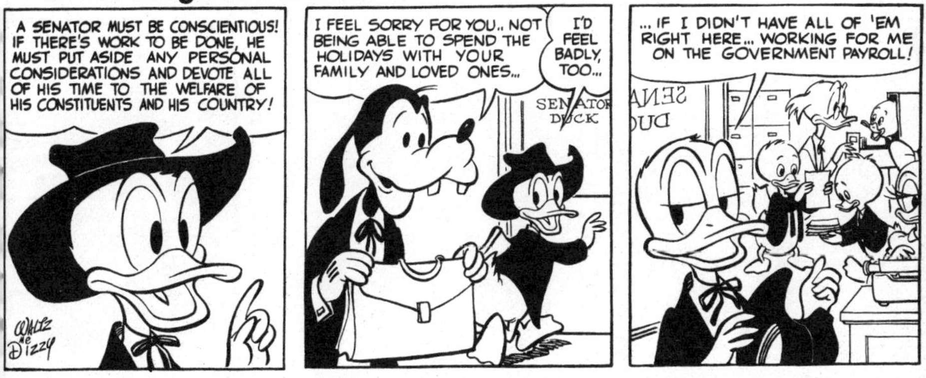
A SENATOR MUST BE CONSCIENTIOUS! IF THERE'S WORK TO BE DONE, HE MUST PUT ASIDE ANY PERSONAL CONSIDERATIONS AND DEVOTE ALL OF HIS TIME TO THE WELFARE OF HIS CONSTITUENTS AND HIS COUNTRY!
I FEEL SORRY FOR YOU.. NOT BEING ABLE TO SPEND THE HOLIDAYS WITH YOUR FAMILY AND LOVED ONES...
I'D FEEL BADLY, TOO...
SENATOR DUCK
...IF I DIDN'T HAVE ALL OF 'EM RIGHT HERE... WORKING FOR ME ON THE GOVERNMENT PAYROLL!

DADDY-O — for Variety

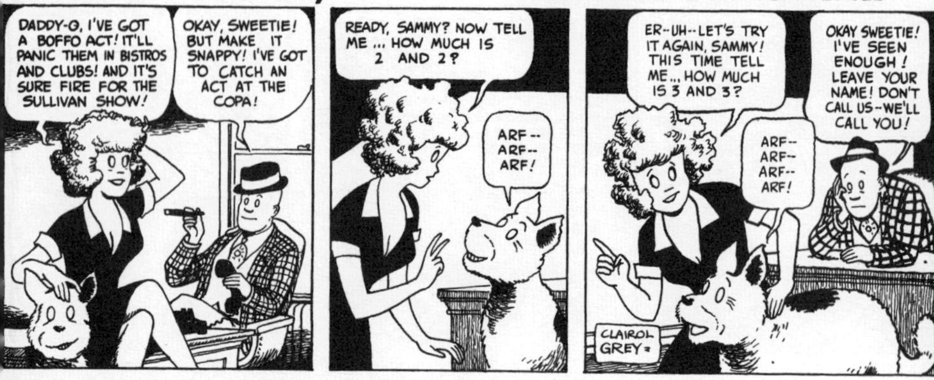

DADDY-O, I'VE GOT A BOFFO ACT! IT'LL PANIC THEM IN BISTROS AND CLUBS! AND IT'S SURE FIRE FOR THE SULLIVAN SHOW!
OKAY, SWEETIE! BUT MAKE IT SNAPPY! I'VE GOT TO CATCH AN ACT AT THE COPA!
READY, SAMMY? NOW TELL ME ... HOW MUCH IS 2 AND 2?
ARF -- ARF -- ARF!
ER--UH--LET'S TRY IT AGAIN, SAMMY! THIS TIME TELL ME... HOW MUCH IS 3 AND 3?
ARF-- ARF-- ARF-- ARF!
OKAY SWEETIE! I'VE SEEN ENOUGH! LEAVE YOUR NAME! DON'T CALL US--WE'LL CALL YOU!
CLAIROL GREY

HY FASHION — for Women's Wear Daily

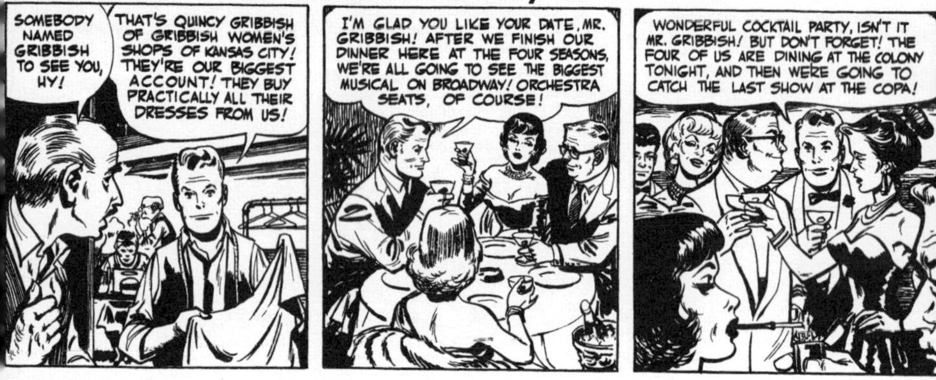

SOMEBODY NAMED GRIBBISH TO SEE YOU, HY!
THAT'S QUINCY GRIBBISH OF GRIBBISH WOMEN'S SHOPS OF KANSAS CITY! THEY'RE OUR BIGGEST ACCOUNT! THEY BUY PRACTICALLY ALL THEIR DRESSES FROM US!
I'M GLAD YOU LIKE YOUR DATE, MR. GRIBBISH! AFTER WE FINISH OUR DINNER HERE AT THE FOUR SEASONS, WE'RE ALL GOING TO SEE THE BIGGEST MUSICAL ON BROADWAY! ORCHESTRA SEATS, OF COURSE!
WONDERFUL COCKTAIL PARTY, ISN'T IT MR. GRIBBISH! BUT DON'T FORGET! THE FOUR OF US ARE DINING AT THE COLONY TONIGHT, AND THEN WE'RE GOING TO CATCH THE LAST SHOW AT THE COPA!

GEN. ABERCROMBIE — for The Army Times

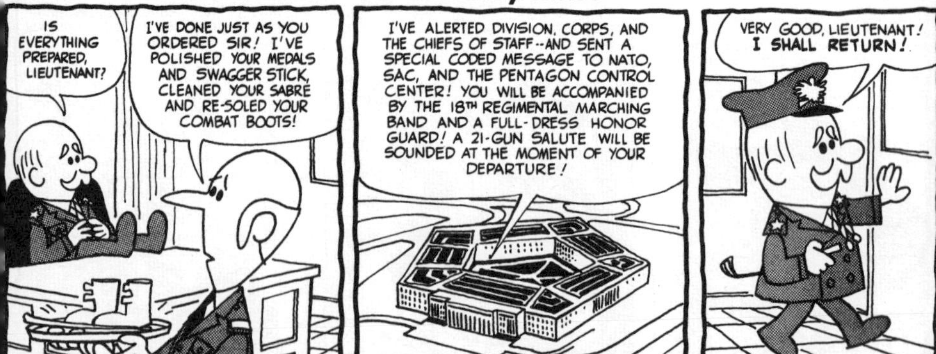

IS EVERYTHING PREPARED, LIEUTENANT?
I'VE DONE JUST AS YOU ORDERED SIR! I'VE POLISHED YOUR MEDALS AND SWAGGER STICK, CLEANED YOUR SABRE AND RE-SOLED YOUR COMBAT BOOTS!
I'VE ALERTED DIVISION, CORPS, AND THE CHIEFS OF STAFF--AND SENT A SPECIAL CODED MESSAGE TO NATO, SAC, AND THE PENTAGON CONTROL CENTER! YOU WILL BE ACCOMPANIED BY THE 18TH REGIMENTAL MARCHING BAND AND A FULL-DRESS HONOR GUARD! A 21-GUN SALUTE WILL BE SOUNDED AT THE MOMENT OF YOUR DEPARTURE!
VERY GOOD, LIEUTENANT! I SHALL RETURN!

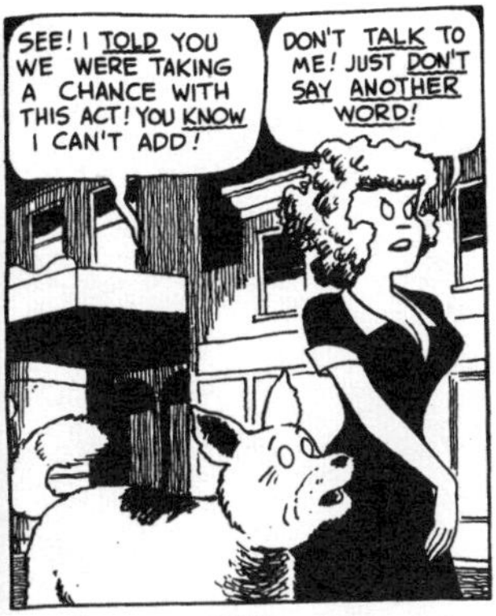
SEE! I TOLD YOU WE WERE TAKING A CHANCE WITH THIS ACT! YOU KNOW I CAN'T ADD!
DON'T TALK TO ME! JUST DON'T SAY ANOTHER WORD!

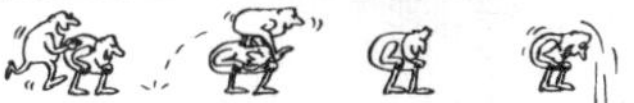

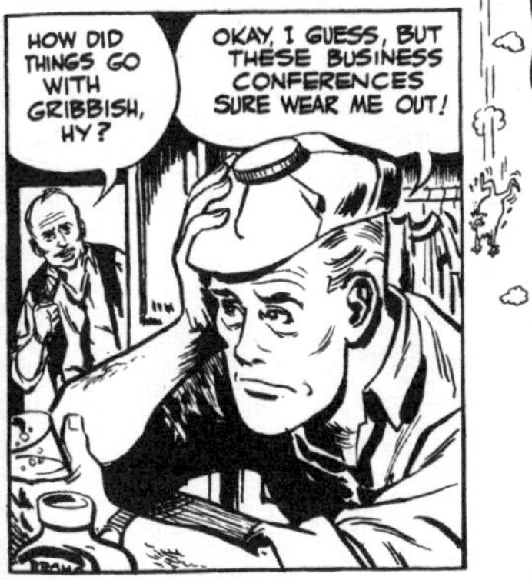
HOW DID THINGS GO WITH GRIBBISH, HY?
OKAY, I GUESS, BUT THESE BUSINESS CONFERENCES SURE WEAR ME OUT!

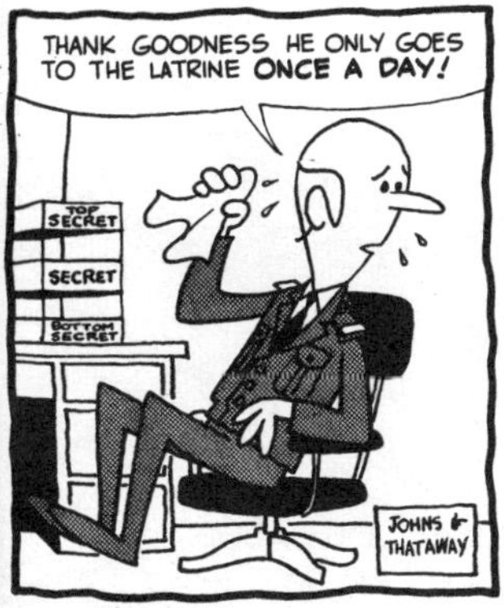
THANK GOODNESS HE ONLY GOES TO THE LATRINE ONCE A DAY!
TOP SECRET
SECRET
BOTTOM SECRET
JOHNS & THATAWAY

TY COON—for The Wall Street Journal

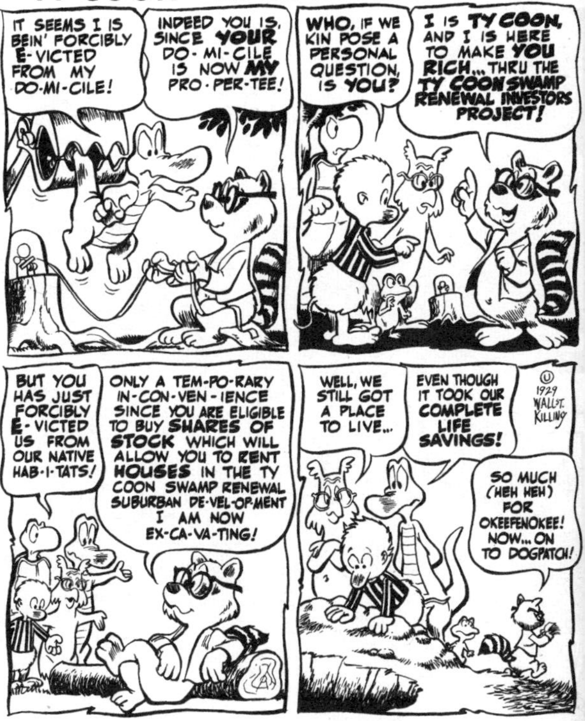
IT SEEMS I IS BEIN' FORCIBLY E-VICTED FROM MY DO-MI-CILE!
INDEED YOU IS, SINCE YOUR DO-MI-CILE IS NOW MY PRO-PER-TEE!
WHO, IF WE KIN POSE A PERSONAL QUESTION, IS YOU?
I IS TY COON, AND I IS HERE TO MAKE YOU RICH... THRU THE TY COON SWAMP RENEWAL INVESTORS PROJECT!
BUT YOU HAS JUST FORCIBLY E-VICTED US FROM OUR NATIVE HAB-I-TATS!
ONLY A TEM-PO-RARY IN-CON-VEN-IENCE SINCE YOU ARE ELIGIBLE TO BUY SHARES OF STOCK WHICH WILL ALLOW YOU TO RENT HOUSES IN THE TY COON SWAMP RENEWAL SUBURBAN DE-VEL-OP-MENT I AM NOW EX-CA-VA-TING!
WELL, WE STILL GOT A PLACE TO LIVE...
EVEN THOUGH IT TOOK OUR COMPLETE LIFE SAVINGS!
SO MUCH (HEH HEH) FOR OKEEFENOKEE! NOW... ON TO DOGPATCH!

COOKIE THE BOOKIE —for The Morning Telegraph

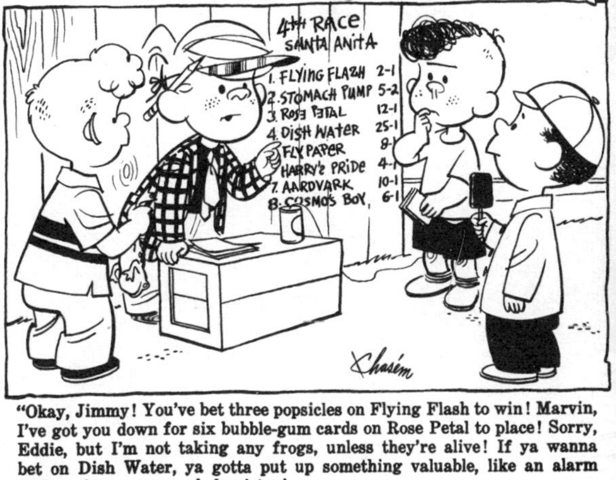
4th RACE SANTA ANITA
1. FLYING FLASH 2-1
2. STOMACH PUMP 5-2
3. ROSE PETAL 12-1
4. DISH WATER 25-1
FLY PAPER 8-1
HARRY'S PRIDE 4-1
7. AARDVARK 10-1
8. COSMO'S BOY 6-1
Chasém

"Okay, Jimmy! You've bet three popsicles on Flying Flash to win! Marvin, I've got you down for six bubble-gum cards on Rose Petal to place! Sorry, Eddie, but I'm not taking any frogs, unless they're alive! If ya wanna bet on Dish Water, ya gotta put up something valuable, like an alarm clock spring . . . or your baby sister!

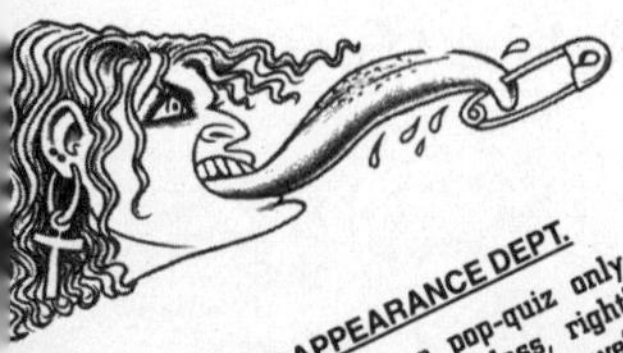

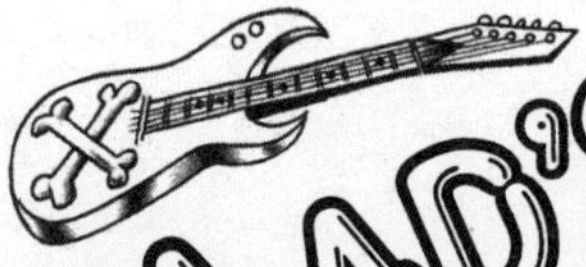

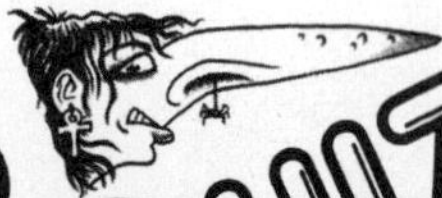

SPECIAL TEST APPEARANCE DEPT.

Surprise! You thought a pop-quiz only happens to you in history class, right? Wrong! It can happen any place! But we're not going to test you on history—it's boring and besides, we know nothing about it ourselves! This quiz is about things they don't teach you in school, but you should know anyway. No, it's not how to pass a roadside sobriety test, it's...

MAD'S HEAVY METAL QUIZ

ARTIST: RICK TULKA WRITER: CHRIS HART

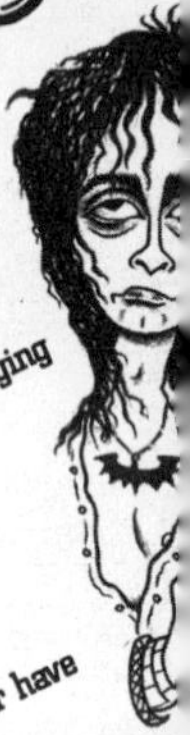

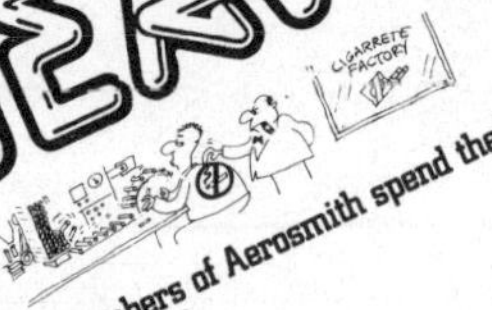
CIGARRETE FACTORY

1. How do the members of Aerosmith spend their time off?

A) Removing their mascara
B) In the Betty Ford Center
C) Helping the deaf to recover from their concerts

2. Heavy Metal singers grab their groins a lot when singing because:

A) Tight leather pants rarely have pockets
B) They need to remember what they're singing about
C) Crab lice itches

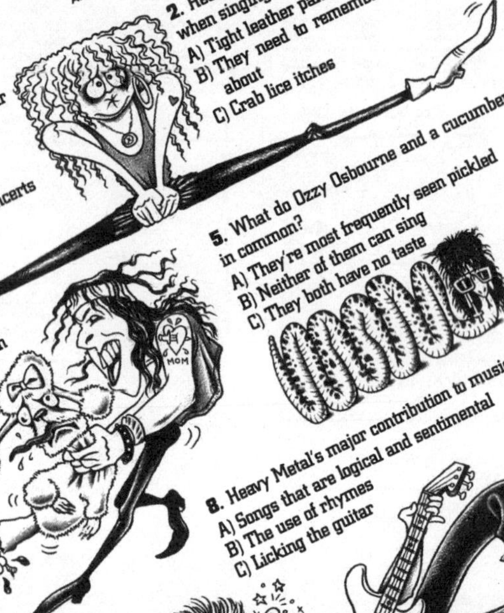
MOM

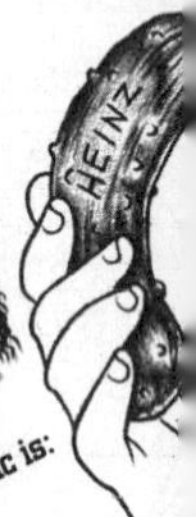
HEINZ

5. What do Ozzy Osbourne and a cucumber have in common?

A) They're most frequently seen pickled
B) Neither of them can sing
C) They both have no taste

4. Complete this Heavy Metal lyric: "I love you with all my heart __________."

A) "But this song won't make the chart"
B) "Tho' my hair will never part"
C) "Kill your dog for Satan"

8. Heavy Metal's major contribution to music is:

A) Songs that are logical and sentimental
B) The use of rhymes
C) Licking the guitar

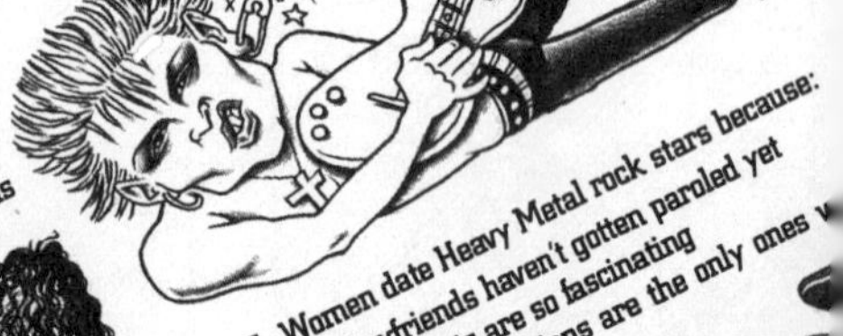

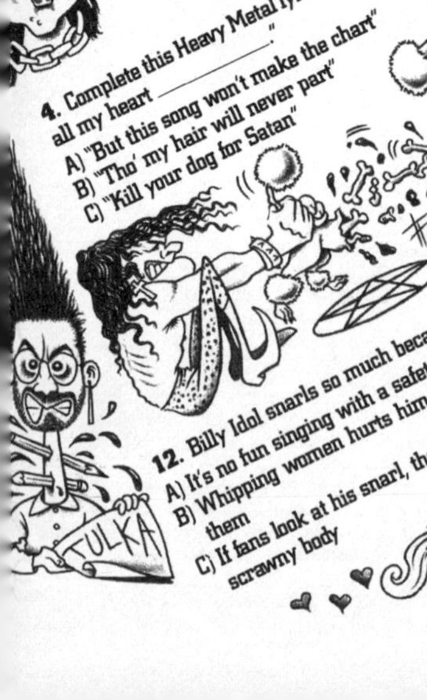
TULKA

12. Billy Idol snarls so much because:

A) It's no fun singing with a safety pin in your ear
B) Whipping women hurts him more than it does them
C) If fans look at his snarl, they might overlook his scrawny body

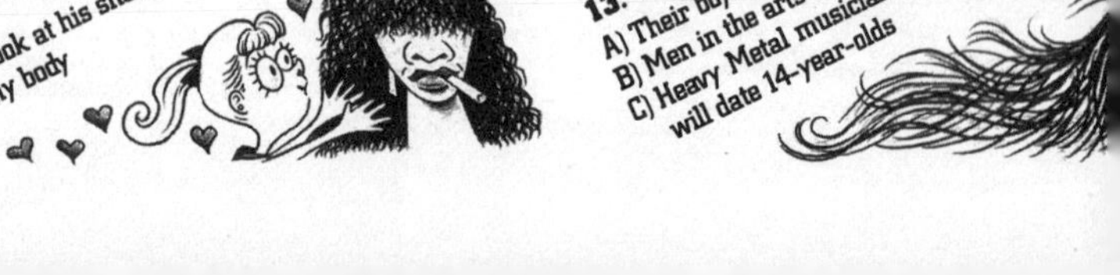

13. Women date Heavy Metal rock stars because:

A) Their boyfriends haven't gotten paroled yet
B) Men in the arts are so fascinating
C) Heavy Metal musicians are the only ones w will date 14-year-olds

3. Organizations that try to censor Heavy Metal lyrics believe that the First Amendment is:
A) Only applicable to people who agree with them
B) An oversight the Founding Fathers made
C) Only a theory, just like evolution

7. Oil is to water the way:
A) Yuppies are to cuisinarts
B) Sugar is to kids' cereals
C) Frank Zappa is to Tipper Gore

6. Heavy Metal stars who do anti-drug commercials are:
A) Pissed at their dealers
B) Starved for T.V. exposure
C) Bigger liars then Joe Isuzu

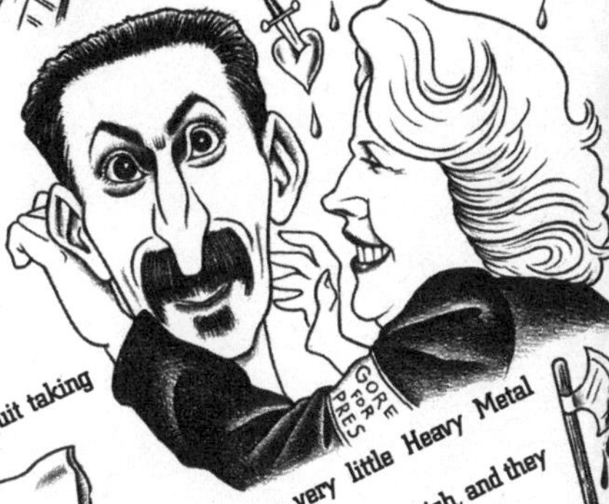
GORE FOR PRES

9. Most parents think that Heavy Metal is:
A) Something to do with uranium
B) Fun for the entire family
C) What good kids will turn to if they quit taking piano lessons

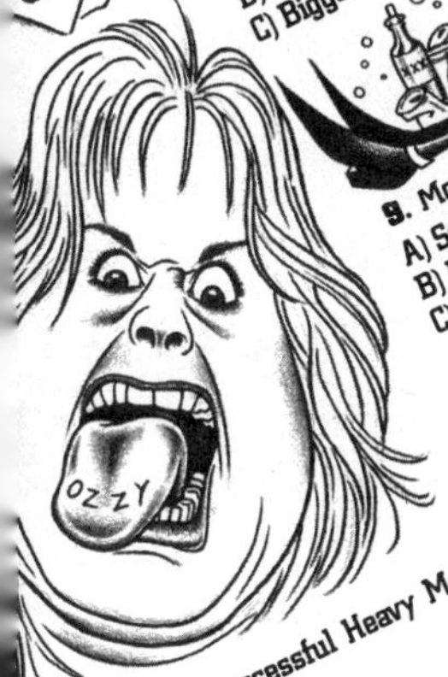
OZZY

11. Radio stations play very little Heavy Metal music because:
A) Most heavy metal listeners are Amish, and they shun radio
B) Their regular listeners would mistake it for static
C) Even disk jockeys have some standards

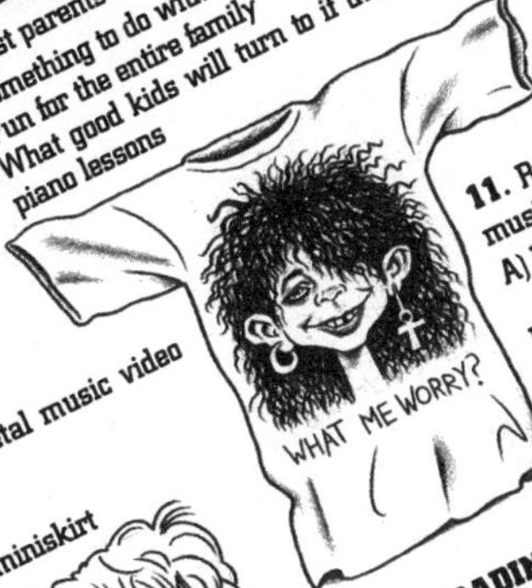
WHAT ME WORRY?

10. Every successful Heavy Metal music video requires:
A) An educational theme
B) A blond babe in a leopard miniskirt
C) A large booze budget

GRADING THIS QUIZ

For questions 1–5 give yourself one point for every "A" answer, two points for every "B" answer, and three points for every "C" answer. For questions 6–10 (except numbers 7, 8, and 9), give yourself one point for every "A" answer, one point for every "B" answer and one point for every "C" answer. For all other questions, give yourself five points for every "A" answer, and deduct five for every "B" or "C" answer. Deduct an additional ten points if, after having read this, you weren't smart enough to change all your "B" and "C" answers to "A"!

14. Heavy Metal album covers never stoop to portraying:
A) Nuns in bondage
B) Men dressed in women's clothing
C) Anything wholesome

INTERPRETING YOUR SCORE:

If you actually took the time to take this little test (let alone figure out your score), congratulations! No matter what you scored, it's obvious you have the kind of mind Heavy Metal music appeals to!

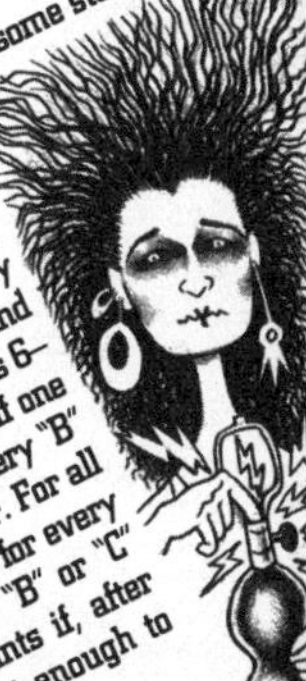
SPIRIN

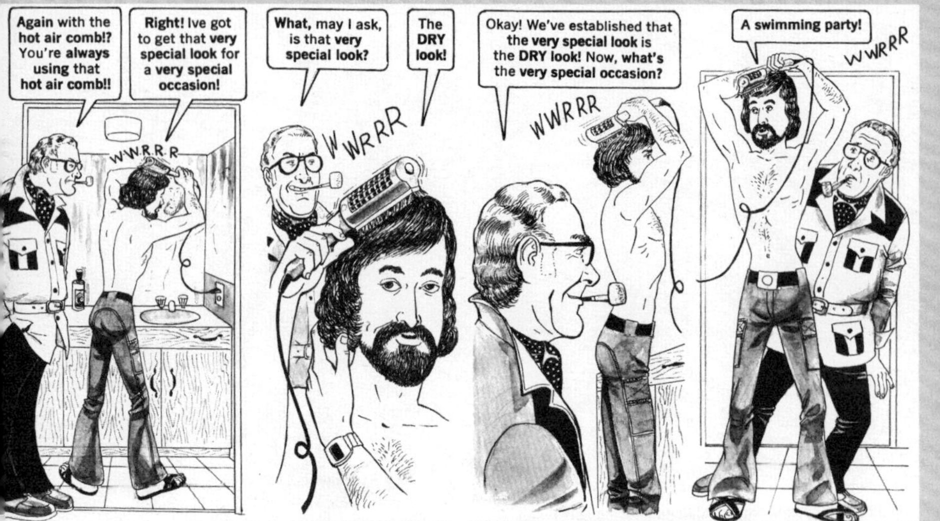

Again with the hot air comb!? You're always using that hot air comb!!
Right! Ive got to get that very special look for a very special occasion!
WWRRR
What, may I ask, is that very special look?
WWRRR
The DRY look!
Okay! We've established that the very special look is the DRY look! Now, what's the very special occasion?
WWRRR
A swimming party!
WWRRR

BERG'S-EYE VIEW DEPT.

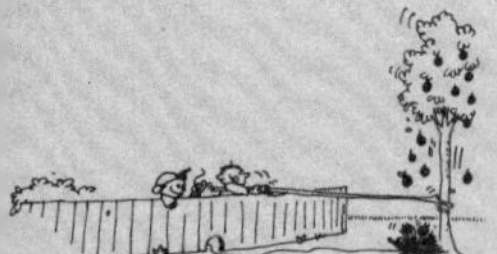

THE LIGHTER SIDE OF...

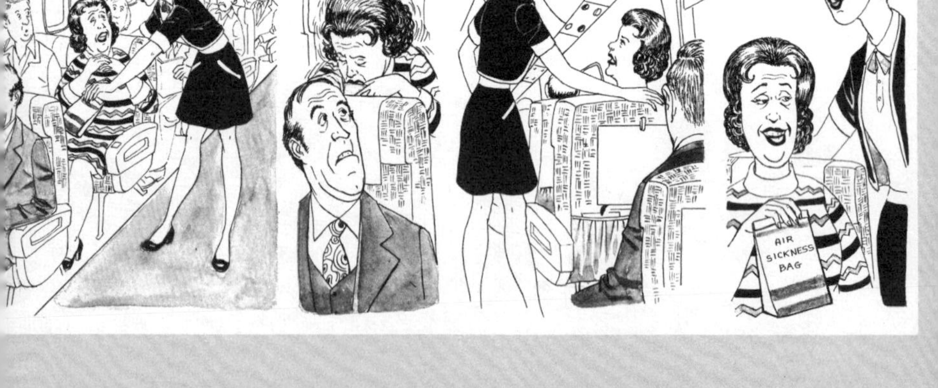

Er . . . oh, Stewardess! I . . . I feel just miserable!
It's probably a touch of air sickness! That's why we have these paper bags! Just put what's bothering you in there!
How do you feel now . . . ?
A little better! I took your advice and put what was bothering me into the paper bag!
My return flight ticket!
AIR SICKNESS BAG

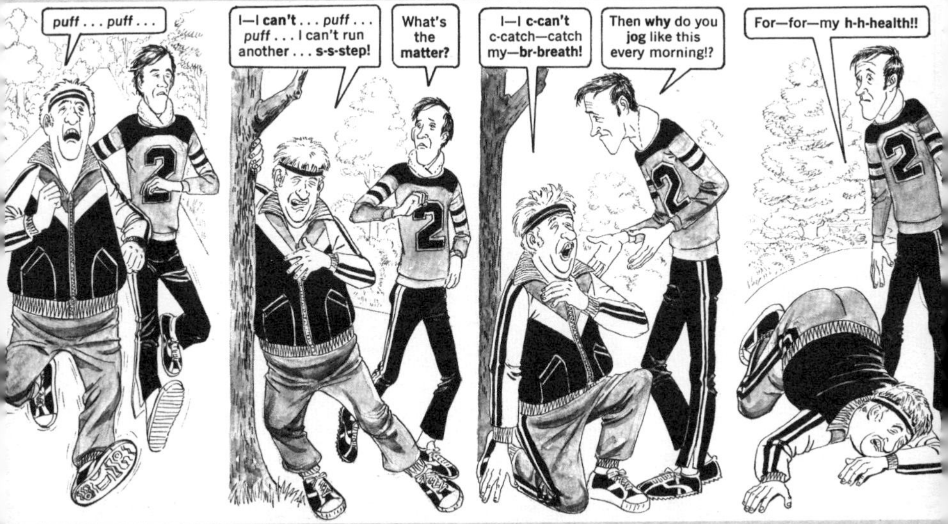
puff . . . puff . . .
I—I can't . . . puff . . . puff . . . I can't run another . . . s-s-step!
What's the matter?
I—I c-can't c-catch—catch my—br-breath!
Then why do you jog like this every morning!?
For—for—my h-h-health!!

AIR AIR AIR

ARTIST & WRITER: DAVE BERG

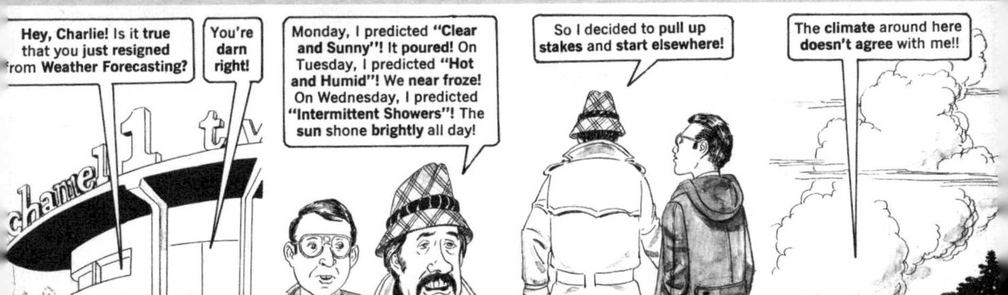
Hey, Charlie! Is it true that you just resigned from Weather Forecasting?
You're darn right!
Monday, I predicted "Clear and Sunny"! It poured! On Tuesday, I predicted "Hot and Humid"! We near froze! On Wednesday, I predicted "Intermittent Showers"! The sun shone brightly all day!
So I decided to pull up stakes and start elsewhere!
The climate around here doesn't agree with me!!
channel 1 t.v

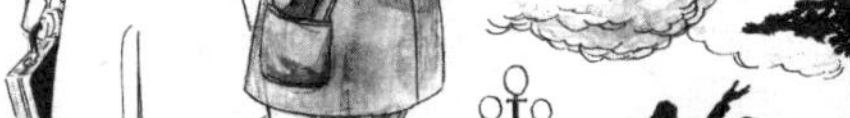

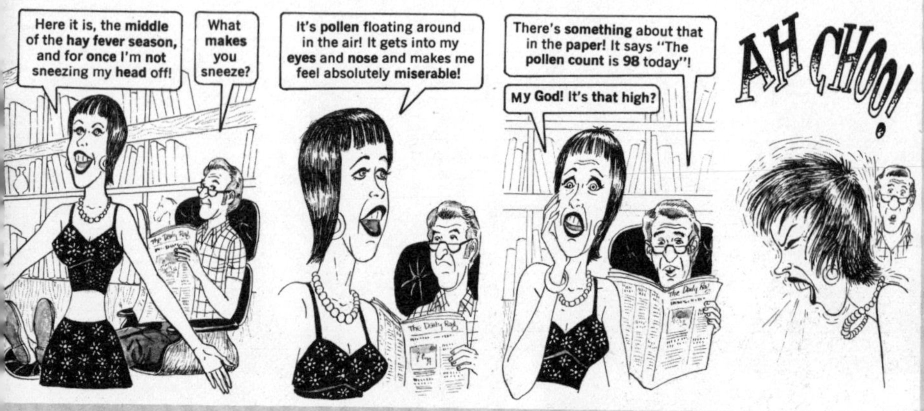
Here it is, the middle of the hay fever season, and for once I'm not sneezing my head off!
What makes you sneeze?
It's pollen floating around in the air! It gets into my eyes and nose and makes me feel absolutely miserable!
There's something about that in the paper! It says "The pollen count is 98 today"!
My God! It's that high?
AH CHOO!

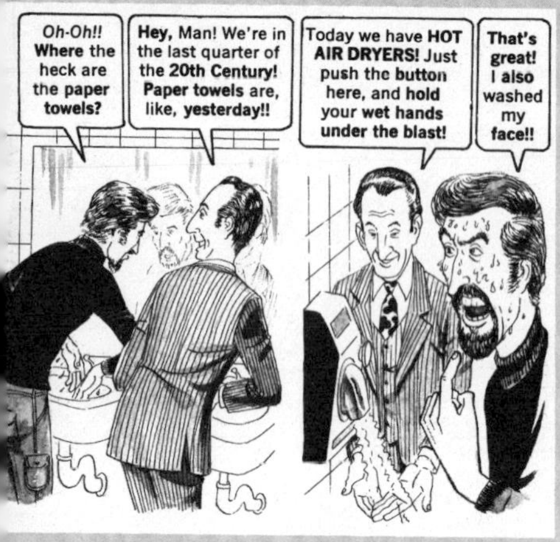
Oh-Oh!! Where the heck are the paper towels?
Hey, Man! We're in the last quarter of the 20th Century! Paper towels are, like, yesterday!!
Today we have HOT AIR DRYERS! Just push the button here, and hold your wet hands under the blast!
That's great! I also washed my face!!

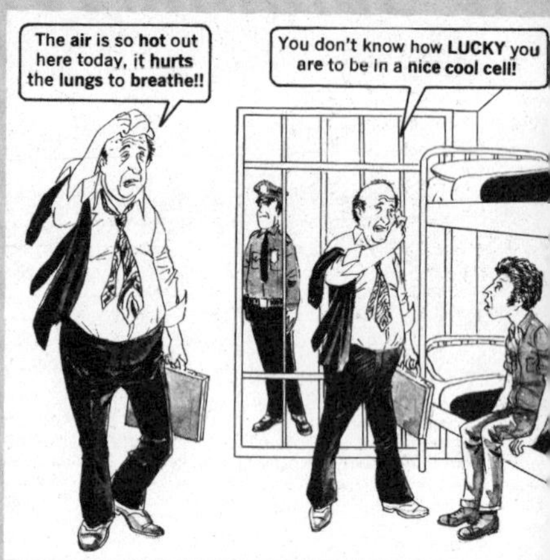
The air is so hot out here today, it hurts the lungs to breathe!!
You don't know how LUCKY you are to be in a nice cool cell!

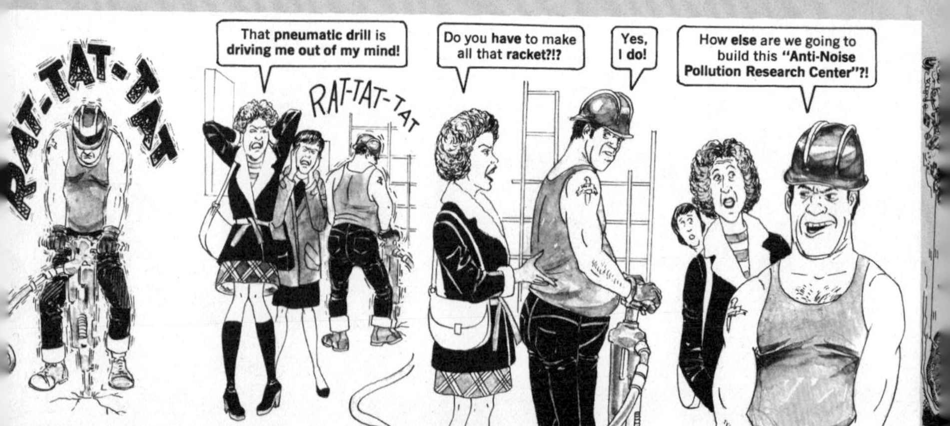
RAT-TAT-TAT
That pneumatic drill is driving me out of my mind!
RAT-TAT-TAT
Do you have to make all that racket?!?
Yes, I do!
How else are we going to build this "Anti-Noise Pollution Research Center"?!

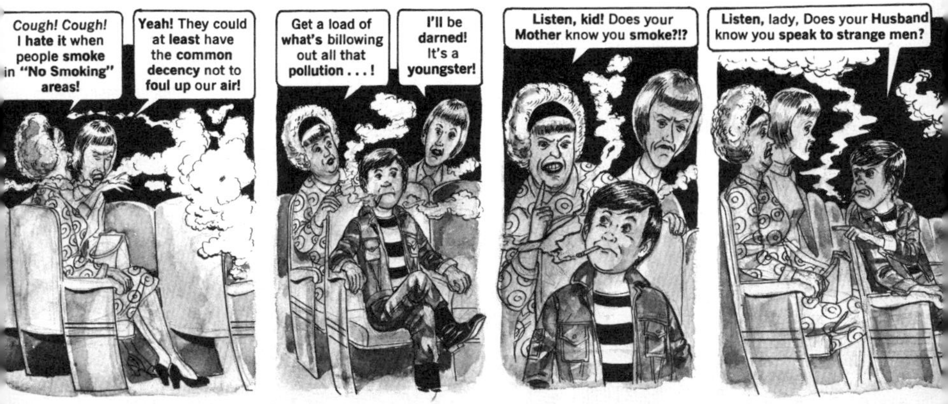
Cough! Cough! I hate it when people smoke in "No Smoking" areas!
Yeah! They could at least have the common decency not to foul up our air!
Get a load of what's billowing out all that pollution . . . !
I'll be darned! It's a youngster!
Listen, kid! Does your Mother know you smoke?!?
Listen, lady, Does your Husband know you speak to strange men?

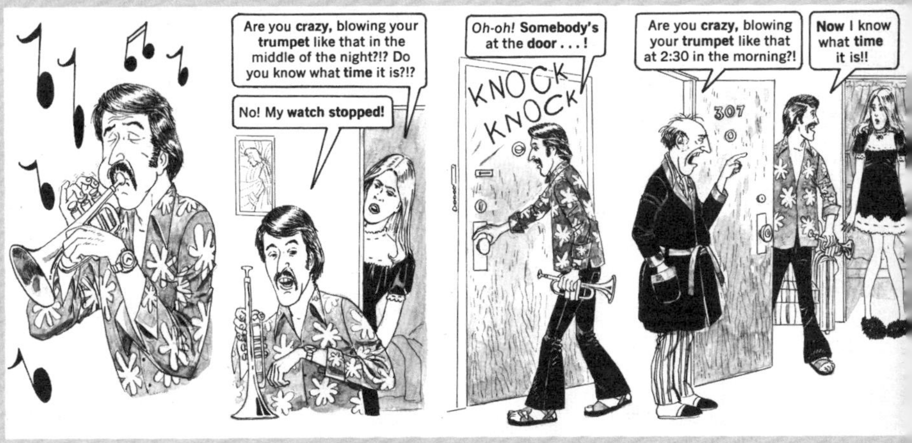
Are you crazy, blowing your trumpet like that in the middle of the night?!? Do you know what time it is?!?
No! My watch stopped!
Oh-oh! Somebody's at the door . . . !
KNOCK KNOCK
Are you crazy, blowing your trumpet like that at 2:30 in the morning?!
307
Now I know what time it is!!

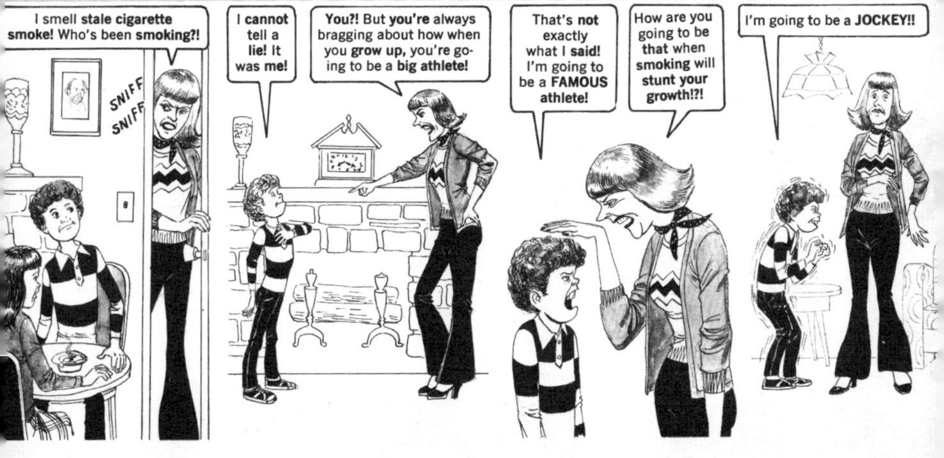
I smell stale cigarette smoke! Who's been smoking?!
SNIFF SNIFF
I cannot tell a lie! It was me!
You?! But you're always bragging about how when you grow up, you're going to be a big athlete!
That's not exactly what I said! I'm going to be a FAMOUS athlete!
How are you going to be that when smoking will stunt your growth!?!
I'm going to be a JOCKEY!!

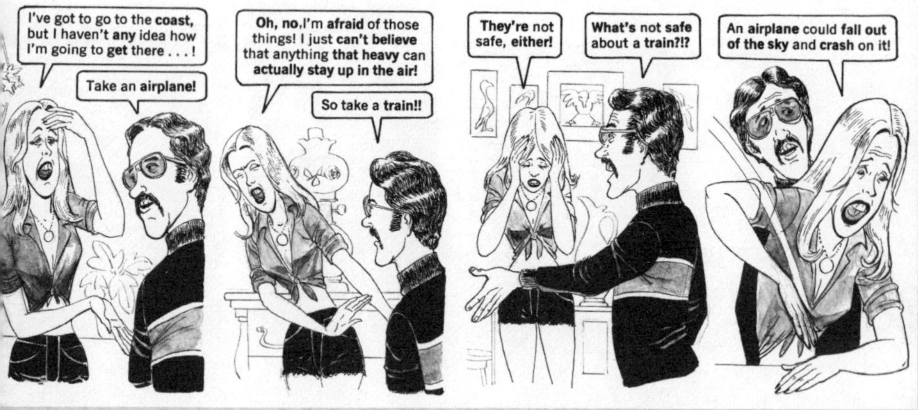
I've got to go to the coast, but I haven't any idea how I'm going to get there . . . !
Take an airplane!
Oh, no, I'm afraid of those things! I just can't believe that anything that heavy can actually stay up in the air!
So take a train!!
They're not safe, either!
What's not safe about a train?!?
An airplane could fall out of the sky and crash on it!

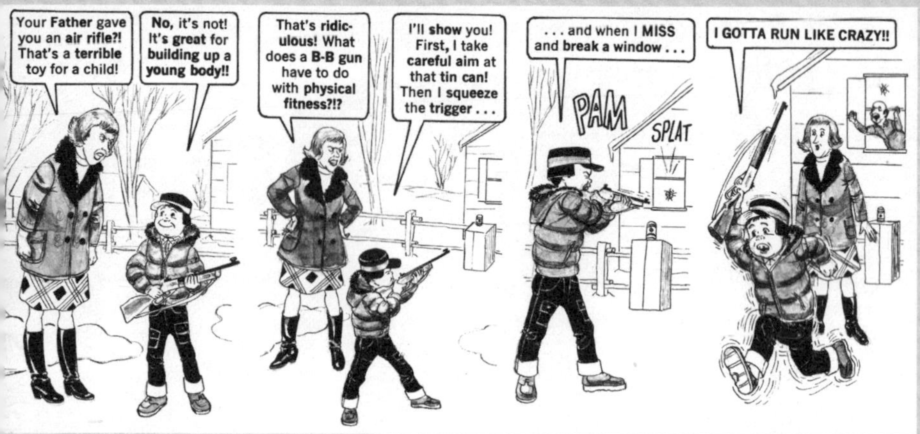
Your Father gave you an air rifle?! That's a terrible toy for a child!
No, it's not! It's great for building up a young body!!
That's ridic-ulous! What does a B-B gun have to do with physical fitness?!?
I'll show you! First, I take careful aim at that tin can! Then I squeeze the trigger . . .
. . . and when I MISS and break a window . . .
PAM
SPLAT
I GOTTA RUN LIKE CRAZY!!

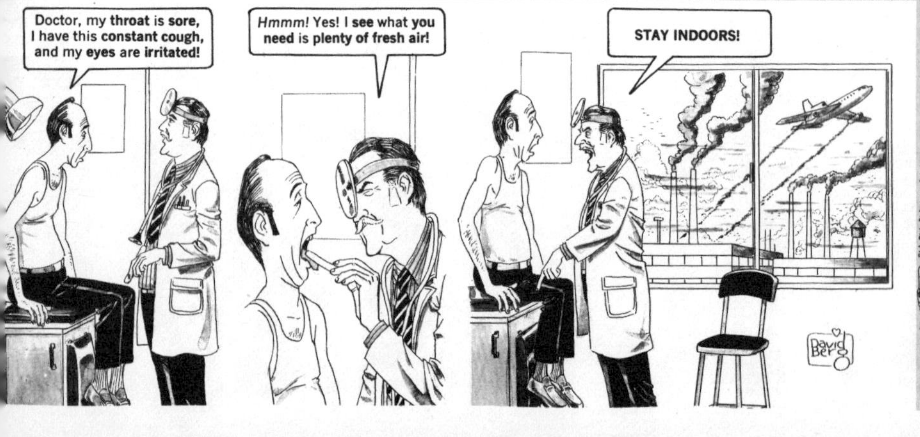
Doctor, my throat is sore, I have this constant cough, and my eyes are irritated!
Hmmm! Yes! I see what you need is plenty of fresh air!
STAY INDOORS!
David Berg

DAILY BREAD DEPT.

A PSALM FOR THE MODERN TELEVISION PREACHER

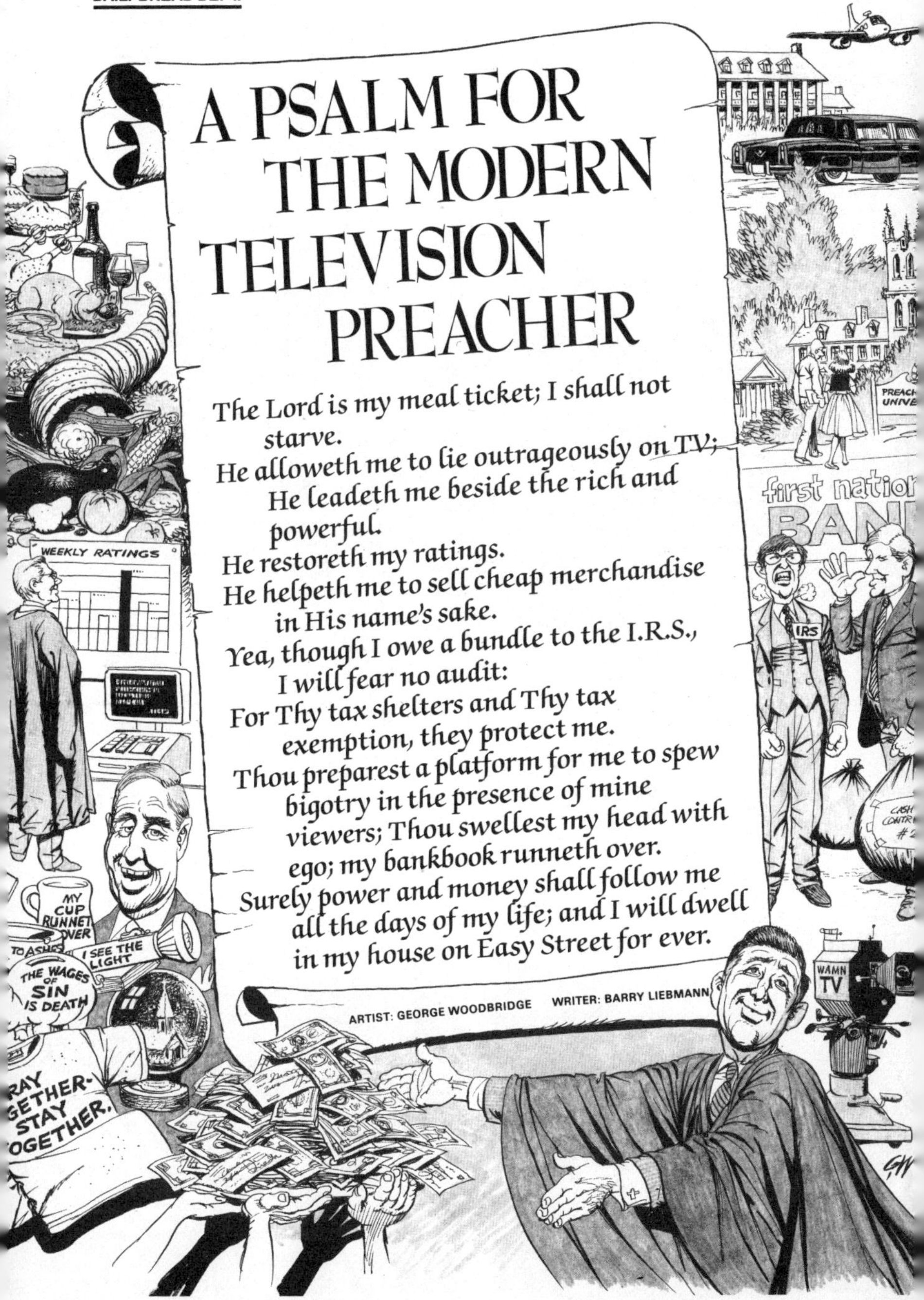

WEEKLY RATINGS
MY CUP RUNNETH OVER
TO ASHES
I SEE THE LIGHT
THE WAGES OF SIN IS DEATH
RAY
GETHER-
STAY
OGETHER.
PREACH
UNIVE
first natio
BAN
IRS
CASH
CONTR
#2
WAMN
TV
GW

The Lord is my meal ticket; I shall not
starve.
He alloweth me to lie outrageously on TV;
He leadeth me beside the rich and
powerful.
He restoreth my ratings.
He helpeth me to sell cheap merchandise
in His name's sake.
Yea, though I owe a bundle to the I.R.S.,
I will fear no audit:
For Thy tax shelters and Thy tax
exemption, they protect me.
Thou preparest a platform for me to spew
bigotry in the presence of mine
viewers; Thou swellest my head with
ego; my bankbook runneth over.
Surely power and money shall follow me
all the days of my life; and I will dwell
in my house on Easy Street for ever.

ARTIST: GEORGE WOODBRIDGE WRITER: BARRY LIEBMANN

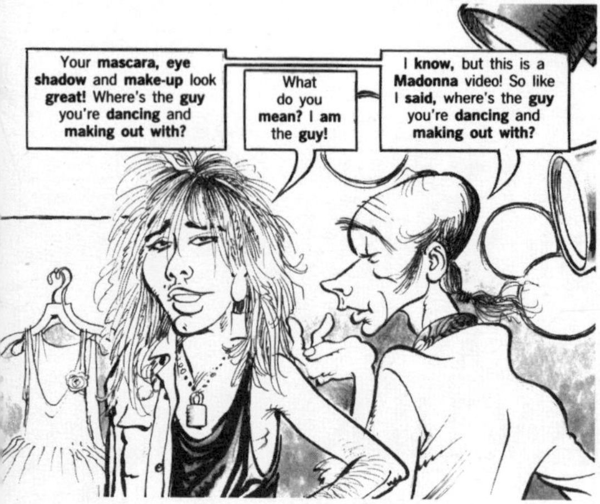
Your mascara, eye shadow and make-up look great! Where's the guy you're dancing and making out with?
What do you mean? I am the guy!
I know, but this is a Madonna video! So like I said, where's the guy you're dancing and making out with?

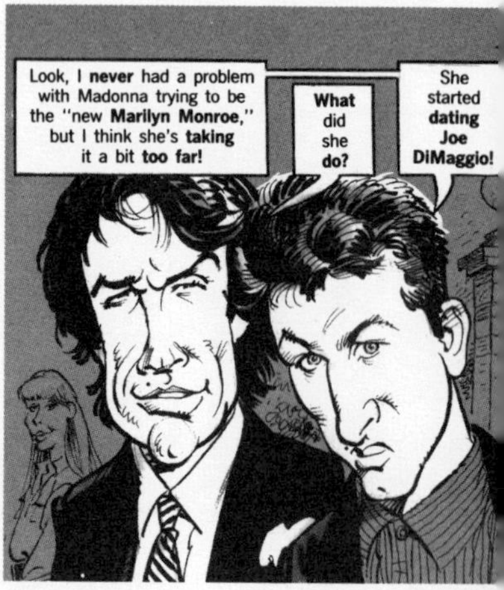
Look, I never had a problem with Madonna trying to be the "new Marilyn Monroe," but I think she's taking it a bit too far!
What did she do?
She started dating Joe DiMaggio!

UNLIKE A VIRGIN DEPT.

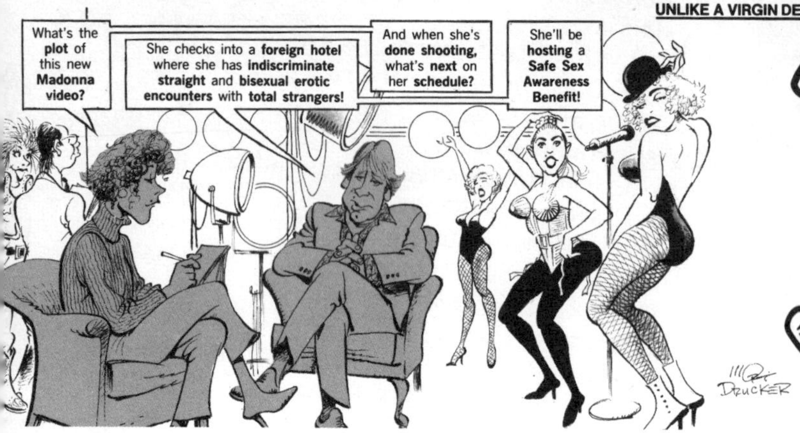
What's the plot of this new Madonna video?
She checks into a foreign hotel where she has indiscriminate straight and bisexual erotic encounters with total strangers!
And when she's done shooting, what's next on her schedule?
She'll be hosting a Safe Sex Awareness Benefit!
DRUCKER

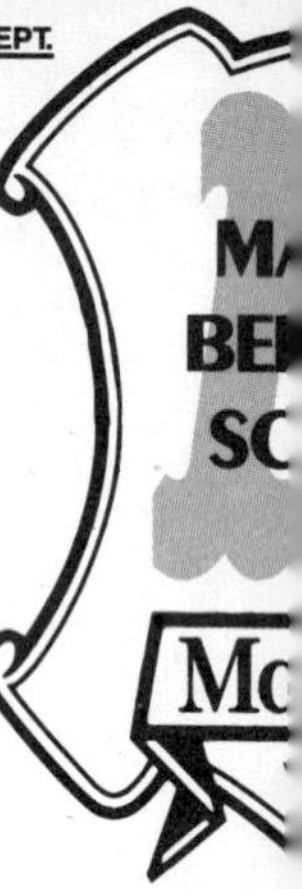

ARTIST: MORT DRUCKE

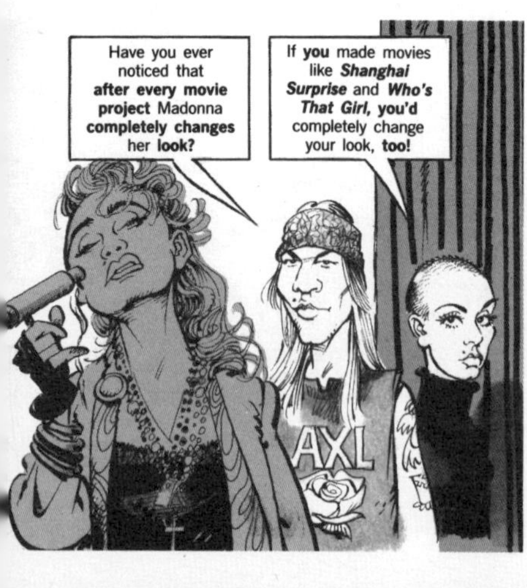
Have you ever noticed that after every movie project Madonna completely changes her look?
If you made movies like *Shanghai Surprise* and *Who's That Girl*, you'd completely change your look, too!
AXL

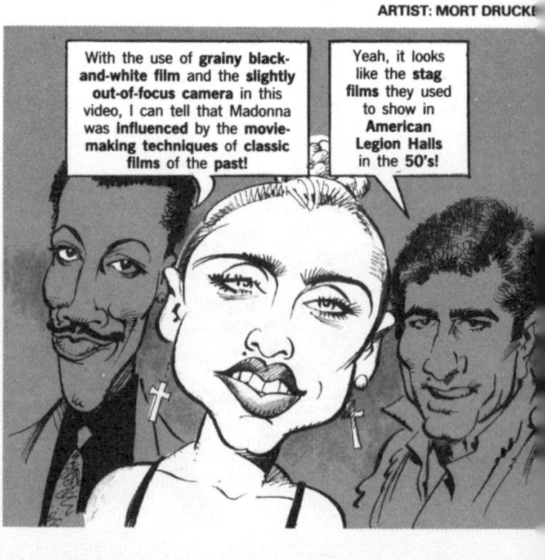
With the use of grainy black-and-white film and the slightly out-of-focus camera in this video, I can tell that Madonna was influenced by the movie-making techniques of classic films of the past!
Yeah, it looks like the stag films they used to show in American Legion Halls in the 50's!

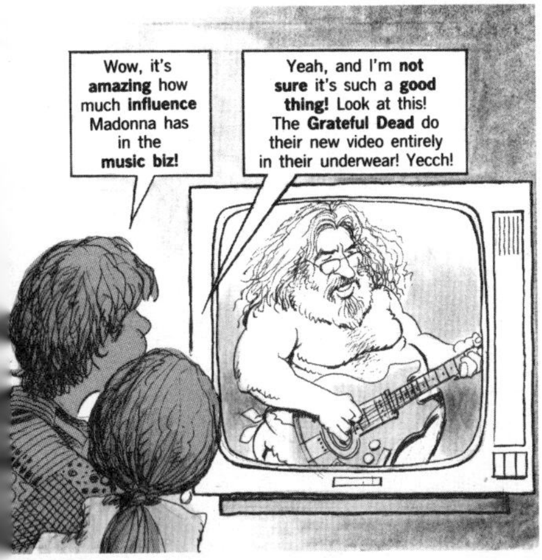
Wow, it's amazing how much influence Madonna has in the music biz!
Yeah, and I'm not sure it's such a good thing! Look at this! The Grateful Dead do their new video entirely in their underwear! Yecch!

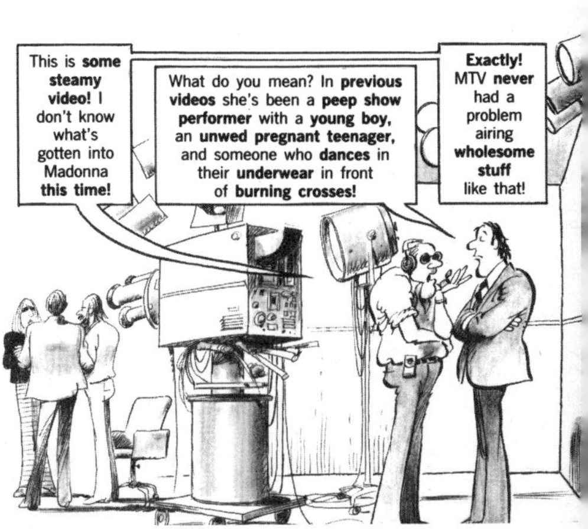
This is some steamy video! I don't know what's gotten into Madonna this time!
What do you mean? In previous videos she's been a peep show performer with a young boy, an unwed pregnant teenager, and someone who dances in their underwear in front of burning crosses!
Exactly! MTV never had a problem airing wholesome stuff like that!

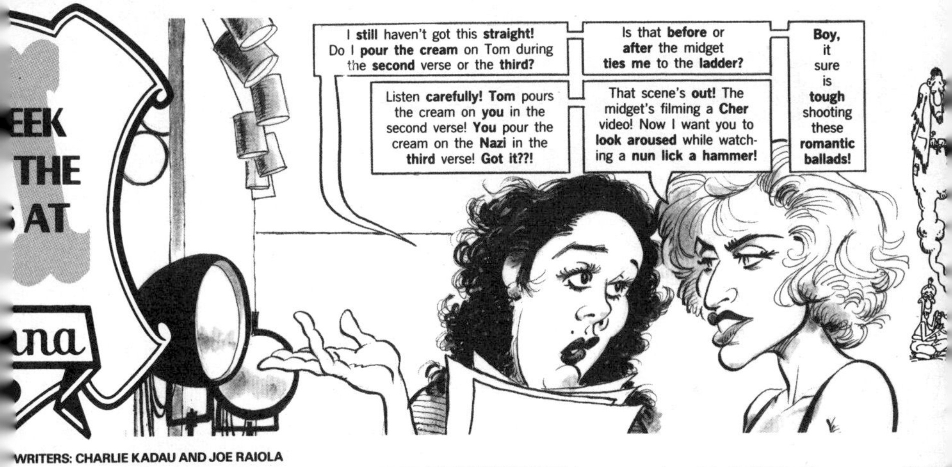
EEK
THE
AT
I still haven't got this straight! Do I pour the cream on Tom during the second verse or the third?
Listen carefully! Tom pours the cream on you in the second verse! You pour the cream on the Nazi in the third verse! Got it??!
Is that before or after the midget ties me to the ladder?
That scene's out! The midget's filming a Cher video! Now I want you to look aroused while watching a nun lick a hammer!
Boy, it sure is tough shooting these romantic ballads!

WRITERS: CHARLIE KADAU AND JOE RAIOLA

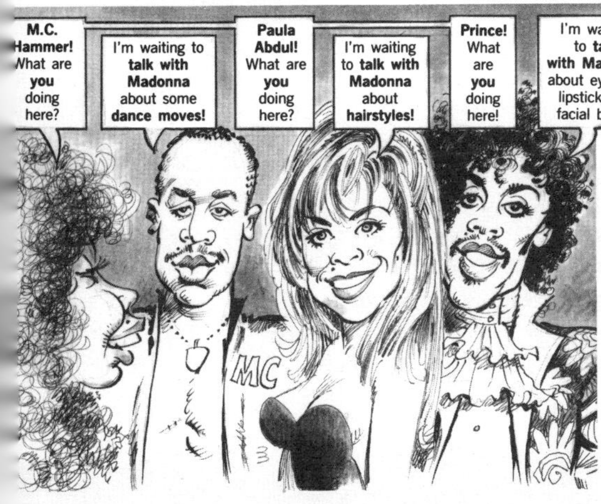
M.C. Hammer! What are you doing here?
I'm waiting to talk with Madonna about some dance moves!
Paula Abdul! What are you doing here?
I'm waiting to talk with Madonna about hairstyles!
Prince! What are you doing here!
I'm waiting to talk with Madonna about eyeliner, lipstick and facial blush!
MC

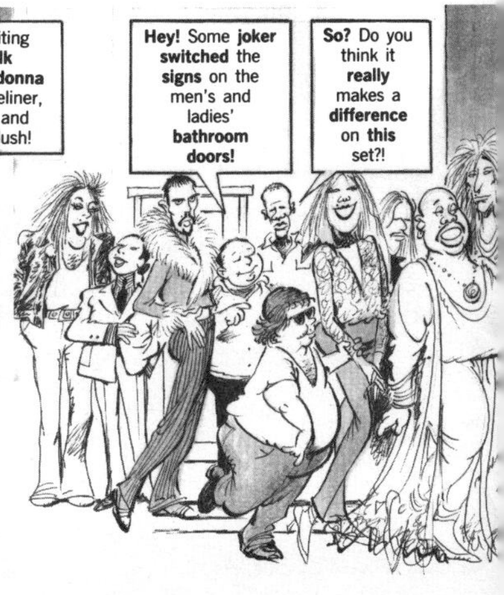
Hey! Some joker switched the signs on the men's and ladies' bathroom doors!
So? Do you think it really makes a difference on this set?!

Whenever a movie-maker wants to make a film look more impressive than it really is, he takes out a big, important-looking ad. This is called "hype" and the ad usually looks something like this . . .

KYLE AND LYLE BRISKET
In Association With
H. SIDNEY MANGOLD
Present
A Monumental Picture
ALEXANDER BARFKIN'S
Production Of
JASON FREEN'S

THE

GREAT DISCO
SPACE WAR

A Frederick Bilge Presentation

STARRING

ELWOOD	MONICA	LANCE
SCURVY	WAXWING	MALOMAR

and FEATURING

VICTOR	BEVERLY	ZOLTAN	KYLE
McSWEEN	NURD	ZANDAR	UNDERFOOT

AXEL VETCH   PHILO E. LODESTAR   SYNDA STAGMIRE

And Introducing DWAYNE OXBLIGHT as "The Visitor"
With HERMAN HERM NADIA OMM J. STUART WANG XERXES SMITH LORD UNKY

And A Special Guest Appearance by MERVYN ELDERTOOTH as himself
SCREENPLAY by TELFORD MUSK, Based on ALVIN TOGGLE'S Novel "Space Boogie"

Costumes by	Miss Waxwing's	Miss Waxing's	Miss Waxwing's Teeth
HILDA HUNGERLIP	Gown by WALTER	Pantyhose by SUPREME	by Milton Beemish, D.D.S.

Filmed on Location in Burma, Morocco, and a Sidewalk in Suburban Knoxville

Color by WILCO	Processing by NILCO	Developing by SILCO	Credits by FORBUSH	Casting by DAPHNE TRIVET	Sound by APEX	Filmed in XZ-47 SUPER VISION

Entire Production Supervised by Elrod Whippet in Association with Warren Scrim and T. Hector Diggs. Not to Mention Waldo C. Erb.

Pretty impressive, huh? But it seems a waste that hype like this is reserved only for movies. There's no reason it couldn't serve us all. By George, let's see some examples of what we'd have...

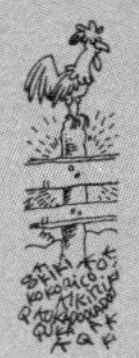

IF "HOLLYWOOD HYPE" WERE USED FOR EVERYDAY DRAMATIC OCCASIONS

ARTIST: JACK RICKARD

WRITER: FRANK JACOBS

FOR A MAFIA VENDETTA

Don Rico Manicotti
in Association with
Salvatore "Fats" Tortoni
Presents
A Manicotti Family Production

WIPE-OUT ON NOSTRAND AVENUE

STARRING

| "BIG LOUIE" LASAGNA | SAL "THE BARBER" SPUMONI | **&** | (by arrangement with Don Carlo Zucchini) | "SID THE SHIV" MANUCCI |

AND INTRODUCING

For the First and Last Time "Shades" Finelli as "The Squealer"

Plus a Milling Throng of Terrified, Uninvolved Onlookers

| Travel Arrangements by Acme Cement | Casting by Don Rico Manicotti | Assisted by Capo Vito Corona | Entire Production Planned, Supervised and Disavowed by Don Rico Manicotti |

St. Ignatius Hospital and
THE SURGICAL TEAM OF OPERATING ROOM B
PRESENT
A Dr. Leon Mishkin Operation
The Grand Opening of

THE STOMACH OF MORRIS PUTTERMAN

STARRING
DR. LEON MISHKIN

with

| Nurse Elvira Quigley | Interne Sidney Birnblatt | and | Dr. Dwayne Farfel as "The Specialist" |

With a Special Guest Appearance by

MORRIS PUTTERMAN

and Introducing
Putterman's Hysterical Wife, Rosalie
Plus a Supporting Cast
of Nurses, Orderlies and
Inquiring Relatives

| **Anesthetics** by Dr. Byron Wimple | **Gauze by** Johnson & Johnson | **Sutures** by Acme |

Financed by Blue Shield and United Major Medical

Entire Production Supervised
by Dr. Leon Mishkin

The State of New York in association with
Justice Felix J. Grumwort Bailiff W. Culpepper
Presents
A Divorce Court Production

HAROLD   **LAURA YURGLE**
SMEED   **SMEED**
in

THE BIG SPLIT

Based On a Scheme by
LAURA YURGLE SMEED
From an Idea of Her Meddling Mother
ELVIRA YURGLE
Co-Starring
ATTORNEY STEVEN WEEDLE
Arguing Greedily Over the Objections Of
ATTORNEY RAMSEY BLIGHT

With a Special Guest Appearance by
STAR WITNESS
LOLA "LEGS" WICKERSHAM
(by arrangement with Private Detective Gump McCall)

And a Tear-Jerking Performance by
SIX-YEAR-OLD BILLY SMEED
Entire Production Paid For Through The Nose By
HAROLD SMEED

Clarabelle Grommet
With Assistance From No One
Presents

WEDNESDAY NIGHT DINNER

Based On A Recipe By Neighbor Dora Mulvaney

STARRING

Clarabelle Grommet   Morris Grommet

WITH   **Sheila Grommet**
as "The Fat One"   **Morris Grommet Jr.**
as "The Finicky Eater"

FEATURING—

Ground Round by Barney the Butcher	Potatoes and Lima Beans by Ernie's Grocery	Bread by Tasty-Fresh	Water from the Town Reservoir	Ice by G. E.	Toothpicks by Supreme	Antacid by Alka Seltzer

Produced in a Hotpoint Oven and Presented On Ajax China
Entire Production Overcooked by Clarabelle Grommet

Marvin Meeg In Close Association With Esther Grush
Presents A Saturday Night Production

"I MADE OUT IN GRIBNEY PARK WITH ESTHER GRUSH"

Scenario by Marvin Meeg
Based On The Teen Age Lust
of Marvin Meeg
Inspired by a $10 Bet With
Charlie Vorch

STARRING

MARVIN MEEG

ESTHER GRUSH

AND

CHARLIE VORCH

as "The Hidden Observer"

Entire Production Staged In The Parking Area of Gribney Park

Automobile by Chevrolet	Recorded Music by Little Stanley And The Aardvarks	Entire Production Plotted and Designed by Marvin Meeg

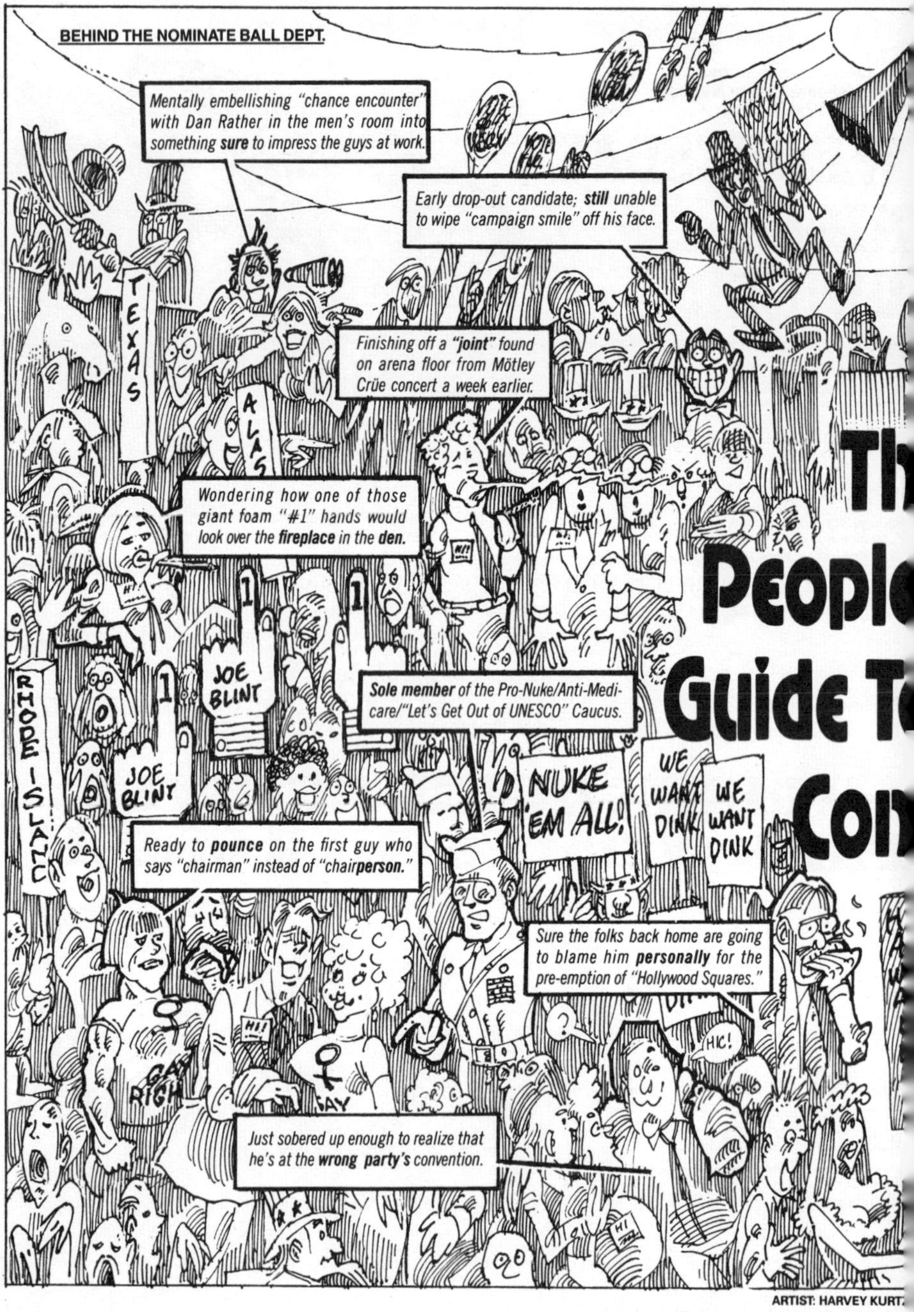
BEHIND THE NOMINATE BALL DEPT.
The
People
Guide To
Con
Mentally embellishing "chance encounter" with Dan Rather in the men's room into something **sure** to impress the guys at work.
Early drop-out candidate; **still** unable to wipe "campaign smile" off his face.
TEXAS
ALAS
Finishing off a **"joint"** found on arena floor from Mötley Crüe concert a week earlier.
Wondering how one of those giant foam "#1" hands would look over the **fireplace** in the **den**.
JOE BLINT
JOE BLINT
RHODE ISLAND
Sole member of the Pro-Nuke/Anti-Medicare/"Let's Get Out of UNESCO" Caucus.
NUKE 'EM ALL!
WE WANT DINK
WE WANT DINK
Ready to **pounce** on the first guy who says "chairman" instead of "chair**person.**"
Sure the folks back home are going to blame him **personally** for the pre-emption of "Hollywood Squares."
HIC!
Just sobered up enough to realize that he's at the **wrong party's** convention.

ARTIST: HARVEY KURTZ

Mad
Watcher's
A Political
ntion

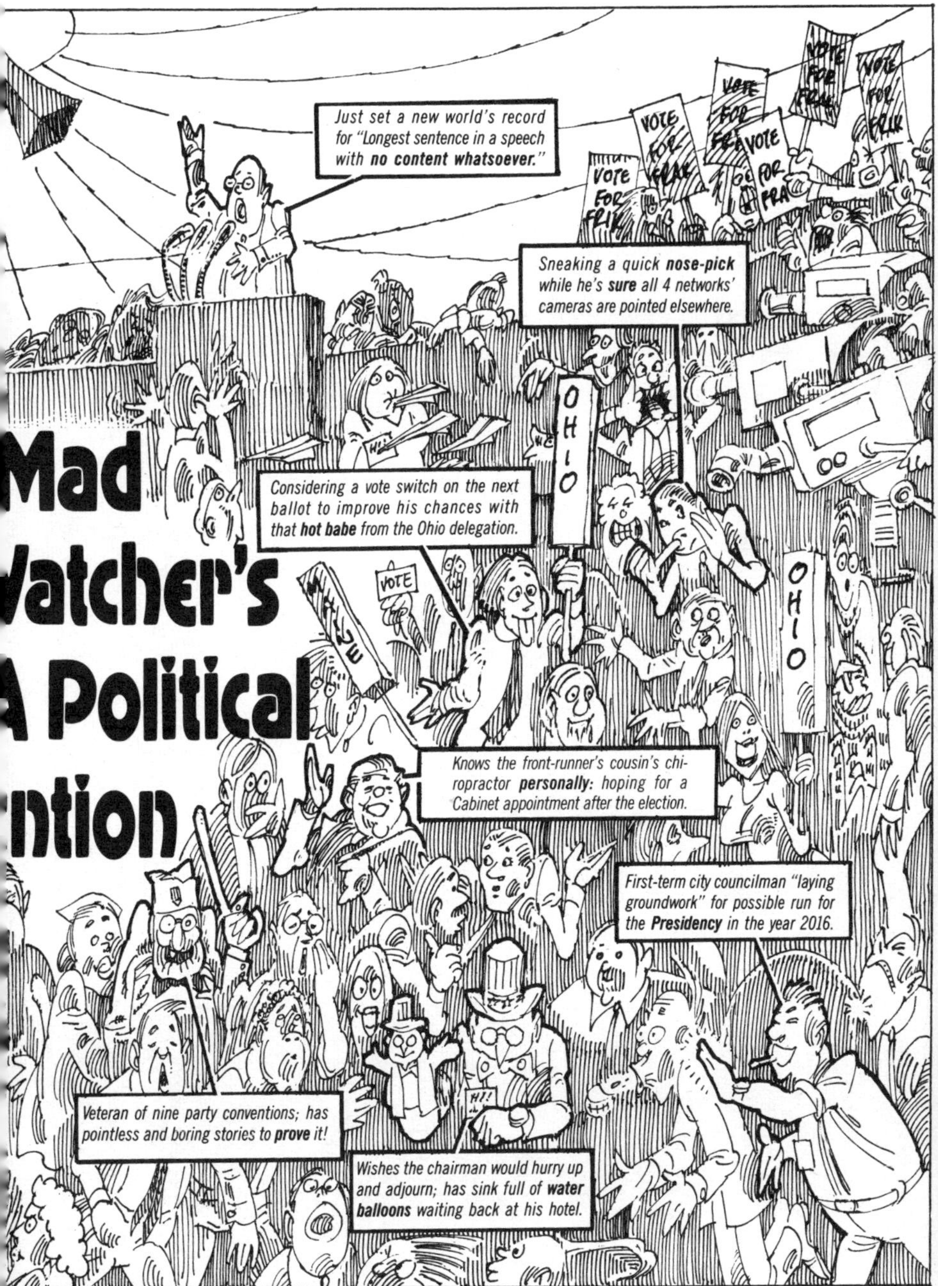
Just set a new world's record for "Longest sentence in a speech with **no content whatsoever.**"
VOTE FOR FRIK
Sneaking a quick **nose-pick** while he's **sure** all 4 networks' cameras are pointed elsewhere.
OHIO
Considering a vote switch on the next ballot to improve his chances with that **hot babe** from the Ohio delegation.
VOTE
OHIO
Knows the front-runner's cousin's chiropractor **personally:** hoping for a Cabinet appointment after the election.
First-term city councilman "laying groundwork" for possible run for the **Presidency** in the year 2016.
Veteran of nine party conventions; has pointless and boring stories to **prove** it!
HI!
Wishes the chairman would hurry up and adjourn; has sink full of **water balloons** waiting back at his hotel.

WRITER: MIKE SNIDER

DON MARTIN DEPT.

LATE ONE NIGHT...

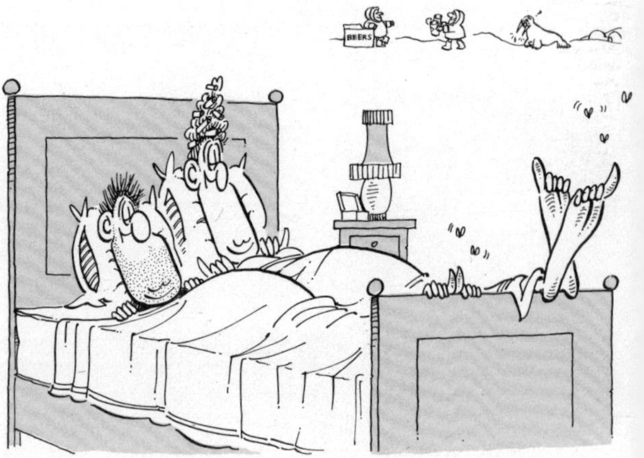
BEERS

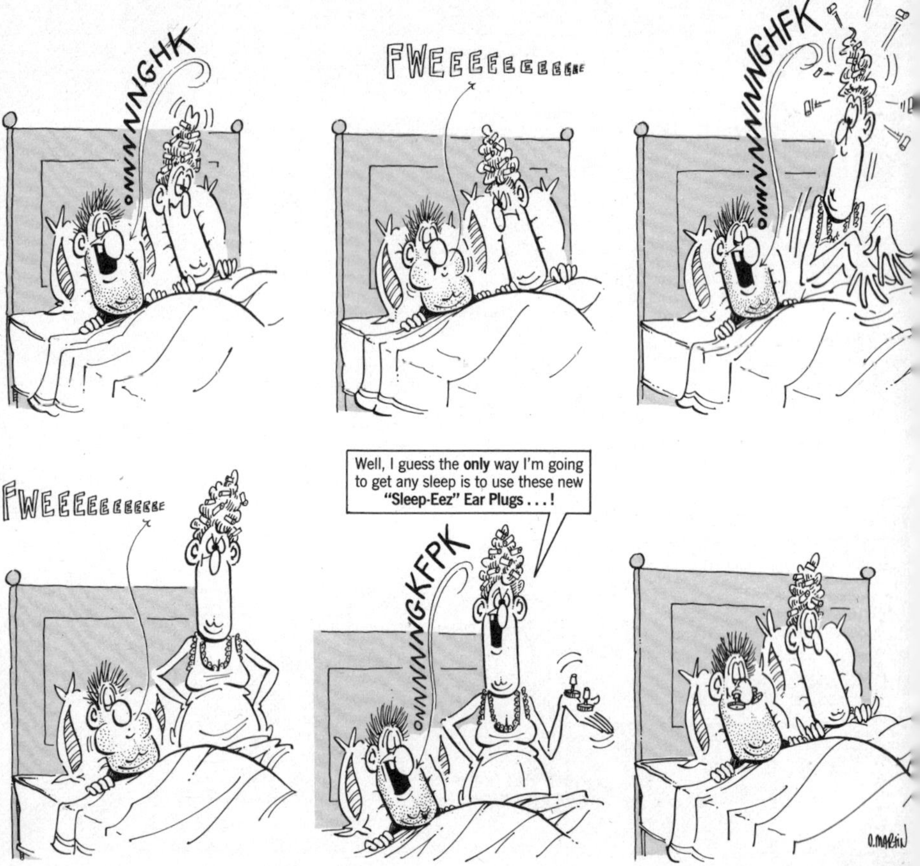
ONNNNNNGHK
FWEEEEEEEEEEE
ONNNNNNNNGHFK
FWEEEEEEEEEEE
ONNNNNGKFPK
Well, I guess the **only** way I'm going to get any sleep is to use these new **"Sleep-Eez" Ear Plugs . . . !**
D. MARTIN

PROMOTION SICKNESS DEPT.

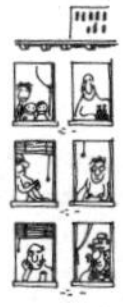

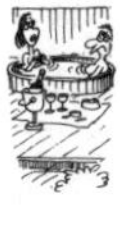

Did'ja ever notice how every few months a new advertising campaign for some product or another bursts onto the scene, takes the country by storm and etches itself into everyone's brain? If you have, then you've probably also noticed how these same campaigns just as quickly arouse everyone's disgust until they eventually wither away and return to the dark empty void from whence they came. If you **haven't** noticed these things, then skip to some other article! The few intelligent and observant people remaining may now enjoy...

STAGES IN THE LIFE OF AN AD CAMPAIGN

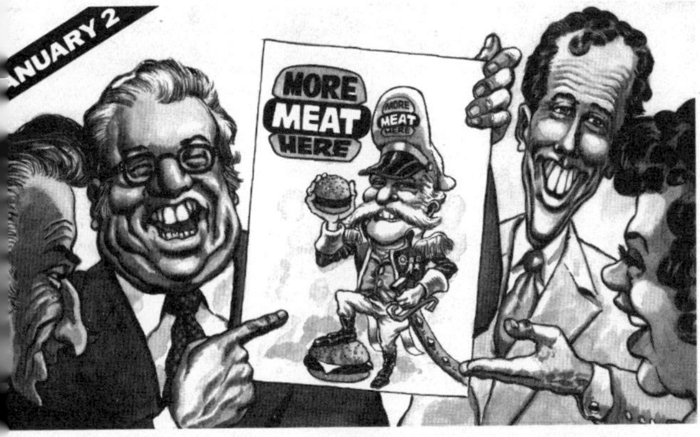
ANUARY 2
MORE MEAT HERE
MORE MEAT HERE

Executives of the McDimple's Hamburger fast food chain announce that the ad agency of Simpson & Hack has been hired to create a new advertising campaign for them. The campaign, featuring the slogan "More Meat Here" spoken by a midget posing as an army general, beat out other proposed slogans, including "From Freshly Killed Cows Right To You!" and "The Home Of America's Biggest Buns!"

ARTIST: BRIAN BUNIAK IDEA: MARC I. WHINSTON WRITER: CHARLIE KADAU

**massive month-long media
tz begins, with 20 million
llars worth of McDimple's
s on TV, radio, billboards,
gazines and hamburger-shaped
mps. Simpson & Hack esti-
tes that every man, woman,
ild and animal in America
ll be exposed to the "More
eat Here" slogan at least 53
nes a day. Also, the midget
my general makes an appear-
ce as a guest referee on
aturday Night's Main Event."**

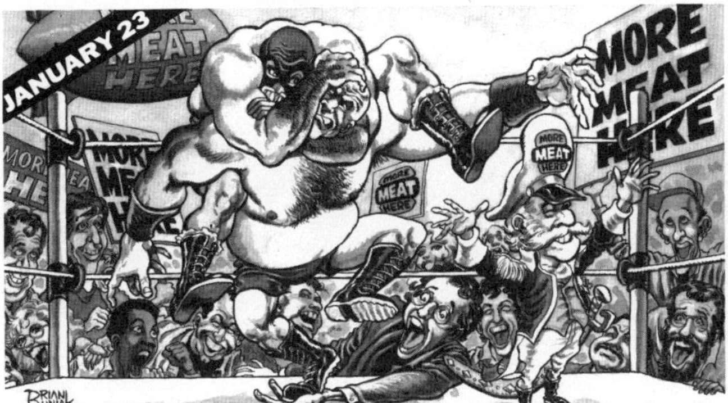
JANUARY 23
MORE MEAT HERE
MORE MEAT HERE
MORE MEAT HERE
BRIAN BUNIAK

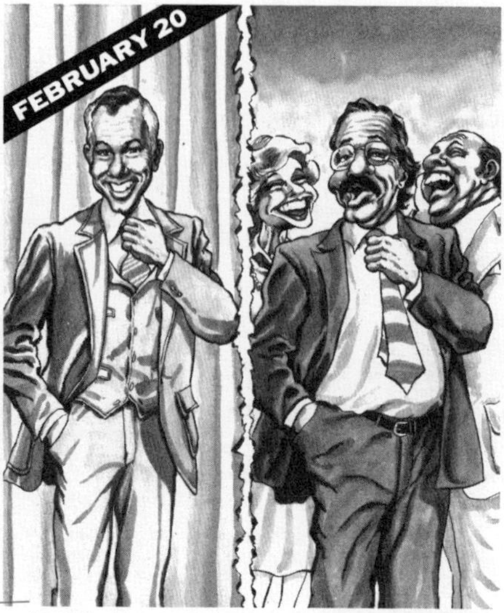
FEBRUARY 20

On "The Tonight Show," Johnny Carson uses "More Meat Here!" as the punch line to the next-to-last joke in his monologue. The next day, office comics from coast to coast are repeating both the joke *and* the slogan. Simpson & Hack is delighted.

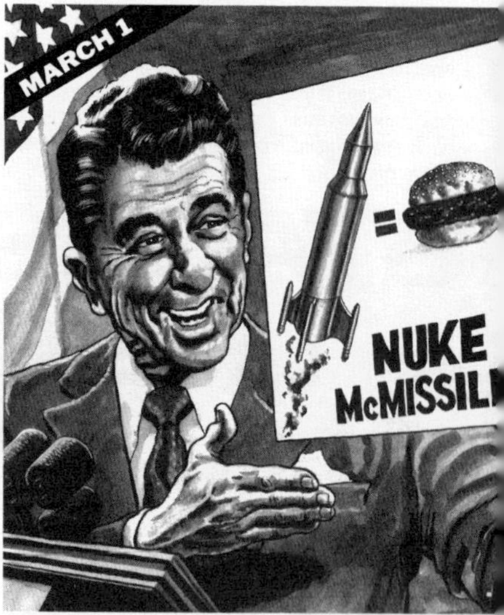
MARCH 1
NUKE
McMISSIL

During an interview, the President uses "More Me Here" to describe his new defense budget proposa His quote makes it to all the nightly news show and the next day politicians from coast to coa are repeating the slogan. Simpson & Hack is *ecstati*

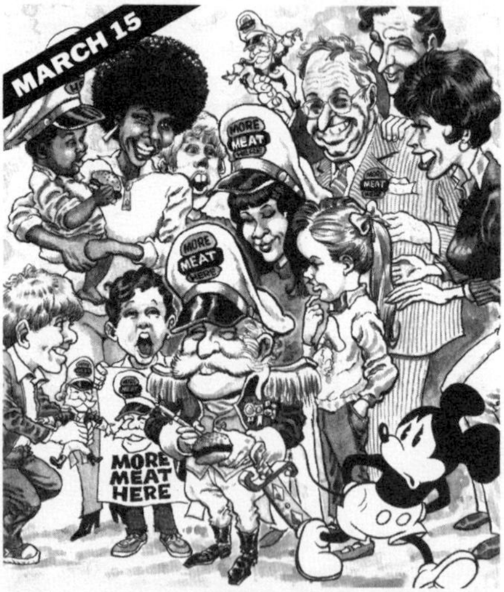
MARCH 15
MORE MEAT
MORE MEAT HERE

Millions of bootleg Korean-made "More Meat Here" T-shirts, hats, key chains and bumper stickers flood the country. A nationwide survey reveals that the midget dressed as an army general is now a more recognizable character than Mickey Mouse.

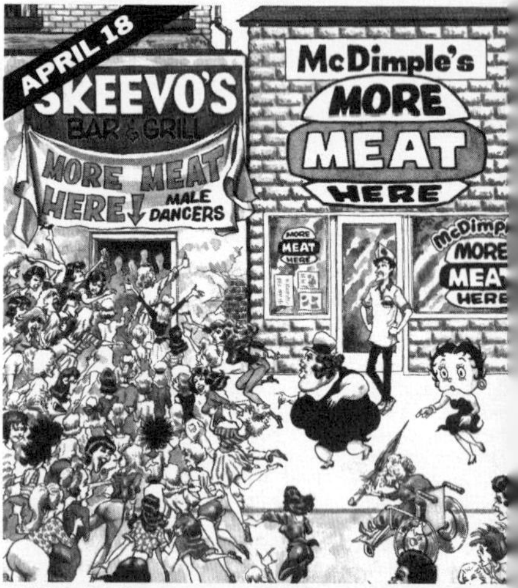
APRIL 18
SKEEVO'S
BAR & GRILL
MORE MEAT HERE
MALE DANCERS
McDimple's
MORE MEAT HERE
MORE MEAT HERE

McDimple's lawyers sue a Toledo, Ohio bar using th "More Meat Here" slogan in promotions for its Frida night ladies-only male dancers show. When the bar owner proves he was using the slogan a year ag McDimple's reluctantly agrees to pay him $50,000 s they can use it too. McDimple's lawyers are fire

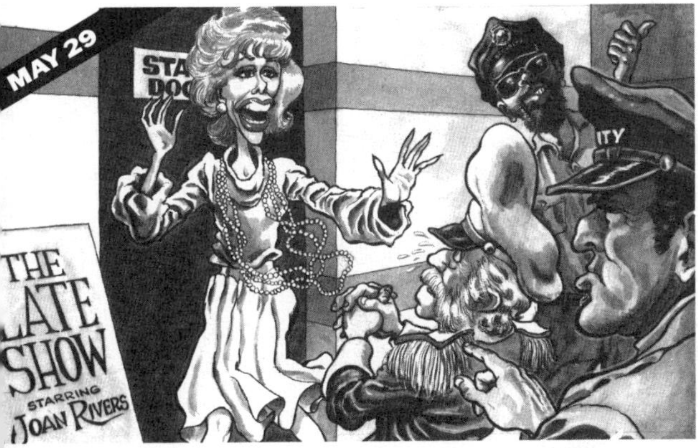

MAY 29
THE LATE SHOW
STARRING
JOAN RIVERS

Simpson & Hack hastily changes the slogan to "Still More Yummy Meat Here" when figures reveal McDimple's hamburger sales have decreased 43% in the past five months. They assure McDimple's owners that this was part of their strategy all along and that sales will be booming by the summer. A scheduled appearance by the midget army general on "The Late Show with Joan Rivers" is mysteriously cancelled. (The very next day Joan herself was mysteriously cancelled, but that's another article !)

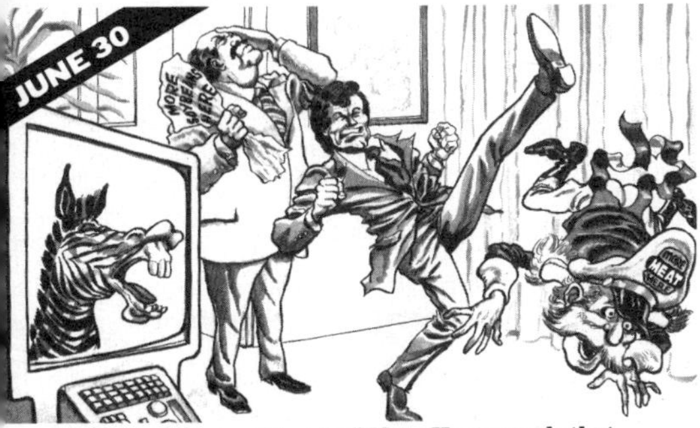

JUNE 30

On "Entertainment Tonight," Mary Hart reveals that Barney Spepple, the midget who appears in the McDimple's commercials, is a vegetarian and has never eaten a hamburger in his life. The next morning, Barney is fired and replaced by an animated zebra.

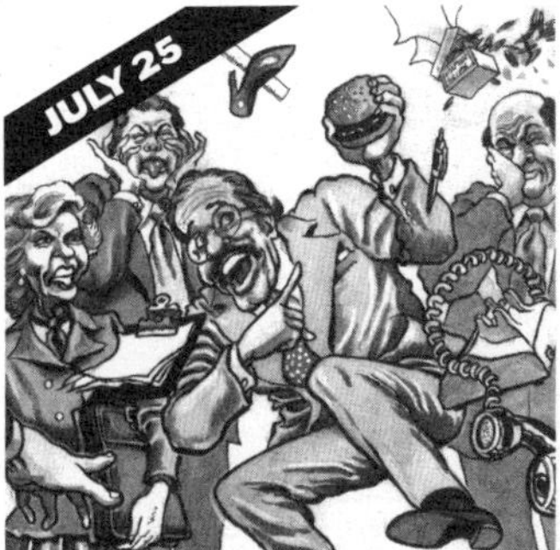

JULY 25

Anyone who utters the phrase "More Meat Here" at any time and in any situation is groaned at and scorned by their friends and family alike.

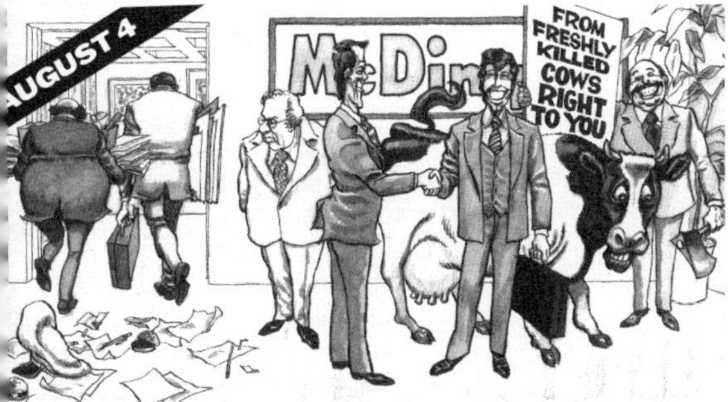

AUGUST 4
FROM FRESHLY KILLED COWS RIGHT TO YOU

As their hamburger sales continue to plummet, McDimple's fires Simpson & Hack and hires the advertising agency of Shmenkin, Berkin & Co. The agency announces McDimple's new slogan will be "From Freshly Killed Cows Right To You."

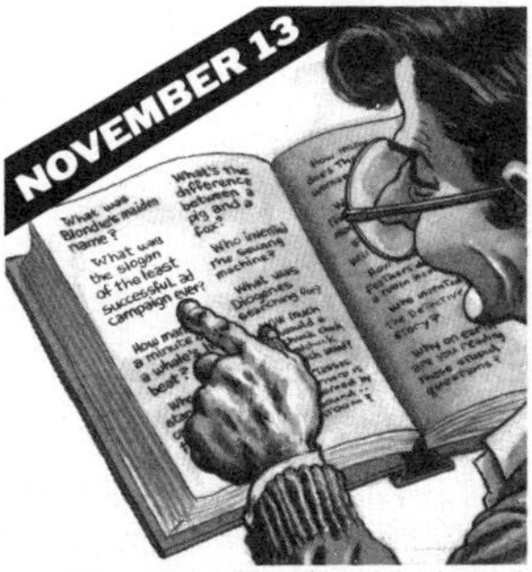

NOVEMBER 13
What was the slogan of the least successful ad campaign ever?

"More Meat Here" appears as the answer to a question on page 87 of *Tom's Big Book of Really Unimportant Trivia.*

A PORTFOLIO OF...
SHAPE-LY

Heave Ho!

Whenever o'er the waves I sail,
Going down, then going up;
You'll always find me at the rail,
Getting sick and throwing up.

Gentleman In Waiting

At bank or post office, I'm easy to spot:

The line that moves quickest is right where I'm not!

Spring's Labor's Lost

I
RAKE
AND SEED,
WATER and WEED,
SPADE AND HOE.
WHAT WILL GROW
AFTER THIS TOIL
IN VIRGIN SOIL?
KENTUCKY BLUE?
NOT IN VIEW.
FESCUE? BENT?
BOTH ABSENT.
WHAT KIND
OF GREEN,
THEN,
WILL BE SEEN? JUST, ALAS, LUSH CRABGRASS

Foul-Up

There's one in every big parade: the guy with lots of pep
Who struts so proud, but, stupidly, is always out of step.

Wedding Reception, Catered

The champagne flows like water,
And Daddy takes some pills.
He's losing a dear daughter,
but gain-
ing
lots of bills.

Profile Of A Dieter

When I started to diet, I had me a plan: To cut down my weight and to get me a man. So I gave up potatoes and ice cream and cake, and I dogged through the days when my stomach would ache. Now my flabby old fat is the thing that I miss— For I ended up looking exactly like THIS!

MAD VERSE

WRITER: WILLIAM GARVIN

Wheel Economy

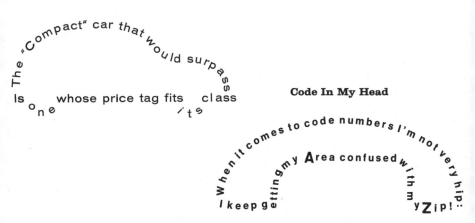

Is The "Compact" car that would surpass Is one whose price tag fits its class

Code In My Head

When it comes to code numbers I'm not very hip: I keep getting my Area confused with my Zip!

Survival Test

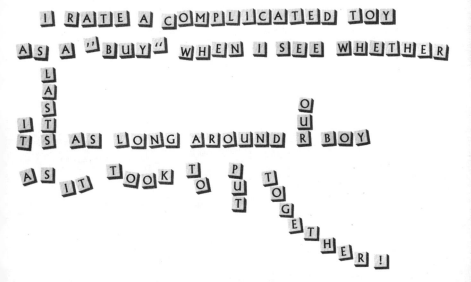

I RATE A COMPLICATED TOY AS A "BUY" WHEN I SEE WHETHER IT LASTS AS LONG AROUND OUR BOY AS IT TOOK TO PUT TOGETHER!

DEVICE SQUAD DEPT.

People who want to write for television waste an awful lot of time reading books that deal with characterization, plot, and other elements that have little to do with the typical TV script! What they *should* read is the one guide that tells them what they *really need* to have a successful career in TV:–

THE MAD WRITER'S

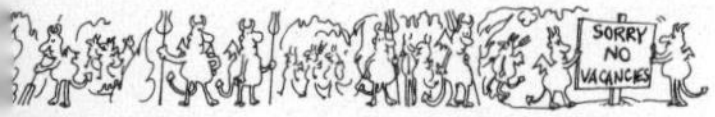
SORRY NO VACANCIES

DRAMATIC

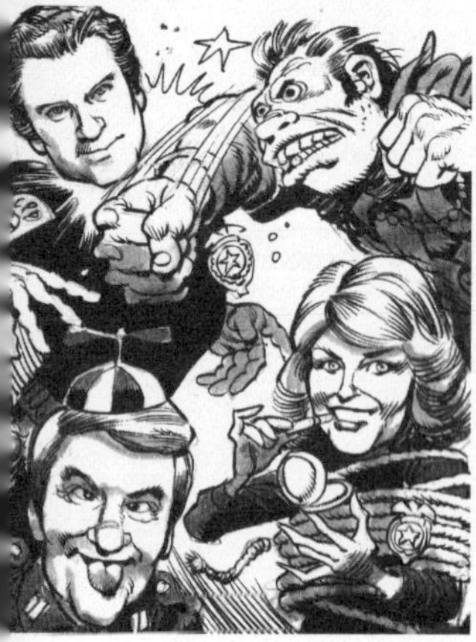

A. Heroes

1. Heroes in all walks of life shall be good looking, no matter how many blows to the face they receive each week. Heroines must never smudge their makeup, even as the result of wearing gags or blindfolds for prolonged periods.
2. Itinerant heroes shall have no difficulty encountering adventure, danger, and romance in every town they pass through.
3. Heroes must in all cases be smarter, more courageous, and more ethical than their superiors or commanding officers. (No explanation need be offered as to why *they* are not the commanding officers.)

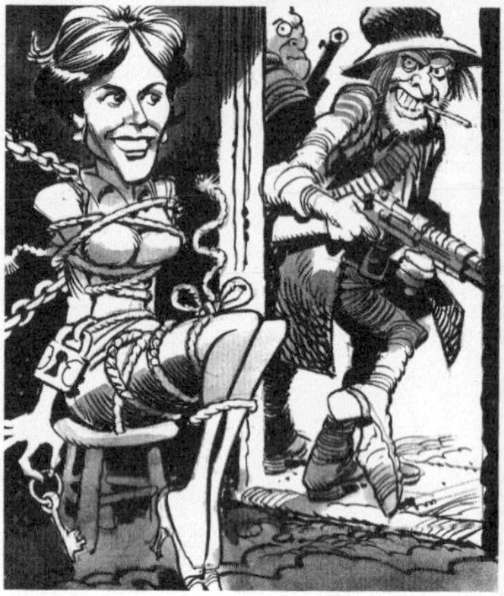

D. Romance

1. A female character shall resist the advances of a male hero only due to some compelling, life-or-death reason, and never simply because she finds the hero unappealing. This situation shall in all cases be resolved before the end of the program.
2. No matter how hard-won the love relationship between a hero and a newly introduced female character, she shall be completely forgotten by the next show.

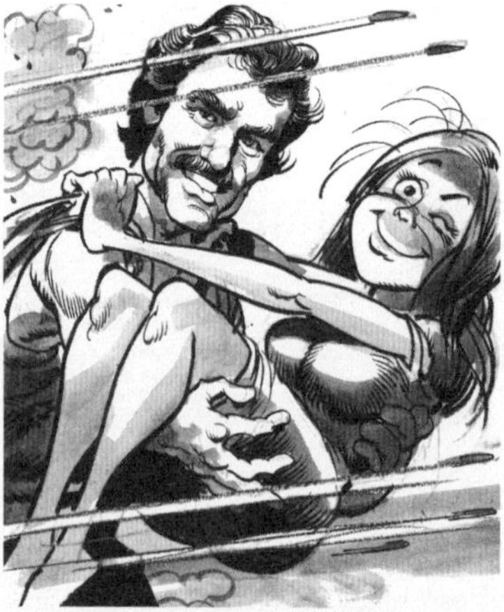

E. Car Chases

1. Characters shall never, even on the busiest New York or Los Angeles streets, encounter traffic jams that prevent the continuation of high-speed auto chases.
2. Firing his revolver at the car he is chasing while simultaneously dodging bullets coming through his windshield shall not prevent a hero from driving without an accident at 90 m.p.h. Villains's cars, however, that skid into highway railings shall in all cases break completely through them, fly over a steep, rocky cliff and burst into flames the moment they reach bottom.

TELEVISION RULE BOOK

ARTIST: JACK DAVIS WRITER: DAVID ALLIKAS

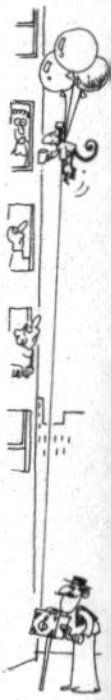

SERIES

B. Villains

1. Villains may not shoot heroes dead upon capturing them. They must first reveal their secret plans, then leave the hero alone in a death trap or guarded room from which he will escape.
2. World-class criminals should subscribe to the moral code which allows them to murder people by the thousands, but prevents them from breaking their word.

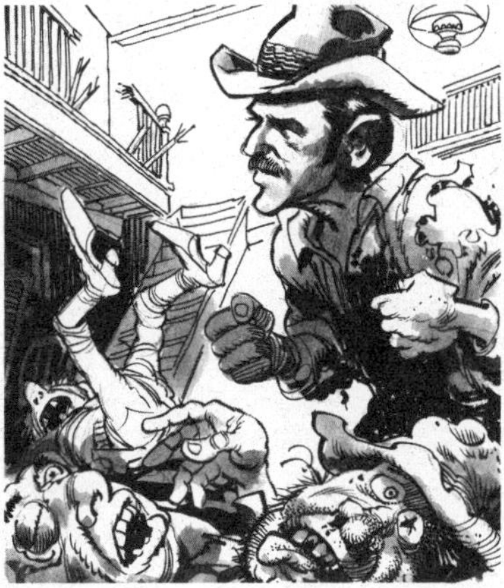

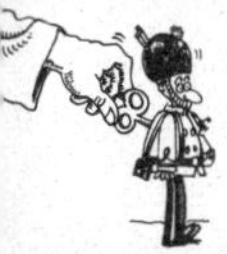

C. Fistfights

1. A hero shall never lose a fistfight against fewer than three opponents.
2. No fistfight shall take place in which each participant does not fall against and break at least one item of wooden furniture. (*Proviso:* in all westerns, at least one such item shall be the railing of a second-floor landing.)

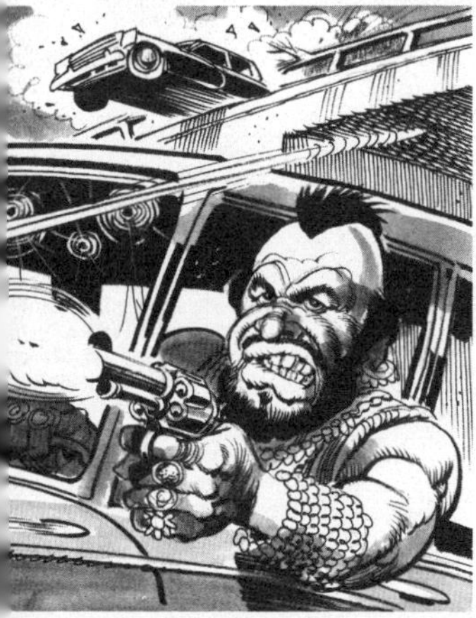

F. Death

A character who falls down a flight of stairs must break his neck and die. (*Adjunct:* any character who is jostled or pushed at the top of a staircase is required to fall down the entire flight.)

2. When a hero in a western series is shot, regardless of by how many outlaws at once and regardless of at what close range, he is "winged." A police detective or private eye similarly shot sustains a "flesh wound."
3. A hero pronounced to be "alive—but just barely" must always pull through.

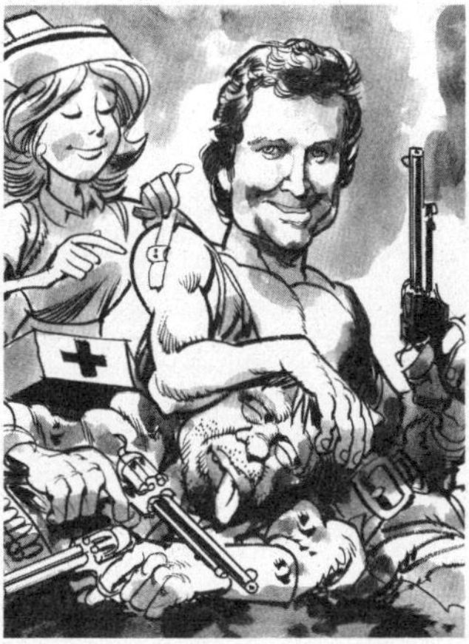

COMEDY SERIES

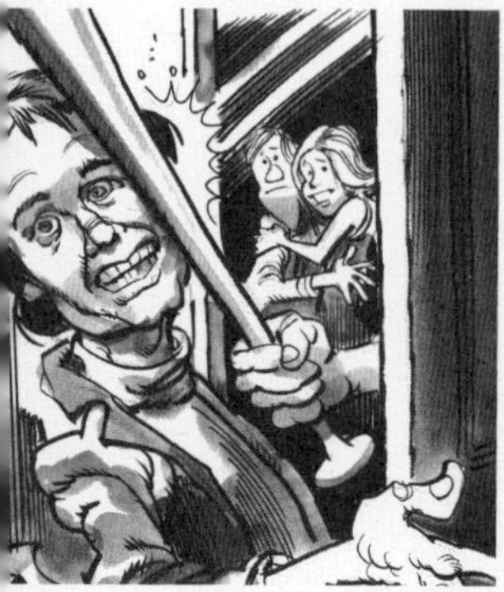

A. Plot Devices

1. A blow on the head shall produce amnesia. A second blow on the head shall relieve the amnesia.
2. Characters who overhear conversations must enter at precisely the right instant to receive a shockingly wrong impression.
3. A pair of handcuffs, within two minutes of being introduced, must be used to lock two characters together. No key must exist, and no reason should be provided as to why a locksmith cannot be found for at least three days.

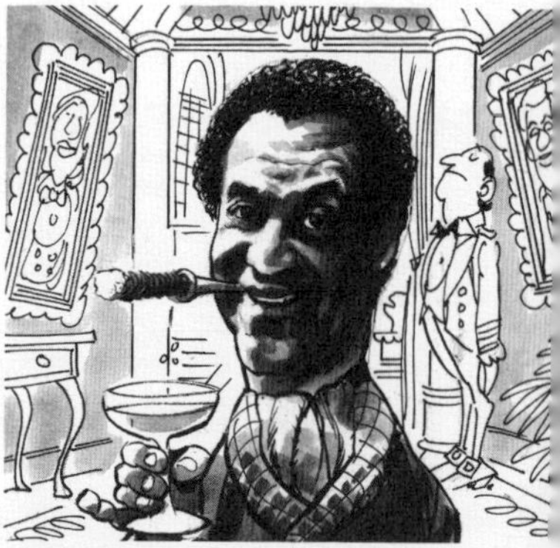

B. Houses and Apartments

1. No character shall be shown living in a house or apartment that is not at least 2½ times as expensive as what he can probably afford on his salary.
2. A couple's best frien shall always be married each other, and live in t same apartment building in the house next door.

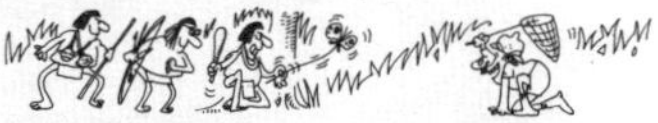

C. Punchlines

1. A joke which is patently corny or unfunny can be used, provided it is followed by 30 seconds of dubbed-in laugh track.
2. No logic shall be employed which would prevent all characters in a show, regardless of age, education, or occupation, to be equally capable of making witty remarks and brilliant puns when the script offers an opportunity.

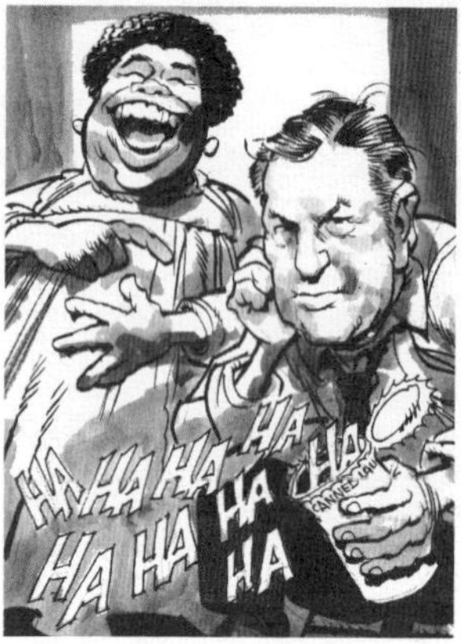
HA HA HA HA HA HA HA HA HA HA

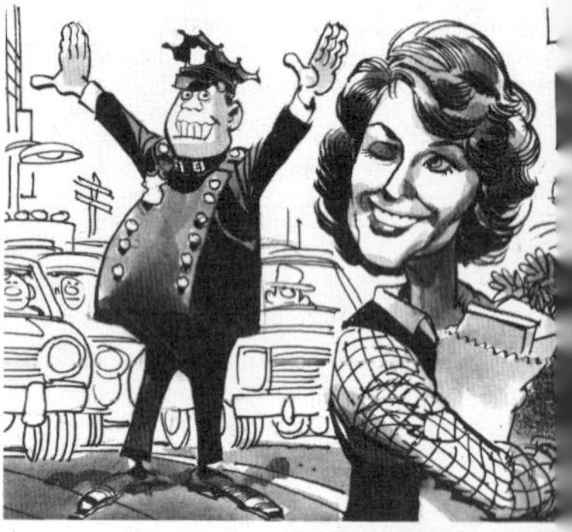

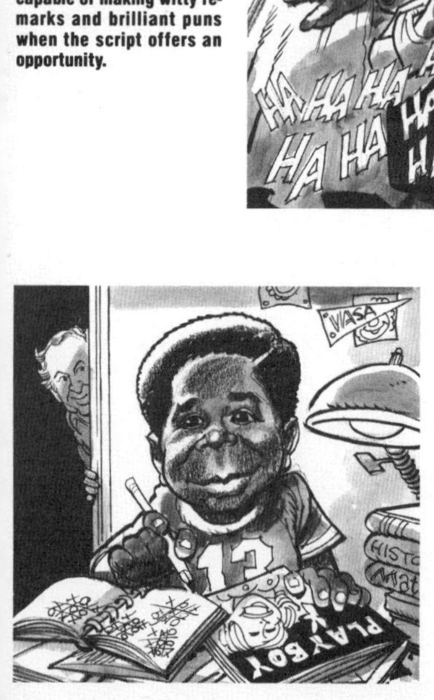
PLAYBOY

D. Kids

1. Children must not be depicted throwing tantrums, crying, telling their parents they hate them, or fistfighting with their brothers and sisters.
2. When a child appears in a school play, he must be crushed because one of his parents is unable to make it. (*Addendum:* the parent must show up at the last minute anyway.)
3. Children above the age of eight should display a knowledge of sex at least equal to that of their parents.

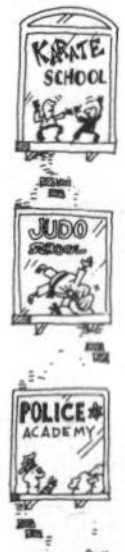
KARATE SCHOOL
JUDO
POLICE ACADEMY

E. Romance and Marriage

1. A divorced mother, r gardless of age, geograph location, or work schedul must have no difficulty fin ing a new handsome an successful boyfriend a least every other week.
2. No logic shall be em ployed which would imped a character from falling love with a newly intr duced romantic interes and finding an incontrove tible reason for a breaku all within 30 minute (minus commercials).
3. At all weddings, the be man must at first be unab to produce the weddin ring.

DON MARTIN DEPT.

THE BRICK LAYERS...

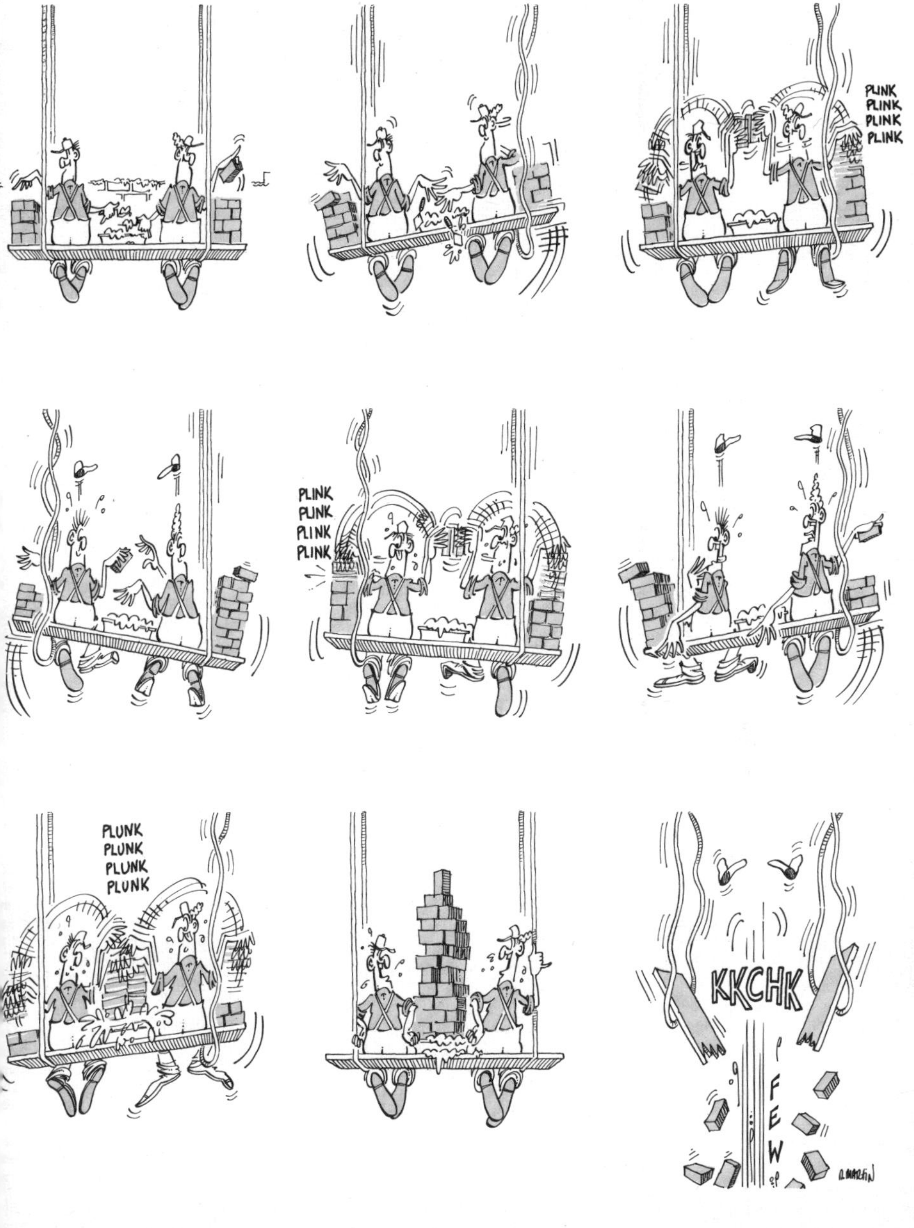

PLINK
PLINK
PLINK
PLINK
PLINK
PLINK
PLINK
PLINK
PLUNK
PLUNK
PLUNK
PLUNK
KKCHK
FEW
D. MARTIN

SERGIO ARAGONES DEPT.

A MAD LOOK AT

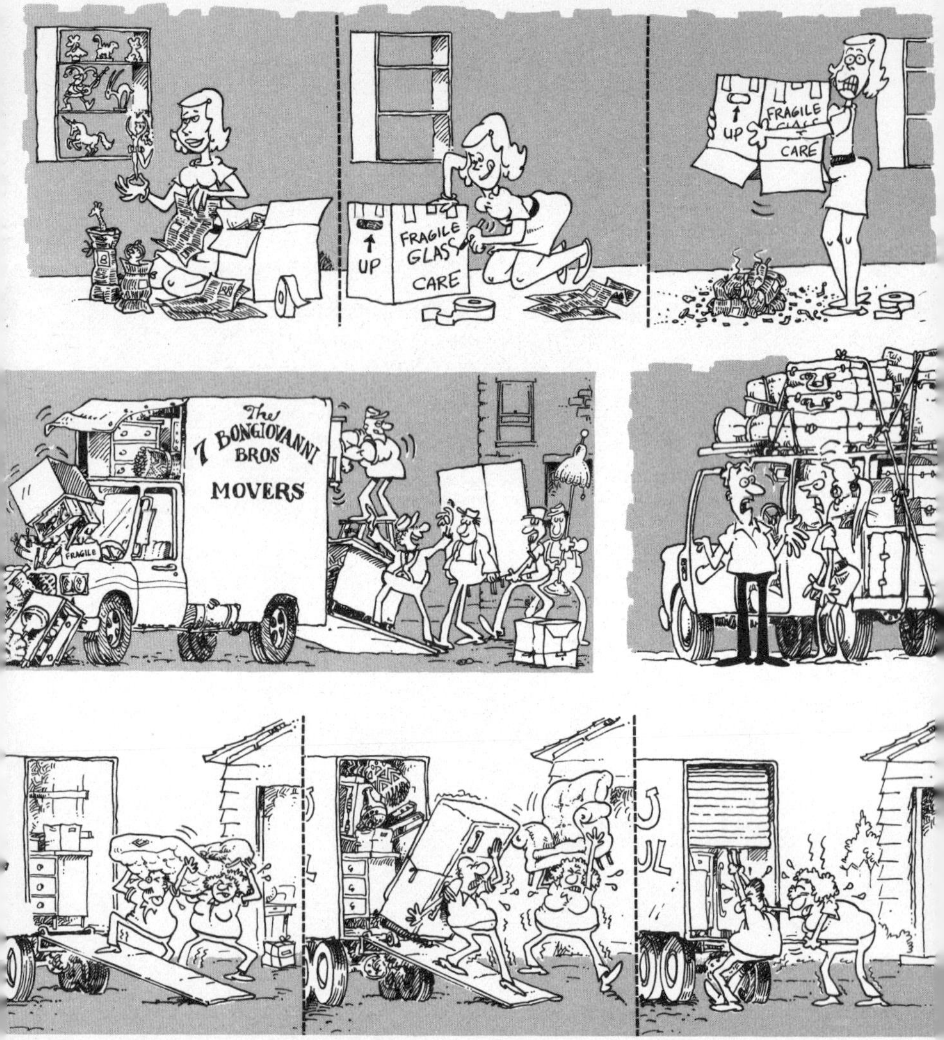

UP
FRAGILE
GLASS
CARE
UP
FRAGILE
CARE
The 7 BONGIOVANNI BROS
MOVERS
FRAGILE

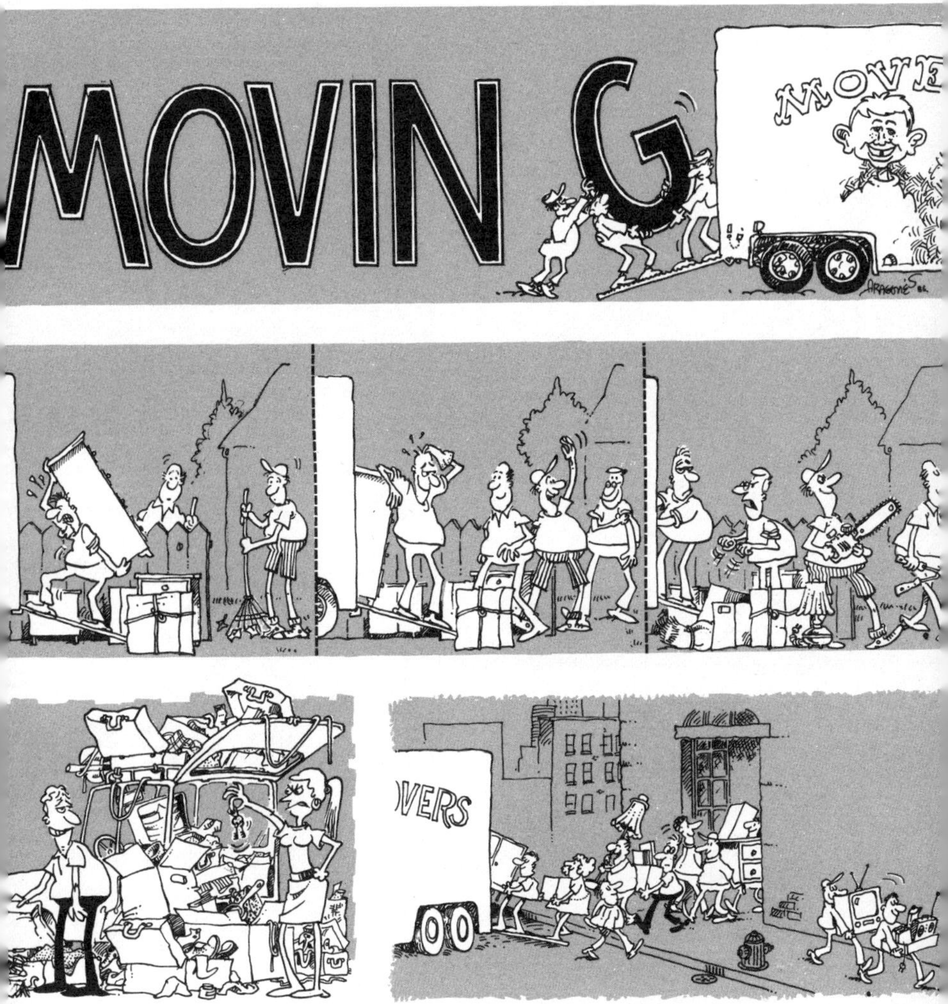
MOVIN G
MOVE
ARAGONÉS
OVERS

ARTIST AND WRITER: SERGIO ARAGONES

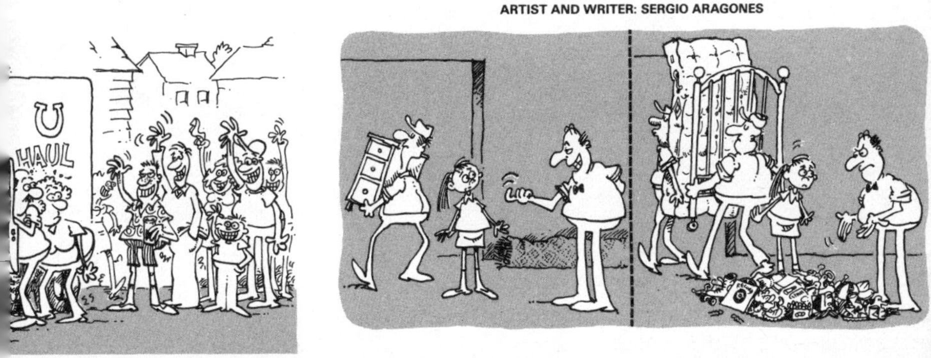
U
HAUL

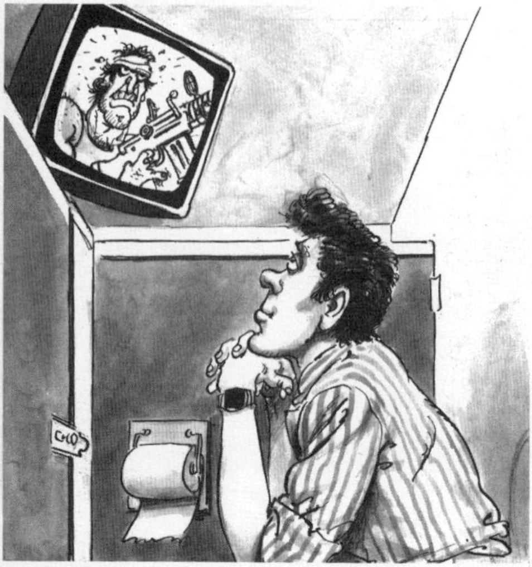
CHO

TV MONITORS *in restroom stalls let you "go" without missing any part of the movie.*

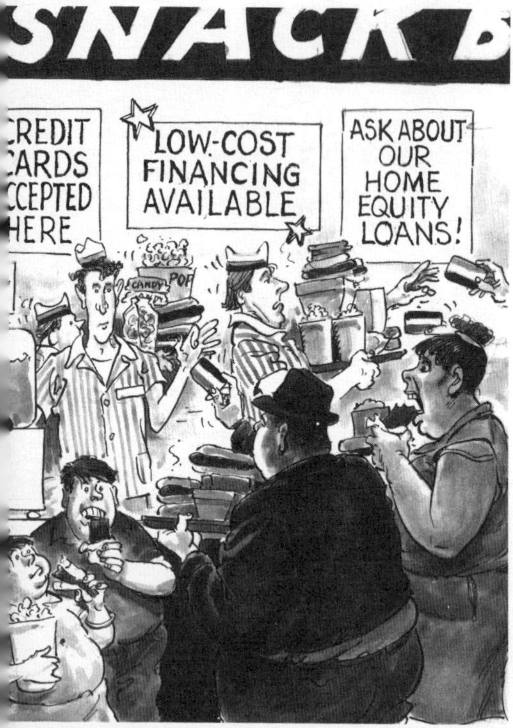
SNACK B
CREDIT CARDS ACCEPTED HERE
LOW-COST FINANCING AVAILABLE
ASK ABOUT OUR HOME EQUITY LOANS!
CANDY
POP

E-Z CREDIT SNACK BAR *allows you to eat like a pig and just say "Charge it!"*

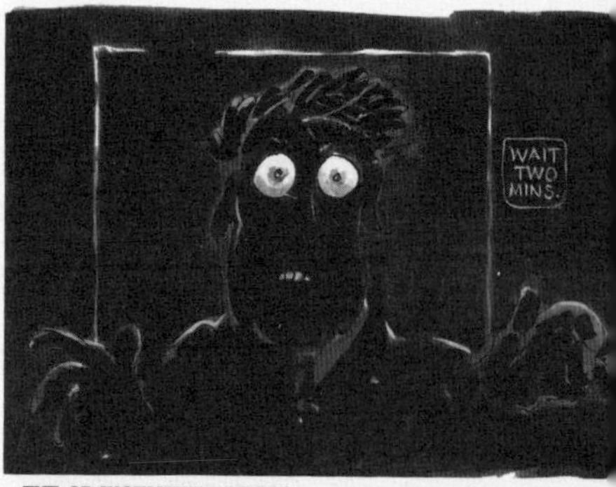
WAIT TWO MINS.

EYE-ADJUSTMENT BOOTH *keeps you from breaking your neck when you stumble into a dark theatre*

GALL OF THE HOUSE OF USHERS DEPT

The growing popularity of VCRs is making harder than ever for movie theatres to get public's dollar . . . well, the public's

MA
PLAN FOR
MOVIE T

ARTIST: HARRY NOR

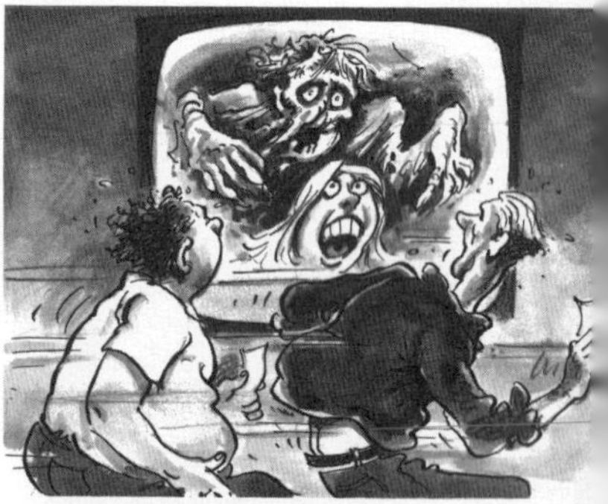

INSTANT-REPLAY SCREEN *helps late-comers catch up on all the action.*

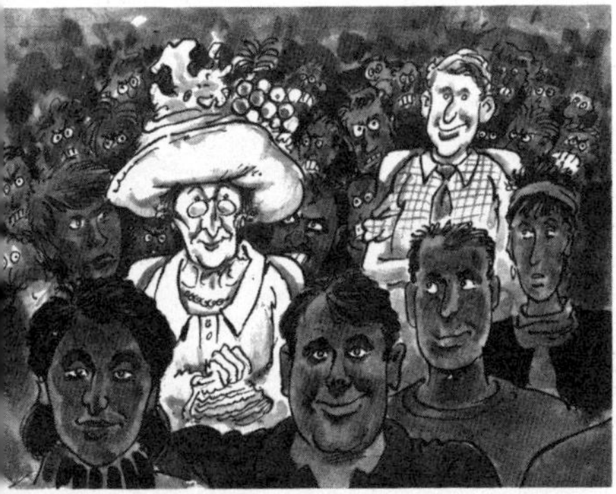

HYDRAULIC-LIFT CHAIRS *raise short viewers over big heads and other obstructions.*

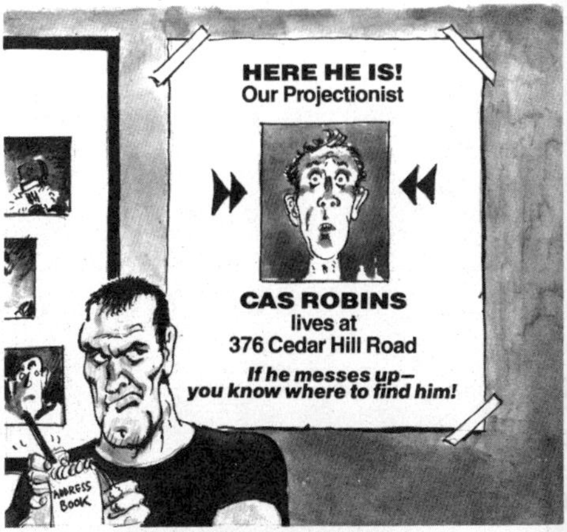
HERE HE IS!
Our Projectionist
CAS ROBINS
lives at
376 Cedar Hill Road
If he messes up—
you know where to find him!
ADDRESS BOOK

"MEET OUR PROJECTIONIST" *poster keeps the film from screwing up.*

llars! But we bet they'd sell more tickets they made a few adjustments! Of course, we ve some suggestions, and they're now playing in

D'S
MPROVING
EATRES

ITER: FRANK JACOBS

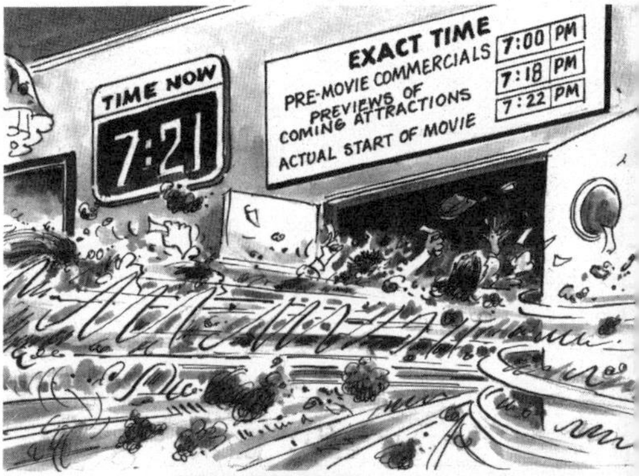
TIME NOW
7:21
EXACT TIME
PRE-MOVIE COMMERCIALS 7:00 PM
PREVIEWS OF COMING ATTRACTIONS 7:18 PM
ACTUAL START OF MOVIE 7:22 PM

EXACT TIMES SIGN *lets you skip boring previews and local ads.*

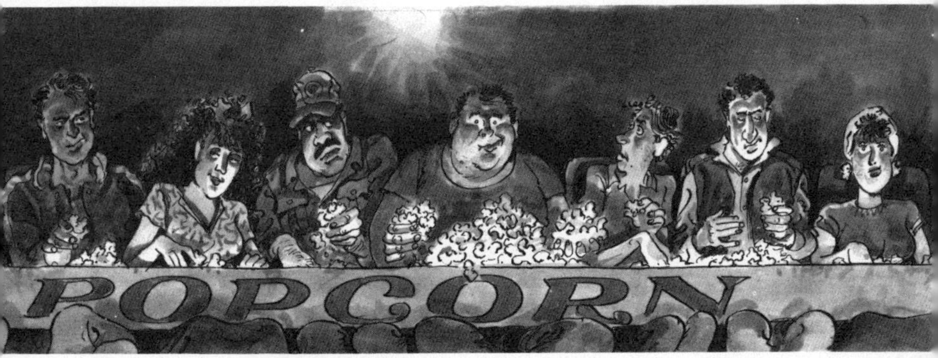
POPCORN

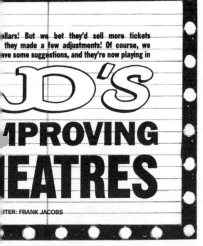

TROUGH-SIZE POPCORN *feeds up to 20 adults in one sitting.*

GIVIN' 'EM A RIBBIN' DEPT.

Why restrict the awarding of medals to the military? After all, Civilians perform heroic acts while fighting life's daily battles as well! Let's recognize them with

THIS ISSUE'S PROPOSED MAD MEDALS

ARTIST & WRITER: AL JAFFEE

. . . TO BE PRESENTED TO DESERVING ACTORS

THE BANKROLL ROLE MEDAL

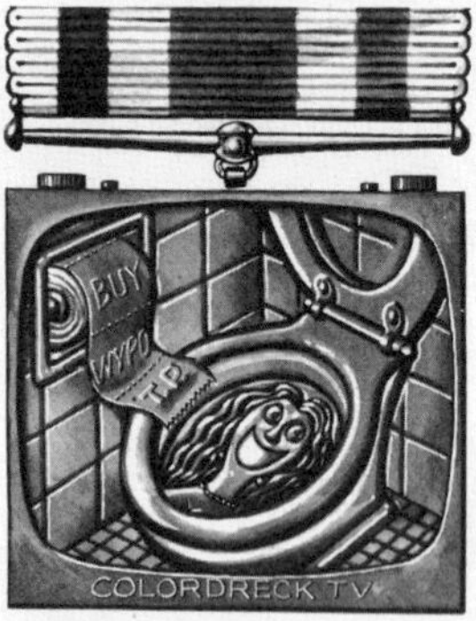
BUY
WYPO
T.P.
COLORDRECK TV

For bravely undergoing years of basic training in classic theater in order to turn out convincingly persuasive and highly profitable TV commercials.

THE AWKWARD "OSCAR" AWARD

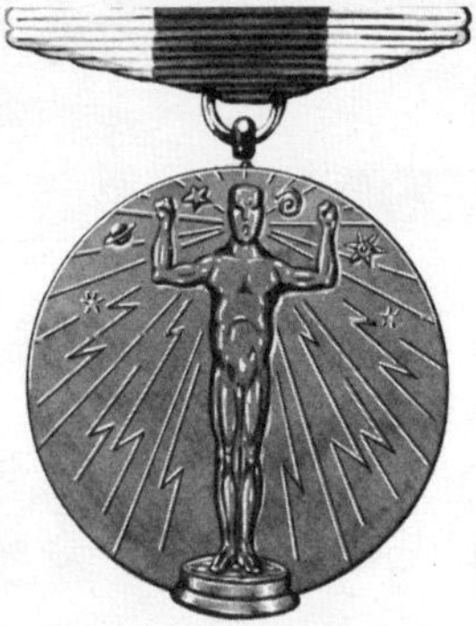

For gallantly awakening and stunning a captive audience by making an inflammatory political acceptance speech at a televised "Academy Awards" ceremony.

THE RINGS OF THE LATTER MEDAL

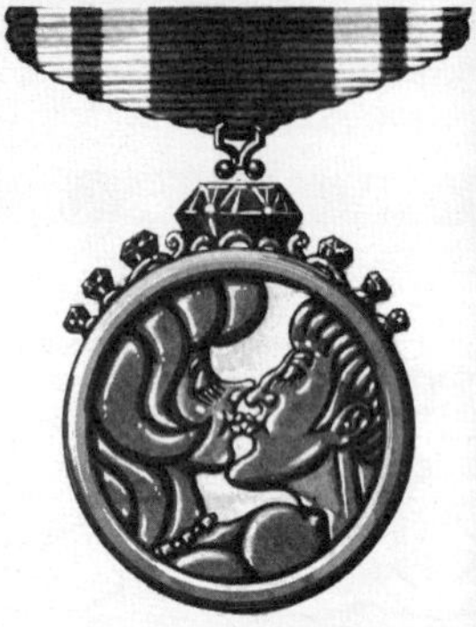

For heroically marrying and divorcing any number of famous and/or notorious people for publicity, resulting in the upward movement of recipient's career.

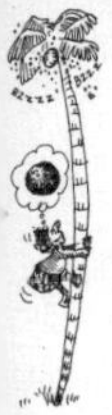

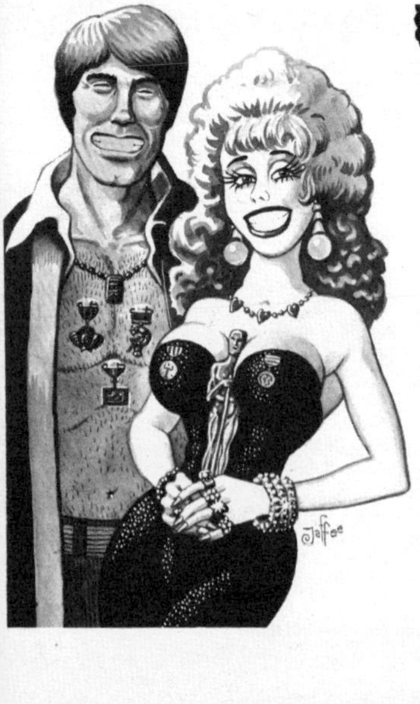
Jaffee

THE MYSTERY GUEST CITATION

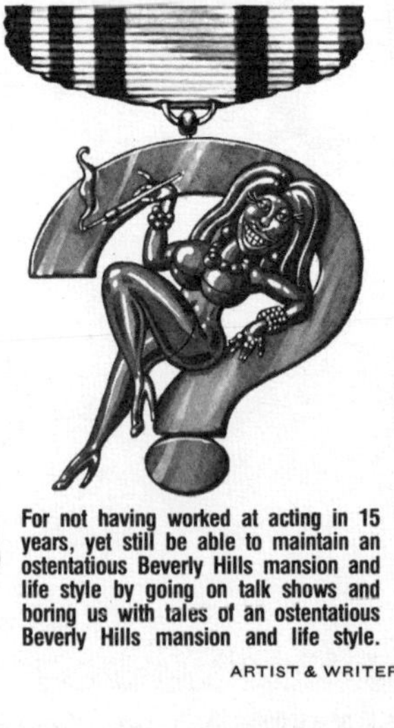

For not having worked at acting in 15 years, yet still be able to maintain an ostentatious Beverly Hills mansion and life style by going on talk shows and boring us with tales of an ostentatious Beverly Hills mansion and life style.

THE HOLIER THAN ANYONE MEDAL

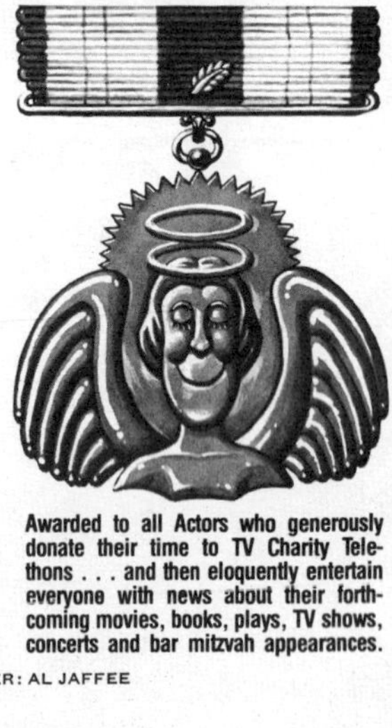

Awarded to all Actors who generously donate their time to TV Charity Telethons . . . and then eloquently entertain everyone with news about their forthcoming movies, books, plays, TV shows, concerts and bar mitzvah appearances.

ARTIST & WRITER: AL JAFFEE

TAIL-ORDER SHOPPING DEPT. —SPECIAL CATALOG INSERT—

For The Pet That Has Everything And Wants More®

PPP
INDUSTRIES

GIFT CATALOG FOR SPOILED ROTTEN PETS

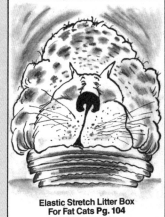

Elastic Stretch Litter Box
For Fat Cats Pg. 104

NEW!

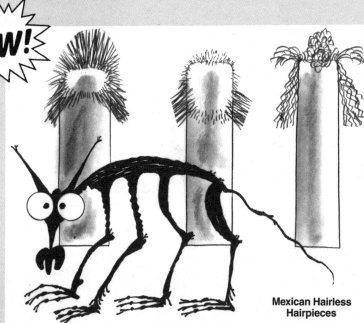

Mexican Hairless
Hairpieces

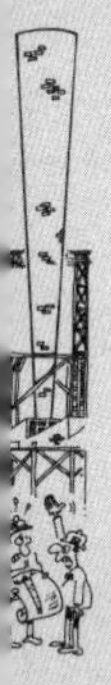

ALSO:

Polka Dot Warm-up Suits for Dalmations...Imported Ten-Speed Gerbil Treadmills...Trained Flea Circus Sets for Puppies...Whirlpool Birdbath Accessories

AND MORE!

ARTIST AND WRITER: PAUL PETER PORGES

A.

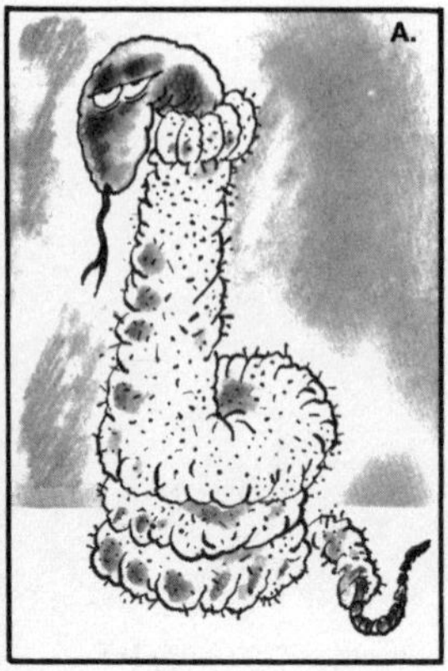

B.

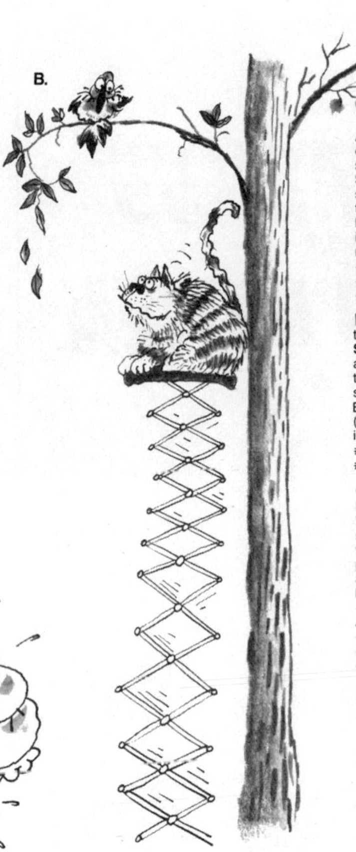

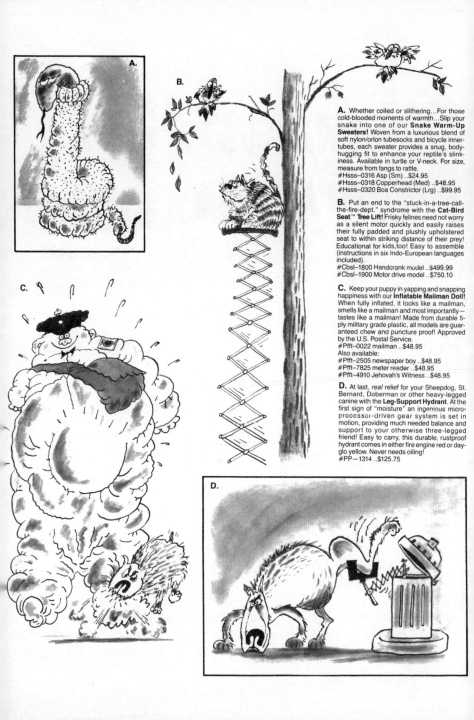

A. Whether coiled or slithering...For those cold-blooded moments of warmth...Slip your snake into one of our **Snake Warm-Up Sweaters!** Woven from a luxurious blend of soft nylon/orlon tubesocks and bicycle inner-tubes, each sweater provides a snug, body-hugging fit to enhance your reptile's slinkiness. Available in turtle or V-neck. For size, measure from fangs to rattle.
#Hsss–0316 Asp (Sm) ..$24.95
#Hsss–0318 Copperhead (Med) ..$48.95
#Hsss–0320 Boa Constrictor (Lrg) ..$99.95

B. Put an end to the "stuck-in-a-tree-call-the-fire-dept." syndrome with the **Cat-Bird Seat™ Tree Lift!** Frisky felines need not worry as a silent motor quickly and easily raises their fully padded and plushly upholstered seat to within striking distance of their prey! Educational for kids,too! Easy to assemble (instructions in six Indo-European languages included).
#Cbsl–1800 Handcrank model ..$499.99
#Cbsl–1900 Motor drive model ..$750.10

C. Keep your puppy in yapping and snapping happiness with our **Inflatable Mailman Doll!** When fully inflated, it looks like a mailman, smells like a mailman and most importantly—tastes like a mailman! Made from durable 5-ply military grade plastic, all models are guaranteed chew and puncture proof! Approved by the U.S. Postal Service.
#Pfft–0022 mailman ..$48.95
Also available:
#Pfft–2505 newspaper boy ..$48.95
#Pfft–7825 meter reader ..$48.95
#Pfft–4910 Jehovah's Witness ..$48.95

D. At last, *real* relief for your Sheepdog, St. Bernard, Doberman or other heavy-legged canine with the **Leg-Support Hydrant**. At the first sign of "moisture" an ingenious microprocessor-driven gear system is set in motion, providing much needed balance and support to your otherwise three-legged friend! Easy to carry, this durable, rustproof hydrant comes in either fire engine red or dayglo yellow. Never needs oiling!
#PP–1314 ..$125.75

C.

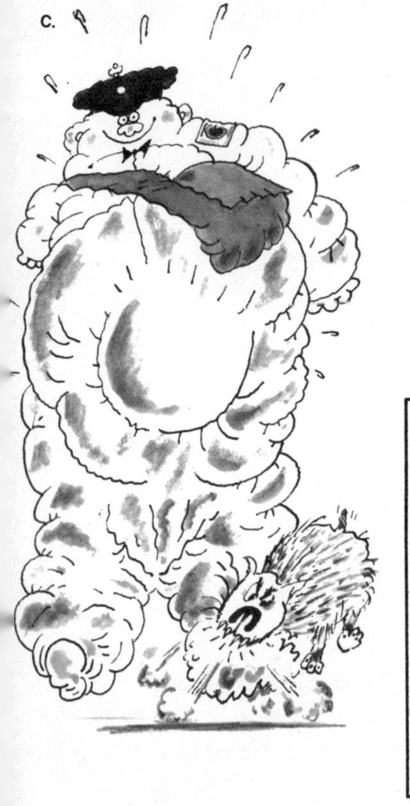

D.

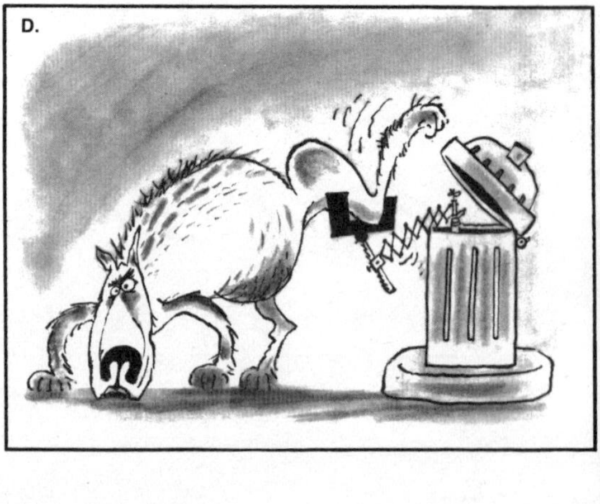

E. Attention, water-shy sport dog owners! Now your beloved setters and retrievers can point without getting their paws muddy and wet with our **Portable Pointers™ Hunting Set!** No more standing frozen on three legs with their tails in the air...water resistant polystyrene signs do all the work! Easy-to-carry arrows are emblazoned with large typefaces for nearsighted hunters. Available in three sets of six signs each.
#Dcoy–1010 Waterfowl ..$79.99
#Bamb–1212 Small game ..$89.99
#Xcon–1414 Prison Escapees ..$99.99

F. Bone of the Month Club—Imagine the happy sight of your dog salivating uncontrollably as a mailman delivers a new assortment of gourmet bones to his doghouse every month! Here's what you get:

Jan:	Imported Himalayan Yak Bones
Feb:	Choice Selection of Bullfight Losers
Mar:	Glorious Bouquet of Spring Bones
Apr:	Hickory-smoked Ham Bones
May:	Bones of All Nations
June & July:	Summer Special Assortment of Bone Jams and Jellies
Aug:	Succulent Ostrich Leg Bone
Sept:	Supreme Bone Meal à la Pekinese
Oct:	Six-Year-Old Aged-in-Dirt Marrow Bone
Nov:	Vermont Turkey Dinner Leftovers
Dec:	Holiday Cheer Moose and Elk Bone Feast

#Woof–2020 Choice of any six months ..$150.00
#Woof–2121 Full Year ..$299.99
#Woof–4032 Ten-Year Order ..$1,999.99

G. Give polly a break with our **Automatic Cracker Dispenser!** Your majestic bird will love you when he no longer has to perform cute tricks or beg just to get a lousy cracker. With this handy device, Polly can pick his own cracker from a variety of choices just a beak's reach away. Posh! Easy ceiling mount included.
#Ritz–1876 Empty dispenser ..$34.95
#Ritz–1928 Cracker Fillers ..$15.95 ea.
(specify Ritz, soda, graham or animal)

H. Keep your spoiled rotten pets trim and in shape with the **Jane Fonda Pet Workout Tapes!** Watch your pets slim down with these frisky aerobic exercises endorsed by Benji, Morris the Cat and Spuds MacKenzie, all of whom owe their good looks to the regular use of these unique tapes! Each 60-minute cassette includes jumping jacks, pushups and tail wagging sections.
#Pant–8804 Dogs ..$19.95
#Psss–8804 Cats ..$19.95
#Twee–8804 Budgies ..$19.95
#Glub–8804 Goldfish ..$19.95
#Gaag–8804 Ferrets ..$19.95

E.

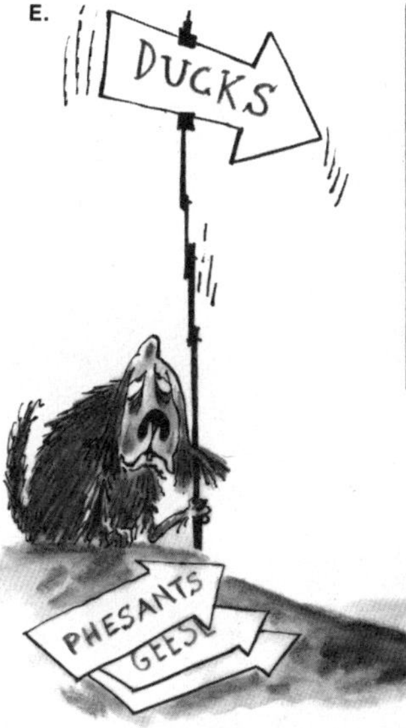
DUCKS
PHESANTS
GEES

F.

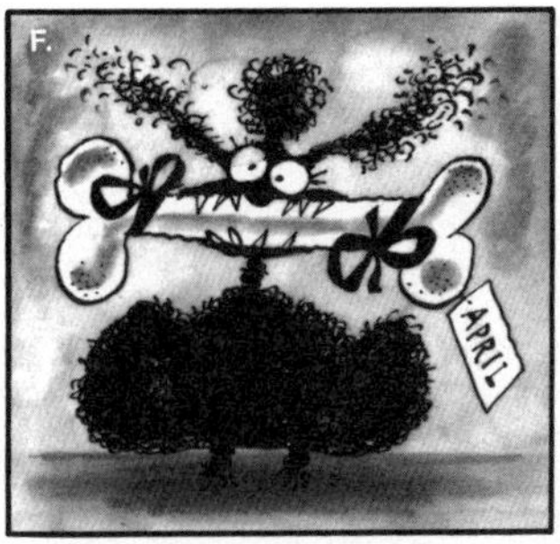
APRIL

G.

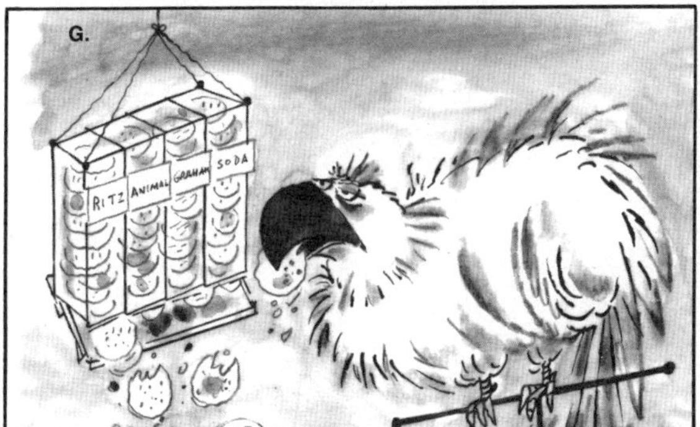
RITZ
ANIMAL
GRAHAM
SODA

H.

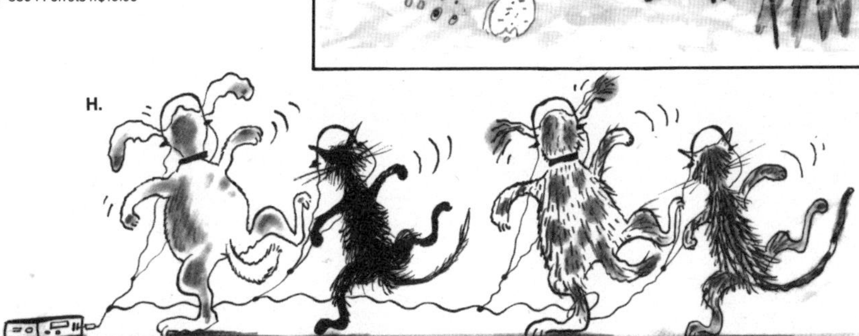
PORGES

HELF CONTROL DEPT.

f you're a consumer (and who isn't?) you must ave noticed that no matter which supermarket ou go to, your shopping experience is pretty nuch the same: LOUSY! Why? Because all super-narkets follow secret, diabolical guidelines nat store employees must swear to never reveal the public. But we at MAD have discovered nem, and expose them here for the first time:

SECRET SU

ARTIST: PAUL COKER

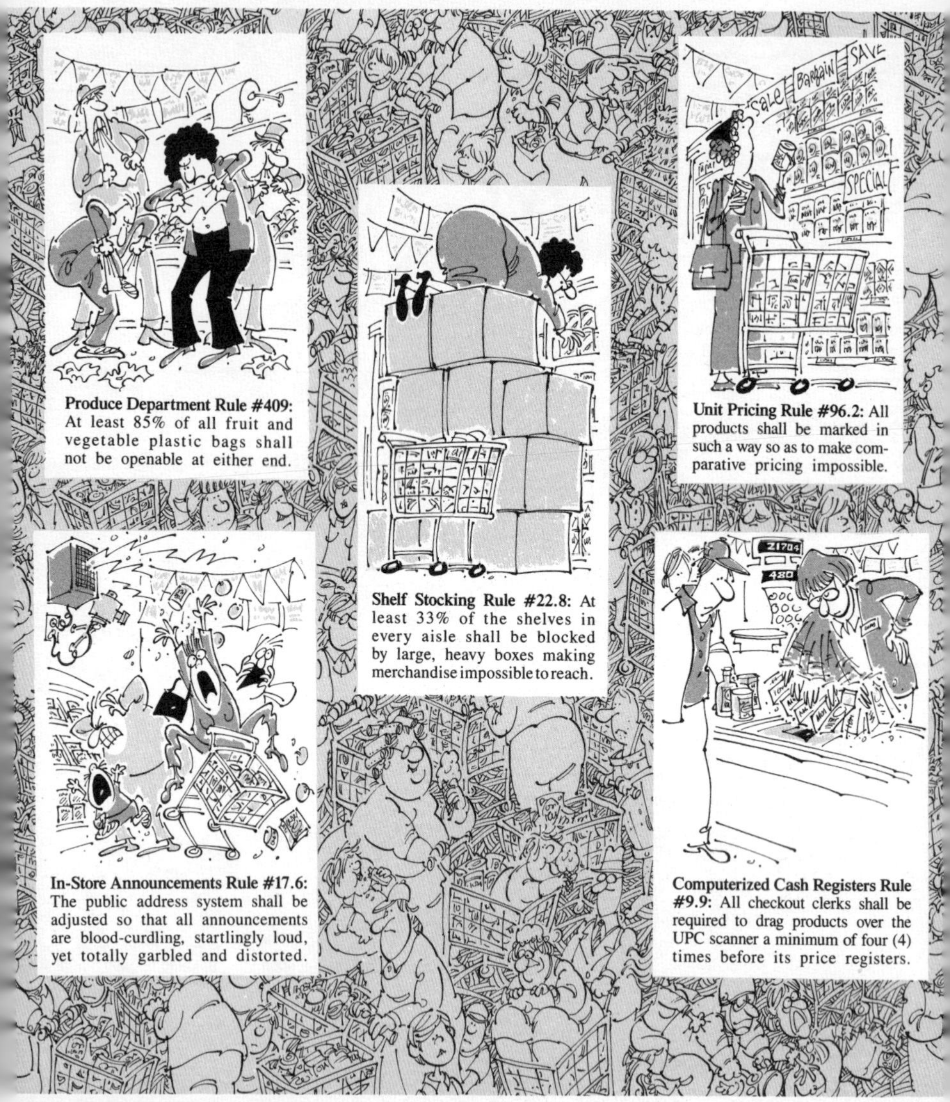
SALE
BARGAIN
SAVE
SPECIAL
21704
480

Produce Department Rule #409: At least 85% of all fruit and vegetable plastic bags shall not be openable at either end.

Shelf Stocking Rule #22.8: At least 33% of the shelves in every aisle shall be blocked by large, heavy boxes making merchandise impossible to reach.

Unit Pricing Rule #96.2: All products shall be marked in such a way so as to make comparative pricing impossible.

In-Store Announcements Rule #17.6: The public address system shall be adjusted so that all announcements are blood-curdling, startlingly loud, yet totally garbled and distorted.

Computerized Cash Registers Rule #9.9: All checkout clerks shall be required to drag products over the UPC scanner a minimum of four (4) times before its price registers.

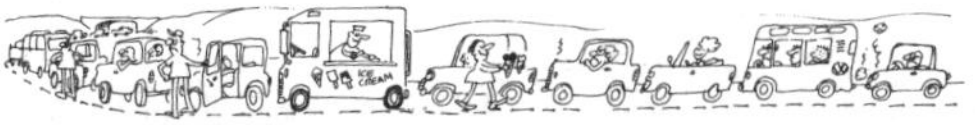

ERMARKET RULES

RITER: CHARLIE KADAU

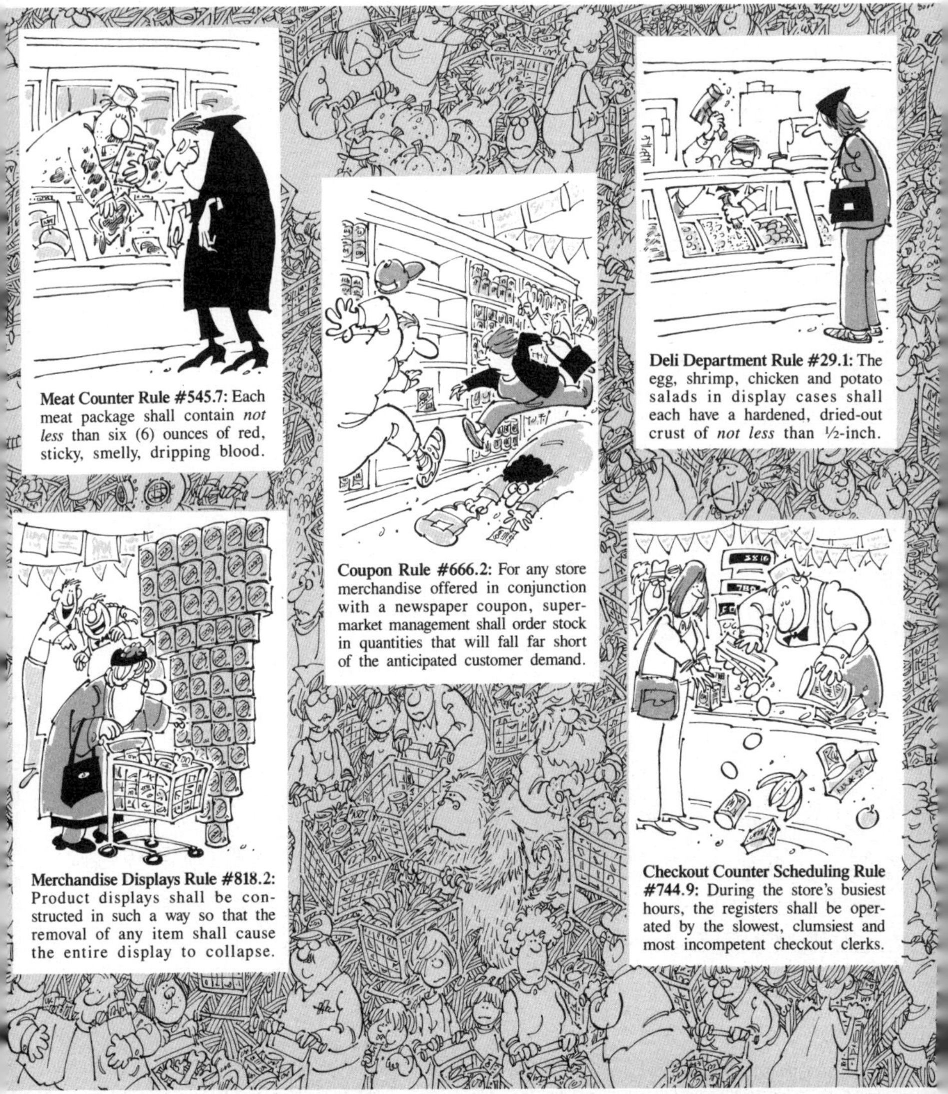

Meat Counter Rule #545.7: Each meat package shall contain *not less* than six (6) ounces of red, sticky, smelly, dripping blood.

Deli Department Rule #29.1: The egg, shrimp, chicken and potato salads in display cases shall each have a hardened, dried-out crust of *not less* than ½-inch.

Coupon Rule #666.2: For any store merchandise offered in conjunction with a newspaper coupon, supermarket management shall order stock in quantities that will fall far short of the anticipated customer demand.

Merchandise Displays Rule #818.2: Product displays shall be constructed in such a way so that the removal of any item shall cause the entire display to collapse.

Checkout Counter Scheduling Rule #744.9: During the store's busiest hours, the registers shall be operated by the slowest, clumsiest and most incompetent checkout clerks.

SEVERENCE PLAY DEPT.

You Know It's REALLY

You Know It's REALLY OVER When . . .

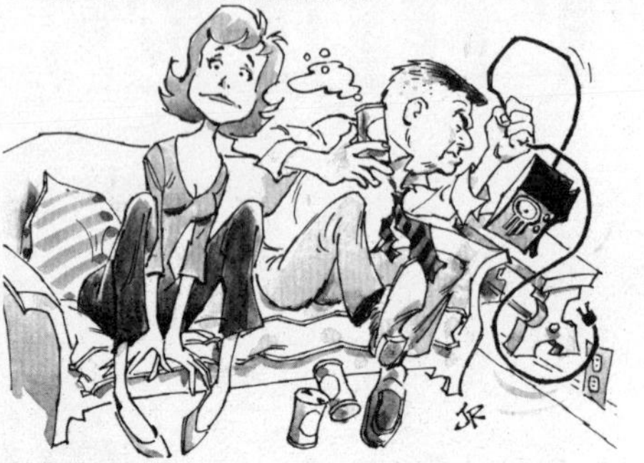

. . . the song you've always considered "our song" comes on the radio, and he snaps it off, saying, "I've always hated that thing!"

You Know It's REALLY OVER When . . .

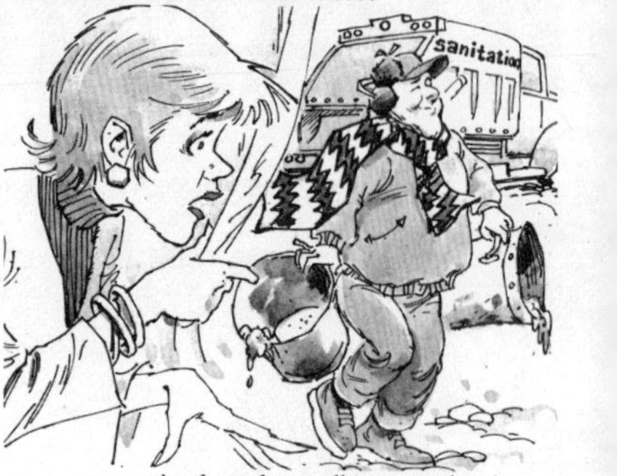

. . . you notice the garbage collector wearing the scarf you spent six months knitting for "him"!

You Know It's REALLY OVER When . . .

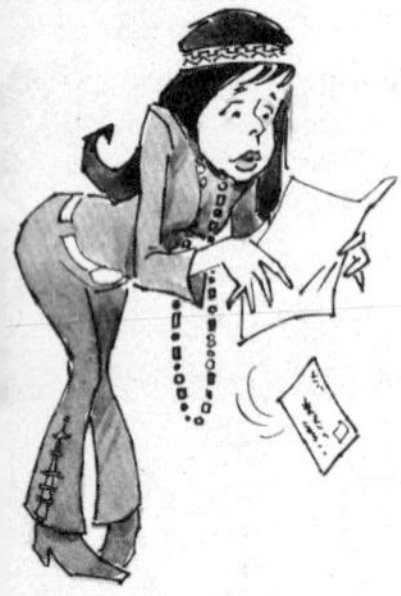

. . . his recent letters end with "Very truly yours,"!

You Know It's REALLY OVER When . . .

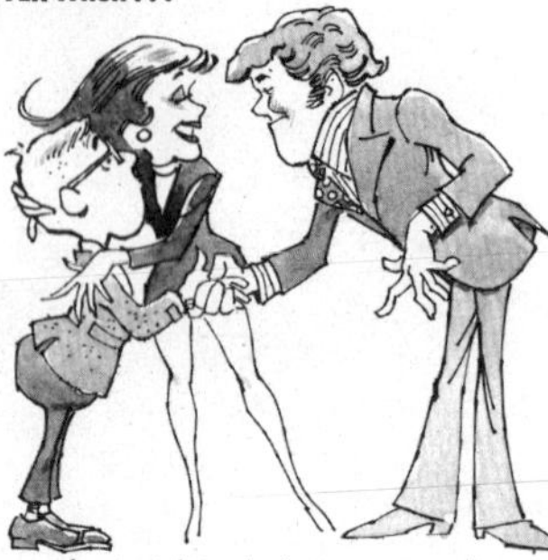

. . . she starts introducing you to people as one of her "oldest and dearest friends!"

You Know It's REALLY OVER When . . .

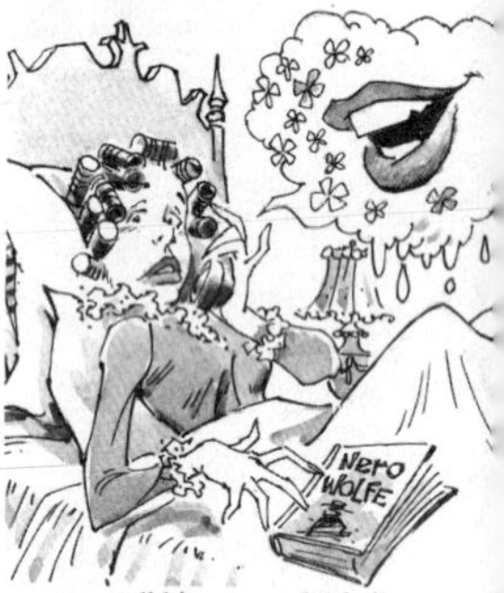
Nero WOLFE

. . . you call him up, and "she" answers

You Know It's REALLY OVER When . . .

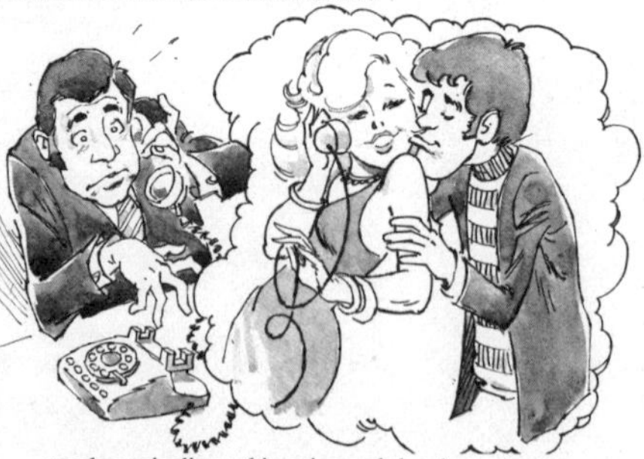

. . . you hear giggling, whispering and slurping noises as she breaks your date because of a headache!

You Know It's REALLY OVER When . . .

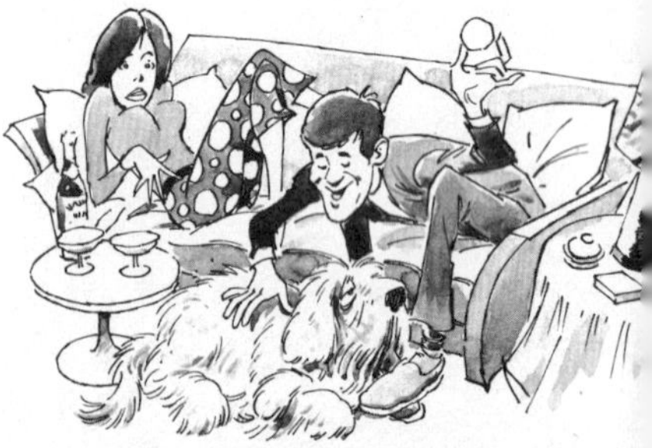

. . . the house is yours, the lights are low, the music is groovy . . . and he spends the night playing with Fido!

OVER When...

ARTIST: JACK RICKARD

WRITERS: AL JAFFEE & GLORIA L. RICH

ou Know It's REALLY OVER When . . .

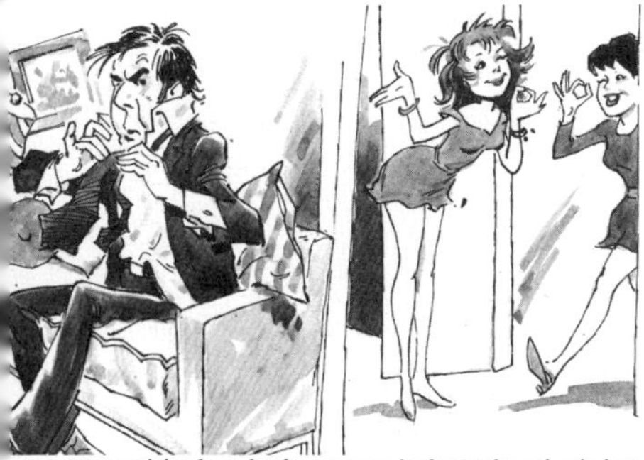

. you start noticing how, lately, someone is always dropping in just hen you think you're going to spend an evening alone in her pad.

You Know It's REALLY OVER When . . .

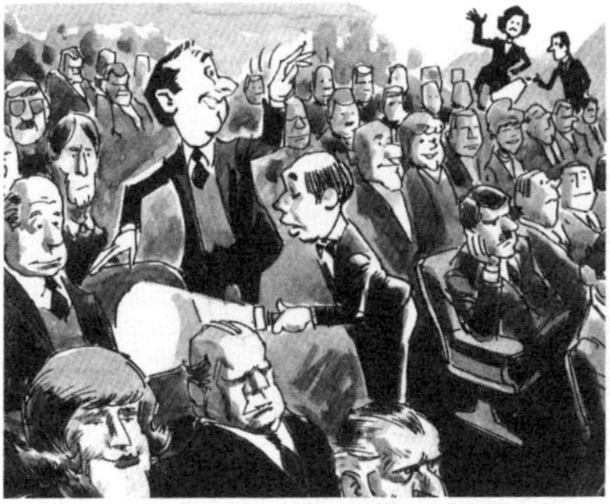

. . . you go to the movies, and he no longer cares about finding "two together"!

You Know It's REALLY OVER When . . .

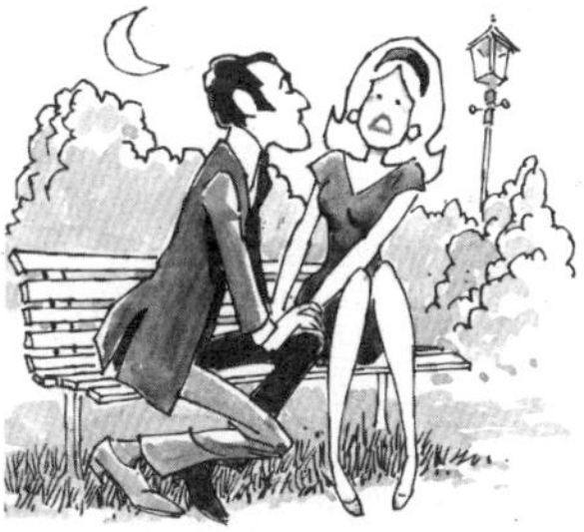

. . . he says, "We can't go on meeting like this!" . . . and you're both single!

You Know It's REALLY OVER When . . .

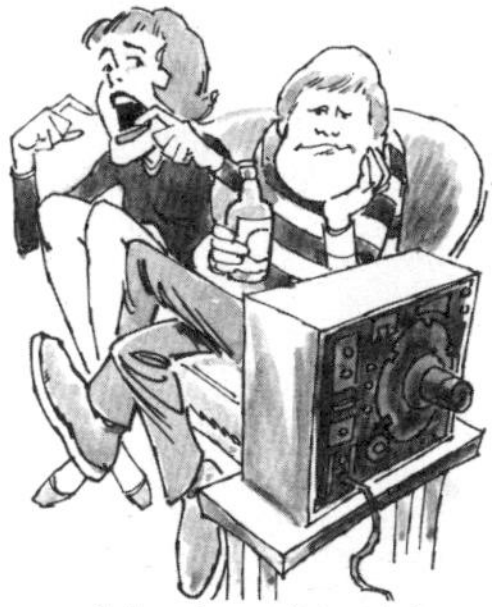

. . . he's no longer interested in your root canal work!

You Know It's REALLY OVER When . . .

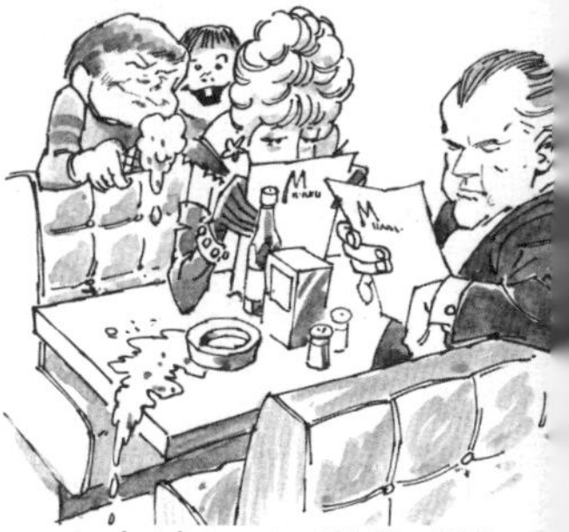

. . . he takes you to a "McDonald's" on the anniversary of your first date.

You Know It's REALLY OVER When . . .

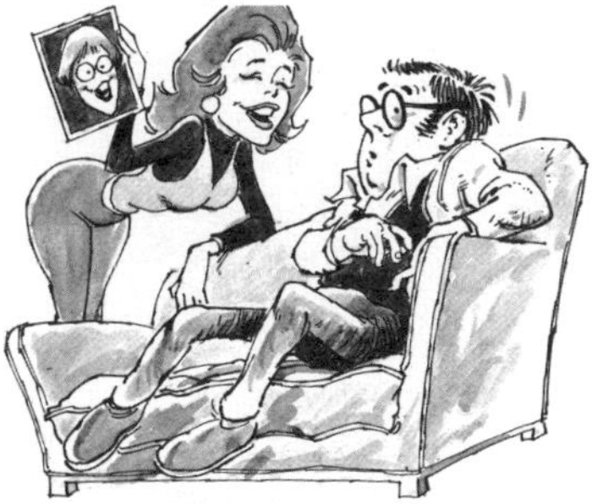

. . . she suddenly announces she has "just the right girl for you!"

You Know It's REALLY OVER When . . .

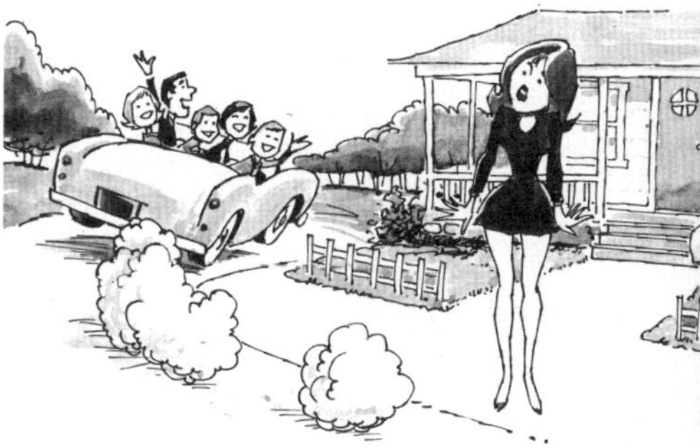

. . . he offers to drive the gang home, and you're the first one he drops off!

You Know It's REALLY OVER When . . .

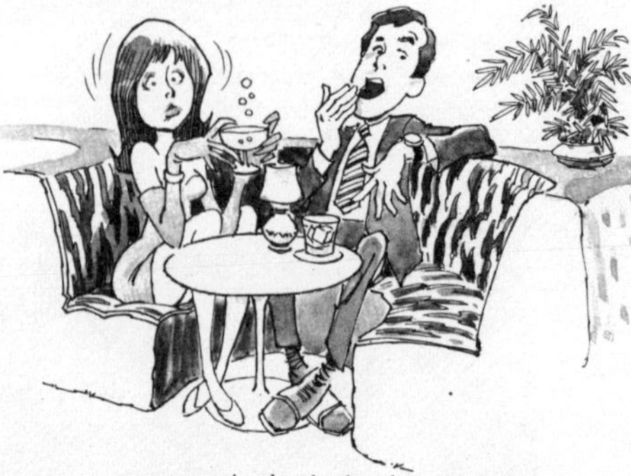

. . . you notice that, lately, whenever you're out together, he yawns a lot and looks at his watch!

You Know It's REALLY OVER When . . .

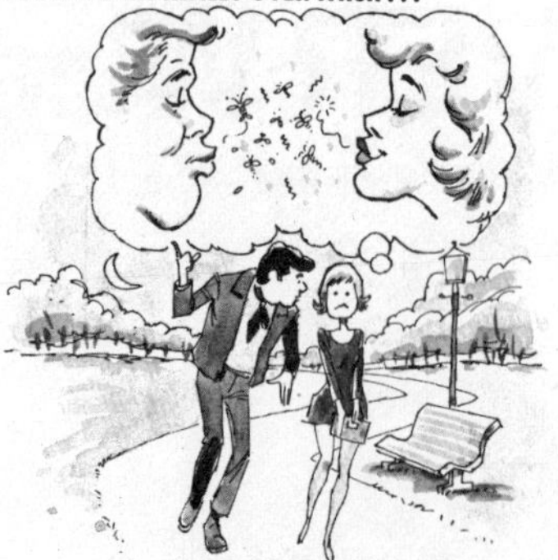

. . . he starts talking about kissing and sex from a hygienic point of view!

You Know It's REALLY OVER When . . .

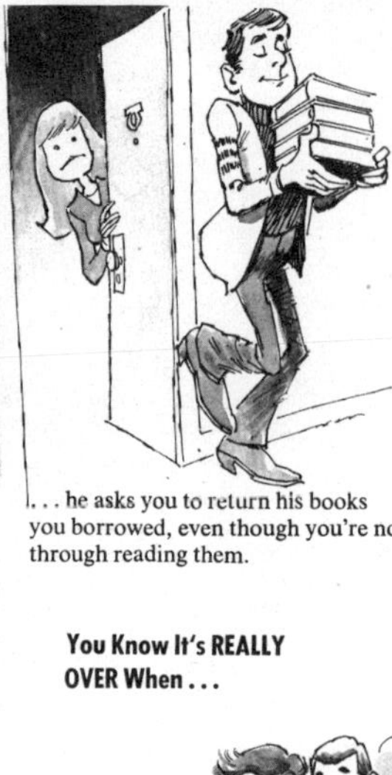

. . . he asks you to return his books you borrowed, even though you're not through reading them.

You Know It's REALLY OVER When . . .

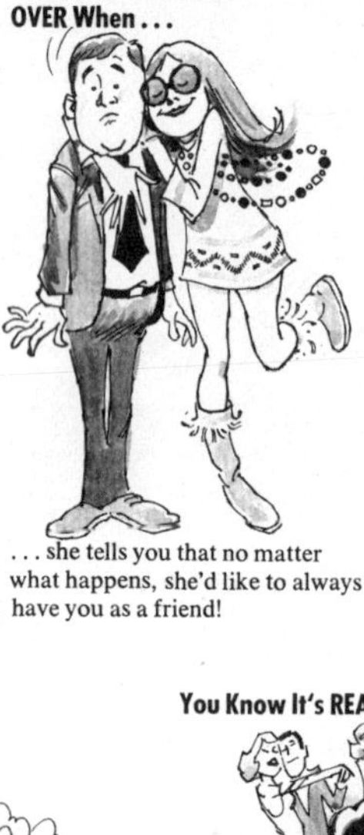

. . . she tells you that no matter what happens, she'd like to always have you as a friend!

You Know It's REALLY OVER When . . .

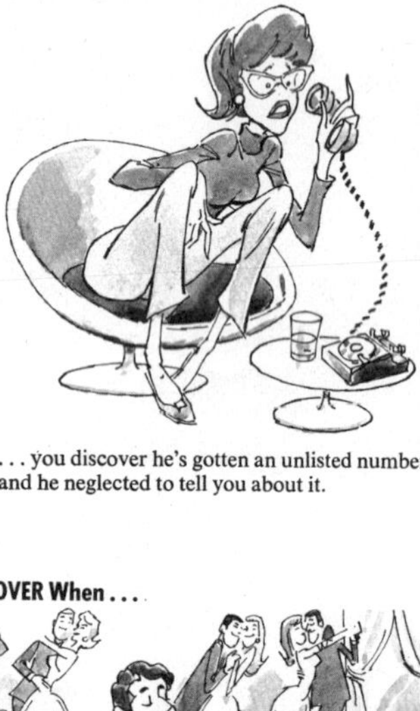

. . . you discover he's gotten an unlisted number, and he neglected to tell you about it.

You Know It's REALLY OVER When . . .

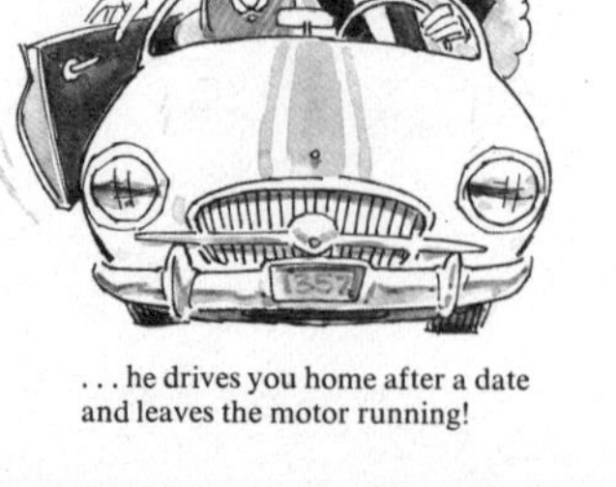
1357

. . . he drives you home after a date and leaves the motor running!

You Know It's REALLY OVER When . . .

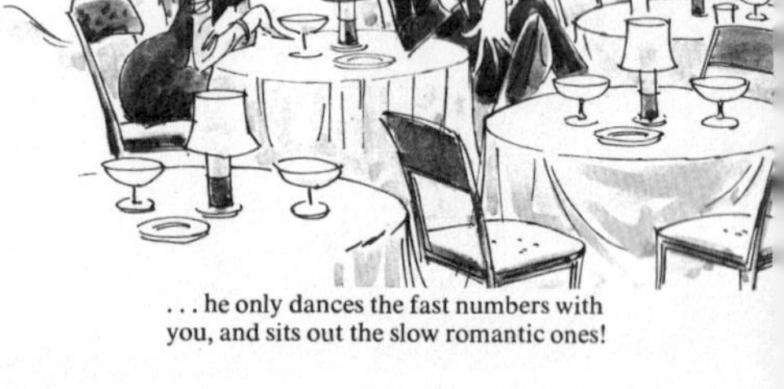

. . . he only dances the fast numbers with you, and sits out the slow romantic ones!

DON MARTIN DEPT.

ANOTHER VISIT WITH A SCULPTOR

Hmmmmm...
Hmmmm—Yes!
CLINK
That's it!! After months of intense study and sketching, it's finally completed! I'll call the Modern Museum Of Art immediately...
LATER...
Well, there it is, J.C.! I call it: "Man's Inhumanity To Man"...
What else could you call it!? You've expressed the thought exquisitely! I'll buy it!!
Could you put it in a bag for me?

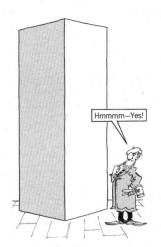

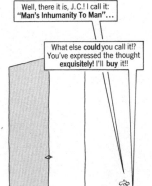

FRANK ON A ROLL DEPT.

The biggest problem in buying greeting car
is finding one that salutes an extraordina

GREETIN
F
Very
Special

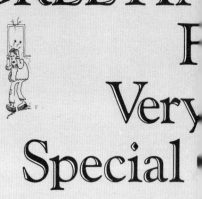

ARTIST: BOB JO

To a Deserted Wife

M.E.

He played around with Kay and Sue,
With Linda, your best friend;
But everytime you always knew
He'd come back in the end;
But now your dreams are swept away,
And though you took it well,
It must have been a shock that day
He left for good—with Mel.

To a Man Who's Been Institutionalized

Last week you were King George the Fourth,
Today you're Aaron Burr;
Tomorrow you'll be Ollie North
Columbus or Ben-Hur;
Your sanity, the doctors say,
There's no hope of restoring;
You're nuts, of course, but what the hey—
At least your life's not boring!

NINA
Bob Jones

To a Man Who's Just Come Out of a 10-Year Coma

Some changes in your life you'll find
Now that you have "come back";
Your business partner's robbed you blind;
Your wife is hooked on crack;
Your daughter lives with seven guys;
Your son is into sheep;
On second thought, it might be wise
If you went back to sleep!

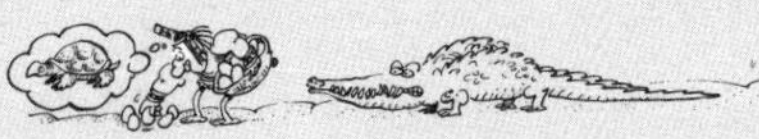

casion. Such cards simply don't exist. At
st till now. Which is our way of introducing

G CARDS

Very

ccasions

JEFFREY L. COHEN   WRITER: FRANK JACOBS

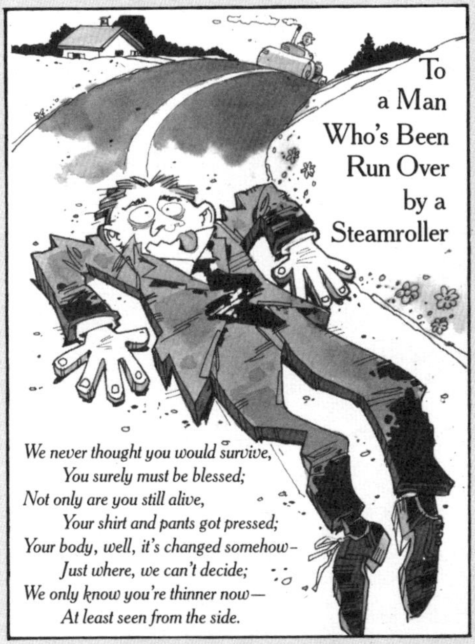

To a Man Who's Been Run Over by a Steamroller
We never thought you would survive,
You surely must be blessed;
Not only are you still alive,
Your shirt and pants got pressed;
Your body, well, it's changed somehow–
Just where, we can't decide;
We only know you're thinner now—
At least seen from the side.

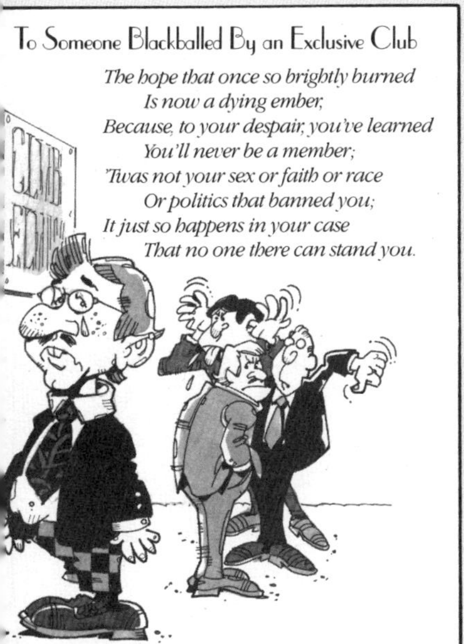

To Someone Blackballed By an Exclusive Club
The hope that once so brightly burned
Is now a dying ember,
Because, to your despair, you've learned
You'll never be a member;
'Twas not your sex or faith or race
Or politics that banned you;
It just so happens in your case
That no one there can stand you.

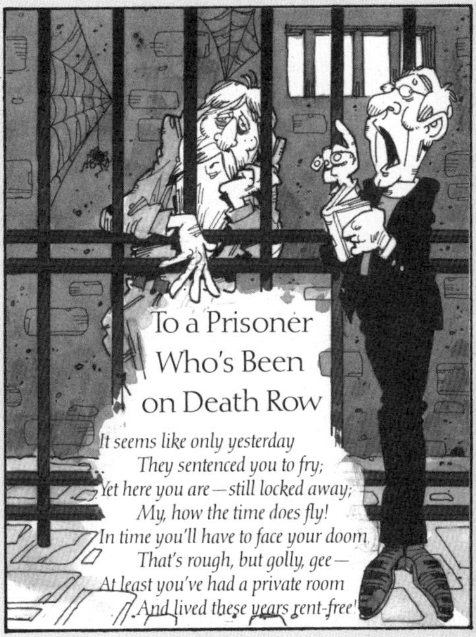

To a Prisoner Who's Been on Death Row
It seems like only yesterday
They sentenced you to fry;
Yet here you are—still locked away;
My, how the time does fly!
In time you'll have to face your doom,
That's rough, but golly, gee—
At least you've had a private room
And lived these years rent-free!

The Let-Her-Know-You're-Hot-For-Her Palm Tickle

ALL JAFFEE DEPT.

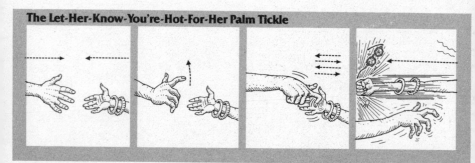

When we're very young, we're taught that shaking hands is the polite thing to do. But as we

MAD LOOKS A

IDEA: FRANK JA

The Prove-You're-A-Member Secret Brotherhood Grab

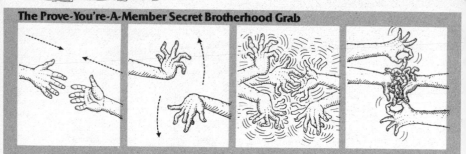

The Let's-See-Who-Cries-"Uncle"-First Macho Knuckle Crunch

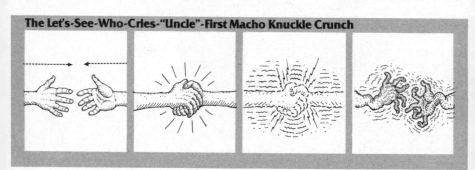

The Phoney-Show-Of-Sympathy Sandwich Crush

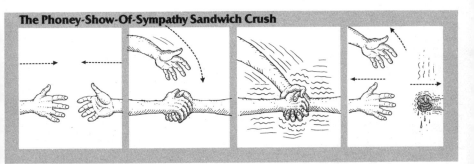

er, we discover that a handshake can have a variety of meanings and uses. As you'll see as...

HANDSHAKES

ST & WRITER: AL JAFFEE

The Show-You're-Cool High Five Slap Shake

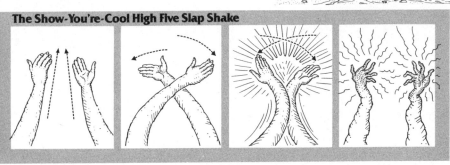

The Man's-Best-Friend Clutch And Squeeze Hold

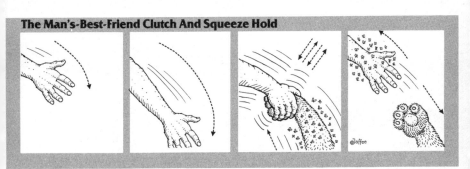

BETTER READ THAN SAID DEPT.

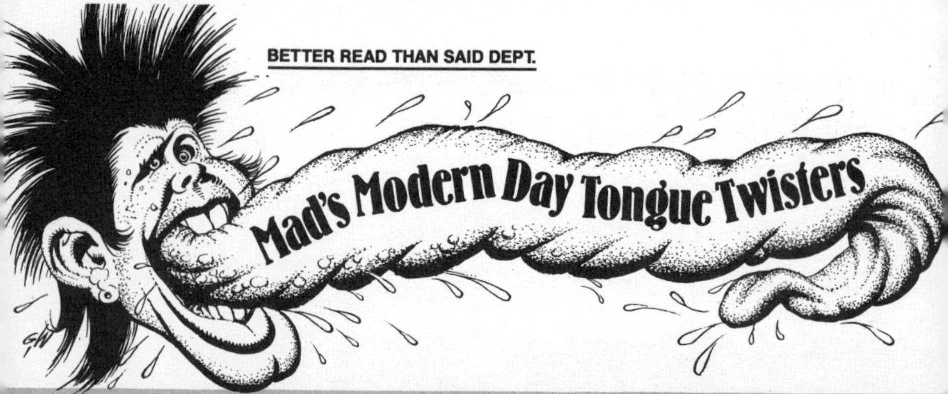
Mad's Modern Day Tongue Twisters
GW

Comic Cosby Coaxes Coke Consumption

Plummeting Pump Prices Plague Persian Petrol Producer

Youths Seek Truth With Sex Sleuth Ruth

Blonde Baby Boomers Buy Bloomingdale's Blue Baby Bloomer

She Smells Slick Smells By The Seashor

How Much Dope Did The Dope Dealer Deal When The Dope Dealer Did Deal Dope

Tots Toying With Toxic Toys Get Totale

ARTIST: GEORGE WOODBRIDGE WRITER: DAVID AMES

SWEAT SUCKS! DEPT.

Wherever you look today, people are into jogging, tennis, marathon-running and other forms of (yecch) exerting pastimes. Mainly, physical fitness has taken over. Which makes it really tough on lazy slobs who hate exercise in any form, but don't want to admit it. What in heck are they supposed to do? Well... as luck would have it, MAD recently came across a catalogue crammed with items expecially designed for the "Non-Athlete." Which is our way of introducing...

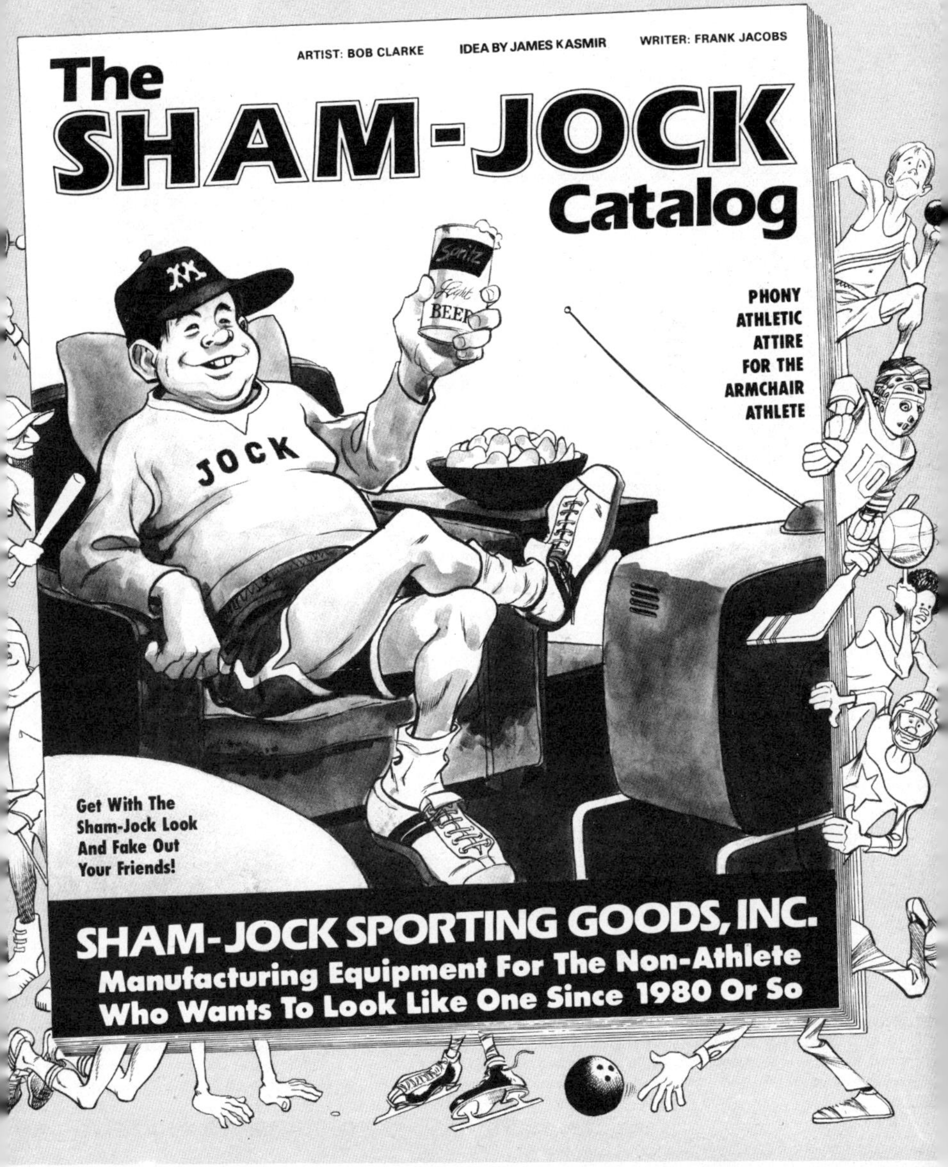
ARTIST: BOB CLARKE
IDEA BY JAMES KASMIR
WRITER: FRANK JACOBS
The SHAM-JOCK Catalog
Light BEER
JOCK
PHONY ATHLETIC ATTIRE FOR THE ARMCHAIR ATHLETE
10
Get With The Sham-Jock Look And Fake Out Your Friends!
SHAM-JOCK SPORTING GOODS, INC.
Manufacturing Equipment For The Non-Athlete Who Wants To Look Like One Since 1980 Or So

OUR "SLOB'S SWEATSUIT" IS DESIGNED TO IMPRESS!

PROPERTY OF
NOTRE
DAME
ATHLETIC DEPT.

NOTE THESE EXCLUSIVE SHAM-JOCK FEATURES!

The "stenciled inscription" makes it look as if you once starred as a first-string college athlete.

The pre-stained underarms gives "evidence" that your sweatshirt has actually been sweated in.

The pre-patched knees convinces your friends that this is a garment that has actually been used for your grueling daily workouts.

The pre-ripped ankle bands backs up wild stories of your "courage" attempting to evade snapping dogs while jogging or marathon-running.

DEPT.

Sweatshirt elbows are triple-layer padded, providing comfy support for those weekends that you spend holding cans of beer while you doze off in your favorite easy chair!

NO. 819 **$39.95**

YOU REALLY GET INTO SHAM-JOCK SOCKS!

Sock it to your chums with our phony footwear! Each pair of our Sham-Jock Socks sports bogus "athletic stripes" at their tops—pre-faded to simulate rugged jock use! Actually, material is heather-soft cashmere for maximum luxuriating while you're goofing off!

FOOT
STENCH
ANOTHER FINE PRODUCT
FROM PUTRID INDUSTRIES

Order 3 pair of socks and get a FREE spray can of our patented Foot-Stench formulated to duplicate the *ulp*-sickening smell of most runners' feet!

NO. 435 **1 PR. $5.50**
3 PR. $15.00

SMELLING IS BELIEVING!

So why work up perspiration when you can spray it on with "Quik Sweat"? Applied to the face, it beads and runs like the real thing! Applied to the underarms, it clings and gives you that unmistakable "work-out odor"!

NO. 297 **PER CAN $5.95**

KEEP ON THE TOP OF YOUR GA

Your game of fakery, that is, when you wear your
Sham-Jock Tennis Hat! Pre-wilted and pre-stained
lifelike bird droppings, it has that authentic "U
Look" coveted by all lazy non-athletes! Order it to

NO. 281 (SPECIFY HAT SIZE) **$6.**

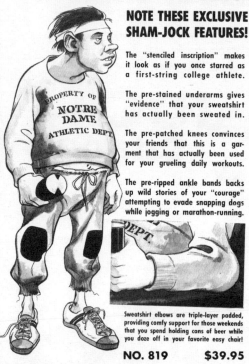

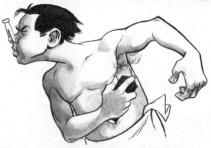

OUR SHAM-JOCK SNEAKERS ARE A REAL "PUT-ON"!

Bending over can be strenuous! Why be "tied down" with ordinary sneakers when you can ease your feet into "Fake Laced" zippered slip-ons!

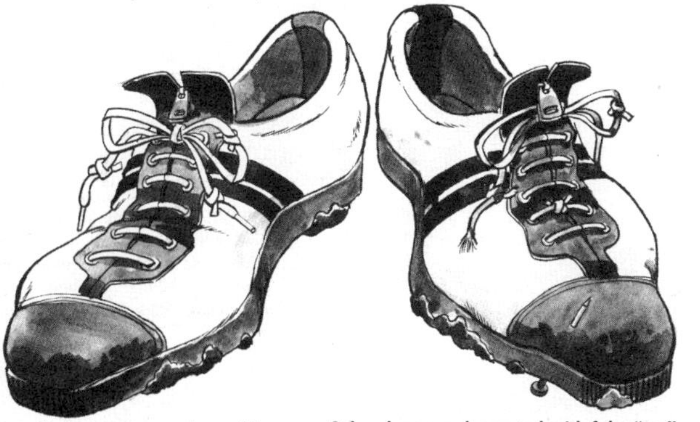

Factory worn soles will prove beyond a doubt that you're into heavy running!

Sole edges are decorated with fake "tar" and "doggie-do" stains... giving more evidence of much rugged street running!

YOU'LL LOVE THESE ADDED "EXTRAS"

Knots in laces will convince your athletic pals that these sneakers have seen plenty tough daily use!

Optional "Imbedded Nail" effect adds to convincing "Run-In Look"!

Cushy heel-base with butter-soft padding guarantees comfort when propping feet on sofas, coffee-tables, footstools and hassocks!

Reenforced multi-layered toe tips resist wear and tear associated with kneeling and tuning TV sets.

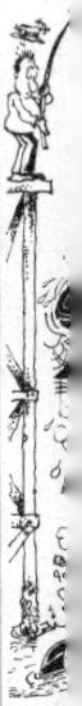

NO. 1015 $32.50 WITH OPTIONAL IMBEDDED NAIL $36.50

FAKE THEM OUT WITH "INSTANT BLOOD"!

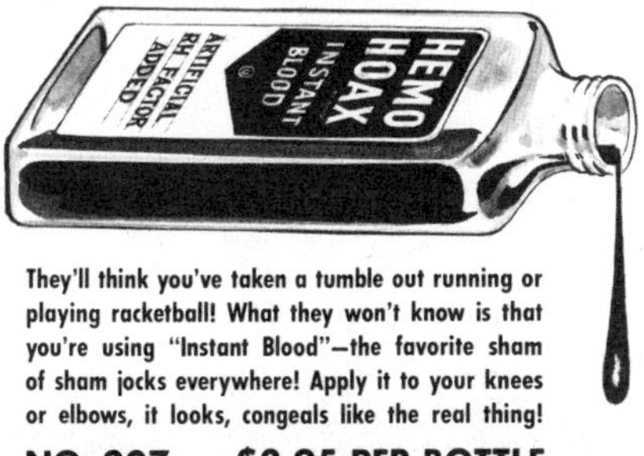
HEMO HOAX
INSTANT BLOOD
ARTIFICIAL RH FACTOR ADDED

They'll think you've taken a tumble out running or playing racketball! What they won't know is that you're using "Instant Blood"—the favorite sham of sham jocks everywhere! Apply it to your knees or elbows, it looks, congeals like the real thing!

NO. 207 $2.95 PER BOTTLE

GET SMASHED OFF THE COURT!

It looks like a can of tennis balls... but actually, it's a sneaky "thermos" that holds 12 oz. of beer or booze or soda or whatever you drink! Now you can have a quick and quite snootful ...while all those other idiots around you are into (yecch) exercising like mad.

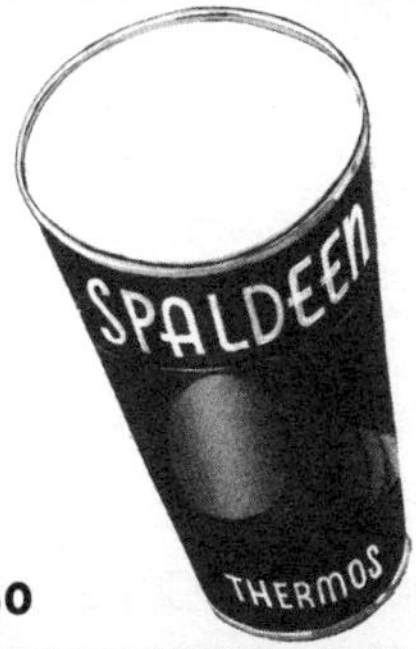
SPALDEEN
THERMOS

NO. 211 $12.50

WHO'S COVERING UP?

You are... when you dress up your library by covering up your old books with our fake jock-sounding jackets! Choose from these exciting titles:

NO. 290 EACH $1.95

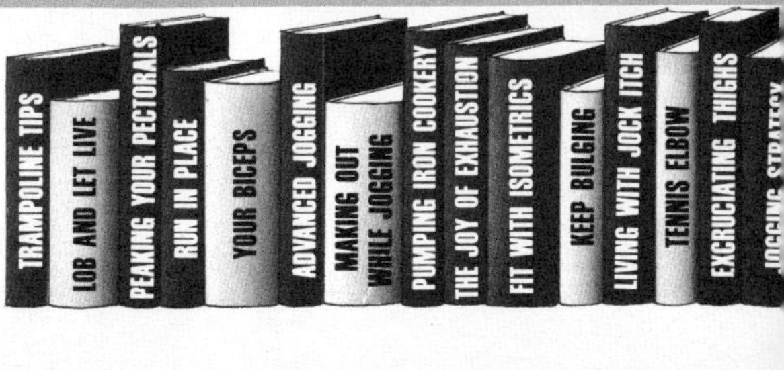
TRAMPOLINE TIPS
LOB AND LET LIVE
PEAKING YOUR PECTORALS
RUN IN PLACE
YOUR BICEPS
ADVANCED JOGGING
MAKING OUT WHILE JOGGING
PUMPING IRON COOKERY
THE JOY OF EXHAUSTION
FIT WITH ISOMETRICS
KEEP BULGING
LIVING WITH JOCK ITCH
TENNIS ELBOW
EXCRUCIATING THIGHS

YOU'LL LOOK GYM-DANDY IN OUR "DO-NOTHING" GYM SHORTS

THE MORE YOU'RE OUT OF SHAPE THE MORE YOU'LL LOVE THEM!

Rip in outer seam adds credibility to the respected "Much-Used Look"!

Discover a new world of non-exercise with the gym shorts favored by out-of-shape "dawdlers" the world over!

The fabric is pre-grimed with road dust mixed with authentic city soot, creating the impression you're into heavy outdoor running like marathons!

Grass stains give "proof" you've taken spills on many a fictitious slope!

Seat is velour-lined for comfy softness while sitting around, and crotch area is double padded to prevent the dreaded "thigh shock" resulting from holding iced drinks between your legs.

NO. 663 $9.95

THE SHAM-JOCK GYM BAG HAS IT ALL!

Our most successful item of athletic fakery! Friends will think you're toting shorts, gym socks and other detestibles! In truth, as the cutaway shows, bag's interior contains compartments for stashing cookies, candy bars, potato chips and similar junk food necessities needed at a moment's notice by the phony jock!

NO. 275	**$12.95**
CHOCK FULL OF GOODIES	**$29.95**

GET INTO AN OLD RACKET!

Carry around this beat-up old tennis racket...and look like a demon of the courts! Pre-scuffed and scratched, its loose strings provide you with the alibi that you're "waiting to have it re-strung!" You're not, of course, and you'll come off as a real tennis fanatic! Off the court, that is, before you can exert yourself!

NO. 244 $27.50

THEY'LL LOVE YOU...IN A PHONY CAST!

A must for the non-skier! Ultra light weight, it fits snugly around your leg as if something was actually broken! It's a sure-fire way to make out in the lodge, while the real skiers are wasting their time on the slopes!

NO. 224 $15.95
PRE-AUTOGRAPHED $25.95

Special Gourmet Supplement

ALF's Celebrity Cat Cookbook

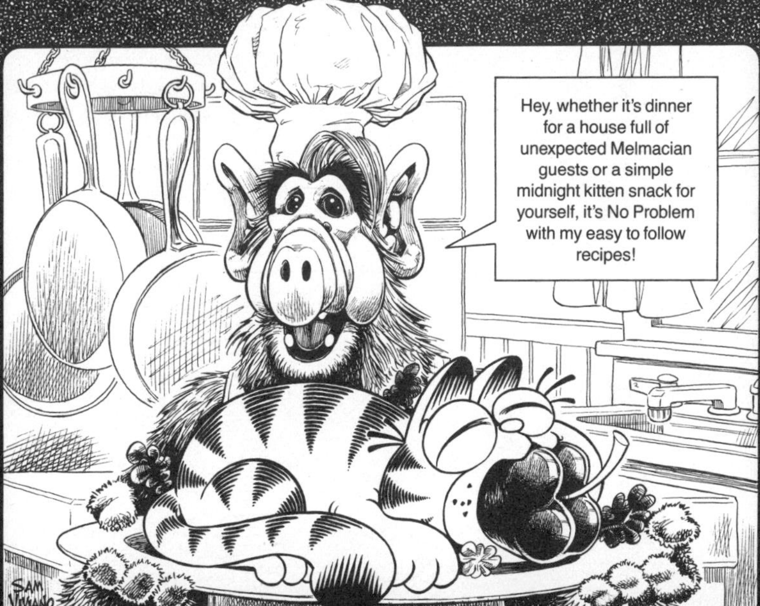
Hey, whether it's dinner for a house full of unexpected Melmacian guests or a simple midnight kitten snack for yourself, it's No Problem with my easy to follow recipes!
SAM VIVIANO

Fabulous Feline Feasts...

...from America's Leading Cat Gourmet!

ARTIST: SAM VIVIANO WRITER: J. PRETE

Hey, thanks for buying the ole Alfer's cookbook! Since most of you have only dreamed about savoring a nice, plump, succulent kitty, I thought I'd start by reciting a little ditty on cat anatomy that was a favorite of mine as an impressionable young Melmacian!

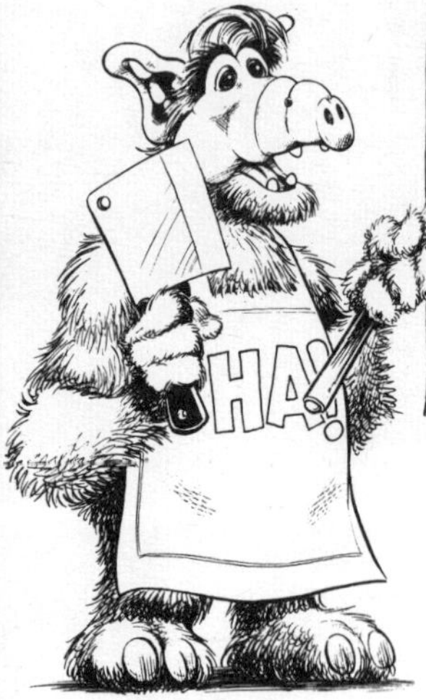
HA!

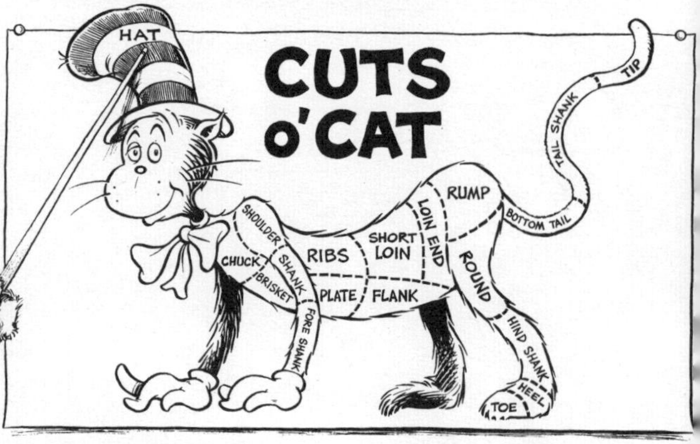
CUTS o'CAT
HAT
SHOULDER
CHUCK
SHANK
BRISKET
FORE SHANK
RIBS
PLATE
SHORT LOIN
FLANK
LOIN END
RUMP
ROUND
HIND SHANK
HEEL
TOE
BOTTOM TAIL
TAIL SHANK
TIP

Juicy, Seussy, poosy cat—
Nothing tastes as good as that!
Boiled or broiled or spread like jam,
Scrambled like green eggs and ham,
No problem in a vat of fat,
Just so long as it's pure cat!

Wanna see a work of art?
Just check out this butcher chart!
Pick your cuisine, pick your style,
Feline is so versatile!
Melmac ground or chopped for stew.
Any cut of cat will do!

GARLIC Garfield

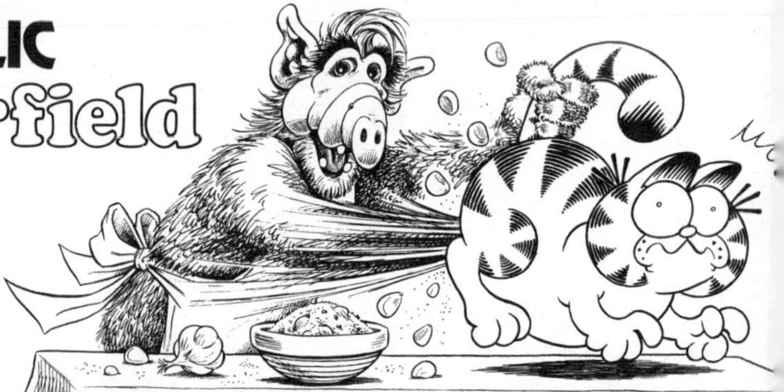

Start by gutting the big fella. Wash 'em good to get rid of an lingering flea powder. (I don't know about you, but that stuff give me cramps!)Next, stuff the Garster with sixty whole cloves of garli mixed in with your favorite stuffing. (I recommend Siamese Stov top Brand Stuffing.) Bake in a 350° oven for about two hours or unt his tail and ear-tips turn golden brown. This dish is the cat's meow Ha! Get it? The cat's meow! Sometimes, I just kill myself!

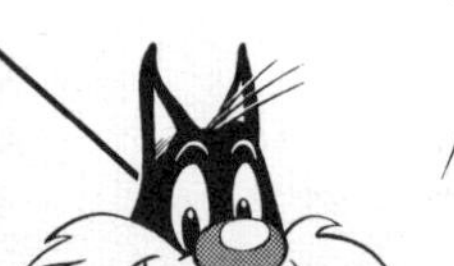

SYLVESTER and SUCCATASH
see page 119.

Whether you're eating a well-prepared Tabby, chocolate cake or left-over linoleum tiles, everything always tastes better when it's smothered in Cat-sup! Yeah! Especially when it's my homemade kind…

Felix the CAT-SUP

Just throw a couple of tomatoes, a basil leaf and Felix in the food processor and let it whiz on high. Within minutes you'll have the purr-fect topping for any dish!

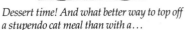

THE *Kliban* CAT-SEROLE

Here's a quick dish that's a big favorite among Melmacians who work part-time. Start by cutting the cat into several parts. Be sure to save any fur that falls out! It makes great soup! Season with a pinch of catnip and surround it with some potatoes and vegetables. Then nuke this baby in the microwave for 17 minutes. (Less if the cat was spayed.) Umm, umm, umm! Ya know, on earth, gluttony is a sin. But on Melmac, it's a gift!

Dessert time! And what better way to top off a stupendo cat meal than with a…

CARMELIZED HELLO KITTY HEAD-ON-A-STICK

Lop off Hello Kitty's head. You can toss out the body. There's so little meat on it, it's not worth saving for stew. Bake in a pre-heated oven for about 10 minutes or until the Kitty's whiskers start to shrivel. Let it cool, then jab in a stick, dip the whole thing in hot melted caramel and that's it! Back on Melmac, kids love these, especially during those long, hot summer years!

REMEMBER! The best thing about all my recipes is that there's never any cleanup! Just do what I do and leave the dirty dishes for somebody else to wash! Ha! What a great idea! I tell ya, I'm a culinary genius!

TRAINING A CLAM TO DO "STUPID PET TRICKS"

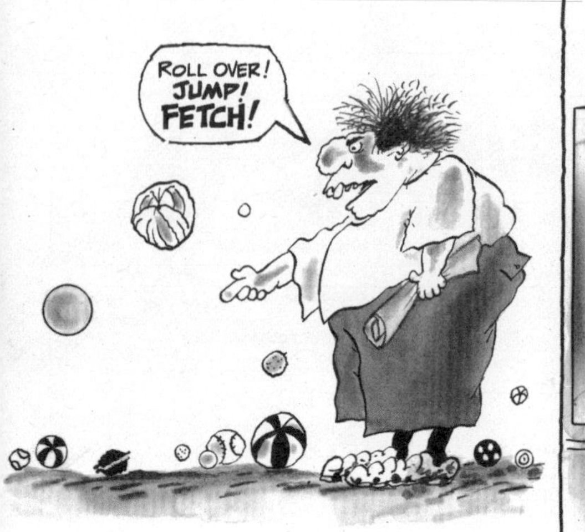
ROLL OVER! JUMP! FETCH!

TIMING EXERCISE SWIMMING LAPS FOR YOUR FAT GOLDFISH

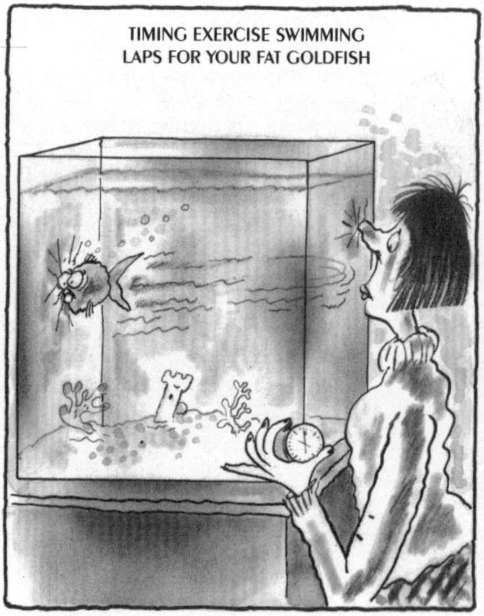

A BOUQUET OF YAWNING GLORIES DEPT.

Some CLASSIC EXAMPLES o

GROWING YOUR FIRST MOUSTACHE WHILE WATCHING THE WEATHER CHANNEL

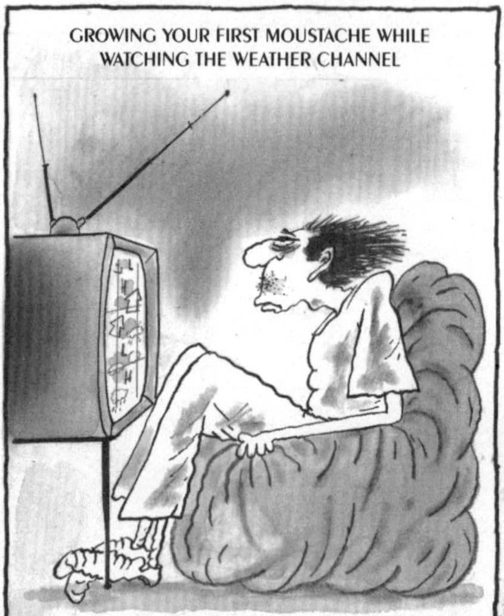

SCORE-KEEPING A SENIOR CITIZEN CHESS TOURNAMENT

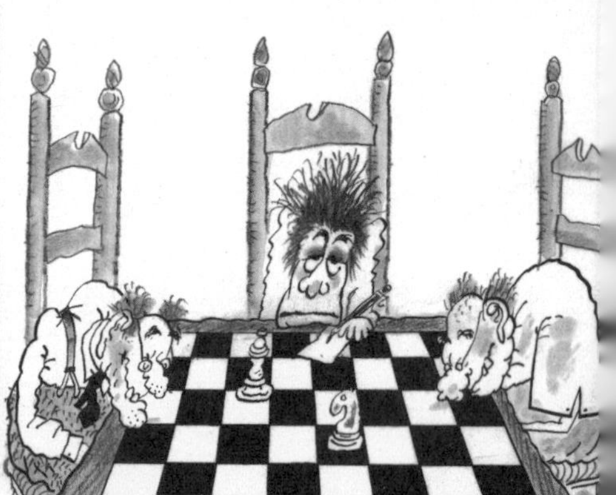

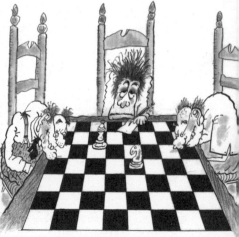

RECONSTRUCTING SHREDDED TEST QUESTIONS

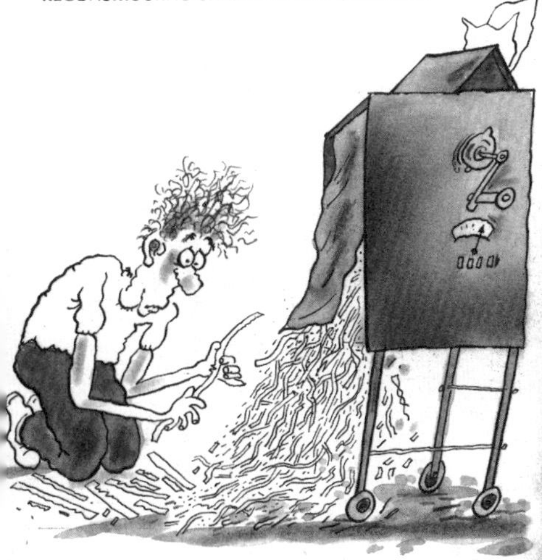

ANSWERING ALL YOUR JUNK MAIL IN CALLIGRAPHIC SHORTHAND

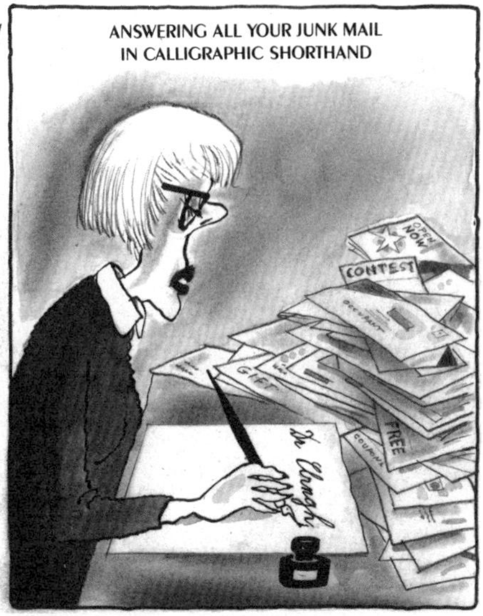
OPEN NOW
CONTEST
GIFT
FREE

WORLD CLASS BOREDOM

ARTIST AND WRITER: PAUL PETER PORGES

CHARTING THE FLIGHT PATTERN OF A PESTY HOUSEFLY

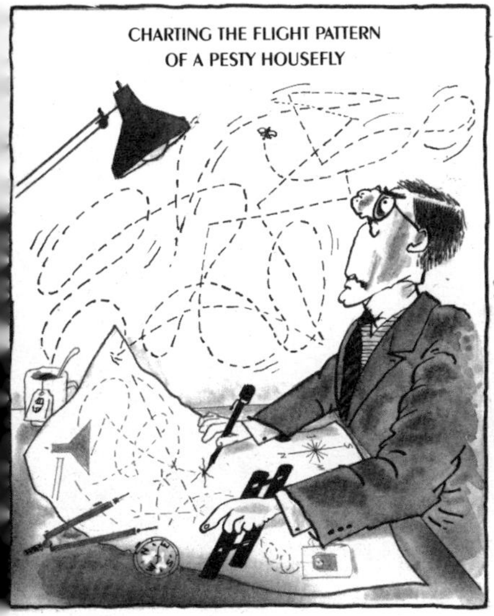

TEACHING YOUR PARAKEET IRREGULAR FRENCH VERBS

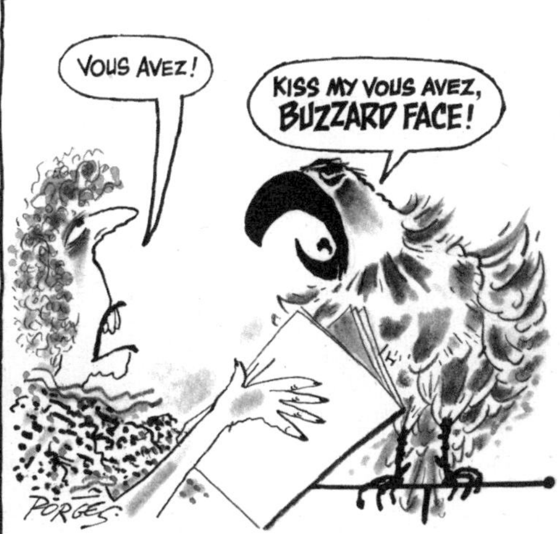
VOUS AVEZ!
KISS MY VOUS AVEZ, BUZZARD FACE!
PORGES

DON MARTIN DEPT.

THE PAPERHANGER

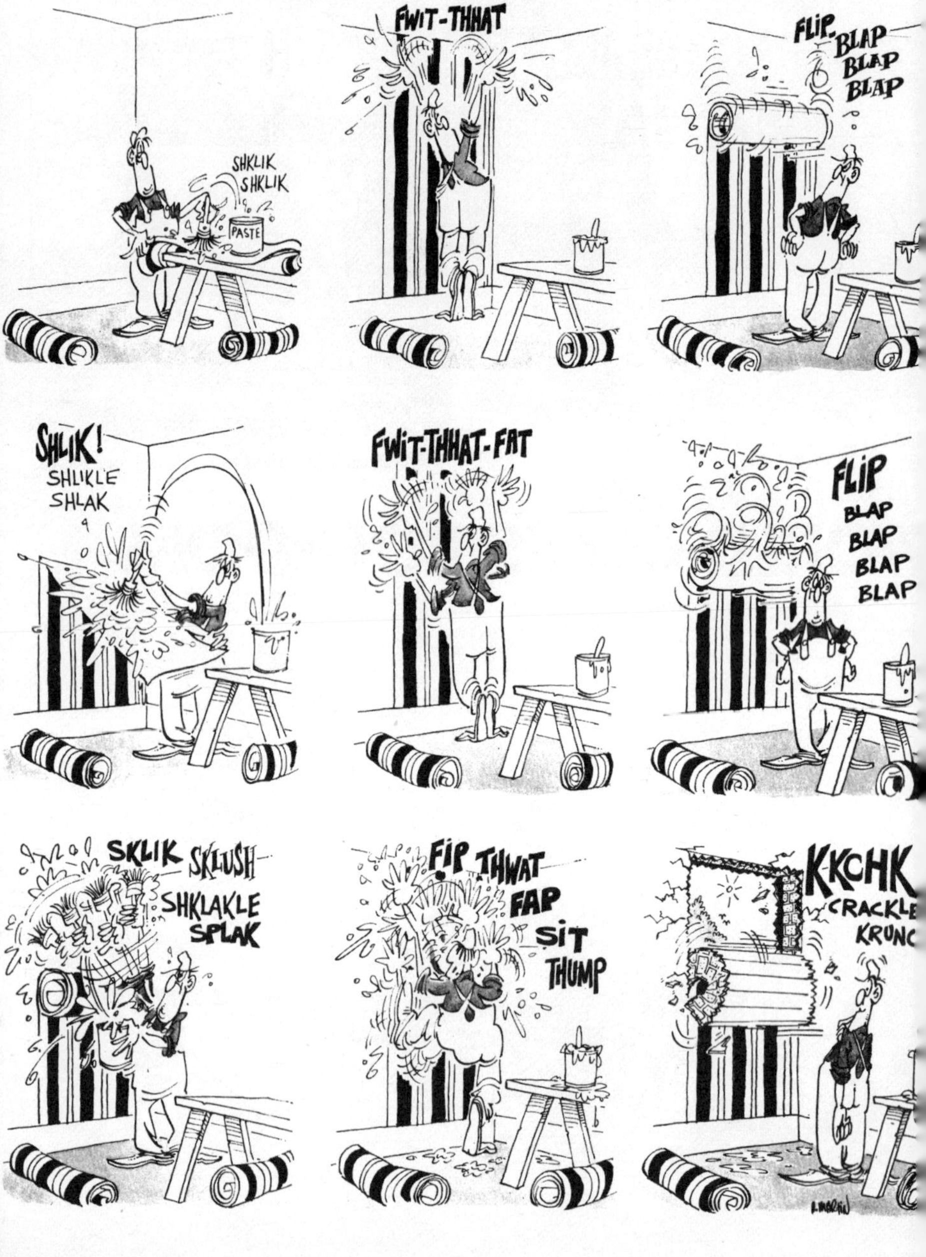
SHKLIK
SHKLIK
PASTE
FWIT-THHAT
FLIP
BLAP
BLAP
BLAP
SHLIK!
SHLIKLE
SHLAK
FWIT-THHAT-FAT
FLIP
BLAP
BLAP
BLAP
BLAP
SKLIK
SKLUSH
SHKLAKLE
SPLAK
FIP
THWAT
FAP
SIT
THUMP
K-KCHK
CRACKLE
KRUNC

TAKE A POWDER DEPT.

You've seen it on television commercials...and you've read about it in newspapers and magazine ads! It's the

AMAZING MIRACLE OF THE 20TH CENTURY!

ARM & HAMMER Baking Soda

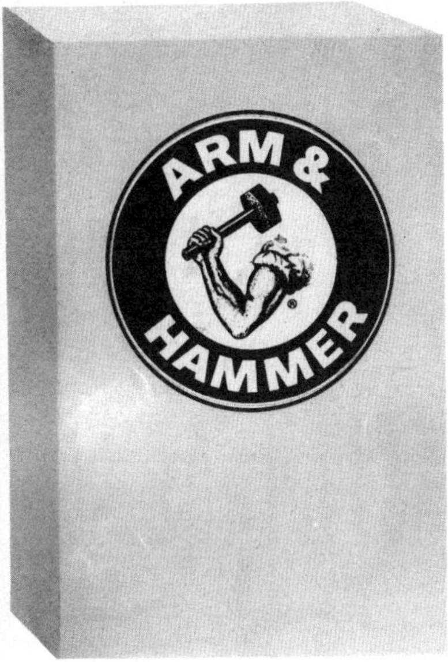
ARM &
HAMMER

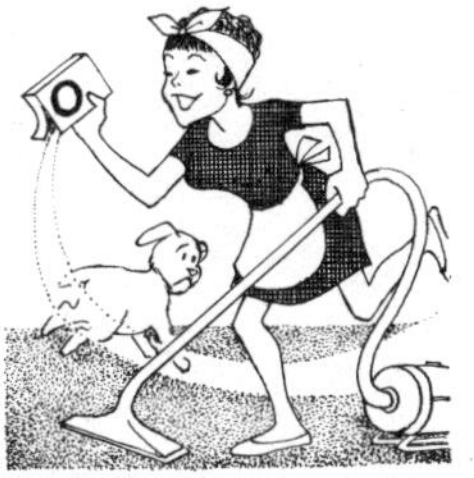

IT FRESHENS YOUR CARPETS!

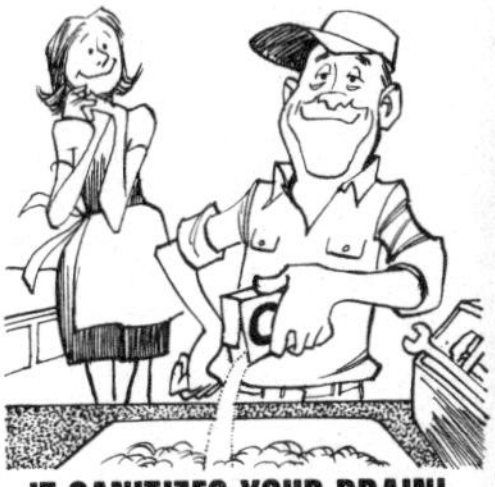

IT SANITIZES YOUR DRAIN!

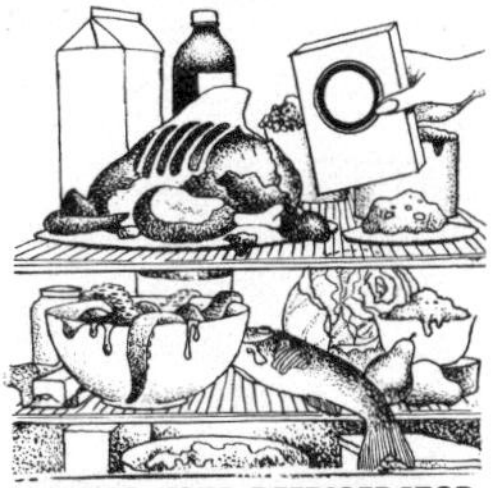

IT KEEPS YOUR REFRIGERATOR SMELLING SWEET AND CLEAN!

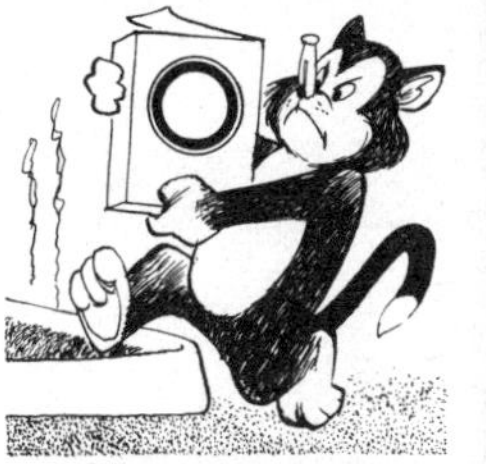

IT DEODORIZES CAT BOXES! IT CLEANS YOUR TEETH...

... IN FACT, IT DOES ANYTHING ARM & HAMMER THINKS WILL MAKE YOU BUY IT! AND EVERY YEAR, THEY MANAGE TO DISCOVER NEW WAYS THAT THEIR BAKING SODA CAN IMPROVE YOUR LIFE! IN FACT, WE CAN ALMOST ASSUREDLY LOOK FORWARD TO THESE...

NEW USES FOR ARM & HAMMER BAKING SODA

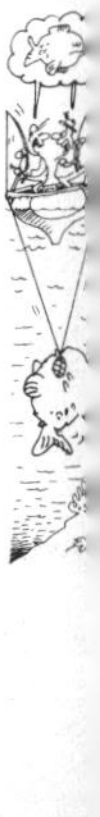

ARTIST: BOB CLARKE WRITER: MIKE SNIDER

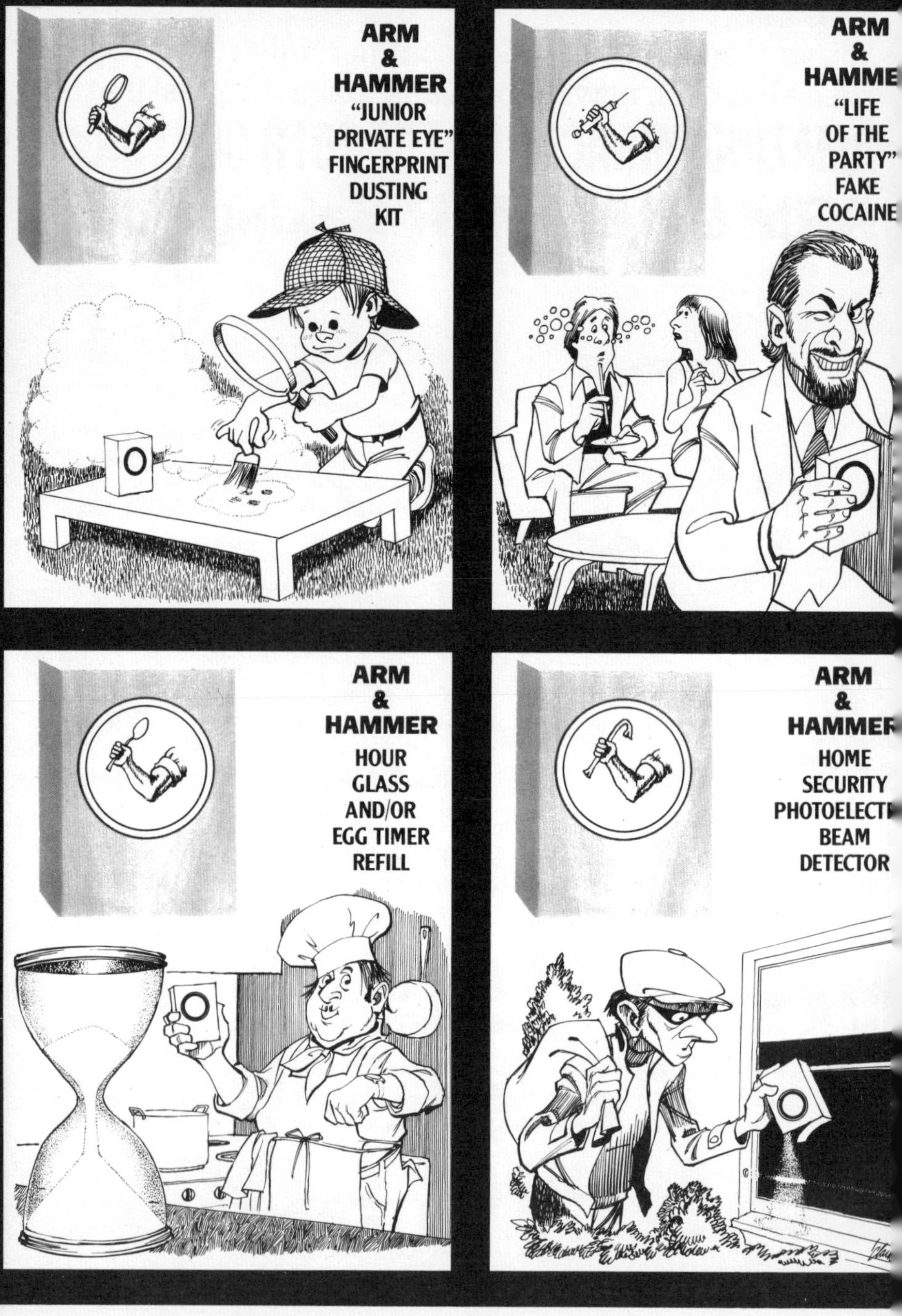

ARM
&
HAMMER
"JUNIOR PRIVATE EYE" FINGERPRINT DUSTING KIT
ARM
&
HAMME
"LIFE OF THE PARTY" FAKE COCAINE
ARM
&
HAMMER
HOUR GLASS AND/OR EGG TIMER REFILL
ARM
&
HAMME
HOME SECURITY PHOTOELECT
BEAM DETECTOR

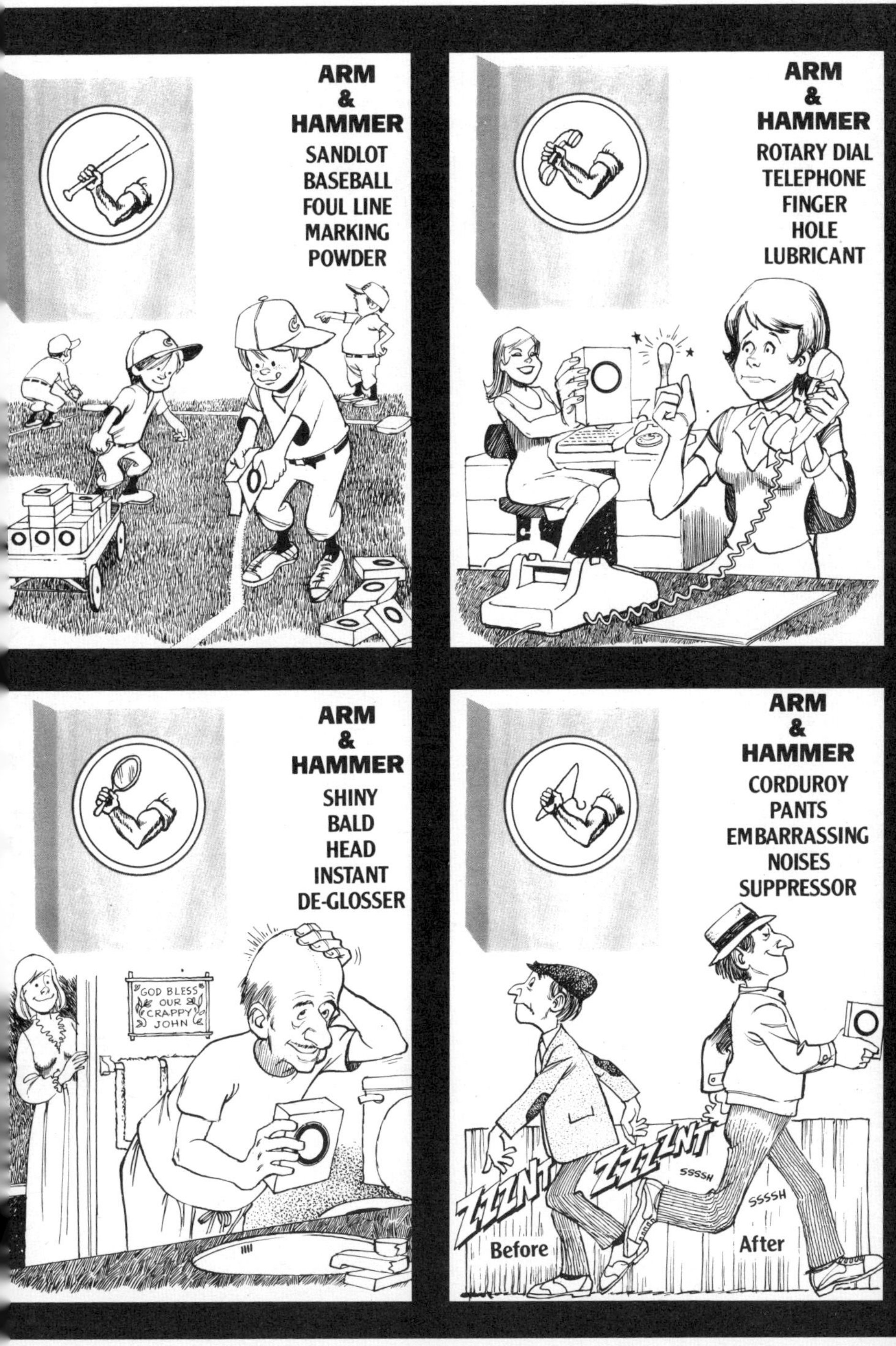

ARM & HAMMER
SANDLOT BASEBALL FOUL LINE MARKING POWDER
ARM & HAMMER
ROTARY DIAL TELEPHONE FINGER HOLE LUBRICANT
ARM & HAMMER
SHINY BALD HEAD INSTANT DE-GLOSSER
GOD BLESS OUR CRAPPY JOHN
ARM & HAMMER
CORDUROY PANTS EMBARRASSING NOISES SUPPRESSOR
ZZZZNT
ZZZZNT
SSSSH
SSSSH
Before
After

WHERE THERE'S SMOKE, THERE'S IRE DEPT.

Here we go with another MAD "Hate Book"... those little gems calculated to make MA readers feel better by blowing off steam about their pet hates. Since non-smokers a the most intolerant people in the world when it comes to smokers, all of you smok

THE MAD NON-SM

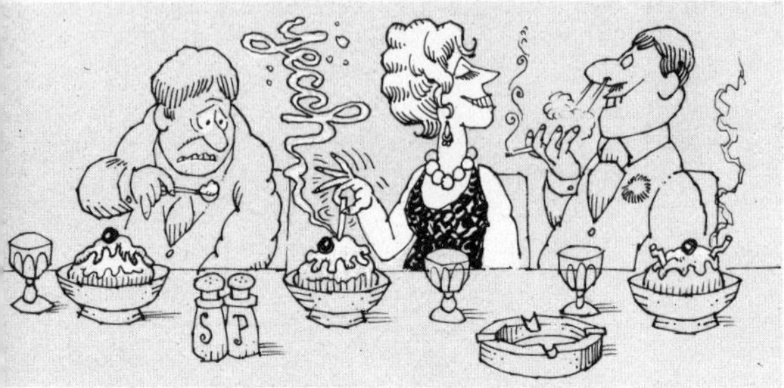
Yecch
S
P

Don't you hate smokers who . . .
. . . put out butts in dishes of food while you're still eating!

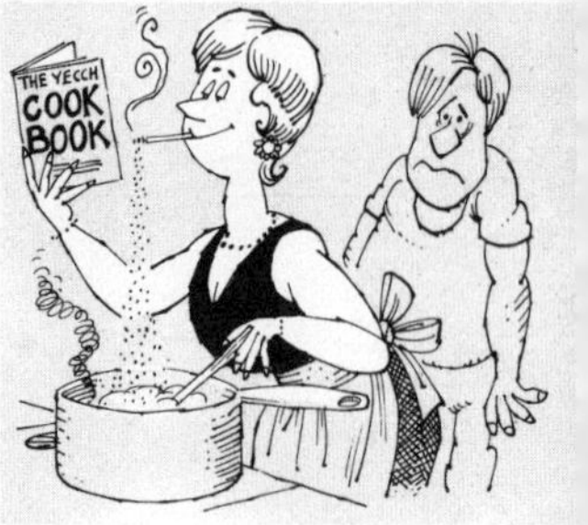
THE YECCH COOK BOOK

Don't you hate smokers who . . .
. . . smoke while they cook!

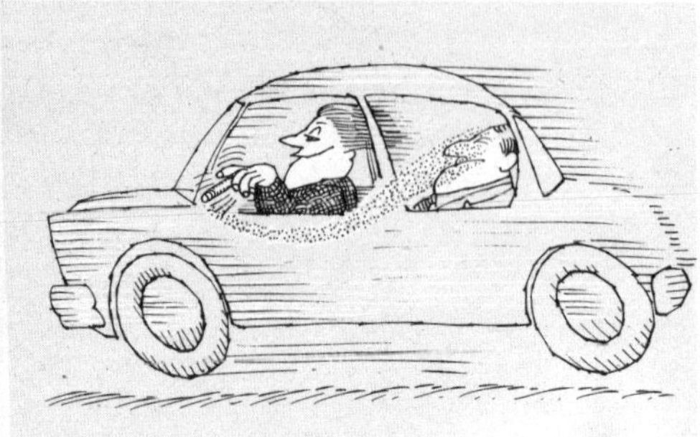

Don't you hate smokers who . . .
. . . flick their ashes out windows of fast-moving cars when you're sitting in the rear seat!

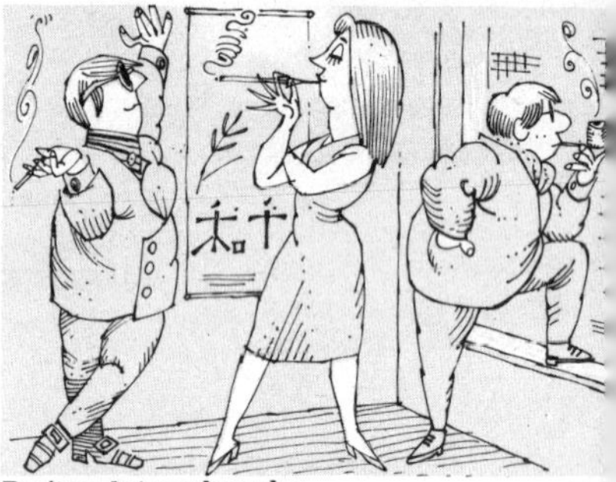

Don't you hate smokers who . . .
. . . affect phony smoking poses that are supposed to make them look smart and sophisticated!

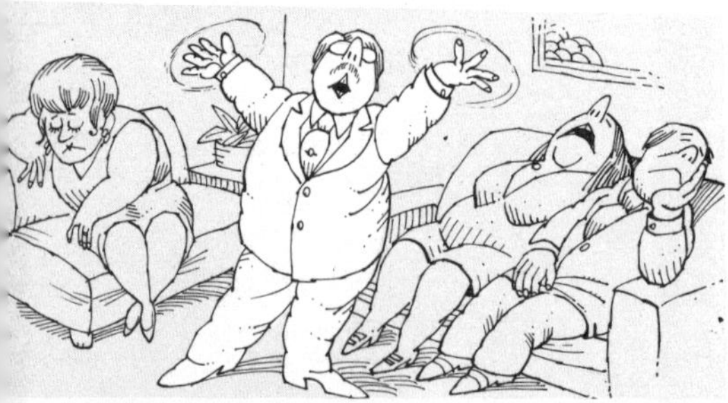

Don't you hate smokers who . . .
. . . bore you with the details of their experiences every time they attempted to give up smoking!

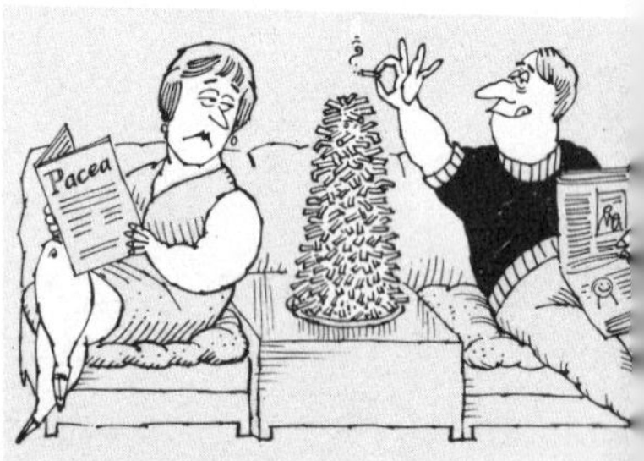
Pacea

Don't you hate smokers who . . .
. . . add yet another butt to a full ashtray without ever once thinking of emptying it!

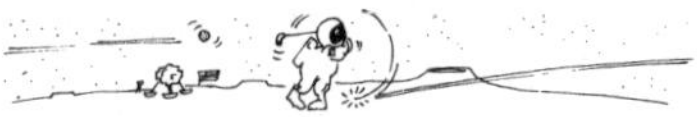

ıtter skip this article. Because it's calculated to make non-smoking MAD readers feel ıtter by blowing off steam about people who, in addition to being addicted to the dis- ısting habit of smoking, also have disgusting smoking habits. Here, then, Gang, is...

)KERS HATE BOOK

ARTIST & WRITER: AL JAFFEE

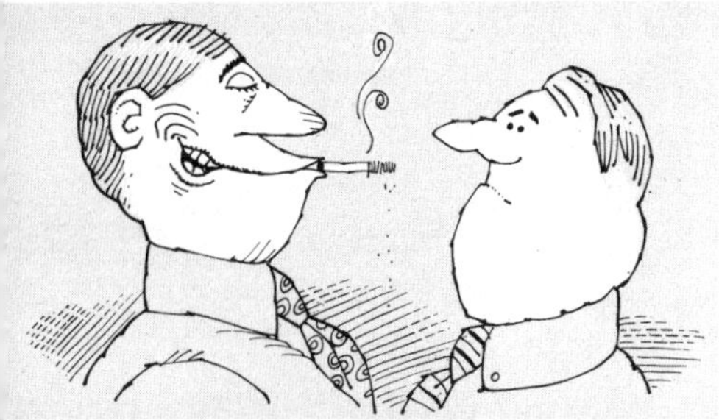

Don't you hate smokers who . . .
. . talk without ever removing their cigarette from their mouth!

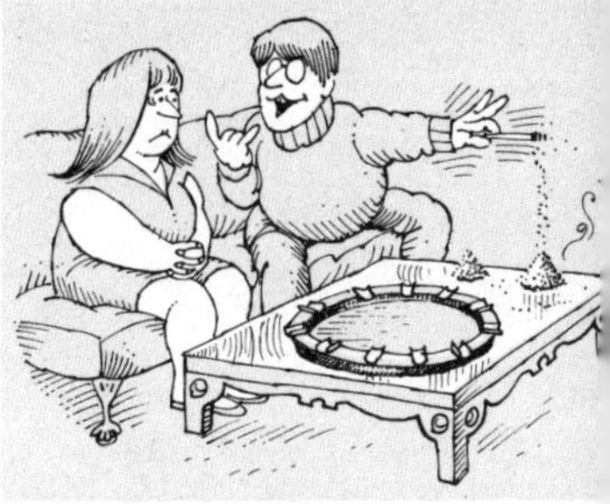

Don't you hate smokers who . . .
. . . never hit the ashtray no matter how big it is!

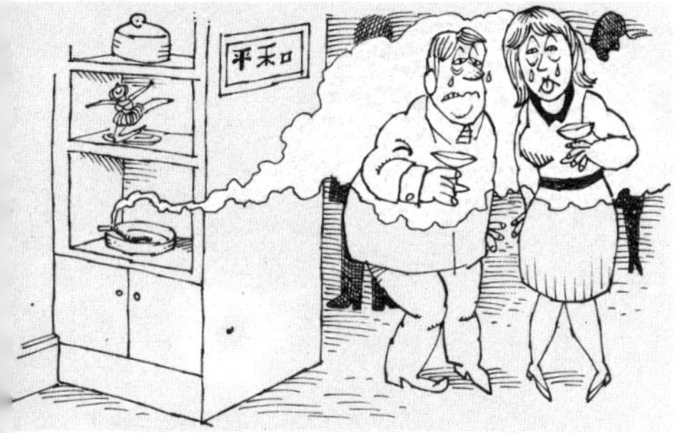

Don't you hate smokers who . . .
. . . let their cigarettes burn out in ashtrays,
causing the nearest thing to a tear gas attack!

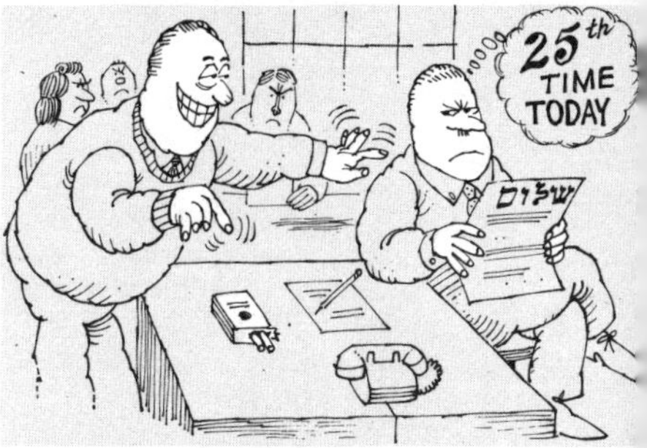
25th TIME TODAY

Don't you hate smokers who . . .
. . . are cutting down on smoking by not carrying any,
but who smoke as much as ever by borrowing!

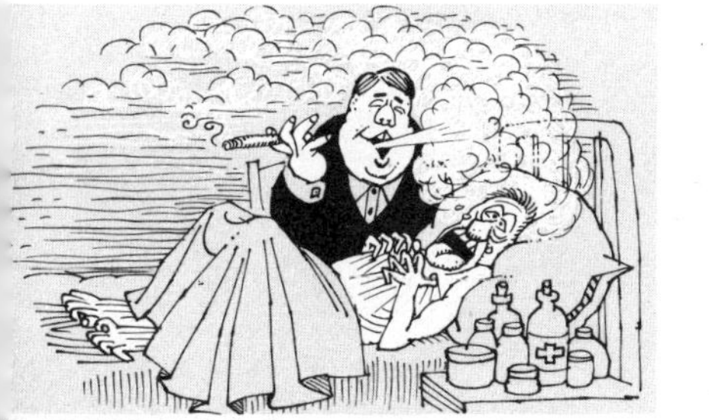

Don't you hate smokers who . . .
. . insist upon lighting up while visiting someone
who's in the hospital with a respiratory illness!

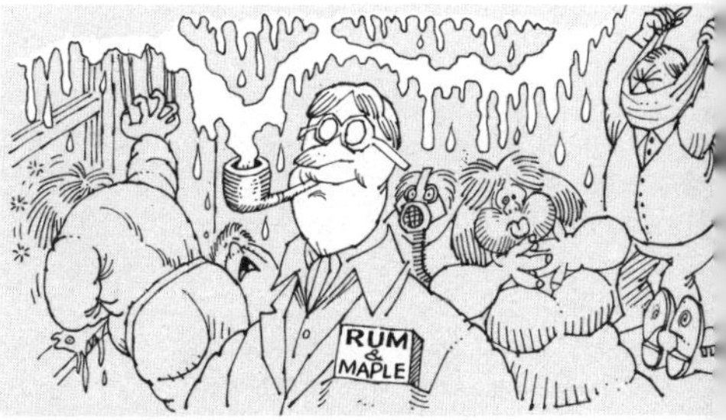
RUM & MAPLE

Don't you hate smokers who . . .
. . . inflict their particular tastes in nauseating
pipe tobacco aromas on an entire gathering!

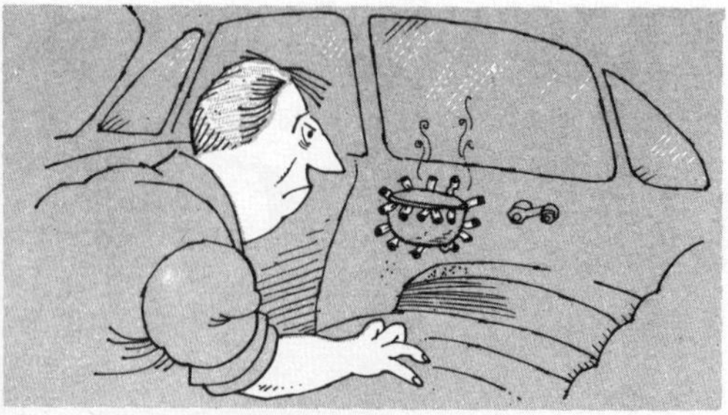

Don't you hate smokers who . . .
. . . stuff auto ashtrays so full they're impossible to remove!

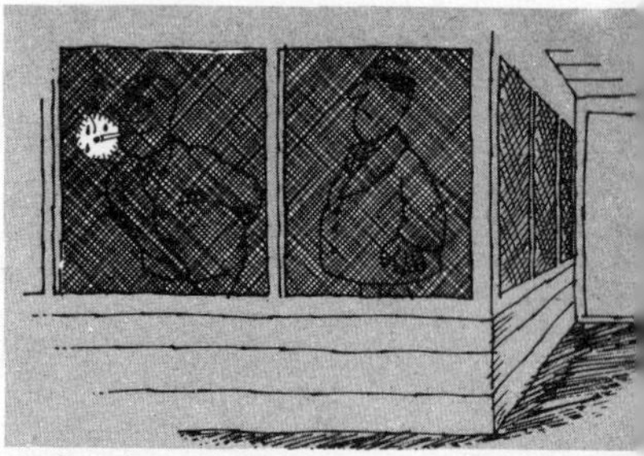

Don't you hate smokers who . . .
. . . stupidly lean into plastic screens!

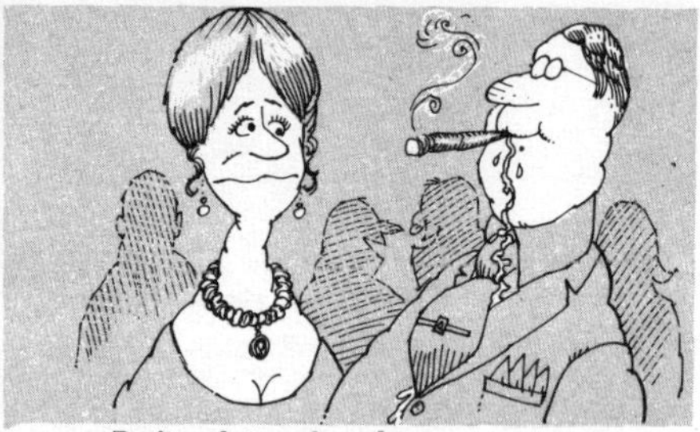

Don't you hate smokers who . . .
. . . always have tobacco spittle running down their chins!

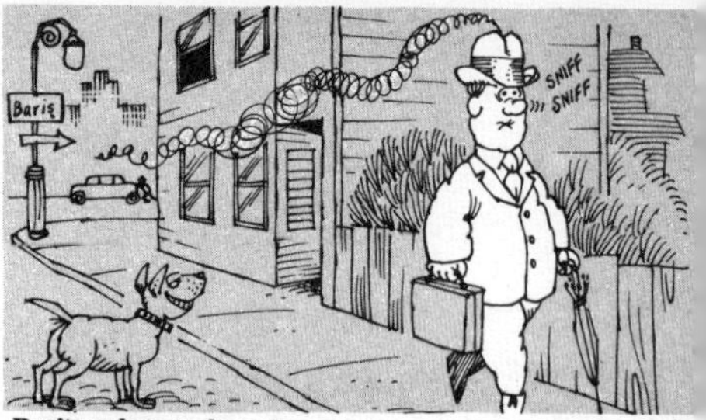
Baris
SNIFF
SNIFF

Don't you hate smokers who . . .
. . . flick cigarette butts out windows!

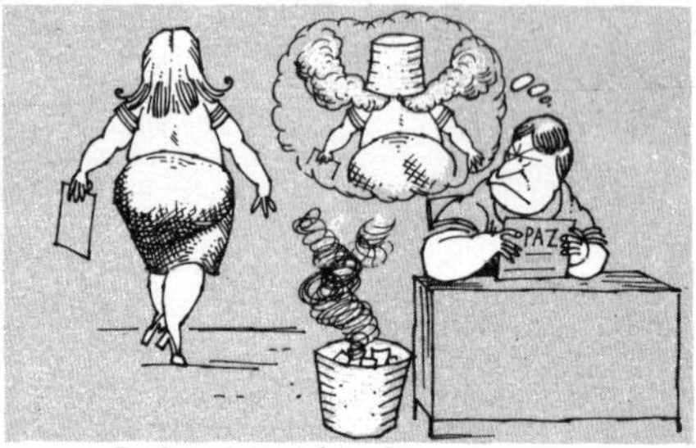
PAZ

Don't you hate smokers who . . .
. . . throw butts that are still alive in wastebaskets!

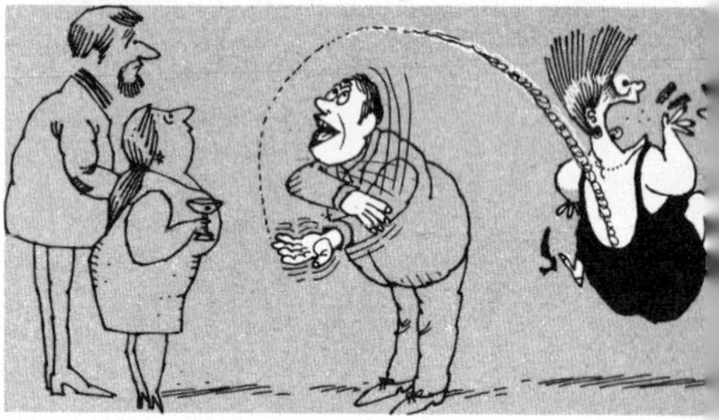

Don't you hate smokers who . . .
. . . do tricks with lighted cigarettes!

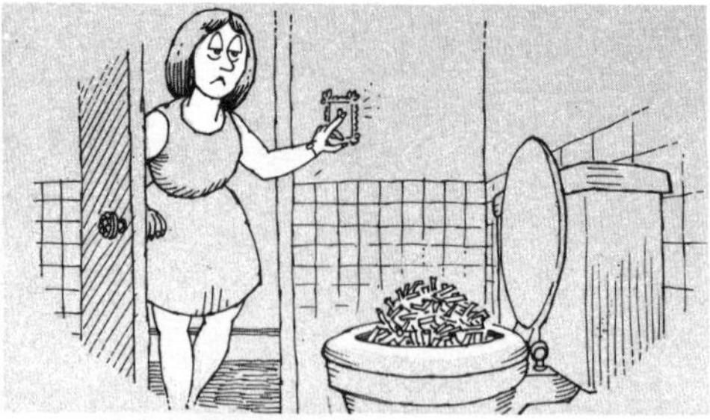

Don't you hate smokers who . . .
. . . dump ashtrays in toilets!

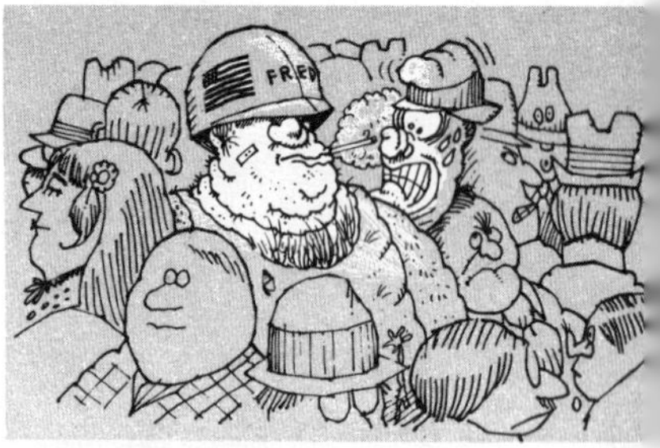
FRED

Don't you hate smokers who . . .
. . . insist upon smoking in crowded places!

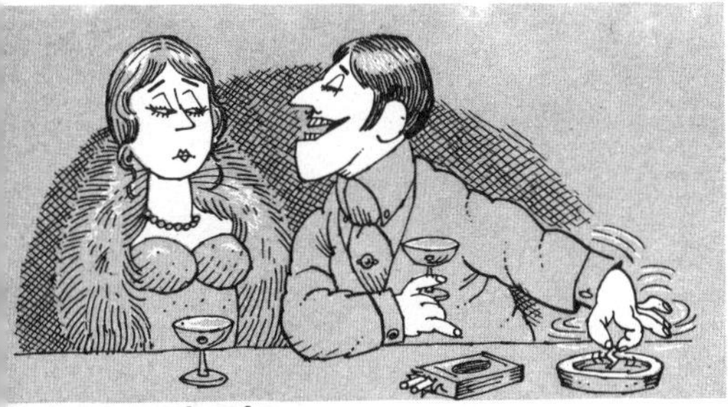

Don't you hate smokers who . . .
. . . keep grinding out a butt till it's time to light another!

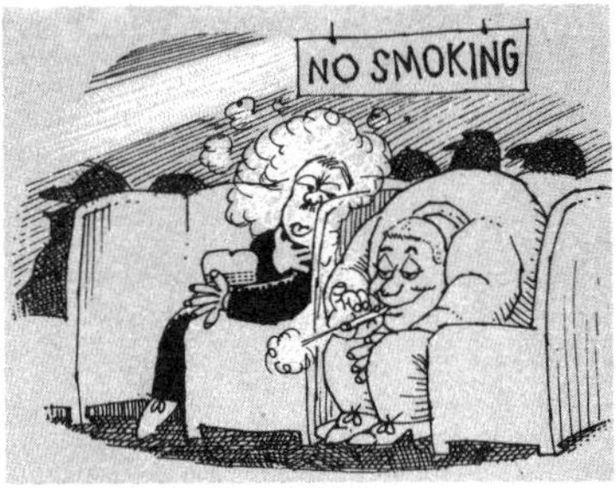
NO SMOKING

Don't you hate smokers who . . .
. . . sneak smokes in "No Smoking" areas!

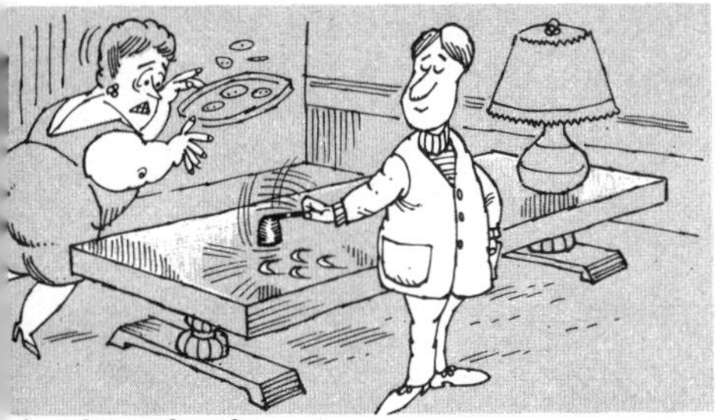

n't you hate smokers who . . .
tap their pipes on any handy surface to clean them!

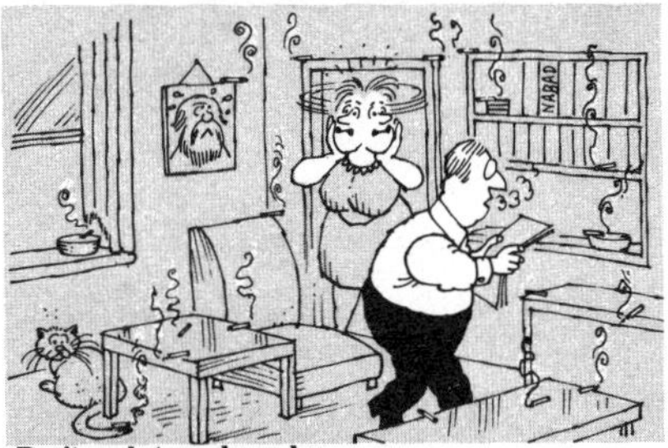

Don't you hate smokers who . . .
. . . never remember where they leave burning cigarettes!

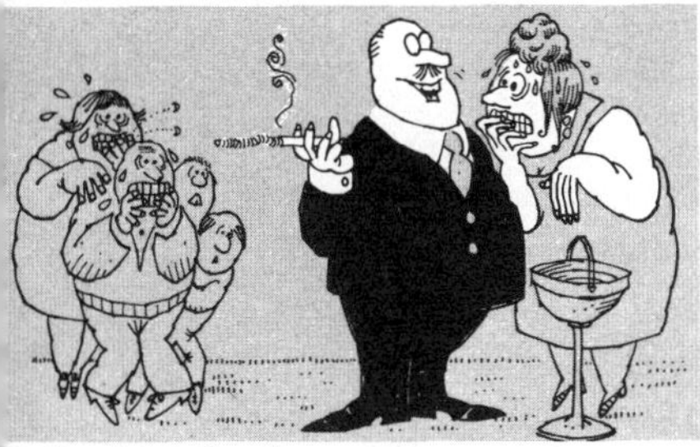

Don't you hate smokers who . . .
. . . wait forever before flicking their ashes!

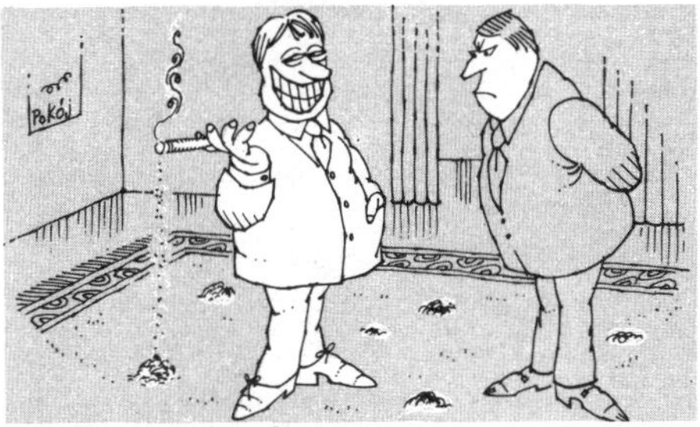

Don't you hate smokers who . . .
. . . always say, "It's good for the rug!"

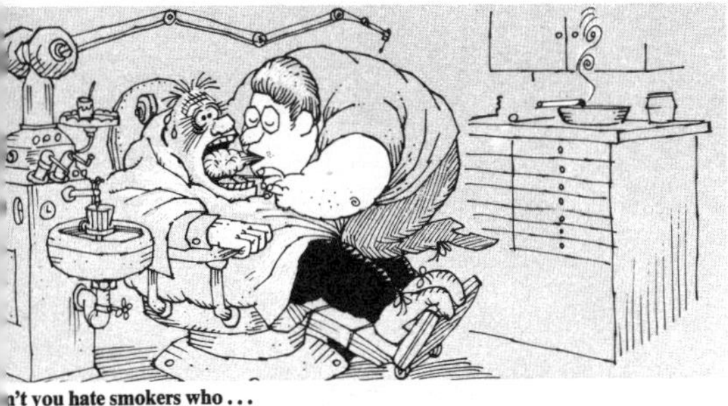

n't you hate smokers who . . .
are dentists or doctors and work on you between puffs!

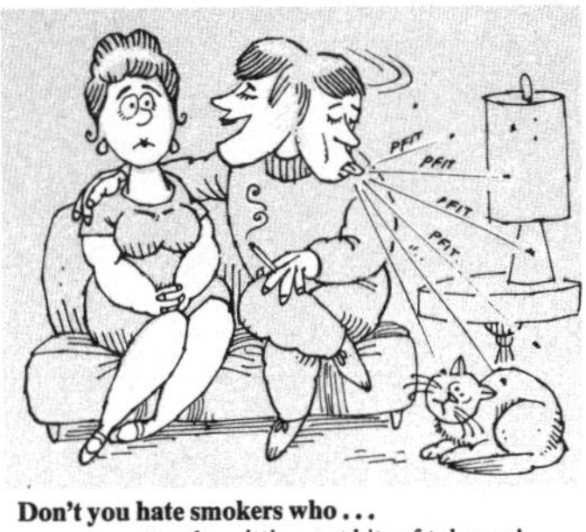

Don't you hate smokers who . . .
. . . are constantly spitting out bits of tobacco!

A few years out of school, most of us are amazed to discover that the biggest clods among our former classmates have somehow latched onto the best jobs. It's just that many under-achievers concentrate on learning the only thing they'll ever need to know, namely how to write hyped up Job Application Letters that will make them seem qualified for cushy, high paying careers. MAD feels that its readers have the potential to be just as boast

MAD'S "Do-It-Yourse

FILL BLANK #1 FROM THIS GROUP

A. it's obvious from the junk you make that you need my advice.
B. your top competitor said I was good enough to work for you.
C. I'm interested in thermal duct deployment, whatever that is.
D. I hear your building is air conditioned, and I sweat a lot.

FILL BLANK #2 FROM THIS GROUP

A. shuffling papers for eight hours a day to look busy
B. filling an executive position as well as the next idiot
C. going potty by myself
D. thermal duct deployment, whatever that is

FILL BLANK #3 FROM THIS GROUP

A. the last Venezuelan ambassador to Latvia.
B. a thermal duct deployer, whatever that is.
C. Chairman of the Board of Packard Motors.
D. presidential campaign advisor to Sergeant Shriver.

FILL BLANK #4 FROM THIS GROUP

A. Oxford, just before the Fire of 1969 destroyed my records
B. the C.I.A. Academy under a secret code name
C. many Ivy League institutions, including Dubuque Jr. High
D. the Zsa Zsa Gabor School of Diesel Mechanics

FILL BLANK #5 FROM THIS GROUP

A. a Ph.D. in whatever your company requires.
B. top honors in Neo-Hegelian philosophy and baton twirling.
C. a bundle playing "Go Fish" at a nickel a point.
D. 66 and lost 13 for an enviable percentage of .835.

Dear Sirs:

I am most anxious to present my job qualifications to your firm because ⑴ .
I feel confident that I have been thoroughly trained in ⑵ and have spent the past year gaining added experience by working as ⑶

I received my higher education at ⑷ , where I won ⑸ . Following my graduation in ⑹ , I went on to do ⑺

Upon entering the field of business, my positions have become increasingly ⑻ . Forever seeking ⑼ , I was ultimately honored to receive ⑽ . As a result, I am currently looked upon by my associates as ⑾ . With this background, I naturally feel ⑿

My starting salary requirement is ⒀ . I sincerely believe that I am well worth this amount because ⒁ . Therefore, I look forward to ⒂

Very truly yours,

FILL BLANK #6 FROM THIS GROUP

A. the upper four-fifths of my class
B. one of the very, very hardest things they taught there
C. front of a cheering throng of admirers
D. a dark blue polyester suit I knitted myself

dishonest in their job seeking correspondence. So we rushing to your aid with a pre-packaged kit that'll ble you to compose your own impressive, sure fire Ap- ation Letter. It's easy to do. Merely give our all-purpose form a personal touch by filling each numbered blank with the attention-getting phrase of your choice. Then sit back and wait for lucrative offers to roll in as dazzled employers rush to respond to your version of

”JOB APPLICATION LETTER

WRITER: TOM KOCH

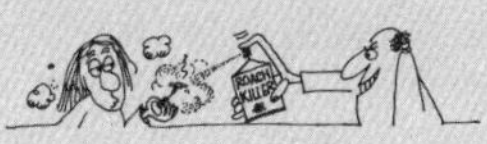
ROACH KILLER

FILL BLANK #7 FROM THIS GROUP

A. advance research on social habits of Las Vegas chorus girls.
B. my impressions of Humphrey Bogart and Walter Mondale.
C. several things which I can only describe to you in person.
D. a dye job on my hair that has done worlds for my popularity.

FILL BLANK #8 FROM THIS GROUP

A. difficult to explain to a layman like yourself.
B. involved with "creative input", and other meaningless terms.
C. hard to master, expecially since I broke my pencil.
D. geared to the natural talents of a water buffalo.

FILL BLANK #9 FROM THIS GROUP

A. to better myself, regardless of who I had to step on
B. a position of trust that would allow me to handle the cash
C. a transfer to our branch office in Miami Beach
D. permission to use the employee washroom

FILL BLANK #10 FROM THIS GROUP

A. a bottle of Listerine from the girls in the typing pool.
B. $35 from a Korean spy who knew I couldn't be bought cheap.
C. several phone calls from people I didn't even know.
D. a Scotch Tape dispenser of my very own.

FILL BLANK #11 FROM THIS GROUP

A. a truly gifted brown nose apple polisher
B. a constant threat to their job security.
C. a person they'd love to catch in the parking lot after dark.
D. the adult who most reminds them of Amy Carter.

FILL BLANK #12 FROM THIS GROUP

A. as qualified as the clods you have working for you now.
B. less ashamed than I once did about sleeping with a Teddy Bear.
C. that I'm a credit to everything I stand for.
D. like someone who literally could tower over Nancy Walker.

FILL BLANK #13 FROM THIS GROUP

A. less than you'd expect to pay each week for a microwave oven.
B. rather high because I'd like to afford a fling at bigamy.
C. naturally more than your cheapskate competitors are paying.
D. just enough to keep the loan sharks from breaking my kneecaps.

FILL BLANK #14 FROM THIS GROUP

A. I am holding your mother hostage.
B. it's only a fraction of what you'd have to pay Robert Redford.
C. I have some choice pictures of you taken at a downtown motel.
D. it'll be on your conscience if I get my kneecaps broken.

FILL BLANK #15 FROM THIS GROUP

A. being invited to your mansion to close the deal over drinks.
B. landing this job so I can stop sharing an apartment with your daughter.
C. next July 16, when I'll begin my first vacation at your expense.
D. getting your company back on its feet while there's still time.

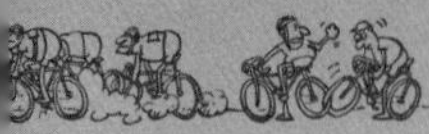

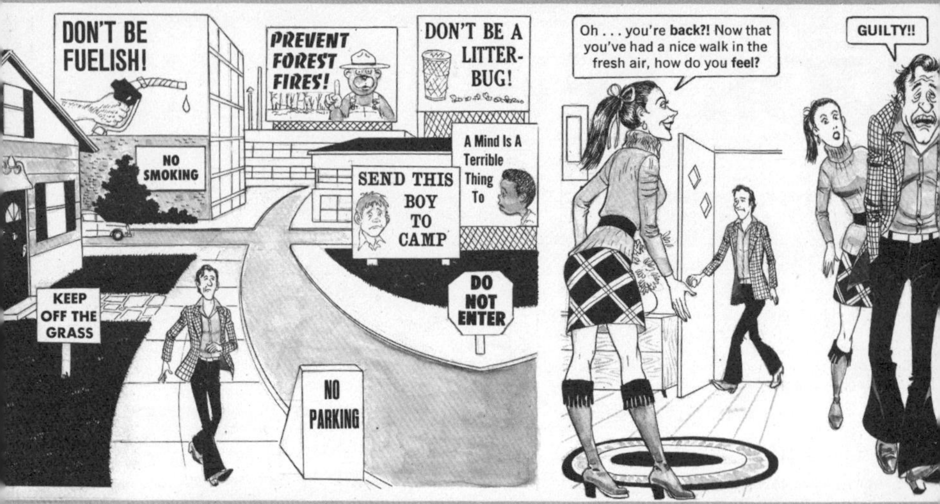

DON'T BE FUELISH!
PREVENT FOREST FIRES!
DON'T BE A LITTER-BUG!
NO SMOKING
A Mind Is A Terrible Thing To
SEND THIS BOY TO CAMP
KEEP OFF THE GRASS
DO NOT ENTER
NO PARKING
Oh . . . you're back?! Now that you've had a nice walk in the fresh air, how do you feel?
GUILTY!!

BERG'S-EYE VIEW DEPT.

THE LIGHTER SIDE OF...

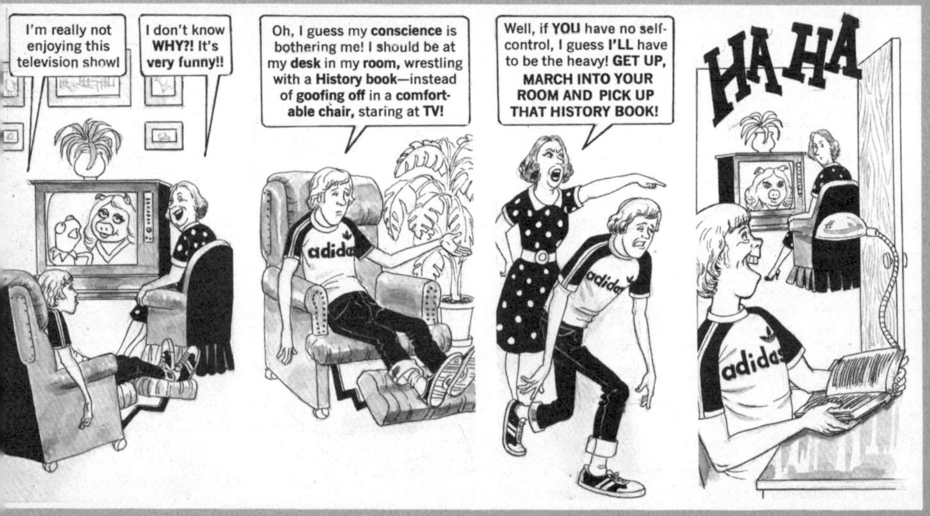

I'm really not enjoying this television show!
I don't know WHY?! It's very funny!!
Oh, I guess my conscience is bothering me! I should be at my desk in my room, wrestling with a History book—instead of goofing off in a comfortable chair, staring at TV!
adidas
Well, if YOU have no self-control, I guess I'LL have to be the heavy! GET UP, MARCH INTO YOUR ROOM AND PICK UP THAT HISTORY BOOK!
HA HA

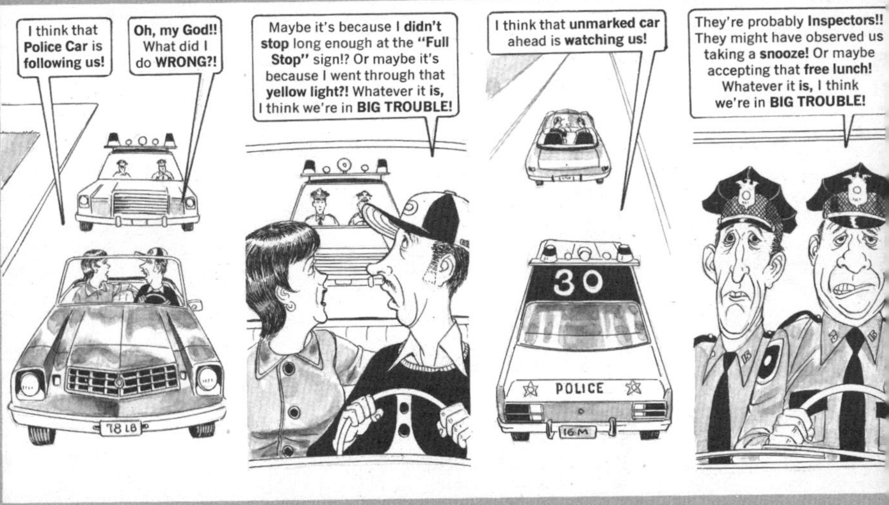

I think that Police Car is following us!
Oh, my God!! What did I do WRONG?!
Maybe it's because I didn't stop long enough at the "Full Stop" sign!? Or maybe it's because I went through that yellow light?! Whatever it is, I think we're in BIG TROUBLE!
I think that unmarked car ahead is watching us!
30
POLICE
They're probably Inspectors!! They might have observed us taking a snooze! Or maybe accepting that free lunch! Whatever it is, I think we're in BIG TROUBLE!

GUILT

ARTIST & WRITER:
DAVID BERG

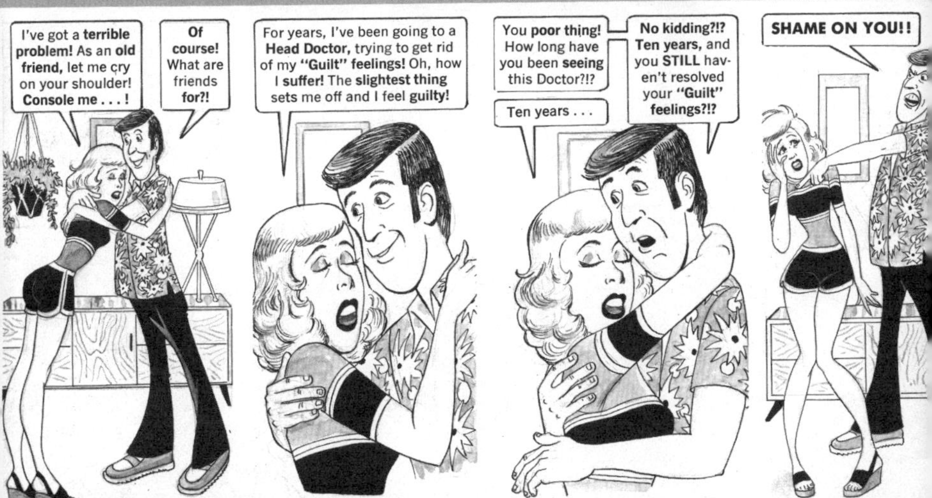

I've got a terrible problem! As an old friend, let me cry on your shoulder! Console me . . . !
Of course! What are friends for?!
For years, I've been going to a Head Doctor, trying to get rid of my "Guilt" feelings! Oh, how I suffer! The slightest thing sets me off and I feel guilty!
You poor thing! How long have you been seeing this Doctor?!?
Ten years . . .
No kidding?!? Ten years, and you STILL haven't resolved your "Guilt" feelings?!?
SHAME ON YOU!!

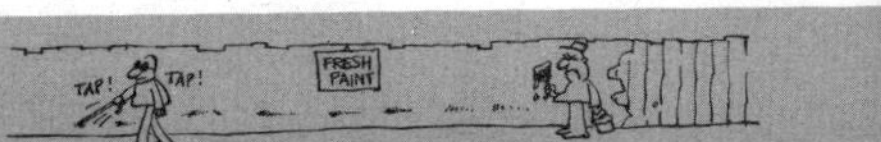

TAP!
TAP!
FRESH PAINT

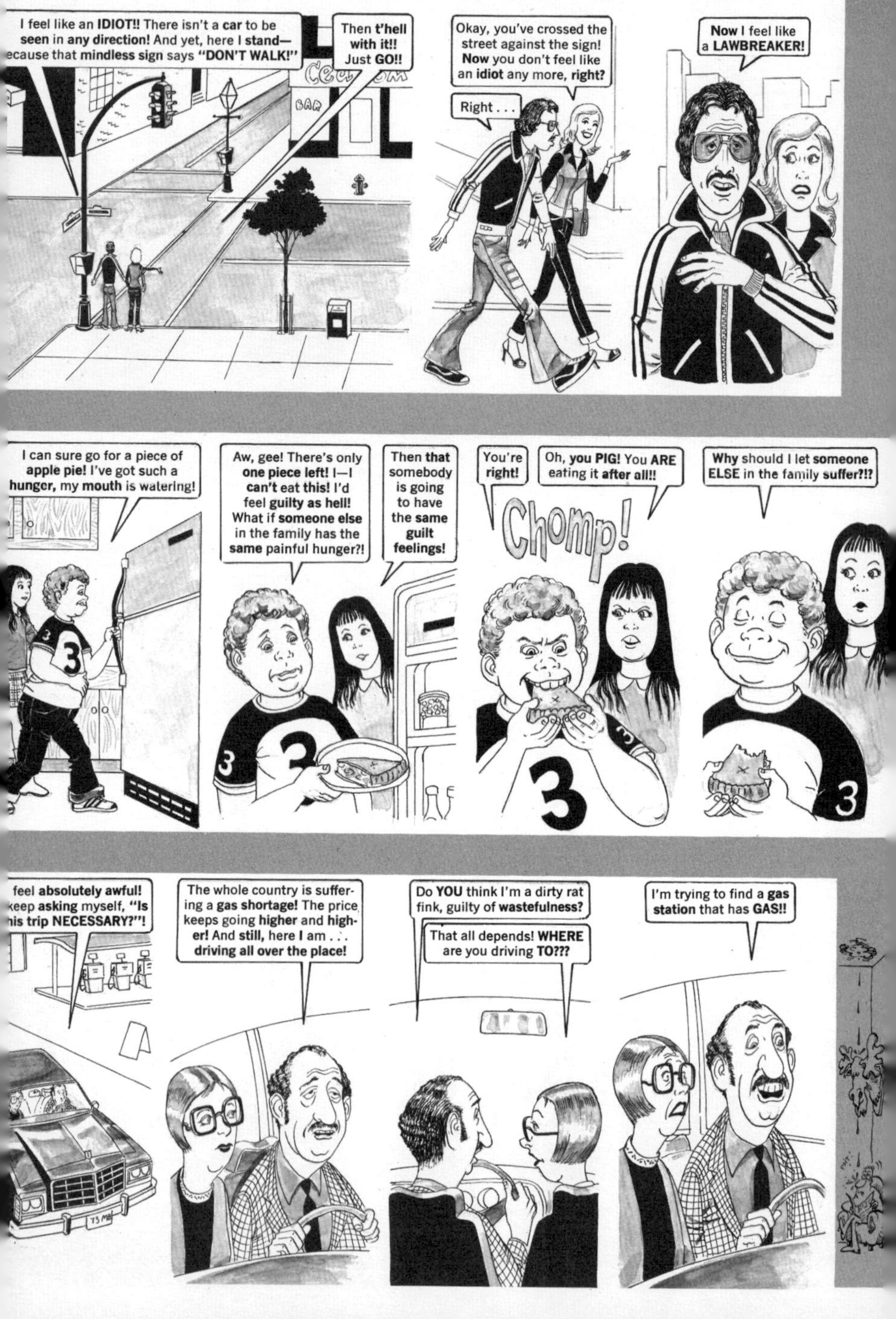
I feel like an IDIOT!! There isn't a car to be seen in any direction! And yet, here I stand— ecause that mindless sign says "DON'T WALK!"
Then t'hell with it!! Just GO!!
Okay, you've crossed the street against the sign! Now you don't feel like an idiot any more, right?
Right . . .
Now I feel like a LAWBREAKER!
I can sure go for a piece of apple pie! I've got such a hunger, my mouth is watering!
Aw, gee! There's only one piece left! I—I can't eat this! I'd feel guilty as hell! What if someone else in the family has the same painful hunger?!
Then that somebody is going to have the same guilt feelings!
You're right!
Oh, you PIG! You ARE eating it after all!!
Chomp!
Why should I let someone ELSE in the family suffer?!?
feel absolutely awful! keep asking myself, "Is his trip NECESSARY?"!
The whole country is suffering a gas shortage! The price keeps going higher and higher! And still, here I am . . . driving all over the place!
Do YOU think I'm a dirty rat fink, guilty of wastefulness?
That all depends! WHERE are you driving TO???
I'm trying to find a gas station that has GAS!!

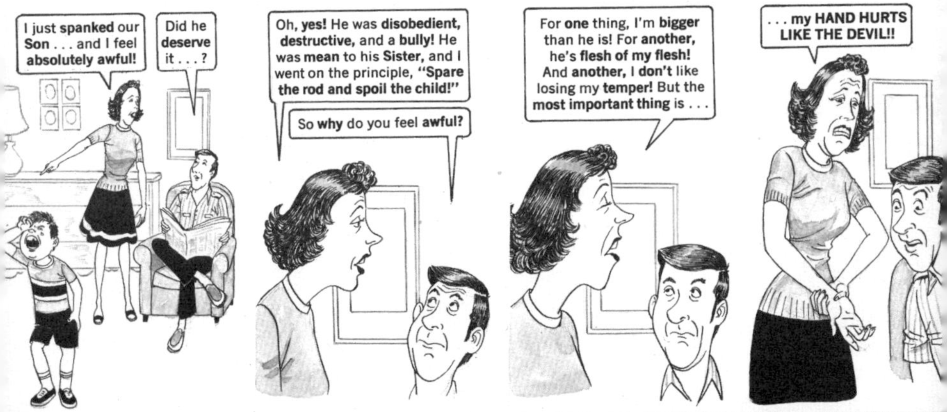
I just spanked our Son . . . and I feel absolutely awful!
Did he deserve it . . . ?
Oh, yes! He was disobedient, destructive, and a bully! He was mean to his Sister, and I went on the principle, "Spare the rod and spoil the child!"
So why do you feel awful?
For one thing, I'm bigger than he is! For another, he's flesh of my flesh! And another, I don't like losing my temper! But the most important thing is . . .
. . . my HAND HURTS LIKE THE DEVIL!!

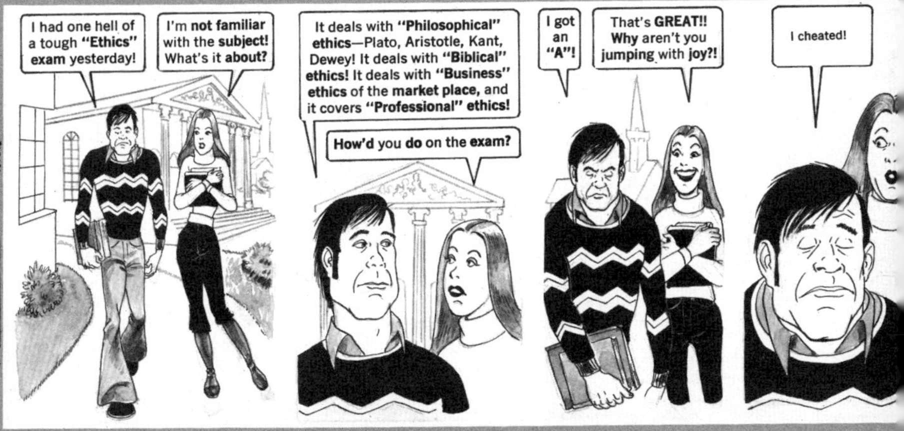
I had one hell of a tough "Ethics" exam yesterday!
I'm not familiar with the subject! What's it about?
It deals with "Philosophical" ethics—Plato, Aristotle, Kant, Dewey! It deals with "Biblical" ethics! It deals with "Business" ethics of the market place, and it covers "Professional" ethics!
How'd you do on the exam?
I got an "A"!
That's GREAT!! Why aren't you jumping with joy?!
I cheated!

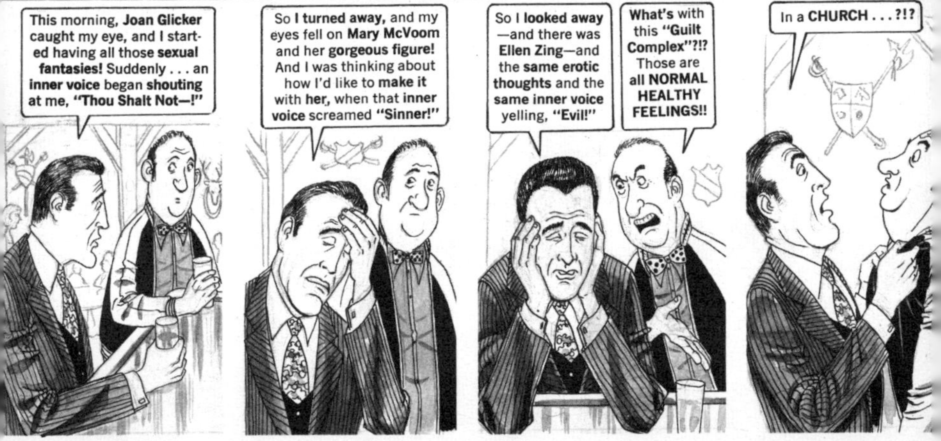
This morning, Joan Glicker caught my eye, and I started having all those sexual fantasies! Suddenly . . . an inner voice began shouting at me, "Thou Shalt Not—!"
So I turned away, and my eyes fell on Mary McVoom and her gorgeous figure! And I was thinking about how I'd like to make it with her, when that inner voice screamed "Sinner!"
So I looked away —and there was Ellen Zing—and the same erotic thoughts and the same inner voice yelling, "Evil!"
What's with this "Guilt Complex"?!? Those are all NORMAL HEALTHY FEELINGS!!
In a CHURCH . . . ?!?

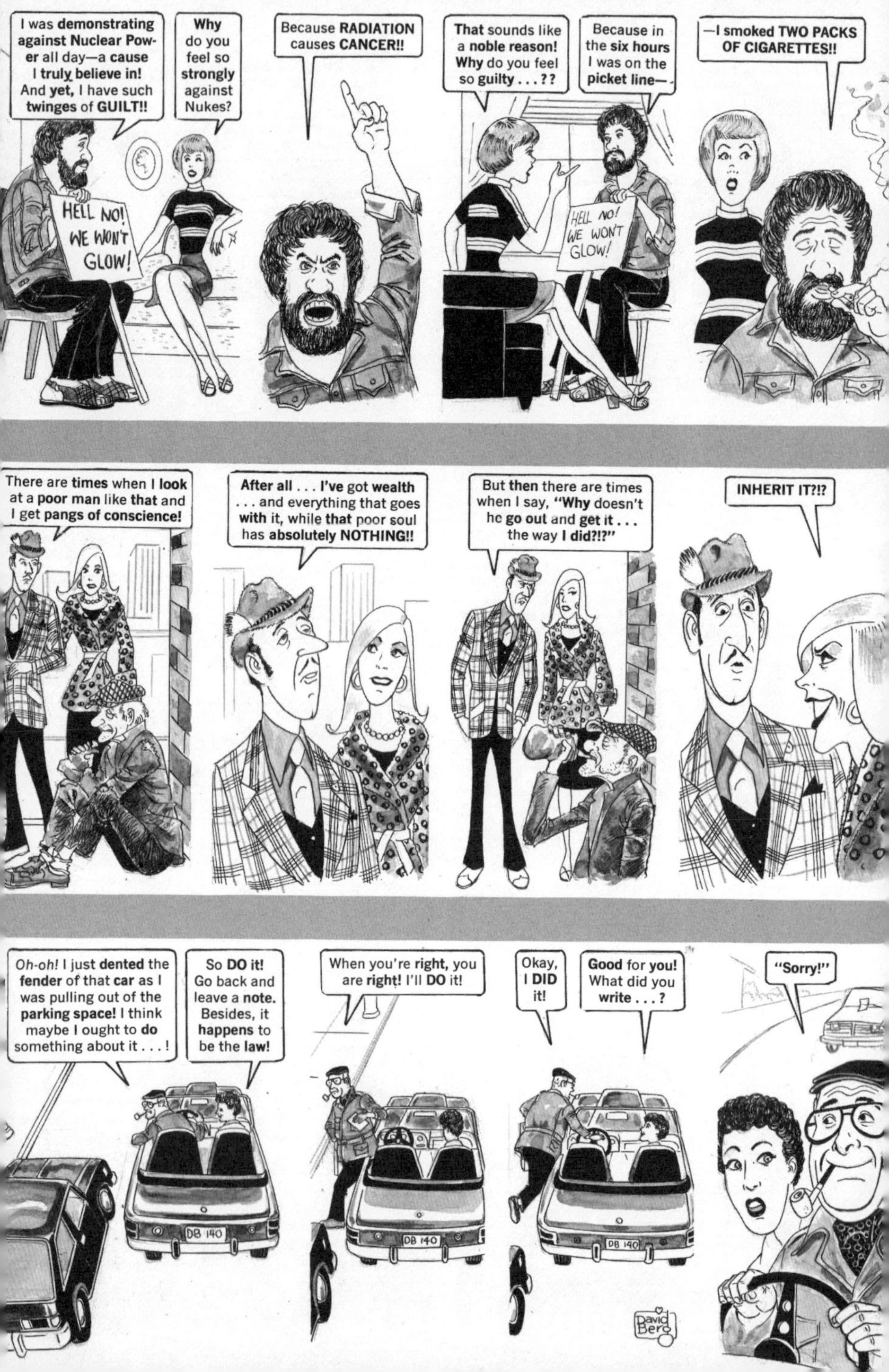

I was demonstrating against Nuclear Power all day—a cause I truly believe in! And yet, I have such twinges of GUILT!!
Why do you feel so strongly against Nukes?
Because RADIATION causes CANCER!!
HELL NO! WE WON'T GLOW!
That sounds like a noble reason! Why do you feel so guilty . . . ??
Because in the six hours I was on the picket line—
—I smoked TWO PACKS OF CIGARETTES!!
There are times when I look at a poor man like that and I get pangs of conscience!
After all . . . I've got wealth . . . and everything that goes with it, while that poor soul has absolutely NOTHING!!
But then there are times when I say, "Why doesn't he go out and get it . . . the way I did?!?"
INHERIT IT?!?
Oh-oh! I just dented the fender of that car as I was pulling out of the parking space! I think maybe I ought to do something about it . . . !
So DO it! Go back and leave a note. Besides, it happens to be the law!
When you're right, you are right! I'll DO it!
Okay, I DID it!
Good for you! What did you write . . . ?
"Sorry!"
DB 140
David Berg

JOKE AND DAGGER DEPT.

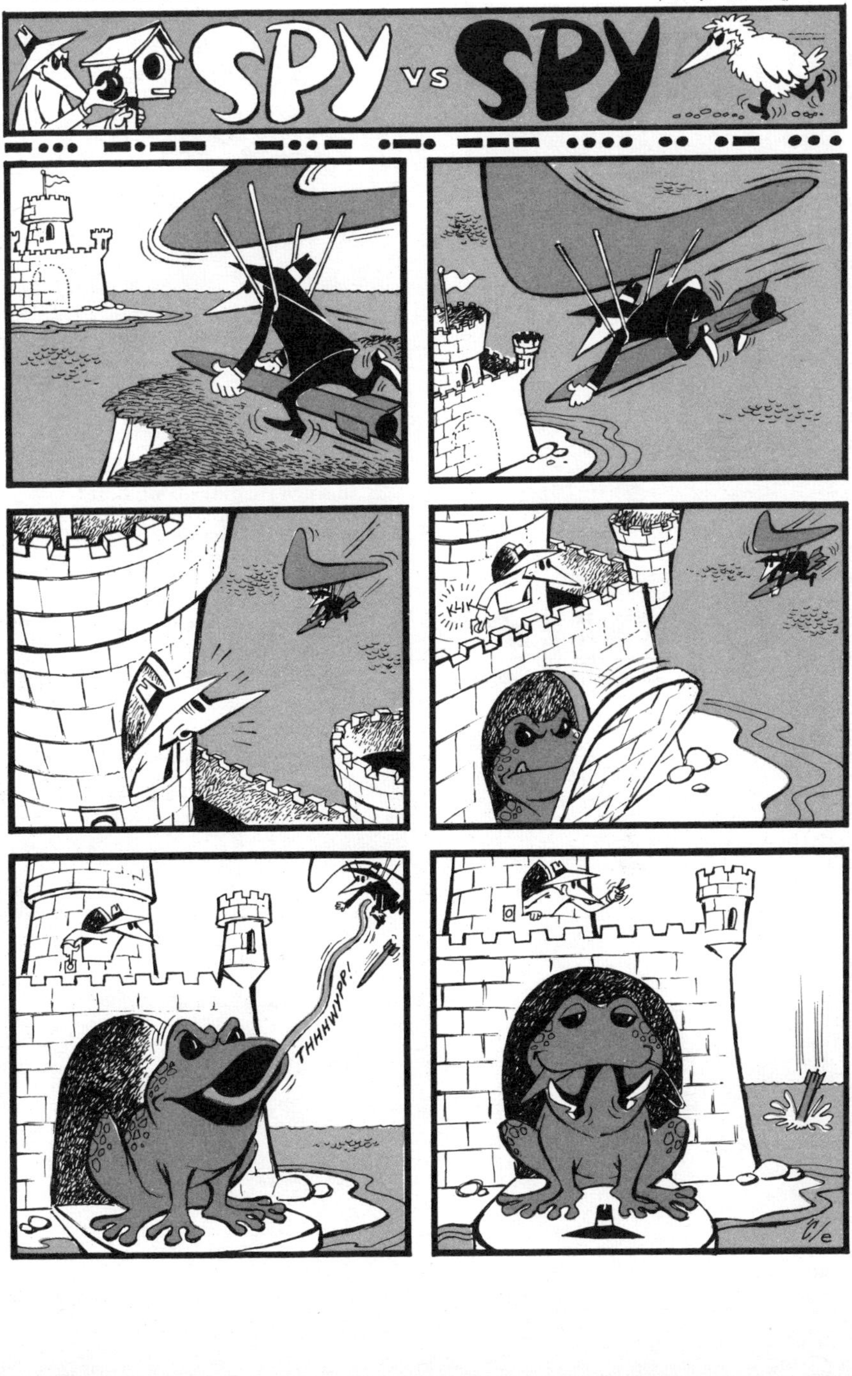
SPY vs SPY
KLIK
THHHWYPP!

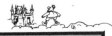

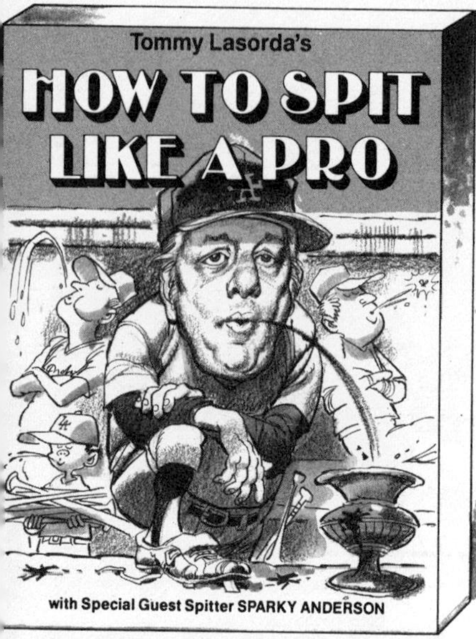
Tommy Lasorda's
HOW TO SPIT LIKE A PRO
with Special Guest Spitter SPARKY ANDERSON

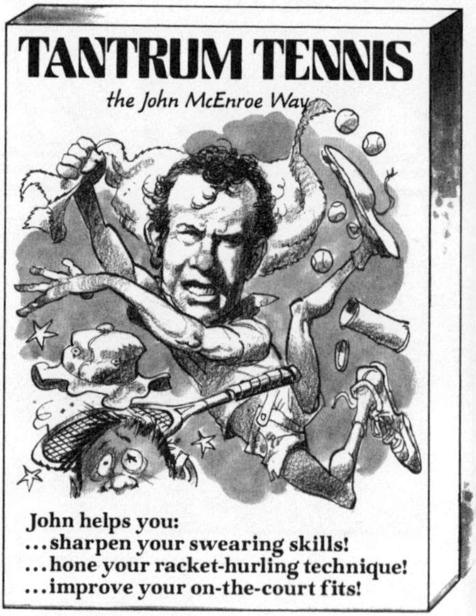
TANTRUM TENNIS
the John McEnroe Way
John helps you:
...sharpen your swearing skills!
...hone your racket-hurling technique!
...improve your on-the-court fits!

TAPE ME OUT TO THE BALLGAME DEPT.

INSTRUCTIONAL SP

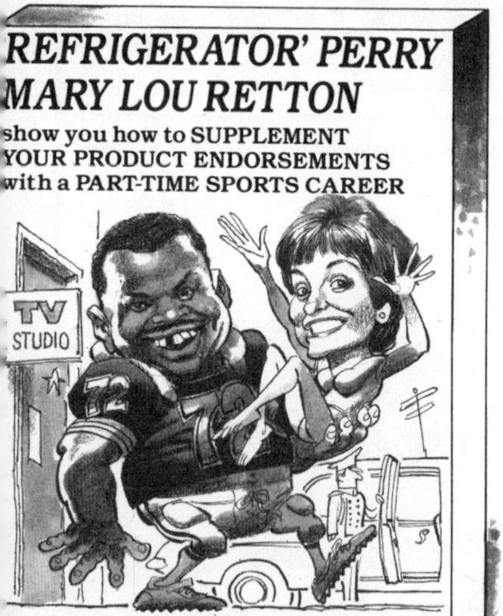
REFRIGERATOR' PERRY
MARY LOU RETTON
show you how to SUPPLEMENT
YOUR PRODUCT ENDORSEMENTS
with a PART-TIME SPORTS CAREER
TV STUDIO
72
Special Added BONUS: The Fridge's "Quick-Weight-Gain Diet"

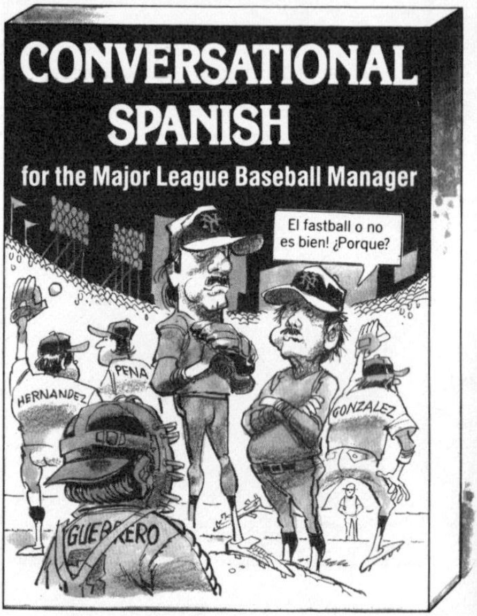
CONVERSATIONAL SPANISH
for the Major League Baseball Manager
El fastball o no es bien! ¿Porque?
HERNANDEZ
PENA
GONZALEZ
GUERRERO

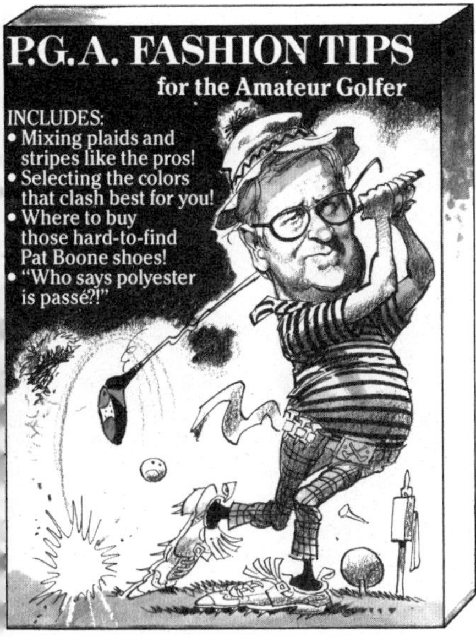
P.G.A. FASHION TIPS
for the Amateur Golfer
INCLUDES:
• Mixing plaids and stripes like the pros!
• Selecting the colors that clash best for you!
• Where to buy those hard-to-find Pat Boone shoes!
• "Who says polyester is passé?!"

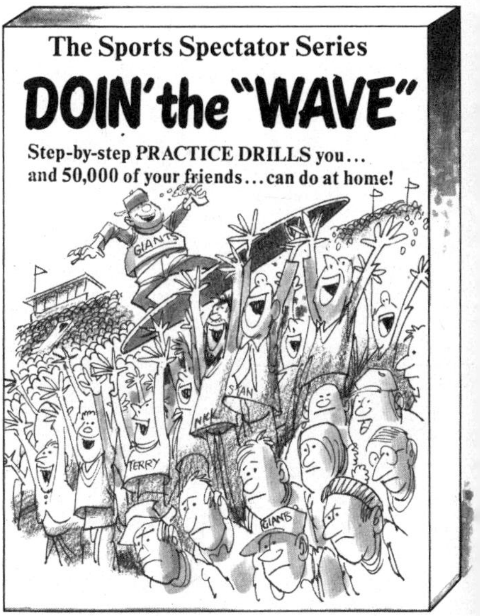
The Sports Spectator Series
DOIN' the "WAVE"
Step-by-step PRACTICE DRILLS you... and 50,000 of your friends... can do at home!
GIANTS
STAN
NICK
TERRY
GIANTS

ORTS VIDEOS we'd like to see

ARTIST: JACK DAVIS WRITER: MIKE SNIDER

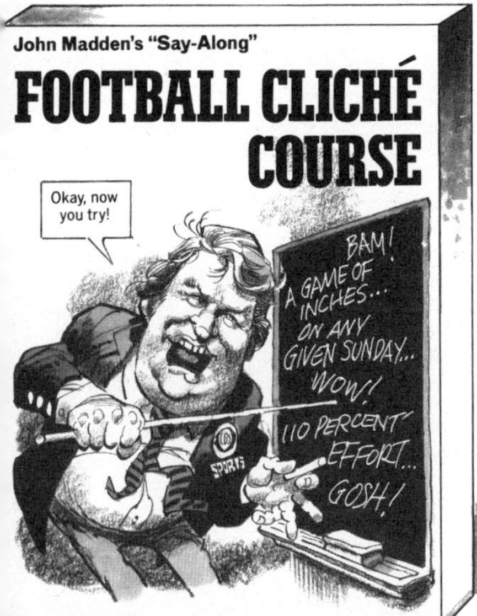
John Madden's "Say-Along"
FOOTBALL CLICHÉ COURSE
Okay, now you try!
BAM!
A GAME OF INCHES...
ON ANY GIVEN SUNDAY...
WOW!
110 PERCENT EFFORT...
GOSH!
SPORTS

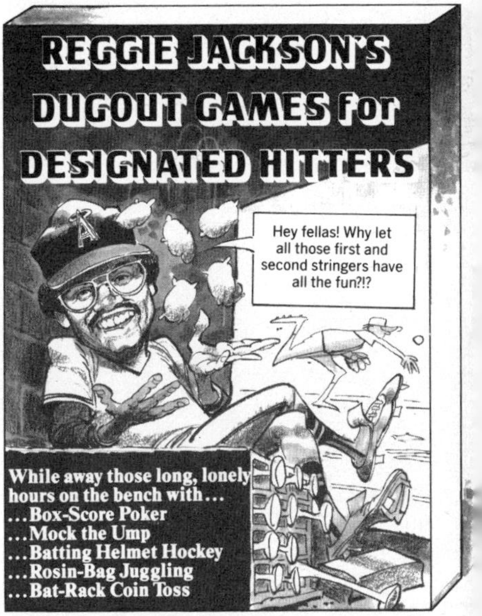
REGGIE JACKSON'S DUGOUT GAMES for DESIGNATED HITTERS
Hey fellas! Why let all those first and second stringers have all the fun?!?
While away those long, lonely hours on the bench with...
...Box-Score Poker
...Mock the Ump
...Batting Helmet Hockey
...Rosin-Bag Juggling
...Bat-Rack Coin Toss

BITING HUMOR DEPT.

A MAD LOOK AT SHA

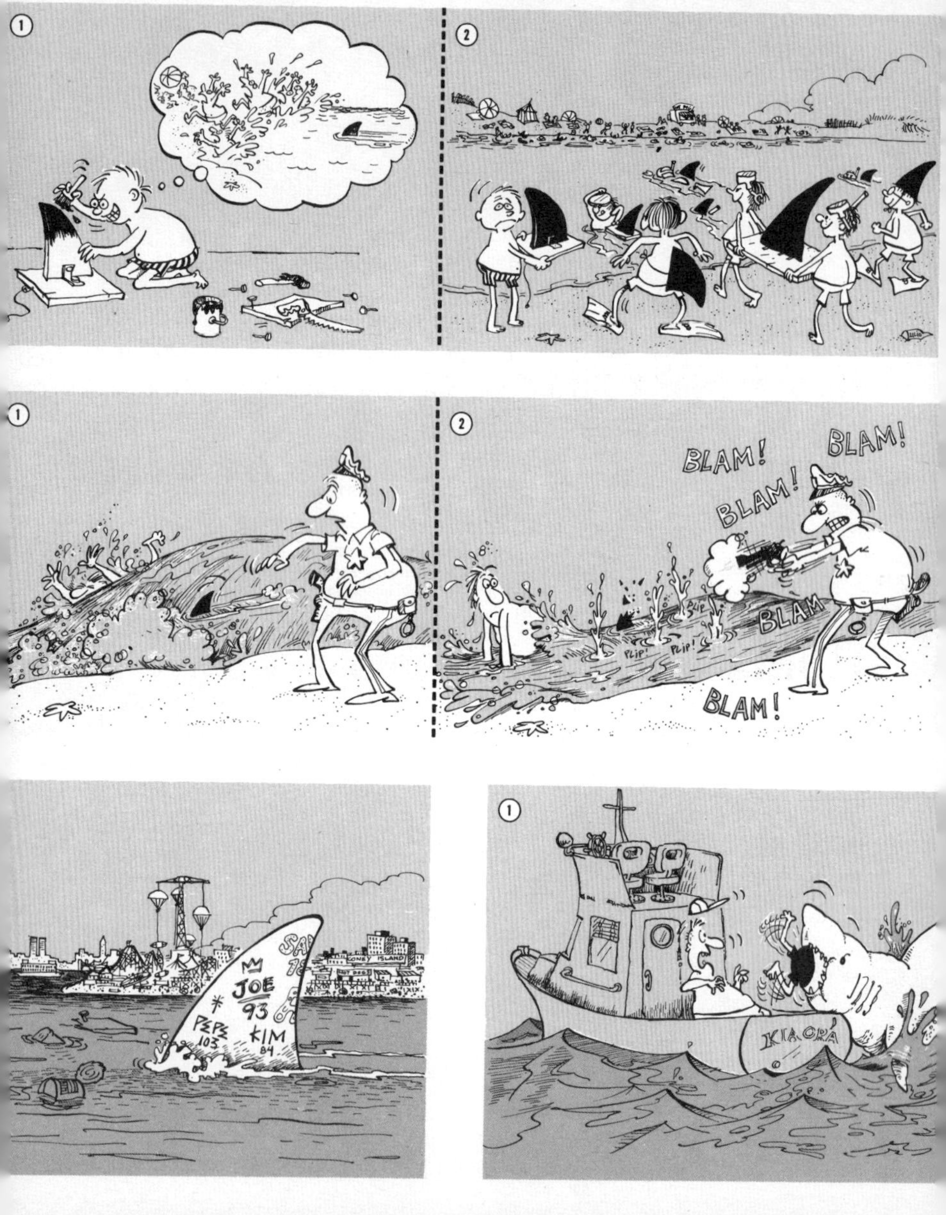

1
2
1
2
BLAM!
BLAM!
BLAM!
BLAM
BLAM!
PLIP!
PLIP!
JOE
93
PEPE
103
KIM
84
CONEY ISLAND
1
KIA ORA

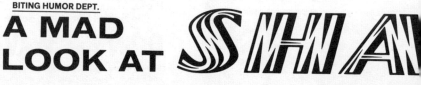

RKS

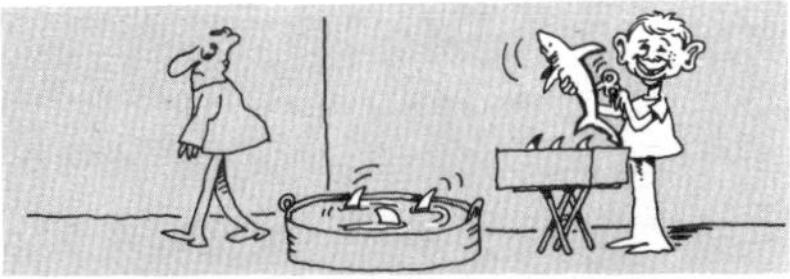

ARTIST & WRITER: SERGIO ARAGONES

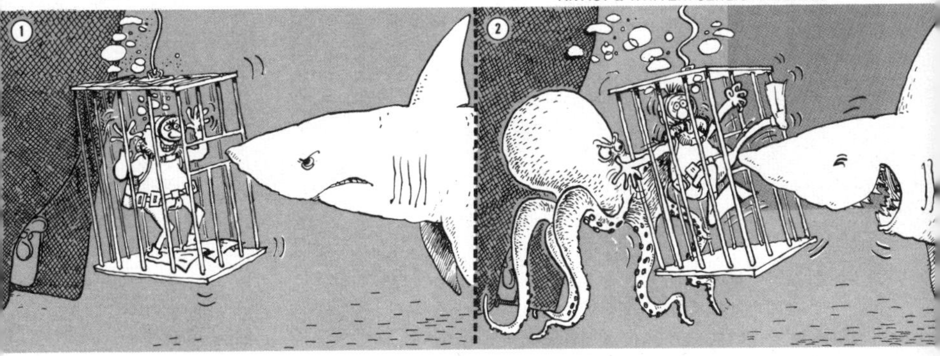

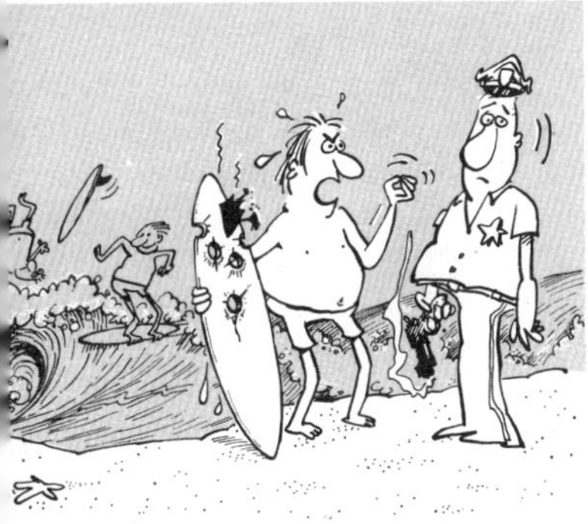

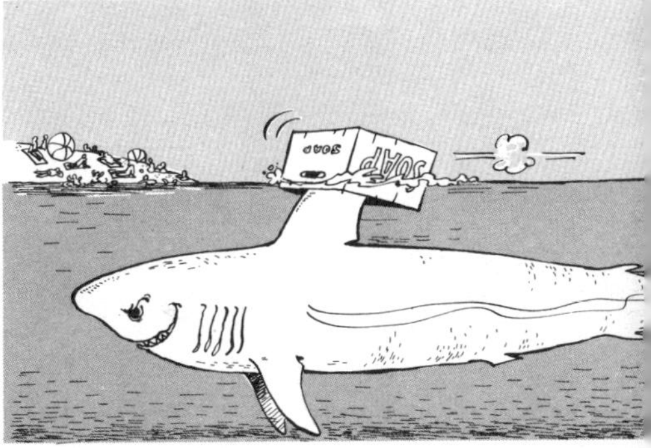
SOAP

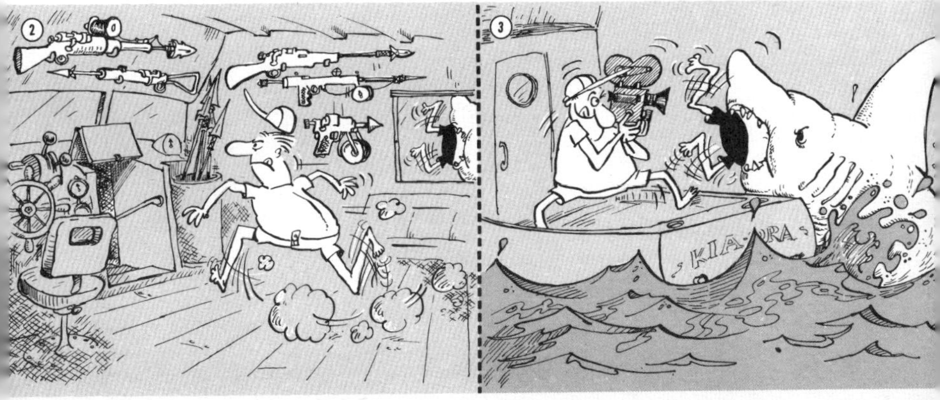

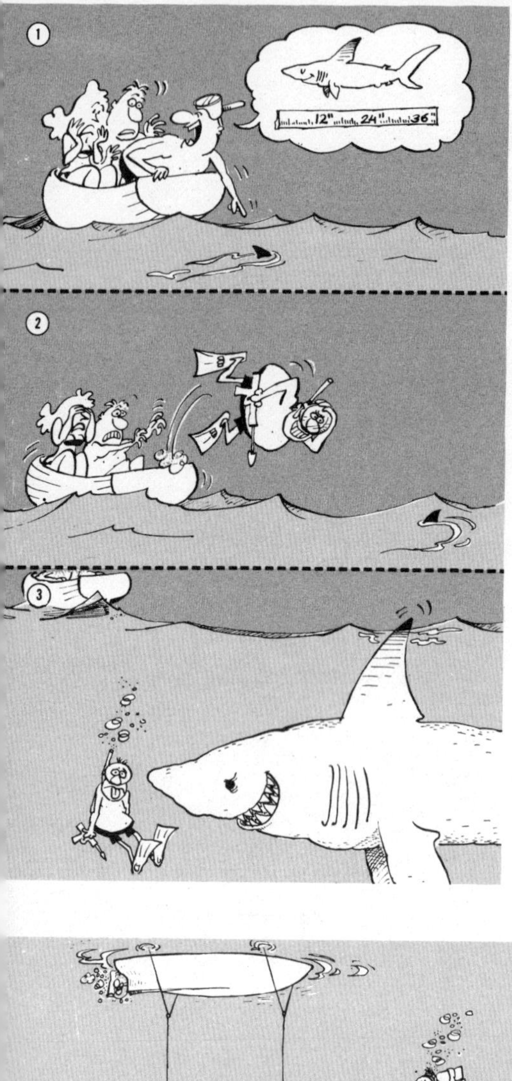
1
12" 24" 36"
2
3

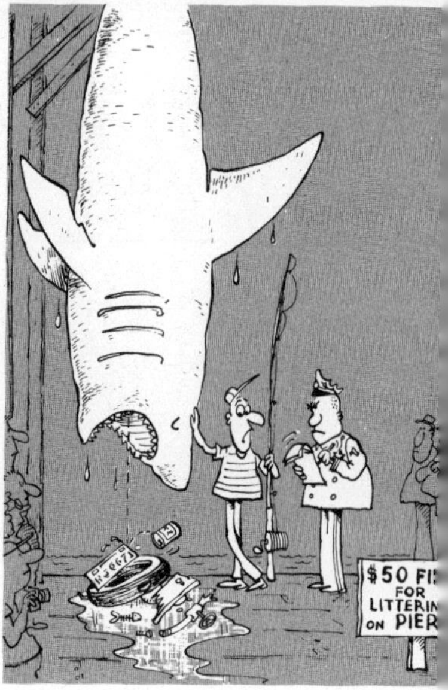
$50 FI
FOR
LITTERIN
ON PIER

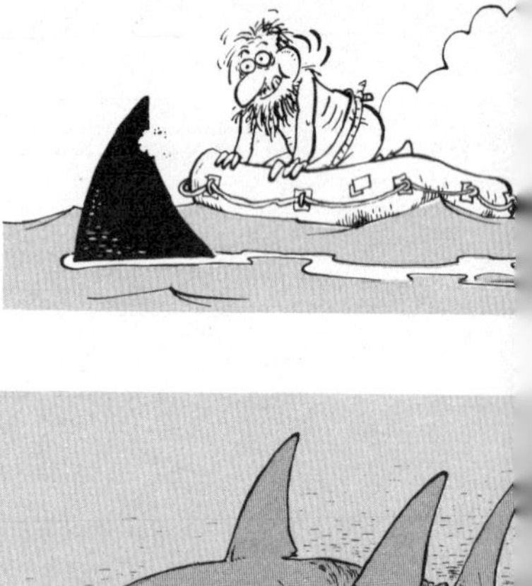

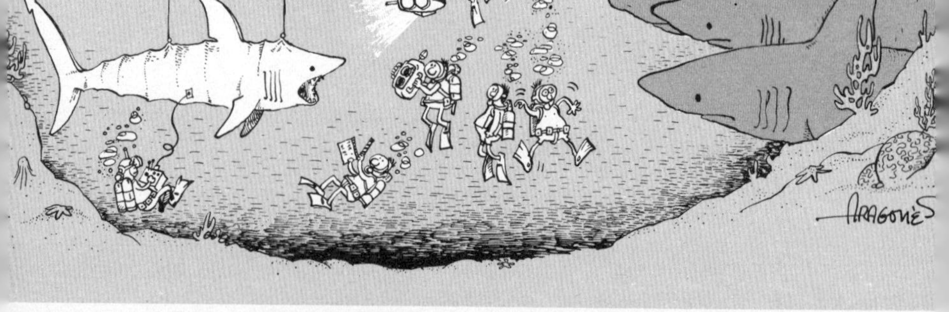
ARAGONÉS

DON MARTIN DEPT.

ONE DAY AT THE OCEAN

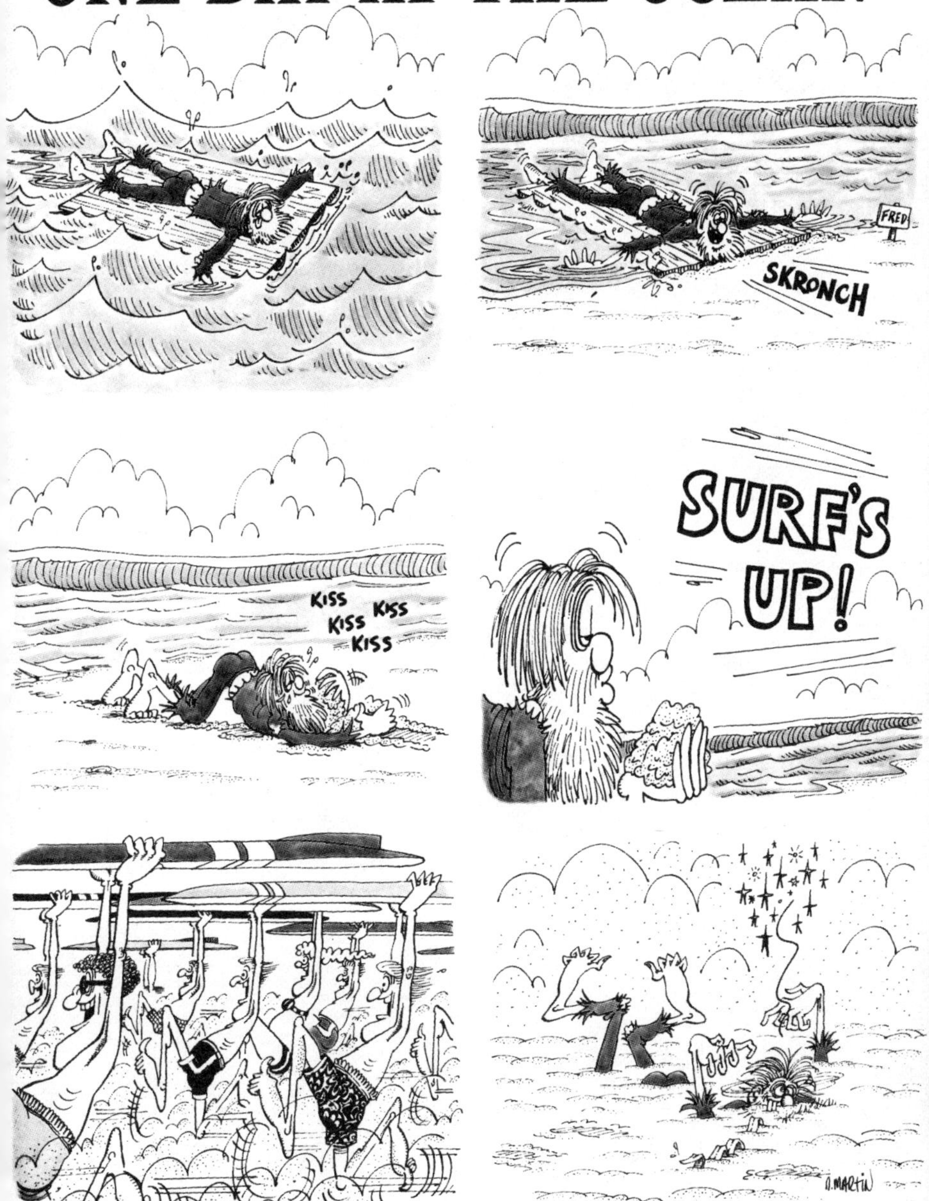
FRED
SKRONCH
KISS
KISS KISS
KISS
SURF'S UP!
D. MARTIN

REACTIONS SPEAK LOUDER THAN WORDS DEPT.

A MAD LOOK AT THE SILENT

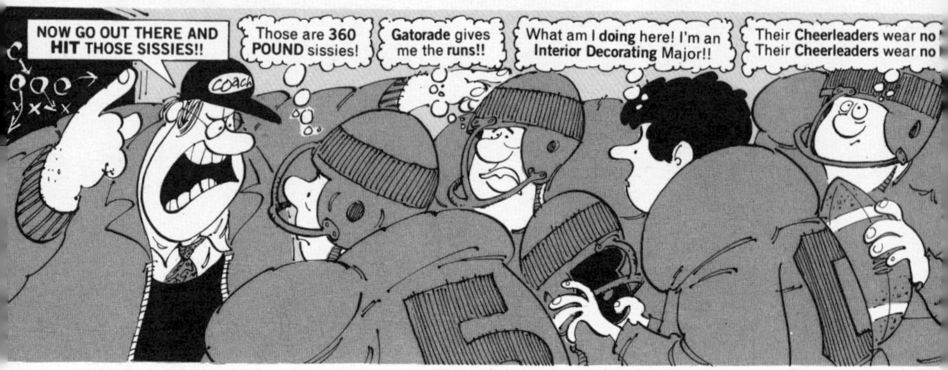

NOW GO OUT THERE AND HIT THOSE SISSIES!!
Those are 360 POUND sissies!
Gatorade gives me the runs!!
What am I doing here! I'm an Interior Decorating Major!!
Their Cheerleaders wear no
Their Cheerleaders wear no
COACH

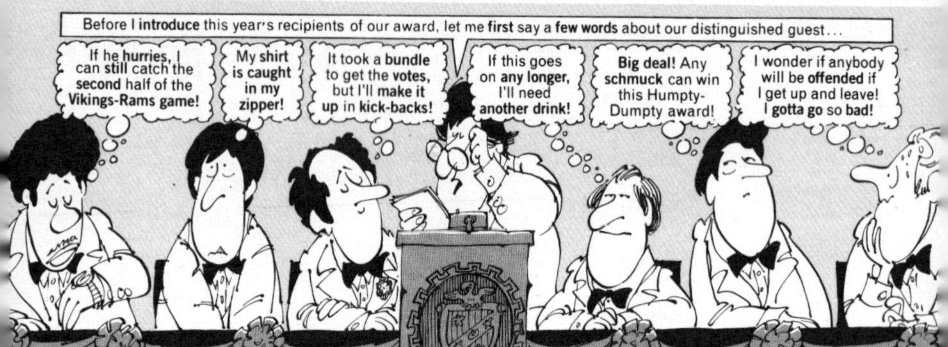

Before I introduce this year's recipients of our award, let me first say a few words about our distinguished guest...
If he hurries, I can still catch the second half of the Vikings-Rams game!
My shirt is caught in my zipper!
It took a bundle to get the votes, but I'll make it up in kick-backs!
If this goes on any longer, I'll need another drink!
Big deal! Any schmuck can win this Humpty-Dumpty award!
I wonder if anybody will be offended if I get up and leave! I gotta go so bad!

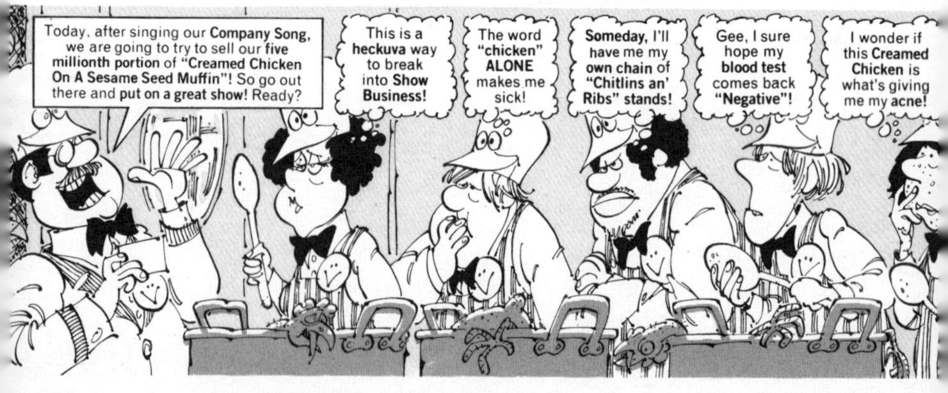

Today, after singing our Company Song, we are going to try to sell our five millionth portion of "Creamed Chicken On A Sesame Seed Muffin"! So go out there and put on a great show! Ready?
This is a heckuva way to break into Show Business!
The word "chicken" ALONE makes me sick!
Someday, I'll have me my own chain of "Chitlins an' Ribs" stands!
Gee, I sure hope my blood test comes back "Negative"!
I wonder if this Creamed Chicken is what's giving me my acne!

thinking AUDIENCE

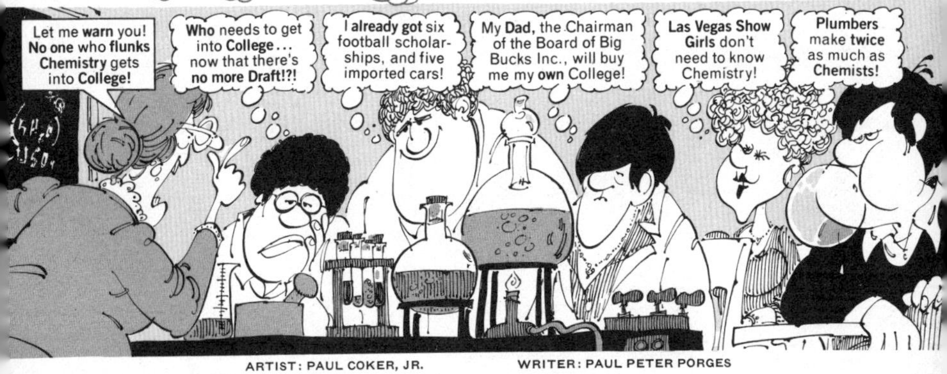
Let me warn you! No one who flunks Chemistry gets into College!
Who needs to get into College... now that there's no more Draft!?!
I already got six football scholarships, and five imported cars!
My Dad, the Chairman of the Board of Big Bucks Inc., will buy me my own College!
Las Vegas Show Girls don't need to know Chemistry!
Plumbers make twice as much as Chemists!

ARTIST: PAUL COKER, JR. WRITER: PAUL PETER PORGES

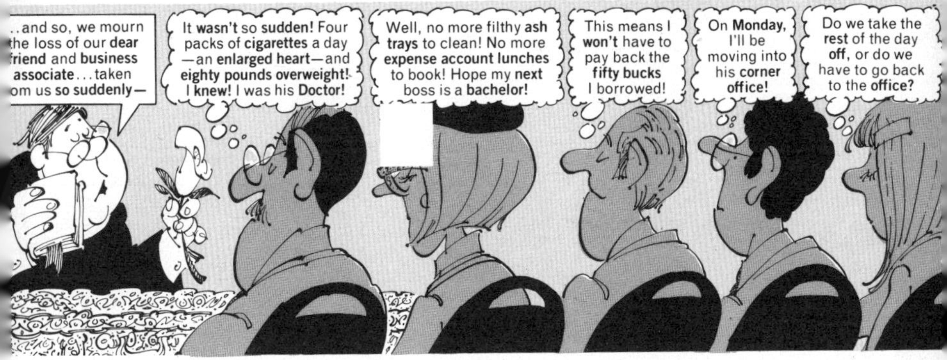
...and so, we mourn the loss of our dear friend and business associate... taken om us so suddenly—
It wasn't so sudden! Four packs of cigarettes a day —an enlarged heart—and eighty pounds overweight! I knew! I was his Doctor!
Well, no more filthy ash trays to clean! No more expense account lunches to book! Hope my next boss is a bachelor!
This means I won't have to pay back the fifty bucks I borrowed!
On Monday, I'll be moving into his corner office!
Do we take the rest of the day off, or do we have to go back to the office?

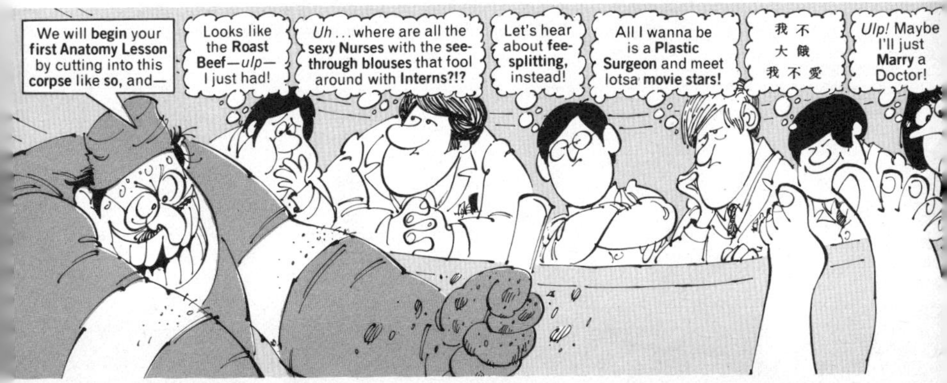
We will begin your first Anatomy Lesson by cutting into this corpse like so, and—
Looks like the Roast Beef—ulp— I just had!
Uh... where are all the sexy Nurses with the see-through blouses that fool around with Interns?!?
Let's hear about fee-splitting, instead!
All I wanna be is a Plastic Surgeon and meet lotsa movie stars!
我 不
大 餓
我 不 愛
Ulp! Maybe I'll just Marry a Doctor!

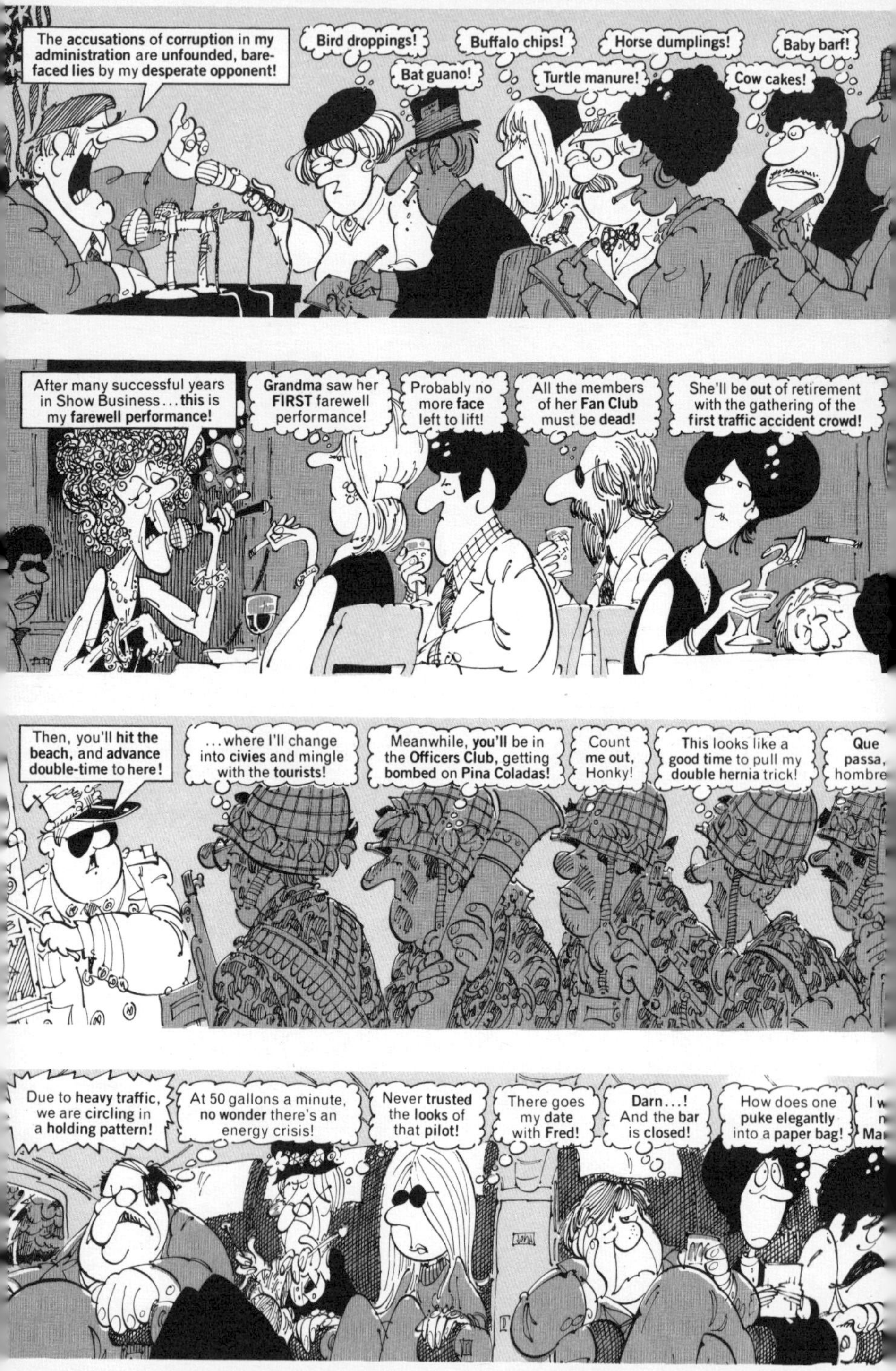
The accusations of corruption in my administration are unfounded, bare-faced lies by my desperate opponent!
Bird droppings!
Bat guano!
Buffalo chips!
Turtle manure!
Horse dumplings!
Cow cakes!
Baby barf!
After many successful years in Show Business . . . this is my farewell performance!
Grandma saw her FIRST farewell performance!
Probably no more face left to lift!
All the members of her Fan Club must be dead!
She'll be out of retirement with the gathering of the first traffic accident crowd!
Then, you'll hit the beach, and advance double-time to here!
. . . where I'll change into civies and mingle with the tourists!
Meanwhile, you'll be in the Officers Club, getting bombed on Pina Coladas!
Count me out, Honky!
This looks like a good time to pull my double hernia trick!
Que passa, hombre
Due to heavy traffic, we are circling in a holding pattern!
At 50 gallons a minute, no wonder there's an energy crisis!
Never trusted the looks of that pilot!
There goes my date with Fred!
Darn . . .! And the bar is closed!
How does one puke elegantly into a paper bag!

HIRE EDUCATION DEPT.

Like it or not, you can't go to school forever. So, in the not too distant future, when you're 25 or so, you're going to wake up one morning and be faced with a momentous decision: either finish high school and go on to college, or go out and get a job. If you decide to go to college, you've got nothing to worry about for another ten years at least. But if you plan to get a job, pay close attention to:

MAD'S GUIDE TO MAKING IT IN THE BUSINESS WORLD

ARTIST: GEORGE WOODBRIDGE WRITER: LARRY SIEGEL

CHOOSING THE KIND OF COMPANY TO JOIN

In the business world, you usually have a choice of two kinds of firms to join, Small or Large.

One Of The Advantages Of Joining A Small Firm

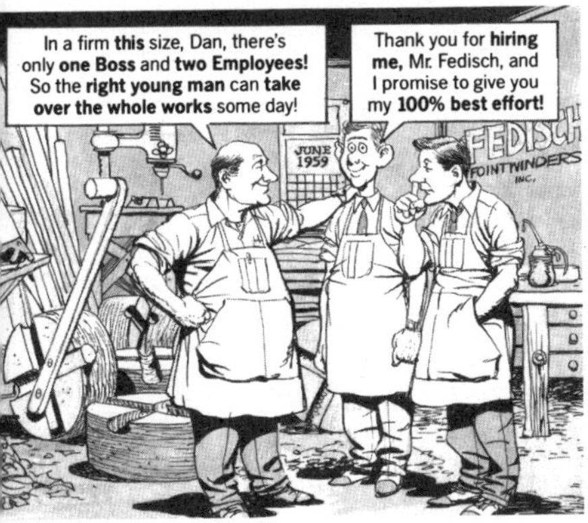

In a firm this size, Dan, there's only one Boss and two Employees! So the right young man can take over the whole works some day!
Thank you for hiring me, Mr. Fedisch, and I promise to give you my 100% best effort!
JUNE 1959
FEDISCH FOINTWINDERS INC.

One Of The Disadvantages Of Joining A Small Firm

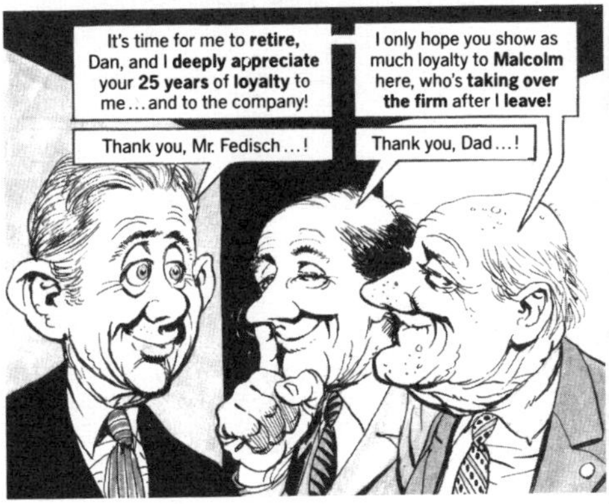

It's time for me to retire, Dan, and I deeply appreciate your 25 years of loyalty to me... and to the company!
Thank you, Mr. Fedisch...!
I only hope you show as much loyalty to Malcolm here, who's taking over the firm after I leave!
Thank you, Dad...!

One Of The Advantages Of Joining A Large Firm

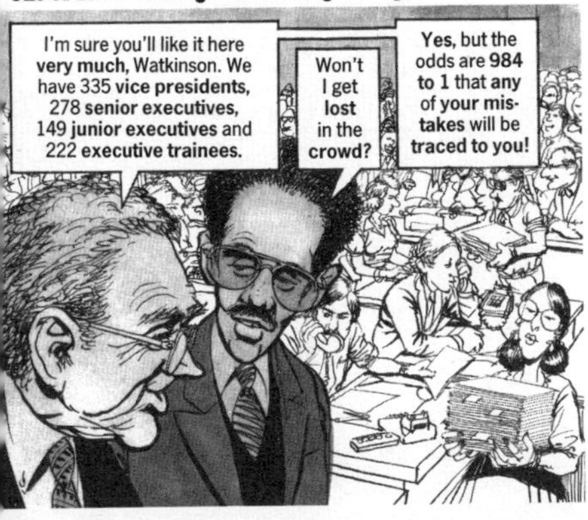

I'm sure you'll like it here very much, Watkinson. We have 335 vice presidents, 278 senior executives, 149 junior executives and 222 executive trainees.
Won't I get lost in the crowd?
Yes, but the odds are 984 to 1 that any of your mistakes will be traced to you!

One Of The Disadvantages Of Joining A Large Firm

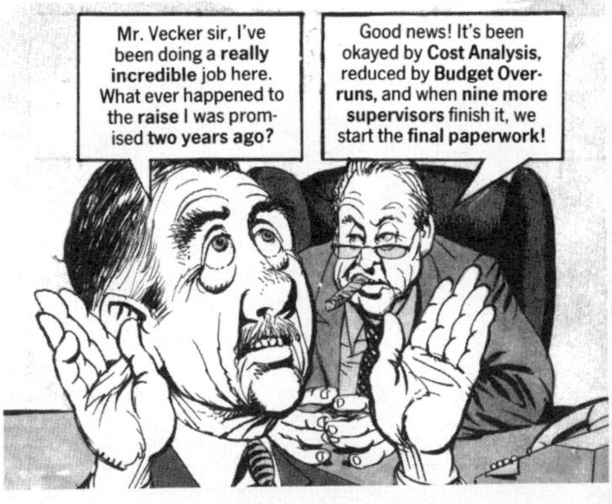

Mr. Vecker sir, I've been doing a really incredible job here. What ever happened to the raise I was promised two years ago?
Good news! It's been okayed by Cost Analysis, reduced by Budget Overruns, and when nine more supervisors finish it, we start the final paperwork!

PATTERN YOURSELF AFTER SUCCESSFUL PEOPLE

The quickest way to achieve success in a large office is to model your behavior after those who are making it, and avoid the mistakes of those who aren't. Here are examples of what we mean...

The Way They Keep Their Desk

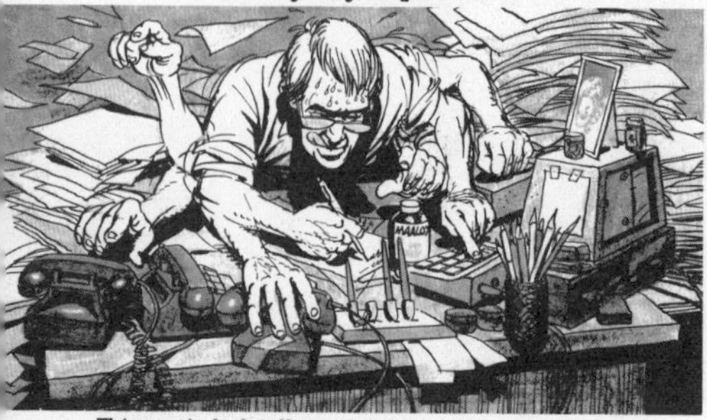

This man's desk tells us that he is a conscientious and tireless worker. It tells us that he has no time for petty politics and no desire to engage in vicious acts like screwing the guy ahead of him on the job scale. It also tells us that this guy is a TOTAL FAILURE IN BUSINESS.

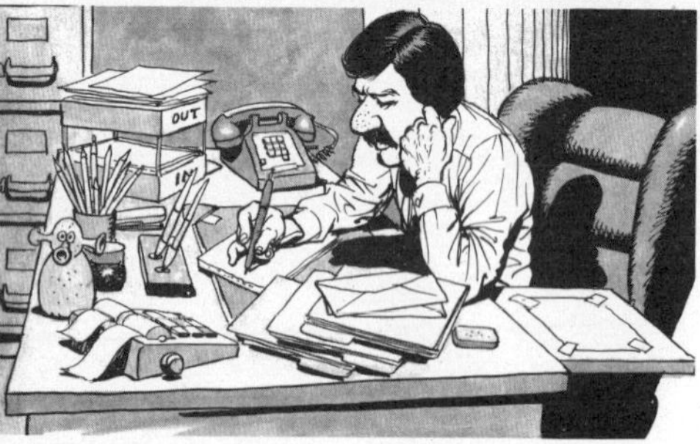
OUT
IN

This man's desk contains only a minimum amount of work. The rest, he either passes on down to underlings, or he destroys. This gives him a free hand to work on important projects. It also gives him his other free hand to knife people in the back who are in his way up the job scale. This guy is obviously a MODERATE SUCCESS IN BUSINESS.

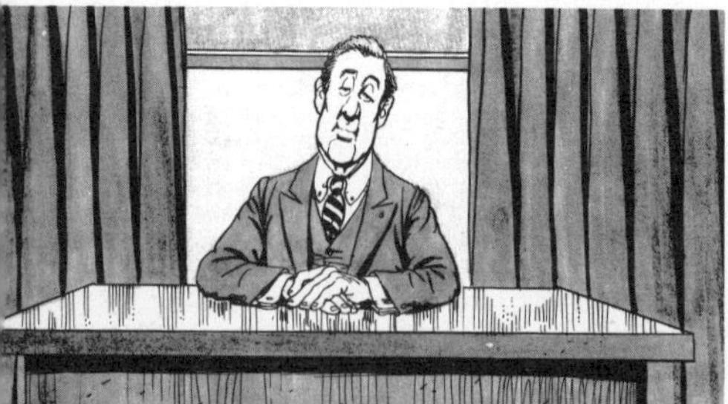

This man's desk is absolutely, totally clean. Everything ...including his work load, his expense account records, and the man he replaced... are in the waste basket under his desk. This guy is obviously CHAIRMAN OF THE BOARD.

The Way They Handle Themselves On The Phone

This man will accept all calls, will talk to anybo the phone, and if he's not at his desk, will return immediately upon his return, which gives him no ti make plans to screw the man ahead of him. Obvic this man is another example of a TOTAL FAILURE IN BUSI

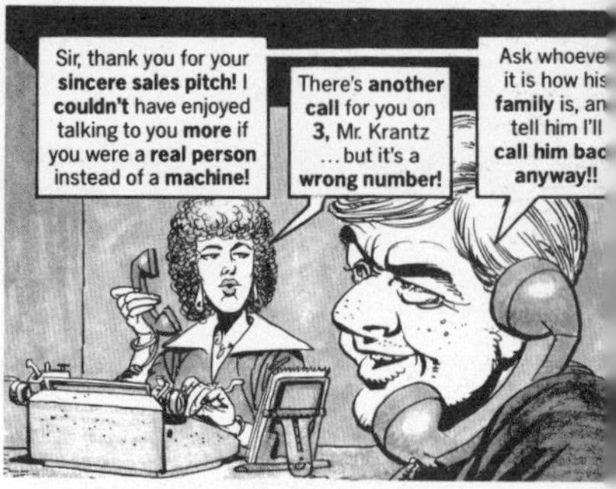
Sir, thank you for your **sincere sales pitch!** I **couldn't** have enjoyed talking to you **more** if you were a **real person** instead of a **machine!**
There's **another call** for you on **3,** Mr. Krantz ...but it's a **wrong number!**
Ask whoeve it is how his **family** is, an tell him I'll **call him bac anyway!!**

This man only speaks to people who can help him, and nores the calls of others. Which gives him time to s around superiors, or make plans to knife them. This is another example of a MODERATE SUCCESS IN BUSIN

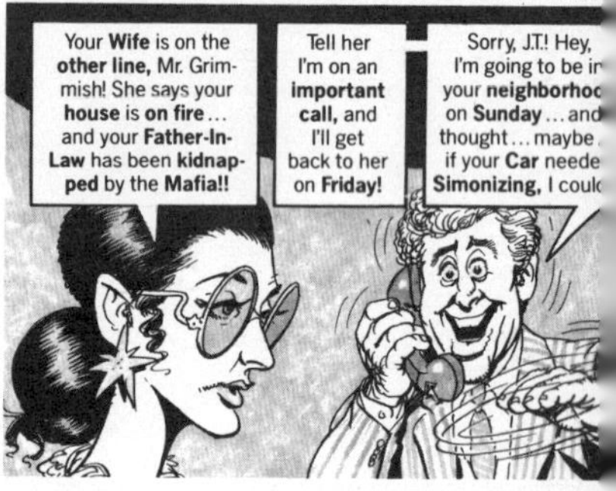
Your **Wife** is on the **other line,** Mr. Grimmish! She says your **house** is **on fire**... and your **Father-In-Law** has been **kidnapped** by the **Mafia!!**
Tell her I'm on an **important call,** and I'll get back to her on **Friday!**
Sorry, J.T.! Hey, I'm going to be in your **neighborho on Sunday**...and thought... maybe if your **Car neede Simonizing,** I coul

Even until his dying day, this guy never accepts ca from anyone! Yep... he's the CHAIRMAN OF THE BOAR

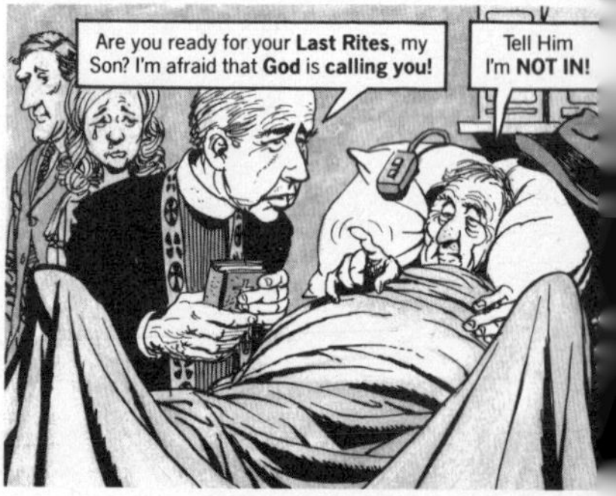
Are you ready for your **Last Rites,** my Son? I'm afraid that **God** is **calling you!**
Tell Him I'm **NOT IN!**

THE VITAL IMPORTANCE OF BUSINESS MEETINGS

usiness meetings are the very lifeblood of y large firm. Following are the "Three W's" siness meetings: "When," "Who," and "Why."

WHEN Should You Call A Business Meeting...? Answer: At Least Twenty-five Times A Day...?

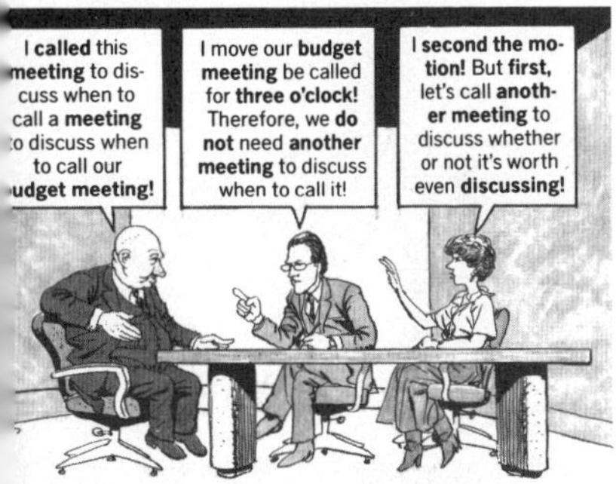

I called this meeting to discuss when to call a meeting to discuss when to call our udget meeting!
I move our budget meeting be called for three o'clock! Therefore, we do not need another meeting to discuss when to call it!
I second the motion! But first, let's call another meeting to discuss whether or not it's worth even discussing!

WHO Should Attend These Business Meetings? Answer: Anybody In The Office! And Remember, There Are Never Too Many Or Too Few People!

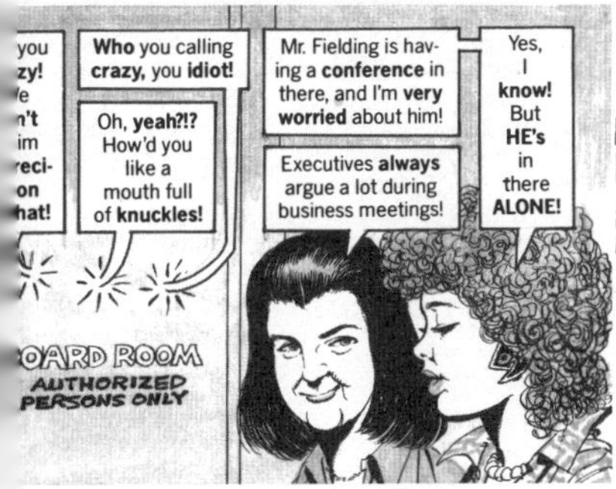

you zy! ve n't im reci- on hat!
Who you calling crazy, you idiot!
Oh, yeah?!? How'd you like a mouth full of knuckles!
OARD ROOM
AUTHORIZED PERSONS ONLY
Mr. Fielding is having a conference in there, and I'm very worried about him!
Executives always argue a lot during business meetings!
Yes, I know! But HE's in there ALONE!

WHY Should You Call A Business Meeting...? Answer: If You Think You Need A Good Reason, You'd Better Get Out Of The Business World!!

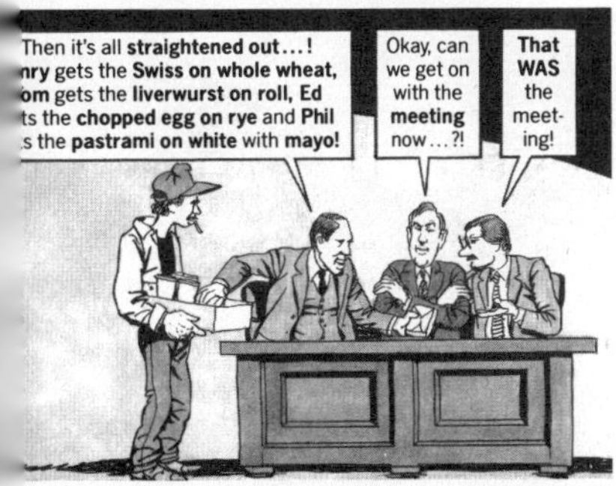

Then it's all straightened out...! nry gets the Swiss on whole wheat, om gets the liverwurst on roll, Ed ts the chopped egg on rye and Phil s the pastrami on white with mayo!
Okay, can we get on with the meeting now...?!
That WAS the meeting!

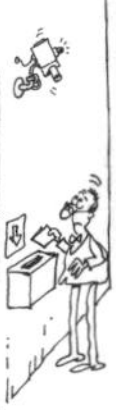

SEX IN BUSINESS

In the business world, you'll come across women of all ages, sizes and shapes! Take warning...!

Back in the old days, the following scene of sexual harassment was very common around most business offices...

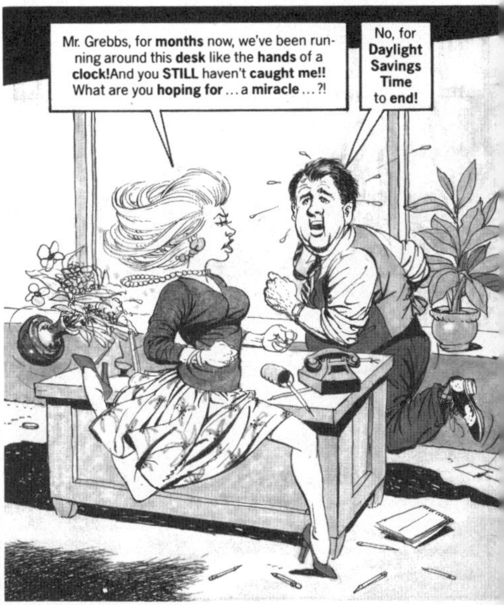

Mr. Grebbs, for months now, we've been running around this desk like the hands of a clock! And you STILL haven't caught me!! What are you hoping for... a miracle...?!
No, for Daylight Savings Time to end!

Today, of course, with the advancement of "Women's Rights," the times... and the scene... have changed dramatically...

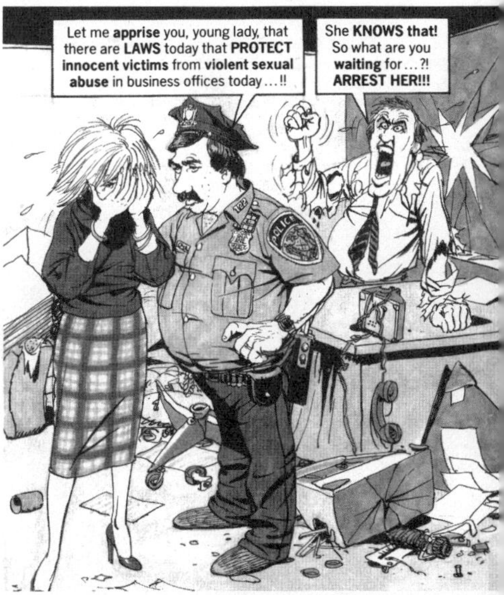

Let me apprise you, young lady, that there are LAWS today that PROTECT innocent victims from violent sexual abuse in business offices today...!!
She KNOWS that! So what are you waiting for...?! ARREST HER!!!

HOW TO DRESS IN THE BUSINESS WORLD

In business, it's important to conform to certain dress codes which coincide with your career

As A Shipping Clerk...

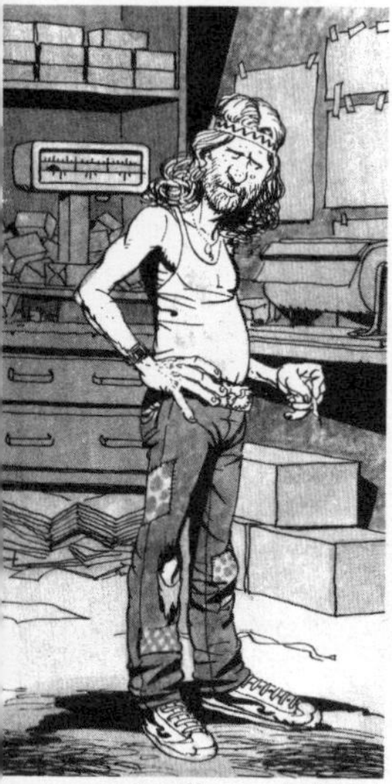

...you will wear battered running shoes, torn jeans, a dirty tank shirt, a beard, a Willie Nelson hair style and an earring. You will be known as a STRANGE WEIRDO SLOB!

As An Executive Trainee...

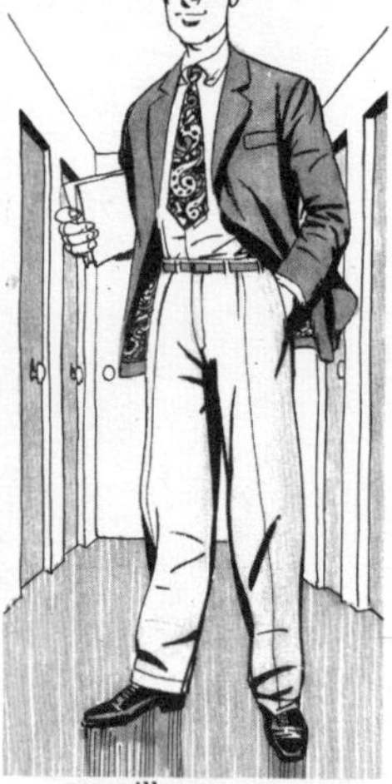

...you will wear a conservative suit, a dark blue shirt, a paisley tie, Italian shoes and short hair. You will be known as a FASHION PLATE ...WITH UPWARD MOBILITY!

As A Vice President...

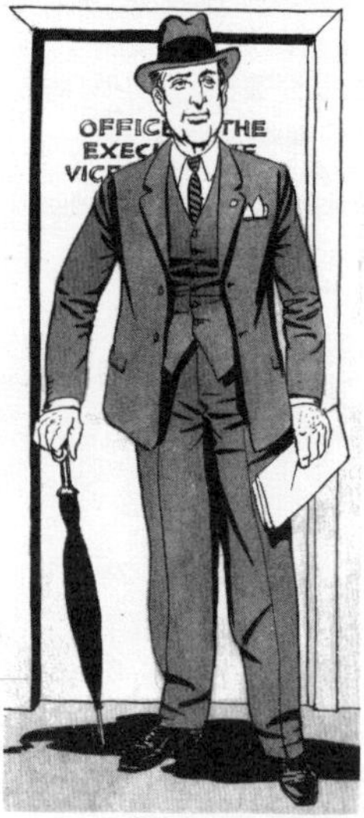
OFFICE THE
EXEC
VIC

...you will be a symphony in black...a black vested suit, black tie and black shoes framing a white shirt. You will be known as an EXECUTIVE WHO'S MADE IT!

As Chairman Of The B

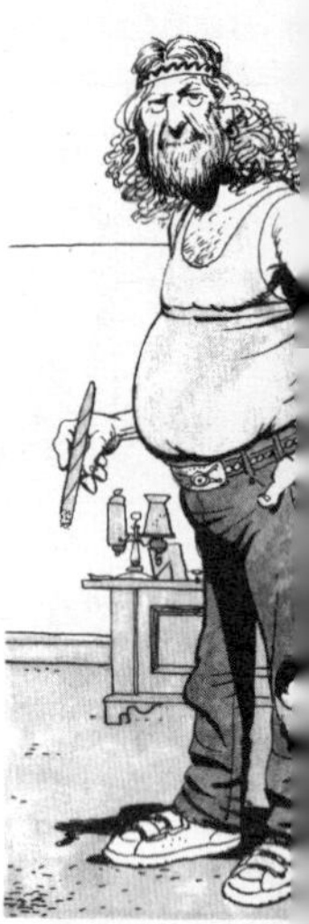

...you will wear b
running shoes, torn
dirty tank shirt, a
Willie Nelson hair st
an earring. You will b
as an ECCENTRIC G

THOSE LEGENDARY OFFICE CHRISTMAS PARTIES

One of the marks of a successful executive is how well and how often he makes out at the Offic Xmas Party. Watch some experts in action and, if you value your career, follow their examples

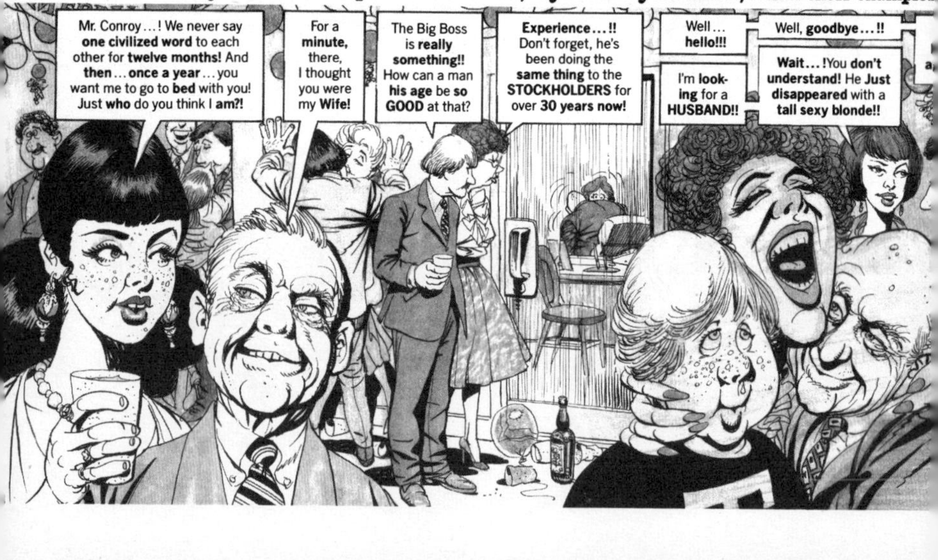
Mr. Conroy...! We never say one civilized word to each other for twelve months! And then...once a year...you want me to go to bed with you! Just who do you think I am?!
For a minute, there, I thought you were my Wife!
The Big Boss is really something!! How can a man his age be so GOOD at that?
Experience...!! Don't forget, he's been doing the same thing to the STOCKHOLDERS for over 30 years now!
Well... hello!!!
I'm looking for a HUSBAND!!
Well, goodbye...!!
Wait...!You don't understand! He Just disappeared with a tall sexy blonde!!

DON MARTIN DEPT.

ONE BEAUTIFUL EVENING LAST MAY

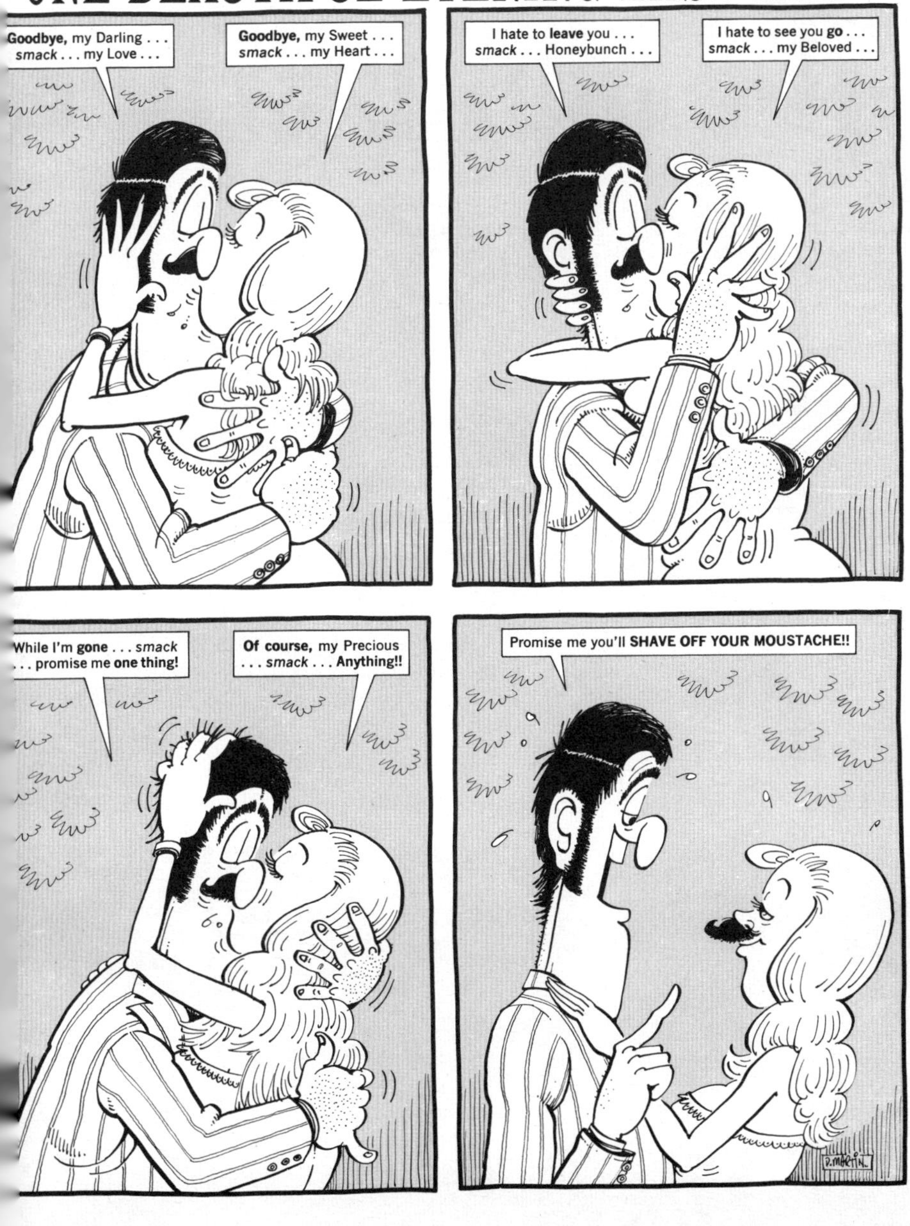
Goodbye, my Darling . . . smack . . . my Love . . .
Goodbye, my Sweet . . . smack . . . my Heart . . .
I hate to leave you . . . smack . . . Honeybunch . . .
I hate to see you go . . . smack . . . my Beloved . . .
While I'm gone . . . smack . . . promise me one thing!
Of course, my Precious . . . smack . . . Anything!!
Promise me you'll SHAVE OFF YOUR MOUSTACHE!!
D. MARTIN

BETTER DEAD THAN BLED DEPT.

If you're like us, you're no doubt waiting with gleeful anticipation for Hollywood to stop producing all those needless and boring movie sequels and just let them die off! Well,

THE MOVIE SEQUE

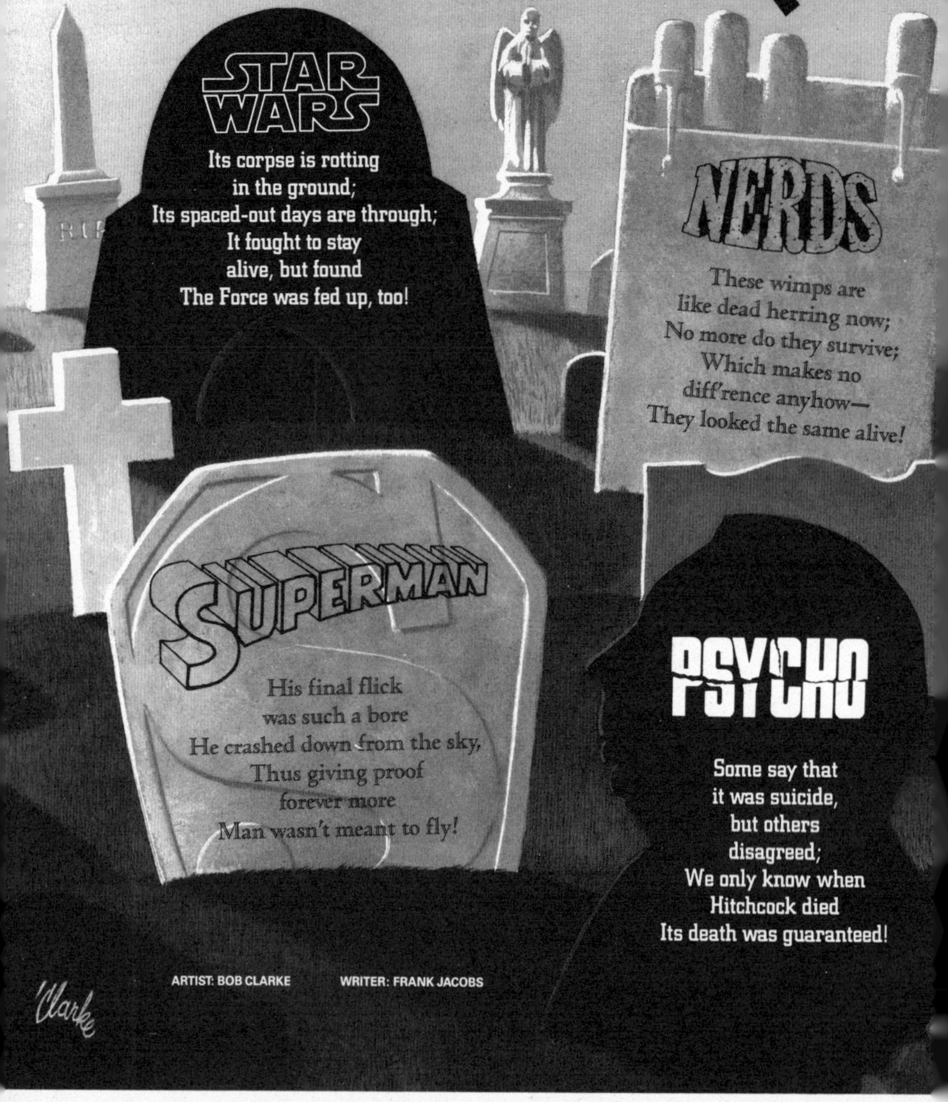
STAR WARS
Its corpse is rotting
in the ground;
Its spaced-out days are through;
It fought to stay
alive, but found
The Force was fed up, too!
RIP
NERDS
These wimps are
like dead herring now;
No more do they survive;
Which makes no
diff'rence anyhow—
They looked the same alive!
SUPERMAN
His final flick
was such a bore
He crashed down from the sky,
Thus giving proof
forever more
Man wasn't meant to fly!
PSYCHO
Some say that
it was suicide,
but others
disagreed;
We only know when
Hitchcock died
Its death was guaranteed!
Clarke

ARTIST: BOB CLARKE WRITER: FRANK JACOBS

en though most of these movie series are still very much alive and kicking, we at MAD
ant to let them know we have some choice plots of ground ready and waiting for them in...

GRAVEYARD

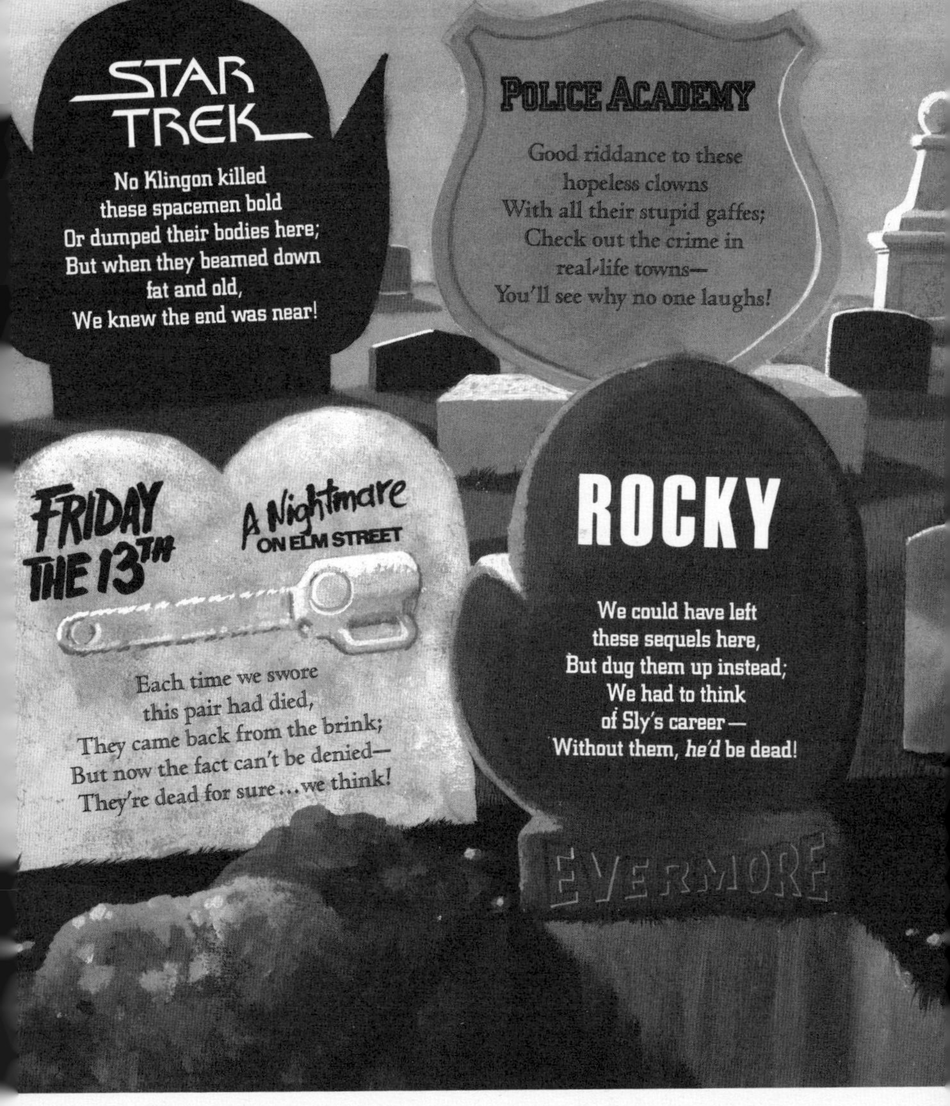
STAR TREK
No Klingon killed
these spacemen bold
Or dumped their bodies here;
But when they beamed down
fat and old,
We knew the end was near!
POLICE ACADEMY
Good riddance to these
hopeless clowns
With all their stupid gaffes;
Check out the crime in
real-life towns—
You'll see why no one laughs!
FRIDAY THE 13TH
A Nightmare ON ELM STREET
Each time we swore
this pair had died,
They came back from the brink;
But now the fact can't be denied—
They're dead for sure...we think!
ROCKY
We could have left
these sequels here,
But dug them up instead;
We had to think
of Sly's career—
Without them, *he'd* be dead!
EVERMORE

A VIEW TO A QUILL DEPT.

PRACTICAL USES FOR WE

SCHOOL CROSSING GUARD

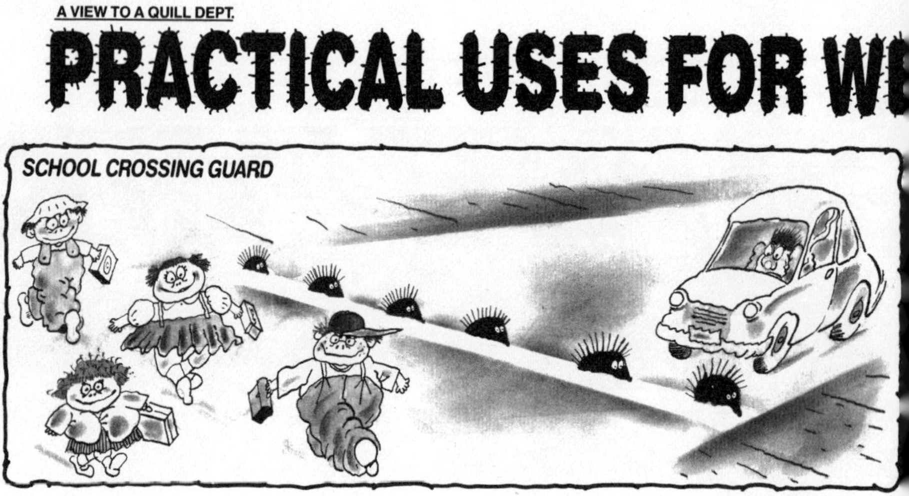

MULTI-HEADED TRASH PICK-UP

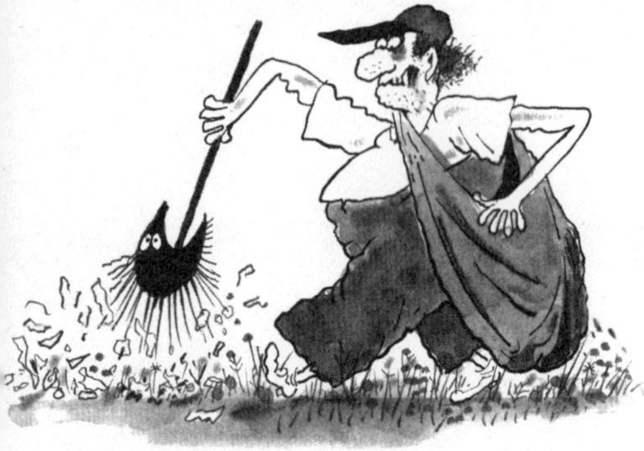

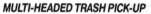

PUNK HAIRPIECE FOR THE BALDING

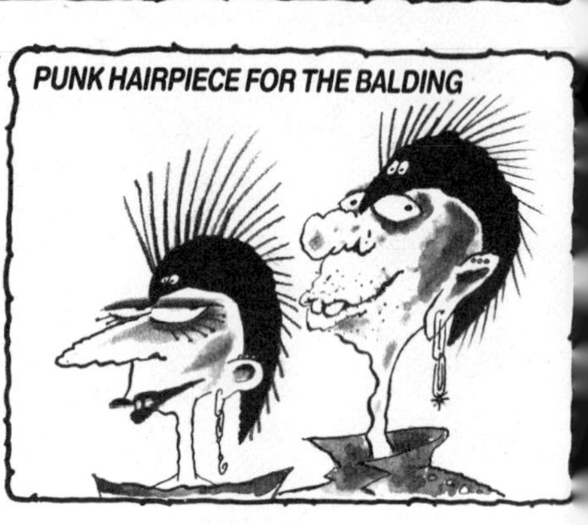

BUFFET TABLE AIDS

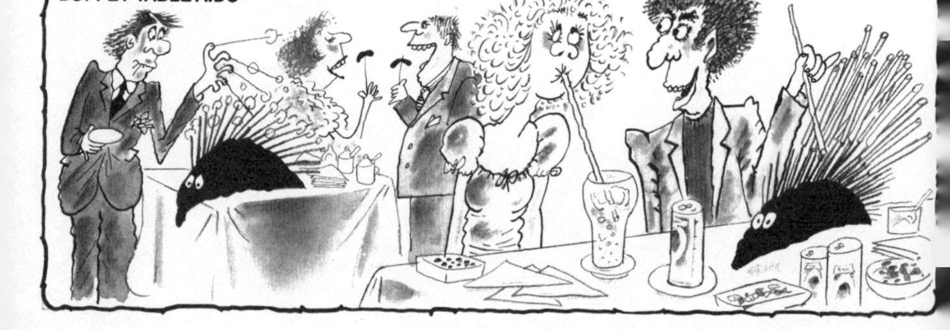

LL-TRAINED PORCUPINES

ARTIST & WRITER: PAUL PETER PORGES

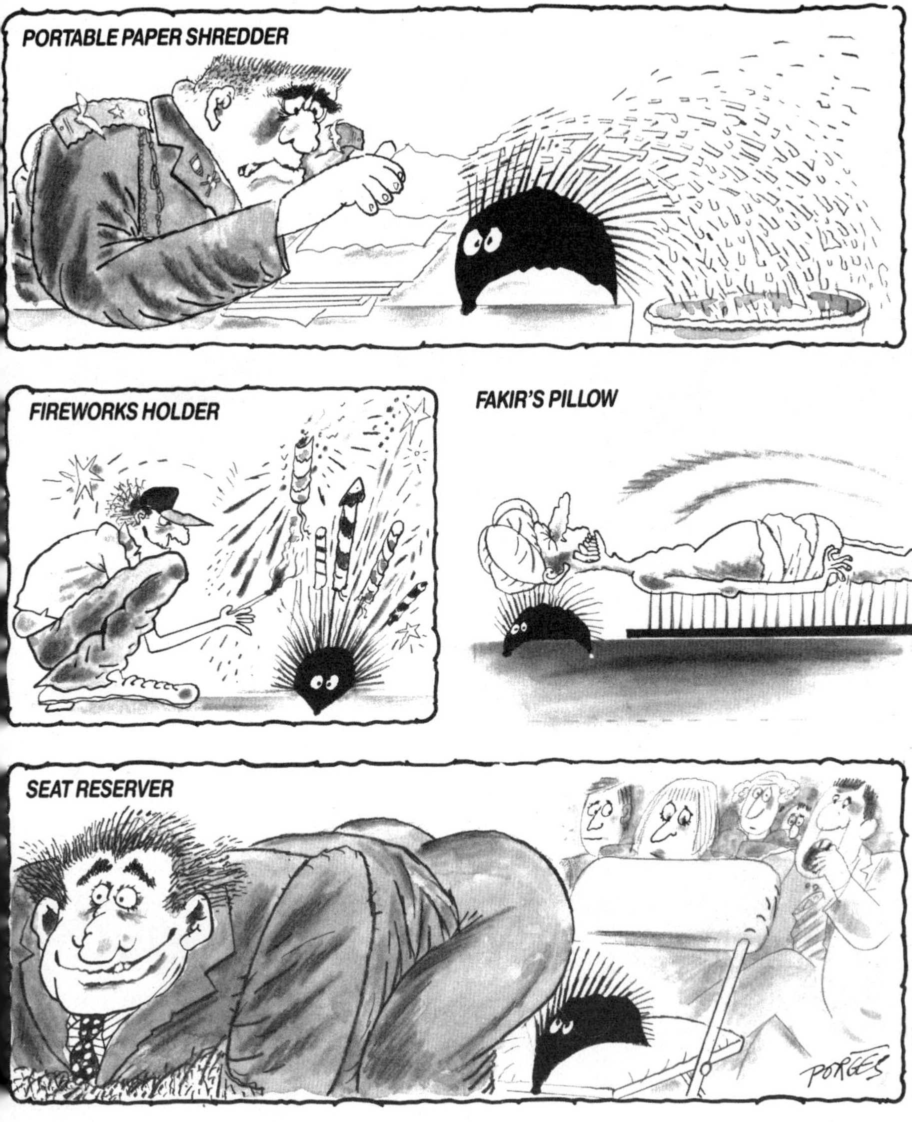
PORTABLE PAPER SHREDDER
FIREWORKS HOLDER
FAKIR'S PILLOW
SEAT RESERVER
PORGES

DON MARTIN DEPT.

THE GREAT ZUCCHINI

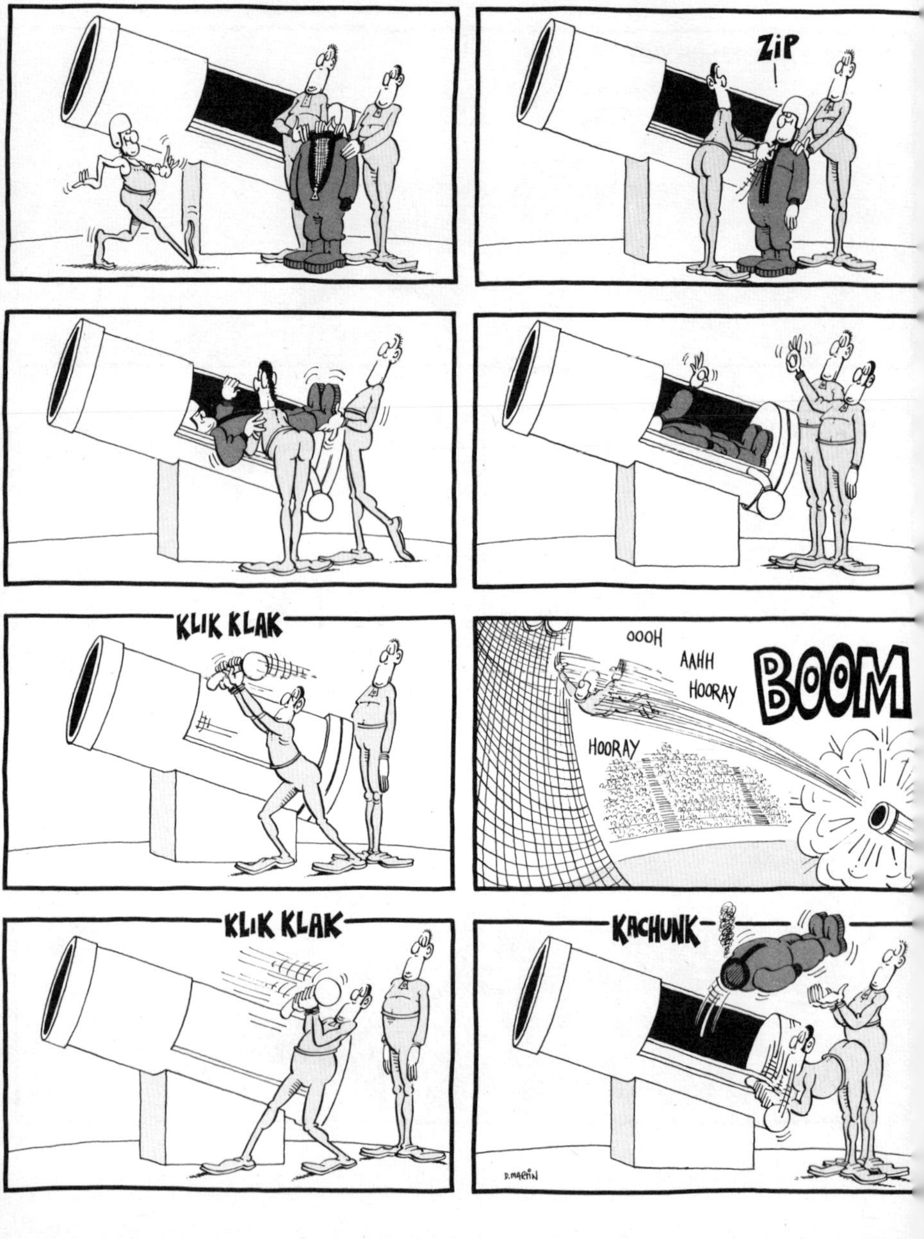
ZIP
KLIK KLAK
OOOH
AAHH
HOORAY
BOOM
HOORAY
KLIK KLAK
KACHUNK
D. MARTIN

CHANGE REACTION DEPT.

GOBOTS and TRANSFORMERS are the hottest toys of the year! As the name implies, these toys transform from one thing into another. For instance, a few deft twists of its moveable parts, and a

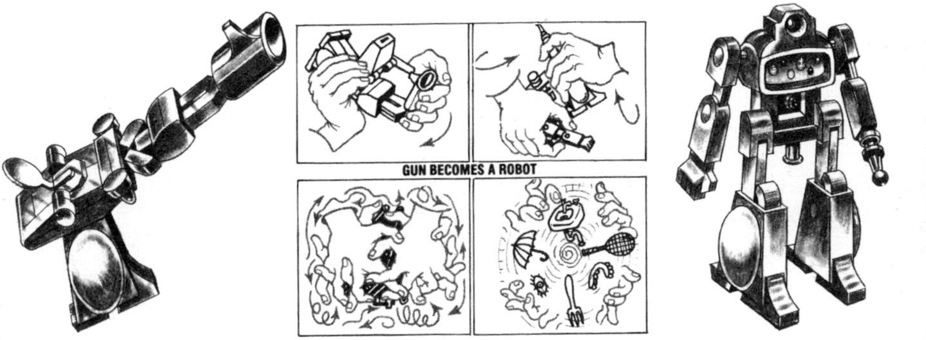

GUN BECOMES A ROBOT

Great! Except they only deal in the fantasy world! What kids need today are toys that deal in the real world! Toys like MAD's...

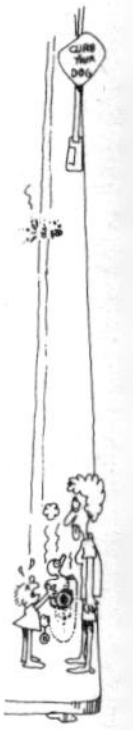

TRULY LOGICAL TRANSFORMERS

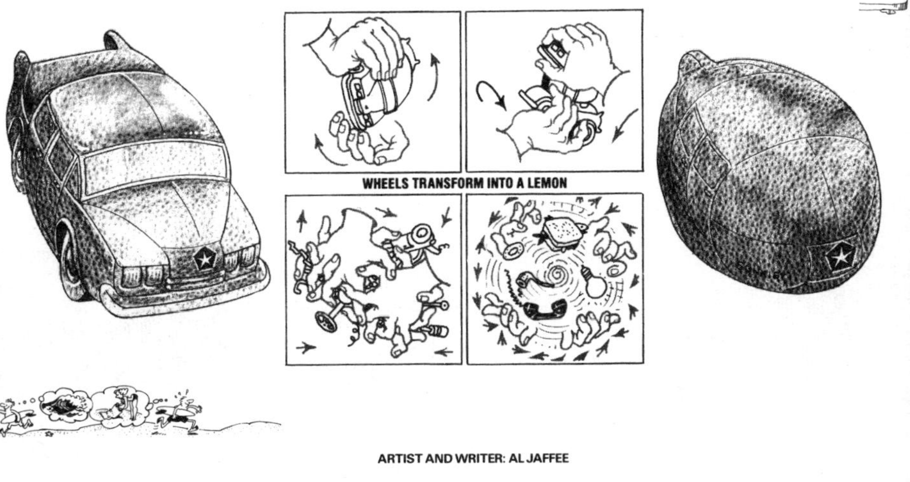

WHEELS TRANSFORM INTO A LEMON

ARTIST AND WRITER: AL JAFFEE

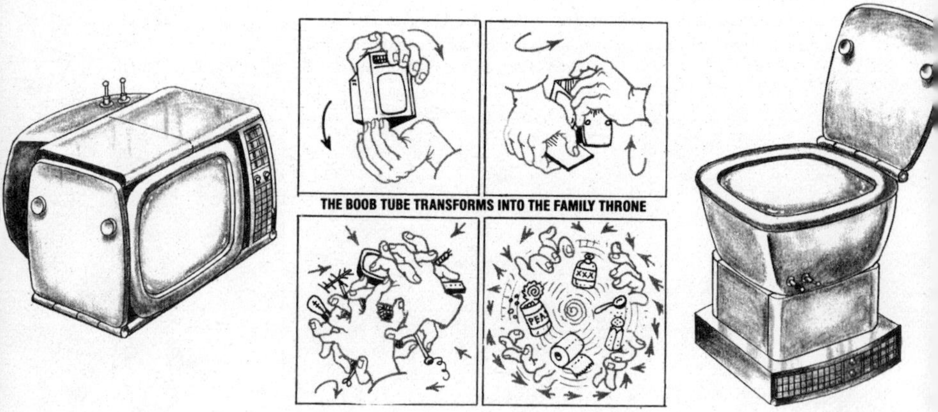

THE BOOB TUBE TRANSFORMS INTO THE FAMILY THRONE

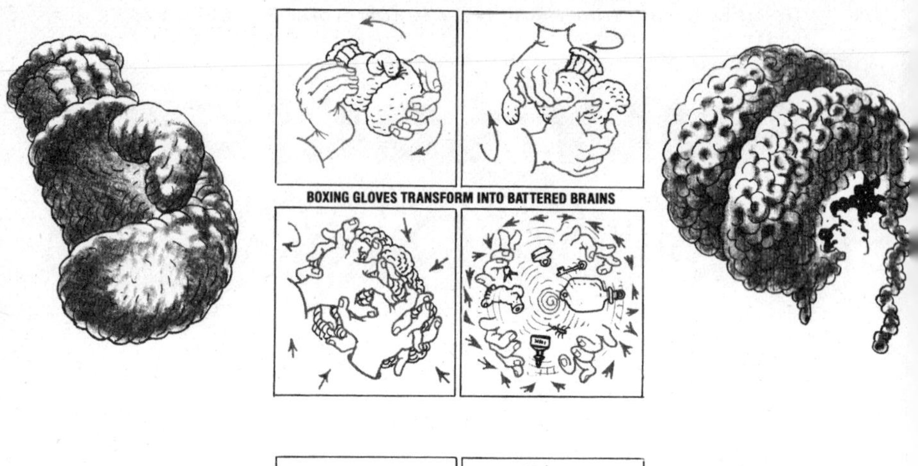

BOXING GLOVES TRANSFORM INTO BATTERED BRAINS

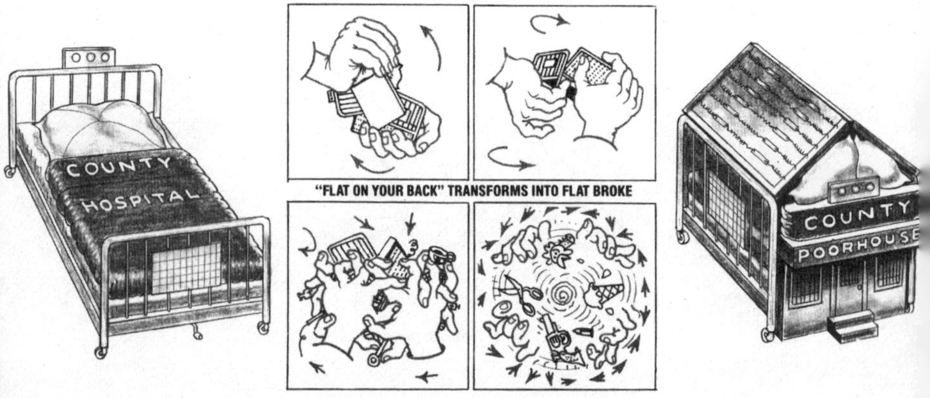
COUNTY
HOSPITAL
COUNTY
POORHOUSE

"FLAT ON YOUR BACK" TRANSFORMS INTO FLAT BROKE

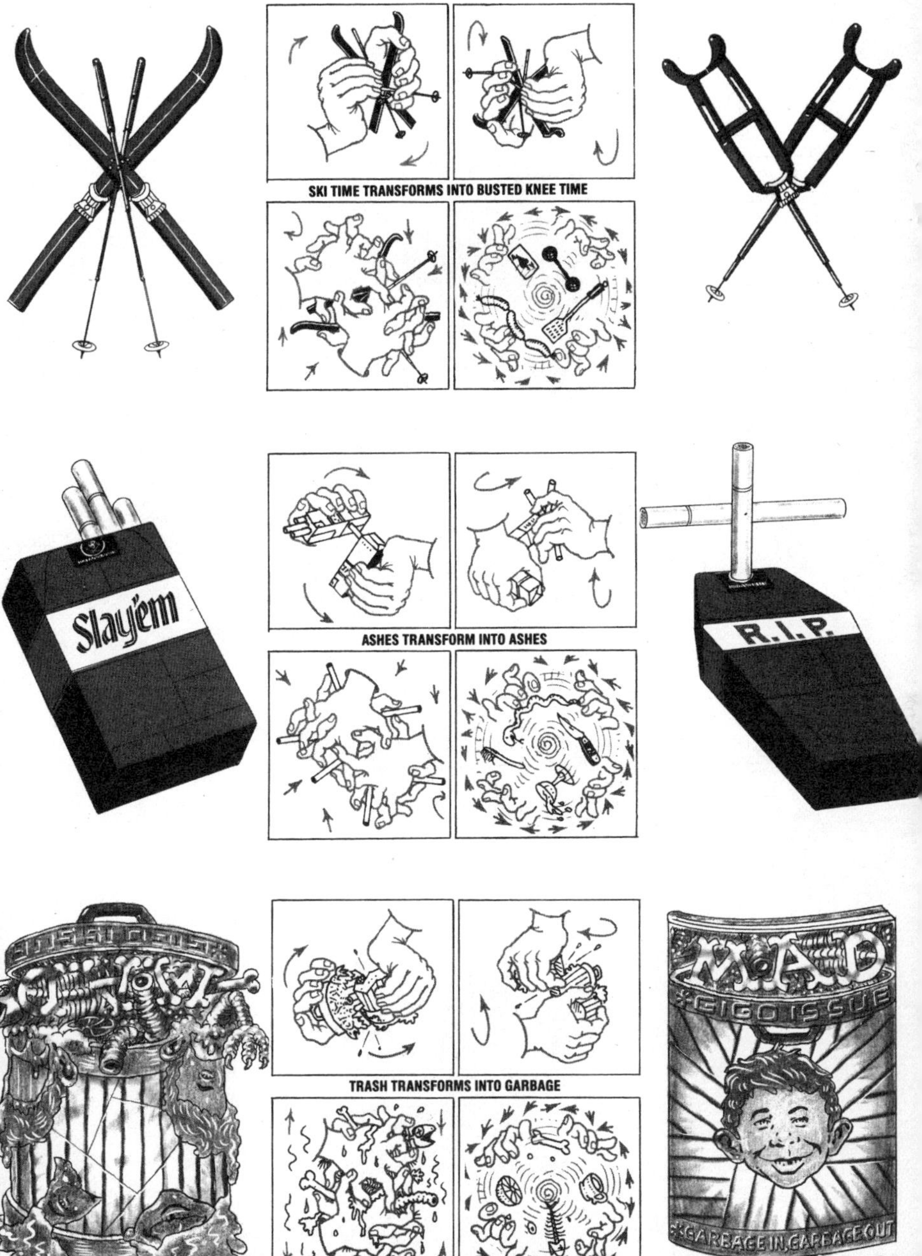
SKI TIME TRANSFORMS INTO BUSTED KNEE TIME
Slay'em
ASHES TRANSFORM INTO ASHES
R.I.P.
TRASH TRANSFORMS INTO GARBAGE
MAD
#GIGO ISSUE
#GARBAGE IN, GARBAGE OUT
Al Jaffee

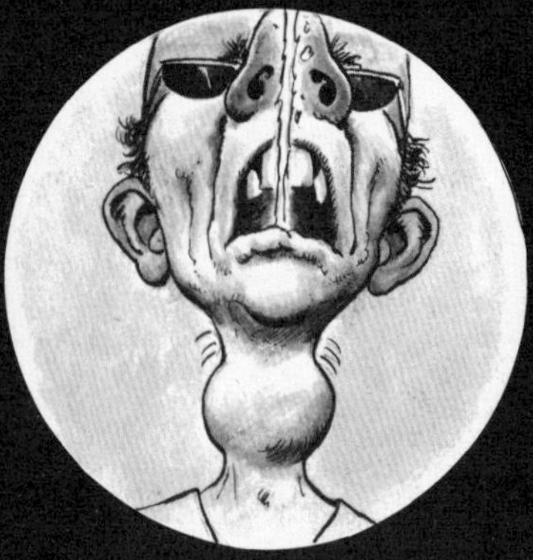

A CENTERFIELDER LOSING THE BALL IN THE SUN

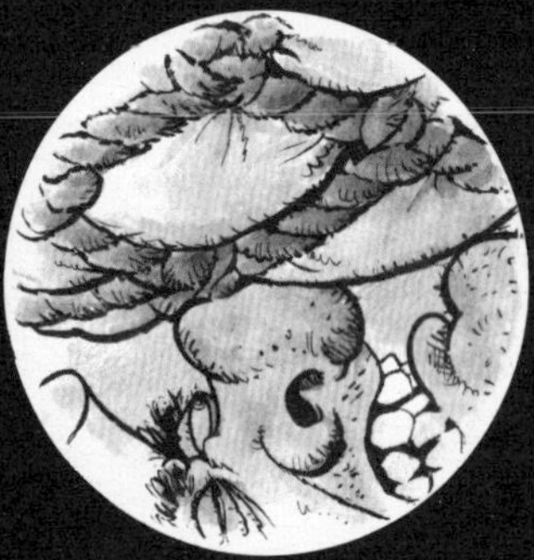

A SAILOR BUNKING UNDER A PORTLY SHIPMATE

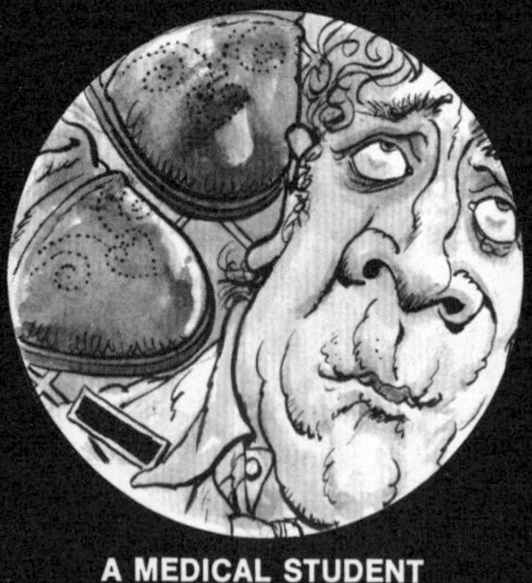

A MEDICAL STUDENT WITNESSING HIS FIRST LIVE OPERATION

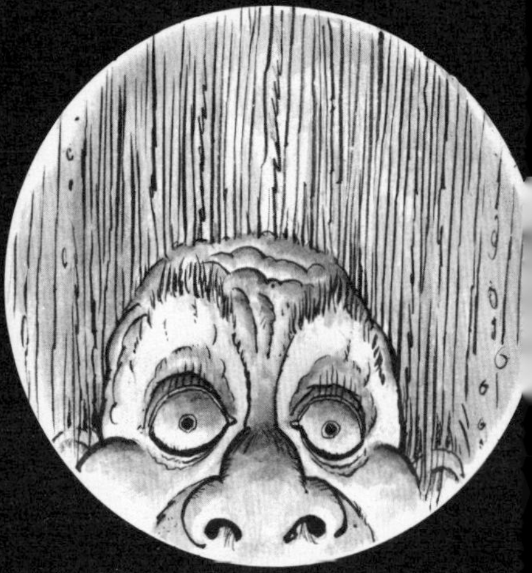

A BALLOONIST RUNNING OUT OF HOT AIR

TELESCOPIC EYE-SORE DEPT.

WITH THE HELP OF A TELESCOPIC L

MAD CI

ARTIST: HARRY NORTH, ES

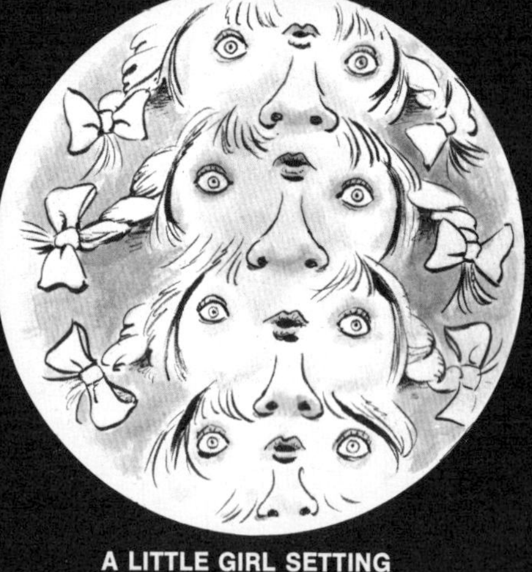

A LITTLE GIRL SETTING THE ROPE-JUMPING RECORD FOR THE GUINNESS BOOK

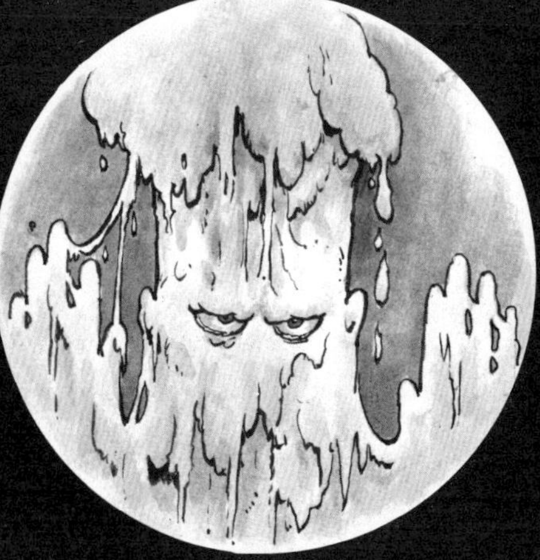

A PIZZA CHEF IMMEDIATELY
AFTER AN UNTIMELY SNEEZE

WE NOW BRING YOU A COLLECTION OF...

OSE-UPS

RITER: PAUL PETER PORGES

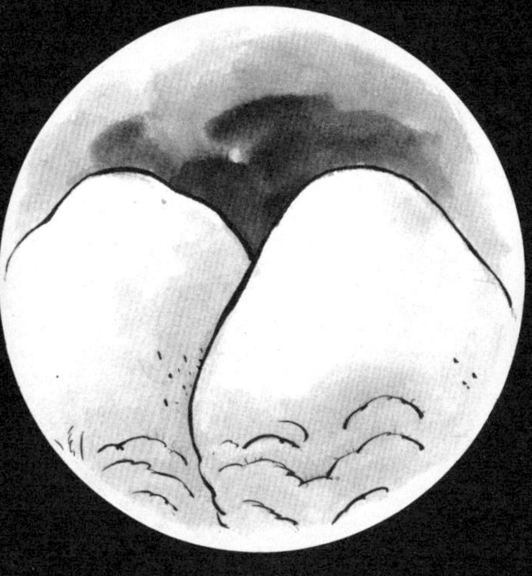

THE WINNER AND THE
RUNNER-UP IN THE "KOJAK"
LOOK-ALIKE CONTEST

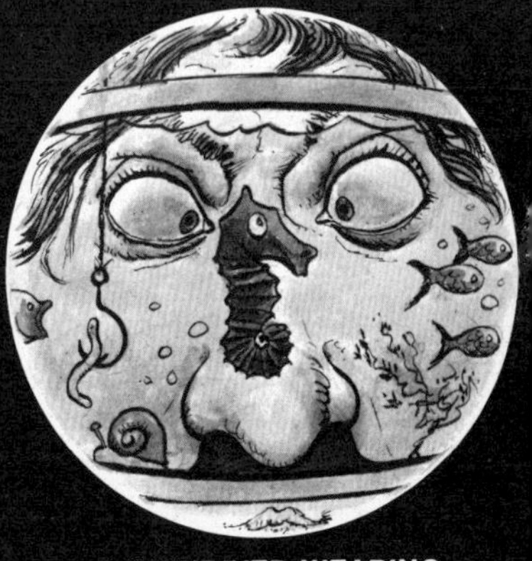

A SKINDIVER WEARING
A LOOSE MASK

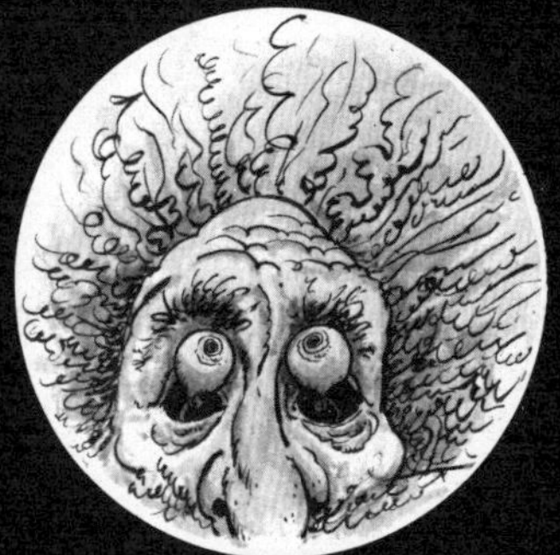

A HOMEOWNER FIXING A
BLOWN FUSE WITH A PENNY

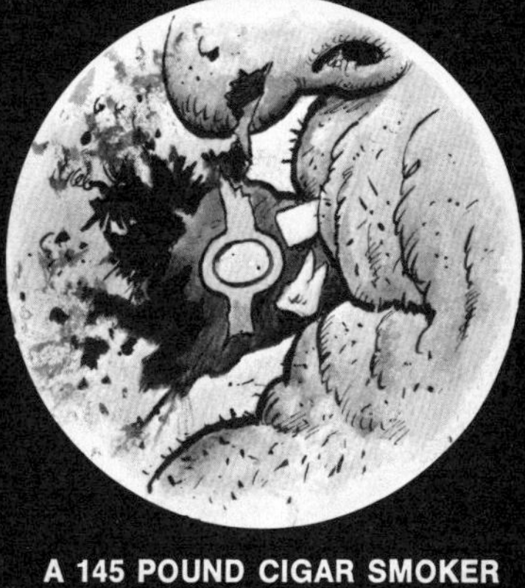

A 145 POUND CIGAR SMOKER
AFTER AN ARGUMENT WITH
A 220 POUND NON-SMOKER

JOKE AND DAGGER DEPT.

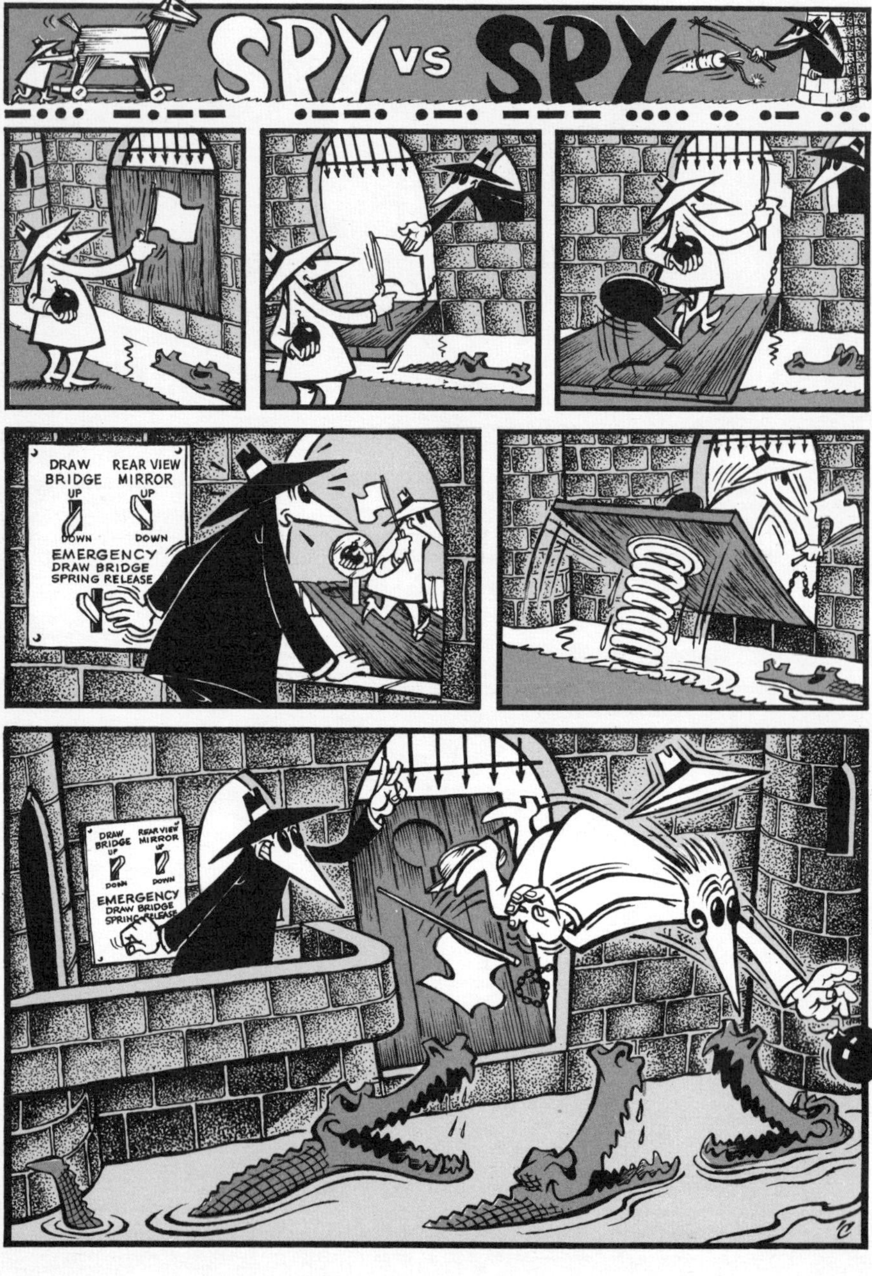
SPY vs SPY
DRAW BRIDGE
UP
DOWN
REAR VIEW MIRROR
UP
DOWN
EMERGENCY DRAW BRIDGE SPRING RELEASE
DRAW BRIDGE
UP
DOWN
REAR VIEW MIRROR
UP
DOWN
EMERGENCY DRAW BRIDGE SPRING RELEASE

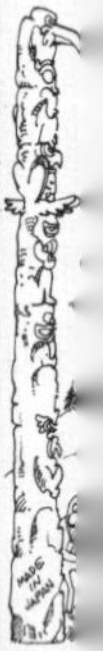

SERGIO ARAGONES DEPT.

A MAD LOOK AT HANDS ACROSS AMERICA

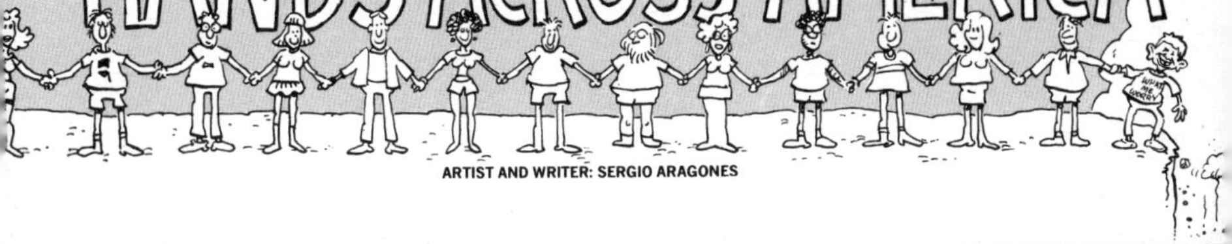

ARTIST AND WRITER: SERGIO ARAGONES

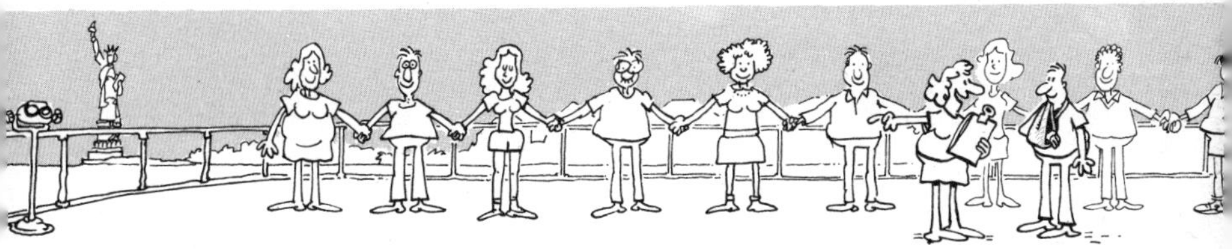

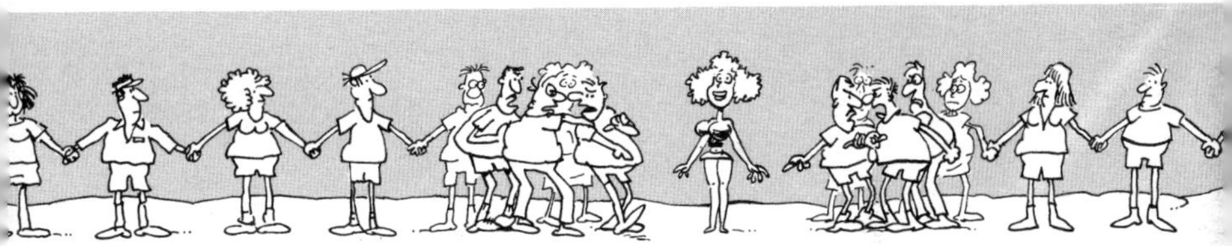

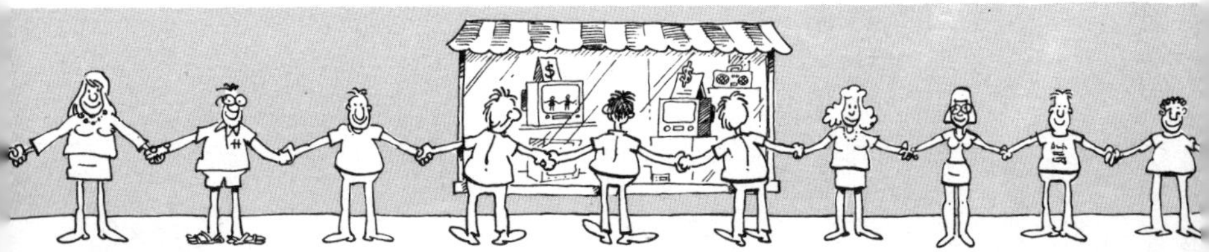

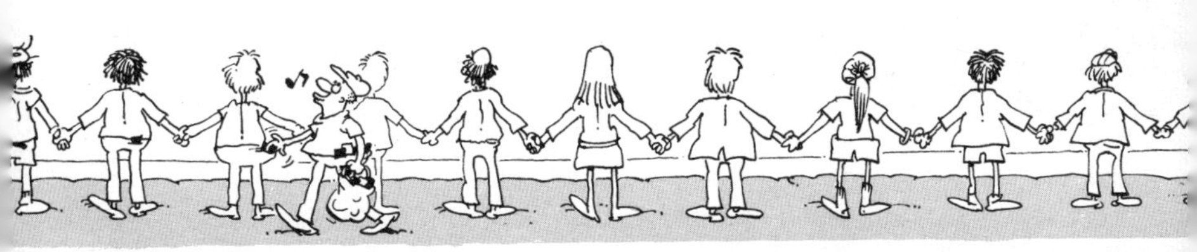

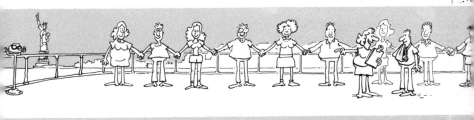

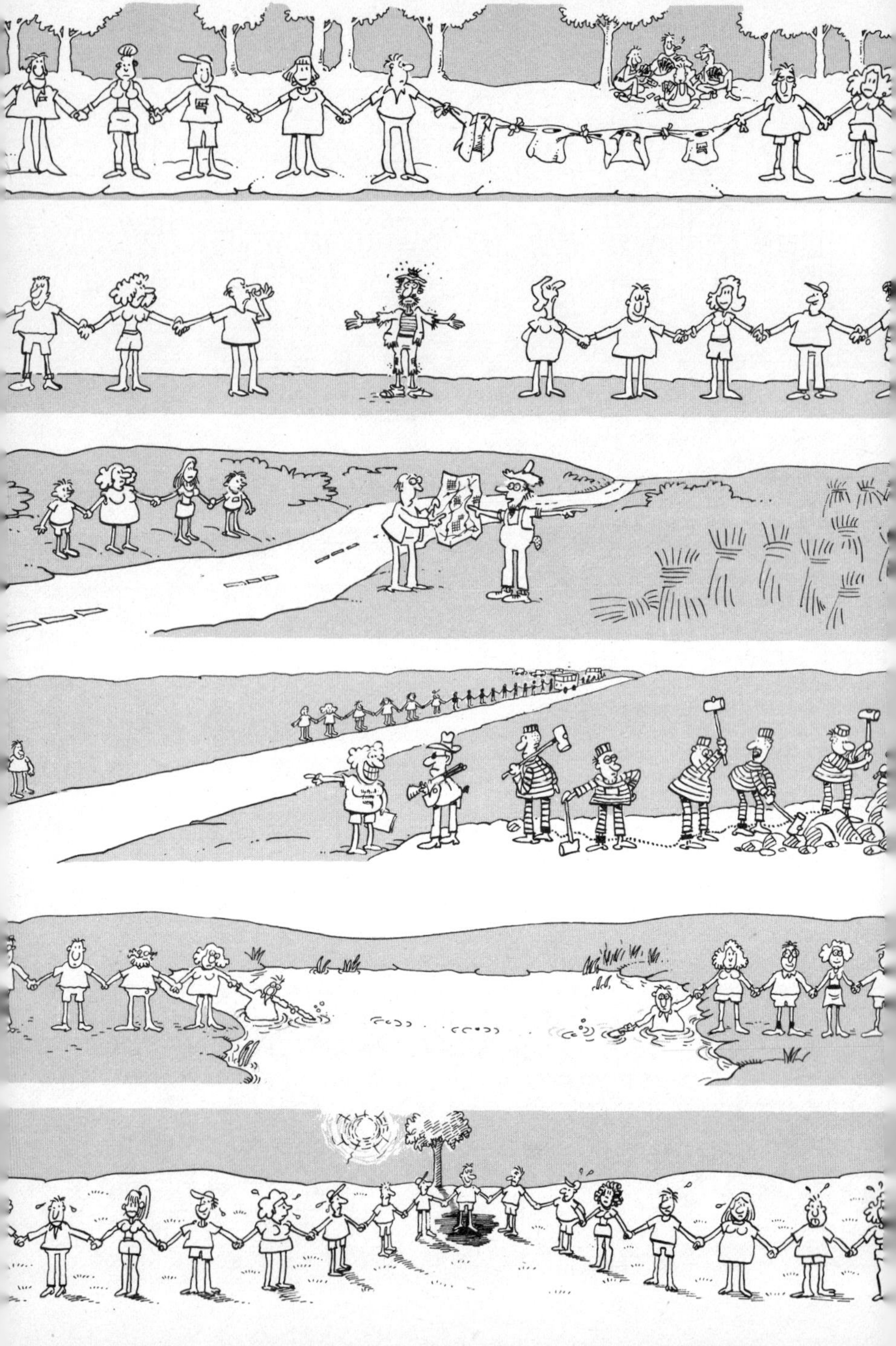

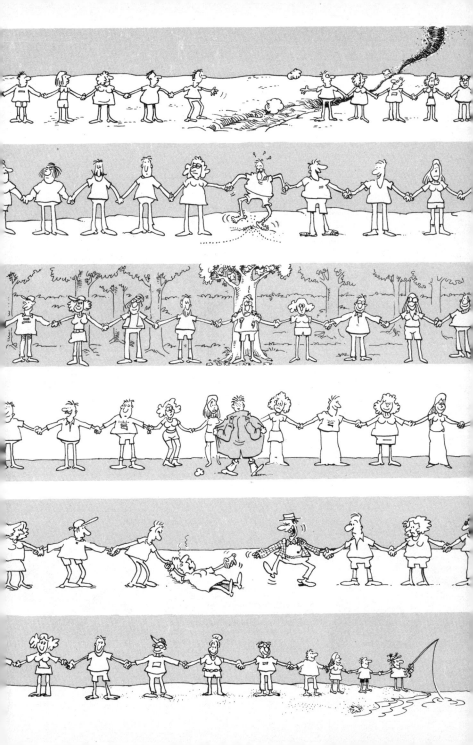

SHELF ABUSE DEPT.

Join MAD's TRENDY BOOK OF

THIS MONTH'S TRENDY BOOK CLUB SELECTION...

THE TRENDY WORLD WAR II NOVEL

THE MARSUPIAL KNISH
by Robert Ludlummox

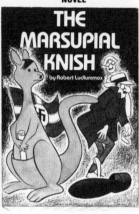

He was a double agent for Iceland and Albania. She was Charles De Gaulle's dental hygienist. Together, they uncover a secret Nazi formula concealed in a kangaroo's pouch at the Berlin Zoo that can transform chicken fat into nuclear energy and seriously endanger the D-Day landings, thereby altering the result of World War II, and possibly destroying the solar system.

THE TRENDY CELEBRITY CHILD-ABUSE BIOGRAPHY

MY FATHER, THE FINK
by George Burns, Jr.

"When he ran out of cigars, he smoked my pacifier!" "I was subjected to off-key frightening lullabies!" "To this day, he still denies he's my Father!" A precocious 2-year-old boy reveals facts about his 88-year-old celebrity father which...if they are true... will make the cruelties suffered by Bing Crosby's son and Joan Crawford's daughter sound like bedtime stories.

THE TRENDY CAT-LOVERS BOOK

CONVERSATIONS WITH CASSANDRA
by Hester Gluck

More sensitive than Garfield and les frivolous than Heathcliff, Cassandr —the world's most knowledgeable cat- chats with her mistress about hibacl cooking, unilateral disarmament, th deterioration of downtown Detroit, plan to feed the world's population the dangers of jogging, and a host o other diverse subjects that will de light and amuse cat-lovers everywhere

THIS MONTH'S TRENDY BOOK CLUB ALTERNAT

THE KANKAKEE 44-HOUR FALAFEL AND CREAM SODA DIET
by
Dr. Ingraham Moorg

THE TRENDY DIET BOOK

From the heartland of Illinois comes this revolutionary new diet, called by its creator "The Diet of the Century!" Learn how the author not only lost 396 pounds in one weekend, but also saw his 280-pound dieting wife vanish completely, and his dieting Cadillac Seville shrink to a Pinto.

JANE FONDA'S
WORKOUT BOOK
FOR DWARVES, LEPERS AND
CROSS-COUNTRY BUS DRIVERS

THE MONTH CLUB

ARTIST: BOB CLARKE   WRITER: LARRY SIEGEL

THE TRENDY
HORROR
NOVEL

THE DEVIL'S NIECE
by Stuart Schvitz

Her father was the brother-in-law of Satan! Her mother was a reincarnated piranha fish! And her Aunt Ann was a comparison shopper for Bloomingdale's! The most horrifying story of all time begins one quiet afternoon in Staten Island, New York, as innocent-looking Belle Zebub wends her way from door to door selling her unique Girl Scout Cookies...made from real Girl Scouts!

THE TRENDY
SEX
BOOK

1001 SEARING
SEXUAL
FANTASIES
by Leon Plunje

A look at the incredibly exciting and unbelievably disgusting sexual fantasies culled from 1001 disturbed minds and recreated in sharp-focus photos. This book has no phony analyses, no long-winded psychiatric explanations and no pompous (but useless) justifications. It's not even written by a Doctor! It's just pure, nauseating no-frills smut for the entire family!

THE TRENDY
ANDY ROONEY
BOOK

...AND STILL YET A
TEENY LITTLE SMIDGIN
MORE FROM ANDY ROONEY
by Andrew J. Rooney

In this week's book, Rooney continues last week's insight into the cosmic significance of belly button lint. He also reveals a life-long sexual obsession for unleavened bread, discusses the problems of keeping a praying mantis as a pet in a singles-only apartment, and tells why he hates manhole covers, the letter "H" and pizza pies. A must for Andy Rooney fans everywhere.

ELECTIONS...

THE TRENDY
EXERCISE
BOOK

Once again, Jane proves that nobody is too handicapped, too sick or too troubled to participate in a healthy daily exercise regimen. This book is a wonderful companion piece for Jane's upcoming "Jane Fonda's Work-Out Book For Migrant Fruit Pickers & Kidnapped Oil Company Executives."

MAD'S TRENDY BOOK OF THE MONTH CLUB
485 MADison Avenue, N.Y., N.Y. 10022

Please enroll me in your club and send me your books at the ridiculously low price of $15.00 each. I understand that if, at any time, one of your books contains a new idea, a new concept or a new thought, all the money that I've sent you will be refunded to me and I will receive a free round-trip cruise for four to Puerto Rico. I also realize that this spread is a satire of those ads for Book Clubs that feature trendy books, and that I'm too smart to fall for a joke. But I'm sending you the money anyway, even though I expect no books in return.

NAME____________________

ADDRESS____________________

CITY__________ STATE__________ ZIP__________

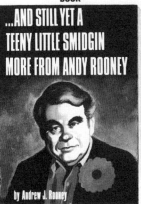

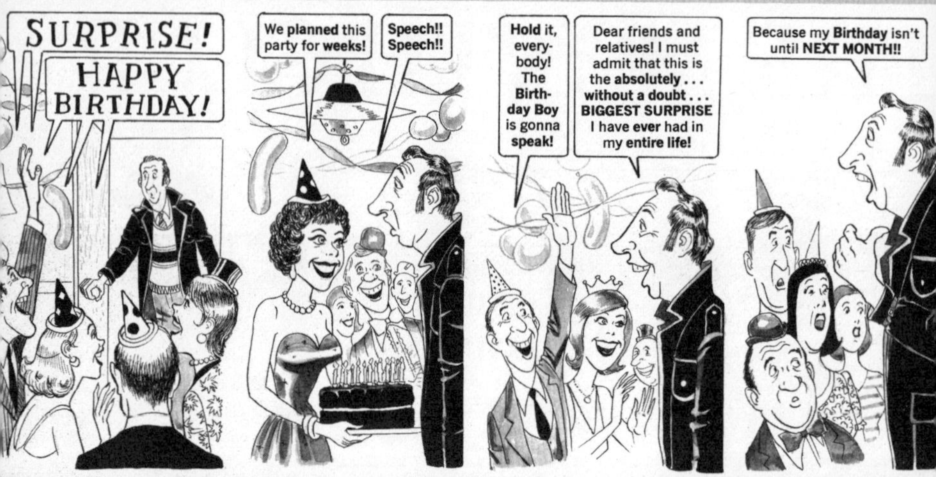
SURPRISE!
HAPPY BIRTHDAY!
We planned this party for weeks!
Speech!! Speech!!
Hold it, every-body! The Birth-day Boy is gonna speak!
Dear friends and relatives! I must admit that this is the absolutely . . . without a doubt . . . BIGGEST SURPRISE I have ever had in my entire life!
Because my Birthday isn't until NEXT MONTH!!

BERG'S-EYE VIEW DEPT.

THE LIGHTER SIDE OF... CEL

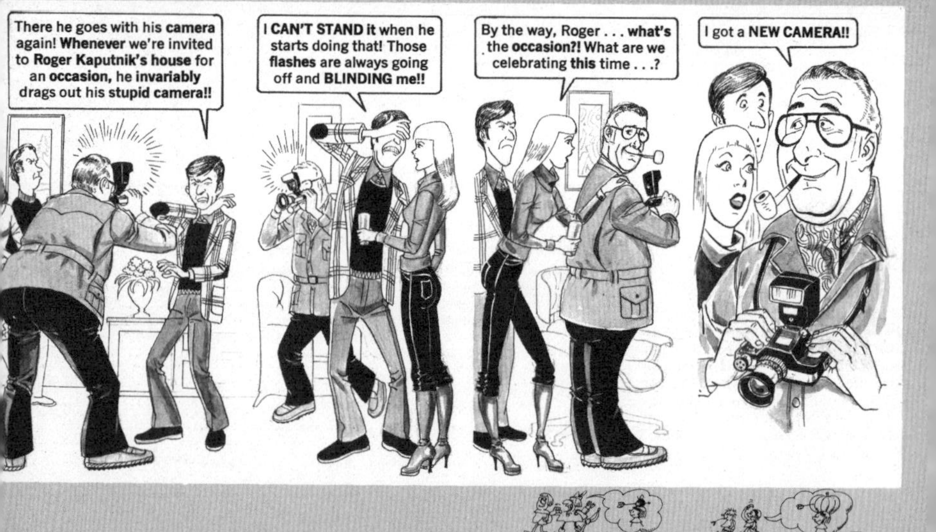
There he goes with his camera again! Whenever we're invited to Roger Kaputnik's house for an occasion, he invariably drags out his stupid camera!!
I CAN'T STAND it when he starts doing that! Those flashes are always going off and BLINDING me!!
By the way, Roger . . . what's the occasion?! What are we celebrating this time . . .?
I got a NEW CAMERA!!

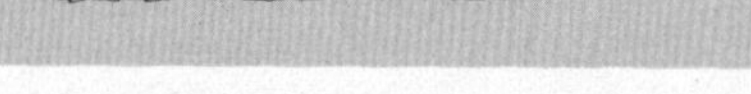

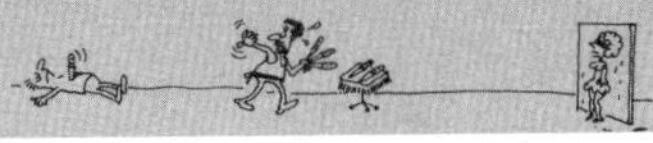

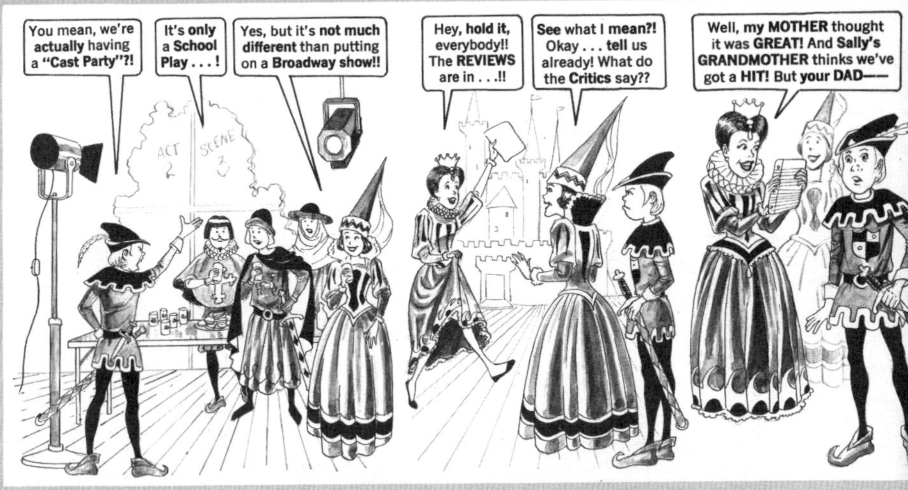

You mean, we're actually having a "Cast Party"?!
It's only a School Play . . . !
Yes, but it's not much different than putting on a Broadway show!!
ACT 2
SCENE 3
Hey, hold it, everybody!! The REVIEWS are in . . .!!
See what I mean?! Okay . . . tell us already! What do the Critics say??
Well, my MOTHER thought it was GREAT! And Sally's GRANDMOTHER thinks we've got a HIT! But your DAD——

EBRATIONS

ARTIST & WRITER
DAVE BERG

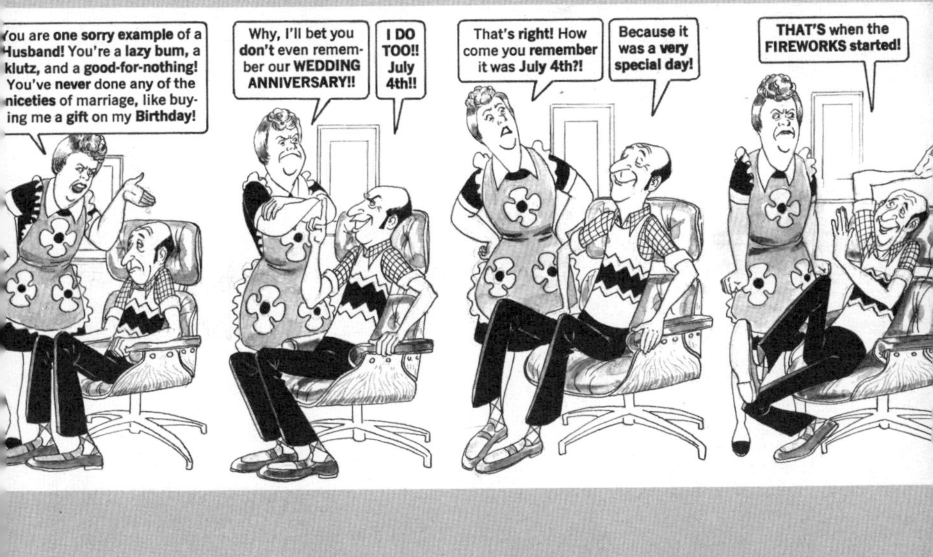

You are one sorry example of a Husband! You're a lazy bum, a klutz, and a good-for-nothing! You've never done any of the niceties of marriage, like buying me a gift on my Birthday!
Why, I'll bet you don't even remember our WEDDING ANNIVERSARY!!
I DO TOO!! July 4th!!
That's right! How come you remember it was July 4th?!
Because it was a very special day!
THAT'S when the FIREWORKS started!

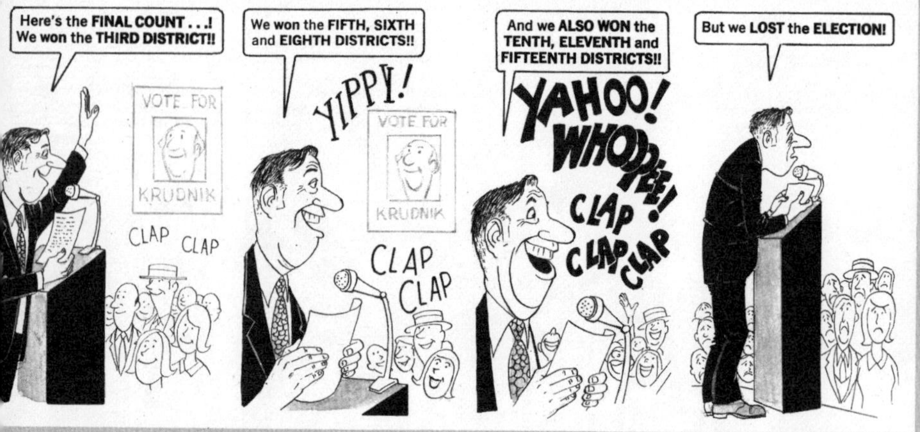
Here's the FINAL COUNT . . .! We won the THIRD DISTRICT!!
VOTE FOR KRUDNIK
CLAP CLAP
We won the FIFTH, SIXTH and EIGHTH DISTRICTS!!
YIPPY!
VOTE FOR KRUDNIK
CLAP CLAP
And we ALSO WON the TENTH, ELEVENTH and FIFTEENTH DISTRICTS!!
YAHOO!
WHOOPEE!
CLAP CLAP CLAP CLAP
But we LOST the ELECTION!

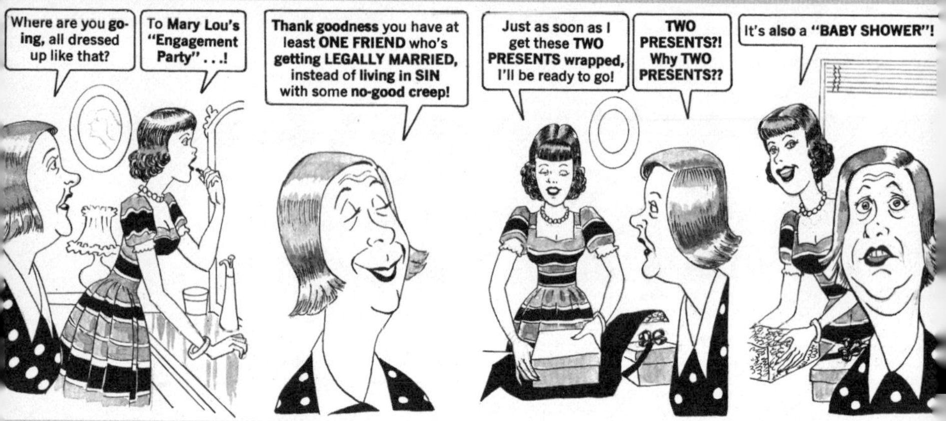
Where are you going, all dressed up like that?
To Mary Lou's "Engagement Party" . . .!
Thank goodness you have at least ONE FRIEND who's getting LEGALLY MARRIED, instead of living in SIN with some no-good creep!
Just as soon as I get these TWO PRESENTS wrapped, I'll be ready to go!
TWO PRESENTS?! Why TWO PRESENTS??
It's also a "BABY SHOWER"!

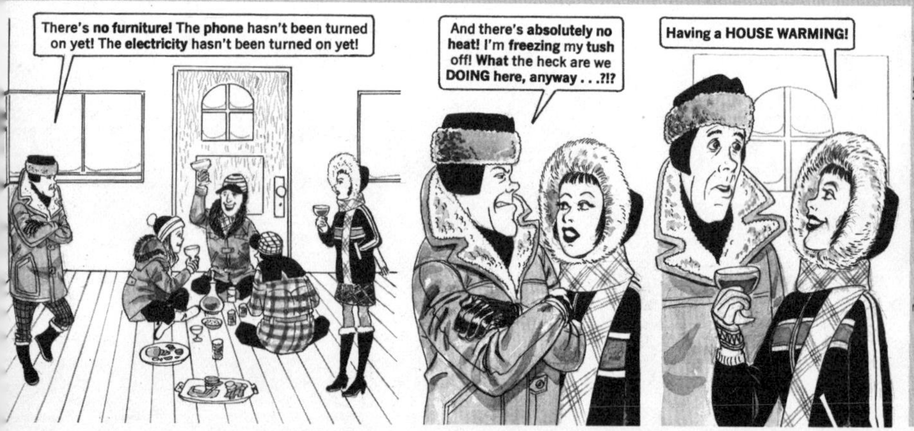
There's no furniture! The phone hasn't been turned on yet! The electricity hasn't been turned on yet!
And there's absolutely no heat! I'm freezing my tush off! What the heck are we DOING here, anyway . . .?!?
Having a HOUSE WARMING!

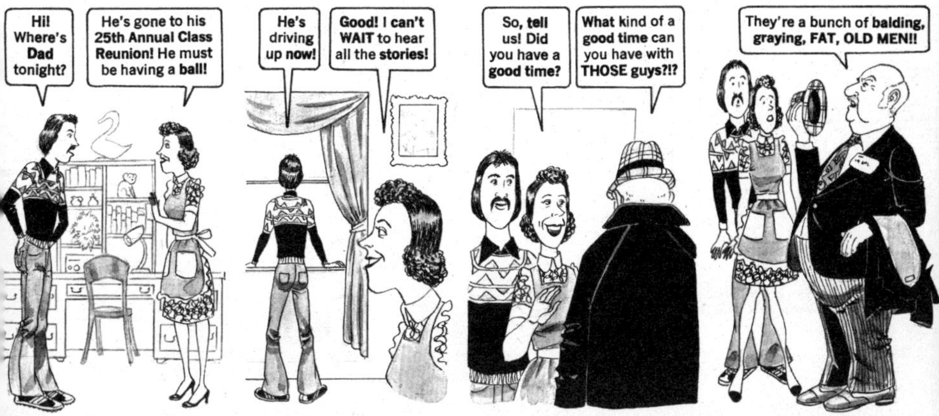
Hi! Where's Dad tonight?
He's gone to his 25th Annual Class Reunion! He must be having a ball!
He's driving up now!
Good! I can't WAIT to hear all the stories!
So, tell us! Did you have a good time?
What kind of a good time can you have with THOSE guys?!?
They're a bunch of balding, graying, FAT, OLD MEN!!

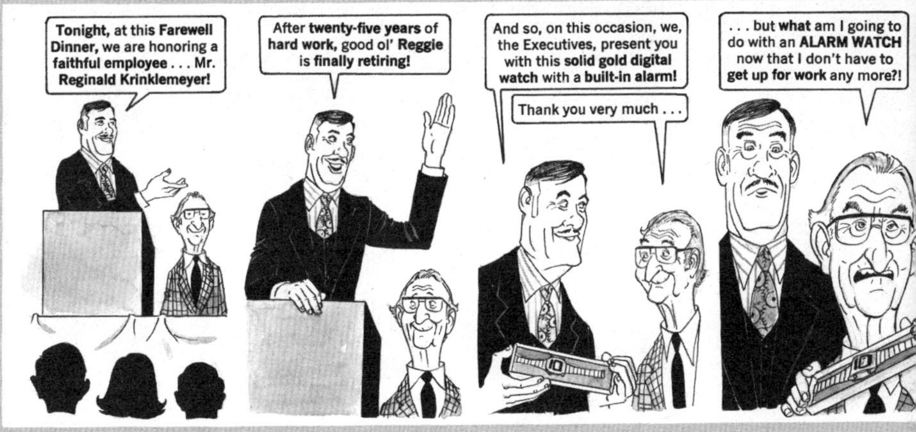
Tonight, at this Farewell Dinner, we are honoring a faithful employee . . . Mr. Reginald Krinklemeyer!
After twenty-five years of hard work, good ol' Reggie is finally retiring!
And so, on this occasion, we, the Executives, present you with this solid gold digital watch with a built-in alarm!
Thank you very much . . .
. . . but what am I going to do with an ALARM WATCH now that I don't have to get up for work any more?!

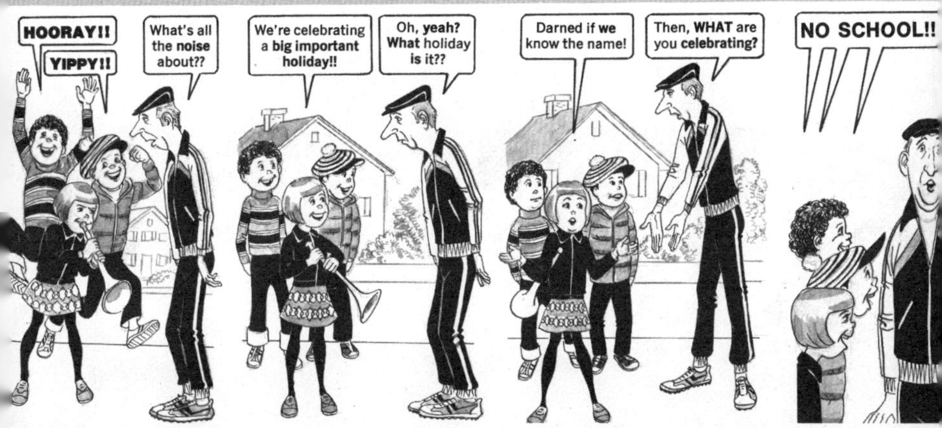
HOORAY!!
YIPPY!!
What's all the noise about??
We're celebrating a big important holiday!!
Oh, yeah? What holiday is it??
Darned if we know the name!
Then, WHAT are you celebrating?
NO SCHOOL!!

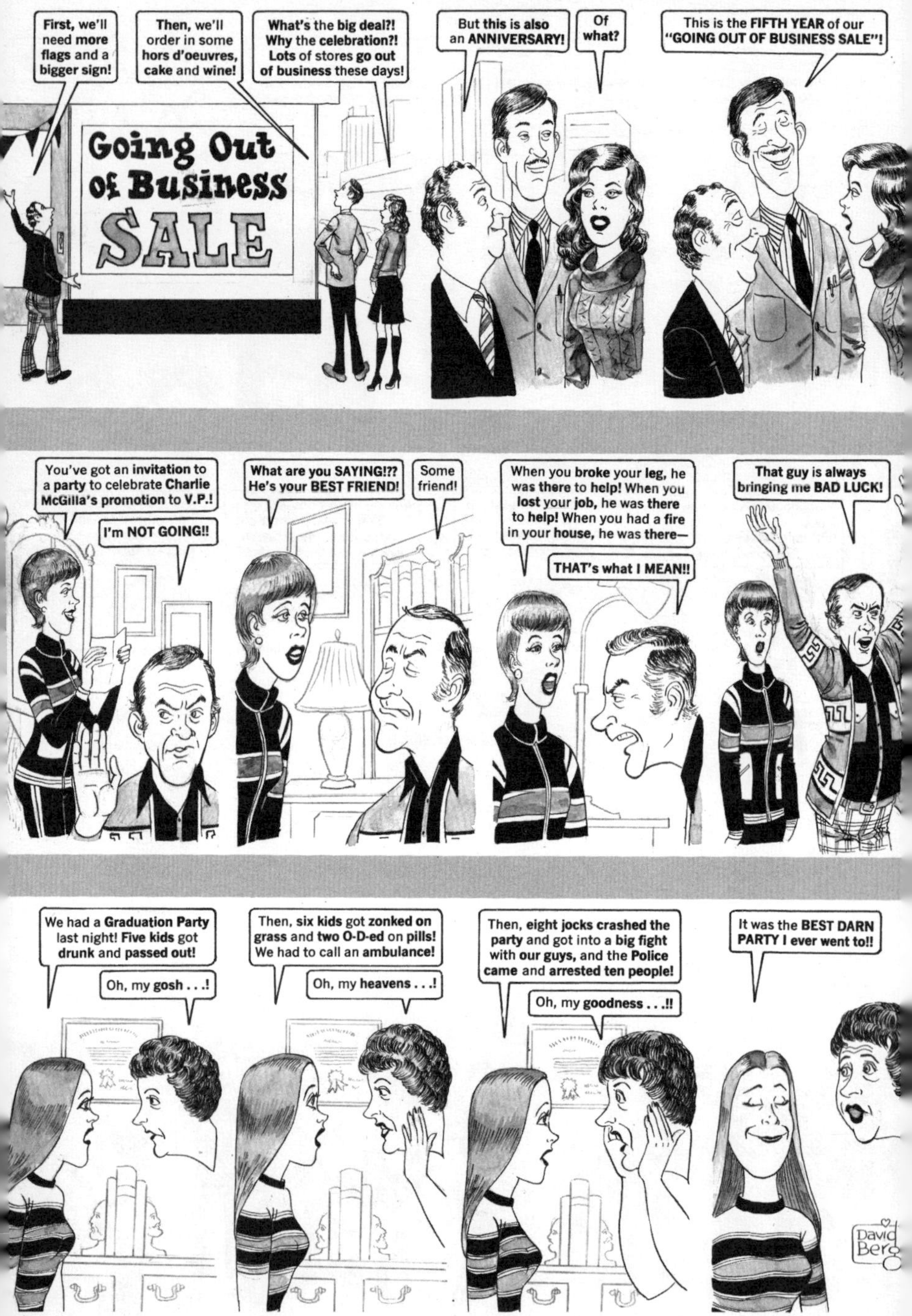
First, we'll need more flags and a bigger sign!
Then, we'll order in some hors d'oeuvres, cake and wine!
Going Out of Business SALE
What's the big deal?! Why the celebration?! Lots of stores go out of business these days!
But this is also an ANNIVERSARY!
Of what?
This is the FIFTH YEAR of our "GOING OUT OF BUSINESS SALE"!
You've got an invitation to a party to celebrate Charlie McGilla's promotion to V.P.!
I'm NOT GOING!!
What are you SAYING!?? He's your BEST FRIEND!
Some friend!
When you broke your leg, he was there to help! When you lost your job, he was there to help! When you had a fire in your house, he was there—
THAT's what I MEAN!!
That guy is always bringing me BAD LUCK!
We had a Graduation Party last night! Five kids got drunk and passed out!
Oh, my gosh . . .!
Then, six kids got zonked on grass and two O-D-ed on pills! We had to call an ambulance!
Oh, my heavens . . .!
Then, eight jocks crashed the party and got into a big fight with our guys, and the Police came and arrested ten people!
Oh, my goodness . . .!!
It was the BEST DARN PARTY I ever went to!!
David Berg

B-S.A.T. DEPT.

ARTIST: GEORGE WOODBRIDGE WRITER: FRANK JACOBS

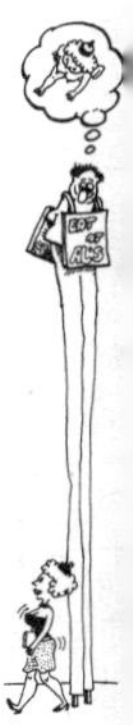

Thinking about what career to get into? Wondering whether or not you'll fit in? Well, here's the third in a series of tests designed to help you choose your future line of work. Mainly, discover your true abilities by taking...

MAD'S APTITUDE TEST NUMBER THREE
WILL YOU MAKE A GOOD ATHLETE?

1. Fill in the blank in this sentence: As a pro athlete, you should never become so successful that you forget the ______ who made it all possible.
   A. agent
   B. tax accountant
   C. investment advisor
   D. All of the above.

2. As a pro, you are swell-headed, alienate your teammates and are the center of controversy. What does this kind of behavior get you?
   A. More newspaper coverage than you ever dreamed of.
   B. An automatic interview on nationwide TV by Howard Cosell.
   C. Praise from the team owner, who knows that controversy improves the gate.
   D. All of the above.

3. 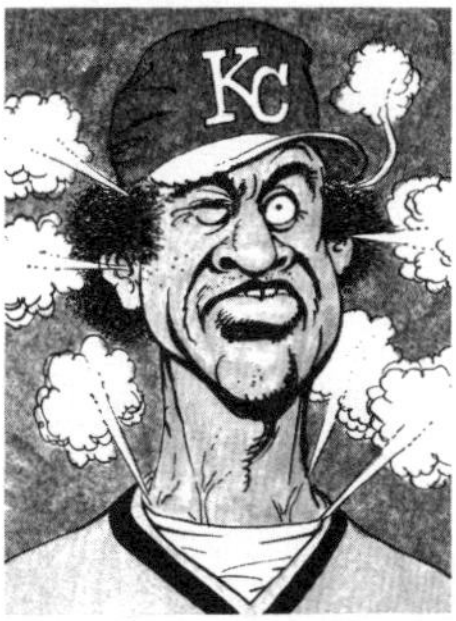
KC

You can tell by the expression on this baseball player's face that:
   A. He's just been turned down for a Miller Beer commercial.
   B. He's just been traded to the Blue Jays.
   C. His wife just learned how he spends his nights on the road.
   D. Any of the above.

4. To quote a famous coach, "Winning isn't everything, it's ______."
   A. the extra $20,000 you get for post-season play.
   B. how you renegotiate your contract.
   C. your name on a candy bar.
   D. All of the above.

5. At contract time, the relationship between a pro athlete and his club's front office can be compared to:
   A. Israel and the Arabs.
   B. Luke Skywalker and the Empire.
   C. Boss Hogg and the Duke Boys.
   D. Any of the above.

6. The expression "playing hurt" means:
   A. It's a big game and the exposure you'll get will more than compensate for the pain.
   B. You healed weeks ago, but you're still faking your injury so the coach will praise you in the press for having guts.
   C. The team doctor has you on so many pain-killers and uppers that you're oblivious to your pain, your injuries, everything.
   D. Any of the above.

7. 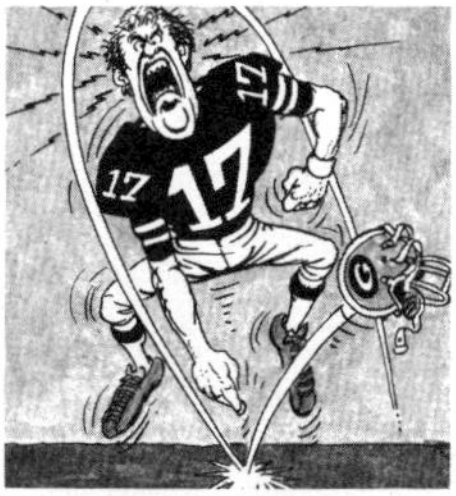
17

This tight end is screaming that the referee made a bad call. Why?
   A. He wants to prove to his agent that he *can* act well enough to get a movie role.
   B. He's on nationwide TV.
   C. The stock he invested in just plummeted and he's got to scream at someone.
   D. Any of the above.

8. 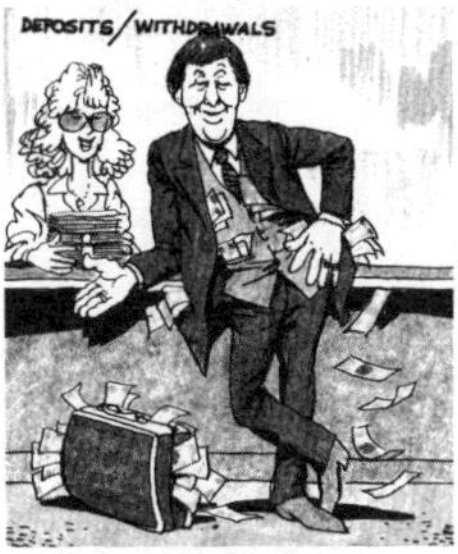
DEPOSITS/WITHDRAWALS

To quote another famous coach, "It isn't that you won or lost, but ______."
   A. how many times your photo gets in Sports Illustrated.
   B. what you pull down as a free agent.
   C. how you do with your tax shelters.
   D. All of the above.

9. You're a baseball player and you end the season hitting over .300. This means that:
   A. Whatever you're making, you're underpaid.
   B. Whatever raise the owner offers, it's not enough.
   C. Whatever you settle on, the publicity will be tremendous.
   D. All of the above.

10. There is a special quality among pro athletes called "hustle." What does "hustle" mean to you?
   A. Pushing for annual cost-of-living increases in your contract.
   B. Making friends with a rich fan who's a Wall Street insider and can give you tips.
   C. Getting out to the stadium early so you can be picked for a pre-game TV interview.
   D. All of the above.

SCORING

If you answered "D." to all the questions, you have the ability to make a good Pro Athlete.

IT STILL DOESN'T ADAGE UP DEPT.

According to the ancient Chinese proverb, "The dead never rise, except on cable TV." True, but to that we'd like to add "and in the pages of MAD," where we've resurrected a lifeless premise from our previous issue—just so we could beat it to death one more time! Yes, once again...

MAD RE-EXAMINES MORE WISE OLD SAYINGS

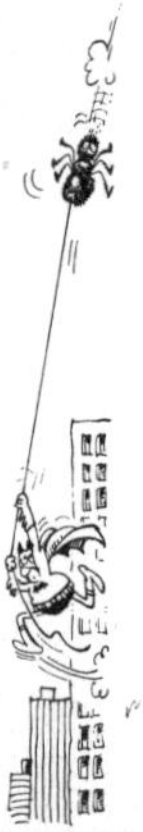

ARTIST: PAUL COKER WRITER: TOM KOCH

"Curiosity killed the cat."

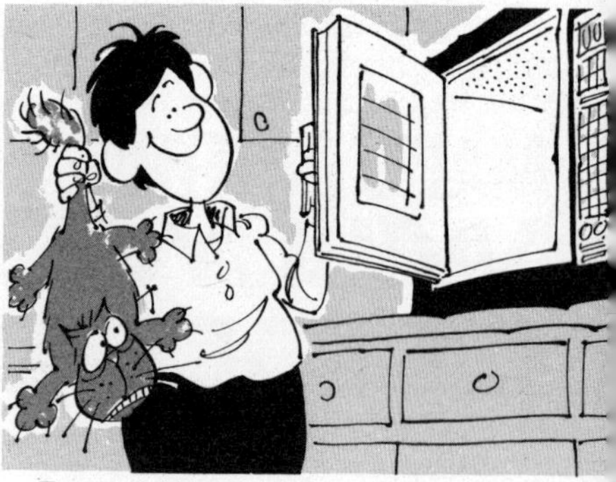

FALSE: A kid with a microwave oven killed the cat!

"13 is an unlucky number."

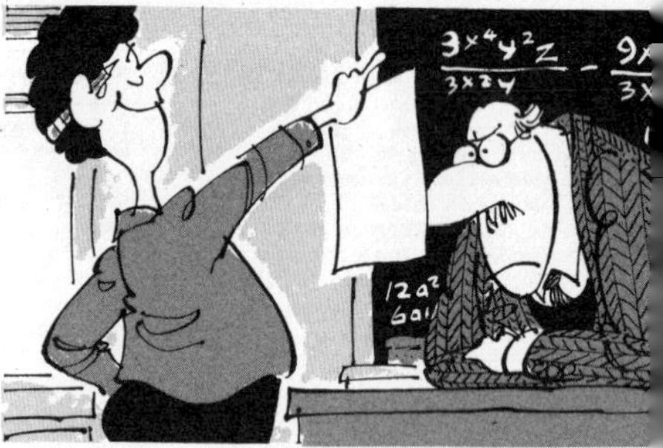

TRUE: Especially for those high school students who put it down on their algebra exam as the answer to the problem, "If $X^2=25$, then X=______."

"The shortest route to a man's heart is through his stomach."

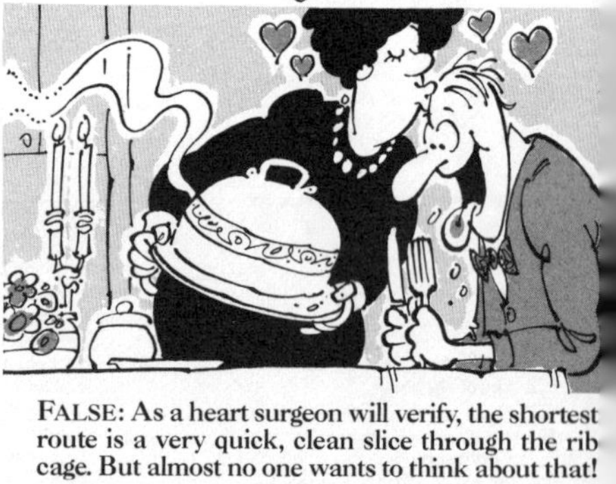

FALSE: As a heart surgeon will verify, the shortest route is a very quick, clean slice through the rib cage. But almost no one wants to think about that!

"An apple a day keeps the doctor away."

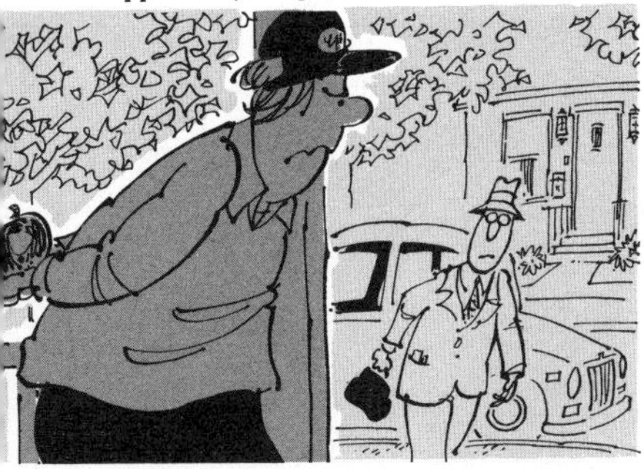

TRUE: But only if your speed and control are good enough to hit him right between the eyes with it!

"If rain starts before 7, it'll end before 11."

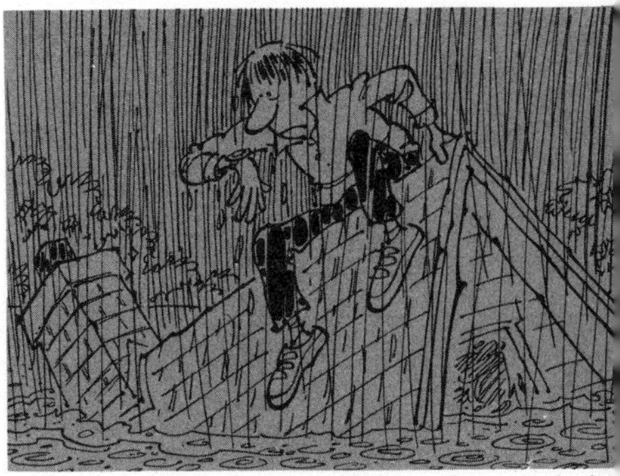

TRUE: It will, but not necessarily on the same day!

"You can't judge a book by its cover."

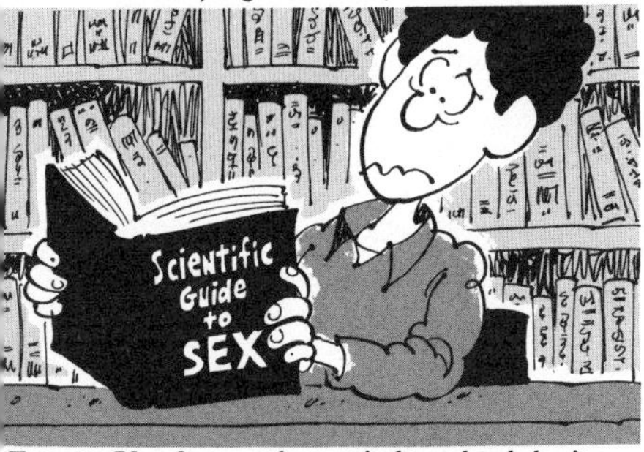
Scientific Guide to SEX

FALSE: You frequently can judge a book by its cover, which is exactly why "The Wit and Wisdom of George M. Steinbrenner" sold only 23 copies!

"A barking dog never bites."

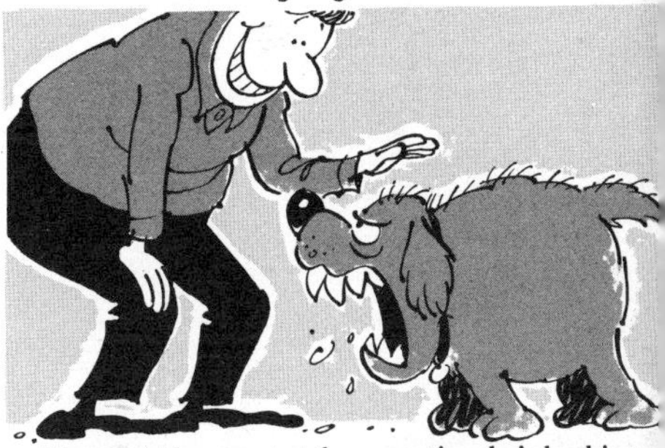

TRUE: At least not at the same time he's barking. There's something about having his mouth entirely filled with your leg that seems to muffle his voice!

"A fool and his money are soon parted."

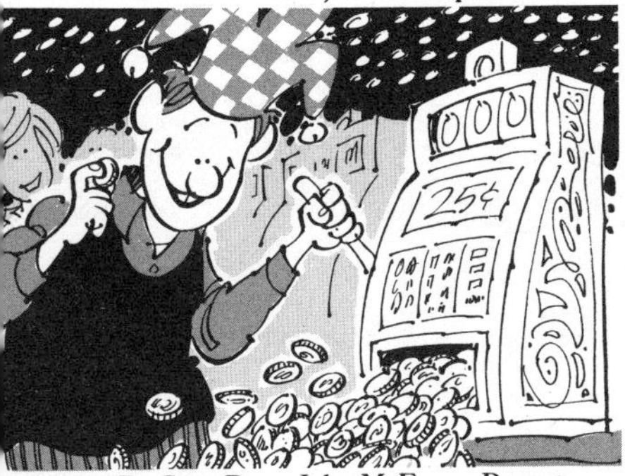
25¢

FALSE: Do Sean Penn, John McEnroe, Rupert Murdoch and Bill Gaines look poor to you?

"A coward dies a thousand deaths; a hero dies but once."

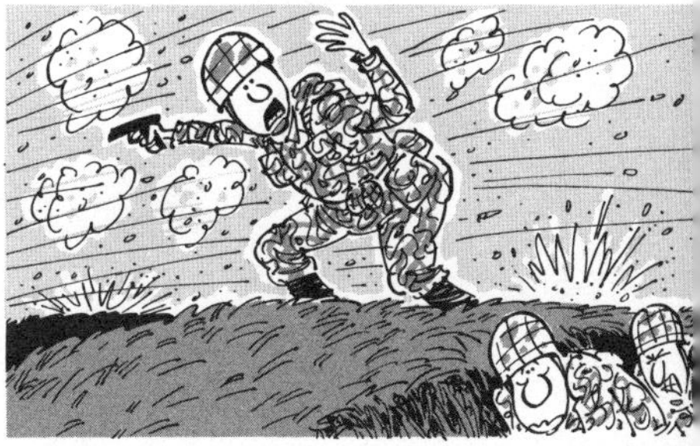

TRUE: But that's only because cowards have about 90 years to work on it, while most featherbrained heroes get themselves knocked off before they're 25!

BYGONE BUY-GONES DEPT.

Despite all the books written about major events in history, we still know ve
little about the way our ancestors lived their normal, every-day lives. Tha
because the world didn't have Classified Telephone Directories in the past. A

THE YELLOW PAGE

ARTIST: BOB CLARKE   WRITER: TOM KOC

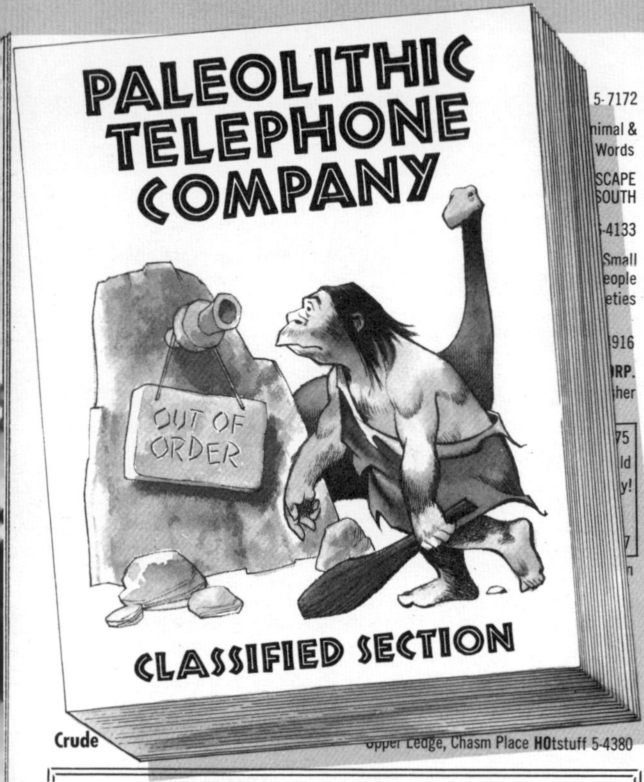

PALEOLITHIC TELEPHONE COMPANY

OUT OF ORDER

CLASSIFIED SECTION

Crude

Upper Ledge, Chasm Place HOtstuff 5-4380

Let A Pong's Professional Help Rid You Of Insect Pests

All Vermin Exterminated by Skillful
Hand Removal From the Hair on Your
Head, Shoulders, Back, Arms & Feet

**SPECIALIZING IN
PAINFUL INFESTATIONS OF**

NITS
LICE
FLEAS
BIG WOLLY THINGS
FORAGING RODENTS

Bring Your Body In For A Free Estimate
Or Call
PRehensile 6-3282

Pong's Pest Riddance 161 Path That's Overgrown

5-7172

nimal &
Words

SCAPE
SOUTH

-4133

Small
eople
eties

916

RP.
her

75
ld
y!

7
n

▶ **Cemeteries**

SHADY ACRES MEMORIAL GORGE

Achieve Lasting Fame By Letting Us
Bury Your Bones Where Future
Archaeologists Will Be Most Likely
To Find Them

427 Road to Where the Sun
Comes Up .... **SToneage 6-909**

Village Burial Mound & Garbage Dump
231 Hilly Path .... **PIitdown 5-217**

▶ **Dating Services**

MURD THE MATCHMAKER

Still Hoping To Meet That "Dream
Girl" You'll Want To Club Over
The Head And Drag Back To Your Cave?

Let Our Personalized Introduction
Service Help You

Upper Ledge, Chasm Place **HOtstuff 5-4380**

▶ **Exterminators**

ORK, AN EXTERMINATOR

Experts Dispatched Promptly To Smoke
The Bats Out Of Your Cave

703 Road Where No One
Passes By .... **AMphibian 4-787**

Pong's Pest Riddance
161 Path That's Overgrown ....**BRutal 6-328**
(See Our Display Ad This Page)

▶ **Firemakers' Supplies**

CLUG & OONG'S RETAIL FLINT SHOP

"Rub Two Of Our Products Together
& Watch The Sparks Fly"

Cave 26, Cliff That's
Crumbling ....**LOwbrow 3-818**

Irg's Stone Quarry
272 Path Running Downhill..**PLiocene 6-527**
(See Our Ad Under "Weapons—Primitive")

▶ **Interior Decorators**

WOG & CHUCKIE

Brighten Up Your Cave Walls With
Hunting Scenes Drawn By
Talented Young Artists

Semi-Lifelike Animals   Somewhat Human Figures
"Good Art Increases In Value Over The Eons"

419 Bare Patch Of Ground ...**PUce 5-6987**

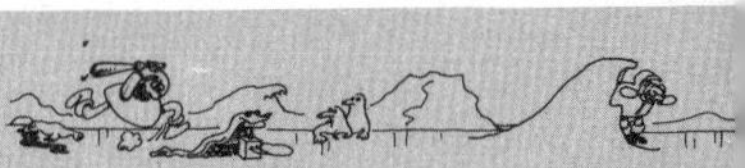

ere's no substitute for reading The Yellow Pages to find out how a community
es and works. So let's suppose the telephones had been invented at the Dawn
Mankind, and phone books appeared a few months later. Here is a MAD look at

S THROUGH HISTORY

*THIS IS PART I OF A CONTINUING SERIES. THE "ANCIENT ROME YELLOW PAGES" WILL APPEAR NEXT.

THE WHEEL—

MANKIND'S HOTTEST NEW INVENTION:

Be The First In Your Neighborhood To Own One While It's Still In The Experimental Stage!

IDEAL FOR USE AS A CONVERSATION PIECE, A LAZY SUSAN OR SOME-
'HING DECORATIVE TO LEAN AGAINST YOUR FAVORITE TREE

For Prices & Specifications
PHONE
BRainstorm 3-9077

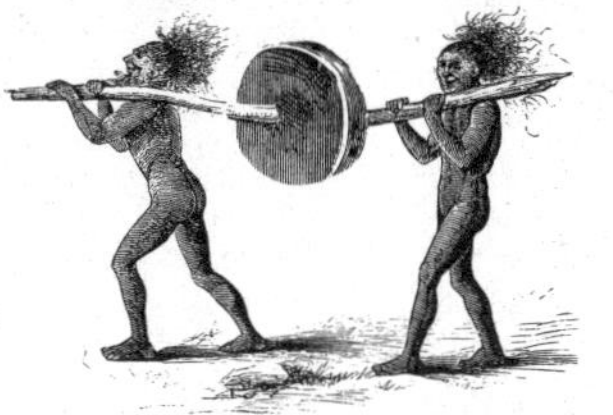

67 Path That's Always Muddy—Futuristic Gadget Company

Ladies' Fashions

LUB'S FUR SALON

FEATURING GORGEOUS SABER TOOTH TIGER PELTS

Many With Skulls Still Attached For Wear As Fashionable Parkas

345 Path Through The Garment District ......**FA**ngsnarl 5-6336

OLY MAMMOTH MART

Enjoy The Splendor Of Warm, Hairy, Dual-Purpose Mammoth Fur

'ear It As A Coat By Day Use It As A Rug By Night

22 Field Where The Sloths Hibernate ......**PA**chyderm 9-4141

Pet Obedience Schools

K'S TYRANNOSAURUS TRAINING

TURN YOUR BIG LOVABLE MUTT INTO A GUARD DINOSAUR!

We Teach Pets to Stomp on Intruders at Your Command!

16 Place of Slimy Green Water .... **RO**ckside 8-2660

Physical Therapists

MEN OF MERCY CLINIC

No Need To Endure Pain When Our Competent Specialists Can Hurl You Off A Cliff And Put You Completely Out Of Your Misery

' Top of The Bottomless Pit ....**AA**rg 5-6175

Real Estate Agents

ntury 13,279 B.C. Realtors
ig Bonfire Circle ....**MI**dden 7-2800

OKK & OKK

OFFERING CHOICE ACREAGE IN THE PRIVEVAL OOZE!

An Investment With A Big Future Profit Potential

The Farthest Hill....**CL**ubswinger 5-4239

▶Religious Organizations

Fellowship of Dirt Worshipers
394 Winding Path ....**AP**elike 7-8192

FIRST CHURCH OF THUNDER FEARERS

Come Join Us In Awaiting The End Of The World During The Next Electrical Storm

146 Trail That Doesn't Go Anyplace . . **TI**medawn 8-9935

SOCIETY OF THE TREE DEITY (ORTHODOX)

See How Worshiping A Lombardy Poplar Can Help You Recover From Toothache, Enjoy A Fuller Love Life And Create Ample Rainfall

Sunday Leaf Raking Ceremonies
Thursday Night Twig Snapping

509 Path Made By Extinct Animals ....**PL**iocene 6-5275

▶Rock Groups

Irg's Stone Quarry
275 Path Running Downhill ..**OO**uch 9-0987
(See Our Ad Under "Weapons—Primitive")

▶Schools—Private

BUR & LITZ LANGUAGE INSTRUCTION

Stop Grunting Like An Animal & Learn To Speak Meaningful Words The Easy Bur-Litz Way!

Cave 8, Cliff by the Gully ......**GR**unt 8-6677

▶Travel Agencies

OVERLAND MIGRATION TOURS

MAKE RESERVATIONS NOW TO ESCAPE THE NEXT ICE AGE BY WALKINC SOUTH

Reach The Tropics In Less Than Four Generations

Nightly Food & Lodging Arranged On Pillage Or Barter Plan

816 Track of the Scary Animals ......**LA**ndbridge 6-4133

▶Weapons—Advanced

Arr's Arsenal
Flat Place Atop The Hill ......**AL**lfours 8-9006
(See Our Display Ad This Page)

GREAT UNITED ARROWHEAD CORP.

MANUFACTURING THE ULTIMATE WEAPON: HAND-SHARPENED POINTY ROCKS!

760 Road to Where the Sun Goes Down ....**JA**vaman 4-4916

▶Weapons—Primitive

IRG'S STONE QUARRY

Many Varieties of Large & Small Rocks for Throwing At Many Varieties of Large & Small People

"We Chisel To Meet Your Requirements"

2 Path Running Downhill **PL**iocene 6-5275

OOM'S HOUSE OF BOULDERS

"Serving The Brontosaurus Squasher Since 1,327,941 B.C."

Free Layaway We Absolutely Don't Deliver

676 Dry River Bed ....**PR**imate 5-7172

▶ Wheels-Crude

Futuristic Gadget Co.,
67 Path That's Always Muddy....**GL**ork 3-9077
(See Our Display Ad This Page)

Want To Survive Your Next Big Game Hunt?

Then Let Us Help You Kill Any-Thing That Moves With Our Complete Selection of Lethal Goods

—Solid Stone Axe Heads
—Polished Hardwood Spears
—Heavy Duty Clobbering Clubs

ARR'S ARSENAL

Also Inexpensive Sharpened Sticks & Other Saturday Night Specials

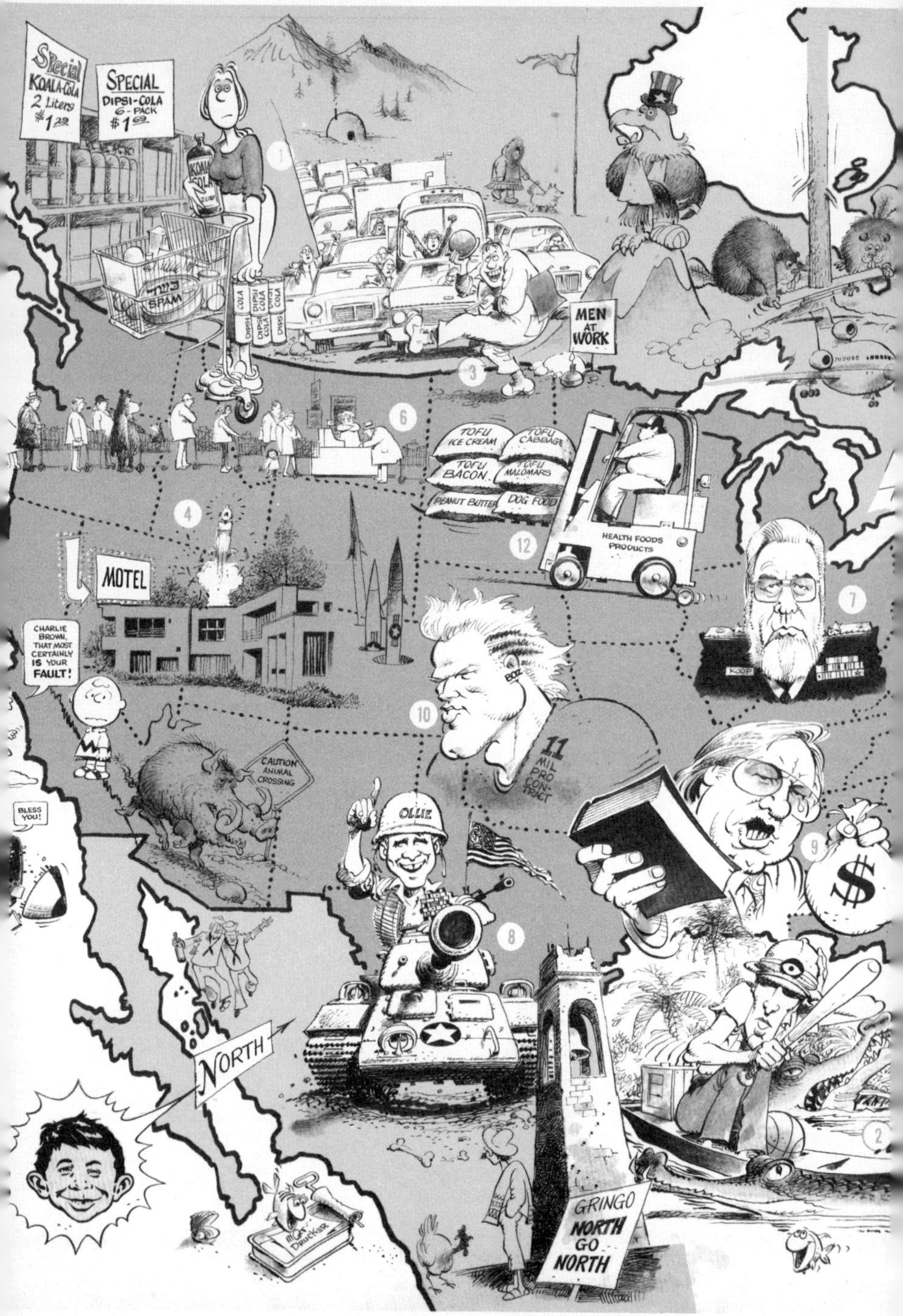

Special
KOALA-COLA
2 Liters
#1.29
SPECIAL
DIPSI-COLA
6-PACK
#1.69
KOALA COLA
SPAM
DIPSI COLA
1
MEN AT WORK
3
6
TOFU ICE CREAM
TOFU CABBAGE
TOFU BACON
TOFU MALOMARS
PEANUT BUTTER
DOG FOOD
HEALTH FOODS PRODUCTS
12
4
MOTEL
CHARLIE BROWN, THAT MOST CERTAINLY IS YOUR FAULT!
7
KOOP
BOZ
10
11
MIL PRO CON-TRACT
CAUTION ANIMAL CROSSING
BLESS YOU!
OLLIE
9
$
8
NORTH
2
GRINGO
NORTH
GO
NORTH

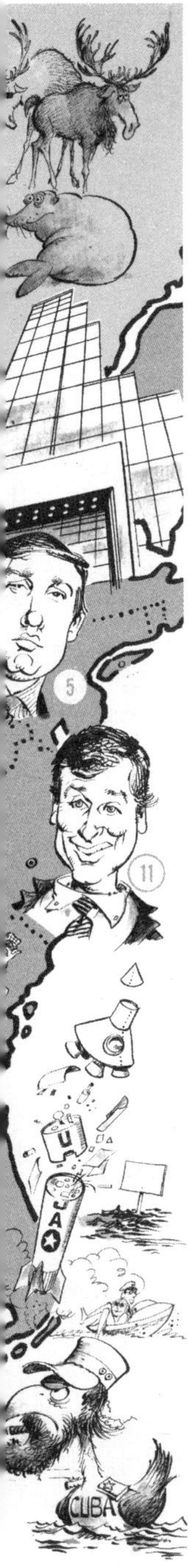
5
11
CUBA

THE UNITED HATES DEPT.

Our nation's in a mess—drugs, pollution, rising crime. In the past we've thrown money c those problems—and we all know what that's gotten us! Crushing debt! Isn't there som way to help our country that doesn't require cash? Why, yes! And we modestly call it..

MAD's 12-POINT PLAN FOR IMPROVING AMERICA

without spending more tax dollars

1. Force soft drink makers to answer the decade's burning question: Are we better off buying 12-ounce cans or 2-liter bottles?

2. Send Brent Musburger to explore a part of the Amazon rain forest fron which no previous explorer has ever returned.

3. Make the highway flagmen who stop us at construction projects entertair us while we wait.

4. Yank out all those modern, hard-to-figure-out motel shower fixtures tha either scald you or freeze you, and melt them down into one huge chro mium glob.

5. Force Donald Trump to name his very next building after some truly grea person—and not himself.

6. Slap a $5.00 Handling Tax on any schmuck who holds up a long super market line to write a check for purchases totalling less than $10.

7. Require that TV commercials for cold remedies tell us we'll get well jus as fast even if we don't take the stuff.

8. Exile Ollie North to Nicaragua so he can try to pull off whatever he has ir mind without involving the rest of us.

9. Make TV evangelists explain in public why the commandment "Thou Shalt Not Steal" doesn't apply to them.

10. Restore confidence in America by forbidding Brian Bosworth to earn more in one week than his former college professors earn all year.

11. Outfit Dan Quayle in a shirt collar and jacket large enough to fit him ir hopes that this may enable more blood to reach his brain.

12. Outlaw tofu.

ARTIST: MORT DRUCKER WRITER: TOM KOCH

DON MARTIN DEPT.

ONE AFTERNOON DOWN HOME

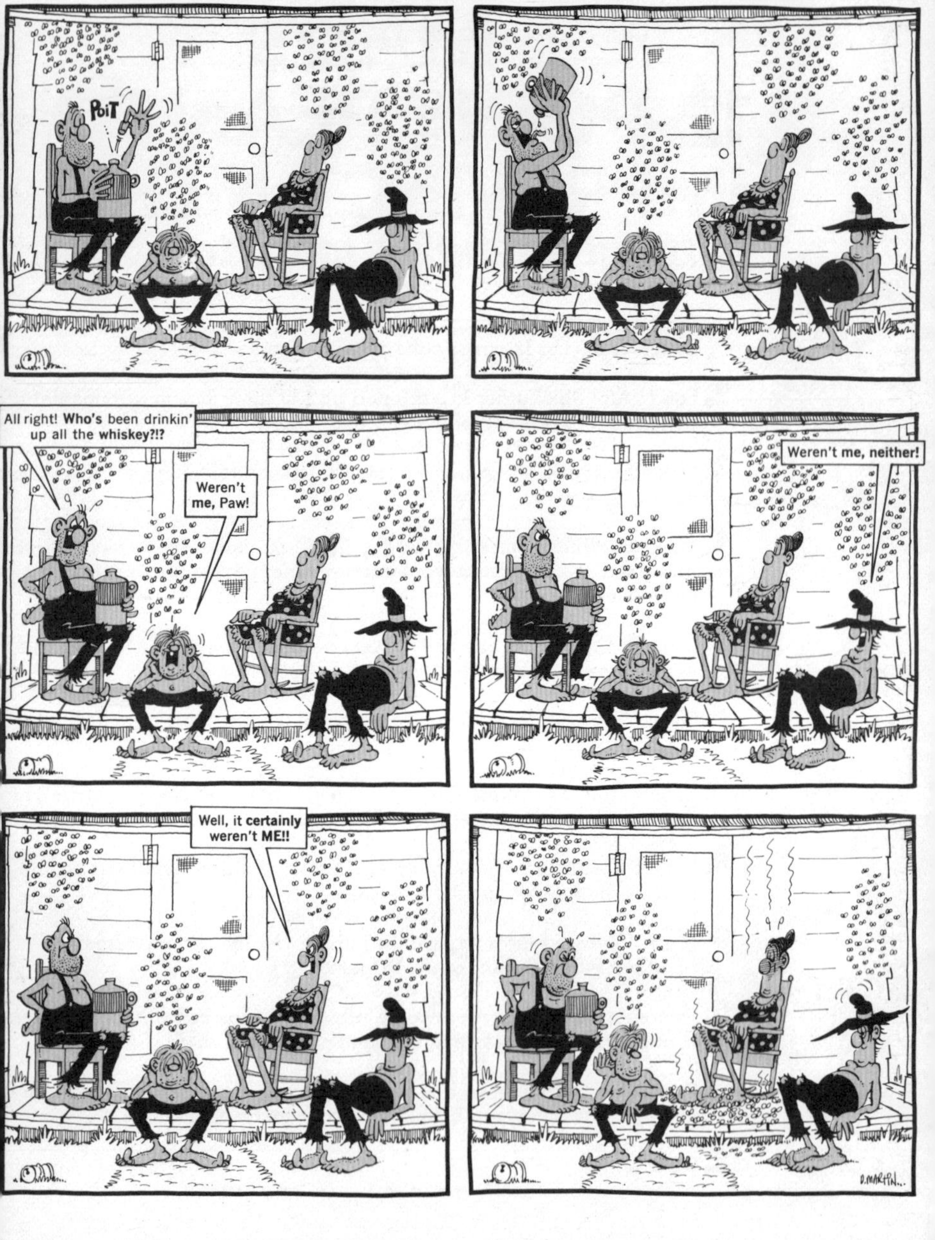
POIT
All right! **Who's** been drinkin' up all the **whiskey?!?**
Weren't me, Paw!
Weren't me, neither!
Well, it **certainly** weren't **ME!!**
D. MARTIN